D1830914

वाणी

हिन्दी-अँगरेज़ी कोश

संकलन-सम्पादन
प्रो. त्रिभुवननाथ शुक्ल
डॉ. भवदेव पाण्डेय

वाणी प्रकाशन

वाणी प्रकाशन

4695, 21-ए, दरियागंज, नयी दिल्ली 110 002

फ़ोन : +91 11 23273167 फ़ैक्स : +91 11 23275710

शाखाएँ

अशोक राजपथ, पटना 800 004, बिहार

कॉफ़ी हाउस कैम्पस, महात्मा गांधी मार्ग, इलाहाबाद 211 001, उत्तर प्रदेश

महात्मा गांधी अन्तरराष्ट्रीय हिन्दी विश्वविद्यालय, वर्धा 442 001, महाराष्ट्र

सुल्तानिया रोड, मोतिया पार्क, भोपाल 462 001, मध्य प्रदेश

www.vaniprakashan.in
marketing@vaniprakashan.in
sales@vaniprakashan.in

VANI HINDI-ANGREZI KOSH
Compiled & Edited by Prof. T.N. Shukla & Dr. Bhavdev Pandey

ISBN : 978-93-88434-10-2
Dictionary

© वाणी प्रकाशन

प्रथम संस्करण 2019

मूल्य : ₹ 995

इस पुस्तक के किसी भी अंश को किसी भी माध्यम में प्रयोग
करने के लिए प्रकाशक से लिखित अनुमति लेना अनिवार्य है।

सिटी प्रेस, दिल्ली-110 095 में मुद्रित

वाणी प्रकाशन का लोगो मक़बूल फ़िदा हुसेन की कूची से

प्रस्तावना

आज हिन्दी ने अपनी परिभाषा बड़ी कर ली है। इस सन्दर्भ में यदि आज हिन्दी को परिभाषित करना है तो इसकी परिभाषा होगी, "जिसे संघ की राजभाषा के रूप में हिन्दीभाषी राज्यों में मातृभाषा के रूप में, अहिन्दीभाषी राज्यों में द्वितीय भाषा के रूप में और विदेशों में अन्य भाषा के रूप में प्रयोग किया जाता है उसे हम हिन्दी कहेंगे।" इस रूप में आज हिन्दी सीमित (हिन्दीभाषी राज्यों के सन्दर्भ में), व्यापक सन्दर्भ में अहिन्दीभाषी राज्यों के सन्दर्भ में, बेहतर रूप में देश के बाहर विभिन्न देशों में व्यवहार किये जाने के रूप में, इस प्रकार से हिन्दी वैश्विक सन्दर्भ में बहुत आगे निकल चुकी है। इन समस्त सन्दर्भों को ध्यान में रखते हुए हिन्दी के सभी अध्येताओं के लिए एक मानक हिन्दी-अँगरेज़ी कोश की आवश्यकता बहुत दिनों से महसूस की जा रही थी। प्रस्तुत कोश इन्हीं आवश्यकताओं को ध्यान में रखकर तैयार किया गया है।

इस कोश में उपलब्ध हिन्दी एवं अँगरेज़ी शब्दों का चयन विभिन्न मान्य एवं प्रामाणिक स्रोतों से किया गया है। अर्थ-निर्धारण की दृष्टि से सभी प्रसिद्ध हिन्दी--अँगरेज़ी कोशों से सहायता ली गयी है। किन्तु सन्दिग्ध स्थलों के निराकरण एवं संगत पर्यायों के चयन की दृष्टि से पूर्व प्रकाशित अँगरेज़ी-संस्कृत एवं अँगरेज़ी-हिन्दी कोशों से भी सहायता ली गयी है। आज के समय में प्रयुक्त हो रहे ऐसे अनेक शब्दों को इस कोश में सम्मिलित किया गया है, जो पूर्व के कोशों में उपलब्ध नहीं होते हैं।

द्विभाषी कोशों में सर्वाधिक कठिन कार्य शब्दों की ठीक और पूर्ण व्याख्या करना है। इस कोश में संगत अँगरेज़ी पर्यायों के साथ ही जहाँ कहीं भी आवश्यकता प्रतीत हुई है, महत्त्वपूर्ण शब्दों को व्याख्यायित किया गया है।

प्रस्तुत कोश में शब्दों के अर्थ-समूहों को संकेतित करने की दृष्टि से संख्याएँ दी गयी हैं और इस बात की सावधानी रखी गयी है कि एक प्रकार का अर्थबोध कराने वाले पर्याय ये कही संख्या के अन्तर्गत आ जायें। कहीं-कहीं अर्थ-व्याप्ति के कारण एक ही शब्द को अन्य अर्थ-समूहों में भी देना पड़ा है। इस कोश को उच्चारण और व्युत्पत्ति की दृष्टि से प्रामाणिक बनाने की पूरी चेष्टा की गयी है। मेरा विश्वास है कि यह कोश हिन्दी के सभी अध्येताओं के लिए उपयोगी सिद्ध होगा।

कोश को यथासमय पूरी तत्परता के साथ प्रकाशित करने के लिए वाणी प्रकाशन के प्रबन्ध निदेशक प्रिय भाई श्री अरुण माहेश्वरी को साधुवाद देता हूँ।

–प्रो. त्रिभुवननाथ शुक्ल

अ-The first letter of the Devnagari script.

अदहैं-will come.

अऊत-a stupid; bachelor; an issueless fellow; a dunce; an idiot.

अऋणी-free from liability.

अंक-a figure; a mark; number; issue (of a publication).

अंकक-an accountant.

अंकगणित-the science of arithmetic; a sum in the science of computation.

अँकड़ना-to curl or to shrink; to become crisp or dry.

अँकड़ा-a hook; hooked implement; an arrowhead.

अँकड़ी-a piece of brick.

अंकन-act or state or marking, writing, drawing etc.

अंकपाली-a nurse; maid female nurse.

अँकवैया-a valuer; appraiser; assessor.

अंकविद्या-mathematics; the science of number; arithmetic.

अंक-संबंधी-numerical; consisting of numbers.

अँकित-spotted; stamped; approved; written.

अंकीय-numerical; concerning numbers.

अँकुड़ी-bent nail; a hook of iron.

अंकुर-an offshoot; germ; bud; hair.

अंकुरक-nest; germination.

अँकुरना-to germinate; to bud.

अंकुश-restraint; control.

अंकुसी-hooked implement; fire-rake; poker.

अंकोड़ा-a large hook.

अँकोर-a bribe; a light meal.

अँकोरना-to embrace; to take to the bosom.

अँखुआ-sprout; shoot.

अँखिया-the eyes; glances.

अंग-body; part of the body; side; aspect; facet; department; part.

अंगज-a daughter.

अंगड़ाई-stretching the limbs; yawning; oscillation.

अंगद-name of the son of Bali.

अंगदान-sacrificing the body; turning the back in battle.

अंगनाई-courtyard.

अँगना-a courtyard from which a house is entered.

अंगन्यास-a religious ceremony in which certain parts of the body are touched and certain are uttered.

अंगभंग-mutilation of some limb of the body.

अंगभूत-constitutive.

अंगरक्षक-body guard.

अंगरक्षा-the protection of body from an attack.

अँगरखा-a long coat worn by men.

अँगरी-protective clothing.

अंगराग-a cosmetic of sandal-wood.

अँगरेज-an inhabitant of England.

अंगलेट-bodily build; physique.

अंगवना-to bear; endure.

अँगवारा-mutual help given in the tillage of land.

अंगविकृति-hysteria.

अंगविक्षेप-twitching of body with a jerk; dancing.

अंग-विच्छेद-amputation; to amputate.

अंगविद्या-physiognomy.

अंगहीन-without a body or its limb.

अंगांगिभाव-the mutual relation of parts of the whole body.

अंगाकड़ी-a small bread-cake baked on hot coal.

अंगार-burning charcoal; embers.

अंगारा-a glowing coal; a spark; cinder; burning matter.

अंगारक-the planet Mars.

अंगारि-a portable fire-pan.

अंगारी-small bits of sugar-cane used for chewing.

अँगिया-bodice; brassier.

अँगरिस-one of the ten Vedic sages.

अंगी-having a body; leading; prominent.

अंगीकरण-adoption.

अंगीकृत-promised; agreed; assured; accepted.

अंगीठी-a pot to keep fire in; furnace; forge.

अंगुल-a finger's breadth; three-fourth of an inch.

अंगुलिपर्व-knuckle.

अंगुलि-finger.

अंगुश्त-pointed out by the finger; famous; notorious; vilified.

अंगुश्ताना-a ring; thimble.

अंगुष्ठ-the big toe.

अँगूठा-the thumb; the great toe.

अँगूठी-finger-ring.

अंगूर-grapes.

अंगेजना-to accept; to endure.

अँगोछना-to wipe the body with a towel.

अँगोछा-towel (for drying the body) a cloth.

अँगोरा-mosquito.

अँग्रेजी-English; British; western.

अँघड़ा-metal toe-ring.

अँघस-an offence; sin.

अँघिया-a sieve with fine mesh.

अँघौरी-prickly heat.

अंचकैं sudden.

अँचड़-stupidity; foolishness.

अँचल-border region; tract; zone; the border or hem at the end of or shawl.

अँचित-adored or respected.

अँचवना-to gargle after eating something.

अँचवाना-to supply water for gargling the mouth after eating.

अँछर-a mystical or magical word or formula; spell; charm.

अँजन-lizard; the elephant of the South West quarter; collyrium applied to the eyelashes; ink; night.

अंजनसार-collyrium.

अंजनहारी-a inflamed gland or sty on the eyelids.

अंजना[1]-the rice crop in the hills which sown in March-April and cut in August-September.

अंजना[2]-a stye on the eye.

अंजना[3]-mythological name of the mother of Hanuman.

अंजनी-delusion; woman perfumed with sandalwood; a small boil on the eyelid; a sty; the mother name of Hanuman.

अंजबार-used medicinally in treating colds and haemorrhage.

अंजली-two handfuls; this cavity is used as a measure which is nearly 16.

अंजवाता-to have collyrium applied to the eyes.

अंजही-the market where corn and cereals are sold.

अंजाम-result; upshot; conclusion; completion; end. to finish; to manage; to carry out (a task).

अंजीर-a fig-tree and its fruits.

अँजोर-full of light; clear; bright.

अँजोरी-moon light; a shining light.

अंजुमन-assembly; a society.

अंजूल-a tear.

अँटना-filled up; to fit in properly.

अंटा-a marble; a skein; a ball; a spool of thread; a bobbin; a billiard bowl.

अंटिया-an egg; upper covering of a fruit.-a small bundle.

अंटी-the space between the fingers; to snatch away another's article by fraud; to cheat or fraud; to deceive.

अंठई-a tick found on dogs.

अंड-testicle; the castor oil plant; the bag containing the testicles; the universe; boundary; the rind or upper covering of a fruit.

अंडगर्भ-vitellus; yolk of an egg.

अंडधारी-oviparous.

अंडवृत्त-an ellipse.

अंडवृद्धि-dropsy of testicle; the disease called.

अंडा-egg.

अंडाकार-egg-shaped; oviform; oval; elliptical.

अंडाकृति-the shape of an egg.

अंडशास्त्र-study relating to birds eggs.

अंडी[1]-a kind of rough silken cloth; castor oil seed.

अंडी[2]-a kind of material.

अँडुआ-animal which is not castrated.

अंडुआना-to castrate a animal.

अंत-the end; finish; completion.

अंतकाल-the time of death; the last breath.

अंतग-a competent person; one who knows everything.

अंतगति-death; final end.

अंतड़ी-entrails; the vitals.

अंतर-difference. & amongst; except; unless; between; without.

अंतरचक्र-a group of relatives; the cardinal points.

अंतरण-transference.

अंतरा-second verse or line of a song. occurring in the midst; or in the interval; except; without; nearly.

अंतरापत-an intermittent fever; tertian ague (fever).

अंतरात्मा-the inward spirit or self; the soul.

अंतराय-difficulty; disturbance.

अंतरालन-spacing.

अंतरासंचार-intercommunication.

अंतरिक्ष-cosmos; the sky; outer space.

अंतरित-secluded; hidden; concealed; placed within.

अँतरिया-tertian ague; an intermittent fever.

अंतरीप-a cape; an island; promontory; headland.

अंतर्गत-internal; included.

अंतर्गृह-inner apartments; harem.

अंतर्गति-mental disposition; emotions of the hearts; earnest desire; inherent feeling.

अंतर्दाह-Cardialgia; heart burn.

अंतर्दृष्टि-clear vision; insight.

अंतर्जात-inland; inbred; inborn; natural; innate.

अंतर्देशीय पत्र-inland letter.

अंतर्देशीय युद्ध-civil-war.

अंतर्जातीय विवाह-endogamy.

अंतर्धान-concealment; evanescence; invisibility.-invisible; vanished.

अंतर्ध्यान-continued thought.

अंतर्निविष्ट-meditated; fixed in the mind.

अंतर्बोध-intuition; knowledge of one's self.

अंतर्भाग-kernel nucleus; internal portion.

अंतर्भाव-internal nature; disposition; inclusion; inherent; concomitance; quietus; final discharge.

अंतर्भावना-deep meditation.

अंतर्भावित-included; hidden.

अंतर्भूत-hidden.

अंत:कोण-internal angle.

अंतर्मुख-having an opening within; opened in the inside.

अंतर्यामी-the Supreme Being; the Almighty.

अंतर्राष्ट्रीय-between different nations; international.

अंतर्लम्ब-a triangle the perpendicular of which falls within it.

अंतर्लीन-drowned; hidden; absorbed; imbibed.

अंतर्वती-a pregnant female.

अंतर्हित-secret; concealed.

अंतस्तप्त-heated; agitated within.

अंतर्सद-a disciple; a pupil; last time.

अंतसमय-a time of death.

अंतस्सलिल-a river whose flow of water is hidden and not visible on the surface.

अंतावरी-the intestines.

अंतावशायी-a ; dwellers on the outskirts of a town; an executioner.

अंतिक-near.

अंतिम-final; last.

अंतें elsewhere.

अंतेवासी-pupil who resides with his tutor; a resident.

अंत:करण-consciousness; the understanding.

अंत:क्षेत्र-enclosure.

अंत:पेटी-the screen which is hung in a theatre.

अंत:प्रवाह-an influx; an infusion.

अंत:पुर-a harem; a seraglio; a thalmus; the inner apartments of a dwelling.

अंत्य-final; last; lowest.

अंत्येष्टि-funeral sacrifice.

अंत्यज-a person of low caste.

अंत्सवर्ण-the final letter of a verse or poem or word.

अंत्याक्षरी-reciting a verse beginning with the same letter which is final letter of a verse recited by another person.

अंत्र-the intestines.

अंदर-inside; within; inwardly.

अंदरून-inner. part of a dwelling; interior.

अंदरी-अंदरूनी-internal; relating to the portion inside.

अंदाज-conjecture; idea.

अंदाजन almost; approximately.

अंदाजा-mental impression; idea.

अंदाज-पट्टी-an estimate of the value of crop.

अंदू, अंदुक-an ornament for the ankles; the chain or rope for fastening and elephant's legs.

अंदेशा-consideration; anxious thought.

अंदोर-disturbance; tumult.

अंदोह-anxiety; trouble.

अंध-darkness; a blind man.

अंधक-a country name; a blind person.

अंधकार-dark.

अंधकूप-a blind well; a well which is over grown with weeds.

अंध खोपड़ी-stupid person.

अंधड़-a violent dust-storm.

अंधतमस-blinding darkness.

अंधता-blindness; folly; benightedness.

अंधपरंपरा-the tradition.

अंधेरी-blind woman.

अँधला-unable to see; blind person.

अंधविश्वास-blind faith.

अंधसैन्य-untrained soldiers.

अंधा-blind; benighted; hoodwinked; foolish; deceived; dim.

अंधाधुंध excessively; ignorantly; unwittingly.

अंधापन-blindness; folly; dimness.

अँधियार-darkness.

अंधियारा-dark; sombre; hazy; obscure; black.

अंधियारी-darkness; storm.

अँधियाला-darkness.

अंधेर-darkness; misfortune; injustice.

अँधेरा-dim; dark.

अँधेरिया-dark night.

अँधेरी-storm; darkness; obscurity; dark night; blinkers.

अँधौरी-prickly heat.

अंध-fowler.

अंब-mango tree or its fruit.

अंबक-bronze; the eye.

अंबर-cloud; clothes; sky.

अँबराई-a mango tree.

अंबरांत-the border of cloth; the horizon.

अंबरीय-war; battle.

अंबरी-resembling ambergris.

अंबल-acid.

अंबष्ट-the offspring of a Brahman father and Vaishya mother.

अंबा-the goddess.

अंबापाली-the dried juice of mangoes in the form of a bread or a flat sheet.

अंबार-heap; store; pile; granary; storehouse.

अंबारी-the canopy or litter used on the back of the elephant.

अंबालिका-a title of the goddess Parvati; mother.

अंबासा-handful of grass or corn cut in reaping.

अंबिका-the title of goddess of Parvati or Durga; mother.

अंबिया-unripe small mango.

अंबु-water plasma; (in hornograms) the figure four.

अंबोह-an assembly; a crowd; a mob; a multitude.

अंभ-water.

अँभोज-the flower of lotus.

अंभोधर-the cloud; the ocean; the sea; the lotus flower.

अँभौरी-prickly heat; water pustules.

अंश-part of the body; part; portion. in part partly.

अंशक-a shearer; a partner; an incarnation; day divider.

अंशपत्र-a deed setting forth the respective shares of property which is allotted to the several members of a family.

अंशांश-sub-division; a degree of latitude.

अंशी-partner; a sharer; a co-heir; one holding a share.

अंशु-rays; ray of light; sunbeam.

अंशुक-upper garment; fine cloth; fine silk wrapper.

अंशुनाभि-the point where pencils of light meet; focus.

अंशुमाली-the sun.

अंस-shoulder; shoulder-blade.

अँसुआ, अँसुवा-tears.

अँसुवाना-filled with tears.

अहं-agitation; sin.

अकंटक-without enemies; free from thorns.

अकंपन-steadiness firmness.

अकंपित-firm; unshaken.

अकच्छ-wearing no loin-cloth; naked.

अकड़-convulsions. crookedness; contortion; pride; strut; conceit. to swagger.

अकड़ैत-an ostentatious person.

अकड़बाई-the cramp in body.

अकड़बाज-pride; strutting.

अकड़ाव-contortion; haughtiness; convolution.

अकथ, अकथनीय-unable to be told or spoken; unspeakable.

अकथक-doubt; suspense.

अकथित-unspoken.

अकथ्य-inexpressible; not to be mentioned.

अकथक-hesitation.

अकन-to listen; to hear.

अकनना-to listen; to hear attentively; to give ear to.

अकना-to be weary of.

अकवक-chatter; nonsense.

अकबत-end of future life; following.

अकबाल-favour; grace; sympathy.

अकर[1]-without hands; exempt from taxes; duty-free.

अकर[2]-difficult; useless; not worth doing.

अकरण-devoid of object; difficult.

अकणीय-not proper.

अकरा¹-costly; best.

अकरा²-a wild grass which chokes young wheat.

अकरास-laziness.

अकरासू-a pregnant woman.

अकर्कस-no hard.

अकर्तव्य-improper or unfit to be done.

अकर्ता-one who does not perform an action.

अकर्तक-without a subject.

अकर्म-bad action.

अकर्मक-intransitive.

अकर्मण्य-unprofitable; useless; good-for-nothing; idle.

अकर्मण्यता-idleness; uselessness.

अकर्मी-a rogue; an evil-does; a sinner; a villain.

अक़ल-mind.

अकलंक-guiltiness.

अकलंकता-spotlessness; purity.

अकल-having no limbs; artless.

अकलखुरा-one who east alone; selfish; jealous.

अकल्पनीय-unimaginable.

अकल्पित-not artificial; real.

अकल्याण-misfortune; unlucky.

अकस-dislike; hatred; ill-will; enmity; hostility.

अकसना-to have ill-will or jealously against; to hate.

अकवाम-communities; peoples; nations.

अकसर generally; often; usually.

अकसीर-highly efficacious or adequate.

अकसरियत-greater part; majority.

अकस्मात accidentally all at once; suddenly.

अकांड-branchless; all of a sudden.

अकांड तांडव-unnecessary frolic.

अकाज in vain; uselessly.

अकाजना-to inflict injury on a person.

अकाट्य-compact; firm; strong; solid; unfit to be rent; incontrovertible.

अकादमी-academy.

अकाम-useless; fruitless; aimless; without desire.

अकामता-freedom from desire.

अकामी-free from desire.

अकाय-unborn; without a body.

अकार-ineffectual; structure.

अकारण-causeless; without reason.

अकारत-of without profit.

अकारथ-useless. in vain.

अकाल-a bad season.

अकाली-a regional political party of Punjab (State of India).

अकास-the sky.

अकासनीम-a parasitic plant found on the tree.

अकासबानी-an oracle; radio; a voice from heaven.

अकिंचन-incapable; stricken; destitute; poor.

अकिल the wisdom.

अक़ीदत-faith; belief.

अकीर्ति-disgrace; infamy; ill-repute; inglorious.

अकुंठ-keen; sharp; quick perception; of nice; indestructible.

अकुताना-to be weary of.

अकुल-without family.

अकुलाहट-unease; weariness; agitation.

अकुलीन-of low birth.

अकुशल misfortune; unlucky; inauspicious.

अकूत-inestimable; unlimited; without idea.

अकृत-not carried through; not made; badly done; not done.

अकृतकार्य-unskilled; unsuccessful.

अकृतज्ञता-ingratitude.

अकृती-incapable; idle.

अकृत्य-a wrongful act.

अकृत्रिम-not made; not artificial.

अकेला alone; merely; simply; singly.

अकेलापन-solitude; singularity; peculiarity; celibacy.

अकेले single; alone.

अकोर-one who receive a bribe or tip from someone.

अकौशल-inaptitude.

अक्कड़-absent-minded; forgetful.

अक्का-an intimate friend; grand sire; father.

अक्खड़-clear-speaking; fearless; quarrelsome; uncivilised.

अक्खा-one of the pair of bags in which grain is packed and put on the back of bullock.

अक्रम-confusion; not in order.

अक्रिय-inactive.

अक्रूर-not cruel; gentle.

अक्ल-intellect; reason; wisdom.

अक्लमंद-intelligent; sensible.

अक्लिष्ट-simple; not difficult to perform.

अक्ली-having to do with mind or intelligence.

अकृत्रिम-not artificial; natural.

अक्ष-a die; axis; yoke; an axle Geog.; latitude.

अक्षपाद-a logician; the name of a sage or Rishi.

अक्षम-incompetent.

अक्षमता-incompetence.

अक्षम्य-unpardonable.

अक्षय-undecaying; permanent; imperishable; external; durable.

अक्षयता-durability; imperishability.

अक्षर-sky; permanent.

अक्षरी-spelling.

अक्षरेखा-axis; axial; terrestrial latitude.

अक्षरौटी-handwriting; alphabet.

अक्षि-the eye (in chrono-grams) the number two.

अक्षिका-eyelet.

अक्षीय-axial.

अक्षुण्ण-whole; entire; unbroken; continuing.

अक्षोनि-an army.

अक्षोभ-calm and quiet; peaceful.

अक्षोहिणी-an army.

अक्स-reverse; shadow; reflection; a reflected image.

अखंडित-not refuted; unbroken; continuous; unlimited.

अखंड़्य-strong; solid.

अखंज-distasteful; unfit to be eaten.

अखड़ैत-wrestler.

अख़नी-a broth made from the juice of boiled meat.

अख़बार-newspaper; newsprint.

अख़बारी-having to do with newspapers; or with journalism; newspaper language.

अखय-imperishable.

अखरना-to irritate; to be disagreeable.

अखरोट-walnut.

अखर्व-long; abundant; large.

अख़लाक़-morals; ethic; friendliness.

अखाड़ा-a place for wrestling; a ring; stadium; circus; amphitheatre; place of assembly; congregation.

अखाद्य-unfit to be eaten; forbidden food; not to be eaten inedible.

अखिल-all-India.

अखीर-completion; end.

अखूट-much; whole; entire; undiminished; imperishable.

अखेट-a sportsman; a hunter.

अखोर-elegant; beautiful; noble.

अखोरा-decanter; a two-handled vessel used for keeping wine; oil.

अखोह-uneven ground.

अख्यात-unknown; infamous.

अख्याति-infamy; obscurity.

अख्यान-a story or tale.

अगड-headless and limbless trunk (of body).

अगंभीर-superficial.

अग-unable to move.

अगज-produced from mountain.

अगट-a butcher's stall.

अगटना-to collect; to assemble.

अगड़बगड़-meaningless; promiscuous; indiscriminate.

अगणनीय-unable to be counted; countless; innumerable.

अगणित-uncounted.

अगण्य-trifling; commonplace; incalculable; innumerable.

अगत-the hereafter; bad state; the future.

अगति-dishonoured; not esteemed; disgraced.

अगतिक-having no shelter; helpless.

अगती-wicked; immoral.

अगनित-innumerable.

अगत्तर-future; coming.

अगम-unattainable; inaccessible; inapproachable; inconceivable; deep; impervious; incomprehensible.

अगर[1]-the aloe-tree and its wood.

अगर[2]-if.

अगरचे-even if; although.

अगराना-to advance; to go forward; to go ahead.

अगरबत्ती-incense-stick.

अगरी-staple of iron or wood attached to a door to fasten it.

अगल-बगल-to put away; to put aside.

अगला-next; following.

अगवना-to go ahead; to go forward; to be ready; to advance.

अगवाड़ा-portion of corn set apart for village; the front part of a house.

अगवान-one who goes forward in welcome.

अगवार-first corn taken from a heap of newly thrashed grain; corn lost during winnowing.

अगस्त-the month of August.

अगस्त्य-a sage of Hindu legend who is said to have drunk off the ocean.

अगह-beyond description; difficult; hard to accomplish.

अगहन-the ninth lunar of the month of Hindu year. (November-December).

अगहनी-having to do with the month Ag'han (as crops).

अगहर-before; in front of; in the presence of.

अगहुँड-forward; further on.

अगाऊ-and advance of money.

अगाड़ी-first action; first attack; advance as pay.

अगाध-bottomless; unfathomable; profound; very deep.

अगार-the front part of a house or a thing; covetousness.

अगासी-a terrace in front of a room of a house.

अगाह-abundant; very deep.

अगाही-previous knowledge.

अगिनित-countless; incalculable.

अगिया-name of a demon ruling over fire.

अगियारी-a receptacle for the sacred fire; kindling the sacred fire.

अगुआ-a leader.

अगुआई-guidance; leadership.

अगुआना-to act as a guide; to appoint a leader.

अगुण-with good qualities; unqualified.

अगुप्त-unconcealed; not hidden.

अगुरु-having no preceptor; light; not heavy.

अगुसरना-to proceed; to go forward or advance.

अगूठना-to cover; to surround.

अगूठा-periphery; boundary; limit; circumference.

अगूढ़-without good qualities.

अगता in front of; before.

अगेटी-brazier; a chafing dish.

अगेही-homeless.

अगोचर-not perceptible; not evident; unseen; mysterious.

अगोट-a support; a screen; to confine.

अगोटना-to accept; to obstruct; to imprison; to conceal; to surround; to select.

अगोड़ी-an advance of money.

अगोर-one who guards a crop.

अगौढ़-the top of sugarcane which is cut up for the sake of seed; advance of money.

अगौर-advance of rent paid by the cultivator to the land-holder in the months of Jeth and Asarth.

अग्नि-the god of fire.

अग्निक-the lady-bird; fireman; an insect of scarlet colour.

अग्नि कीट-a salamander; an insect supposed to live in fire.

अग्निकुमार-the son of fire.

अग्नि कुंड-a fire-pit; hearth.

अग्नि कोण-the South-East quarter.

अग्निक्रिया-cremation; the burning of the dead.

अग्निक्रीड़ा-firework.

अग्निज-digestive; appetising; produced from fire.

अग्नि-जिह्व-a god.

अग्नि ज्वाला-the goddess of hearth; flame of fire.

अग्नि त्रेता-the three sacred fires of the Hindus taken collectively.

अग्निदाह-burning of a corpse; burning.

अग्नि दीपक-improving digestion.

अग्नि देवता-Vulcan; the god of fire.

अग्नि परीक्षा-checking the purity of silver or gold by putting them in fire.

अग्निपूजक-a fire-worshipper.

अग्निपूजा-fire-worship.

अग्निपूर्ण-full of fire; fiery.

अग्निप्रस्तर-flint; fire-stone.

अग्निबाव-erysipelas; an eruptive disease.

अग्निबोट-a steam boat.

अग्निभोजक-a fire-eater.

अग्निमंथ-the Arani wood which is used for kindling fire by means of attrition.

अग्निमुख-a Brahman; a god.

अग्निरक्षक-not burnt by fire; fire proof.

अग्निलिंग-divination by the colour of the flame of fire.

अग्निशाला-a place where consecrated fire.

अग्निष्टोम-a ceremony in which oblations are given to fire.

अग्नि संस्कार-purifying a thing by burning it in fire; the burning of a dead body.

अग्निहोत्र-the ceremony consisting of offering oblations to the consecrated fire.

अग्निहोत्री-a surname of Brahmans; one who performs oblations to sacrificial fire.

अग्न्यस्त्र-a missile which emits fire; artillery.

अग्यारी-throwing incense and other things in fire.

अग्र-first; prior; foremost; beginning.

अग्रणी-a leader.

अग्रिम-first; chief.

अघ-guilt; crime; wickedness; suffering.-sinful.

अघट-impossible; difficult; not happening; unworthy.

अघटित-which has not happened; improbable; unit; unworthy.

अघन-no compact or solid.

अघनाशक-destroyer of sin; expiatory; purifying.

अघवाना-to feel to the fill; to gratify fully; to satiate.

अघहर्ता-the remover of sin.

अघाई-surfeit; satiety; fullness.

अघाट-land which is held in perpetuity but is not alienable.

अघारि-an epithet of Lord .

अघी-wicked; guilty; sinful.

अघोर-a title of Shiva; fine; splendid; not terrible.

अघोरी-a member of the ashore community.

अघोष-without sound; noiseless.

अचंभा-surprise bewilderment; a wonder.

अचक-astonishment.

अचकन-a long coat.

अचकरी-sportiveness; wickedness; wantonness.

अचक्का-unknown.

अचक्षु-blind; without eyes.

अचगरी-lasciviousness; misbehaviour.

अचण्ड-gentle; not passionate.

अचतुर-not cunning or clever; unskilful.

अचना-to wash and cleanse the mouth after eating anything.

अचपल-clam; not unsteady; still.

अचपली-playfulness; flirtatiousness.

अचर-inanimate; constant; immovable.

अचरज-surprise; a miracle.

अचरा-fixed; not moving; changeless; firm; constant.

अचल-tenement; immovable property.

अचला-the earth.

अचव-to sip water; to rinse the hands and mouth before or after eating.

अचवन-same as the act of sipping water.

अचाका suddenly.

अचानक all of a sudden; unexpectedly; suddenly.

अचारी-a kind of pickle made of peeled mangoes; a pot of keeping pickles.

अचालन-operation of a project or a scheme.

अचाहा-loveless; disinterested.

अचाही-disinterested.

अचिक्कन-rough; un-polished.

अचिंत-heedless; free of care.

अचिना-freedom from care or anxiety; slight; heedlessness; neglect.

अचिंता-heedlessness; disregard.

अचिन्त्य-unimaginable; inconceivable.

अचित्-soon; devoid of sense.

अचिर-not of long date; near (future); brief; recent.

अचूक-unfailing; certain; infallible; unerring.

अचेत-stupid; senseless; dead; unaware; thoughtless.

अचेतन-state of unconsciousness.

अचेष्ट-inert.

अचैतन्य-irrational; without sensation or consciousness.

अचैन-uneasy restless.

अचोना-a drinking pot; a cup.

अच्छ-the clean; good; the eye; a rosary.

अच्छा-good; excellent; fine; nice.

अच्छाई-goodness; virtue.

अच्छापन-virtue; quality; excellence.

अच्छाविच्छा-robust; hale and hearty; selected.

अच्छोत in plenty; much.

अच्छर-a syllable; a letter.

अच्युत-fixed; not fallen; imperishable; immortal.

अछक-hungry; not satiated.

अछकना not to be satisfied.

अछत-crownless.

अछताना-पछताना-to repent.

अछन-long duration of time.

अछरा-a fairy.

अछरौटी-the alphabet.

अछवाना-to cleanse; to decorate.

अछूत-untouched; untouchable.

अछूता-not used; fresh; unpolluted.

अछेव-

अछेह-continuous; plenty.

अछोप-coverless; naked; mean.

अजंट-an agent.

अज-unborn.

अजगर-a large snake; a dragon; a python; a boa-constrictor.

अजगरी-an indolent life.

अजगुत-marvellous.

अजगैब-an unknown place; future condition.

अजड़-a living body.

अजन-self-existing; eternal.

अजनबी-a stranger; a foreigner.

अजन्म-unborn.

अजपा-unpronounceable; ineffable; unutterable.

अजब-astonishing.

अजमूद-celery.

अजमोद-a green culinary herb; parsley; caraway.

अजय-not victorious; defeat.

अजया-the intoxicating hemp shrub.

अजय्य-invincible; insuperable.

अजर-not subject to age or decay; ever young.

अजरायल-long-lived.

अजस-scandal; ill repute.

अजसी-scandalous; disreputable.

अजस्त्र-unbroken; continual.

अजहू-immediately; even today.

अजा-a she-goat; a nanny goat; the unreality of the universe.

अजात-undeveloped; unborn.

अजान-inattentiveness; simplicity.

अजानी-innocence; ignorance.

अजामिल-a sinful Brahman mentioned in the who obtained salvation by uttering the name of his son Narayan at the time of his death.

अजाय-unfit; improper.

अजायब-in wonders.-museum.

अजार-sickness; illness.

अजित-invincible; unconquered; unsurpassed.

अजितेन्द्रिय-sensual; lewd; one who has no control over his mind and senses.

अजिन-the hide of an antelope.

अजिर-the courtyard of a house.

अज़ीज़-dear; beloved; excellent.

अजीब-wonderful; strange.

अज़ीम-great; large; vast.

अजीर्ण-indigestion; surfeit.

अजीव-lifeless; dead; deprived of life.

अजेय-not to be subdued; unconquerable.

अजोत[1]-uncultivated (land).

अजोत[2]-not bright; dim; dull.

अजोता-the last day of the month of on which bullocks are not yoked to work.

अजौं-even now; up till now.

अज्ञता-ignorance; stupidity; dullness of perception.

अज्ञात-unknowing; unsophisticated; unexpected.

अज्ञान-ignorance; insensibility; stupidity.

अज्ञानी-a foolish person; unwise; ignorant.

अज्ञेय-unknowable.

अझर-not raining or dropping.

अटंबर-a crowd; multitude.

अटक-affair; check; stoppage.

अटकना-to be stopped; to falter; to delay; to linger; to hindered.

अटकरना-to guess to estimate.

अटकल-conjecture; an unsupported estimate; guessing. by guess; at random; approximately.

अटका-earthen vessel in which food is prepared for the public at the door of the Jagannath temple in Puri; cooked rice or money offered at the temple of Jagan-nath.

अटखट-nonsense; meaningless.

अटखेल-playful; wanton; coquettish; trifling in love.

अटट्-coarse; strong.

अटन-journey; going about; wandering.

अटना-to fill up; to be contained in; to wander or walk about.

अटपट-nonsensical; restless; confused.

अटपटी-naughtiness.

अटब्बर-vain show; pride; household; family.

अटल-fixed; unchangeable; steadfast; lasting.

अटा-heap; pile; an upper room.

अटाटूट-unbroken.

अटाल-tower; minaret.

अटाला-pile; lumber; miscellaneous effects.

अटूट-not liable to be broken; strong; inexhaustible; not fragile.

अटेक-unsupported.

अटेरन-a reel or skein of thread; the lounge or circle of horse.

अटोक-unrestricted; unhindered; unquestioned; unrestrained.

अटोल-rude; uncivil.

अट्टहास-a horse-laugh.

अठंग-a combination of eight things.

अठ-eight.

अठकौसल-a conference; a council; a meeting.

अठखेलपन-playfulness; flirtatiousness.

अठखेली-playfulness; wantonness; gaiety.

अठगुना-eightfold; octuple.

अठत्तर-seventy-eight.

अठपहला-octagonal.

अठपाव-mischief; vexatious.

अठमासी-a gold-coin weighing eight mashes.

अठहत्तर-seventh-eight.

अठाई-naughty; wicked.

अठान-work unfit to be settled; quarrel; enmity; difficult work; harassment.

अठाना-to harass; to vex; to tease.

अठेल-stalwart; not to be pushed out of place; or pushed about.

अठोठ-vain show; pomp.

अठोतरी-a rosary of 108 beads used for counting mantras.

अड़ंग-a warehouse where goods are sold wholesale.

अड़ंगा-a mode of wrestling with the feet; obstacle; obstruction.

अड़ंगी-unyielding; obstinate.

अड़काना-to cause to obstruct.

अड़गड़ा-place for halting bullock carts; a stall for cattle.

अड़गोड़ा-a piece of wood tied to the neck of cattle (to prevent them straying).

अड़चन-obstacle; hindrance.

अड़दार-obstinate; spurred; haughty.

अड़ना-to stick; to stop; to be obstinate; to intervene; to jib.

अड़बग-crooked; difficult; uneven; inconvenient; arduous.

अडसट्टा-estimate; rough calculation.

अड़हाया-tares; oats; weeds.

अड़ा-a birds perch; roost.

अड़ाड़-a bank of a river or pond; an outhouse for cattle; a heap or pile.

अड़ान-a halting or resting place; encampment.

अड़ाना-by force.

अड़ारी-heap; heap of fire-wood for sale; pile.

अड़ार-pile; a heap.

अड़ारी-heap; pile; mass.

अडिग-firm; unshakable; immovable.

अड़ियल-an obstinate person.

अड़ी-stop; a check; halt.

अडुआ-jibing as a horse; mulish; obstinate.

अडूसा-used medicinally; a shrub.

अड़ोल-fixed; immovable.

अड्डा-a place of meeting; a prominent place; a resort; a halting place; stand.

अढ़तिया-an agent.

अढाई-two and a half times.

अढिया-a hod; an iron port for carrying mortar.

अढोना-an assigned task.

अढक-a stumble; to take support of.

अणि-edge or point of a sharp instrument or weapon.

अणु-an atom; a molecule.

अणुक-microscope; atomic; minute.

अणुवीक्षण यंत्र-a microscope.

अतक distress; trouble.

अतंद्रिक-restless; nimble; agile; smut.

अतएव-therefore; whereas; thence.

अतट-precipitous; very steep.

अतनु-bodiless; ; the god of love; the bodiless one.

अतर-perfume box; scent (of flowers); fragrance.

अतरसों-next to the day after tomorrow.

अतर्क-illogical.

अतर्क्य-beyond thought or reason (as the supreme being).

अतर्कित-not within the province of logical inquiry; sudden; unexpected.

अतर्पित-unsatisfied; dissatisfied; not contended.

अतल-bottomless.

अतलसी-made of satin; like satin.

अतसी-linseed.

अतवार-Sunday;

अता-to give; to grant.

अताई-musician or dancer; a self-taught singer.

अति-supreme; exceeding; very much.

अतितापन-overheating.

अधिक-overmuch.

अतिकाय-of huge size; gigantic.

अतिकाल-protracted time.

अतिकृच्छ-a great trouble; a fast of six days.

अतिक्रम-beyond limit; lapse; contrary behaviour; trespass; deviation.

अतिक्रान्त-surpassing; overstepping; exceeding.

अतिक्रुद्ध-spitfire; wrathful.

अतिगर्वित-arrogant; very proud.

अतिगुप्त-hidden from view; very secret; closely concealed.

अतिगूढ़-abstruse; concealed; not obvious.

अतिघृणा-to hate intensely; abomination; detestation.

अतिचकित-extremely curious.

अतिजीवन-survival.

अतिजीवी-living very long; surviving; a survivor.

अतिजीर्ण-decayed; very old.

अतितीव्र-towering; the highest female voice.

अतित्रस्त-rack rent.

अतितीक्ष्ण-very keen; pungent; severe; sharp; piquant.

अतिथि-a guest; hospitable.

अतिदयालु-very kind; indulgent; very yielding.

अतिदरिद्र-very poor; needy.

अतिदान-a munificent gift; munificence.

अतिदाह-great inflammation in the body; violent heat.

अतिदीन-very distressed or needy; very miserable.

अतिदुखी-despicable; miserable; contemptible.

अतिदूर-most remote; ultimate.

अतिद्वेष-intense; malignity; hatred; virulence.

अतिदुष्ट-very wicked; atrocious; horrible; outrageous.

अतिदोष-a great crime or fault committed by a person.

अतिधनाढ्य-very wealthy or rich; multi-millionaire.

अतिधृति-a metre of nineteen syllables in Sanskrit.

अति नम्रता-subservience.

अति निकट close by; very near.

अति निपुण-adroit; adept.

अति निष्ठुर-diabolical.

अति न्यून-rock bottom.

अति पराक्रम-great strength; valour; intrepidity; courage.

अति परिचय-intimacy.

अति पवित्र-a Puritan.

धअति प्रतिष्ठा-worship.

अति प्रमुदित-rapturous.

अति प्रवण-steep.

अति प्रशंसा-to exalt; to extol; to panegyric.

अति प्रसन्न-to rejoice greatly; wreathed in smiles.

अति प्राचीन-very old; immemorial; very ancient.

अतिप्रिय-honey-sweet.

अतिप्रेम-adoration.

अतिपात-breach; lapse trespass; disorder; obstacle; obstruction.

अतिपातक-a heinous sin.

अतिपातकी-one who is guilty of a heinous crime; a heinous or great sinner.

अतिपान-excessive drinking; intoxicating.

अतिपीड़ा-excessive pain; suffering; great agony.

अति पूज्य-venerable; sacrosanct.

अति बल-very powerful.

अतिबार very frequently.

अतिबेल-excessive; extremely; unlimited.

अतिभक्षक-gluttonous; a voracious person.

अतिभार-great burden.

अति भोग-time of mirth; excess of enjoyment.

अतिभोजन-surfeit.

अतिमुक्त-having attained final beatitude or salvation.

अतिमपुर-luscious; very sweet.

अतियोग्य-very worthy; very deserving; most suitable.

अतिरंजन-exaggeration.

अतिरंजित-exaggerated.

अतिरथी-one who can fight a host of men.

अतिरिक्त-exceeding; extra; surplus.

अतिरेक-excess; surplus.

अतिलोलुप-insatiable.

अतिवक्ता-a great talker; loquacious;

अतिवाद-vain glory; boasting; bragging; ostentation.

अतिवादी-extremist.

अतिविकट-very fierce; horrible; formidable.

अतिविनी-very much.

अतिविद्वान-profound (scholar).

अतिवृद्ध-dotard.

अतिविष-an antidote to poison.

अतिविषा-a medical plant.

अतिविस्तृत-much extended; oceanic.

अतिवृष्टि-a great flood.

अतिव्यग्र-restless; perturbed; impatient.

अतिव्ययी-lavish; prodigal.

अतिशक्त-very powerful.

अतिशक्ति-great strength.

अतिशय-very much; excessive.

अतिश्रम-overwork.

अतिशीघ्र quickly; presently.

अतिशेष-balance.

अतिशयता-abundance; excess.

अतिसंचय-great accumulation; a large quantity.

अतिसतर्क-meticulous.

अतिशेर-loin-hearted; brave.

अतिश्रेष्ठ-transcendent.

अतिशोध्य-overdue.

अतिसंसर्ग-intimacy.

अतिसंधान-transgression; deception; violation of trust.

अतिसमीप-approximate.

अतिसामान्य-common place; hackneyed; used too much.

अतिसार-dysentery; diarrhoea.

अतिस्फीति-hyper inflation.

अतिस्पष्ट-glaring; explicit.

अतिहर्ष-great joy.

अतिहानि-immense or great loss.

अतिहास-a violent laugh; a horse-laugh.

अतिसूक्ष्म-imperceptible.

अतीत-past; former.

अतीव[1]-& very much; exceedingly; excessively; much.

अतीव[2]-dull; stupid.-a stupid or dull person.

अतुरा-impatient; to be restless.

अतुराई-hurry; haste; fickleness; quickness.

अतुराना-to be in a fix; to be in hurry or haste.

अतुल-immeasurable; unequalled.

अतुलित-not weighed boundless; incomparable.

अतुल्य-dissimilar; unequalled; immeasurable.

अतूथ-extraordinary; queer.

अतृप्त-unsatisfied; restless.

अतेज़ा-dim; dark; dull.

अतोर-unbreakable; strong.

अत्तार-a druggist; an apothecary; a perfumer.

अत्यल्प-trivial; insignificant.

अत्यंत-endless; vest; excessive; extreme.

अत्यतिक-wandering.

अत्यधिक-extreme; excessive.

अत्यय-passing away; death.

अत्यर्थ-exorbitant; excessive.

अत्यल्प-very little; a small particle.

अत्यम्ल-very acid (in taste).

अत्याचार-aggression; outrage; crime; offence; atrocity.

अत्याधुनिक-sophisticated.

अत्यानन्द-ineffable bliss; ecstasy.

अत्यावश्यक-extremely urgent; vitally important.

अत्याज्य-unfit to be abandoned.

अत्युक्त-described at length.

अत्युक्ति-hyperbole; exaggeration.

अत्युत्तम-best; rare; good; first class; superfine; superlative.

अत्युग्र-very difficult; very violent; very keen or sharp.

अत्र in this place.

अत्रक-pertaining to this world; terrestrial; wordily.

अतृप्त-insatiable.

अतीत-fore time.

अतुल्य-unrivalled; incomparable.

अथ-further; so; thus. however.

अथऊ-food which Jains takes before sunset.

अथक-unwearied; vigilant indefatigable.

अथरा-a large earthen tub or wide mouthed vessel.

अथवा or rather; or even.

अथाई-a place where people hold a meeting.

अथाना-to sound the depth of water; to make a search of.

अथाह-imponderable; beyond a man's depth; bottomless.

अथित-wavering; unstable.

अथिर-unfixed; vacillating.

अथोर-much; not little.

अदंक-fear; dread.

अदंड-not deserving; exempt from punishment; unpunished.

अदंत-having no teeth; toothless.

अदंभ-devoid of ostentation or arrogance; natural; true.

अदग-pure; clear; untouched; unpolluted.

अदद-a number; a figure.

अदन-the act of eating; food; the garden of Eden.

अदना-low; humble; base; insignificant.

अदब-politeness; good breeding; etiquette; respectfulness. intentionally; knowingly; certainly.

अदम-non-existence; lack.

अदम्य-irrepressible.

अदंभ्र-exceeding; very much.

अदय-merciless; cruel; unfeeling.

अदया-cruelty; mercilessness.

अदरक-green ginger.

अदराना-to boast; to act in an affected.

अदरावन-persuasion.

अदर्श-unseen.

अदर्शन-invisibility; disappearance; absence.

अदर्शनीय-clumsy; ugly.

अदल-justice.

अदवान (अदवायन)-the string which is used for tightening up the tape of a bedstead.

अदहन-water set to boil for the purpose of cooking food in it.

अदांत-toothless; without teeth (said of a beast).

अदा-(manner of) performing; performance.

अदाई-deceitful; misleading.

अदाय-without blemish; defectless; clear; unspotted; spotless.

अदान-unknown; ignorant; greed; miser.

अदानी-stingy; miserly; illiberal; niggardly.

अदालत-a court of justice; tribunal.

अदावँ-difficulty; doubt.

अदावत-ill-will; hatred; malice. maliciously.

अदाह्य-fire-proof; incombustible; unable to be burnt.

अदित-the Sun.

अदिति-the earth; name of goddess; boundless.

अदिन-an inauspicious or unlucky day; misfortune.

अदिव्य-worldly; common.

अदिस्टि-invisible.

अदीठ-unseen; secret.

अदृढ़-not fixed or firm.

अदियमान-unfit to be given.

अदृन्द-calm; without an equal; matchless.

अदूरदर्शिता-improvidence.

अदूरदर्शी-pure; spotless; uncontaminated.

अदृश्य-invisible; not to be seen.

अदृष्ट-unforeseen; secret.

अदेख-not seen; hidden.

अदेखी-unseen; jealous.

अदेय-not to be given. improper or unfit to be given; or transferred.

अदोष-innocent; guiltless; without blemish; faultless.

अद्‌र्ध-half of anything.

अद्‌धा-a half; a halfbottle; a half piece of counterfoil.

अद्‌भुत-wonderful; supernatural; astonishing; a marvel; remarkable; strange.

अद्य-now; today.

अद्यापि even; toady.

अद्रक-ginger.

अद्रि-mountain; rock; stone.

अद्रिकी-knob.

अदृढ़ संधि-rickets.

अदृश्य-viewless; invisible.

अदृष्ट-fortune; luck.

अद्रावत्व-indissolubility.

अद्रोह-moderate; peaceful; innocuous.

अद्‌वन्द्‌व-free from strife; tranquil; quiet; undisturbed.

अद्‌वितीय-unique; unequalled; incomparable; without a second.

अद्‌वेष-inoffensive; harmless.

अद्‌वैत-single; undivided; peerless.

अध: down; downward; below.

अधंग-palsy affecting only one half of the body.

अध:पतन-the fall of a thing from a height; downfall; ruin.

अधपात-misfortune; downfall; destruction.

अध-in compound-half.

अधकचरा-half-ripe; incomplete; incompetent.

अधाकपारी-pain in the side of the head; hemicrania.

अधकरी-half the tax or rent which is remitted at a fixed period; an instalment of eight annas in the rupee.

अधकहा-half-uttered; indistinctly spoken; half-spoken.

अधखिला-half-bloomed (flower); half-open.

अधखुला-half-open.

अधगदरा-half-ripe.

अधघट-not fully understood.

अधचरा-half-grazed or eaten.

अधड़ा-baseless; without foundation; groundless; nonsense; disconnected.

अधन-not having wealth; destitute; needy.

अधन्य-unfortunate; infelicitous; prosperous.

अधपई-a weight consisting of two .

अधपका-half-cooked; half-ripe.

अधपन्ना-counterfoil.

अधबटाई-division of produce in equal shares.

अधबना-half-made; incomplete; unfinished; partly accomplished; imperfect.

अधवा-the middle portion of a thing; half way.

अधम-vile; inferior; lowly; wretched; base.

अधमरा-half (almost); dead.

अधमर्ण-a debtor.

अधमाधम-extremely wicked or sinful; most mean; roguish.

अधमुआ-half dead.

अधर[1]-not able to be caught; not caught or held.

अधर[2]-an empty space; the space between heaven or earth; suspended at a distance.

अधरज-the redness of lips.

अधरपान-the kissing of the lower lip of a female.

अधरम-impiety.

अधरामृत-the moisture of the lower lip.

अधर्म-crime; sin; guilt; impiety; unjustly; immorality.

अधर्मचारी-of irreligious behaviour.

अधर्मात्मा-wicked; vicious; irreligious; immoral; sinful.

अधर्मी-sinful; immoral; criminal; wicked; irreligious.

अधस्-below; downward; down.

अंधाधुंध-blinding; excessive.

अधावट-so much thickened (said of milk) that only half the quantity remains.

अधार-support.

अधार्मिक-wicked; unjust; iniquitous.

अधिक-utmost; more; additional; excessive; abundant; plentiful.

अधिकतम-maximum; huge; greatest.

अधिकतर-frequently; greater.

अधिकत्व-अधिकता-aggravation; superiority; affluence.

अधिकमास-an intercalary month in the year.

अधिकरण-support; base; section; a tribunal; commission.

अधिकर्म-management; supervision.

अधिका-to increase.

अधिकांग-having an extra limb in the body.

अधिकांश-greater part or portion; extensively; majority; for the most part.

अधिकाई-great amount; abundance; supremacy.

अधिकाधिक-more and more.

अधिकाना-to increase; to augment; to aggrandise.

अधिकायत-to exceed; to be plentiful.

अधिकायु-over-age.

अधिकार-freedom of action; power; government rule; authority.

अधिकारी-a proprietor; ruler; an officer; an authority.

अधिक्रम-hierarchy.

अधिकृत-taken in occupation.

अधिकृति-possession of authority; or right.

अधिगत-acquired; known; learnt or studied.

अधिगम-acquiring; knowledge; finding judgement (in law).

अधिग्रहण-requisition.

अधिचित्र-overlay.

अधिनायक-lord; chief; commander; leader.

अधिनियम-act.

अधिनियमन-enactment of legislation.

अधिनिर्णय-adjudication; award.

अधिपति-monarch; leader; lord; sovereign.

अधिप्रमाणित-authenticated.

अधिप्रभार-surcharge.

अधिप्रौढ़-advanced.

अधिमत-verdict.

अधिमांस-a fleshy excrescence; a cancer of the eye.

अधिया-ownership of one-half of a village; half portion.

अधियाना-to halve; to divide; to be halved.

अधियार-the sharer of half the land.

अधिरथ-supreme ruler; emperor; a suzerain; a potentate.

अधिराज-monarch; an emperor.

अधिरोपण-imposition (as of a charge).

अधिवक्ता-advocate; lawyer.

अधिवर्ष-a leap year.

अधिवास-a dwelling fragrance; a house; domicile; residence.

अधिवेशन-a sitting; meeting; session; a conflux.

अधिशासी-executive.

अधिशेष-a surplus.

अधिशोषण-absorption.

अधिष्ठाता-a ruler; founder; the supreme being; a protector; governor; one who superintends or guides.

अधिष्ठान-place of dwelling; abode; residence; condition.

अधिष्ठित-residing; placed.

अधिसंख्य-supernumerary; very numerous.

अधिसूचना-notification.

अधिस्फोटक-detonator.

अधिसंख्यक-supernumerary.

अधीक्षक-superintendent.

अधीक्षिका-matron.

अधीत read; studied.

अधीन-obedient; submissive; subordinate; servile; docile.

अधीनस्थ-subordinate.

अधीमान्य-preferred.

अधीर-distracted; hasty; unstable; irresolute; restless; fickle.

अधीश-master; lord; ruler; king.

अधीश्वर-supreme lord or king; emperor.

अधुना even; now; exactly at this moment.

अधूत-a thief; unflinching; fearless.

अधूरा-unfinished; not fully formed; an adolescent; incomplete.

अधेड़-midway between youth and old age; middle-aged.

अधेला-a small copper coin; equal to half a piece.

अधो-down; downward; descent.

अधोतर-a kind of thick cloth.

अधोगम-very low or mean.

अधोभाग-lower; bottom; part.

अधोमार्ग-passage going in an underground cell; the anus.

अधोमुख-topsy-turvy; downcast; headlong.

अधोवर्ती-subjacent.

अधोवायु-emission of wind from anus.

अधोहस्ताक्षरी-undersigned.

अधोबिन्दु-Nadir.

अध्यक्ष-a chief; master; lord; head; superintendent; director; chairman; supervisor; controller; governor; man of rank; ruler.

अध्ययन-perusal; tuition; learning study.

अध्यवसाय-enterprise; resolution; undertaking; diligence; assiduity.

अध्यवसायी-assiduous; persevering.

अध्यात्म-knowledge; spiritual.

अध्यादेश-ordinance.

अध्यापक-a teacher; instructor.

अध्यापकी-the work of teaching.

अध्यापन-instruction; the act of teaching.

अध्यापिका-a governess.

अध्याय-section; chapter; lesson.

अध्यारोप-falsely attributing the attributes of one thing to another.

अध्यारोपित-superimposed.

अध्यास-a false knowledge of a thing; false accusation.

अध्यासित-occupied.

अध्याहार-an ellipsis; understood.

अध्यासीन-seated on the ground.

अध्याहृत-inferred; supplied.

अध्येय-worth studying.

अध्रुव-unfixed; inconstant; uncertain; doubtful.

अनंगना-to lose control over senses and body.

अनंत-infinite; endless; eternal; infinity; everlasting.

अनंतता-boundlessness; eternity; endlessness.

अनंतिम-provisional; not final.

अनंतर-after; next; afterwards.

अनंतरित-not separated; whole; entire.

अनंतराशि-infinite quantity.

अनंत्य-eternity; infinity.

अनंता-boundless; infinite; the Anant cord tied round arm.

अनंद-pleasure.

अनंदना-to be happy or pleased.

अनंदी-happy.

अनंभ-without impediment or obstruction.

अनंत रूप-multiform.

अनंतवीर्य-of infinite strength.

अनंश-excluded from an inheritance; without a share.

अन in sense of without; other; next in place or time.

अनअहिवात-widow-hood.

अनऋतु-change of season; improper season; bad time.

अनकहा-unuttered; untold.

अनक्षर-illiterate.

अनख-wickedness; enmity; malice; depression.

अनखना-to be angry or displeased with anyone.

अनखाहट-anger; displeasure.

अनखी-displeased; angry.

अनगढ़-unformed; disorganised; unfinished; crude; uncouth; misshapen; awkward.

अनगन-countless; not counted; innumerable.

अनगवना-to delay knowingly.

अनगिनत-unnumerable; uncounted.

अनगी-allowance or discount of one in the rupee.

अनगौरी-foreign; not known.

अनघ-pure; without sin.

अनघेरी-an inopportune time; improper time.

अनघोर-oppression; tyranny; tumult; severity.

अनचाहत-not desired; not wishing.

अनचाहा-not desired.

अनचीता-not thought of; not desired; unforeseen.

अनचेना-valuation of a standing crop.

अनछेड़-untouched; unmolested.

अनजना-not born.

अनजला-unscorched; not burnt.

अनजाई-mongrel; a hybrid animal.

अनजामा-unproductive barren.

अनझिप-not blinking.

अनट-oppression; hardship; wrong; injustice.

अनडीठ-unseen; unobserved.

अनत-elsewhere.

अनति-a little; pretension.

अनदेखा-invisible; unseen; undiscovered; unexampled.

अनधिक-more.

अनधिकार-taking place without right or authority; unauthorised.

अनधीन-not dependent.

अनधीनता-insubordination.

अनधोया-not cleaned; not washed with water.

अनध्यवसाय-laziness; slothfulness.

अनध्याय-cessation from work; payday; a holiday; intermission.

अनन्त-illimitable; immediate; inexhaustible; sempiternal; limitless; infinite.

अनन्नास-the pineapple plant and its fruit.

अनमोल-invaluable.

अनन्य-having no other; being only one; single; whole; incomparable.

अनन्यता-engrossment; absorption.

अनपच-indigestion.

अनन्वित-disconnected.

अनपढ़-illiterate; uneducated.

अनपत्य-having no issue; childless; integrity.

अनपराध-innocent.

अनपरिचय-non-acquaintance.

अनपाय-indestructible; imperishable; enduring.

अनपेक्ष-disregardful; neglecting; careless.

अनपेक्ष्य-not to be wished for; unexpected.

अनप्रतीती-having no trust; unfriendly; unbelieving.

अनबन-discord; enmity.

अनबनाव-dissension; misunderstanding.

अनबियाहा-unmarried.

अनबिधा-unpierced.

अनबूझ-hard to understand; a riddle.

अनबेधा-unperforated; unpierced.

अनबोल-speechless; mute.

अनबोला-unspoken.

अनबोया-unsown; wild.

अनब्याहा-an unmarried person; unmarried.

अनभल-bad fortune.

अनभला-not good; bad.

अनभाया-disagreeable; displeasing.

अनभिज्ञ-foolish; ignorance; insensible; silly; not knowing.

अनभिलाषी-lacking desire.

अनभोरी-wontless; deception; fraud.

अनभ्यस्त-unpractised; unaccustomed.

अनभ्यास-want of practice.

अनभ्र-cloudless.

अनमापा-unfit to be measured.

अनमारग-an evil path.

अनमिल-heterogeneous; discordant; incoherent.

अनमीलना-to open the eyes.

अनमुख-having the face formed away; in other direction.

अनमेल-discordant; inharmonious; unsuitable; inappropriate; unmixed.

अनमोल-priceless; very costly; invaluable; costly.

अनय-misfortune; misconduct; injustice.

अनयश-ill-fame; infamy; disrepute; public disgrace.

अनर्थ-useless; pointless; meaningless; senseless.

अनर्थी-a wrong-does; transgressor.

अनरना-to disrespect; to dishonour.

अनरस-dryness; disgust; trouble; absence of flavour; distaste; sorrow.

अनराता-not fallen in love; not coloured; plain.

अनरूप-ugly; deformed.

अनर्गल-useless; continuous; free.

अनर्घ-priceless; valuable.

अनल-fire; flame.

अनल्प-not little; much.

अनलमुख-a god or Brahman.

अनलस-agile; quick; smart.

अनलसित-vigorous; not fatigued or enervated.

अनलायक-incapable; worthless.

अनवकाश-not having free time; or opportunity; inopportune.

अनवच्छिन-not broken up; entire.

अनवट-toe-ring.

अनवद्य-blameless; faultless.

अनवधान-indifference; inattentive; inadvertent.

अनवधानता-inadvertence.

अनवधि-limitless. always.

अनवरत-unremittingly; continuously; incessantly; always.

अनवसर-want of leisure or opportunity; unseasonable; inopportuneness.

अनवस्थ-unstable; incontinent.

अनवाँसा-sheaf of corn; first harvest.

अनवाँसी-a very small measure of land;

अनशन-hunger strike; fasting.

अनश्वर-not perishing; immortal; eternal; immanent.

अनसखरी-food which is cooked in ghee only.

अनसमझ-uneducated; untrained.

अनसहत-unbearable.

अनसुना-unheard; disregarded; to pretend not to hear what is said.

अनसूय-not spiteful; not envious.

अनसोच-thoughtless; inattentive.

अनहंकार-absence of pride; humility; modesty.

अनहंकारी-humble; not proud.

अनहित-ill-disposed; bringing misfortune.

अनहोता-poor; wonderful; peculiar; uncommon.

अनहोना-in want; unexampled; not to be.

अनहोनी-something impossible. improbable.

अनाकानी-conniving; overholding.

अनाकार-without form; shapeless.

अनाक्रमण-non-aggression.

अनाक्रांत-not attacked.

अनाखर-shapeless; ugly.

अनागम-non-arrival; non-appearance.

अनागम्य-not obtainable; not approachable.

अनाचरण-unprincipled; improper or dishonest conduct.

अनाचार-improper; conduct; indecorum; malpractice.

अनाचित-inattentive; heedless.

अनाज-grain; corn.

अनाज्ञाकारी-insubordinate.

अनाड़-not discovered; secret.

अनाड़ी-unskilfulness; silliness; stupidity.

अनात्म-lifeless; soulless.

अनातुर-not restless; not distressed.

अनात्मक-unreal; of short duration.

अनाथ-without a helpless; ownerless.

अनाथालय-an asylum for the poor and helpless.

अनादर-affront; disrespect; slight.

अनादरणीय-not to be respected; unworthy.

अनादि-eternity.

अनादृत-insulted; abused; disrespected.

अनादित्व-without beginning; eternity.

अनाप-शनाप-meaningless talk; disconnected prattling.

अनाप्त-incompetent; untrue.

अनाम-anonymous; obscure; nameless.

अनामय-healthy; defect-less; uninjured.

अनायक-having not protector or leader.

अनायास-easy.

अनायोजित-impromptu.

अनायासिक-done without effort.

अनार-a pomegranate; a kind of firework.

अनारक्षित-unreserved.

अनाराध्य-inexorable; implacable.

अनारी-colour of a pomegranate.

अनार्थिक-uneconomical.

अनार्य-not noble; not respectable.

अनावश्यक-needless; redundant; insignificant.

अनावर्ती-non-recurrent.

अनावृष्टि-want of rain; drought; dryness.

अनावृत-not hidden; bare; uncovered; unveiled.

अनावृति-not-return; release from rebirth.

अनाश्य-indestructible; imperishable.

अनाश्रमी-devoid of caste; of low caste.

अनाश्रय-without a support; poor destitute; helpless.

अनासक्त-disinterested.

अनास्था-want of faith or respect in a deity.

अनाहक-uselessly.

अनाहत-unwounded; unhurt.

अनाहार-without taking food; fasting; absence from food.

अनाहारी-fasting.

अनाहूत-not called or invited.

अनिंदनीय-blameless; irreproachable.

अनिंदित-not blamed.

अनिच्छा-absence of desire; unwillingness.

अनिच्छित-undesired.

अनित्य-transient; frail; perishable; provisional; adventitious; fleeting.

अनिद्र-wide awake; not sleeping; sleepless.

अनिन्दित-irreproachable.

अनिप-the commander of an army.

अनिपुण-unskilled; unqualified; inept; incompetent.

अनियत-not fixed; uncertain; indefinite.

अनियम-absence of rule; disorder; disorderly; anomaly.

अनियमानुरूप-informal.

अनियमित-irregular.

अनियार-pointed (as shape of eyes).

अनियारा-sharp; pointed.

अनिरुद्ध-unobstructed; restrained.

अनिर्णय-indefiniteness; uncertainty.

अनिर्णीत-pending.

अनिर्मल-dirty; impure; foul.

अनिर्देश्य-indefinable; indescribable; explainable.

अनिल-wind; air.

अनिवारित-unopposed; unchecked.

अनिवार्य-compulsorily; necessarily.

अनिवारक-passive.

अनिवार्यता-inevitability; compulsory or essential nature.

अनिश-continuing; constantly.

अनिश्चय-indecision; uncertainty; suspense.

अनिश्चित-indefinite; uncertain; doubtful.

अनिष्ट-obnoxious; ominous; evil; inconvenient; undesired; forbidding.

अनी-depression of body; disgust; multitude.

अनीक-host; edge; army; point.

अनीकिनी-a small army.

अनीठ-bad; incoming; unfavourable.

अनीति-improper; injustice; wrong; impropriety.

अनीश-without a master; helpless.

अनीश्वरवाद-atheism.

अनीस-helpless; without a master.

अनु-a prefix denoting 'each'; 'according to'; 'every'; 'in imitation of'; 'together'; 'similar'.

अनुकंपा-compassion; sympathy.

अनुकंपित-conversation; narrative.

अनुकथन-concurrent speech.

अनुकरण-imitation; mimicry.

अनुकरणीय-deserving to be emulated.

अनुकर्त्ता-an imitator; obedient.

अनुकारी-imitating; obedient.

अनुकूल-favourable; pleasure; agreeable; suitable; helping.

अनुकूलक-adapter.

अनुक्रमणी-index.

अनुक्रम-sequence.

अनुक्रमी-serial.

अनुकृत-imitated or copied.

अनुकृति-imitation or copy.

अनुकूलन-adoption; adjustment.

अनुक्त-not spoken; told or mentioned; not expressed.

अनुक्रम-order; succession; series.

अनुगूँज-echo.

अनुगृहीत-grateful; favoured; obliged.

अनुग्रह-kindness; patronage; support.

अनुग्राहक-supporter; showing favour; kind.

अनुचर-dependent shadow; footman; lackey; a companion; escort; henchmen.

अनुचित-unbecoming; wrong; unsuitable; undesirable.

अनुचरित-sought; followed; pursued.

अनुचार-adherence; allegiance.

अनुचिह्न-trail.

अनुच्छेद-article.

अनुज-born afterwards.

अनुजा-a younger sister.

अनुजीवी-living by or upon dependent; following adhering to.

अनुज्ञप्त-sanctioned; permitted.

अनुज्ञा-mandate; order; command; permission.

अनुज्ञप्तिधारी-licensee.

अनुज्ञापक-making known.

अनुज्ञेय-permissible.

अनुताप-remorse; repentance; distress.

अनुतापित-troubled in mind.

अनुतापी-remorseful; troubled; penitent.

अनुतारा-a satellite.

अनुतोष-relief.

अनुतोषिक-gratuity.

अनुत्तर-having no superior; having no answer; excellent.

अनुत्क्रमणीय-irreversible.

अनुदिन-grant.

अनुदेश-instruction; directive.

अनुद्योग-inaction.

अनुद्वाह-an indolent person.

अनुधावक-chaser.

अनुधावन-investigation; the act of following or running behind.

अनुनाद-resonance.

अनुनासिक-nasal.

अनुनति-courteous.

अनुपकार-disservice; harm.

अनुपत्ति-absurdity.

अनुपपत्ति-incongruity.

अनुपपन्न-unbecoming; out of place; inadvisable.

अनुपम-incomparable.

अनुपमित-uncompared.

अनुपयुक्त-unsuitable; unfit.

अनुपयोगी-useless; unfit.

अनुपलभ्य-inappre-hensible.

अनुपलक्षित-unnoticed; unknown.

अनुपलब्ध-not extant; not obtained.

अनुपलब्धि-non-availability.

अनुपस्थित-not pre-sent.

अनुपात-proportion; rule of three ratio.

अनुपातक-a heinous offence.

अनुपातन-sorting; grading.

अनुपाती-proportionate.

अनुपान-anything taken with a medicine after it.

अनुपालन-compliance.

अनुप्रयोग-application; use of procedure and rules.

अनुप्रास-assonance; repetition of words.

अनुपूरक-supplementary.

अनुबंध-agreement; connection; correlation; stipulation.

अनुबल-the rear of an army.

अनुभव-experience perception; consciousness.

अनुभवना-to feel; to experience.

अनुभवी-experienced; traveller.

अनुभाग-section.

अनुभावक-causing to perceive or to feel.

अनुभावन-expression of the feeling by look or gesture.

अनुभावी-possessing experience.

अनुभूत-tried; felt; guessed; know; perceived; experienced.

अनुमतांकन-rating.

अनुमति-permission; assent; approval; counsel.

अनुमन्य-permissible; admissible.

अनुमरण-death by burning of a Hindu widow.

अनुमस्तिष्क-cerebellum.

अन्यगोत्र-pertaining to another family or lineage.

अन्यचित्तज्ञान-telepathy.

अन्यजन्म-another birth; regeneration.

अन्यतः-from any other place or person.

अन्यत्र-located elsewhere.

अन्यथा-wrong; otherwise; contrarily; improper.

अन्याय-outrage; wrong; oppression; injustice.

अन्यारा-not different; not separate; queer.

अन्योक्ति-another's precept.

अन्योदर-born from other womb; a step brother.

अन्वय-lineage; leisure; mutual relation of cause and effect; empty space; interpretation.

अन्वयांतर-paraphrase.

अन्वह-continuous; consecutive.

अन्वीक्ष-microscope.

अन्वीक्षण-enquiry; thinking; meditation; investigation.

अन्वेषक-an investigator; carrying out investigation.

अन्वेषण-to find out; investigation; enquiry; quest; viewing.

अन्वेषित-investigated.

अन्वेषी-an enquirer; investigator.

अन्हवाना-to cause to bathe.

अन्हाना-to bathe; to wash.

अप-water.

अपंग-infirm; maimed; helpless.

अपंथी-without a path; on a bad path.

अपक-green; crude; raw; unripe.

अपकर्त्ता-one who does harm; a sinner; a wrong-doer.

अपकर्ष-disrespect; descent; dishonour; degradation; reduction; fall.

अपकलंक-an indelible disgrace.

अपकाजी-selfish.

अपकार-detriment; harm; disadvantage; damage; injury; maltreatment; mischief.

अपकीर्ति-scandal; dishonour; disgrace; discredit; reproach; ill-fame; bolt; ill-repute.

अपकृत-dishonoured; discredited; disgraced.

अपकृष्ट-deteriorated; inferior; base; abhorrent.

अपक्व-dishonoured; discredited; disgraced.

अपक्रम-disorder; turmoil.

अपगत-strayed; gone away or amiss.

अपगति-ill-repute; discredit; evil.

अपघटन-decomposition.

अपघर्षण-abrasion.

अपघात-murder; treachery; deception; suicide.

अपच-indigestion.

अपचयन-reduction.

अपचार-bad behaviour; offence; unwholesome; diet.

अपचाल-misbehaviour; misconduct; naughtiness.

अपिजयं-defeat.

अपजस-dishonour; disgrace; ill-repute; ignominy.

अपजसी-infamous.

अपटु-unskilled; awkward; not deft.

अपठ-illiterate; ignorant; unlearned; foolish.

अपडंर-fear; anxiety.

अपड़ाना-to higgle; to quarrel.

अपड़ाव-quarrel.

अपत-leafless; shameless; naked.

अपताई-shamelessness.

अपतुष्टि-appeasement.

अपति-husbandless; widowed.

अपत्य-offspring; descendant.

अपथ-a wrong road; an evil course; wicked means.

अपथ्य-unwholesome; indigestible.

अपद-insects having no feet; that creep.

अपदस्थ-dismissed; deposed.

अपदेखा-self-exulting; proud; vain.

अपद्रव्य-bad loathsome object; wealth.

अपनयन-removal; transfer; withdrawal.

अपना-self; personal; own; my.

अपनाना-to make a person or thing one's own.

अपनाम-ill repute; bad name.

अपनिन्दक-a blasphemer; abuser.

अपभय-unreasoning or blameworthy fear.

अपभाषा-obscene or vulgar language.

अपभ्रष्ट-degenerate.

अपमान-disgrace; disrespect; insult.

अपमानित-insulted; shown disrespect; shamed; dishonoured.

अपमानी-disreputable.

अपमान्य-deserving disrespect; dishonour.

अपमृत्यु-a sudden or untimely death; violent death.

अपयश-disgraceful; disreputable; infamous.

अपरंच moreover; also; too.

अपरंपार-boundless; infinite.

अपर-other; another; second one; opposite; additional.

अपरछन-without covering; hidden; secret.

अपरता-indifference; selfishness; neutrality.

अपरती-selfishness; deceit.

अपरत्व-adverseness; oppositeness; posterity.

अपरस-untouchable; untouched.

अपरा-worldly wisdom; materialism.

अपराजय-invin-cibleness.

अपराजित-undefeated; invincible.

अपराध-wrong-doing; offence; crime; default; sin.

अपराधी-offending; malefactor; guilty.

अपराह्ण &-afternoon.

अपरावर्त-hyperbola.

अपरिग्रह-non-acceptance of charity; renunciation.

अपरिच्छिन-undividable; boundless; connected.

अपरिणामी-unchangeable; useless.

अपरिपक्व-immature; unripe.

अपरिपूर्ण-ungratified.

अपरिमित-unmeasured; unlimited.

अपरिमेय-countless; innumerable; infinite.

अपरिवर्ती-constant.

अपरिष्कृत-not purified; impure.

अपरिहार्य-unavoidable; inalienable; obligatory.

अपरीक्षा-unable to be examined; want to trial.

अपरीक्षित-untested; unproved.

अपरूप-deformed; distorted.

अपरूपण-shearing.

अपरोक्ष-not remote; present.

अपर्याप्त-immeasurable; short; insufficient.

अपलक-fixed; unblinking.

अपलक्षण-ill-oman; bad sign of something to happen.

अपलोक-disgrace; dishonour.

अपवचन-abuse; slander.

अपवर्ग-final beatitude; completion.

अपवर्जन-exclusion; getting rid of.

अपवर्जित-got rid of; excluded.

अपवर्तक-a factor.

अपवश-independent; uncontrolled; unconstrained.

अपवाद-an exception; accusation.

अपवादात्मक-exceptional.

अपवादिक-exceptional; occurring as a special case.

अपवादित-refuted; slandered; censured.

अपवारण-impediment; obstruction; disappearance.

अपवाह-drainage.

अपवित्र-unclean; impure; unholy.

अपव्यय-expenditure; waste; prodigality; extravagant; dissipation.

अपविद्ध-pierced; abandoned.

अपव्ययी-extravagant.

अपशकुन-an unlucky omen; portent.

अपशिष्ट-waste.

अपशेष-waste product.

अपसंचय-hoarding.

अपसना-to flee; to run away in a secret manner.

अपसमायोजन-maladjustment.

अपसर्जन-relinquishment.

अपसव्य-the right side of body; opposite.

अपसारिता-divergence.

अपसौन-bad omen.

अपस्नान-bathing on the death of a relative.

अपस्मार-epilepsy.

अपस्वर-discord.

अपस्वार्थी-selfish.

अपह-wasting or destroying.

अपहत-killed; ruined; removed; destroyed.

अपहरण-hijacking; robbing; taking as plunder; kidnapping; stealing; carrying off.

अपहरना-to abduct; to snatch away; to embezzle.

अपहर्ता-a thief; a plunderer; a pilferer.

अपहृत-taken away; stolen; plundered.

अपह्नव-refusal; pretext.

अपक्व-raw; unripe; immaturity.

अपांग-disembodied; bodiless.

अपाढ़-difficult to perform.

अपादान-the ablative case in grammer; separation; removal.

अपान-not to be drunk.

अपामार्ग-a medical plant.

अपाप-guiltless; sinless.

अपाय-injury; helpless; destruction.

अपार-impassable; unbounded; infinite.

अपारदर्शक-opaque.

अपारदर्शी-immaterial.

अपास-excessive; boundless; extravagant; unlimited.

अपार्जित-extracted; expelled.

अपार्थ-immaterial.

अपाल-without a patron or supporter; shelterless.

अपावन-impure; not holy; polluting.

अपाव-injustice; exercise of power; tyranny.

अपाश्रय-without support; destitute; helpless.

अपाश्रित-sequestered; indifferent; retired from the world.

अपास्व-deserted; expelled; forsaken; abandoned.

अपाहिज-a maimed person; a cripple; a disabled person.

अपाहण-attraction.

अपितृ-fatherless; without father.

अपिधान-wrapper; a cover; envelope.

अपिनद्ध-bound up; covered.

अपीड़-without pain.

अपीन-not stout; thin; lean.

अपीनस-loss of smell; dryness of nose.

अपील-appellant.

अपुंस्त्व-want of sexual power; impotence.

अपुच्छ-tailless.

अपुण्य-wicked; impious; inholiness; irreligiousness.

अपुत्र-not having a son. childless.

अपुनीत-devoid of son.

अपुरुष-efferminate; impotent.

अपूजक-irreligious; irreverent.

अपूत-without offspring; childless.

अपूर-full; complete.

अपरदन-erosion.

अपूरा-filled up; extended.

अपूर्ण-not full; continuous; imperfective; incomplete; insufficient.

अपूर्व-novel; new; strange; uncommon; extraordinary.

अपेख-unseen.

अपेय-not to be drunk; not drinkable.

अपेल-immovable; unalterable.

अपेक्षण-hope; expectation.

अपेक्षा-comparison; in view of; hope; necessity; expectation.

अपौरुष-unmanly; impotent.

अप्रकट-not apparent; not manifested; hidden form view.

अप्रकाश-hidden; secret; not evident.

अप्रकृत-not cultivated; artificial; false; unnatural.

अप्रतिदेय-non-refundable.

अप्रतिपत्ति-absence of esteem.

अप्रतिबंध-free; not restricted; undisputed.

अप्रतिभ-not ready-wetted; bashful; dull; blunt.

अप्रतिम-unique; unparalleled; matchless.

अप्रतिष्ठा-ill-repute; disgrace; disrespect; dishonour.

अप्रतिहत-unchecked; uninjured; undamaged; unimpeded.

अप्रतीत-not deserving; credence; improbable; unclear.

अप्रतीति-lack of confidence; mistrust; implausibility.

अप्रत्यक्ष-absent; not present; secret.

अप्रत्यय-doubt; distrust; incredulity; misbelief.

अप्रधान-secondary; subordinate.

अप्रभावी-without effect; ineffectual.

अप्रमेय-endless; limitless; boundless; immeasurable; unable to be proved.

अप्रमादी-unerring.

अप्रमाण्य-want of proof.

अप्रमाणित-invalid.

अप्रयोज्य-inapplicable.

अप्रयुक्त-forward in used; not brought; unused.

अप्रवीण-unskilled; inexperienced.

अप्रवेश्य-impervious; impenetrable; not to be passed through.

अप्रशिक्षित-untrained; uninstructed.

अप्रसन्न-dissatisfied; displeased; umbrage.

अप्रसाद-regard; disfavour; unfavourable.

अप्रस्तुत-foreign; out of mark; irrelevant; not to the point.

अप्राकृत-unnatural; not common; contrary to nature.

अप्राचीन-recent; of late origin; up-to-date; modern.

अप्राण-not conscious; inanimate.

अप्राप्त-not having attained puberty; unobtained.

अप्राप्य-not available; unobtainable.

अप्रामाणिक-inauthentic; not genuine.

अप्रासंगिक-out of connection or topic; irrelevant.

अप्रिय-unloved; unfriendly; unpleasant.

अप्रीति-want of love; dislike; enmity; aversion; unfriendliness.

अप्रेम-want of love; hatred; dislike; enmity.

अप्रेषण-non-despatch.

अप्रैल-April.

अप्रौढ़-immature.

अप्सरा-celestial nymph; fairy; angel; damsel; siren.

अफरना-to gormandize; to eat to the full; to swell out.

अफराना-to satiate; to glut.

अफल-unproductive; ineffectual.

अफ़लातून-a boastful or haughty man.

अफलित-not in fruits.

अफ़वाह-rumour; hearsay.

अफ़सर-an officer.

अफ़साना-a tale; a story.

अफ़सोस-regret; sorrow.-a pity.

अफेन-without foam or froth.

अब-just now; at the present time.

अबख़रा-vapour; steam.

अबतक by this time; as yet; hitherto.

अबतर-deteriorated; ruined; bad; spoiled; base.

अबद्ध-unbound; unrestrained; disordered; disorganised.

अबध-certain; unerring; sure.

अबधूत-unwise; ignorant.

अबध्य-inviolable; not to be killed; sacred; not deserving death.

अबर-feeble; weak.

अबरक-talc; mica; make-up; cosmetic.

अबरन-colourless; without shape; indescribable.

अबरू-the eyebrow.

अबल-weakness.

अबलख-piebald; black or white; mottled.

अबला-the wicker vessel; a woman.

अबल्य-frailty; weakness.

अबसन-naked; not clothed.

अबही hitherto; yet; even now.

अबा-a kind of loose cloak.

अबाती-not moved by wind; windless; burning within.

अबादान-inhabited; filled.

अबाधित-unobstructed; free.

अबान-unarmed; without weapons or arms.

अबाबील-a swallow.

अबार-delay; lapse of time.

अबास-place or residence; habitation; dwelling.

अबिन्दु-without a dot or point.

अबीज-bad seed.

अबीर-the red power which the Hindus sprinkle on one other's face on the Holi festival.

अबुद्धि-want of understanding; ignorance; undesigned.

अबेर-delay.

अबोध-ignorance; puzzled; boundless.

अबोधगम्य-uncom-prehensible.

अबोध्य-inexplicable.

अबोल-mute; dump; silent; speechless.

अब्ज-the lotus; conch; a millions; the moon.

अब्जा-the goddess Laxmi.

अब्द-cloud; sky.

अब्धि-sea; ocean.

अब्बा-father.

अब्रह्मण्य-what is unfit for Brahmans.

अभंगुर-unbreaking; lasting; unbreakable; indestructible.

अभक्त-undivided; ungodly; irreligious; non-transient.

अभक्ष्य-not fit to be eaten.

अभग्न-unbroken; complete; perfect.

अभद्र-indecent; crude.

अभय-courageous; amnesty; fearless; undaunted; bold.

अभरन-ornaments; jewels.

अभरम-not deluded; fearless; undoubtedly; unconfounded.

अभल-wicked; not good; bad.

अभव्य-wonderless; queer; inauspicious; unimposing.

अभाऊ-unbecoming; distasteful.

अभाग-misfortune; ill-fate.

अभागा-luckness; accursed; unlucky; unfortunate.

अभाज्य-ill-fate; misfortune.

अभार-not heavy or ponderous; of light weight.

अभाव-absence; nothingness; destitution.

अभाववर्थक-privative.

अभावी-not destined to exist; non-existent.

अभाव्य-impossible; improper; not to be.

अभि-denoting priority in place or time; with; towards; against.

अभिकथन-assertion; allegation.

अभिकरण-agency.

अभिकर्ता-an agent; intermediary.

अभिकलन-computation.

अभिकल्पन-designing; planning.

अभिक्रम-attack; assault; undertaking; an enterprise.

अभिक्षमता-aptitude.

अभिगम-access.

अभिगमन-a going near or approaching; sexual intercourse.

अभिगृहीत-reception; seizure; occupation.

अभिगामी-cohabiting; coming near; approaching.

अभिग्राहित्र-receiver.

अभिजनन-breeding.

अभिजित-beautiful; well-born; noble; wise; fit; respected; lovely.

अभिज्ञ-skilled informed; versed knowledgeable.

अभिज्ञान-recognition (by a distinctive mark or token).

अभिदान-contribution; subscription.

अभिधा-literal sense; purport.

अभिधान-appellation; nomenclature; a dictionary; a vocabulary.

अभिधारणा-a pustular; hypothesis.

अभिधायक-denominative.

अभिधेय-a predicable.

अभिनन्दन-compliment; praise; greeting; congratulation; approbation.

अभिनय-acting.

अभिनव-up-to-date; fresh; new; recent.

अभिनवन-innovation.

अभिनवीकरण-modernization.

अभिनिर्धारण-identification.

अभिनिविष्ट-engrossed.

अभिनिषिद्ध-proscribed.

अभिनीत-just performed dramatically; brought proper; staged nearer; suitable; decorated.

अभिनेता-the actor in a play.

अभिनेत्री-an actress.

अभिनेय-stageable.

अभिन्न-undivided; not separated; integral.

अभिन्नता-identity; unity; integral.

अभिपुष्ट-confirmed.

अभिपूर्ति-implementation.

अभिप्रेरण-impulse; motivation.

अभिप्रेत-desired; intended.

अभिभावक-guardian (as of a minor).

अभिभावकता-status of guardian.

अभिभाषण-formal or ceremonial address.

अभिभूत-in subjection; overwhelmed; defeated.

अभिमंचन-staging.

अभिमंत्रण-purifying with the help of mantras.

अभिमत-opinion; idea; desired; approved; accepted; agreeable.

अभिमति-opinion; pride; desire.

अभिमन्यु-name of Arjun's son.

अभिमतता-desire.

अभिमान्य-proud; conceited.

अभिमान-conceit; unjustifiable; arrogance; pride.

अभिमानी-a proudly person.

अभिमुख-facing; turned towards.

अभियंता-an engineer.

अभियंत्रण-engineering.

अभियाचना-demand.

अभियान-expedition.

अभियुक्त-accused.

अभियोग-an accusation.

अभियोजक-prosecutor.

अभिरक्षक-custodian.

अभिरक्षण-keeping in custody.

अभिरक्षा-custody.

अभिराधन-appeasement.

अभिराम-beautiful; charming; delightful; bewitching.

अभिरुचि-inclination; desire; interest.

अभिलंब-normal.

अभिलक्षण-characteristic.

अभिलषित-desired.

अभिलाष-desire; wish; option; appetite; craving; pleasure.

अभिलाषा-desire; longing.

अभिलाषी-desirous; wishing.

अभिलिखित-recorded.

अभिवक्ता-pleader (at law); a speaker.

अभिवन्दन-salutation; obeisance; praise.

अभिवचन-a plea (at law).

अभिविन्यास-orientation.

अभिवृद्धि-growth; increase.

अभिवृत्ति-attitude.

अभिव्यंजक-expressive.

अभिव्यक्त-manifested; revealed.

अभिशंसा-recommendation.

अभिशप्त-accused; imprecated.

अभिशाप-allegation; curse; false.

अभिशासन-governing; rule.

अभिषद-syndicate.

अभिषंग-defeat; false; accusation; baptised; enthroned; invested.

अभिष्यन्द-flow of water.

अभिसंधि-alliance; deceit.

अभिसमय-settlement; convention.

अभिसरण-convergence.

अभिसर-a companion; a follower; a retainer.

अभिसार-meeting; attack; lovers' meeting or assignation; union.

अभिसारी-assistant keeping a tryst or assignation.

अभिस्वीकृति-acknowledgment.

अभीक्ष्य frequently.

अभीक-fearless; hardhearted; eager; cruel; intrepid.

अभीत-not fearful; fearless.

अभीप्सा-desire; longing.

अभीष्ट-desired.

अभुक्त-not eaten; not used.

अभूत-not past; improbable; non-existent.

अभेद-absence of difference; identity; sameness; impenetrable; inseparable; united.

अभेद्य-unbreakable; unshakable; impenetrable.

अभेरना-to set together; to mix.

अभेरा-rubbing; concussion; hand-to-hand.

अभोग-unenjoyed; unfit; unpossessed; for use.

अभोजन-abstention from food; fast; taking no food.

अभौतिक-immaterial.

अभ्यंग-smearing; anointing oil over the body.

अभ्यंतर-interior; internal.

अभ्यर्थन-

अभ्यर्थित-earnest request; prayer.

अभ्यर्पण-surrender.

अभ्यस्त-repeated; learnt by heart; accustomed; invertebrate; experienced.

अभ्यागत-a visitor; a guest; visiting officer.

अभ्यागम-presence; proximity; arrival.

अभ्यागमन-visitation.

अभ्यापत्ति-protest.

अभ्यारोपण-indictment.

अभिवेदन-representation.

अभ्यास-repetition; practice; repeated reading; study; habit; practice; to acquire familiarity; to inure oneself.

अभ्यासी-studious; exercising; practising.

अभ्युत्थान-rise; rising; revolt; progress; elevation; increase.

अभ्र-the sky; a cloud.

अमंगल-inauspicious; evil; ill omen; disastrous; unlucky.

अमंद-not dull or slow; fast; keen; sharp; diligent; loud.

अमचूर-mango pairings dried in the Sun.

अमड़ा-a tree which yields small sour fruits of which pickles are made.

अमद-not maddened or prideless; sober; intoxicated.

अमन-tranquillity; peace.

अमनिया-pure; clean; not touched.

अमनुष्य-unmanly; inhuman.

अमनुष्यता-inhumanity.

अमनोगत-not in mind; not consciously intended.

अमनोज्ञ-disagreeable; uninteresting.

अमनोनीत-depraved; disapproved; reprobate.

अमनोयोग-inattentive or thoughtless person.

अमनोहर-unattractive; disgustful; displeasing.

अमम-want of interest; stoicism; disinterestedness; unselfishness.

अममता-disinterestedness.

अमर-exempt from death; deathless; everlasting; immortal; undying.

अमरख-worrow; wrath; perplexity; anger.

अमरण-undying.

अमरपद-immortality; salvation; the status of being immortal.

अमरपुर-heaven; the abode of gods; paradise.

अमरबेल-a parasitic plant which has neither leaves nor root; an airplant or dodder.

अमरलोक-immortals; heaven; the region of the paradise.

अमरस-mango juice.

अमराई-mango grove.

अमरालय-heaven.

अमरावती-city of Gods.

अमरी-the abode of immortals; the city of Indra.

अमरू-a kind of silk cloth.

अमरूद-the guava tree and its fruit.

अमरेश-the lords of gods (in Heaven).

अमर्ध-inestimable.

अमर्त्य-immortal.

अमर्याद-affronted; improper beyond limits; dishonoured.

अमर्ष-anger.

अमर्षण-wrath.

अमर्षी-wrathful; intolerant; angry; indignant.

अमल-without stain; pure; clear; guiltless; sinless.

अमलता-cleanness; brightness; purity.

अमतासी-orange-yellow.

अमलदारी-sway; government.

अमलपट्टा-a writ of authority.

अमलबेल-sorrel; a sour medicinal plant.

अमला-the goddess Lakshmi; agents.

अमलाक-estates; lands; possessions.

अमलिन-stainless; pure; clean.

अमली-exercising; practical; an effect.

अमलोनी-a kind of saltish grass used as vegetable.

अमहर-dried pairings of unripe mangoes.

अमहल-without place.

अमानता-to invite; to entertain.

अमात्य-minister (of a government); counsellor.

अमात्र-without measure; limitless.

अमानत-charge; deposit; anything given in trust.

अमाना-be held; to go into; fit.

अमानी-without pride; inattentive; incredulous.

अमानुष-inhuman; not human.

अमानुषी-superhuman; devilish; inhuman; supernatural.

अमान्य-not acceptable; not to be respected or honoured.

अमान्यकरण-invalidation.

अमामा-a large turban.

अमाया-fraudless; deceitless.

अमार-pile; heap.

अमार्ग-bad conduct; evil course.

अमवट-mango-juice.

अमावस्या-the last day of the dark; half of the month; the junction of the Sun and Moon; lunar conjunction.

अमाह-the red flesh from the eyeball; nail.

अमिट[1]-not erased; indestructible; irrevocable; indelible.

अमिट[2]-limitless; too much; undefined; immeasurable; endless.

अमितव्ययी-uneconomical.

अमिताभ-Lord Buddha.

अमित्र-friendless; having no friend.

अमिय-nector.

अमिया-a mango; a unripe mango.

अमिल-unconcerned; dissimilar.

अमिश्र-not mixed; simple.

अमिश्रित-pure; unmixed; not adulterated.

अमिष-absence of deception; with not pretext.

अमा-sweet one; nectar; darling.

अमीन-a trustee; an officer of the court entrusted with outside work.

अमीर-chief; a grandee; rich.

अमुक-(some) one or another; a certain (person or thing).

अमुख्य-not chief; secondary; ordinary; subordinate.

अमूर्त-unembodied; shapeless.

अमूर्ति-shapeless.

अमूल-rootless; baseless.

अमूलक-without a base or foundation.

अमूल्य-invaluable; costing nothing; priceless; gratis.

अमृत-immortal; nectar.

अमृत्व-release from rebirth; immortality.

अमृत्यु-immortal.

अमृतवान-a pot with a lid to keep and preserve food.

अमृततांबु-the moon.

अमेजना-to union; to mix.

अमेध्य-an impure substance; substance which is not fit for sacrifice; excrement.

अमेय-unlimited; boundless.

अमोघ-unfailing (a stragem); unerring.

अमोल-valuable; priceless; unpurchasable.

अमोला-a small mango-plant (used for grafting).

अमोही-hard-hearted; indifferent; disinterested.

अमौआ-dark green; mango-coloured.

अम्मा-mamma; mother (used in calling).

अम्मामा-a kind of turban.

अम्मी-colloq. mother.

अम्ल-sourness; acidity.

अम्लजन-oxygen.

अम्लपित्त-acidity; pyrosis.

अम्लसार-essence of lemon.

अम्लता-sourness; acidity.

अम्लान-clean; not fading; pure; not dejected.

अम्हौरी-clean; pure; not dejected or sad; not fading.

अय-iron; weapon; fire.

अयतन-without effort or pain.

अयथा-not true; false; unworthy; improper.

अयन-a road; path; a place of motion.

अयनान्त-solstice.

अयश-detraction; disgrace; odium.

अयशस्वी-disreputable; disgraced; infamous.

अयस्-iron.

अयस्क-ore.

अयस्कहीन-barren.

अयस्कांत-a magnet.

अयाचक-unsoliciting; satisfied.

अयाच्य-fully satisfied.

अयान[1]-ignorant; foolish.

अयान[2]-natural disposition; not moving.

अयाल-lock of hair on the nect certain animal (horse or lion); a horse's mane.

अयुक्त-illicit; unseemly; undue; unift; incimpatible; preposterous.

अयुत-a myraid; ten thousand.

अयोग-trouble; difficulty; bad time; improper.

अयोग्य-incompetent; incapable; undeserving; unsuitable; inappropriate; unqualified.

अयोध्य-not to be contended; not to be warred against.

अयोनि-unborn; constant.

अरकट-cleverness; dexterity; ingenuity.

अरक्षणीय-indefensible.

अरक्षित-naked; unguarded; unprotected; bare.

अरंग-flow of fragrance.

अरंभना-to make a noise; to begin; to commence; to cry.

अर-obstinacy.

अरई-a goad.

अपकना-बरकना-to wander about.

अरक्षित-unprotected; undefended.

अरगजा-a kind of yellow perfume.

अरगट-separate; different; distinct; unique.

अरगनी-a rope or cord; a dejected face; or bamboo.

अरगला-obstruction; a bolt.

अरगाना-to be separate; to remain silent.

अरघ-libation.

अरघान-fragrance; scent.

अरचन-worship.

अरचना-to worship; to adore.

अरज-breadth; request; solicitations.

अरजी-petition; representation; memorial.

अरण्य-wild green scrub jungle; forest.

अरत-listless; uninvolved; detached; passionless.

अरति-disownment; renunciation; indifference.

अरथ-to explain.

अरथी-to bier; to begin; a (Hindu) funeral to take place.

अरथाना-to explain.

अरदब-a frustrating or vexatious situation.

अरदना-to trample under foot; to destroy by crushing.

अरदली-an orderly; an attendant.

अरदास-a gift to god; a present; a donation.

अरधंग-half of body.

अरधंगी-paralytic.

अरध-half.

अरन-a forest.

अरना-a wild buffalo.

अरपन dedication.

अरब-a hundred million; a myriad.

अरबर-confused talk.

अरबी[1]-Arabian; Arabic.

अरबी[2]-the Arabic language.

अरबोला-innocent; simple.

अरमान-desire; ambition; wish; craving.

अरर-Oh! (expressing dismay).

अरराहट-crash; roar; rumble.

अरवन-first cutting of the crop (offered to family gods and Brahmans); grain cut when still unripe.

अरविंद-a lotus.

अरवी-a species of Arum the root of which is used as food.

अरस-languor.

अरसठ-a monthly account of revenue.

अरसना-to be dull; to be slow.

अरसा-intervening a space of time; delay; interval; time.

अरसाना-to cause to be lazy.

अरसिक-not savouring; dull.

अरसीला-drowsy; full of laziness.

अरसीलो-languid (the body).

अरहट-a wheel fixed at the top of a well for drawing water with.

अरहर-a type of pulse.

अराजकता-anarchy; anarchist.

अराज़ी-detached portions of land; lands.

अराति-an enemy; anger.

अराधना-to worship; to adore.

अरारूट-arrowroot.

अराल-victorious; destroying the enemy. poet.

अरि-an enemy; an antagonist; a wheel.

अरित्र-rudder.

अरिष्ट-not hurt; name of demon killed by Krishna.

अरियाना-to despise; to express words of disgust.

अरिहा-destroyer of enemies.

अरी used to girls or women.

अरुंधती-the small star Alcor in the plough.

अरुचि-lack of appetite; lack of interest; aversion; dislike; unappetising.

अरुज-free from disease; healthy; in sound state.

अरुणाप्रिया-a fairy.

अरुणाई-the colour seen at the time of the dawn.

अरुणित-caused to glow; glowing red; reddened.

अरुणिमा-reddish; flush; glow.

अरुणोदय-the early dawn; early morning; daybreak.

अरुणोपल-a ruby.

अरुप-shapeless; without form.

अरूलना-to have wound or pain.

अरूस-a bride.

अरे say! hullo! oh! expressing astonishment or concern.

अरेरना-to rub; to chafe.

अरोधना-to strangle.

अरोचक-nasty; insipid.

अरोहना-to ascend; to climb up.

अलझाना-to entangle.

अहरना-worship.

अर्क-swallow-worth; the sun.

अर्कज-the god of death; Yama.

अर्कजा-daughter of the Sun.

अर्कदिन-a solar day; Sunday.

अर्कमंडल-the disc of the Sun.

अर्कवर्ष-a solar year.

अर्कव्रत-the borrowing of money of a king from his subjects for their benefit.

अर्काश्मन्-crystal lens; ruby.

अर्कोपल-the sun-stone; a crystal; a ruby.

अर्गनी-a rope which is stretched for hanging or drying clothes; towel-rail.

अर्गल-a wooden bar for fastening a door; an impediment.

अर्गला-obstruction; bolt; the chain with which an elephant is tied; a bar.

अर्घ-a respectful offering; of water (in which substances such as rice; curds; or milk may be mixed) a libation; worth; value; price.

अर्घा-a boat shaped vessel used for performing libations.

अर्घ्य-costly; of worth; article offered respectfully to a deity; or to a guest.

अर्चक-worshipping; adoring; adorer.

अर्चा-adoration; an image or a deity; worship.

अर्चि-brightness; flame; light; radiance; splendour.

अर्चित-adored; revered.

अर्ज-request; representation; petition.

अर्जन-earning; accumulation; collection.

अर्जित-acquired; earned leave; gained.

अर्जी-an application.

अर्जुन-a large deciduous tree.

अर्जुनी-a white cow; a procures; a bawd.

अर्ण-water; the Sal tree; a letter of the alphabet.

अर्णव-ocean; sea.

अर्तला-a patron; a protector; a supporter.

अर्थ-signification; purpose; intention; meaning.

अर्थवाद-words uttered in the form of an aphorism with a view to excite some emotion.

अर्थात् that is to say; in other words.

अर्थान्तर-difference of interpretation; exposition.

अर्थाना-to explain.

अर्थित-requested; after demanded; sought.

अर्थी[1]-a petitioner; a plaintiff; a claimant.

अर्थी[2]-a bier.

अर्दन-wounding; killing; request; covetousness.

अर्ध-half (in compound).

अर्धगोल-hemisphere.

अर्धचन्द्र-a semicircle; the symbol of; crescent.

अर्धचक्र-semicircle.

अर्धन-bisection.

अर्धनयन-the third eye in the forehead of God Shiva.

अर्धपारदर्शक-translucent.

अर्धमास-a fortnight.

अर्धरात्रि-midnight.

अर्धांग-hemiplegia; half the body.

अर्धांगिनी-one's wife.

अर्धाली-single line of a couplet.

अर्धांश-half the portion or share; a moiety.

अर्पण-sacrifice; entrusting; placing in or upon; to present; to offer.

अर्पित-delivered; offered; entrusted.

अर्भक-child; the young of an animal; son; lean.

अर्मान-hope; desire; inclination; disposition.

अर्यमा-the Sun; one of the constellations.

अर्वाक-behind; toward; near.

अर्वाचीन-or recent origin; new; up-to-date; modern.

अर्श-heaven; throne; highest.

अर्हता-qualification.

अर्हणा-worship.

अर्ह्य-respected; adorable.

अलं-sufficient; enough.

अलंकरण-decoration; ornamentation; ornamenting.

अलंकार-finery; decoration; ornament; schema.

अलंघनीय-inviolable; strict.

अलंघ्य-inviolable; not to be injured; insurmountable.

अलक-a lock of hair.

अलक्ष-unseen; invisible; unobserved.

अलक्षणी-unfortunate.

अलक्षित-imperceptible; invisible; unseen; sudden.

अलक्ष्य-invisible; indescribable.

अलख-imperceptible; invisible.

अलग-aside; aloof; several; astute; distinct; separate; apart; a piece.

अलगरजी-carelessness.

अलगाव-separate state; aloofness; segregation; detachment.

अल्हड़-not grown up; imperfect.

अलड़ाना-to scream; to shriek.

अलता-varnish (as used on the fingernails); lac dye.

अलफा-a kind of long cloak.

अलफाज-words.

अलबत्ता-of course; certainly; surely.

अलबल-very strong; almighty.

अलबिलल-very foolish; vain; fruitless.

अलबेट-turn; twist; bend.

अलबेलापन-charm.

अलभ्य-precious; rare; unattainable.

अलम-enough.

अलमस्त-intoxicated; free form anxiety.

अलमारी-cupboard; wardrobe; bookcase.

अलमास-diamond.

अलर्क-white swallow worst; rabid dog.

अलल-chiefly in cheerful; frisky.

अललाना-to cry aloud; to roar.

अलवाँती-a woman who has lately given birth to a child.

अलवाई-a cow which has given birth to a calf a month or two before.

अलवान-shawl (of wool); shawl cloth

अलवाया-soft; gentle; tender.

अलविदा-the last Friday in Ramazan. Goodbye.

अलस-slothful; lazy; slack; drowsy.

अलसान-laziness; idleness; drowsiness.

अलसानि-languor.

अलसेट-deception; discrepancy; duplicity.

अलहदा-aloof; separate.

अलाहदी-lazy; slothful.

अलात-fire brand.

अलान-a post for tying an elephant; chain or rope used to tie an elephant; a fetter.

अलापना-to speak; to converse; to tune the voice before singing; to utter words.

अलाव-pot made of dried gourd.

अलाभ-unprofitably; loss.

अलाभ-one who makes pretence or pretext; a liar.

अलामत-sign; mark.

अलायक-unworthy; unfit.

अलाल-good for nothing; sluggish; worthless.

अलाव-a fire lit in the open (as on winter nights to warmth).

अलिंग-unknowable, without sign.

अलिंजर-an earthen pot for storing water; water-pot.

अलिंद-terrace; balcony.

अलि-wine; dog; a crow; a large black bee; a scorpion.

अलिक-the forehead.

अलिनी-a bumble bee.

अलिफ़-the first letter of the Arabic alphabet.

अली-a female friend; row or line.

अलीक-disrespected; false; untrue.

अलीन-a side pillar of a building; the long piece of wood forming the frame of a door.

अलील-unwell; ill.

अलुटना-to stumble; to totter.

अलूला-flame; bubble.

अलेख-indescribable; incalculable.

अलेखी-useless; unaccountable.

अलोकना-to look; to see.

अलोकित-unseen; unnoticed.

अलोना-tasteless; insipid; without relish.

अलोप-extinct; vanished; disappeared; concealed.

अलोभ-ungreediness.

अलोल-supernatural; superhuman.

अलौलिक-occult; transcendental.

अलौह-non-ferrous.

अल्प-insignificant; summary.

अल्पक-very small; minimal; minimum.

अल्पजीवी-short-lived.

अल्पज्ञ-knowing little; foolish; unwise; ignorant.

अल्पतर-less; lesser.

अल्पता-small size or amount; insignificance; inferiority.

अल्पदृष्टि-myopia.

अल्पप्रभाव-a little consequence; insignificant.

अल्पप्राण-an unaspirated consonant.

अल्पबल-feeble; of little strength.

अल्पबुद्धि-lacking in understanding; shallow-minded; foolish; unwise.

अल्पभोजन-smack.

अल्पभाषी-reserved; uncommunicative; taciturn.

अल्पमत-minority.

अल्पमात्र-only a little; remote; smack.

अल्पमूल्य-of little or small value.

अल्पवय-of short duration; ephemeral; young.

अल्पवयस्क-of short duration.

अल्पव्यय-less expense; to spare.

अल्पवेश-wearing insufficient dress; dishabille.

अल्पशः-little by little; by degrades; slightly.

अल्पस्थायी-temporary.

अल्पहास-snigger.

अल्पायु-of short duration or age.

अल्पांश-less numerical value; modicum; a small quantity.

अल्पार्थक-a diminutive.

अल्पाहार-eating a little; temperateness; moderation of food.

अल्लाना-to cry out loudly; to scream; to shriek; to groan.

अल्लाह-the Almighty God.

अल्हजा-stray talk; gossip.

अल्हड़-ignorant; youthful; childish; inexperienced; carefree.

अव-used in the sense of certainty; diminution; depression; disjunction.

अवकल-differential.

अवकलन-ascertainment; collecting; collection; observation.

अवलित-observed; ascertained.

अवकाश-interspaced; empty space; interval of time; leisure; opportunity.

अवकिरण-diffusion; scattering; spreading.

अवकीर्ण-spread out; diffused; strewn; dispersed; prolix.

अवकेशी-barren; unfruitful.

अवगतना-to fall down; to think out; to understand.

अवगति-awareness; decline; knowledge; comprehension; deterioration.

अवगारना-to explain; to elucidate; to illustrate.

अवगाहन-ablution; understanding; examination; immersion.

अवगुंठन-hiding; covering; a mask; a veil for the face.

अवगुण-defect; fault; vice.

अवग्रह-embankment; nature; obstruction; curse.

अवघट-inaccessible; rugged; steep; uneven; precipitous.

अवचट with difficulty; unexpectedly; all of a sudden.

अवच्छेद-distinction; section; boundary; feature.

अवज्ञा-defiance; despite; contempt; insubordination.

अवज्ञात-neglected; disregarded.

अवज्ञेय-fit to be discarded; contemptuous.

अवटना-to wander; to ramble.

अवडेर-to abandon; to forsake.

अवडेरा-quarrelsome; wicked.

अवतंस-a wreath; ornament for the head; tiara; garland.

अवतत-widely spread.

अवतमस-dusk.

अवतर-to be born; to appear.

अवतरणिका-introduction (to a book); preface.

अवतरना-to incarnate; to cross over; to be born; to assume human form.

अवतरित-incarnate; landed; excerpted; crossed over.

अवतल-concave.

अवतार-to produce; to give birth to.

अवतारण-descending; bringing down.

अवदशा-ill-luck; misfortunate.

अवतीर्ण-descended; become failed; excerpted; cited; incarnate.

अवदात-white; pure; clear; beautiful; spotless; yellow.

अवदान्य-powerful; strenuous; niggardly; stingy.

अवदारण-a lever; a breaking; a spade.

अवद्य-sinful; wicked; faulty.

अवध-the province of Oudh.

अवधान-vigilance; care; caution; attention.

अवधारण-definition; ascertainment; conception.

अवधारित-ascertained; decided; determined.

अवधारना-to hold; to grasp.

अवधावन-running of following after.

अवधि-set time; period; extent; limit.

अवधिमान-the ocean.

अवधूत-shaken off; discarded.

अवनत-generated; fallen; less; bent; deteriorated.

अवनति-decline; downfall; retrogression; deterioration.

अवनमन-depression.

अवनि-the world; the earth.

अवनीश-a king; sovereign.

अवन्तिका-the city of Ujjain.

अवपात-bathing at the end of a sacrifice.

अवमंदन-damping.

अवम-inferior; lowest; base.

अवमान-disrespect; detestation.

अवमानता-downgrading; disregard.

अवमृदा-subsoil.

अवयव-part; limit; member; a term.

अव्यवहृत-obsolete.

अव्यवसायिक-amateur.

अवर-hinder; under; inferior; low.

अवरत-separate; constant; extended; distinct.

अवराधन-adoration; homage; worship.

अवरुद्ध-restrained; kept secret.

अवरोध-blockade; obstacle; restriction; confinement; siege.

अवरोह-a descent; fall; decline; origin; birth.

अवरोही कर-regressive tax.

अवर्णनीय-indescribable; unspeakable; ineffable.

अवर्षण-absence or rain; aridity.

अवलंब-support; shelter; protection.

अवलंबना-to stay; to take shelter; to adopt; to halt.

अवलक्षण-ill-favoured; unfortunate; of ill omen.

अवली-flock (of birds).

अवलीक-faultless; sinless; pure.

अवलेखना-to scratch; to dig; to mark; to scrape.

अवलेप-unguent; ointment; vanity; pride.

अवलेह-jelly (medicinal).

अवलोकन-the looking at an object; view; perusal.

अवलोकनि-eye sight.

अवलोकित-perceived; seen; looked; inspected.

अवलोचना-to remove an object.

अवश-powerless; not under control; in subjection; without choice; unveiling.

अवशिष्ट-remaining; left; surviving.

अवशेष-remains; limit in space; residue; the end; termination; remnant.

अवशोषक-absorber.

अवशोषण-absorption.

अवश्य-without doubt; uncontrolled; unrestrained.

अवसन्न-troubled with misfortune; bad; sad; lazy.

अवसंरचना-infrastructure.

अवसर-opening chance; opportunity; venture.

अवसर्पण-downfall descent.

अवसाद-weakness; poverty; destruction; sediment; annihilation.

अवसान-destruction; death; boundary; conclusion; limit; evening.

अवस्त्रवण-seepage.

अवसि-of course.

अवसेचन-watering; extracting blood from the body; oozing; perspiring.

अवसेद-care; obstruction; anxiety; entanglement; delay.

अवसेर-anxiety; delay.

अवयस्क-minor.

अवस्तु-unreal; trivial; inessential; insubstantial.

अवस्तुता-nonessential nature; unreality.

अवस्था-condition; situation; trim; job; stage; way; mood; state; position; circumstance; fettle; predicament; age.

अवस्थापन-location; setting.

अवस्थित-situation.

अवतर-middle; intermediate.

अवसी-portion of the new crop first reaped for being eaten; mouthful.

अवाक-speechless; taken aback; nonplussed.

अवाची-the south.

अवाच्य-not to be uttered; inexpressible; not to be spoken of.

अवांछनीय-undesirable.

अवाज-sound.

अवाम-the common people.

अवार-the part or river's bank; toward us.

अवारना-to obstruct; to detain.

अवि-the Sun.

अविकल-whole; complete; entire; stagnant; calm.

अविकल्प-without hesitation or doubt; to alteration; definite; decided; fixed.

अविकार-flawless; without change; not libel to change; faultless.

अविकृत-unchanged; not deformed; not altered.

अविगत-not gone away; present; existent.

अविचल-motionless; unmoved; resolute; unshaken.

अविचार-thoughtless.

अविचारी-wanting in judgement.

अविच्छिन्न-ceaseless; continuous; uninterrupted.

अविच्छेद-undivided; continuous.

अविजित-unconquered.

अविज्ञात-not distinguishable or to be known.

अविज्ञेय-unknowable.

अवितत-opposite; inverted.

अवितरित लाभ-corporate savings.

अविदित-not known; not evident; mysterious.

अविवादित-not understood; unknown.

अविद्यमान-untrue; not present; false; inexistent.

अविद्या-ignorance; illiteracy; false understanding.

अविधिमान्य-in-valid.

अविनय-pertness; insubordination; disrespect; immodesty; rudeness.

अविनश्वर-eternal, undecaying.

अविनाभाव-concomitance; mutual relation.

अविनाश-indestructibility; imperishability.

अविनीत-preocious; ungracious; wanton; immodest.

अविभक्त-solid; undivided; same.

अविमर्शी-rapid.

अविरत-constant; continually; without interruption; uninterrupted.

अविरति-want of peace.

अविरल-dense; close.

अविराम-continuous; without rest; without repose.

अविरुद्ध-favourable; permitted; not discordant or at variance.

अविरोध-harmony; concord; peace; tranquillity; quietness; consistency.

अविलंबित-not delaying prompt.

अविवाहित-single; not married; bachelor; wifeless; celibate.

अविवेक-lack of judgement; imprudence.

अविशेष-identity; similar; without a difference; alike; similarity.

अविश्रान्त-not stopping; not weary.

अविश्वसनीय-unreliable; untrustworthy; unbelievable.

अविश्वास-want of confidence; discredit; doubt; disbelief; mistrust.

अविष-not poisonous; anti-toxic.

अविसन-unindustrious.

अविहड़-imperishable; indestructible; not broken.

अविहित-nonstatutory.

अवीर-impotent; weak; helpless.

अवीरा-a widow who has no issue; a childless widow.

अवेक्षक-caretaker.

अवेक्षण-retaliation.

अवेस-excitement.

अवैतनिक-unpaid for one's services; honorary.

अवैदिक-contrary of Vedas.

अवैध-illegal.

अव्यक्त-unmanifested; unknown; unclear; imperceptible.

अव्ययी-unchangeable; a kind of compound (in Sanskrit grammar).

अव्यर्थ-not useless or fruitless.

अव्यवस्था-lack of organisation; disorder.

अव्यवहार-disuse.

अव्यवहित-united; immediate; jointed; direct.

अव्याकुल-calm; not perplexed; composed; quiet.

अव्यापक-not pervading the whole; restricted; limited.

अव्याप्त-not pervading; not diffused.

अव्याप्ति-diffusion.

अव्याप्य-non pervasive.

अव्याहत-not alarmed; repelled; true; not obstructed.

अव्युत्पन्न-rude; illiterate; not proficient; not experienced; ignorant.

अव्वल-first; excellent; chief; best.

अव्वीन-first; former; ancient.

अशंक-fearless; without doubt; undaunted.

अशकुन-inauspicious.

अशक्त-powerless.

अशक्तता-disability.

अशक्य-beyond the power of; impracticable; impossible.

अशन-food; eating.

अशनि-without shelter; helpless.

अशरफ़-nobler; very noble; eminent.

अशरफ़ी-a gold coin; a sovereign of gold; yellow boy.

अशरा-the first ten days of the month of Muharram.

अशराफ़-persons of aristocratic family.

अशरीर-bodiless; disembodied.

अशनाया-desire of eat; hunger.

अशांत-disturbed; anxious; restless; inquiet.

अशास्त्र-unlawful; illegal; contrary to the rules of law.

अशिक्षा-ignorance; lack of education.

अशिक्षित-philistine; unread; untaught; savage.

अशिव-inauspicious; malign; not prosperous.

अशिष्ट-uncouth; crude; uncultivated; impolite.

अशील-of bad character; behaved; badly.

अशुच-impure.

अशुद्ध-imperfect; corrupt; impure; incorrect; faulty.

अशुभ-sinister.

अशेष-all; endless; without remainder; infinite; entire; complete; finished.

अशोक-name of the emperor Asoka; the tree.

अशोचनीय-fathomless.

अशोभा-dire (as circumstances); boding; unattractive.

अश्क-a tear.

अश्मंतक-covering; a kind of grass of which girdle for the waist were made in ancient times.

अश्मक-an old name of Travancor State.

अश्मरी-the disease called 'the stone' calculus.

अश्रद्धा-want of faith; lack of reverence or esteem; disbelief.

अश्रद्धेय-not to be believed; incredible unrespectable.

अश्रान्त-untried. indefatigable.

अश्राव-unaudible; unheard.

अश्रु-a tear.

अश्रुत-peculiar; unheard; inexperienced.

अश्रुति-deprived of hearing.

अश्लील-wretched; base; indecent.

अश्लेष-without a double meaning.

अश्व-a horse.

अश्वकर्ण-a kind of sal tree.

अश्वतर-a mule.

अश्वत्थ-the sacred tree.

अश्वत्थामा-the name of the son of .

अश्वपाल-a groom.

अश्वमेघ-the horse-sacrifice.

अश्वरक्षक-a groom.

अश्वशाला-a stable for keeping horses.

अश्वा-a mare.

अश्वारूढ़-mounted on horseback.

अश्वरोही-a cavalier; an equestrian.

अश्विनी-the first lunar mansion in Aries.

अष्टकुल-the eight races of serpents according to Puranas.

अष्टद्रव्य-the eight articles which are used in sacrifices.

अष्टधाती-strong; prepared from eight metals; irascible; quarrelsome.

अष्टधातु-the eight metals; lead; gold; silver; copper; tin; brass.

अष्टपाद-an insect with eight feet; a spider.

अष्टपहर-the whole day and night.

अष्टमी-the eight day of a lunar half month.

अष्टमूर्ति-who manifests himself in eight different forms. the God Shiva.

अष्टलोक-the eight words.

अष्टसिद्धि-the eight ; which when attained help a man to fulfil his desires.

अष्टादश-eighteen; eighteenth.

अष्टांगी-of eight limbs.

अष्टास-octagonal.

अष्टि-a fruit stone; kernel.

असंक्राम्यता-immunity.

असंख्य-countless; innumerable.

असंगत-inappropriate; bizarre; not connected; incoherent; inconsistent.

असंत-wicked; roguish.

असंतित-childless.

असंतान-without child.

असंतुष्ट-querulous; reluctant; disgruntled; dissatisfied; discontented.

असंतोष-dissatisfaction; displeasure; discontentment; grudge.

असन्दिग्ध-undoubted; unambiguous; unquestionable; authentic.

असंपूर्ण-incomplete; defective; imperfect.

असंभार-great boundless; unsupportable; limitless.

असंभव-impossible; improbable; inconceivable.

असंभावी-not to happen.

असंभ्रम-absence of mind.

असंभ्रान्त-imperturbable.

असंभाष्य-adverse; dissentient; inconsistent.

असंमत-adverse; contrary; inconsistent; dissentient.

असंयत-unrestrained; unbridled.

असंयमित-unrestrai-ned; undisciplined.

असंयुक्त-not connected; separate.

असंमान-disgraced; disrespect.

असंसारी-unearthly; weird.

असंशय-absence of doubt.

अस-similar; so; thus.

असकत-inactivity; laziness.

असकृत often; frequently.

असगन्ध-the medicinal plant.

असज्जन-not virtuous; not good; not respectable; wicked.

असत्कार-inhospitality.

असत्ता-non-existence; badness.

असत्य-untrue; false; ungodly.

असत्याभास-a paradox.

असदृश-dissimilar.

असफल-crash; failure; unsuccessful.

असबग-a kind of long grass used in colouring silk.

असभई-incivility; rudeness.

असभ्य-impolite; uncouth; uncivilised; rude.

असमंजस-hesitation; uncertainty; difficult situation; disparity; suspense; disharmony.

असम-unequal; not leave; dissimilar; uneven.

असमझ-without understanding; foolish; thoughtless; ignorant.

असमता-inequality; unevenness; dissimilarity.

असमर्थ-incapable; weak; helpless; incompetent; powerless; unfit incompetent.

असमशर-the God Cupid.

असमान-not even; unequal; incomparable; dissimilar.

असमानता-disparity.

असमायोजनीय-non-adjustable.

असमाप्ति-incompleteness.

असमीप-not near; remote.

असयाना-simple.

असर-effect; mark; sign; consequence; influence.

असरल-intricate.

असल-original or real nature.

असली-real; original; basic; genuine; actual; pure; inherent; essential.

असहन-impatient; unbearable; intolerant.

असहमति-disagreement; dissent.

असहयोग-non-cooperation.

असहाय-without help or assistance.

असहायता-helpless state.

असत्य-untrue.

असहिष्णु-intolerant; peevish.

असही-jealous.

असांच-untrue; false.

असाँचा-false.

असा-a staff; rod; mace.

असाइत-an unlucky moment; inauspicious.

असाई-rude; uncivilised.

असाक्ष्य-want or testimony or witness.

असाढ़-the fourth month of the Hindu year; June-July.

असाध-wicked.

असाधारण-uncommon; enormous; signal; unusual; special; private.

असाधु-unrighteous; immoral; wicked; not proper; corrupt.

असाध्य-weak; incapable; unable; beyond one's reach; incorrigible.

असामयिक-immature; untimely; ill-timed.

असामंजस्य-disharmony; disproportion.

असामान्य-uncommon; peculiar; unusual; abnormal.

असार-hollow; worthless.

असार्वजनिक-private; not public.

असालत-firmness; integrity; truthfulness.

असावधान-careless; inattentive; neglectful.

असावन्त-timid; unquiet.

असासा-goods and chattels; property.

असाहसी-spiritless; cowardly.

असित-black; crooked; not white.

असिद्ध-incomplete.

असिपत्र-the blade of a sword.

असींचा-not irrigated or water plot of land.

असीम-absolute; unlimited.

असीस-blessing; benediction.

असु[1]-breath; affection; life.

असु[2]-a horse.

असुखी-unhappy; distressed.

असुप्त-not a sleep; awake.

असुविधा-inconvenience.

असुर-an evil spirit; demon.

असुरक्षित-insecure.

असुरारि-a god; Lord Vishnu.

असूत-contrary; opposite.

असृक-blood.

असेवन-disregard; neglect.

असेवा-disregard; neglect.

असेग-laborious; unbearable; difficult; arduous.

असेसर-an assessor; a juryman; an inspector.

असैला-acting against fixed rules of conduct; wicked.

असों this year.

असोच-carefree; heelless.

असोभा-graceless.

असोस-not dried; not drying.

असौध-putrid smell.

असज्जित-unfurnished.

अस्तगत-setting (of Sun) descending; coming down.

अस्त-decline; fall.

अस्तबल-a stable.

अस्तब्ध-not firm; unsteady.

अस्तमन-the setting of heavenly bodies.

अस्तव्यस्त-perturbed; preoccupied; in disorder; dishevelled.

अस्ति-existence; present reality.

अस्तीन-sleeve.

अस्तु-so be it; very well.

अस्तुति-an anthem; praise; eulogy; prayer.

अस्तरा-a shaving razor.

अस्तेय-not stealing the property of others.

अस्त्र-a weapon armament.

अस्थल-a place.

अस्त्री-person who is wearing arms.

अस्थि-a skeleton; a borne.

अस्थित[1]-unfixed; unsettled.

अस्थित[2]-settled.

अस्थल-lean and thin; not fat.

अस्थैर्य-instability; fickleness; unsteadiness.

अस्नेह-unkindness; want of feeling.

अस्निग्ध-uneven.

अस्पताल-a hospital; pharmacopeia.

अस्पृश्य-untouchable; intact; unfit to be touched.

अस्पष्ट-unclear; not understood; indistinct.

अस्पृष्ट-untouched; pure; virgin.

अस्पृह-without desire; disinterested.

अस्फुट-indistinct; not clear.

अस्मरण-forgetfulness; oblivion.

अस्मृति-forgetfulness.

अस्त्र-a corner; blood; water; tears; saffron.

अस्त्रप-a demon; louse.

अस्वादित-not tasted; without taste or flavour.

अस्वाभाविक-unnatural; artificial.

अस्वार्थ-unselfishness;disinterestedness.

अस्वीकार-negation; refusal; repulsion; rebuff.

अस्सी-eighty.

अहं-egotism; pride; ego; self-conceit; arrogance.

अहंकार-squirt; vain; arrogant; egoist; haughty.

अह exclamation of astonishment; pain.

अहक-desire; wish.

अहत-one; unity.

अहद-period; promise; contract; reign; time; lifetime.

अहर्दी-habitually lazy or slothful; idle.

अहन-a day.

अहम-important.

अहमक-a fool; a dunce; a blockhead.

अहमियत-importance; stress.

अहमेव-vanity; self-conceit; pride.

अहरन-an anvil.

अहरना-to turn a piece of rough wood into shape.

अहरा-fuel made of cow-dung in the form of cakes.

अहरी-a small tank or pond.

अहर्निश day and night.

अहर्ष not happy; sorrowful.

अहलकार-an official; an officer; an agent.

अहला-unploughed.

अहवाल-obligation; sympathy; kindness.

अहस्तांतरणीय-not transferable; non-transferable.

अहह-exclamation of astonishment; grief; awe; pain.

अहा exclamation of pleasure also pain.

अहाता-boundary; enclosure.

अहार-diet.

अहारना-to fasten or paste with; to paste; starch.

अहिंसा-non-violence; benevolence; in-offensiveness.

अहि-a snake.

अहित-unfriendly; enmity; inimical; injurious.

अहिफेन-the saliva or venom of a spent; opium.

अहिबेल-the betel creeper.

अहिवात-married happiness; married state of a woman whose husband is alive.

अहिटा-to ensure that dues are paid; a field watchman who supervises crops until they are threshed.

अहीश-the king of serpents.

अहुटान-to remove oneself.

अहुटाना-to remove.

अहुठ-three and a half.

अहे-expressing sorrow.

अहेड़ी-a fowler; a hunter.

अहेतु-causeless; groundless; without reason; fruitless.

अहेर-chase; the animal hunted; game; hunting.

अहरी-one who hunts.

अहै-is.

अहो[1]-O!; Oh!.

अहो[2]-& day and night.

अहोई-when women pray for children name of a rite held before Dewali.

अहोभाग्य-& good fortune; good luck.

अहोरात्र-day and night.

अह्वान-var; pronun.

आ

आ The second vowel of the Devnagari alphabet.

आँकड़ा-accurate and detailed information in figures; data; statistics; a hook.

आँकन-grain of Indian maize or corn.

आँकर-extreme, deep; dear, very costly.

आँकल-bolt; a branded bull.

आँकरी-a hoot; a barb of an arrow.

आँकू-estimation; valuation; one who sets or estimates value of thing.

आँख[1]-vision, sight; eye; glance.-to look; to see; to try to harm.

आँख[2]-sprout in a sugarcane joint; shoot; eye of potato.

आँखफाड़वा-a midge; a grasshopper.

आँग-limb.

आँगन-court; square; quadrangle; a courtyard; the open space within a house.

आँगिक-pertaining to the body.

आँगा-a fine sieve.

आँगुल-breadth of a finger.

आँधी-a sieve made of fine wire or cloth.

आँच-flame; sexual desire; heat; brilliance.

आँचना-to burn; to heat.

आँचल-the end of sari; the border or hem at the end of a sari, which usually covers a woman's breast.

आँचलिक-zonal.

आँचू-bramble; blackberry; raspberry.

आँजन-collyrium applied to the eyes.

आँजनेय-a title of Hanuman.

आँजि-hem; selvage.

आँट[1]-the portion of the palm of hand between the forefinger and the thumb.

आँट[2]-to be sufficient.

आँटना-to be filled in.

आँटी-skein (of thread); bundle (of grass, wood).

आँटसाँट-intrigue; secret alliance; conspiracy.

आँठी-a knot; coagulation; the stone of a fruit.

आँड-any round object; testicle.

आँडू-having testicles.

आँत-entrails; bowels; intestine.

आंतर गुणनफल-inner product.

आंतरिक-inner; internal.

आंद-mud; mire.

आंदू-a ring of iron; fetters.

आंदोलन-a movement; swinging.

आंधना-to make a sudden assault; to attack.

आँधी-a dust-storm; whirlwind.

आँय-बाँय-nonsense talk; useless gossip.

आँब-mango.

आँव-looseness of the bowels; diarrhoea; dysentery.

आँवड़-border.

आँवड़ना-to overflow.

आँवड़ा-very deep.

आँवन-an iron band which round the nave of a wheel.

आँवल-the membranous; covering of a womb; placenta.

आँवला-dried myro-balan; or a wind fallen one.

आँवले-twins.

आँवा-the potter's kiln.

आंशिक-pertaining to a part; partial; fractional.

आँस-agony; fibrous part of anything; rope; pain.

आँसी-sweetmeats which are distributed among relatives and friends on festivals.

आँसू-a tears to come; to weep or to flow.

आँहड़-an earthen pot.

आँहाँ a word of disapproval.

आइंदा in future.

आइना-a mirror; a looking-glass.

आई-period of life; death; appointed hour.

आईन-law; rules and regulations; statute.

आऊस-rice sown in month of April-June.

आकंप-shaking; trembling.

आक-the medicinal plant.

आकबत-the condition after death.

आकन-weeds or grass collected from a ploughed field.

आकबाक-incoherent gossip.

आकर-a mine; treasury; a rich source; variety; store.

आकरी-the work of digging a mine.

आकई-extended up to ears.

आकर्ष-magnet; attraction; fascination; lodestone.

आकर्षक-attractive; appealing; fascinating.

आकर्षण-attracting; charm; attraction.

आकर्षित-attracted.

आकलक-estimator.

आकलन-seizing; estimate; counting; accumulation; search; investigation.

आकला-peevish.

आकाली-agitation; embarrassment; perplexity.

आकस्मिक-casual leave; sudden; unexpected; occurring by chance.

आकांक्षक-expatiator.

आकांक्षा-wish; desire; intention prospect; expectation.

आकांक्षित-desired; expected.

आक़ा-master.

आकार-structure; appearance; magnitude.

आकारण-invitation.

आकारित-sketched; outline.

आकाश-the sky; heavens; the vault of heaven; the atmosphere.

आकाशकुसुम-an impossibility.

आकाशगंगा-the heavenly Ganga, the galaxy; the Milkway.

आकाशचारी-an aeroplane; moving in the sky (aeroplane, bird etc.).

आकाशतीर-antenna.

आकाशधुरी-the axis of the universe.

आकाशबेल-a parasitic plant.

आकाशमंडल-the celestial or heavenly sphere.

आकाशमुखी-the class of devotees who practise austerity with their faces towards the sky.

आकाशवाणी-a divine communication; an oracle; a revelation.

आकाशी-having to do with space or with sky; atmospheric; aerial.

आकिंचन-poverty.

आकिंचन्व-poverty.

आकिल-wise; intelligent; sensible.

आकीर्ण-full of diffusion; scattered in different places.

आकुंचन-contraction.

आकुंठन-becoming clogged or knotted; shame.

आकुल-anxious; eager; distressed; agitated; confused.

आकुलित-made agitated.

आकृति[1]-intention.

आकृति[2]-form; feature.

आकृष्ट-attracted; drawn.

आक्रिन्दन-lamentation; weeping.

आक्रम-invasion.

आक्रमण-an attack; invasion; aggression.

आक्रमित-attacked; invaded.

आक्रम्यता-predisposition (to infection).

आक्रान्ता-surrounded; besieged; occupied; invaded; covered; defeated; frustrated.

आक्रान्ति-overpowering; attack; rising; assault.

आक्रामक-aggressive; attacking.

आक्षेप-censure; throwing away.

आक्षेपण-the act of throwing away.

आखत-unbroken rice used in oblations.

आखता-castrated (bull, horse).

आखन continually; without interruption; incessantly.

आखना-to describe; to look at; to relate; to wish.

आखर-letter.

आखा-a sieve; a riddle; a pair of bags used as a pannier.

आखिर-eventually; at last; finally; in the end; after all.

आखु-a dig; a mouse; a rat.

आखेट-hunting; terror; the chase.

आखेटक-one who hunts; a hunter.

आख़ोर-leaving; refuse.

आख्या-name; renown; title; report; fame; account.

आख्यात-renowned; said; famous.

आख्यान-description.

आख्यानक-a short tale.

आख्यायिका-a tale; narrative; an episode; a story; a romance.

आगंतुक-a newcomer.

आग-heat; jealously; fire.

आगजनी-arson; criminal act of setting fire.

आगत-happened; arrived; present.

आगति-arrival.

आगमजानी-an augur; a prophet.

आगमन-induction; coming; arrival; approach; origin; appearance.

आगमति-mastered (a topic); learned.

आगमविद्या-the science of Vedas.

आगमसोची-foresighted; foreseeing; looking carefully; forward.

आगमी-one who tells the future; an astrologer.

आगर[1]-a mine, a store; a wise or skilled person; a salt-pit; treasury.

आगर[2]-abode.

आगरी-a person who prepare salt, a salt-maker.

आगा[1]-front portion of a house; face; breast; forehead; chest.

आगा[2]-lord; owner; master.

आगाज़-beginning.

आगान-news; talk; context.

आगामी[1]-coming; impending; future.

आगामी[2]-a fortune-teller.

आगार-treasury; house; place; store.

आगाह-futurity; aware; acquainted with.

आगाही-foreknowledge; information, knowledge.

आगि-fire.

आगु-forthwith.

आगुआ-pommel (of saddle, sword).

आगे forwards; beyond, more; farther; ahead; in future; onwards.

आगोश-embrace.

आग्नेय-volcanic; igneous; glowing; incendiary (weapon).

आग्रह-earnestness; insistence; pressure; urgency; persistence; zeal; importunity; pertinacity.

आघ-cost; price.

आघात-a blow; shock; injury; slaughter; gust; blast; killing; stress.

आघूर्ण-oscillating; rotating; moving; wandering.

आघ्राण-smell; satiety; gratification; satisfaction.

आचमन-the rinsing of mouth with water before religious ceremonies; slipping of water.

आचरना-to behave; to practise.

आचरित-performed.

आचार-conduct; behaviour; manner of life; tradition; rite; ceremony.

आचारिक-customary; traditional.

आचारज-a preceptor.

आचारजी-precep-torship.

आचारवान-of good moral character; leading pure life.

आचार-विचार-religious; observance.

आचार्य-a religious instructor; the priest who invest the pupil with sacred thread and instructs him the Vedas; a preceptor; the annotator of the Vedas.

आचार्या-a spiritual; the wife of an .

आचार्याणी-the wife of a holy instructor or preceptor.

आच्छादन-one who covers; anything that covers.

आछत in the presence of before; except; in the existence of remaining.

आछना-to be; to remain.

आछ-well; thoroughly.

आछेप-objection.

आज-today; now; modern.

आजन्म-throughout the life.

आजमाइश-test; trial; examination.

आजमाई-to test

आजमाना-to test; to try; to examine; to experiment.

आज़मूदा-proved; tested; tried.

आजा-parental grand-father; the preceptor of a preceptor.

आजाद-light-hearted; carefree.

आजानु-reaching up the knee or thigh.

आजार-distress; sickness; trouble; disease.

आजी-parental grandmother.

आजीव-subsistence; profession; livelihood.

आज्ञप्ति-decree; an order.

आज्ञा-licence; permission; sanction; instruction; commandment; flat.

आज्ञान-perception.

आज्ञापक-one who orders; a director; a master.-mandatory.

आज्ञापत्र-warrant; a permit; written order; a passport.

आज्ञापन-mandate; known; order making.

आज्ञाभंग-defiance; insubordination; law-breaking.

आज्ञार्थक-imperative; permissive.

आटना-to fill full.

आटा-flour; meal; any grain ground to powder.

आटोप-covering; pomp; show.

आठवारा-a period of eight days a week.

आडंबर-show; arrogance; tinsel; eclat; parade; affectation.

आड़-support; obstruction; covering; protection.

आड़न-a shield.

आड़ना-to shelter; to obstruct; to forbid; to put in pawn; to stop; to check.

आड़ा-oblique; horizontal; transversal; crooked.

आड़ी[1]-a fellow-member of a team.

आड़ी[2]-a coot.

आड़ी-टेड़ी-obstinacy; crossness.

आड़ू-a peach; of the form of a peach.

आढ़[1]-a kind of fish.

आढ़[2]-a hidden movement; dissembling.

आढ़क-horse bean; a weight of eight seers (near about eight kg.)

आढ़त-brokerage; warehouse; goods held by an agent.

आढ़तिया-an agent.

आढ़्य-rich; excellent; wealthy.

आढ़ा-a measure of grain.

आढ़े-rich; respected.

आणविक-atomic; molecular.

आतंक-apprehension; fear; awe; terror.

आतंकित-apprehensive; awe-struck; fearful; terror-stricken.

आत-the custard-apple.

आत् forms some adverbial expression of cause, by chance or fate.

आततायी-felonious; thievish; incendiary; murderous.

आतप-heat of the sun; burning heat.

आतपी-the sun.

आतपत्र-an umbrella.

आतम, आतमा-soul.

आतश-fire.

आतशदान-furnace; a grate; a chafing dish.

आतशपरस्त-a fire worshipper; a Parsi.

आतशबाजी-display of fireworks.

आतशी-fiery, fireproof; producing fire; pertaining to fire.

आतापी-a kite; a demon.

आतिथेय-host.

आतिथ्य-hospitality.

आतिशक-syphilis; venereal disease.

आतिशय-exaggeration; excess; abundance.

आती-पाती-game similar to hide-and-seek.

आतुर-restless; sick; grieved; perplexed; wounded; agitated.

आतुरी-perplexity; commotion; agitation.

आत्म-pertaining to self; one's own; personal.

आत्मक-having the nature or character of; format.

आत्मकल्याण-one's own good or advantage.

आत्मकार्य-concern; personnel.

आत्मकृत-done by himself.

आत्मग्रही-selfish; avaricious.

आत्मज-one's own off-spring; a son.

आत्मज्ञ-one who knows the supreme spirit.

आत्मज्ञान-self-knowledge; the knowledge of spirit.

आत्मज्ञानी-a mental philosopher.

आत्मतुष्टि-self-satisfaction.

आत्मत्याग-renunciation; renouncement; self-sacrifice.

आत्मानिंदा-self-reproach.

आत्मनिवेदन-self sacrifice.

आत्मप्रशंसा-self-praise.

आत्मबल-initiative.

आत्मरक्षा-self-defence; self-protection.

आत्मरत् (ति)-one who have knowledge of supreme spirit.

आत्मविक्रय-selling of one's self.

आत्मविद्या-the science of the knowledge of soul.

आत्मश्लाघा-egotism; self-applause; to heckle; to quack.

आत्मसमर्पण-capitulation; surrender.

आत्मसंशयी-diffident; wanting self confidence.

आत्मसंसूचन-auto-suggestion.

आत्महत्या-suicide.

आत्महित-good for self.

आत्मा-the reasoning faculty; ego; self; mind; the soul; oneself.

आत्मानंद-the pleasure of being one with supreme soul.

आत्माभिमान-egotism; self-conceit; arrogance.

आत्माभिमानी-self-conceited.

आत्मावलंबी-self-supporting; standing on one's own legs.

आत्मसात्करण-assimilation.

आत्मिक-having to do with the self.

आत्मिकी-study of the psyche.

आत्मीय-pertaining to one's own self; cognate; proper; intimate.

आत्मोन्नति-self-realisation.

आत्यधिक-abundant; plenty.

आत्रेय-of the family of Atri.

आथी-capital; money; steadiness.

आदत-habit; manner; custom; knack.

आदती-customary.

आदम-the first man created on earth.

आदमियत-humanity; civility.

आदमी-a husband; an adult; a man.

आदर-preference; honour; reverence; consideration; estimation.

आदरना-to honour; to revere.

आदर्श-a specimen; ideal; paragon; standard; prototype; model.

आदा-fresh ginger.

आदान-accepting; fees; receiving; acceptance as of taxes.

आदाता-payee.

आदाव-decency; compliment; salutation; ceremony; etiquette.

आदि-early; prior; first; original; beginning with; and so on.

आदिक and so forth, et cetera.

आदिकारण-the primary or first cause; nature; God.

आदित्य-one of various deities; sons of Aditi; a deity.

आदि-existing in the beginning; first.

आदिपुरुष-the first progenitor; the supreme soul; God.

आदिम-prior; original; first; primitive.

आदिशेष-opening balance.

आदी-ginger.

आदूणन-setting.

आदृत-honoured; respected.

आदेय-gratifying; acceptable; fit to be taken.

आदेश-directive; writ; instruction; order.

आदेशक-directing.

आदेशन-directing; instructing.

आदेशी-one who directs; a fortune-teller.

आद्यंत-from beginning to end.

आद्य-first.

आद्यक्षर-initials.

आध-one of the two equal parts.

आधा-a half.

आधान-surety; pregnancy; conception.

आधार-base; foundation; premise; basis.

आधारिक-fundamental;infrastructure.

आधारित-supported; based.

आधारी[1]-format; supported by living on.

आधारी[2]-supporting; resting.

आधासीसी-pain affecting half of the head.

आधि[1]-anxious; thought; expectation; distress.

आधि[2]-pawn; pledge; site; location.

आधिक-half.

आधिक्य-abundance; excess; surplus.

आधिपत्य-control; ownership.

आधिभौतिक-(affliction, pain) caused by animal; material.

आधी-mental; agony; a pawn; perplexity; location; a pledge; situation.

आधीन-in the custody of.

आधुत-shaken, agitated.

आधे-in the middle; half-way.

आधेय-able to be pledged; supportable; support.

आन[1]-modesty; boundary; reputation; way; manner; self-respect.

आन[2]-other.

आन[3]-instant; moment.

आनन्द-glee; jocosity; pleasure; happiness; enjoyment; joy; pleasantry.

आनन्दता-state of joy or bliss.

आनंदित-cheerful; joyful; delighted.

आनन्दी-joyful.

आनक-a large drum; a small tabor; a roaring cloud.

आनद्ध-bound; covered.

आनन-face, mouth.

आनना-to bring.

आनयन-the initiation of the sacred thread; bringing.

आनरेरी-honorary.

आनर्त-a dancing-room.

आन्तरिक-intrinsic; internal.

आन्दोलन-perturbation; agitation; oscillation.

आना-the sixteenth part of a rupee; to return; to come; to appear; an .

आनाकानी-not acknowledging; overlooking; pretence; turning a deaf ear; whispering; conniving; excuse.

आनाह-inflation of stomach.

आनुतोषिक-gratuity.

आनूपूर्वी-serially; in a series; one after another.

आनुभविक-empirical.

आनुभाविक-regular; probable; conjectural; regular.

आनुवंशिक-hereditary.

आनुवंशिकी-genetics.

आनुश्राविक-traditional.

आनुषंगिक-inherent; consequent; incidental (to); connected; concomitant.

आन्विक्षिकी-the science of logic; metaphysics.

आप[1]-one's self; my self; your self; himself.

आप[2]-water.

आपत्-misfortune; disaster.

आपत्काल-disaster; distress; accident; calamity; misfortune.

आपत्ति-a happening; an objection; a query; adversity; misfortune.

आपत्य-having to do with offspring; patronymic; parental.

आपद-disaster.

आपदा-disaster; distress; misfortune.

आपद्धर्म-the action enjoined to be performed only in times of extreme distress.

आपन-one's self.

आपन्न-unfortunate; afflicted; distressed; fallen into.

आपनिक-an emerald.

आपराधिक-criminal.

आपया-river.

आपरिवर्तन-modification.

आपरूप-self-formed; wonderful; peculiar; own-formed; strange.

आपस reciprocally; in common; in concert; mutually.

आपा-one's own existence or reality; arrogance; to lose vanity.

आपात-attack; effect; an emergency; falling upon.

आपनक-a drinking-bout.

आपाती-stand-by.

आपातोपयोगी-stand-by.

आपाधोपी-personal (individual) personal anxiety; grudge.

आपापंथी-depraved; wicked.

आपीड़-a head-dress.

आपूरना-to fill in.

आपूर्ति-supply.

आवेक्षिक-interdepending.

आप्तकाम-self-satisfied; whose desires are fulfilled.

आप्ति-gain; acquisition.

आप्यायित-satisfied.

आप्रवास-immigration.

आप्रवासी-immigrant.

आप्लिव-a dip; a plunge.

आप्लावन-inundation.

आफ़त-misfortune; calamity; disaster; wretchedness.

आफरीन bravo!

आफ़ियत-well-being.

आबटन-allotment.

आब-brilliance; splendour; sharpness; lustre; elegance; honour.

आबजोश-raisin which has been boiled in water.

आबताब-splendour; lustre; brilliance; sheen.

आबदस्त-washing oneself after eating nature.

आबदाना-subsistence; to have no means of livelihood subsistence; livelihood.

आबदार-lustrous; brilliant.

आबदारी-lustre; splendour; brilliance.

आबद्ध-constrained; bound.

आबनूस-ebony.

आबपाशी-irrigation.

आबरू-honour.

आबाल-a blister; a pustule.

आबहवा-weather; climate of a place.

आबाद-settled; under cultivation.

आबादी-cultivated; a habitation; a village; population; place of abode.

आबी-pale; having to do with water; aquatic; watery.

आबेरवाँ-flowing water; a fine muslin.

आबोताब-brilliance.

आबोदाना-means of livelihood.

आबोहवा-climate.

आब्दिक-yearly, annual.

आभरण-nutriment; maintaining.

आभा-tinge; light; splendour; beauty; gleam.

आभार-obligation; burden of household; favour; burden; responsibility.

आभास-reflection; shadow; suggestion.

आभासित-bathed in light; shining.

आभास्वर-shining; radiant.

आभूषण-a piece of jewellery; decoration; an ornament.

आभोग-fullness; plenty; abundance; surfeit.

आभोग्य-not to be used; unfit for use.

आभ्यंतर-internal; interior.

आभ्यंतरिक-internal.

आभ्यासिक-habitual.

आमंत्रण-an invitation; a call; solicitations.

आम[1]-common; general; public (as a meeting, an election); everyday.

आम[2]-the mango tree; its fruit.

आमद-arrival; coming; income; approach; revenue.

आमदनी-income; revenue; proceeds; profit.

आमदिया-a wholesaler in imported goods; one whose income is large.

आमनिया-cleaned grain.

आमय-disease; sickness.

आमरक्तातिसार-bloody dysentery.

आमरण throughout one's life; till death.

आमर्दन-rubbing; violently.

आमर्ष-anger; rancour; envy; intolerance.

आमातिसार-dysentery.

आमात्य-minister.

आमादनी-alertness; readiness; briskness.

आमादा-prepared; ready; come; roused; alert; disposed.

आमालक-land near a mountain.

आमीन amen; so be it.

आमुख-the prelude of a drama; introduction.

आमूल-or to; from; the root.

आमेजना-to dought; to mix.

आमेख्ता-learnt.

आमोद-pleasure; odour; orgy; joy; fragrance; amusement.

आम्र-the mango.

आम्ल-acidity.

आय-receipts; revenue; profit; income.

आयंदा in future.

आयत-wide; long.

आयतन[1]-a place of worship; an alter; a house; a mansion; a resting place.

आयतन[2]-volume.

आयत्त-dependent on; subject to.

आयस-an armour for the protection of body, iron.

आयसु-command; order.

आया-lady's mind; an ; children's nurse.

आयात-imported goods.

आयातक-an importer.

आयाम-extension; regulation; length.

आयामन-extending; extension.

आयास-a labouring long or hard; exertion; effort.

आयीता-ready; prepared.

आयु-age, duration of life.

आयुध-weapon; ornament; sheath; armour; defensive.

आयुर्वेद-the science of medicine in Sanskrit.

आयुष्-prolonging life.

आयोग-commission.

आयोगव-the carpenter's tribe.

आयोजक-organiser.

आयोजन-organising; convening; organisation; arranging.

आयोजित-organised.

आरंभ-beginning; to begin; dawn.

आरंभिक-introductory; unadvanced; undeveloped; primary; elementary.

आरंभी-initiating; beginning.

आरंभना-to begin.

आर[1]-spike; a spoke a pointed implement; a goad; awl.

आर[2]-a kind of ladle used in making of sugar.

आर[3]-worn by women on the forehead; an ornament.

आर[4]-a boundary between two fields.

आरक्त-rosy; slightly red.

आरक्षक-providing protection or security; a guard.

आरक्षण-reservation.

आरक्षित निधि-reserve fund.

आरक्षा-security; protection.

आरक्षी-guard.

आरजा-disease; illness.

आरजू-wish; longing; eagerness; hope; eager; request; entreaty.

आरण्य-wild; a forest.

आरत-tortured.

आरति-distress.

आरती-a ceremony performed during worshipping a God; a dish of lamp.

आरन-a jungle; a forest.

आरना-to hesitate; to stop.

आरपार over; astride; across; athwart.

आरम्भ-begun; commenced.

आरभती-a highly ornate style of composition.

आरव-strongly audible noise.

आरस-laziness.

आरसी-a mirror; thumb-ring containing a mirror.

आरस्य-insipidity; dullness (of nature); spiritlessness.

आरा-a shoemaker's awl.

आराइश-preparation; decoration; good arrangement.

आराति-enemy; foe.

आराध-to propitiate; to adore; to worship; to gravity.

आराम-a pleasure; ease; a grove; pleasure; rest; peace; solace; comfort.

आरास्ता-embellished; adorned; decorate.

आरि-a wise man; holy man.

आरेखण-delineation; drawing; sketch.

आरुँधना-to squeeze neck; to strangle.

आरुढ़-stagnant; bent; mounted; determined; ascended.

आरो-nose, sound.

आरोगना-to take one's meals during the day; to eat.

आरोग्य-freedom from disease; health.

आरोधना-to stop; to obstruct.

आरोप-allegation; charge; false knowledge; transmutation; predication.

आरोह-the buttocks; mounting on a elephant or horse.

आर्जव-sincerity; candour; honesty.

आर्त-distress; injured; hurt; afflicted.

आर्तव-timely; opportune; produced in season.

आर्ति-pain; distress; affliction.

आर्थिक-monetary; financial; pecuniary.

आर्द्र-moist; humid; wet.

आर्द्रता-moisture; humidity.

आर्द्रा-the sixth lunar mansion.

आर्य-honourable; noble; excellent.

आर्या-mother-in-law; grandmother; the goddess Parvati.

आलंकारिक-figurative; rhetorical.

आलंग-sexual passion arising in mares.

आलंब-shelter; base; protection; foundation; support.

आल-tears; moisture.

आलकस-lazyness.

आलक्षण-ill-fated; unfortunate.

आलत-implement; equipment; apparatus.

आलन-mud mixed with straw used in plastering or brick-making.

आलपीन-a pin.

आलम-the world; the universe; condition; time; multitude; mankind.

आलमारी-an almirah.

आलमी-of the world.

आलय-residence; house; dwelling; abode.

आलस्य-indolence; torpor; inaction; laziness; idleness; sloth; trounce.

आला-a small recess in a wall; a niche; excellent.-an instrument; a tool.

आलान-a rope.

आलाप-speaking; conversion; a dialogue; the prelude to singing.

आलिंगन-an embrace; endearment.

आलि-a female friend; a female bee; row; line; scorpion.

आलिम-knowing; learned; a learned man.

आली[1]-a woman's female friend.

आली[2]-exalted; high; noble.

आलू-yarn; potato.

आलूचा-a type of small plum.

आलेख-script; writing; graph.

आलेखक-conspirator; plotter.

आलेख्य-picture; painting.

आलेप-liniment; plaster.

आलेपन-smearing; applying (embrocation) plastering.

आलोक-brightness; lustre; splendour; moonlight.

आलोचन-seeing; review; criticism; survey.

आलोच्य-to be considered; under consideration; review.

आलोड़ना-to stir; to chum.

आवंटित-allotted; divided.

आव[1]-life-time; age.

आव[2]-to arrive; to come.

आवटना-unsteadiness; uproar.

आवधिक-periodical.

आवन-coming; approach.

आवभगत-entertainment.

आवरण-a cover; a shield; the protective covering of a book; obstruction.

आवर्त-returning; turn; turning motion; cyclical movement or progress.

आवर्तक-recurring; recurrent.

आवर्ती-recurring.

आवली[1]-series; row; range; dynasty; lineage.

आवली[2]-danger; disaster; calamity; mortal.

आवश्यक-needful; exigent; necessary; compulsory; essential; emergent.

आवा[1]-a potter's kiln.

आवा[2]-furnace.

आवागमन-coming and going; metempsychosis; transmigration.

आवाज-report; sound; voice; whisper.

आवाजा-jeers; taunting.-innuendoes.

आवाजाही-coming and going; thoroughfare.

आवारजा-ledger.

आवारा-without house and home; wandering; separated from family.

आवास-place of residence or habitation; housing; abode.

आवासन-immigration.

आवासित-habitat; resident.

आवासीय-residential.

आवास्य-habitable.

आवाह-to call; to summon.

आवाहन-invocation of a deity; respectful invitation; summoning; address.

आविद्ध-pierced; ripe.

आविर्भाव-appearance; emergence; rise; manifestation.

आविर्भूत-visible; apparent; created; manifested.

आविल-poet; muddied; impure.

आविष्करण-inventing; invention.

आविष्कार-an invention; contrivance; manifestation; a discovery.

आवीक्षण-reconnaissance.

आविष्ट-covered; covered over; enclosed; surrounded.

आवृत्त-occurred; repeated; recurred.

आवेक्षण-watch observation.

आवेग-haste; surge; fit (of anger).

आवेजा-pendant; ear-ring.

आवेदन-an application (form).

आवेष्ट-epilepsy; fury; excitement; tantrum.

आवेश-frenzy; fit; access.

आशंसा-hope; desire.

आशंका-doubt; fear; apprehension; awe; danger.

आशंकित-suspected; fearful; alarmed; feared; apprehended.

आशना-an acquaintance; a friend; a mistress; a lover.

आशय-purpose; intention; drift; aim; meaning; end; design; sense; purport; import; opinion.

आशा-trust; hope; expectation.

आशोधन-alteration; modification.

आशिक-a suitor; a lover.

आशिक़ा-sweetheart; mistress.

आशिक़ाना-amorous; erotic; loving.

आशियाना-nest; small dwelling.

आशिष-benediction; blessing.

आशी-eater; devourer.

आशीर्वाद-benediction; blessing.

आशीष-blessing.

आशु-swiftly; quickly; speedily.

आश्चर्य-wonder; surprise; astonishment.-astonishing.

आश्रम-hermitage an

आश्रय-reliance; retreat; stand; behalf.

आश्रित-a dependant; a servant; adherent.

आश्लेष-connection; embrace; intimate.

आश्लेषण-mixture.

आश्वस्त-reassured.

आश्वस्ति-warranty.

आश्वास-breath; comfort; chapter; consolation; breathing.

आश्वासन-comfort; consolation; assurance; reassurance.

आषाढ़-a month of Hindu year.

आसंग-means; ability; association; instrumentality; contact; attachment.

आस-faith; hope; expectation; desire; longing; confidence.

आसकत-indolence.

आसकती-lazy; idle.

आसक्त-strongly attached; engrossed; devoted; infatuated.

आसते slowly.

आसन-posture; a seat; mat of cloth.

आसनी-a small carpet or skin.

आसन्न-impending; drawn near; contiguous; immediate; on the point of imminent.

आसमन्तात on all sides; all round; wholly.

आसमान-heaven; the sky; paradise.

आसरतू-dependant.

आसमुद्र-up to the sea coast.

आसरना-to give shelter; to take shelter.

आसरा-decoction; distillate; liquor; potion.

आसरैत-dependent.

आसवन-distillation; distilling.

आसवनी-a distillery.

आसाइश-comfort; ease; repose; facility; enjoyment.

आसान-convenient; manageable; simple; easy.

आसाम-Assam; a state of India.

आसमी-Assamese.

आसामी[1]-the language of Assam.

आसामी[2]-a customer.

आसार-symptom; sign.

आसिख-benediction.

आसिन-var.

आसीन-sitting; seated.

आसु quickly.

आसुर-devilish; pertaining to a demon.

आसुरी-a surgery.

आसूदा-prosperous; tranquil; satisfied; opulent; calm.

आसिन-same as the month of .

आसों this year.

आस्तिक-a pious man; one who believes in God; religious.

आस्ति-a (financial) asset property.

आस्ते slowly.

आस्त्र-armed.

आस्थगन-postponement.

आस्थगित-deferred.

आस्था-regard; belief; consideration; faith; a session; respect.

आस्थान-footing; place of sitting; pedigree; assembly; birth.

आस्थानी-auditorium.

आस्थित-staying.

आसाद-place; birth; rank; dignity; situation; footing; pedigree; site.

आसादन-procurement.

आस्पद-rank; place; community; situation; abode; status.

आस्य-visage; face.

आस्वाद-good taste; relish; flavour.

आस्वादन-relishing; trying; tasting.

आस्वादित-tasted; relished.

आह sorrow; indicating pain.

आहट-the sound of footsteps; light sound; noise.

आहत-wounded; offended; injured.

आहन-iron.-blacksmith.

आहनी-made of iron.

आहर-a small pond; a drain, a trough for watering; a salt-pit.

आहर-जाहर-coming and going.

आहरण-seizing; the carrying of an object from one place to another place.

आहल-freshness of soil.

आहलाना-to rejoice.

आहवन-a sacrifice; oblation; an offering to a God.

आहाँ-call, a cry for help; proclamation.

आहा joy; expressing wonder, aha! alas! bravo! alas! well done!

आहार-foodstuffs; nourishment; food; food and drink.

आहार्य-artificial; accepted eatable; consumable.

आहित-placed; tenderly; pawned; stationed.

आहिस्तगी-slowness.

आहिस्ता slowly; gently; softly; tenderly.

आहुत-hospitality; sacrifice; offering oblations to a deity in fire.

आहुति-sacrifice; burnt; oblation; offering.

आह्निक-diurnal; pertaining to a day.

आह्लाद-delight; mirth; festivity; joy.

आह्लादक-causing joy.

आह्वान . cry; summon; call (to).

इ-The third vowel of the Devnagari alphabet.

इंगलिसिया-pensioner; an invalid soldier.

इंगित-indication; gesture; hint; sign; motion.

इंगुर-vermillion.

इंगुरौटी-a small box in which vermilion is kept.

इंच-the twelfth part of a foot.

इंचाव-drawing, pulling, attraction.

इंजर-पिंजर-skeleton.

इंजील-the Bible, the holy scripture of Christian.

इँडुरी, इँडुवा-a circular fold of cloth put on the heat while carrying a burden.

इंतकाम-reprisal; revenge; retaliation.

इंतकाल-transfer of one's right to another; destruction; death.

इंतखाब-election; selection; choice.

इंतजाम-arrangement.

इंतजार-expecting; waiting.

इंतहा-end; limit; utmost.

इंतिकाल-death.

इंतिख़ाब-election; selection.

इंतिज़ाम-arrangement.

इंतिज़ार-waiting.

इंतिहा-limit; end.

इंदराज-entry.

इंदारा-a large masonry well.

इंदिरा-the goddess Lakshmi.

इंदीवर-the blue lotus.

इंदु-the moon; camphor.

इंदुर-a rat; a mouse.

इंद्र-the king of Gods; ruler; Jupiter; the god of rain; glorious.

इंद्रजाल-trickery; magic; illusion; juggling; deception; stratagem.

इंद्रधनुष-a rainbow; bow in heaven.

इंद्रनील-sapphire.

इंद्रप्रस्थ-old name of modern Delhi.

इंद्रलोक &-the abode of Indra.

इंद्राणी-the wife of God Indra; a kind of creeper; name of a medicine or plant;

इंद्रायन-wild gourd; a beautiful creeper with bitter fruits; colocynth.

इंद्रायुध-the rainbow; thunderbolt of Indra.

इंद्रिय-the genitals; the senses; the organs of sense.

इंद्रियाजित-one who has control over his all senses.

इंद्रीजुलाब-a diuretic medicine which produces profuse urination.

इंधन-fire wood; fire.

इंसाफ-justice; decision; equity; impartiality.

इक[1]-forms adjective and derived agent nouns from nominal roots with or roots or initial vowel.

इक[2]-one.

इकजोर at the same time; together; simultaneously.

इकट्ठा-collected; totalled; assembled; taken together.

इकतर-collected.

इकता-unity.

इकताई-matchlessness; singleness; solitariness.

इकतान-steady; uniform; harmonious; similar.

इकतारा-one-stringed musical instrument like guitar.

इकत्र-together.

इकदाम-going forward; endeavour; effort.

इकबाल-dignity.

इकमुश्त सौदा-package deal.

इकराम-honouring; complementing; remuneration; respect.

इक़रार-promise; agreement; attestation; acknowledgement; assurance.

इकला-alone.

इकलाई[1]-a single fold of material; single sheet; a verity of cotton;

इकलाई[2]-loneliness.

इकलौता-single.-an only son.

इकहाई together; all of a sudden; immediately.

इकाई-unit.

इकी forms-nouns serving as name of sciences and technical fields.

इकौज-a woman who has born only one child.

इकौना-of one kind, pure.

इकौसो-alone.

इक्कस-envy; jealousy.

इक्का-alone; unequalled; a champion who fights alone; stray; unique; cattle.

इक्षु-sugar-cane.

इक्ष्वाकु-bitter gourd; name of a king.

इखराज-charge; expense.

इखलाकी-moral; ethical.

इखलास-friendship; intimacy; attachment devotion; love.

इख्तियार-right option.

इख्तिलाफ-discord; opposition.

इखु-an arrow.

इगर-दिगर-disarranged; in disorder.

इच्छना-to wish; to desire.

इच्छा-appetite; will; yearning; wish; view; desire; to incline; to yearn.

इच्छित-wished for.

इजतिराब-anxiety; distress.

इजमाल-abridgment; an abstract; synopsis; joint possession (of a property).

इजरा-causing to circulate; issuing; or giving effect to.

इजराय-performance; occupation; execution.

इजहार-disclosure; display; declaration; statement.

इजाज़त-permission; sanction; consent; order.

इज़ार-trousers.-lecherous.

इजारा-letting of something on lease.

इज्जत-esteem; honour; grandeur; dignity.

इठलाना-to walk affectedly; to speak other than in a normal way as pertly.

इठाई-intimacy; love, friendship; desire.

इडली-a steamed rice-cake; a south-indian dish.

इत here; this way; hither.

इत forms passive past participle adjectives from verb roots and from modified forms of verb stems.

इतक-so much; this much.

इतना, इतने-this much; so much, so many; as much.

इतमाम-completion; accomplishment.

इतमीनान-confidence; ease; comfort; satisfaction.

इतर-remaining; other; inferior.

इतर (इत्र)-perfume; scent bottle; perfume-box.

इतराजी-enmity; objection; opposition.

इतराना-to behave with pride; to exult or conceit or arrogance; to strut.

इतरेतर mutually; reciprocally.

इतवार-Sunday.

इताअत-obedience; submission; homage.

इति-end; finish; conclusion.

इतिहास-thus indeed it was; history; annals; account; tradition.

इतेक-so much.

इतै-hither.

इतौ-so much.

इतफ़ाक़-fortune; concord; incident; similarity; friendship; accident.

इत्तला-information; knowledge; intimation; acquired.

इत्तहाद-union; league.

इत्थं-in this manner; in this way.

इत्यादि-etc.

इत्रीफल-a purgative medicine.

इदमित्थं-truly; indeed.

इदानीं-at this time; now.

इधर-उधर-here and there; back and forth; hither and thither.

इनकलाब-transformation; change; revolution; turn.

इनकार-to disavow; to deny; denial; refusal.

इनफ़िसाल-(law) decision (of a case).

इनसान-man; mankind.

इनसाफ-fair decision; justice.

इनहिसार-encirclement; blockade.

इंधन-fuel; fire wood; timber.

इनाम-prize; gift; reward; need.

इनायत-favour; gift; bounty; obligation.

इनारा-a well.

इनेगिने-a few; the selected few.

इन्कार-denial.

इफ़रात-abundance; profusion; extravagance.

इबरत-warning; example.

इबरानी-Jewish.

इबलीस-the devil; Satan.

इबादत-adoration; worship.

इबारत-structure; article; essay; diction; sentence; style.

इब्तिदा-beginning.

इब्रानी-Hebrew; Jewish.

इभ-an elephant.

इम in this way.

इमकान-practicability; power; possibility; capacity.

इमदाद-donation; assistance; help; subsidy.

इमरती-a sweet made from pulse; a small type of melon.

इमला-correct writing; orthography; dictation.

इमली-the tamarind tree; its fruit.

इमानदार-simple; honest; incorrupt; upright.

इमाम-a religious letter; patriarch.

इमामदस्ता-a mortar of iron or brass for producing things.

इमामा-turbon.

इमामबाड़ा-the yard in which Mohammedans of the sect keep and bury their Tazias.

इमारत-building; a building; structure; superstructure.

इमारती-used in building (material), having to do with building.

इमि-in this way.

इम्तहान-test; examination.

इम्तियाज़-distinction; discernment.

इम्तिहान-examination.

इरषा-envy.

इरशाद-direction; order; instruction.

इरसाल-sending; sent; a remittance; despatch.

इरादतन-intentionally.

इरादा-wish; inclination; desire; intention; plan; purpose; effect; design.

इर्द-गिर्द-all around; round about; around; in the vicinity.

ईर्षना-ardent desire.

इलज़ाम-charge; censure; calumny; libel; accusation.

इलहाम-inspiration; revelation.

इलाका-estate; attachment; connection; region; holding connection.

इलाज-medical treatment; remedy; cure.

इलाम-order; an official notice; order.

इलायची-cardamom.

इलाही-the Almighty; God.

इल्जाम-assured belief; blame; conviction; reproach.

इल्तमास-petition.

इल्तिजा-a request; assured belief; solicitations.

इल्तिफ़ात-attention; regard; courtesy.

इल्म-knowledge; learning.

इल्लत-defect; pretext; perplexity; disease; dispute; bad habit.

इल्ली-caterpillar.

इव-similar; resembling.

इशरत-enjoyment; pleasure.

इशारा-command; sign; wink; symbol; hint; suggestion; symbol.

इश्क-love; passion; craze; to have a love affair.

इश्किया-erotic; amatory.

इश्तहार-notification; advertisement; promulgation; publication.

इषा-shaft (of plough or vehicle); pole.

इषु-an arrow.

इष्ट-wished; beloved; favourite.

इष्टदेव-a tutelary deity; the favourite god.

इष्टांश-quantum.

इस-is, this, it.

इसपात-steel which is hard and rough.

इसबगोल-seed of the flea-wort; horse's ear.

इसराज-a kind of lute.

इसराफ़-excess; extravagance.

इसरार-act of concealing; keeping secret; disclosure.

इसलाम-Islam (a religion).

इसलाह-correction.

इसारत-hint.

इसुमसीह-Jesus Christ.

इसे-objective case of

इस्टंट-assistant.

इस्तक़बाल-welcome; reception.

इस्तगामा-calling for help; demanding justice; complaint.

इस्तदुआ-request; entreaty.

इस्तरी-an iron; ironing.

इस्तिंजा-wiping or washing the private parts after satisfying nature.

इस्तिक़बाल-welcome.

इस्तिहकाम-firmness; confirmation.

इस्तरारी-permanent; perpetual.

इस्तिरी-a smoothing iron.

इस्तिलाह-phrase; usage; idiom; a technical term.

इस्तिसनाई-exceptional.

इस्तीफा-resignation.

इस्तेदाद-abilities; capacity; readiness.

इस्तेमाल-employment; use; application.

इस्पात-steel.

इस्पाती-made of steel; tempered.

इस्म-name.

इस्लाम-the Mohammedan religion.

इह here; in this place; in this world.

इहलौकिक-of this world; worldly.

इहाँ-here.

इहि-this, it.

ई The fourth vowel of the Devnagari alphabet.

ईंगुर-cinnabar; red lead; vermilion; mercuric oxide.

ईंघे-hither; here.

ईंचना-to attract; to allure; to pull to draw.

ईंट-a brick; a tile.

ईंटालारी-laying of bricks.

ईंडवा-same as above.

ईंडवी-turban.

ईंढ़-equal; tantamount; similar.

ईंदुर-a mouse; a rat.

ईंधन-fuel (chemical, mineral, wood).

ईक्षक-an onlooker; an observer.

ईक्षण-superintendence; the act of seeing; sight.

ईक्षणिक-an astrologer.

ईक्षित-understood; observed; seen.

ईख-sugar-cane.

ईखना-to look; to see.

ईछन-the eye.

ईछना-to wish; to desire.

ईजा-injury; harm; molestation.

ईजाद[1]-an invention; created; approbation.

ईजाद[2]-addition; increase.

ईजादी-one who invent; inventive.

ईठ-a friend.

ईठना-to desire; to intend.

ईठि-lance; spear.

ईडा-invocation; admiration; praise.

ईढ-persistence; obstinacy.

ईढी-obstinate.

ईतर-impertinent; giving oneself airs.

ईति-drought, any seasonal disaster (as flood, plague of insects).

ईद-a Mohammedan festival.

ईदी-money given to children on

ईदृश in this way; this; such.

ईप्सा-wish; desire.

इप्सित-desired; longed for.

ईबीसीबी-the hissing sound coming from the mouth.

ईमान-faith; truth; confidence; belief; conscience.

ईरखा-jealously.

ईरित-urged; directed; impelled.

ईर्षणा-jealously.

ईश-master; king; leader; mercury; Shiva.

ईशान-a title of Shiva.

ईशा-power; dominion.

ईशानी-an epithet of .

ईशिता-divine or supernatural power; supremacy.

ईश्वर-ruler; ; providence; lord; owner; king; god.

ईश्वरत्व-supremacy.

ईष-master; lord; king; god.

ईषत-very little.

ईषार-a small quantity; a little; a bit.

ईषदुष्ण-lukewarm.

ईषद्दर्शन-side look; ogle.

ईषद्धास-smile.

ईषना-ardent desire.

ईसवी-Christian.

ईसा-Jesus Christ.

ईसाई-Christian.

ईसार-an offering; presenting.

ईस्वी-century.

ईहाँ here.

ईहा-energy; wish; effort; exertion; greed; desire.

उ

उ-The fifth vowel of the Devnagari alphabet.

उँकारी-a curve mark resembling the Arabic letter

उँगनी-smearing; greasing.

उँगल-finger.

उँगुली-the finger.

उँघाई-same as

उँघाना-to be drowsy; to doze.

उँचान-height.

उँचाना-to raise; to lift.

उँचास[1]-height.

उँछ-gleaning of a field; gathering grain of a field after harvesting.

उँछवृत्ति-to make livelihood by collecting grains from field.

उँजाना-light.

उँजियार-shining.

उँडेलना-to pour.

उँदुर-a rat; a mouse.

उँह expressing refusal, contempt.

उऋण-out of debt.

उअना-to grow.

उकठा-dry; sapless.

उकडूँ-squatting with the feet flat on the ground.

उकताना-to fret; to tired of; to be dejected or melancholy.

उकतारू-instigator; plotter.

उकताहट-boredom.

उकलना-to open a flower; to boil up over; to be unfolded.

उकलाना-to vomit.

उकलाई-vomiting; nausea.

उकवत-a kind of disease in which pustules appear on skin and there is itching.

उकना-to feel nausea; to feel sick; to vomit.

उकवथ-a skin disease.

उकवाँ at a guess; roughly.

उकसोंहाँ-rising or swelling up.

उकाब-an eagle.

उकासना-to excite; to lay open; to open; to dig out and throw above.

उकेरक-engraver.

उकेलना-to remove the folds; to tear off; to remove peel.

उकेला-the strands used in forming a rope.

उक्त-aforesaid; said; spoken.

उखड़ना-to be rooted up; to be raised; to be torn asunder; to slip out.

उखट-to break off; to tear off.

उखटना-to stumble.

उखमज-mischief; turmoil.

उखली-a mortar; of wood or stone for pounding grain.

उखाड़-rooting up; eradication.

उखाड़ी-a field of sugar-cane.

उखारी-a field of sugarcane.

उखाड़ू-rooting up; eradicating.

उखेलना-to write something; to paint a picture.

उगटना-to abuse; to revile.

उगना-to germinate; to spring up; to grow; to rise.

उगसाना-to excite.

उगसारना-to express; to narrate; to describe.

उगाना-to create; to germinate; to expose; to raise; to cause.

उगारना-to save; to rescue; to clean to sediment from a well.

उगालदान-a spitting-pot; a spittoon.

उगाही-realization; levy.

उग्र-fierce; extreme; harsh; dire; terrible; cruel; overpowering.

उघटना-to disclose a secret; to revile a man by reference to his defects; to vilify.

उघठा-one who repeatedly mentions favours shown by him.

उघाड़ा-opened; uncovered.

उघेलना-to open; to lay bare.

उचकन-a support.

उचकना-to stand on tip-toe; to spring up; to leap; to bound; to snatch a thing by pouncing upon it.

उचक्का-a wicked person; a thief; a swindler; a pickpocket; a rogue.

उचना-to rise; to ascend.

उचाने-rise; elevation.

उचरंग-a moth.

उचलना-to peel (as skin); to be separated.

उचा-to raise; to elevate.

उचाट-want of interest; sorrow; uneasiness; indifference; dejection; restlessness.

उचाटी-sorrow; indifference.

उचाड़ना-to tear off.

उचाना-to raise; to elevate.

उचार-voicing (of a name); utterance.

उचावा-talking in one's sleep; nightmare.

उचित-suitable; expedient; sufficient.

उचितता-appropriateness.

उचौहाँ-raised up; elevated.

उच्च-lofty; higher; superior.

उच्चत on high; aloft.

उच्चतम-highest; most eminent; maximum.

उच्चर-to pronounce.

उच्चावचन-fluctuation.

उच्चाट-uprooting.

उच्चाटन-driving away (by magical means); estranging; alienating.

उच्चायुक्त-High Commissioner.

उच्चार-pronunciation; utterance.

उच्चारण-enunciation; expression; voice; deliverance; utterance.

उच्चारित-uttered; pronounced; spoken.

उच्चार्य-to be pronounced.

उच्छन्न-uprooted; torn up; destroyed.

उच्छलना-to leap.

उच्छव-festival.

उच्छाह-agitation.

उच्छिन-cut off; waste; ruined; laid; destroyed.

उच्छ-cough which appears on the stoppage of something in the throat.

उच्छू-cough made to clear the throat; choking.

उच्छ्वसित-living in full blooming state.

उच्छ्वास-breathing out; a breath.

उछंल-lap; bosom.

उछंकना-to regain senses after intoxication.

उछटना-withdraw.

उछलना-to leap; to rebound; to jump; to spring up; to start up.

उछाल-leap; jump; hop; vomiting.

उछाह-desire; glad occasion; festival; enthusiasm; eager.

उछाही-zealous; ardent; enthusiastic; merry-making.

उछीर-opportunity; room; favourable time; place.

उजरत-wages; remuneration.

उजराना-to make bright; to cleanse.

उजलत-haste; quickness.

उजला-radiant; white; shining; splendid; clear; luminous.

उजागर-bright; shining; gaudy; renowned; splendid.

उजाड़-laid waste; a ruined place; deserted; divested.

उजाड़ू-destructive; wasteful; squandering; laying waste.

उजान upstream.

उजाला-splendour; light of moon or stars; daybreak; daylight; moonlight.

उजाली-moonlight.

उजास-light; splendour; luminosity; brightness.

उजियार-light; bright.

उजियारना-to brighten; to make bright.

उजियाला-light.

उजीर-minister.

उजूबा-wonder.

उजेला-light; sheen; brightness; moonlight.

उज्जल-bight.

उज्जगरी-manifest.

उज्जयिनी-the name of the old capital of Malwa.

उज्जैन-an old city in Madhya Pradesh.

उज्र-*mas.* objection; opposition.

उज्ज्वल-beauty; bright; clear; beautiful; splendid; splendour; refulgent.

उझकना-to jump; to be startled; to stand on tip-toe; to peep.

उझर[1]-to flow; to flood.

उझर[2]-to pour out.

उझरना-to rise aloft.

उझलना-to pour or throw a fluid from one vessel to another.

उझाँकना to peep.

उटंगन-an edible grass; a king of four-leafed plant.

उटंग-high on the leg; not long enough (trousers).

उटक-to guess; to guess at.

उटकना-to make a conjecture.

उटज-a hut of leaves; cell of a hermit; a hermitage.

उठँगन-support; wedge (used to raise).

उठँगना-to rest upon for support; to lean against.

उठंगल-dull-wetted; stupid.

उठना-to get up; to rise; to stand up; to heave; to accrue; to arise.

उठ-बैठ-to stand up; to rise.

उठल्लू-not having any fixed abode movable.-a wanderer; vagrant.

उठवाना-to be lifted by another; to be removed from a place; to cause.

उठवैया-one who rises or helps to raise (a load).

उठाईगीरा-petty thief; a pilferer; a rascal.

उठाऊ-extravagant; portable; lavish.

उठान-disbursement; swelling; growth; beginning; rise; expense; first stage of motion; act or rising.

उठा-बैठी-kneeling and standing.

उठाव-ablation; support; expenditure; disbursement.

उठौवा-one who does not stick to a place; roving.

उड़नछू-vanishing; passing from view; disappearing.

उड़नफल-fruit, when eaten by someone then he will supposed to get power to flying.

उड़ना-to soar; to take a fly; to explode; to vanish; wing.

उड़प-a raft; a kind of dance; the moon.

उड़ाऊ-extravagant; dispensable; wasteful.

उड़ाका, उड़का-a flyer; an aviator.

उड़ान-a leap; flying; bound; flight.

उड़ायक-flying.

उड़ास-place of residence; a palace; abode.

उड़िया-the Oriya language.

उड़ीसा-Orissa.

उड़बर-a wild fig tree.

उड-a planet; a star; a bird; a water; a boatman.

उडुप[1]-lord of the stars; the moon.

उडुप[2]-a kind of dance.

उडुपति, उडुराज-the common bedbug; the moon.

उडेलना-to pour out; to empty (the contents of a vessel); to pour out (as emotions).

उड़ेनी-the fire-fly.

उड़ाहाँ-a flyer; an aviator.

उढ़क-crying; wailing.

उढ़कना-to upset; to recline a thing against another; to turn over.

उढ़री-a woman taken by a man to live with; a second wife.

उढ़ावनि-shawl.

उढ़ावनी-a coverlet.

उढ़ीक-a support; wedge.

उत-there; thither.

उतंग-lofty; high; elevated.

उतंत-there; thither; at that position or place.

उतन-on that side; thither.

उतना-as much as that; as many as that.

उतपानना-to germinate; to produce in the earth.

उतरंग-the wooden arch surmounting a door.

उतरना-to come down from a height; to fall; to get down; to fall in value.

उतरहा-northern.

उतराई-the toll which is paid for crossing a river; a slope; descent.

उतरायल-second-hand.

उतराहाँ towards the north.

उतलाना-to make haste.

उतान, उताना-lying on the back; supine; upright.

उतायल-hasty.-haste.

उतार-descent; decrease; fall (as of price or flood-water); reduction.

उतारना-to descend; to lower; to cause; to bring down.

उतारा-toll; (to ariver); landing-place; crossing.

उतारू-bent on; determined.

उताल quickly; hurriedly.

उताली-quickness; rashness; hastiness.

उतावला-impatient; rash; headstrong.

उऋण-freed from obligation; out of debt.

उत in that place; there.

उत्कंठा-longing; sorrow; ardour; uneasiness; craving; care; impatience.

उत्कंठित-longing; eagerly; desirous.

उत्कट-keen; fervid; excessive; difficult; furious; boisterous; fervent; intense.

उत्कर्ण-having the ears raised or cocked (an animal).

उत्कर्ष-excess; elevation; increase; superiority; excellence; eminence; rise.

उत्कर्षक-elevating; raising; developing; increasing.

उत्कर्षता-excess; exaltation; excellence; superiority.

उत्कल-the province of Orissa.

उत्कलित-blossoming; loosened; unbounded.

उत्कीर्ण-carved; engraved; cut.

उत्कुण-a bug; a louse.

उत्कोच-a bribe.

उत्कृष्ट-excellence; superior; excellent; outstanding; superiority; good.

उत्कृष्टता-excellence; superiority.

उत्क्रम-reverse.

उत्क्राम-turn out.

उत्केन्द्र-eccentric.

उत्खनक-excavator.

उत्खनन-excavation.

उत्खात-a hole; a cavity.

उत्तंगक-prostrative.

उत्तंस-an ornament of ears.

उत्त-amazement; wonder; doubt; astonishment.

उत्तप्त-excited; anxious; well heated; very desirous.

उत्तम-excellent; highest; choice; supreme; best.

उत्तमतया thoroughly; well.

उत्तर[1]-an answer; superiority; a reply; best; power; defence.

उत्तर[2]-the north.

उत्तरता-posterity.

उत्तरण-taking over or across (to the far bank); landing.

उत्तरकोशल-the old name of modern Oudh.

उत्तरक्रिया-funeral rites.

उत्तरजीवी-surviving.

उत्तरदाता-a responsible person.

उत्तरदायित्व-responsibility; burden.

उत्तरपक्ष-the principal premise in logic.

उत्तरपद-the last work of compound in Sanskrit.

उत्तरमीमांसा-another name for Vedanta philosophy.

उत्तरवादिता-liability.

उत्तरा-wife of Abhimanyu.

उत्तराधिकार-reversion; inheritance; succession.

उत्तराधिकारी-an heir; reversioner; a successor; inheritor.

उत्तराभास-a false answer.

उत्तरार्ध-the northern part; a ; the upper part of the body; the latter part of a book.

उत्तराषाढ़ा-the twenty-first lunar mansion.

उत्तरी-north hemisphere; northern.

उत्तल-convex.

उत्तान-inverted; lying on the back; upside down.

उत्ताल-towering; huge.

उत्ताप-intense heat; perplexity; sorrow; warmth; excitement; affliction; embarrassment; affliction.

उत्तीर्ण-passed; crossed over; liberated; successful.

उत्तुंग-very high; conspicuous; prominent.

उत्त-an instrument for making folds on cloth.

उत्तेजक-exciting; irritant; incentive; stimulating; burning; rousing influence; stimulant.

उत्तेजना-excitement; instigation; actuation; thrill; stimulation; flurry.

उत्तेजित-stimulated; excited.

उत्तोलक-lever.

उत्तोलन-raising; lifting.

उत्तोलित raised.

उत्किरक-engraver.

उत्थवना-to begin; to commence.

उत्थान-awakening; rising up; the awakening of Vishnu; progressive.

उत्थापन-the act of raising up; awakening; erection; moving; stretching.

उत्पत्ति-produce; origin; articulation; production; birth.

उत्पन्न-secured; produced; born.

उत्पल-a species of blue lotus; a louts.

उत्पाटन-uprooting; plucking off; extirpating.

उत्पाटित-uprooted; eradicated.

उत्पात-oppression; injury; a portent; disturbance; plague; confusion.

उत्पादक-productive; having to do with production.

उत्पादन-giving birth to; creation; generation; production.

उत्पादित-produced.

उत्पीड़क-an oppressor.

उत्पीड़न-oppression; vexation; trouble; harassing.

उत्पीड़ित-oppressed.

उत्प्रवासी-emigrant.

उत्प्रेक्षा-fancy; metaphor; comparison; simile; conceit; illustration.

उत्प्लवन-a jumping up; keeping afloat; buoyancy.

उत्फाल-leaping; jumping.

उत्फुल्ल-wide open (the eyes); fully open (a flower); radiant (the face).

उत्स-a spring.

उत्संग-the upper portion; lap; central; bosom; a roof.

उत्सर्ग-waste; resignation; excretion; gift; secretion; resignation.

उत्सर्गी-dedicating; devoting.

उत्सर्जन-emission; excretion; donation; abandonment; resignation; a gift.

उत्सर्वण-ascending; a crossing over; ascent.

उत्सव-festivity; rejoicing; festival; ceremony.

उत्सादन-abolition.

उत्साह-strength; morale; enthusiasm; effort; zeal.

उत्साहक-encouraging; inspiring.

उत्साहित-ardent; zealous.

उत्साही-energetic; enthusiastic; encouraged; inspired.

उत्सुक-earnest; wistful; keen; eager; ardent; whole-hearted; concerned.

उथपना-to be upset; to be in motion; to totter; to linger.

उथला-facile; shallow; low-lying; superficial.

उथलापन-shallowness.

उड्डयन-flying; flight; aviation.

उदक-the pouring of water (a funnel rite), water.

उदकना-to come out; to ooze; to protrude; to appear.

उदग्ग-high; lofty; violent; tall; arrogant.

उदघटना-to be visible; to see the light; to appear.

उदघाटन-to view; to open; to expose; to bring; to exhibit.

उदघोषक-announcer.

उदघोषण-proclamation.

उदड़-गुदड़-tattered clothes; rags.

उदथ-the Sun.

उदधि-holding water; the ocean.

उदबंधन-sling.

उदबस-a nomad; a wanderer; desolated, deserted.

उदमद-intoxication.

उदमदना-to be mad; to be intoxicated.

उदमिद-flora.

उदय-appearance; advent; light; prosperity; rising.

उदर-the abdomen; stomach; interior.

उदर्व (रोग)-the disease scarlatina; scarlet fever.

उदरीय-abdominal.

उदात्त-lofty; high or sharp; beloved; great; generous; illustrious.

उदायन-a garden.

उदार-noble; moderate; munificent; generous; illustrious; liberal.

उदावर्त-prolapses of the anus.

उदास-indifferent; being indifferent; sitting apart.

उदाहरण-premise; exemplification; instance; assumption; illustration; example; lesson; major case; citation.

उदियान-to be agitated; to be disturbed; to be perplexed.

उदित-risen (as the sun); conspicuous; evident.

उदीयमान-rising; promising.

उदीची-the north direction.

उदीच्य-residing in the north; pertaining to the north.

उदुम्बर-the fig-tree and its fruit.

उदूलहुक्मी-violation or infringement of a command; disobedience of an order.

उदोत-light.

उदोती-giving light.

उद्गम-rise; appearance; outlet; centre; foundation; emanation; ascension; cause; cradle; spring.

उद्गत-cast up; vomited.

उद्गाता-one of the four priests who chants Sama Veda while performing a sacrifice.

उद्गार-vomiting; spitting; abundance; roar; a loud cry; exhalation; ejaculation; belching; effervescence.

उदत-arisen; sprung up; emerged.

उदम-venting (feelings); welling up; an expression of strong feeling; boiling up or over.

उद्ग्रहण-a levy.

उद्ग्रीव-with neck raised; with head held high.

उद्घाटन-inauguration; disclosing; publishing; opening; unfastening.

उद्घात-one who pushes stroke; commencement; blow.

उदधार-salvage.

उद्दंड-in revolt; refractory; arrogant; insolent; wilful.

उद्दाम-free from restraint; splendid; self-willed; magnificent.

उद्दिम-employment.

उद्दीपन-illumination; glowing; exciting.

उद्द्योत-radiance; light.

उद्धत-indigestion; asthma.

उद्धव-the sacrificial fire of Hindu festival.

उद्धार-discharge; removing; amelioration; salvation; deliverance.

उद्धवस्त-broken up; tottered.

उद्धधृत-vomited; uplifted; quoted.

उद्धबुद्ध-regaining sense; awakened; risen up; having attained; full-blown.

उद्भट-great, eminent; magnanimous; powerful; noble.

उद्भव-birth; production; origin; appearance; source; springing up.

उद्भावना-imagination; thought; fancy; conception.

उद्भासित-visible; shining forth.

उदभिज-vegetation; plants that sprout up from the earth.

उदभूत-a public exhibit; exposition; sprouting up.

उदभौति-a marvel; miracle.

उद्भ्रान्त-amazed; rotating; astonished; going astray; wonder-struck.

उद्यत-held up; prepared; raised; eager; active.

उद्यम-business; strenuous effort; employment; operation; pursuit.

उद्यमी-active; energetic; engaged in trade; commence or industry.

उद्यान-a garden.

उद्यापित-brought to a conclusion.

उद्युक्त-engaged in some kind of work, preserving.

उद्योग-enterprise; diligence; industry; essay; labour.

उद्योत-brilliant; lustre; light; radiance.

उद्रेक-increase; excess; affluence; abundance.

उद्वह-son; one of the seven vital airs in the body.

उद्वहन-pulling up; marriage; lifting; wedding.

उद्वासन-removing from a place; killing or murdering.

उद्विग्न-dejected; perturbed; anxious; confused.

उद्वेग-agitation of feelings; fear; passion; tempered; anxiety.

उद्वेगी-perplexed; solicitous; anxious; agitated.

उद्वेलित-made to overflow; stirred up (emotion).

उधड़ना-to be opened out; to be untwisted; to be unrolled.

उधम-alarm; uproar; terror; anarchy.

उधरा-unrolled; untwisted; undone; opened.

उधली-lustful.

उधार-credit; debit; loan; liability.

उधेड़बुन-reflection; meditation; perplexity.

उनंत-sloping; down; bending.

उनदा-sleepy.

उनमाथना-to churn; to agitate.

उनमान-weight; conclusion; power; capacity; measure; strength.

उनमुगा-mute; silent; taciturn.

उनमूलना-to uproot; to pull up.

उनरना-to rise up; to walk in a hopping gait; to protrude.

उनवना-to hang; to gather up; to be surrounded; to be bent.

उनहानि-uniformity; similarity.

उनहार-alike; similar.

उनहारि-resemblance; likeness.

उनाना-to engage; to bend; to apply.

उनींदा-sleeping; dozy.

उन्नत-elevated; prosperous; advanced; well-developed; tall; high; lofty.

उन्नति-rising; progress; increase.

उन्नतोदर-convex; convexity.

उन्नयन-development; raising; uplift.

उन्नावी-jujube-coloured; dark red.

उन्नायक-raising; lifting; increasing.

उन्निद्र-sleepness.

उनींदा-drowsy; sleepless; sleepy.

उन्मत्त-wild; rabid; furious; fanatic, enthusiastic.

उन्मत्तता-madness; frenzy.

उन्मना-absent-minded; vexed; agitated; impatient.

उन्माद-madness; frenzy; passion.

उन्मादक-making frenzied; intoxicating.

उन्मादन-one of the five arrows of Cupid (God of Love); act of intoxicating.

उन्मादी-frenzied; insane.

उन्मार्ग-measure of size or quantity; volume; estimate.

उन्मान-a measure (of weight, amount or size).

उन्मानी-conjectural.

उन्मीलन-to open; to expand.

उन्मीलना-to open; to expand.

उन्मुक्त-made loose; freed; released; opened; unconstrained; undone.

उन्मुख-looking upwards; ready; eager; intent.

उन्मूलक-ruining; destroying; devastating.

उन्मूखर-noisy; ringing.

उन्मुद्र-beside oneself; unsealed.

उन्मूलन-rooting up; abolishing; eradicating.

उन्मेष-looking upwards; ready; intent.

उन्हार-appearance; type; kind.

उपंग-a type of musical instrument.

उपकंठ-nearness; vicinity; proximity.

उपकथा-episode in a larger story.

उपकरण-instrument; apparatus; equipment; implement; utensil; device; insignia (of royalty); materials.

उपकरना-to do good; to oblige.

उपकार-beneficence; kindness; favour; benefit; help; protection; preservation.

उपकारी-aiding; beneficent; assisting; salutary; subsidiary.

उपकृत-benefited; obliged.

उपकृति-favour; obligation.

उपकूल-bank; sore.

उपकेंद्रीय-centrifugal.

उपक्रम-undertaking; preparation; commencement.

उपक्रमणिका-preface; introduction.

उपखंड-sub-division.

उपगत-approached; turned; comprehended; agreed.

उपगति-acquisition; acquiring; knowledge.

उपगम-approach.

उपग्रह-a satellite; encouragement.

उपग्रन्थ-a minor work.

उपगुरू-an assistant teacher; the monitor (of a class).

उपगिरी-hillock.

उपगोल-spheroid.

उपंग-a kind of musical instrument.

उपघातक-offensive.

उपचय-growth; collection; accretion; accumulation; increase.

उपचार[1]-service; traditional; attendance or formal usage (as that of welcoming a guest); medical care; remedy; any of various individual rites in worship; the process of treatment.

उपचार[2]-to perform (as a tradition or formal usage, or as a rite).

उपचारिका-a nurse.

उपचारी-a servant.

उपचित-accrued.

उपछाया-penumbra.

उपज-produce; production (of goods, assets); invention; crop; yield; original idea; fancy.

उपजात-produced; propagated.

उपजीवन-defence on others for livelihood.

उपजीवी-dependent for support.

उपटन-unction; a mark made by pressure.

उपटाना-to have unction rubbed over the body.

उपठना-to be fatigued; to be tired of a business.

उपत्वचा-cuticle.

उपदंश-syphilis; relish; an appetiser; venereal disease; flavour.

उपदल-the calyx of a flower.

उपदान-allowance; subsidy; a grant.

उपदिशा-the intermediate quarter between the four cardinal points; angle.

उपदिष्ट-having received spiritual instruction; referred to.

उपदेश-indicating; instructing; to exhort; advice; counsel.

उपद्रव-making trouble; causing riot.

उपद्वीप-a tiny island.

उपधरना-to acknowledge; to admit; to accept; to confess.

उपधा-fraud.

उपधारा-sub-section.

उपधान-cushion; a pillow; a support.

उपनति-trend.

उपनदी-an influent river.

उपनना-to be born; to be begotten; to be generated.

उपनगर-a suburb.

उपनय-the minor premise in logical syllogism; bringing near.

उपनाम-nickname; pseudonym.

उपनिदेशक-Deputy Director.

उपनिधि-a deposit or pawn.

उपनिविष्ट-settled in another country; a colonist.

उपनिवेशन-colonising.

उपनिवेशी-colonial.

उपनीत-acquired invested with the sacred thread; earned.

उपनेता-a religious guide; one who conveys or brings forward, a preceptor.

उपन्यायाधीश-Sub Judge.

उपन्यास-fiction; a novel; romance.

उपन्यासकार-novelist.

उपनेत्र-spectacle; eye-glasses.

उपपन्न-fugitive; come; suitable; acquired; proper.

उपपातक-a crime or sin which can be expiated.

उपपादन-performance; completion of work; establishing; proving by arguments demonstrating by proofs.

उपपाद्य-proved or demonstrated.

उपबंध-provision (of regulations).

उपबाहु-the lower arm.

उपभाषा-a dialect.

उपभोग-consumption (as of goods); enjoyment.

उपभोक्ता-one who enjoys; to use.

उपमा-similarity; a simile; comparison.

उपमाता-a wet-nurse; a foster-mother.

उपमान-comparison; similarity.

उपमित-the thing which is compared (in a simile).

उपमिति-analogy;picture;resemblance; image; comparison.

उपमेय-to be compared; comparable.

उपयंत्र-machine tools.

उपयंना-to turn away; to flee.

उपयुक्त-fit; appropriate; proper; suitable; worthy (as of a post).

उपयोग-avail; use; employment; subservience; utility.

उपरत-disinterested; impartial; indifferent; dead.

उपरत्न-a covering; a scarf.

उपरना-a shawl.

उपरला-upper; superficial.

उपरफट-useless; superficial.

उपरस-a secondary material.

उपरांत-eclipse; colour; darkening; coloration.

उपराचढ़ी-emulation; rivalry; competition.

उपराज-to produce; to earn; to acquire; to create.

उपराला-help; aid; support; assistance.

उपराहना-to extol; to elate; to praise; to commend.

उपराही-excellent.

उपरि-above; over; upon.

उपरिभूमि-upland.

उपरिशायी-overlay.

उपरी-उपरा-rivalry.

उपरैनी-a woman's scarf.

उपरोध-partiality; hindrance; covering.

उपरोधक-obstructing.

उपरोधी-disturbing.

उपरौटा-the upper portion of a garment.

उपल-a rock; a jewel; cloud; stone; a precious stone.

उपलक्षक-inferring; denotational; deducing.

उपलक्षण-a type of metaphorical or elliptical expression; indication.

उपलक्षित-implied.

उपलब्ध-available; received; known; gained; acquired.

उपला-dried cow dung cakes used as fuel.

उपलाना-to rise to the surface (of water); to float.

उपलिप्त-smeared; anointed.

उपल्ला-the upper portion or fold of a thing.

उपवन-a grove; a garden.

उपवाद-censure; blame.

उपवास-fast; to starve; starvation; fasting.

उपविष-a narcotic; a drug.

उपविष्ट-sitting; seated.

उपवीत-invested with the thread; sacred thread.

उपवेद-the science deduced from the Vedas.

उपवेशन-the act of sitting.

उपवृत्ति-avocation.

उपशम-becoming calm or stilled (the aroused sense) tranquillity; patience; calm.

उपशमन-appeasing; calming; allaying.

उपशांत-pacified; tranquil.

उपसम्पादक-a sub-editor; an assistant editor.

उपसंहार-an epilogue; concluding chapter of book in which the summary of the entire work is put down.

उपस-bad smell.

उपसर्ग-a particle, prefixed to a root (in grammer).

उपसागर-a sea; part of an ocean; strait.

उपसाधन-accessory.

उपसाना-to cause to rot or putrefy; to stale.

उपसेचन-juice; watering; a wet thing; sprinkling with water; soup.

उपस्कर-an appliance; equipment.

उपस्थ-genitalia male or female; lower part.

उपस्वत्व-the right or claim in the income of a property.

उपहत-fallen in difficulty; impaired; destroyed.

उपहार-gift; present.

उपही-foreigner; and unknown person; an alien.

उपांग-something supplementary; sectarian mark which is made on the fore-head of a devotee.

उपांत-margin; suburbs of a city or town; neighbouring small border.

उपांत्य-penultimate.

उपा-to devise; to create; to produce.

उपाऊ-measure; way; device.

उपाख्यान-a story; a tale; a narrative; a legend.

उपाचार्य-reader.

उपाट-to root out (a tree).

उपाड़-pulling up or out by the root.

उपाति-produce; birth; origin.

उपादान-raw material substance; acquisition of knowledge; substance.

उपाध-violence; tumult.

उपाधि-nickname; attribute; title; rank; diploma; decoration; degree.

उपाधी-mischievous; violent; tyrannical.

उपाध्यक्ष-Vice President; Vice Chairman.

उपानह-shoes; foot-wear.

उपान्त्य-last but one; penultimate.

उपाना-to beget; to produce.

उपापचय-metabolism.

उपाय-means; contrivance; plan.

उपायन-a gift; a present.

उपार्जन-acquisition; earning; amassing.

उपालंभ-railing; scolding; reproach; complaint.

उपास-fast.

उपासक-a worshipper; devotee.

उपासा-fasting; keeping fast.

उपाहार-refreshment.

उपेन्द्र-the God Vishu.

उपेक्षक-ir-responsive.

उपेक्षण-indifference; hatred; animosity.

उपेक्षणीय-to be neglected; negligible.

उपेक्षा-contempt; indifference; neglect.

उपेक्षित-slighted; disdained; discarded; neglected.

उपैना-naked; opened.

उपोद्घात-prolegomena; introduction; exordium; forward.

उफ़ colloq. oh! (expressing distress, regret, irritation, pain).

उफड़ना-to simmer; to boil up; to boil; to ferment.

उफनना-to foam; to boil over; to froth; to boil up.

उफान-boiling up; surge; froth; burning; eagerness; turmoil; foam.

उबकाई-vomiting.

उबटन-a paste (made up of turmeric, an ointment, oil and perfume) rubbed on the body when clean and soften the skin.

उबना-to shoot; to grow; to germinate.

उबसना-to become stale; to smell unpleasant; to rot.

उबहना-to pull out sword from its sheath; to throw out water; to lift up.

उबाऊ-tiring; boring.

उबाकना-to vomit; to reject.

उबांत-vomiting; nausea.

उबार-deliverance; liberation; salvage; release.

उबाल-fury; boiling; rage.

उबासी-a yawn.

उबीधना-to be entangled; to be ensnared; to be stuck in.

उबेना-without shoes on; bare-footed.

उभरना-to be vain or arrogant.

उभड़ना-to be excited; to go away; to increase; to rise; to swell; to overflow.

उभय-amphibious.

उभयत:-in both conditions or cases, on both sides.

उभाना-to disturb (as by gestures or movement); to alarm.

उभरौं-protruding; effervescing.

उभाड़-uprise; heave; height; lift; jut; protuberance; salience; ridge.

उभार-swelling; rising; plumpness; fullness.

उभिट-to be hateful; unpleasant.

उभियाना-to rise up.

उभिरना-to stop short.

उमंग-transport; rapture; ecstasy; ambition; gust; exultation.

उमंगी-ambitious; desirous; elated.

उमग-to flow; to exultant; to be elated.

उमचना-to jump on a thing for pressing it; to be alert.

उमड़-swelling; rising; flooding; overflowing (of emotion); gathering (of clouds).

उमदना-to be stirred; to be intoxicated; to be excited.

उमर-age.

उमराव-rich man.

उमस-humid heat.

उमह-to exult; to well up; to swell.

उमाकना-to dig out; to destroy.

उमापति-the God Shiva.

उमाहना-to swell.

उमाहल-filled with excitement; excited encouraged.

उमूमन commonly; generally.

उमेठन-a twist; spiral state.

उमेठना-to twist.

उमेठवाँ-twisted; spiral.

उमेलना-to lay open; to open; to expose; to describe.

उम्दगी-worth.

उम्दा-fine; nice; good; excellent.

उम्मीद-dependence; hope; expectation; trust.

उम्मीदवार-an applicant.

उम्मेद-hope; expect.

उम्मेदवार-an expectant; a candidate.

उम्र-age; lifetime; life.

उर-the heart; bosom; breast.

उरकना-to stop.

उरग-a snake; breast-goer.

उरण-a ram.

उरद-a kind of pulse.

उरम-to hang down.

उरमना-to be supported; to be hung on something.

उरमा-to hang; to suspend.

उरला-strange; belonging to this side; mysterious; boundless.

उरलाना-to caress; to embrace.

उरजिस-the female breast.

उरहन-reproach.

उरहना-complaint.

उरा-the earth.

उरारा-magnificent; wide.

उरु-vast; ample; broad.

उरुवा-a kind of own which makes a harsh sound.

उरूज-increase; growth; enlargement; rise.

उरे more distant; on the farther.

उरेह-to apply; to draw.

उरोज-the female breast.

उरोरित-the sternum.

उर्जा-energy.

उर्दू-a type of language.

उर्फ-common parlance; known as alias.

उर्मिला-the wife of Lakshman.

उर्वरक-fertiliser.

उर्वरा-fertile soil.-fertility.

उर्विजा-the planet Mars.

उर्वी-the earth; ground; wide.

उलंग-naked.

उलँग-cross over.

उलंघन-violation.

उलचना-to pour off; to throw out; to bale out; to drain.

उलछना-to spread asunder; to drain off; to throw out.

उलझन-complication; disorder; turn; twist; problem; confusion; anxiety.

उलझा-complicated; entangled.

उलझाव-entanglement; dispute; quarrel; dispute.

उलझेड़ा-entanglement.

उलझेड़िया-a quarrelsome person.

उलट-change; inversion; reversal; overturning.

उलटवाँसी-suggestive paradox.

उलटा-reversed; opposite.

उलटान-to interchange; to upset; to overturn; to reverse.

उलटी-vomiting; somersault; nausea.

उलटे conversely; contrarily.

उलथना-to agitated; to oscillating; to undulate.

उलथा-a type of dance incorporating rhythmical leaping movements.

उलद-incessant fall of rain.

उलदना-to pour out.

उलमना-to be confused; to slope; to be disarranged.

उलफत-affection; friendship; love.

उलरना-to be upside down; to leap; to attack; to jump.

उलसना-to be confused; to be disarranged; to slope.

उलह-to be reproachful; to shoot; to spring up.

उलाँघना-to leap over; not to perform bidding; to disobey.

उलार-depressed by weight on the back side.

उलारना-to throw off water.

उलू-an owl.

उलूक-an owl; a firebrand.

उल्का-a meteor; comet; a spark; flame; fire.

उल्था-version; translation.

उल्लंघन-infraction; transgression; contravention; violation; infringement.

उल्लसन-enjoyment; merry-making.

उल्लेख-mention; to give an account.

उल्लेखन-writing; inscription; painting of a picture.

उल्लू-an owl; the night bird; a simpleton; an idiot; a stupid fellow.

उल्व-the outer membrane of a foetus; womb.

उवना-to grow.

उषसी-twilight; dawn.

उषा-early morning; dawn; day-break.

उष्ट्र-a camel.

उष्ण-hot; tropical; warm; active; caustic; pungent; sharp.

उष्णक-the hot season; fever.

उष्णत्व-heat; warmth.

उष्णीष-crown; turban; diadem.

उष्णोत्स-geyser.

उष्म-the hot season.

उष्मता-heat.

उष्मा-heat, sunshine; warmth; anger.

उसकन-grass; leaves used in cleansing and polishing vessels of metal.

उसकाव-excitement; stimulation.

उसनना-to be boiled; to simmer.

उसना-boiled; cooked.

उसमा-anointing; twisting.

उसास-to breathe; to sigh.

उससना-to retreat; to breath.

उसरबगेरी-a kind of bird.

उसाना-to separate chaff from the grains to winnow.

उसालना-to remove; to uproot.

उसास-a sigh; breather; breath; groan; a respite.

उसासी-leisure; opportunity.

उसीजना-to cook slowly.

उसीरा-the upper-portion of a bedstead; a pillow.

उसीसा-a pillow; head of bead.

उसूल-roots; causes; principles; settles motive.

उसेर[1]-yearning; anxiety; remembering with regret; solicitude; pining.

उसेर[2] to pine; to yearn; to delay.

उस्तरा-razor.

उस्ताद-a skilled craftsman; a teacher; master (of an art); a rogue.

उस्तुरा-a razor.

उस्त्र-a ray of light; a bull.

उहदा-a rank.

उहताँ, उहाँ there.

उहित-discussed subject.

उहापोह–reasoning; arguing; full consideration of a subject.

ऊ

ऊ-The sixth vowel of the Devnagari alphabet.

ऊँग-drowsiness.

ऊँगा-the plant used in medicine.

ऊँगन-& doze; to nap.

ऊँघ-a brief light sleep; snooze.

ऊँघना-to slumber; to doze.

ऊँघाई-doze; drowsiness.

ऊँच-high; eminent.

ऊँचा-upper; high (rank, birth, quality); ranking above others in caste, importance etc.; great; lofty; elevated; loud.

ऊँचाकानी-deafness.

ऊँची-lofty; high; an upland.

ऊँछना-to comb (the hair).

ऊँट-a camel.

ऊँटनी-a female camel.

ऊँदर-a rat.

ऊँहूँ-no; denoting refusal or denial never.

ऊअना-to rise; to germinate.

ऊआबई-of no avail; useless.

ऊई-fear, expression of pleasure (used by women); surprise; pain.

ऊक-a firebrand; burning; a shooting star; a meteor.

ऊकना-to forget; to neglect; to mistake; to miss; not to aim.

ऊकार-the letter or its sound.

ऊकारांत-(word) ending in

ऊख-sugar-cane.

ऊखम-hot.

ऊखल-a large wooden pot for husking rice etc.; mortar.

ऊगना-to grow.

ऊजड़-deserted; ruined; waste; desolate.

ऊजरा-white.

ऊटक-haphazard; a pointless or misconceived task or project.

ऊटना-to argue; to discuss; to be excited; to be encouraged.

ऊड़ा-loss.

ऊड़ी-decrease; annihilation; destruction; dearness; loss.

ऊढ़-to marry (a wife); to cause to be led (home).

ऊत-an unhoused spirit man who dies childless; a fool.

ऊतर-pretext; answer.

ऊतला-agile; quick.

ऊदा-brownish blue; of the colour of a brinjal.

ऊदेस-track; pointing out; search.

ऊधम-uproar; disturbance; turmoil; bustle; agitation; rebellion; hubbub.

ऊन[1]-wool.

ऊन[2]-disaffected (towards); deficient; less; minus; defective; displeased.

ऊना-a small sword.

ऊनी[1]-less; deficient.

ऊनी[2]-woollen.

ऊपर-on top; overhead; above; additionally; up; over; upwards; superficially.

ऊब-agitation arising from continuous work; feeling of aversion; perplexity; tedium; irksomeness.

ऊभ[1]-surliness; elevated; high; zeal; ardent; protruding.

ऊभ[2]-languor; inertia; sultry heat.

ऊभना[1]-to rise.

ऊभना[2]-to fell languid; to suffer from the heat.

ऊँमक-rise; quickness.

ऊमी-an ear of half-ripe corn.

ऊरु-the thigh.

ऊर्ज-the mouth of ; powerful, strong.

ऊर्जस्वी-potent; powerful; glorious; strong.

ऊर्जा-power; energy.

ऊर्जस्वल-powerful.

ऊर्जस्वित-vigorous.

ऊर्ण-wool.

ऊर्णनाभ-a spider; wool-bodied.

ऊर्ध्व-above, on hight.

ऊर्ध्वगामी-attaining emancipation, rising above.

ऊर्ध्वपात-up-throw.

ऊर्ध्वपुण्ड्र-a perpendicular marking in the forehead delineated by Vishnu's worshippers.

ऊर्ध्वरेता-an abstinent person; one who always remains chaste and never indulges in sexual intercourse.

ऊर्ध्वलोक-the sky; the heaven.

ऊर्ध्वश्वास-a deep respiration or gasp.

ऊर्मि-a wave.

ऊलना-to active; spirited.

ऊषण-black pepper; dry ginger.

ऊषर-sterile; fallow.

ऊषा-early morning; redness of dawn.

ऊष्म-warmth; heat.

ऊष्मा–heat; vapour; the summer season; the hot season.

ऊसर-sandy fallow land, sterile; fallow; prolific.

ऊह[1] exclamation of pain or astonishment; distress.

ऊह[2]-reasoning; inference; deliberation.

ऊहित-subject; guessed; concealed; discussed.

ऋ

ऋ-The seventh vowel of the Devnagari alphabet.

ऋक्ष-a bear; a planet; a constellation (fixed star).

ऋक्षपति-the moon.

ऋग्वेद-the first of the four Vedas.

ऋचा-an aphorism of the Veda; a hymn; an incantation.

ऋजु-simple; straight; forward; honest; sincere.

ऋजुता-honesty; sincerity; happiness; straightness.

ऋण-loan; a debit; debt of gratitude; obligation; negative; minus.

ऋणग्रस्त-owing money; indebted.

ऋणी-indebted; beholden.

ऋत-a fixed order; order; cosmic.

ऋतु[1]-sky; season of the year; the right time.

ऋतु[2]-menstrual discharge; menses.

ऋतुचर्या-regiment according to season (of the year).

ऋतुमती-a woman in her courses; menstruating.

ऋतुराज-the spring season.

ऋतुस्नान-a bathing of woman after the menstruation period.

ऋत्विज-a sacrificial priest.

ऋद्ध-prosperous.

ऋद्धि-success; prosperity.

ऋभु-a deity.

ऋषभ-the second note of the Indian musical scale; a bull.

ऋषि-author of sacred hymns; recited; or remembered.

ऋष्टि-sword; weapon; swear.

ऋष्य-a white-footed antelope.

ए

ए-The eight vowel of the Devnagari alphabet.

एँड-spur (attached to the heels of shoes).

एँडी-silk produced from this worm; coral; a silkworm which eats leaves of the castor seed plant.

एँडुआ-a round folded cloth on the head when carrying a burden.

एकंग-alone; single.

एक-similar; single; equal; alone; one; singular; someone.

एकंतरा-next but one.

एककालन-synchronisation.

एककाल-the same time; one time.

एकचक्र-the supreme monarch; the chariot of the Sun.

एकचित-like-minded; concurring.

एकछत्र-absolute; government by one king alone.

एकज-one who is not twice-born.

एकजद्दी-belonging to the same race or parents; born of the same ancestors.

एकजातीय-cognate.

एकट्ठा-united; collected; together.

एकठा-a small boat rowed by sculling.

एकड़-an acre.

एकड़ा-the figure.

एकडाल-a dagger.

एकता-harmony; sameness; unity; identity.

एकतान-attentive; intent.

एकतारा-a musical instrument having one wire only.

एकत्र-emotions; accumulated; concentrated thoughts; collected together.

एकत्रित-collective; in one place.

एकत्व-a unit; unity.

एकदंत-an epithet of the God Ganesha.

एकदम-quite; in a moment; immediately; in a breath; at once; completely.

एकदा-once; at one time; occasionally; once upon a time.

एकदिन-lasting only for a day; transitory; ephemeral.

एकनिष्ठ-attached or devoted to a single individual or God.

एकमेक-one, homogeneous; jumbled; mixed; quite; confused.

एकमेव-only; single,

एकपक्ष-an adherent; a partisan; an associate.

एकपक्षीय-one-sided; unilateral; prejudicial.

एकपद-single leg; one who has only one leg.

एकपार्श्विक-unilateral.

एकपिण्ड-consolidated.

एकबार once; at one time.

एकभुक्त-eating only once in twenty-four hours.

एकमत-agreeing; rapport; consensus; unanimous.

एकमुखी-with one mouth.

एकमुश्त-lump sum.

एकमेव-only; single.

एकरस-similar; alike.

एकरसता-monotony.

एकरार-agreement.

एकरूप-uniform; having the same shape or form; similar; unbroken.

एकरूपता-uniformity; similarity.

एकलपंक्ति-single file.

एकलिंग-an epithet of Shiva.

एकलौता-single (a child); only.

एकवचन-number (in grammer); singular.

एकवाक्यता-harmony; concord; agreement.

एकवेणी-female recluse or hermit; a widow.

एकसमान-constant.

एकसर-alone; one-folded.

एकसाँ-similar; sort; identical; alike; of the same equable.

एकसाथ-one and all; together; simultaneously.

एकसुर-consonant.

एकस्व-patent.

एकहत्था-working with one hand only.

एकांगी-partial; resolute; one-sided; obstinate.

एकांतता-secrecy.

एकांतर-alternate.

एकांश-item; unit.

एका-unity; league; union; unanimity; combination; conspiracy.

एकाएक suddenly; unexpectedly.

एकांश-one part or portion.

एकाकार-likeness; identical; uniformity.

एकाकी-solitary; isolated; alone; single.

एकाक्षरी-of only one letter; monosyllable.

एकाग्र-attentive; concentrating; single-minded; intent in one point.

एकांक-a unit.

एकात्मक-unitary.

एकादश-eleventh.

एकादशी-the eleventh day in the fortnight of a lunar month.

एकाध-some; a few.

एकाधिकार-exclusive; right; monopoly.

एकाधिपति-a king; a sovereign; an emperor.

एकार्थक-of similar meaning.

एकान्तवासी-a recluse.

एकाह-finishing a work in single day; ephemeral.

एकाहार-eating only once during the day.

एकीकरण-accumulation; integration.

एकीकृत-accumulated.

एकीभूत-amalgamation.

एकेन्द्रिय-a vermin having only one limb.

एक्का-an ace of playing card; a stray animal; a two-wheeled conveyance to carry three passengers.

एक्की-an ace of playing cards.

एखनी-broth.

एजेंट-an agent.

एड़क-a kind of firework.

एड़-गज-the medicinal plant

एड़ी-heel.

एतकादी-having faith in; believing.

एतमाद-faith; reliance; trust.

एतराज-objection; disapproval; opposition.

एता-so much; this much.

एतादृश of this sort; such.

एतादृशता-similarity.

एतावत्-such a quantity.

एतिक-so much.

एमन-a kind of song.

एरंड-the castor-oil plant.

एलची-an emissary; an ambassador.

एला-small cardamom.

एलान-declaration; proclamation; announcement; manifesto; slogan.

एलवा-wormwood.

एवं-and; thus; so.

एव-also, too.

एवज़-requital; in return; a substitute or exchange.

एवज़ी-a substitute; one officiating for another.

एवड़-a flock of sheep or goats.

एषणा-desire.

एहतियात-caution; care; abstinence; precaution; warning.

एहद-pledge.

एहसान-kindness; beneficence; favour; sense of obligation; gratitude.

एहसानात-favours; kindness.

एही-used for calling a person.

ऐ-The ninth vowel of the Devnagari alphabet, it is placed on the top of the letter and assumes the form when combined with a consonant.

ऐंच-pulling; dearth; dragging; scarcity; tightening; delay; holding aloof.

ऐंछना-to comb one's hair; to remove impurities; to cleanse.

ऐंठ-pride; twist; wrench; opposition; cramp; contortion; distortion.

ऐंठनी-pride; peevishness.

ऐंठुआ-curled; tortuous.

ऐंठू-affected; haughty; proud; blackmailer.

ऐंठूपन-affectation; pride; hauteur.

ऐंड-strut; pride; twist; a whirlpool.

ऐंडाना-to be proud; to show affected airs; to stretch the limbs.

ऐंडालना-swaggering.

ऐंद्री-Indra's wife; cardamon; the goddess Durga.

ऐ to call someone.

ऐकाहिक-lasting one day ephemeral.

ऐक्य-oneness; concord; harmony; unity.

ऐगुन-defect; blemish; stupidity.

ऐच्छिक-according to wish; voluntary.

ऐज़न the same; ditto.

ऐतरेय-a portion of Rigveda.

ऐतवार-Sunday.

ऐतिहासिक-history-making (event).

ऐन-precise (of time); exact; just.

ऐनक-spectacles for weak eyes; an eye-glass.

ऐने-to this place; hither.

ऐपन-a mixture of pounded rice and turmeric used by Hindu women in some religious functions.

ऐब-a vice; defect; shortcoming; fault.

ऐबी-wicked; naughty; faulty; with defective limbs; squint-eyed.

ऐयार-crafty; a cheat; cunning; a swindler.

ऐयाश-fond of luxury; voluptuous person.

ऐरावत-the name of Indra's elephant; a thunder-cloud.

ऐल-an old man; turmoil; confusion; lenity.

ऐल-फ़ैल-abusive language; chatter.

ऐलान-announcement.

ऐवान-gallery; hall; chamber; portico.

ऐश-luxury; pleasure; to enjoy; delight.

ऐश्वर्य-supremacy; divine; pomp; dominion; majesty; grandeur.

ऐषीक-made of reeds.

ऐस, ऐसन-similar.

ऐसा-so much; like; after this manner.

ऐसे-in this way or manner; similarly.

ऐहिलौकिक-of this world.

ऐहिकीकरण-mundane; worldly.

ऐहैं-Ah me! alas! expressing sorrow.

ओ

ओ-The tenth vowel of the Devnagari alphabet.

ओइंछना-to propitiate; to appease; to sacrifice.

ओंकार-the sound ॐ.

ओंटना-to boil (a liquid) for long time; to gin.

ओंठ-the lip.

ओक[1]-the palm hollowed to drink from water; drunk from the hollowed palm.

ओक[2]-vomiting; nausea.

ओक[3]-house; refuge; dwelling; dwelling-place.

ओकना-to vomit; to cry like a buffalo; to nauseate.

ओकाना-to vomit; to retch.

ओखली-a small mortar.

ओखा-not compact; dry; crooked; wicked; impure; difficult.

ओग-tribute; levy.

ओगरा-a kind of gruel; pottage.

ओगल-moisture in the soil.

ओगार-to drain; a well.

ओघ-tax; subscription.

ओछा-insignificant; light; frivolous; silly; superficial; narrow-minded.

ओज-brilliance; light; fervour; lustre; splendour.

ओजना[1]-to ward off (a blow).

ओजना[2]-to pour out.

ओजस्विता-lustre; brilliance; splendour.

ओजस्वी-vigorous; powerful; nervy.

ओझ-entrails; paunch.

ओझड़ी-ribs.

ओझर-the stomach.

ओझल-screen; shelter; concealment.

ओझा-a wizard; a charmer; a witchcraft; a necromancer; a magician; a diviner; an occultist.

ओट-partition; shelter; screen; protection; shade; under; concealment; cover.

ओटल-screen; cover.

ओठ-lips.

ओड़-protection (as from a blow); to shelter from the wind.

ओड़चा-a wooden tub used in irrigating.

ओड़न-shield.

ओड़ना-to expand; to describe; to stop; to stretch.

ओड़ा-a big wicker-work; deficiency; basket; a pannier.

ओड़ी-a small basket.

ओढ़ना-to cover the body with something; to put on.

ओढ़नी-a woman's sheet or shawl.

ओढाना-to cover someone with cloth.

ओत[1]-surplus; advantage; gain; recovery (from sickness); benefit.

ओत[2]-woven.

ओद[1]-wetness.

ओद[2]-wet; damp; moist.

ओदन-boiled rice.

ओदा-wet, moist; damp.

ओदराना-to tear asunder; to demolish; to destroy.

ओध-to join (as battle); to bind.

ओधा-position; office; post.

ओना-the outlet for draining of a tank's water.

ओनाना-to hear; to attend.

ओनामासी-the beginning.

ओप-lustre; polish.

ओपची-a warrior wearing coat of mail; a body guard.

ओपना-to be polished; to be lustrous.

ओपनिवारी-glittering; shinning.

ओपनी-the process of polishing sword or dagger.

ओबरा-excessive.

ओबरी-tasteless; insipid.

ओर-side; boundary; origin; limit; direction.

ओरमना-to support; to hang.

ओरमा[1]-hemstitching; seam.

ओरमा[2]-to hang down.

ओराना-to bring to an end; to be finished; to be completed.

ओरालना-statement of dissatisfaction or disapproval; complaint.

ओरी-protector; supporter.

ओलंबा-complaint.

ओल[1]-pawn; hostage; security; bail; pledge.

ओल[2]-to ward off; to take upon oneself; to bear; to endure.

ओलट-screen; cover.

ओलन-a plumb-line.

ओलना-to stop; to endure; to screen.

ओलमना-to be suspended; to be hung.

ओलरना-to lie down; to repose.

ओला[1]-hailstone; a loaf-sugar ball (type of candy).

ओला[2]-screen; secrecy.

ओलौनी-an example; an illustration.

ओल्यो-pretext.

ओष्ठ-the lip.

ओष्ठी-a creeper; having a red flower with which the lip is compared.

ओस-dew.

ओसनना-to knead dough or moistened flower.

ओसर-a heifer.

ओसरी-turn; time.

ओसाई-work of winnowing or fanning.

ओसाना-to separate grains from husk.

ओसार-width; girth; breadth.

ओसारा-a shed; porch; portico.

ओह pain; expressing wonder; carelessness.

ओहट-obstruction.

ओहर towards.

ओहरुवा-curtain; frill.

ओहदा-an office; position; duty.

ओहार-covering of a cart; housing.

ओहो-expressing regret Alas! Heigh-ho!

औ

औ-The eleventh vowel of the Devnagari alphabet.

औंगन-axle grease.

औंगा-dump; silent.

औंगी-dumpness, silence.

औंघना-to feel sleepy; to be half asleep; to doze.

औंघाई-a short sleep; nap.

औंडाई-depth.

औंजना-to be agitated; to be perplexed.

औंठ-projecting border or rim of something.

औंड-a labourer who digs earth with a spade.

औंडा-deep; not shallow; deep.

औंधना-to be overturned; to be emptied; to lower (the sky with clouds).

औ-and.

औकल restless; uneasy.

औकात-riches; capacity; wealth; season; time; means; opportunity.

औकान-a pile of grain and chaff ready for winnowing.

औकाल-untimely; premature.

औगत-ill-luck; misfortune; calamity; disaster.

औगी[1]-ornamental edging (on shoes), goad; a whip made of twisted cord.

औगी[2]-pit for catching large animals.

औघट-steep; inaccessible; arduous.

औघड़-misshapen; uncouth; strange; ungainly; awkward.

औघर-unshaped; queer.

औचक sudden; unexpectedly.

औचित्य-suitableness; aptness; fairness; rightness; justification; fitness.

औज़ार-having to do with equipment.

औटन-boiling; heat.

औटाना-to boil (as milk); to boil down; to cause to boil.

औढ़र-consulting one's own inclination.

औत्कर्ष्य-excellence; superiority.

औत्सर्गिक-coming about by nature; natural.

औद्सुक्य-impatience; ardent desire; eagerness; longing; regret.

औदकना-to startle in fear.

औदमिक-a cook.

औदस-ill-renown; bad fame.

औदसा-dire state; calamity.

औदान-thrown in; given gratis.

औदार्य-liberality; open minded-ness; munificence.

औदासीन्य-sadness.

औदास्य-sadness; solitude; loneliness; isolation.

औदेस-foreign region or country.

औद्धत्य-impertinence; rudeness; rashness; incivility.

औद्योगिक-industrial.

औध-limit.

औधान-womb.

औधिया-a thug; a thief.

औनि-earth.

औपकाय-house; a tent.

औपचारिक-formal; pertaining to service or employment; ceremonial.

औरंग-throne.

और-besides; and; but, also.

औरना-to be leader.

औरस-legitimate.

औरस-चौरस-all around.

औरसना-to be insipid; to get angry; to be irritated.

औरासा-peculiar; extraordinary.

औरी-बौरी-crazy; mad.

औलना-to be sultry.

औलाद-children; offspring; descendants.

औलिया-a saint.

औलू-new, difficult; peculiar; extraordinary; queer.

औवल-best; chief; first; eminent.

औशि definitely, certainly.

औषध-medicine.

औषधालय-a place where medicine are prepared; pharmacy; dispensary.

औसत-mediate; the middle; moderation; medium; average.

औसतन on average.

औसती-moderately.

औसना-to be sultry; to putrefy; to become musty; to rot.

औसर opportunity; chance.

औसेर-delay; care; solicitude; anxiety.

क-The first consonant of the Devnagari alphabet.

कंक-the white kite (white vulture); flesh eating bird; a heron; the name of during .

कंकड़ी-small fragment (as of sugar; salt); a small stone.

कंकण-a bracelet which is tied round the wrist of the bridegroom and the bride at the time of marriage.

कंकाल-having the body wasted to a skeleton.

कंकालशेष-a person whose body become a skeleton.

कंकालिन-a witch.

कंखवारी-a tumour in the armpit.

कंखौरी-inflamed or boil swelling in the armpit.

कंगन-bracelet of precious metal (worn by women); an iron bangle (worn by Sikh.

कंगनी[1]-a scalloped or toothed edge; a small bracelet.

कंगनी[2]-a millet.

कंगलटर-vain-glorious.

कंगला-a pauper; a beggar.

कंगाल-penniless; beggarly; poor; famine stricken; miserable; penurious.

कंघा-a big comb.

कंघेरा-a maker of comb.

कंचन-gold; wealth.

कंचनी-a dancing-girl.

कंचली-a snakes's slough.

कंचुक-a serpent; a door-keeper; an attendant who serves in the harem.

कंचुकी-bra.

कंचेरा-a glass worker.

कंज-hair (of the head); a lotus; .

कंजर-the member of which make and sell string; metal goods; a scattered itinerant community.

कंजा-a thorny bush used in medicine.

कंजिया-a small sty.

कंजूस-skinflint; a miser.

कंटक-a source or hurt or trouble; a troublesome person; a thorn.

कंटिया-a fishing hook; a small nail; a pointed hook; an ornament for the hair.

कंटोप-a cap with which the head and ears are covered.

कंठ-the neck; throat.

कंठला-a necklace of piece of gold or silver; such a necklace as put on children to avert evil.

कंठा-an ornament for the neck; the collar of a coat.

कंठी-a necklace of small beads.

कंडरा-a big artery of blood under the chest; tendon.

कंडा-a piece of dry dung.

कंडाल-a trumpet; a clarionet.

कंडी-a small basket; a container for burning cow-dung fuel.

कंडु-itch; scratching.

कंडुआ-a fungus that attacks cereals.

कंथा-a patched cloth or garment.

कंद-an esculent tuber root; coagulated sugar; a cloud; sugar-loaf.

कंदर-cavern; a cave.

कंदर्प-the god of live; a title of .

कंदल-young shoot or sprig; war; battle.

कंदसार-a deer; a stag.

कंदा-sweet potato; squill.

कंदीय-tuber.

कंदुक-a betel; a ball; a round pillow.

कंदैला-dirty; filthy; foul.

कंदोरा-a cord worn round the waist; waist-band.

कंध-branch of a tree; the shoulder.

कंधर-the neck.

कंधा-shoulder.

कंधेला-the part of the wrapper or garment which female lies on her shoulder.

कंप-tremor; trembling shaking.

कंपनी-a trading or banking corporation.

कंपाना-to show fear; to swing; to oscillate; to wag.

कंपास-the bamboo of a carriage; compasses.

कंपित-made of tremble or to shake; tremulous; fear-stricken; fearful.

कंपू-a camp; encampment; temporary abode or residence; cantonment.

कंबल-a blanket; a rug.

कंस-bellmetal; a cup; a pitcher; a cymbal brozen.

कंसताल-cymbals.

कंसार-an engraver on metal.

कंसुआ-a caterpillar that attacks young shoots of sugar-cane.

कई-a few; several.

ककड़-vegetable marrow; a long fleshy fruit; cucumber.

ककना-weed which chokes crops; a metal bangle.

ककहरा-the alphabet.

कका-paternal uncle.

ककुद-insignia of royalty; the hump of a bull.

ककुभ-a part of ; the tree Arjun high.

ककोरना-to scoop out; to scratch.

कक्कड़-leaves of dried tobacco which people smoke with the help of pipe.

कक्ष-house; compartment; belt; the armpit; sin; a jungle; side; earth.

कक्षा-orbit (of a heavenly body); class; rank; class (school; university).

कक्षोन्नति-promotion.
कखरी-the armpit.
कगर-on the bank of a river; uneven border; projecting portion in a wall.
कगारा-precipice; scrap.
कच-cloud; hair; a dried sore; sound of piercing or crushing; cicatrix.
कचक-shooting pain; a jerk; a strain; shock.
कचकोल-begging bowl made of a big cocoanut.
कचड़ा-rubbish.
कचदिला-having no courage to endure; feeble-hearted; pain or misery.
कचनार-tree; a moderate-sized deciduous;
कचपच-numerous objects in small space; packing up.
कचपेदिया-un-settled opinion.
कचमच-colloq. babble; gibberish.
कचरना-to crush with feet.
कचरा-rubbish; straw; an aromatic root of the genus; a small unripe melon.
कचरी-dried vegetable which are fried and eaten.
कचलोन-a ball of uncooked meal.
कचवा-to be irritated.
कचहरी-a court of justice; assembly; meeting.
कचाई-unripeness; uncooked; inexperience.
कचाना-to lose courage; to be frightened; to recede.
कचायँध-smell of rawness.
कचालू-a kind of a salad.
कचिया[1]-shy; timid.
कचिया[2]-a sickle.
कचियाना-to be timid; to draw back (from); to shy.
कचूमर-sweet fruit pickle.
कचूर-the medicinal plant ant its roots.
कचोका-blow; piercing; slab.
कचोट-vexation; galling feeling.
कचोना-to penetrate.
कचौड़ी-a kind of having a filling of lentils or vegetables.
कच्चा-crude; inexperienced; immature; uncooked.
कच्छ-low-lying ground (by a river or the sea).
कच्छप-a tortoise; a turtle.
कच्छपी-female tortoise.
कच्छा-a big boat with two rubbers; a fleet of boats.
कछ-side; flank.
कछना-shorts.
कछनी-lower garment reaching up to knees; a skimming vessel.
कछवाहा-name of a Rajput community.

कछार-wet land (by a river); alluvial land.

कछारना-to rinse; to wash.

कछारी-alluvial.

कछुआ-a turtle; a tortoise.

कछुई-a female tortoise.

कछोटा-cloth worn between the legs.

कछौहा-land in low situations.

कज-crookedness; perversity; defect; deficiency.

कजइ-the iron bit of a bridle put in a horse's mouth.

कजरा-lampblack; a bull with deep black eyes.

कजराई-blackness.

कजली-a type of sung song in the month of ; blackness.

कजलौटी-a small pot for lampblack.

कज़ा-fate; death; destiny.

कजावा-the pack-saddle placed over the back of camel.

कजिया-a dispute; a legal case.

कजी-crookedness; defect.

कज्जाक-a robber; a ruffian.

कटक-a bracelet; middle part of a mountain; a legion; an army.

कटकई-an army.

कटखना-prone to bite.

कटघरा-a stockade; balustrade; a large cage; a palisade; pillory; railing.

कटड़ा[1]-market; local bazar.

कटड़ा[2]-a buffalo calf.

कटती-sale of a commodity.

कटना-to be wounded by a sharp blade of something; to be cut.

कटनास-a kind of bird with blue neck.

कटनी-act of cutting; the harvest time; a cutting appliance; time of reaping.

कटर-a king of grass.

कटरा-a market surrounded on all sides of walls; a buffalo calf.

कटवाँसी-a knotty bamboo.

कटवाना-to cause to be cut.

कटसरैया-a thorny bush.

कटहा-liable to bite.

कटा-murder; slaughter; blooded.

कटाई-cutting; harvest-time; reaping; trimming; mowing; price for cutting.

कटाऊ-sharp; cutting (as remarks); biting.

कटाकट-a broil; a quarrel.

कटाक्ष-a sidelong glance; an aspersion; a flirtatious glance.

कटान-cutting; style; cut.

कटायक-one who cuts.

कटार-a type of dagger; plant of the genus or

कटारी-a small dagger.

कटाव-flowering designs on cloth; intersection; a cut; hack; nick.

कटावन-cutting; the portions cut off; the work of cutting.

कटास-an animal of the weasel family.

कटाह-a caldron; a high mound of earth; a tortoise shell; a well; hut.

कटि-the waist; the loins.

कटिया-a kind of ornament for the waist; a fishing-hook.

कटियाना-to stand (of hairs) on end.

कटिसूत्र-a girdle for the waist; a waist-band.

कटी-a slashing stroke (with a sword).

कटीला[1]-bewitching; thorny; enchanting; pointed; exciting.

कटीला[2]-thorny; pointed.

कटु-cutting; sharp; impetuous; fierce; pungent; hot; unpleasant.

कटुता-wickedness; bitterness; irritability; pungency; impetuosity.

कटूक्ति-a bitter or unfavourable remark.

कटैया-one who cuts; cutter.

कटोरदान-a brass pot with a lid for keeping articles of food.

कटोरा-cup (of a flower).

कटोरी-a small cup or bowl; the round top portion of the hilt of a sword.

कटौती-discount.

कटौसी-reduction.

कट्टर-a blind follower; dogmatic; prone to bite; a conservative.

कट्टरता-fanaticism.

कट्टा-stout and plump; robust; powerful.

कठंदर-swelling of the stomach.

कठकेला-a kind of plantain whose fruits are insipid and dry.

कठघरा-a palisade.

कठड़ा-a fence of skates; a large wooden box.

कठपुतली-a puppet; wooden toy.

कठफोड़वा-a woodpecker.

कठबंधन-the wooden ring with which an elephant is tied to a peg.

कठमलिया-a false or ascetic or quack saint.

कठमस्त-plump and stout; dissolute; licentious.

कठरा-wooden board; pot; a wooden saddle for a came; wooden platter.

कठला-a charm which is put on a child's neck.

कठिन-difficult; hard; cruel; abstruse; tough; knotty; uphill; long; severe.

कठिनी-a piece of chalk which is used for writing.

कठिया- a snare.

कठुवाना-to be benumbed; to be chilled by coal; to be hard as wood by being dried.

कठुमर-a wild-fig tree.

कठेठ-hard; strong; bitter; robust; powerful; sturdy; difficult.

कठोर-harsh (of manner); uncouth; arduous (toil); unfeeling.

कठौता-a large shallow wooden tub.

कड़-the seed of safflower.

कड़क-crack; thunder; agility; sharp noise.

कड़कनाल-a wide-mouthed gun of old type.

कड़का[1]-crash; report; crack.

कड़का[2]-colloq. broke.

कड़खा-martial music.

कड़खत-one who sings a martial song; a bard; a herald.

कड़ड़ा-an instrument to pick up something.

कड़ना-to pierce.

कड़वा[1]-bitter; pungent; sour; harsh; acrid; disagreeable; saline.

कड़वा[2]-myrrh.

कड़वी-plant of Indian corn (without seeds).

कड़ा-hard; powerful; firm; vigorous; tight; hard; tough; strong; rigorous.

कड़ाई-harshness; tightness; hardness; rigidity; stiffness; unbearableness.

कड़ाका-the crack of anything breaking; a rigid fast.

कड़ापन-stiffness; firmness; hardness.

कड़ाबीन-a carbine.

कड़ारा-steep; high bank (of a river; tank); a precipice.

कड़ाह-pan.

कड़ाहट-rigidity; stiffness; a shallow.

कड़ाही-a cauldron; a pan; a stew.

कड़ी[1]-difficulty; portion of a song.

कड़ी[2]-a beam; a squared rafter.

कड़ीदार-full of links.

कड़ुआ-bitter; sharp; pungent; harsh; sharp; keen; arduous; acid; mordant.

कड़ुआना-to get angry; to become bitter; to feel sore (as of eyes).

कड़ेर-hard; stiff.

कड़ोड़ा-one who has high post in service.

कड्डी-a metal pin or nail.

कढ़ना-to be drawn or extracted; to be increased; to escape; to be pulled up.

कढ़ाई-embroidery; pulling or drawing out; payment for embroidery.

कढ़ावली-a pain.

कढ़ाव-needlework; embroidery; drawings in relief worked on cloth.

कढ़ी-pulse meal with spices and sour milk ; particular a dish.

कढ़ेलड़-a child born to a widow who has remarried.

कढ़ैया-one who takes out; a seller.

कढ़ोरना-to pull; to drag.

कण-a grain; small fragment; a granule; a particle; seed; drop.

कणिका-small fragment; a grain (as of corn).

कणिश-spike.

कत-where; whither? by no means; why?

कतई-wholly; entirely; finally; altogether.

कतना-to be spun.

कतनी-a small straw basket; spinning.

कतर-cutting; clipping.

कतरन-pairings; shavings.

कतरनी-nippers; scissors.

कतरवाँ-crooked; zigzag.

कतरवाई-cost of cutting or price paid for cutting.

कतरा-fragment (as of stone); clipping; chip; a piece (as of sweet); paring.

कतराना-to cause to be cut; to avoid.

कतरी-a brass ornament for the twist or pewter.

क़तल-assassination; killing; murder; execution; slaughtering.

कतला-a slice of anything.

कतलाम general massacre.

कतली-sweetmeat in the form of a lozenge.

कतुहूँ somewhere; anywhere.

कताई-payment for or cost of spinning.

क़तार-order; row; series; a line.

कतारा-a variety of thick red-coloured sugarcane.

कति-several; a few.

कतिक how much; how many.

कतीरा-a large deciduous tree; an insoluble gum obtained from deciduous tree.

कतोरा-the gum used in medicine.

कतौनी-spinning; wages paid for spinning.

कत्तर-a small piece of cloth.

कत्तल-a small piece of stone; a chip.

कत्ता-an implement for tearing bamboos; a small dagger.

कत्ताल-a murderer.

कत्थई-of the colour of catechu.

कत्थक-a South-Indian dance.

कत्था-the tree from the bank of which catechu is extracted by boiling it.

क़त्ल-murder.

कथ-to compose (oral poetry); to expound; to recite; to tell.

कथक-a teller of old stories; a narrator.

कथड़ी-a tattered or patched garment or quilt.

कथन-mention; speech; utterance; narration; statement; recital.

कथनी-verbal quarrel; narration.

कथा-story; tale; report; said; sacred legend or tale; narration; legend.

कथाचित perhaps.

कथानक-a small story or narrative; narration.

कथामुख-introductory part of a story book.

कथावस्तु-the plot of a story; drama or play.

कथिक-narrate; told; said.

कथाद्घात-introduction of a story; the prelude of a drama.

कथोपकथन-discussion; conversation.

कथ्य-worth narrating or saying.

क़द-height; stature.

कदंब-aggregate; assembly; sum total; a kind of tree whose fruits are eaten.

कद[1]-insistence; importuning; persistence.

कद[2] when.

कद[3] defective; useless.

कदधव-wicked path.

कदन-destruction; slaughter; destroying.

कदन्नन-bad corn; bad food.

कदम-the foot; the sole; a foot's length; step measure; a pace.

क़दर-value; worth; respect; appreciation.

कदरमस-timidity; idleness.

कदरो-an Indian bird like the

कदर्थ-refuse; sweepings.

कदर्थना-bad luck; misfortune; miserable condition.

कदर्थित-involved in miserable plight.

कदर्य-miser; niggardly.

कदली-the plantain tree and its fruits.

कदा when?

कदाच perhaps.

कदाचार-wicked behaviour; evil conduct; misconduct.

कदाचित् at some time; perhaps; hardly even.

कदापि likely; seldom; perhaps.

कदी-obstinate; persistent.

कदीम-ancient.

क़दीमी-antiquated; traditional; very old; ancestral.

कदुपयोग-misuse.

कदुष्ण-slightly warm; lukewarm.

कदूरत-foulness; affliction; impurity; resentment; distress; depression of spirits; trouble.

कद्दावर-of tall stature; giantlike; gigantic.

कद्दी-obstinate.

कद्रुज-a snake; serpent.

क़द्दू-a pumpkin; gourd.

कद्र-worth; merit.

कन-small fragment; a particle.

कनई-new shoot of a plant.

कइउड़-disgraced.

कनक-wheat; gold; the thorn-apple.

कनकफल-the plant the fruit of thorn-apple.

कनकी-scrap; fragment; a piece of broken rice.

कनकूत-an estimate for the price of standing crop.

कनकौवा-to fly kites against each other; a large square paper kite.

कनखजूरा-a centipede.

कनखी-wink; ogling; a side-glance.

कनखोदनी-an ear-pick.

कनगरिया-the little finger.

कनछेदन-the ceremony of piercing a boy's ear.

कनटोप-a cap with flaps covering the ears.

कनतूतुर-a kind of poisonous toad.

कनपटी-the area between the temple and the ear.

कनपेड़-mumps; swelling of glands between throat and ears.

कनफटा-a designation of members of the sect.

कनफुसकी-whisper; murmur.

कनमनाना-to show signs of being awake from sleep; to speak something against or act against another's will.

कनय-gold; wheat.

कनरस-a taste of music; pleasure from music.

कनवाई-piercing the ears.

कनसलाई-a worm like the centipede.

कनसाल-the transverse mortise of a bedstead.

कनसार-one who inscribes on a copper plate.

कनसुई-secret watching; espionage.

कनस्तर-canister.

कनहार-boatman.

कनहाई-valuation of standing crop.

कना-a particle.

कनावड़ा-grateful; obliged.

कनात-the wall of a tent.

कनिका-the little finger.

कनिको-a tiny piece; a little bit.

कनिगर-one who takes care of his status in society.

कनियाँ-the lap.

कनियाना-to dodge; to go to one side avoiding the sight of anyone.

कनियार-a kind of tree that bear yellow flowers.

कनियाहट-timidity; avoiding; shyness.

कनिष्ठ-small; junior; younger; inferior; smaller.

कनिष्ठा-a less-favoured wife; a junior wife.

कनीनिका-pupil of the eyes.

कनीज़-a female-servant.

कने-under the sway of; near; towards; on the side of; in the vicinity of.

कनेठा-squint-eyed; one-eyed.

कनेठी-chastising by pulling or twisting the ears.

कनेर-oleander.

कनेरिया-an oleander of blackish red.

कनौजिया-belonging to Kanauj.

कनौड़-shame; diffidence; shyness.

कनौड़ा-one-eyed; a grateful person.

कनौती-the ear of an animal; pricking up the ear.

कन्ना-particle of rice; part of the kite to which string is tied; end; border.

कन्यका-a maiden; an unmarried girl; daughter.

कन्या-virgin; daughter; a lass; maid; maiden; girl.

कन्हाई-lord.

कप-trembling.

कपट-dissembling; trick; insincerity; trickery; deceit.

कपटी-designing; deceitful; dissembling; insincere; malicious.

कपड़द्वार-a store-room for garments; a wardrobe.

कपड़धूलि-fine silken glossy cloth; crepe.

कपड़ा-cloth; clothing; clothes; garment.

कपड़ागंद-the smell of burnt cloth.

कपर्द-locks of hair on 's head; a cowrie.

कपर्दिका-a small cowrie.

कप्तान-a captain.

कपाट-a door; a valve; leaf of a door.

कपाल-a broken water-pot; destiny; a beggar's bowl; head; the brow.

कपालिनी-an epithet of .

कपाली-one who wears skulls as a necklace.

कपास-the cotton-plant.

कपिंजर-a kind of Cuckoo.

कपि-monkey; the Sun; elephant.

कपिश-light-brown; tawny.

कपीश-an epithet of Hanuman; the lord of monkeys.

कपीशा-a kind of liquor; the name of a river.

कपूत-a bad son.

कपूर-camphor.

कपूरा-testicles (of ram; buffalo; goat)

कपोत-a pigeon; a dove.

कपोतव्रत-silently enduring the affront of others.

कपोती-a hen pigeon.

कपोल-cheek.

कप्तान-captain (of a crew; a team).

कफ-phlegm; one of the constituent of the body.

कफ़-cuffs of the sleeves of a garment; foam; froth.

कफ़चा-a skimmer or stirrer.

कफ़न-coffin; shroud.

कफ़नखसोट-miserly; very greedy; avaricious.

कफ़नाना-to wrap (a dead body) in a shroud.

कफ़स-a bird's cage; imprisonment; cell.

कबंध-belly; cloud; stomach; torso; headless trunk of a creature; a tub.

कब-when; rhetor; indeed?

कबक-a kind of partridge or quail.

कबड्डी-an Indian outdoor game of boys who plays the game by forming two parties; a fowler's stick for catching.

कबर-a tomb; a grave.

कबरा-spotted; variegated or different colour.

कब्रिस्तान-cemetery.

कबल before; previously; since.

कबा-a kind of ling robe.

कबाड़-worthless; articles; rubbish; useless material; useless enterprise.

कबाब-sliced meat stuck on skewers to be roasted.

कबाबचीनी-cubeb.

कबार-profession; broken furniture; business.

कबारना-to disengage; to pull up; to extricate.

कबारू-work; occupation (as of a boatman).

कबाला-a bill of sale of immovable property; a title-deed.

क़बाहट-inconvenience; difficulty; perplexity; defect.

कबीर-noble; great; name of a north Indian of the late 15th century.

कबीला-wife; better-half.

क़बीला-a tribe family.

क़बुली-a sacrificial (animal).

कबूतर-a pigeon; a dove.

क़बूल-agreement; approbation; consent; favourable reception.

कब्ज-constipation; seizing; taking possession.

क़ब्ज़ा-hinge; a handle; possession; clutch; tenure; grip; grasp; hasp.

क़ब्जियत-constipation.

क़ब्र-a grave; a tomb; a sepulchre.

क़ब्रिस्तान-a graveyard; burial ground; churchyard; a tomb; cemetery.

कमंडलु-an wooden or earthen pot used by mendicants; a spout for keeping water.

कमंद-rope; scaling-ladder; lasso.

कम-short; little; scanty; few; spare; scant; under; less.

कमअसल-crossbred; hybrid.

कमकर-deprived.

कमखव-brocade; silk embroidered with silver or gold.

कमचोर-malingerer; shirker.

कमची-a slender stick; a strip of bamboo or wood; twigs for making baskets.

कमजोर-feeble; week; ineffectual; deficient.

कमठ-a tortoise; a turtle.

कमतर-lesser.

कमताई-a state of minimisation or reduction; shortage; scarcity.

कमना-to be decreasing; to be lessened; deficiency.

कमनत-an archer.

कमबख्त-unlucky; cursed; ill-fated; unfortunate.

कमर-the loins; the waist; waist (of a garment).

क़मर-the moon.

कमरख-a particular small tree.

कमरा-a room hall; compartment; chamber (of a public building).

कमरिया-a small blanket; a strong elephant of small stature.

कमल-the lotus plant and its flower; jaundice; copper; a tumour in the uterus; a kind of antelope; a crane.

कमलबाई-a form of jaundice.

कमला-the goddess ; a king of big orange.

कमलासन-the god ; a special mode of sitting.

कमांडर-commander.

कमसिन-of under age; young.

कमाई-the act of earning or acquiring; earning; gain; profit.

कमाऊ-industrious; earning of livelihood; laborious.

कमानची-hoop (of a cask).

कमाना-to work; to earn; to accumulate.

कमार-a blacksmith.

कमानिया-an archer.

कमानी-a spring (in a mechanism).

कमाल-a miracle; excellence; perfection; completion; conclusion.

कमासुत-a earner.

कमी-poverty; deficiency; extenuation; reduction; failing; scarcity; shortfall.

कमीज़-a shirt.

कमीना-vile; wicked; base; mean.

कमेटी-a committee.

कमेड़ी-a dove; a ring dove.

कमेरा-a servant; a workman; a labourer.

कमोदनी-the white water-lily.

कमोदिनी-a lily flower.

कमोदी-sweet rice.

कमोरा-a big jar of clay; wide-mouthed earthen jar.

कमोरी-a small wide-mouthed earthenware pot (as used for making curds).

कयपूती-a kind of perennial plant from which scented oil is extracted.

क़याम-stability; certainty; residence; state of rest.

क़यामत-calamity; lamentation.

क़यास-imagining; conjecture; conception; measuring; fancy; though.

करंक-pod made of coconut shell; head; skeleton.

करंग-skeleton.

करंजा-quaint-eyed.

करंड-a bee-hive; a sword; a bamboo basket; a kind of swan.

करंतीना-quarantine.

कर-tribute; tax; toll.

करई[1]-a small earthen pot with a spout.

करई[2]-a granary; store house.

करक-the drinking pot of an ascetic; pomegranate; pain in scanty urination.

करकच-a fragment; made of evaporation; sea-salt.

करकसा-a termagant woman; boisterous; a shrew.

करका-hail.

करकाना-to break; to strain.

करख-to incite.

करग-Rhinoceros.

करगस-a kind of arrow.

करगह-a weaver's loom; a hand-loom.

करगहना-bricks or stone placed over a door; lintel of wood.

करग्रह-marriage.

करग्रहण-to marry.

करचंग-a micro-tome.

करण-the instrumental case; an action.

करतब-performance; jugglery; work; a feat; skill; exploit.

करतरी-one who performs feats.

करतार-author; the creator; master.

करताल-a kind of small cymbal; clapping of hands.

करतूत-manner of life; action; business; work; conduct.

करद-helper; assistant; dependent; a tax-payer.

करधनी-a chain of silver or gold worn round the waist.

करधर-the cloud.

करनफूल-an ornamental ear-ring worn by ladies.

करनल-colonel.

करनवेध-the ceremony of piercing a child's ear.

करना-to work through; to do; to act.

करनाई-a small trumpet.

करनाल-a kind of trumpet or horn; a kind of gun; a kind of big drum.

करपर-the skull.

करपीड़न-marriage.

करपृष्ठ-the back portion of the palm of the hand.

करबर-speckled; the cheetah.

करबरना-to be restless; to be agitated.

करबस-the strap in the saddle of a cavalier on which weapons are hung.

करबी-the hollow stalk of a plant.

करभ-a young camel; the back portion of the palm of the hand; the waist; young one of an elephant.

करम-grace; kindness; generosity; favour; fortune; luck.

करमकल्ला-a cabbage.

करमचन्द-fate; destiny; luck.

करमट्ठा-miserly; niggardly.

करमाली-an epithet of the Sun (full of rays).

करमी-working; active; laborious.

करमुँहा-a big boiling pan.

करवट-the side (of the body) on which one rests; the position of lying or sleeping on the side.

करवत-a saw.

करवर-disaster; trouble; distress.

करवरना-to make a noise.

करवा-a pot made of metal or earth with a spout.

करवार-pole used as a rudder; a sword; paddle; an oar.

करवाल-a finger-nail; a sword; a scimitar.

करवाली-a small sword; a scimitar.

करवैया-an operative; a worker.

करश्मा-a wonder.

करष-agitation; anger; a pulling; tension; excitement; hostility; envy.

करसना-to attract.

करसायल-an antelope; black buck.

करह-a camel.

कराँत-a saw.

कराँती-a small saw.

कराइत-the black cobra.

कराई-cost of getting done.

करात-a carat; weight of four grains (about four grams).

कराधान-taxation.

करामात-feat; exploit.

करायल-resin.

क़रार-stability; contract; rest; firmness; undertaking; satisfaction; promise.

करारा-strong; firm; heavy (as price); crisp; high priced; of full weight.

कराल-formidable; with big protruding; huge; teeth; lofty.

क़रावल-watchman; vanguard; guard; hunter; sentry.

कराह-a moan; groan.

कराहत-dislike; disgust; aversion.

कराहना-to sigh; to moan; to groan.

कराही-a frying pan.

करिंद-the elephant of the god ; a beautiful big elephant.

करि-an elephant.

करिखा-a female elephant.

करिया-black.

करिल[1]-the new tender leaf of a plant.

करिल[2]-cauldron.

करिवर-a splendid elephant.

करिश्मा-glance; wonderful; a wonder; phenomenon; talisman.

करिहाँव-loin; the waist.

क़रीब-near (in time or place).

करीम-gracious; munificent; bountiful; kind; benevolent; generous.

करीर-the shoot of bamboo plant.

करीश-a very big elephant; the king of elephants.

करीष-dry cow-dung found scattered in jungles.

करुण-God.-merciful.

करुणा-pity; mercy; of feeling; tenderness; compassion.

करुना pity; mercy.

करुवा bitter.

करूला-a bangle.

करेजा-bosom.

करेणु-an elephant.

करेम-an eatable vegetable grass which is cooked.

करेर-vehement; hard; stiff.

करैत-very poisonous; name of a black snake.

करैल-black earth found on the banks of river or lakes; a raven; a jackdaw.

करैला-bitter gourd.

करोड़-of vast wealth; ten millions; a crore.

करोड़ा[1]-famine; distress; drought; disaster; trouble.

करोड़ा[2]-tax-gatherer; inspector; overseer (as of a market).

करोदना-to scrape; to scratch.

करौछा-somewhat black; of blackish colour.

करौंदा-the horny plant ; the gooseberry.

करौत-a large saw.

करौता-a hand-saw; a phial or glass for keeping oil.

करौल-a hunter.

करौली-a dagger.

कर्क-a crash; a mirror; fire; a sing of zodiac-cancer.

कर्कट-a crab; the sign Cancer.

कर्कटी-cucumber; a snake; a female tortoise; silk-cotton tree.

कर्कर-hard; stiff; rough.

कर्कवृत्त-Tropic of Cancer.

कर्केतर-a kind of quartz.

कर्कोट-the tree.

कर्चूर-the plant the gold.

कर्ज़-a debt; a loan.

कर्ज़दार-indebted.

कर्ण-helm of a ship or boat; the ear; hypotenuse.

कर्णकुहर-the hole of the ear.

कर्णधार-a helmsman; a steersman.

कर्णनाद्र-buzzing in the ears.

कर्णमूल-a swelling in the ear.

कर्णाटक-the Karnataka region of South India.

कर्णामूल शोध-mumps.

कर्णिका-a fruit-stalk; the pericarp of a lotus; ear-ring; an ear ornament; the middle finger.

कर्णिकार-name of a mountain; having large eyes; having ears or projections.

कर्तन-cutting of thread; weaving.

कर्तनी-scissors.

कर्तरी-shears of a goldsmith; scissors; a small sword; a scimitar; a dagger.

कर्तव्य-duty; to be done; task.

कर्ता-creator of world; doer; performer.

कर्तार-creator; God; doer.

कर्तृक-done; performed.

कर्त्तृत्व-state of acting; management; action; rule; agency.

कर्तृन-shearing.

कर्तृवाचक-doing the work of a subject.

कर्द-mire; mud.

कर्दम-mud; sin; mire; flesh; lime; dregs; filth; clay.

कर्नता-a species of horse.

कर्पट-worn out clothes; rags.

कर्पर-skeleton; skull; a weapon; tortoise-shell; cranium cauldron; pan.

कर्बुर-water; gold; a demon.

कर्म-destiny; deed; occupation; business; act; work; fate; Hindu sacrifice; worship; funeral rites.

कर्मकर-a worker.

कर्मकांड-that part of the which relates to ceremonial acts and sacrificial.

कर्मकारी[1]-a bull; an artisan; labourer; a servant; a goldsmith.

कर्म कौशल-workmanship.

कर्मक्षेत्र-sphere of functions or duties.

कर्मचारी-an official; an employee.

कर्मच्युत-dismissed from office.

कर्मत्व-objectivity (in grammar).

कर्मठ-industrious; assiduous.

कर्मणा by action; by deed.

कर्मण्य-enjoined by or scripture; energetic; industrious.

कर्मनिष्ठा-performing religious ceremonies daily.

कर्मभूमि-a place of devotion.

कर्मभोग-fulfilment of fortune; result of past birth.

कर्मयुग-the age of action; the present epoch.

कर्म-रेख-mark of fate on the body; fortune; destiny.

कर्मवाच्य-passive voice.

कर्मवान्-engaged in work.

कर्मविपाक-the consequence of action done.

कर्मशाला-workshop.

कर्मशील-assiduous.

कर्मशूर-industrious; laborious.

कर्मसंन्यास-relinquishment or resignation of action.

कर्मसाक्षी-an eye-witness of work performed.

कर्मिष्ठ-assiduous laborious; active.

कर्मेन्द्रिय-an organ of action (the foot; the hand; anus and generative organs; organ of voice).

कर्राना-to be stiff or hard.

कर्ष-attraction; astringency; pulling.

कर्षक-one who pulls; cultivator of the soil; a tiller; a tiller of the soil.

कर्षण-haulage; pulling; attraction.

कर्षना-to drag; to pull.

कलंक-blemish; reprehension; shame; taint; ignominy; scandal; foulness.

कलंदर-an itinerant Muslim ascetic; a monkey-dancer; a bear-dancer.

कलंब-stalk of a green vegetable; an arrow.

क़ल-sweet (of a sound); charming soft; low.

कल[1] yesterday; the recent past.

कल[2]-bud.

कलई-thin coat of tin on an object; gilt; external grandeur; white-wash; tin.

कलकंठ-a swan; a cuckoo; a pigeon.

क़लक़-keen regret; distress.

कलकना-to make a shrill noise; a cry aloud.

कलकल-a rippling sound; quarrel; din of crowd.

कलकादि-difficulty; obstacle; trouble; anxiety.

कलकी-the name of the tenth and future avatar of .

कलकूजिका-a female with a sweet voice or tone.

कलगा-crest.

कलगामा-the flower the coxcomb.

कलगी-an ornament for the head; coxcomb; a king of song; a prince's feather plume; crest.

कलछा-a ladle with long-handle.

कलछी-a large bowl spoon with a long handle.

कलझँवा-tawny; black.

कलत्र-wife; better-half.

कलदार-fitted with accessory parts.

कलधूत-silver.

कालधौत-sweet harmonious sound; gold; silver.

कलन-preparing; a morsel; a mathematical process; a connection; conduct; a conception; an idea.

कलना-created; creation.

कलप-starch; hair-dye.

कलपना-to be distressed; to lament.

कलफ़-starch.

कलबंद-a variety of aloe.

कलबल-contrivance; device; uproar.

कलबूत-body; frame (of a man or woman); mould.

कलबूद-mould.

कलभ-a young elephant.

क़लम-pen; hand-writing.

कलमल-agitation; restlessness; disquiet.

कलमकारी-paining with brush; engraving; etching.

कलमतराश-a pen-knife.

कलमदान-an inkstand; a small box used for keeping ink, pencil, pin.

कलमना-to cut off; to pare; to lop.

कलमलना-thrilling of body owing to external pressure; writhing.

कलमा-confession of Mohammedanism; a statement.

कलमुँहा-unlucky; stained; unfortunately.

कलरव-a pigeon; sweet notes; din; hubbub; a cuckoo.

कलल-the bubble-shaped primary formation of an embryo.

कलविक-a sparrow; a watermelon.

कलश-an ornament on the top of summit of a dome; a water-pot; a pitcher; hydra; a dome; top; spire.

कलसा-the steeple over a temple; a water-pot.

कलसी-

कलह-quarrel; strife.-quarrelsome.

कलहटी-tumbling; acrobatics.

कलहारी-quarrelsome; termagant.

कलही-contesting; quarrelsome.

कला-a digit of the moon; a small part of anything; an art; a sixteenth part; trick; juggling.

कलाई-the fore-arm; the wrist; a skeing of thread.

कलाकंद-a sweet made of or with sugar.

कलाकार-a skilled performer; an actor.

कलाना-to winnow; to shake up; to shake together.

कलानेत्री-a woman artist.

कलादा-a seat on elephant's head on which diver sits for guiding.

कलाधार-the moon; an epithet of ; one who is proficient in any art.

कलनिधि-the moon.

कलाप-lamentation; sorrow.

कलापनी-the peahen; night.

कलापी-a peacock; having a mass of (tall) feather.

कलाबतून-gold or silver thread.

कलाबत्तु-gold or silver thread which is twisted on cotton or silk thread.

कलाबाज़-a juggler.

कलाबाज़ी-tumbling; acrobatic feat of somersault.

कलाम-speech; discourse; a composition; word; a complete sentence.

कलाल-one who distils liquor; a caste.

कलावती-a juggler; a singer; an artist; an acrobat; a musician.

कलावा-a red and yellow colour thread which worn on the wrist on auspicious occasions.

कलावान-skilful; competent; moon.

कलिंग-the name of a region along the South-East of India.

कलिका-a kind of musical instrument; a bud.

कलिकाल-present age.

कलित-made with art of skill.

कलिया-boiled or fried meat with any dressing; a meat curry.

कलियाना-to blossom; to bud.

कलियारी-a kind of plant with poisonous roots.

कलियुग-the fourth age of Hindu mythology; present age.

कलिंहारी-quarrelsome.

कलिंदा-a water-melon.

कली-a flower bud; an unopened bud.

कलीट-deep black.

कलीराम-a kind of wreath which is worn during the marriage ceremony.

कलील-moderate; little; scanty; barely sufficient.

कलीसा-a church.

कलुष-dirty; impure; foul; sinful; dirtied.

कलुषाई-profanity; wickedness; impurity.

कलेउ-breakfast for bridegroom given by brides father.

कलेजा-hear; spirit; the liver; bosom; magnanimity.

कलेजी-the liver (of an animal); lungs and lever (of an animal).

कलेवर-to pass from one body to another; structure of the body.

कलेशियाया-truculent; quarrelsome.

कलेस-distress; calamity; affliction; trouble.

कलैंडर-a calender.

कलैया-somersault.

कलोर-sport; gaiety and mirth; frolic; amusement.

कलौंजी-black; a kind of vegetable; black cummin.

कलौंस-slightly black; stain.

कल्ल-fraud; powder; medicine in the form of paste; wickedness.

कल्प-practice; age; an aeon; rule.

कल्पक-a barber; creator.

कल्पना-something imagined; a conjecture; hypothesis; making.

कल्पवृक्ष-a mythological tree that is supposed to grant all desires.

कल्पनीय-imaginable; conceivable.

कल्पित-supposed; formed; fabricated; contrived; artificial; false.

क़ल्ब-inner part; core; the heart.

कल्पष-uncleanness; filth; sin; impurity.

कल्पाष-black and white; variegated; spotted; black.

कल्य-early morning; honey; early; dawn; wine.

कल्याण-good fortune; welfare; auspicious; action.

कल्लर-non-fertile land.

कल्ला-the upper jaw; cheek boasting.

कल्लोल-pleasure; sensation; happiness; merry-making.

कल्लोलिनी-a river.

कल्हरना-to be fried; to be cooked in a pan.

कल्हारना-to fry in a pan; to cry in grief; to wail; to make a wailing sound.

कवक-fungus.

कवच-coat of mail; armoured; lucky charm.

कवची-wearing armour.

कवयित्री-a poetess.

कवर-mouthful; morsel; gulp; gobbet; a braid of hair.

कवरी-a braid of hair.

कवर्ग-the five consonants.

कवल-a species of good horse; a kind of bird; a gargle; mouthful; morsel.

कवलित-taken in the mouth; eaten swallowed up.

कवि-a poet.

कविका-bit of bridle.

कविता-poetry; a poem.

कविताई-poetry making; composition of poetry.

कवित्त-a poem; poetry; a Hindi syllabic meter having four line with thirty-one syllables per line.

कविराज-a title of physicians of Bengal; the prince of poets.

कविलास-heaven; paradise.

कवेला-the small crow.

कव्य-offering of food to dead ancestors.

क़व्वाल-a musician (a Muslim) who sing religious songs to an accompaniment; speaking (by occupation); a professional story-teller.

कश-a whip; drawing in the smoke tobacco into the mouth; straining; lash; pulling.

कशिश-attraction; power; charm.

कशीदगी-tension; ill-feeling.

कशीदा-needlework; floral designs worked on cloth.

कश्चित्-any one; some one; any; some.

कश्ती-narrow tray; a boat.

कश्मीर-Kashmir.

कश्यप-one of the stars in the Great Bear; a tortoise; a kind of antelope.

कश्शाफ़-very clear; explicit.

कष-a wheatstone; a touchstone; tria; criterion; test; testing the purity of gold by rubbing it on a touchstone.

कष्ट-difficulty; wretchedness; inconvenience; suffering; trouble; effort; hardship; pain; affliction; labour.

कष्टी-afflicted; distressed.

कस[1]-a mean of binding; strength; power; tenacity.

कस[2]-a small mattock or pickaxe.

कसक-elasticity of a sword; trial; test; power assay; obstruction; strength.

कसकुट-an alloy of copper; tin and zinc.

कसन-strain; rope for tightening.

कसना-to tighten; to press down to against; to draw tight.

कसनी-string or strap which is used for tying pillow-case or bodice; touch-stone.

कसब-task; toil; exertion; labour; employment.

कसबल-power; vitality; energy.

क़सबा-a small town.

कसबिन-a whore; prostitute; an adulterous.

कसबी-one who grains or earns; a prostitute.

कसम-to make some one swear; an oath; to perform nominally.

कसर-deficiency; violence; revenge; malice; animosity; enmity.

कसरती-sportive; athletic.

क़साइन-a butcher's wife.

कसाई-a butcher.

कसाना[1]-to cause to be tightened.

कसाना[2]-to cause to be tested; to put to proof.

कसार-wheat meal mixed with sugar and fried with ghee.

कसाला-to labour; pains.

कसाव-astringency; pungency; causticity.

कसावर-struck with a stick; a metal plate; cymbal.

कसीर-numerous; abundant.

कसीला-strong (a person or animal); well built.

कसीस-green-vitriol; iron-sulphate.

क़सूर-error; to commit a fault; fault.

कसेरा-a brazier; a tinker.

कसेरु-an edible tuber of the plant

कसैला-astringent; pungent.

कसोरा-a cup of baked clay.

कसौदी-an oil pickle.

कसौ-what sort of?

कसौटी-touchstone; criterion; proof; an assay; a test.

कस्तूर-the musk-deer.

कस्तुरिया-the colour of musk.

कस्तूरी-musk; the Indian blackbird; the musk deer (a small brownish-grey deer).

क़स्द-attempt; intention; wish; resolve.

क़स्बा-town.

कस्सा-a kind of liquor.

क़स्साब-a butcher.

कहं-where.

क़हक़ह-peal of laughter.

क़हक़हा-a boisterous laugh; a horselaugh.

कहगिल-mud plaster which is applied on walls.

कहत-utter scarcity; famine.

कहता-a person who speaks.

कहना-to repeat; to say; to utter; to tell; to remark; to observe.

क़हर-calamity; rage; violent or dire.

कहल-trouble; indolence; languor.

कहवाँ where; in which place.

कहवैया-to cause to tell; to end word.

कहाँ in what (possible) case? where? how?

क़हाक़ा-peal of laughter.

कहाना-to be said.

कहानी-tale; a short story; story.

कहालत-remissness; sloth; inactivity.

कहावत-byword; proverb; dictum; saw maxim; motto; dictum; parable.

कहिया-when; on what day.

कहीं-anywhere; somewhere.

कहुं-to some one.

कहुं-some where.

कांइया-cunning; rogue.

कांकड़ी-a small stone.

कांक्षा-longing; desire.

कांक्षी-desiring; desirous.

काँख-armpit; side (of the body).

काँखना-to grunt; to make a groaning sound; to stain (at stool); to cry in pain.

काँगड़ी-an earthenware pot of coals.

काँगनी-a millet;

काँच-glass; end of the lower garment which is tucked on waist; a disorder of the rectum.

काँचन-gold.

काँचरी, काँचली-the slough of a snake.

काँचा-unripe.

कांची-girdle worn by woman.

काँचुली-a bodice; a snake's slough.

काँजी-rice-water; a kind of vinegar made from rice or mustard seed.

काँट-sour gruel; curry.

काँटा-thorn; spine; a fishing hook; spicule; nail.

काँटी-small thorn; small hook; or nail.

काँठा-red and blue ring round a parrot's throat; shore; throat; edge.

कांड-part; from one joint to another; part of sugar-cane.

काँड-to pound; to trample; to crush (as grain).

काँडली-purslane.

काँडी-a big piece of wood; a rafter; the yoke of a plough.

कांत-lovely; beloved; husband.

कांता-a beautiful woman; beloved; wife.

कांतार-a forest or desolate region.

कांति-lustre; beauty; gloss; decoration; splendour.

काँदना-to weep or lament.

काँदा-an edible root or bulb; an onion.

काँदो-mud; mire.

काँधना-to take upon oneself; to lift up; to assume responsibility; to accept; to support; to determine.

काँधर[1]-the neck.

काँधर[2]-shoulder.

काँप-an ornament for the ear; a thin flexible stick.

काँपना-to shiver; to quiver; to tremble.

काँवर-a bamboo having slings or baskets suspended at each end for carrying loads.

काँवरा-perplexed; confused.

काँवरिया-a pilgrim who carries his luggage.

काँवरू-exciting.

काँसा-pewter; bismuth; bronze; a kind of begging bowl.

कास्य-bronze.

काई-lichen; moss.

काक-crow; a cork.

काकड़ा-stiff leather; a large or stiff wick.

काकतालीय-occurring accidentally; by chance; at random.

काकदन्त-something remarkable and wonderful; a miracle.

काकपक्ष-a sing of caret made below; a line to show the place for words omitted.

काकबन्ध्या-a woman who has born only one child.

काकरी-a pebble.

काकली-a low soft sound.

काकलोद-longing; attachment.

काका-a paternal uncle.

काका कौआ-a cockatoo.

काकिणी-a small coin worthy twenty cowries; a cowrie shell.

काकु-a figure of speech; a taint; a sneer; a sarcasm.

काकुल-a curling lock; tuft of hair on the head.

काकोली-a medicinal plant.

काख-the armpit.

काग-a crow; plug for a bottle cork.

कागज़-a paper; document; an account; bond; note.

कागज़ात-legal deeds; written documents.

कागज़ी-made of paper; done on paper.

कागर-wing.

कागरी-worthless.

कागारोल-tumult; hubbub.

काच-a disease of the eye; alkaline ashes; crystal; glass.

काचक-glazier.

काची-a pot which is used for keeping milk or curd.

काछ-shorts.

काछनी-cloth worn over a

काछी-a gardener who cultivates and sells vegetables; tortoise.

काछे-near; nearby.

काज-a matter in hand; task; affair; occupation; matter; work; activity.

काजर-soot.

काजल-lampblack; soot.

काजी[1]-occupied; busy; employed.

काजी[2]-a Mohammedan judge or law-officer.

काट[1]-slice; piece; a cut; slash; bite; bit; chip.

काट[2]-edge (of a blade).

काटना-to clip; to interrupt; to retrench; to bite; to fillet; to carve.

काटू-prone to bite (an animal); corrosive; irritable; pungent.

काठ-a block; timber; a scabbard.

काठड़ा-a big shallow wooden vessel.

काठिन्य-difficulty; roughness.

काठी-scabbard; shape; structure; form; body; appearance; pad; saddle.

काड्-the cod fish.

काड़ी-a dry stalk.

काढन-embroidery.

काढ़ना-to work figures on cloth; to draw out; to draw lines or figures; to embroider; to borrow; to boil; to sift.

काढा-a medicinal extract.

कात-the spur of a cock.

कातना-to spin (cotton; thread; cord); to twist or to wrap round.

कातर-timid; distressed; frightened; afraid; nervous.

कातिब-a writer of documents; a scribe; a clerk.

क़ातिल-murderous; killing.

काती-scissors; a small sword; a knife; a scimitar.

कात्यायन-a sage who was the descendant of Kat.

कादंबरी-wine; the moon.

कादंबिनी-a row of clouds.

काद-mud.

कादर-perplexed; distressed.

क़ादिर-mighty; omnipotent.

कादिरी-a kind of bodice.

कान-the ear; shame; helm of a boat; rudder; the handle of a vessel; modesty; heed; respect; regard.

कानन-a group of tree; wood; forest; grove.

काना[1]-one-eyed; worthless.

काना[2]-distorted in shape.

कानाकानी-a whispering in the ear; idle talk; gossip.

कानाफूसी-whispering; tales; whispered words; intrigue; a sudden noise made in a child's ear.

कानि-modesty; regard; shame; regard; retaliation.

कानी[1]-the little finger.

कानी[2]-a woman with one eye.

कानीन-one who is born of a unmarried woman.

क़ानून-a law.

क़ानूनियत-legality.

क़ानूनजदाँ-one who is conversant with laws; a lawyer.

क़ानूनिया-a litigious or legalistic person.

कान्त-a husband.

कान्ता-a wife; sweet-heart.

कान्ति-effulgence; decoration; lustre; gloss; light; splendour.

कान्यकुब्ज-name of a community of Brahmans.

कान्हड़ा-name of a

कापना-to shiver; to trebmle.

कापिल-tawny; pertaining to or the philosophy.

कापी-a notebook; an exercise book; a copy.

कापुरुष-a contemptible person.

काफ़िर-impious; not believing (in Islam).

काफ़िला-a multitude of travellers; a caravan.

काफ़ी-enough; sufficient; considerable amount.

काफर-to run away; to flee; to disappear.

काफरी-pertaining to the colour of camphor; a large dish.

काफूर-to take to one's heels; to vanish; camphor.

काब-a large dish.

काबर-mottled.

काबिल-clever; skilful; fit; qualified.

कबिस-a colour which is applied to vessels of clay before being caked.

काबीना-cabinet.

काबुक-pigeon-house.

काबुली-produced in Kabul or belonging to Kabul.

काबुली-the language of Kabul.

क़ाबू-grasp; control; hold; authority.

काम-task; duty; cupid; wish.

कामकला-sexual intercourse; wife of Cupid; an epithet of .

कामकाजी-active; busy; industrious; laborious.

कामगार-worker.

कामचोर-shrinking from work; inactive; lazy.

कामज-amorous.

कामज्वर-a fever occurring in perfect celibacy.

क़ामत-bodily shape; stature; desire.

कामदहन-an epithet of who burnt Cupid to ashes.

कामदा-a cow that fulfils one's all desires.

कामदार-an agent; a manager.

कामधाम-work; occupation.

कामना-wish; lust; desire.

कामप्रवृत्ति-sexual instinct.

कामभावना-sex feeling.

कामयाब-successful.

कामरी-a blanket.

कामल, कामला a disease in which entire body becomes climbing plant jaundice.

कामवती-a woman desiring sexual intercourse with a man.

कामवान्-a lust-loving person.

काम विचलन-sexual deviation.

कामशास्त्र-sexual science.

काम-शिक्षा-sex education.

कामाक्षी-a form of the goddess .

कामातुर-lustful; love-sick; agitated by lust.

कामर्त-love-iron.

कामायनी-a book; novel.

कामिल-complete; entire; expert; perfect; accomplished; able.

कामी-twigs for basket-making; an ingot of precious metal.

कामुक-sensual; amorous; salacious; lecherous; erotic; rakish.

कामुकी-a sensual woman.

कामेश्वरी-one the five idols of the lewdness.

कामोद-a kind of musical note sung at nigh.

काम्य-desirable; beautiful; lovely; self-interested.

काम्येष्टि-the sacrifice which is performed to fulfil a definite desire.

काम्यदान-a desirable gift.

काय-the body.

कायदा-law; order; practice; custom; established order; good manner.

कायम-firm; settled; fixed; established; durable.

कायर-cowardly; timid.

कायल-to convince; to imbued; convinced by argument.

काया-the body.

कारबार-business occupation.

कारवाँ-a convoy; caravan (of travellers).

कारसाज-an inventor; a doer of efficient work.

कारस्तानी-cunningness; trickery.

कारिका-a gnome; an acrobat's wife; an aphorism.

कार्कश्य-harshness.

कार्पण्य-miserliness.

कार्पास-cotton.-made of cotton.

कार्मिक-personnel.

कार्मुक-a bow.

कार्य-function; act; affair; action; business; profession; avocation.

कार्यकलाप-activity.

कार्यकर्ता-an official; a worker; a factor; a functionary.

कार्यकारी-acting; working.

कार्यकुशलता-workmanship.

कार्यकाल-tenure; session.

कार्यकेन्द्र-focus (of work).

कार्यक्रम-schedule; programme; scale; campaign.

कार्यक्षेत्र-scope.

कार्यगृह-station.

कार्यतत्पर-occupied in a work; engaged in work.

कार्यदिवस-working days.

कार्यनियोजक-a taskmaster.

कार्यपरीक्षा-inspection of work.

कार्यपंजी-log book.

कार्यपालक-executive.

कार्यभंग-destruction; tampering.

कार्यभार-duty; charge.

कार्यरत-serving.

कार्यशाला-workshop.

कार्यसमय-business hours; working hours.

कार्यसमिति-working committee.

कार्यसाधक-efficient; telling; efficacious; working; telling; competent.

कार्यसिद्धि-success in one's enterprise; efficiency.

कार्यसूची-agenda.

कार्याधिकारी-a responsible officer; one who is entrusted with a specific work.

कार्यान्वयन-execution.

कार्यार्थ छुट्टी-duty leave.

कार्यार्थी-desirous; of success in an undertaking.

कार्यालय-factory; office.

कालंगड़ा-a king of song.

कार्षापण-an old Indian coin.

काल-time; season; date; period.

कालकूट-a deadly poison.

कालकंठ-a peacock; an epithet of ; a wagtail; a blue-jay.

कालकेतु-the name of a demon.

कालकोठरी-a very dark dungeon in any prison where criminals are shut up.

कालक्षेप-loss of time; to procrastinate.

कालखंड-God.

कालगडेत-the spotted cobra.

कालचक्र-cycle; a period of time; the wheel of time; a missile.

कालज्ञ-an astrologer; one who knows time changing in future.

कालतुष्टि &-the satisfaction that time will fulfil everything.

कालदंड-God of death.

कालपूर्व-premature.

कालमान-time scale.

कालमापी-time keeper; chronometer.

कालयापन-passing away of time.

कालवाचक-an adverb in time; pertaining to tense (in grammar).

कालस-blackness.

कालसर्प-the deadly cobra.

कालसार-a black antelope.

कालाक्षरी-very lear-ned; very intelligent.

कालातिल-black sesame.

कालातीत-time barred; the proper time of which has elapsed.

काला बाजार-black market.

कालावधि-time; period; limit.

कालि-period or time.

कालिक-relating to time.

कालिक-soot.

कालिकाल often; sometime.

कालिब-the body; figure; a mould; a last.

कालिया-darkness; blemish; stigma; calumny; blackness.

काली[1]-black colour or mark; a title of the goddess .

काली[2]-name of a snake that lived in the river ; that was killed by.

कालीन-a carpet.

कालुष्य-foulness; blackness; impurity.

कालेश्वर-an epithet of or.

कालोचित-expedient.

कालौंच-blackness.

काल्पनिक-imaginary; unreal; visionary; imaginative; fabulous; quixotic; fictitious; weal; chimerical.

कावर-two hanging slings at the both sides of a bamboo stick.

कावा-the lounging of a horse.

काव्य-a literary composition in verse by a single author; a poem; belles letters.

काव्यत्व-poetic quality or style.

काश-a kind of long reed; asthma; cough; catarrh.

काशीफल-the sweet fruit of the tree

काश्मीरा-a rough woollen cloth prepared in Kashmir.

काषाय-the colour of riddle.

काष्ठ-wood; ligneous; wood used as fuel.

कास-cough.

कासा-a cup; a bowl; a goblet; a pot for food made of a big coconut used by mendicant.

कासार-a tank; small pond.

क़ासिद-a messenger.

काह-what.

काहल-lazy; dull.

काहिल-indolent; slack; negligent.

काहाँ-in what place; where.

काही-blackish green; of the colour of grass.

काहे-wherefore; with what aim; why.

किंकर-a servant.

किंरता-bondsmanship; service.

किंकर्तव्यविमूढ़-perplexed; in a fix.

किंगरी-a stringed instrument of medium size having a box-like wooden frame.

किंगी-a kind of small fiddle.

किंचन-a small quantity.

किंतु-but; otherwise.

किंपुरुष-a tribe of Indians of old times.

किंदन्ती-a rumour; hearsay.

किंशुक-the tree and its red colour.

कि-since; why; what; wherefore; which; what; that.

किचड़ाहा-muddy.

किछ-some.

किड़-a worm.

किण्व-seed or drug used as ferment in making spirits.

कित-whither; how much; where; towards.

कितक-how many in number; how much.

कितना-how much; how many?

कितब-a cheat; a gambler; a cunning fellow; a wicked person.

किता-a piece; a cut-off portion.

किताब-a book; work register; account book.

किताबी-of the form of a book.

किति-renown; fame; celebrity.

कितीक-how many.

कितेक-how may (particular items)?

कित्त-where.

किदार-a name of *kidar.*

किधर-where? whither?

किन-scar; a wound.

किनका-broken grain; broken rice.

किनवानी-light shower of rain.

किनार-a shore.

किनारा-end; limit; margin; edge; side; shore; bank; beach; a border.

किनारी-edge; gold or silver; border; jabot; lace; tatting.

किन्तु without; but; only.

किफ़ायत-abundance; advantage (by saving); sufficiency; profit.

किफ़ायती-economical; thrifty.

किम् how? what? why?

किमरिख-cambric.

किमाम-yeast or fermenting agent; a thickened juice.

किमाश-in what way; how.

किस्मत-device; skill; artifice.

कियात् how much.

किया-performed.

किरंटा-Christian of low social status.

किरकिटी-dust; or dirt fallen into the eye.

किरका-mote of dust; a fragment; a small bit.

किरकिर-the sound of anything gritty under the teeth; grittiness; grating; creaking (as of a door).

किरकिराहट-a grating noise; a cracking noise.

किरकिल-the chameleon.

किरकी-a type of ornament.

किरच-a bit; grain; a straight sword; metal; a splinter of glass.

किरचा-to cut to pieces.

किरण-a beam; stream; ray of light.

किरणन-irradiation.

किरतनिया-a singer of devotional songs.

किरदार-character (of a literary work).

किरन-a frill of gold thread.

किरम-a small insect; grub or larva; a maggot.

किरमाल-a dagger; a sword.

किरमिच-a type of cloth; cochineal (the insect; a former source of scarlet and crimson dye).

किरमिज़-a species of horse; a kind of red colour.

किरवान-scimitar; a sword.

किराँची-a two-wheeled covered cart.

किरात-the jeweller weight; 'carat' equal to 3.17 grams.

किराना-to sift.

किराया-charge or payment for hire; rent or lease; freight charge.

किरायेदार-the tenant of a house; a hirer.

किराव-a soldier who glides along an army which goes forward to prepare the battle-field.

किरासन-paraffin; kerosene.

किरिच-a bayonet.

किरिया-duty; work; an oath.

किरिस्तान-a Christian.

किरीट-crest; any ornament used as a crown; diadem; a tiara.

किरोना-to scratch; to scrape.

किरौना-a worm.

क़िल-indeed; certainly; really; of course; verily.

किलकना-to shout in joy.

किलकार-shout of joy.

किलकिंचित्-gestures; amorous.

किलना-to obstruction motion; to be brought under subjection.

किलनी-a tick; an insect found on animals.

किलबिलाना-to creep; to crawl.

किल्बिषी-sinning; culpable.

किलवारी-a small oar of a boat; a rudder.

किलसना-to weep; to feel pain; to curse.

किलसाना-to cause to weep.

किलहँटा-a bird like starling.

किला-a palace; a castle; fort; tower.

किलिक-reed pen; a piece of reed.

किल्लत-scarcity; deficiency; difficulty; poverty.

किल्ली-a handle; a peg; a rod.

किल्विष-fault; disease; crime; sin; defect.

किवाँच-the edible seeds of the plant

किवाड़-door; leaf of the door.

किशमिश-currants; small stoneless raisins.

किशोर-a minor in age; a son; a child; adolescent; juvenile; boy aged eleven to fifteen years; sun.

किश्त-instalment; checkmate in the game of chess.

किसब-craft; acquirement; trade; gain.

किसबी-a craftsman.

किसमत-fate; fortune; luck.

किसमी-a workman; a coolie; a labourer.

किसलय-sprout or shoot of new foliage.

किसान-a cultivator; an agriculturist; a ploughman; a farmer.

कीकना-to cry out shrilly; to scream.

कीकर-a type of tree found chiefly in dry regions.

कीच-mud; sewage; mire; filth; dirt.

कीचक-the hollow part of a bamboo from which a kind of sound comes out when air passes through it; the name of 's brother-in-law.

कीचड़-mud; mire; ooze; gummy matter in eyes.

कीट-a grime; an insect.

कीटज्ञ-Entomologist.

कीड़ा-a grub; a snake; insect; a worm; maggot; reptile; leech; vermin.

कीड़ी-an ant; a small worm.

कीन-done.

किनना-to purchase; to buy.

कीना-spite; malice; rancour; grudge.

कीप-a diminishing or funnel for transferring fluids from one part to another.

कीमत-worth; value; price.

क़ीमती-valuable; precious; expensive.

कीमा-minced flesh.

कीमिया-chemistry; alchemy.

कीमुख्त-valuable; costly; precious; of great value.

कीर-a fowler; a parrot.

कीर्तन-group singing of hymns to a deity

कीर्ति-fame; glory; mention.

कील-a nose-pin or stud; a nail; spike.

कीलक-a spike; a cleat; a peg; a gnomon.

कीलन-act of stopping; obstruction; stoppage.

कीलना-to spike (a canon); to close up (the mouth); to silence (one).

कीला-a wedge; a peg; a tack; a spigot.

कीलाल-water; blood; nectar; a beast; honey.

कीली-spike in the yoke of a harness; pivot; axis.

कुँकुम-the red powder which is used by Hindus in worshipping; saffron.

कुचन-bending; curvature; contraction.

कुंज-a grove; an arbour; bower.

कुँजक-bower; arbour; alcove; pergola; clump; grove.

कुँजगली-a narrow land of a city; an arbour.

कुँजड़न-a women who sells vegetables.

कुँजड़ा-a green-grocer; one who sell fruits and vegetable.

कुँजर-an elephant.

कुंजबिहारी-an epithet of God .

कुंजी-key; fair version (as of a book).

कुंठ-foolish; silly; dull; knotty; blunt.

कुंठा-dullness; stupidity; bluntness; frustration.

कुंडड़ा-heap; pile; a stack (as of corn).

कुंडरा-a big wide-mouthed earthen pot to keep oil.

कुंडल-a large ear-ring; any ring shaped ornament (for ears); snake's coil.

कुंडली-a coil; a peacock; a spotted deer; nativity or horoscope; a serpent.

कुंडा-a big wide-mouthed earthen pot to keep water.

कुंडी-a hasp or staple; a small shallow earthen or wooden pot.

कुंत-a lance; a spear.

कुंती-name of the wife of ; mother of the five princes by five gods; a king of bee.

कुंथना-to be severely beaten.

कुँद-a lotus flower; a kind of Jessamine.

कुंदन-fine gold; pure gold; gold leaf.

कुंदरू-a creeper whose fruits are used as vegetable called .

कुंदा-wooden rifle (used by recruits in training); block of wood stock (as of rifle); a log.

कुंदेरना-to turn an article on a lathe; to scratch.

कुंदेरा-a turner.

कुंबी-name of a particular community of cultivators.

कुंम्भ-protuberance on an elephant's head; the tenth sign of the zodiac; a pot of clay.

कुम्भक-the process of suspending breath in

कुम्भार-a potter.

कुँभिका-a small earthen pot; a lily; a disease of the eye; sty.

कुँभिला-shrivelled.

कुँवर-a body; youth; an unmarried youth; a son; a prince.

कुँवरी-young girl; unmarried girl; daughter; princess.

कुँनकुँह-saffron.

कुँहड़ा-ash gourd.

कुँअर-the son of a king; a prince; a son.

कुअँरेटा-a young child; a boy.

कुआँ-a well.

कुआँरा-unmarried.-bachelor.

कुआर-a Hindu calendar month.

कुइयाँ-a small well.

कुक-कुक-the clucking of a hen.

कुकटी-a cotton plant which yields cotton of rosy colour.

कुकड़ी-hank; thread on the spindle of a spinning-wheel.

कुकरी-a wild hen.

कुकरोंदा-a plant whose leaves are used medically.

कुकरौंधा-the plant

कुकर्म-misconduct; a bad or wicked action; vice; sin; villainy; fornication.

कुकर्मी-wicked; deprived; miscreant.

कुकुर-a dog.

कुकुही-a wild hen.

कुक्कुट-a cock.

कुक्कुटी-a hen.

कुक्कुर-a dog.

कुक्ष-stomach; belly.

कुक्षि-womb.

कुखेत-an evil spot; bad condition; a bad place.

कुख्यात-bad condition; defamed.

कुगति-sad plight; miserable condition; affliction.

कुगहनि-stubbornness; obstinacy; perverseness.

कुघात-tricky; bad opportunity; improper time; deception; evil practice.

कुच-the female breast.

कुचंदन-sandlewood.

कुचकुचवा-an owl.

कुचना-to be contracted.

कुचक्र-bad circle; a plot; intrigue.

कुचक्री-a strategist; a plotter; an intriguer.

कुचर-a vagabond; a worthless fellow; a calumniator.

कुचली-a canine teeth.

कुचलाई-misconduct; depraved conduct.

कुचाल-coarse cloth; bad clothing.

कुचील-filthy; dirty.

कुचेल-bad clothing; coarse cloth.

कुचेष्ट-of bad manners.

कुचेष्टा-bad demeanour of face; evil intention; to cause injury.

कुचैला-dirty; filthy; ill-clad; dressed in filthy clothes.

कुछ-something; any; a little; anything.

कुछेक-some; little; few.

कुजोग-bad company; bad occasion or opportunity.

कुट-a fort; a water-pot; a small bit; a house; something pounded.

कुटका-a piece; fragment.

कुटकी-a gnat which infests dogs and cattle; a medicinal plant.

कुटकुट-sound of nibbing.

कुटनहारी-the woman who pounds, paddy or other corn.

कुटन-a backbiter; a mischief maker; a procurer; a pander; an implement for pounding.

कुटनी-a bawd.

कुटम्मस-beating-up; rough reception; a beating.

कुटाई-price paid for pounding.

कुटिया-a hut; a cottage.

कुटिलता-crookedness.

कुटी-hut; hermitage; cottage.

कुटीचर-a deceitful person.

कुटीर-hut; cottage.

कुटुम्ब-family; household; kith and kin; race.

कुटुर-a crunching or munching sound.

कुटेक-evil obstinacy or persistence; perseverance.

कुटेव-a bad habit.

कुट्टनी-procures.

कुठला-a large earthen bin for grain; limekiln.

कुठाँव-an evil state; a bad place; beating on the vital parts of the body.

कुठार-a sort of hoe or spade; an axe; hatchet.

कुठाली-a jeweller's crucible.

कुठियार-a storehouse, granary.

कुठियारी-keeper of a storekeeper.

कुठौर-bad occasion; a wrong place; to misplace something.

कुड़क-a hen that has finished laying; clucking (a hen); a clucking hen.

कुड़माई-betrothal; the celebration of an engagement.

कुड़व-a pot used in ancient times of measure corn.

कुड़ी-a hearth; a hut; hearth-tax.

कुडुक-a coil; a wire.

कुढंग-boorishness; bad conduct; misdemeanour; rudeness; ill-manner.

कुढंगा-unmannerly; ill-bred; rude; boorish.

कुढ़क . fretting.

कुढ़न-resentment; jealously; vexation; disgust; distress; sorrow; fretting.

कुढ़ब-misshapen; uncouth; ill-shaped; ill-mannered.

कुढ़ानी-annoying; teasing; vexing.

कुणपाशी-a carrion-eating animal or bird.

कुतका-a mace; a small thick staff; a cudgel.

कुतना-to be estimated (as revenue, produce).

कुतप-noon time; the eight part of the day.

कुतरन-to gnaw; to bite.

कुतर्क-a wrong reasoning; illogical reasoning.

कुतिया-a bitch.

कुतुब-the pole star.

कुतुबनुमा-a mariner's compass.

कुतूहल-anything curious; eager interest in unusual; curiosity.

कुत्त where? whither?

कुत्ता-a dog; a hand vice; ratchet; the trigger of a gun.

कुत्सा-calumny contempt; reproach; censure.

कुत्सित-censured; base; blamed.

कुथरा-filth; rotting.

कुथुआ-an inflammation of the eyelids (in children).

कुदकना-to jump.

कुदरत-power; creation of the Universe; God; authority; nature; omnipotence.

कुदरा-a pick-axe.

कुदर्शन-ill looking; ugly.

कुदलना-to toss; to jump; to walk; leaping.

कुदशा-dire state.

कुदाँव-ill-condition; bad situation; treachery; deceit; bad place.

कुदाई-jumping.

कुदान-distance covered by some one in a jump; mode or act of jumping; vault.

कुदाम-a counterfeit coin.

कुदाय-improper way; deceit.

कुदाल-a spade; a grub-hoe; a one-sided pick axe.

कुदृष्टि-malicious glance; evil eye; lascivious glance.

कुदेव-a Brahman.

कुद्रव-a kind of small grain eaten by the poorer people.

कुद्दल-a mountain ebony.

कुद्दूस-pure, holy.

कुधर-a mountain.

कुधातु-iron, base metal.

कुनकुना-lukewarm; warm; tepid.

कुनबा-kindred; family.

कुनमुनाना-to whimper; to whine; to be restless or agitated; to demur.

कुनवा-a turner.

कुनह-malice; spite; grudge.

कुनाई-scrap; a bit; corner.

कुनाम-ill repute; infamy.

कुनैन-quinine obtained from bark; a kind of medicine used to cure .

कुप-heap of chaff; pile (of hay, straw).

कुपंथ-prohibited conduct; wicked path; bad path doctrine.

कुपढ़-uneducated, illiterate.

कुपथ-evil conduct; a bad path; a bad way.

कुपना-to be angry.

कुपाठ-evil advice.

कुपात्र-unworthy.

कुपार-the ocean.

कुपित-angered.

कुपुत्र-a disobedient son; a wicked son.

कुपती-mother of an unworthy son.

कुप्रयोग-rough, misuse; usage.

कुप्रबंध-mismanagement.

कुफ़र-blasphemy, unbelief.

कुफ्र-any religion against Mohammedanism; unbelief heathenism.

कुफ्ल-a lock.

कुब-hump of the back.

कुबन्ड-a bow.

कुबजा-a hunch-backed woman.

कुबड़ा-hunch-backed; crook-backed.

कुबत-censure; bad conduct; disapproval.

कुबानि-evil habit.

कुबानी-bad profession.

कुबुद्धि-foolish, wicked.

कुबेला-bad time, evil opportunity, evil occasion.

कुभा-bad lustre, the shadow of the earth.

कुमंत्रणा-evil counsel; bad advice; intrigue.

कुमठी-a splint of wood.

कुमुक-assistancehelp;reinforcements; aid; support.

कुमत-stupidity.

कुमति-stupidity; indiscretion; folly; error.

कुमया-severity; harshness.

कुमरिया-a species of elephant.

कुमरी-a kind of bird.

कुमाच-a kind of silken cloth.

कुमारतंत्र-part of Indian medical science which deals with disease of children.

कुमारभृत्य-treatment of a pregnant woman; the science of easy child-birth.

कुमुख-having an ugly appearance.

कुमुद-a water lily.

कमेरु-the South Pole.

कुम्मत-very expert; cunning; a horse of deep red colour.

कुम्हलाई-drooping; blighted; dejected appearance; withering.

कुम्हार-a potter.

कुम्हारन-a potter's wife.

कुम्हारी[1]-a woman of community.

कुम्हारी[2]-a wasp like insect which builds its nest of clay.

कुरंग-a copper-coloured antelope.

कुरंगति-a female deer; the female of an antelope.

कुरंटक-a medicinal plant.

कुरंड-corundum store.

कुरकुर-sound produced by breaking a crisp object.

कुरता-a shirt of without collar.

कुरती-a jerkin; blouse; smock.

कुरबान-scarified; to be sacrificed as a victim.

कुरर-an osprey.

कुरवक-flowers of different species; the red amaranth.

कुरसी-chair; throne; seat.

कुरा-the tumour which grows in an old word.

कुराई-a beam; stocks (for the feet).

कुरान-Mohammedan's sacred book.

कुराय-evil course; bad conduct; misconduct.

कुराह-improper or wrong course.

कुराही-a bad or depraved person; one on a wrong course.

कुरी-a millet.

कुरीज-evil habit; moulting of birds; moult.

कुरीति-evil habit; bad custom; misconduct.

कुरुचि-inclination; distaste; depraved; perversion; aversion.

कुरुन-emery stone also called pumice.

कुरुल-lock (of hair); a curl.

कुरुवक्र-the flower of crimson amaranth.

कुरुप-ugly; hard-featured; grotesque; featureless.

कुरेदना-to scratch; to scrape.

कुरोचना-to erase.

कुरैया-a wild tree called as ; a wild tree which bears beautiful flowers.

कुरौना-to heap uo.

कुर्क-confiscated; attached; distraint; an official of the court who attaches property of a debtor.

कुर्बान-sacrifice.

कुलंग-a cuckoo; a cock.

कुर्सी-chair.

कुल-birth, blood, caste; race; parentage; generation; tribe.

कुलंग-a crane.

कुलकुना-to jump in joy or merriment; to be delighted.

कुलकलंक-a disgrace of family.

कुलकान-family respect.

कुलकुला-to make sound like gargling; to feel hungry.

कुलक्षण-bad temper; an evil omen; misconduct.

कुलचा-a small rounded bread made of milk, butter and flour.

कुलच्छन-bad habits.

कुलच्छनी-a woman of evil disposition; a hag.

कुलट-a man of loose character; an adulterer.

कुलदेव-the household (tutelary) god.

कुलदेवी-the family goddess.

कुलद्रोही-one who brings disgrace to his family.

कुलना-to feel throbbing pain.

कुलपति-patriarch; head of a family; paterfamilias; vice-chancellor.

कुलपूज्य-reverened by the members of a family.-the priest of a family.

कुलफ़ी-ice-cream; a mould (as for jellies, ice-cream).

कुलबोरन-one who ruins family prestige.

कुलवधू-the virtuous woman of a noble family.

कुलवंत-of noble family; to noble birth or descent.

कुलवान-pure of noble blood; genteel.

कुलह-cowl of falcon.

कुलही-a cap for babies.

कुलांगार-one who ruins his family.

कुलाँच-leap; a bound.

कुलाचार्य-a family preceptor.

कुलाधिपति-chancellor (of a university).

कुलानुशासक-proctor (of a university).

कुलाबा-an iron ring; link; hasp; a hook.

कुलाल-a potter.

कुलाह-cap, hat.

कुलिंग-a sparrow; a fork-tailed bird called snipe.

कुलिक &-a nobleman; the head of a family; an artist;

कुली-a coolie; a labourer.

कुलुफ़-a padlock; a lock.

कुशलता-expertness; well-being; skilfulness; deafness; welfare.

कुशा-rope.

कुशाग्र-penetrating and sharp as the point of a grass.

कुशादा-extensive; wide; expended; uncovered; opened.

कुशासन-bad government; mal-administration.

कुशील-of bad disposition or character.

कुशीलव-an actor; a poet; a singer; an epithet of .

कुसलई-skill; expertness.

कुसली-the stone of a mango.

कुसाइत-unfortunate time; evil moment; inopportune season or occasion.

कुसीद-sum lent on interest; interest.

कुसंभ-safflower.

कुसुम-a flower.

कुसुमित-ripe; in a state of bloom; full-blown.

कुसुमी-reddish-yellow.

कुसूत-mismanagement; a wicked son.

कुस्वप्न-bad dream, nightmare.

कुस्वभाव-a wicked or bad nature.

कुहक-the crowing of cock; stratagem; cunningness; deceit; illusion; a juggler.

कुहप-a giant.

कुहर-a cavity; chasm; hole.

कुहरा-damp; mist; fog; haze.

कुहराम-wailing or weeping; lamentation.

कुहाना-to fret; to be angry.

कुहासा-mist; fog.

कुही-a pony; a kind of bird to prey; a species of horse.

कुहु-the cry of peacock or cuckoo; the last day of lunar month when the moon is invisible.

कुहेलिका-haze; fog; mist.

कूखना-to give a hollow groan.

कूँचा-a broom.

कूँची-a painter's brush; a small broom.

कूँज-crane.

कूँडी-a small earthen trough; a small cup of stone.

कूँथना-to strain; to groan.

कूढ़-foolish; stupid.

कूत-weight of an article; an estimate of the value.

कूद-jump; leap; a spring.

कूदना-to jump.

कून-the rope with which a boat is tugged in water; a hawser.

कूप-a well; pit; a hole; an oil-well.

कूबड़-hunch; hump.

कूम्हल-housebreaking; burglary; a hole made by a thief in the wall of house.

कूर-cruel.

कूरा-portion; share; part; a heap; allotment.

कूर्म-a tortoise.

कूल-bank; shore; a canal; a pond; a big waterway; rear of an army.

कूला[1]-& hip; haunch.

कूला[2]-an irrigation channel.

कूल्हा-the bones of the hip.

कूवत-power; strength.

कूह-the trumpet of an elephant.

कूहड़-uneven; rough.

कृकर-the air in the head which causes sneezing.

कृच्छ-causing pain.

कृछ-trouble; difficulty; sin; pain; scanty urination accompanied with pain.

कृत-prepared; done; performed; made; composed.

कृति-performance; act; deed; action; a stroke; sorcery; jugglery.

कृती-skilful; successful; satisfied; contented.

कृते-per pro.

कृत्तिका-the third lunar mansion.

कृत्य-to be done; an act; a service; function.

कृत्रिम-artificial; man-made; synthetic (a product); counterfeit; feigned.

कृपण-pinch-fist; stingy.

कृपया favourably; kindly.

कृपा-favour; grave.

कृपाण-a sabre; a rapier; a small sword; a scimitar.

कृपाणी-a small dagger.

कृपालु-kind; compassionate; showing favour.

कृमि-an insect; a grub; a maggot; a worm.

कृमिरोग-the accumulation of worms in the intestines.

कृमिहर-worm-killer.

कृश-small; lean; emaciated; slenderness; spareness; leanness; smallness.

कृशता-weakness; thinness.

कृशार-a kind of pea; rice cooked with sesame.

कृशान-fire.

कृशित-enfeebled; emaciated.

कृशोदरी-a woman with slender waist; a woman having slim waist.

कृषक-a cultivator; a farmer; a peasant.

कृषि-ploughing; cultivation; agriculture.

कृष्ट-ploughed.

कृष्ण-black; dark.

कृष्णा-the name of river ; name of the companion of .

केंकड़ा-& crab.

केंचुआ-an earthworm; an intestinal worm.

केंचुली-the slough of a snake which it casts off yearly.

केन्द्र-middle part; centre.

केंद्रित-centred.

केउ-some one.

केका-the cry of peacock.

केकिनी-a peahen.

केत-a house; a place of residence; a flag of a country, banner; habitation.

केतन-invitation; place, sign; flag, symbol, house.

केतली-a kettle.

केता-how much.

केतु-sign of recognition; splendour; a banner; a comet; a meteor.

केतुमान-resplendent; lustrous; wise; intelligent; luminous.

केतो how many; how much.

केदार-a name of ; a field.

केबिस-a red clay.

केमरा-a photographic apparatus.

केयूर-an armlet (worn on the upper arm).

केराना-grocery; commodities which a grocer sells.

केराव-a small type of pea.

केरी-a small raw fruit of mango tree.

केला-Banana.

केलि-amorous play; dalliance; sexual intercourse.

केवका-the spices which are administered to lying-in females.

केवट-a boatman.

केवल-alone; only; sheer; absolute.

केवा-the lotus; the water lily; pretext.

केवाड़-door.

केश-a ray; an epithet of ; the Sun; hairs on the head.

केशव-having long or much or beautiful hair; a title of or .

केशांत-the tonsure ceremony among Hindus.

केशिनी-the woman with long beautiful hairs; a fairy.

केशी-hairy; name of an killed by lord.

केस-a case for keeping jewels; a law suit; an accident.

केसरी-a lion; a horse name.

केहरी-a lion.

केहा-a peacock.

केहूँ-in what way; how.

केहू-some body; some one.

केचा-squint-eyed.

केड़ा-method; mode; trick; cunning; dexterity; scale.

कृेंची-scissors; shears.

कै[1]-how many?

कै[2]-vomit.

कैकप-a giant; a demon.

कैतब-treachery; fraud; deceit.

कैतून-kind of fine lace.

कैद-imprisonment; confinement; incarceration.

कैकद-a file used for keeping papers.

कैदखाना-prison; jail.

कैदतनहा-solitary confinement in a cell.

कैदमहज-confinement of simple imprisonment.

क़ैदिन-a female prisoner.

क़ैदी-a prisoner; a captive; convict.

कैन-a bamboo twig.

कैफ़-intoxication.

कैबा-how many times; how often.

कैरव-lotus; a white water-lily.

कैरा-brown colour.

कैरु-morsel.

कैलाश-a mountain.

कैवर्त-a boatman; a fisherman.

कैवल्य-absolute singleness of state or unity.

कैसर-an emperor; the former emperor Kaiser.

कैसा-of what kind? what sort of? in what condition?

कोंई-a water lilly.

कोंच-stab; prick.

कोंढा-hasp; metal ring.

कोंत-a spear; barb.

कोंपर-a ripe mango which drops from the tree.

कोंपल-shoot; sprout; a new leaf.

कोंहड़ौरी-a dish of pulse mixed with slices of pumpkin.

कोई-anyone; someone; some; any; a person.

कोउ-some body; some one; a few.

कोक[1]-flower of the red water-lily.

कोक[2]-a treatise of sex.

कोकटी-a kind of cotton having a reddish colour (source of a fine cloth).

कोकदेव-the expounder of the science of coition.

कोकनद-red lily; red lotus.

कोकना-a kind of dye.

कोकाह-a white horse.

कोकिल-a swallow; charcoal; a shade of sapphire; the Indian cuckoo.

कोकीन, कोकेन-cocaine.

कोख-womb; stomach; abdomen.

कोखा-abdomen.

कोगा-a hunting creature which is similar to dog.

कोच-a four wheeled carriage; a padded seat or chair.

कोचवान-driver of a carriage; a coachman.

कोटला-a small fort; muniments.

कोटा-quota.

कोटि-class, rank; order; point of a weapon.

कोटिक-millions; myriads; innumerable.

कोटिशः-excessive; much. in several ways.

कोठ-a kind of leprosy with large round spots.

कोठरी-cabin; a small room; compartment; closet; chamber; cell.

कोठा-storehouse; a large room; granary; the flat top; roof of the house.

कोठार-granary; store-house; a barn.

कोठी-a large house or brick or stone; a bungalow.

कोठीवाल-a banker; a wholesale merchant; a script in which bankers write their account books.

कोड़ंड-a bow.

कोड़ा-a lash; a whip; warning; exciting or piercing talk.

कोड़ाई-cost of digging up.

कोड़ी-a core; twenty.

कोढ़-leprosy.

कोढ़ना-to trouble; to tease; to vex; to torment.

कोढ़िन-a female leper.

कोढ़ी-a leper; a lazer.

कोण-an angle.

कोतल-a red horse; horse of a king's personal riding.

कोतवाल-chief police officer of a town or city.

कोताह-deficient; small.

कोथमीर-coriander.

कोथला-stomach; a large bag.

कोथली-a deep money-bag; a small bag; bag of sweet sent as a gift.

कोदंड-a bow; the ninth sign of zodiac; an eyebrow.

कोद-corner; direction.

कोना-an angle; a corner; point (as of a geometrical figure); an angular piece.

कोप-to be or to become angry.

कोपन-provocation; excitement.

कोपि any one, some one.

कोफ्त-sadness; vexation; tedium.

कोफ्ता-a dish prepared from pounded meat.

कोब-a small mallet.

कोबी-cabbage.

कोबर-a mango fruit which is ripe on the tree.

कोमलता-delicacy; tenderness; softness; effeminacy; softly; plasticity; flabbiness; gently.

कोमलास्थि-a cartilage.

कोयल-the Indian Cuckoo; the creeper which is called

कोयला-coal; charcoal; a live coal.

कोया-the ball of the eye; ripe pulpy seeds of a jack fruit.

क़ोरमा-a lightly spiced fried curry.

कोरा-unwashed; unhandled; fresh; brand new.

कोरी-a weaver.

कोरो-a bamboo rafter or pole; a prop.

कोलतार-coal tar.

कोला-a small field.

कोला-a jackal.

कोलाहल-uproar; din; shouting; noise of festivities.

कोलिया-a narrow lane.

कोल्हाड़-site of a sugar-mill.

कोल्हू-mill (of sugar-cane or oil-seeds); a press.

कोविद-learned; an experienced person; versed; a scholar.

कोश-treasury; store-room.

कोशकार-a lexicographer; a scabbard maker; silky case of a silk worm.

कोशवृद्धि-the enlargement of the scrotum; hydrocele.

कोशागार-a treasure room.

कोशिका-cell.

कोशिश-endeavour; attempt; trail; exertion.

कोष-a fund.

कोषाध्यक्ष-a bursar; a treasurer; a financier.

कोष्ठ-an enclosed place (as a granary); any abdominal organ (stomach, intestine, bowels).

कोष्ठक-a wall or line encircling something; a case with several holes; a bracket.

कोष्ठबद्ध-costiveness (of howels); constipation.

कोस-a measure of distance (approximately two miles).

कोसना-to curse; to accuse; to imprecate; to execrate; to damn.

कोसा[1]-a kind of big earthen pot; a kind of silk.

कोसा[2]-to curse.

कोसा[3]-a kind of silk made in .

कोसाकोटी-a curse in the form of an abuse.

कोफ्त-grief; beating; anguish.

कोहँडौरी-a mixed dried dish made of pulse and bits.

कोहनी-elbow.

कोहराम-loud noise.

कौंध-to dazzle.

कौंधना-to flash (as lightning).

कौंआ-crow.

कौटिल्य-fraud; crookedness; cunningness.

कौटुंबिक-pertaining to a family; forming a family; having a family.

कौंडा-a fire lit in the open to give warmth.

कौड़िया-of the colour of a shell; of the form of a cowrie.

कौड़िल्ला-the king-fisher.

कौड़ी-a cowrie (formerly in use as a barter token of very low value); a small shell.

कौणय-a sinner; a demon.

कौणप-a demon or gobin.

कौतिक-wonder.

कौतुक-any event arousing curiosity or interest; eager; curiosity.

कौतुकिया-festive; joyous; sportive; one who arranges marriage connections.

कौतूहल-desire; curiosity; wonder.

कौथ-which day of the month, what connection.

कौथा-which number in the process of reckoning.

कौन-who.

कौपीन-a small piece of cloth from which one can cover the private parts.

क़ौम-caste; sect; house; tribe; family.

कौमार्य-state of youthfulness, virginity.

क़ौमियत-nationality.

कौर-a mouthful; a morsel.

कौरना-to bake slightly; to fry.

कौरव-connected with Kuru.

कौरी-bosom; lap.

कौलंज-the pain in the lower part of the ribs.

कौल-a mouthful; born in a high family.

कौंली-embrace; bosom; lap; armful.

कौवा-a crow; a cunning fellow; the tonsils; an anchor; a fish with duck-like mouth.

कौशेय-silken.

कौस्तुभ-name of the jewel worn by on his chest.

कौसीस-sulphate of iron; green vitriol.

क्या what, way, how.

क्यारी-a bed (of vegetables or flowers).

क्यों-why, how, wherefore; well, what, then.

क्योंकर-how? for what reason, why?

क्योंकि-because.

क्रदंन-a war cry; lamentation; weeping and wailing.

क्रकच-a saw.

क्रम[1]-ordered; sequential; graded.

क्रम[2]-sequence.

क्रमशः-step by step; by degree.

क्रमण-gradation.

क्रमागत-traditional; attaining a gradual change.

क्रमावली-a programme.

क्रमिक-serial; successive hereditary.

क्रमुक-the betel-nut; the name of an ancient country.

क्रमेलक-camel.

क्रय-purchase; buying.

क्रयी-a purchaser; a buyer.

क्रय्य-a commodity which is set for sale.

क्रव्य-flesh.

क्रांत-ascending; covered; going ahead; surmounting.

क्रांति-progress; revolution.

क्रिकेट-the game of cricket.

क्रिमिजा-lac.

क्रियमाण-what is being done; present performance of work.

क्रिया-action; activity; work; motion; job.

क्रियाचतुर-skilful; dextrous.

क्रियान्वयन-implementation.

क्रियानिष्ठ-regular in performing daily religious duties.

क्रियायोग-worships of Gods.

क्रियाविशेषण-an adverb.

क्रिस्तान-a Christian.

क्रीड़ा-amusement; sport; play.

क्रीड़ित-one who sports; a gambler; a player.

क्रीत-bought; purchased.

क्रुद्ध-angry; fierce.

क्रूर-cruel; ruthless; harsh; heartless; oppressive; destructive.

क्रेता-purchaser; a buyer.

क्रोड़-the portion between arms while embracing; bosom; breast.

क्रोध-anger; fury; heat; fury; spleen; flame; tantrum.

क्लांत-wearied; languid; tired.

क्लांति-weariness; languor; fatigue.

क्लिष्ट-weary; afflicted, distressed; dissimilar.

क्लीम-the right lung.

क्लीव-impotent.

क्लेद-humidity; moisture; wetness; sweat.

क्लेश-suffering; affliction; anguish; strife.

क्लेव्य-absence of virility; unmanliness; timidity; impotence.

क्वचित् a few; rarely; rarely some one.

क्वणित-sounded; resounding.

क्वथनाँक-boiling point.

क्वाँरी-an unmarried girl.

क्वार-a name of the seventh lunar month.

क्वारछल-virginity.

ख

ख-The second consonant of the Devnagari alphabet.

खँखड़-hard; shrivelled; dry and crackling; withered.

खँखरा-a big cauldron of copper.

खँखार-the sound of clearing the throat; phlegm; spittle.

खँग-a sword; a rhinoceros.

खँगड़-any dry or hard substance of object.

खँगना-to decrease; to lessen.

खँचना-to mark; to imprint.

खँचाना-to mark; to write in a hurried manner.

खँचिया-a small wicker basket.

खँची-decrease; diminution.

खँज-a lame man; a limping person; a cripple.

खँजन-a wagtail.

खँजर-a dagger.

खँड-part; segment; section.

खंडन-negation; denial; disproof; recantation.

खंडपरशु-an epithet of .

खंडपूरी-a kind of pudding.

खंडवरा-a kind of sweet of pudding.

खंडरा-a kind of sweet made from flour and pulse.

खँडला-a slice; a piece.

खँडहर-a ruin; a dilapidated building.

खंडा-a fragment; broken rice.

खंडिता-a woman whose husband or lover has been unfaithful.

खंतरा-angle; hollow; corner; a breach in wall.

खंता-a mattock; a spade.

खंदक-trench; moat; ditch; shelter.

खंधक-moat; trench; ditch; shelter.

खंधवाना-to cause to empty or vacate.

खँधार-encampment; suzerain; an overload; a chieftain; cantonment.

खंभ, खंभा-a pillar; a pole; a post; a column.

खंभार-anguish; distress.

खई-quarrel; destruction; demolition; fight.

खक्खा-loud laughter.

खखार-phlegm.

खखेटना-to wound; to press.

खखोलना-to search out among many objects; to search for.

खग-a bird; a planet; a star that moves in the sky; a god; the Sun; the moon; air.

खगना-to pinch; to pierce; to be rooted in the mind; to be engaged; to be imprinted; to be stuck.

खगपति-the gigantic crane; the Sun.

खगहा-a rhinoceros.

खगोल-the vault of the heavens; the sky.

खगोलीय-astronomical; celestial.

खग्रास-the total eclipse of the Sun of the Moon.

खचड़ा-packed to full; crowded.

खचन-the work of binding, setting or marking.

खचरा-wicked; cunning; cross-bred; ingenious.

खचाखच-filled up to the brim; stuffed together; overcrowded.

खचेड़ना-to drag along; to drag.

खच्चर-a mule.

खज-fit to be eaten; eatable.

खजहजा-a palatable fruit.

ख़जानची-cashier; treasurer.

खजाना-hoard; treasury; exchequer; repository.

खजूरा-the cord for plaiting locks of hair.

खजूर-a kind of tree.

खट-sound produced by two objects striking together.

खटक-suspense; doubt; apprehension; suspicion; disgust; anxiety; danger.

खटकाना-to knock.

खटखीड़ा-a bug.

खटना-to spend money; to be engaged in a work.

खटपट-quarrel; strife; wrangling; contention; noise made by two objects striking together.

खटबुना-a weaver of bedstead.

खटमल-a bed-bug.

खटमिट्ठी-mixed state of being sour and sweet.

खटराग-trouble; wrangling; useless and worthless articles; perplexity.

खटला-household; wife and family; baggage.

खटाई-sourness; tartness.

खटाक-a crashing noise.

खटाना[1]-to become sour; acid or tart.

खटाना[2]-to maintain oneself; to find a resting-place or support; to exist.

खटिया-a small bedstead or bed.

खट्टा-a citron.

खट्टापन-acidity; sourness; tartness.

खट्टी-a very sour lemon.

खट्टू-colloq. industrious.

खटत्-a labourer.

खटवा-a bedstead.

खड्ग-a sword.

खडंजा-a pavement made with upright bricks.

खड़क-an abyss; a valley; the fragment of a gem.

खड़-grass; rough (ground or way).

खड़कना-doubt.

खड़का-suspense.

खड़काना-to alert.

खड़गी-a rhinoceros.

खड़तल-rude; uncivil; spoiled; quarrelsome.

खड़बड़-tumult; noise; confusion.

खड़बड़ी-disorder; tumult.

खड़बीहड़-rugged; uneven; rough.

खड़मंडल-wrangling; confusion.

खड़ल-mortar.

खड़हर-laid waste.

खड़ा-erect; upright; standing; straight; vertical; perpendicular; high.

खड़ाऊ-a wooden-soled sandal.

खड़ाका-noise made in breaking; a crash.

खड़िया-white clay; chalk.

खडुवा-type of women's metal bracelet.

खडग्-scimitar; sword.

खड्ड-low ground between hills; a pit; a gap; a pass; saddle.

खड्डा-depression; hollow; cavity; a pit.

खत-a note; hand-writing; a line; a letter.

खतखोट-incrustation over a wound on surface of body.

खतना-circumcision.

खतम-end, conclusion; complete; finish.

खतमी-the marsh mallow.

खतरनाक-dangerous; risky.

खता-a mistake; fault; oversight; miss (as of an arrow).

खतिका-furrow.

खतियाना-to enter in an account-book or ledger.

खत्तरी-khatri cast.

खत्ता-a grange; a cavity in the ground for storing grain; granary; gamer; bin.

ख़त्म-end; complete; done; exhausted (as a commodity); finish.

खदखदाना-to boil; to simmer.

खदबद-the sound of boiling or bubbling.

खदान-a quarry; a ditch dug for some purpose; a mine.

खदानकार-quarry man.

खदिर-the tree

खदेड़-chase-out.

खदेड़ना-to chase; to pursue; to hunt; to drive away.

खद्दड़, खद्दर-hand-spun cloth.

खद्योत-a firefly; a light in the sky.

खनक-a miner; a geologist; one who digs the ground.

खनता-crowbar; a digging implement; shovel.

खनिज-mineral.

खनित्र-shovel.

खनी-a pit in which grain is stored.

खपच्ची-sliver (of wood or bamboo); a splinter; skewer; splint; a lath.

खपड़ा-an earthen begging pot; a roofing tile; a crocodile shell.

खपड़ी-skull; the head; a small earthen pot.

खपत, खपती-consumption; demand; sale; vent; expenditure.

खपना-to be expended; to sell; to enter; to penetrate.

खपरिया-a mineral in the form of tile.

खपरैल-titled shed.

खपाच-a splinter of wood of bamboo.

खपाट-a large piece of spilt wood; branch broken; wooden side-piece of a bellow; broken off a tree.

खपाना-to spend; to waste; to destroy; to dispatch.

खपाव-expenditure; consumption; use; assimilation; absorption; adjustment (as to a new situation); destruction.

खपुर-the betel tree.

खपुष्प-the sky-flower; an impossibility; a castle in the air; something impossible.

खप्पर-coconut or other vessel used as a begging bowl or dish; gourd; skull.

खफ़गी-anger; displeasure; wrath; hot displeasure.

ख़फा-displeased.

ख़बर-report; news; intelligence; account; rumour.

ख़बरदार-painstaking; careful; watchful; cautious.

ख़बीस-wicked; bad; foul.

ख़ब्त-obsession; madness; craze; whim.

ख़ब्ती-insane; mad; crazy; eccentric; wicked.

खब्बा-left.

खभार-trouble; encumbrance; perplexity.

ख़म-curve; coil; curl; bent or crooked; bend; reverse.

खमदम-courage; valour.

खमध्य-vertex; meridian; Zenith; highest altitude.

खमस-humid.

ख़मसा-a kind of song.

ख़माची-a wicker.

ख़मियाज़ा-punishment; stretching.

ख़मी-crookedness.

ख़मीर-kneaded and leavened dough; yeast; the stuff of (one's) nature.

ख़म्माच-a kind of song.

खयानत-breach of trust; to be unfaithful to a trust.

ख़याली-imaginary; illusory; fanciful; to build castles in the air.

ख़र[1]-a crow; a mule; an ass; grass; straw.-hard; stiff; sharp.

खर[2]-harsh, severe; hot; biting.

खर[3]-grass.

खरका-a toothpick; a straw.

खरकौकी-eating (consumption) straw; fire.

खरखरा-rough.

खरखशा-quarrel; wrangle.

खरगोश-a hare; a rabbit.

ख़रच-expenditure.

खरचना-to use; to spend; to expend.

खरचा-expenses, cost (in law suits).

खरछरा-uneven; rough.

खरता-very sharp.

खरदुक-a kind of tattered and old garment.

खरपा-side seam.

खरब-a billion; one thousand million.

खरबूज़ा-a musk-melon.

खरमस्ती-wickedness; mischief.

खरमिटाव-refreshment; breakfast; a light repast of early morning.

खरल-a mortar.

खरसा-a kind of food cooked with spices.

खरसान-a wheatstone.

खरसैला-mangy (of animals); scabby.

खरहरा-a curry-comb.

खरहा-cony; rabbit; hare; puss; bunny.

खरही-a stack or heap (of grass, straw).

खरा-plain speaking; true; excessive; of the best quality.

खराद-a lathe.

खरापन-goodness; genuineness.

खराब-poor; bad; miserable; depraved.

खराबी-defect; deficiency.

ख़रामाँ-walking in a stately or graceful way.

ख़रायँध-foul smell (as of urine); smell of an acid.

खराश-irritation or hoarseness of the throat; scratch; scraping.

खराहंद-an offensive smell; the smell of urine.

खरिका-a piece of leaf fibre.

खरिया-a knap-sack; a net for binding chaff.

खरीता-purse; pouch; bag (of letters).

ख़रीद-shopping; purchase.

खरीदना-to bring upon oneself; to buy.

खरीदार-a vendee; a purchaser; a buyer.

ख़रीफ-the crop which is reaped in autumn.

खरौंटा-a scratch which is made on the body.

खराहा-saltish; slightly acid.

खर्च-expenditure; disbursement; outlay; charge.

ख़र्चना-to bring into use; to use.

ख़र्चीला-expensive (an object); extravagant (a person).

खजूर-the date tree, its fruit; scorpion; silver.

खर्पर-an earthen hod; a chaffing dish; a begging-bowl; head; cranium.

खर्बूजा-a musk-melon.

खर्व-maimed.

खर्रट-vigorous; forceful.

खर्राटा-to snore while sleep; to be in deep sleep.

खलंगा-a reception area (near a house).

खल-vile; malignant; mischievous; cruel; wicked; low.

खलड़ी-a small hide or skin (as of a sheep).

खलता-malice; wickedness; villainy; ill-will.

खलना-to be disgusting or displeasing; malicious.

खलबली-commotion; alarm.

खलल-interruption; disturbance; confusion; injury; damage.

खलसा-a kind of fish.

खलार-low ground.

ख़लास-finished; fallen free; released; liberated.

खलासी-porter.

ख़लासी-a sailor; porter; crew member; tent-pitcher.

खलाल-a toothpick.

खलित-moving; fallen; fickle.

खलियान-a granary; a barn.

ख़लिश-pain; a sting.

खलीज-bay; gulf.

खलीफा-successor; senior person.

खलोक्ति-wicked language; abuse; reproach.

ख़ल्क-the creation of the world; mankind.

खल्लड़-a mortar for grinding drugs; a large bag of leather.

खल्ला-old shoes.

खल्व-baldness of head.

खवैया-an eater.

खशख़श-poppy-seed; poppy.

ख़स-a type of scented root of the grass.

खसकंत-slipping or slinking.

खस-खस-a sound of grating; chewing.

खसखसाना-to grind the teeth.

खसना-to run away; to fall.

ख़सम-master; husband.

ख़सरा-eczema; scabies; itch.

खसलत-habit; nature; mode; property.

खसाना-to throw down; to let fall.

खसिया-impotent; castrated.

ख़सीस-stingy; miserly; parsimonious; frugal.

खसोट-plucking or tearing out; tear; a scratch.

ख़स्ता-broken; wounded; brittle; fragile; crisp.

खस्सी-a castrated animal (a goat). -castrated.

खहर-the quantity in arithmetic whose divisor is zero.

खाँग-spike; spur (of cock); horn of rhinoceros; tusk (of boar).

खाँगना-to lessen; to decrease.

खाँगी-deficiency; loss; deficit.

खाँचना-to draw; to mark; to scratch a line; to scribble.

खाँचा-a basket; a pannier; a crate; a hencoop.

खाँड-unrefined sugar; molasses; treacle.

खाँप-a piece; slice.

ख़ातून-lady (title occurring finally in many Muslim female names).

खाद-manure; dung; waste.

खादक-*adj.* &-eater; user.

खादन-taking food; eating.

खादिम-a servant; attendant.

खादी-a coarse, thick type of cotton cloth.

खादुक-violent; murderous.

खाद्य-edible; eatable.

खाधु-anything edible.

खान-a quarry; a mine; a store; source; treasury; ample store; abundance.

खानक-a digger; a mason; a prospector.

ख़ाना-to embezzle; to eat; to get; to experience; to harass.

खानि-a mine.

खाप-sheath; stalk; tribe; group a slice of fruit; stem (of plantain).

खाब-a dream.

खाबड़-uneven (ground); rough.

खाम-pillar; a post.

ख़ाम-immature; unripe.

खामना-to shut up the mouth of a pot by means of wet mud; to seal an envelope.

खामोश-taciturn; silent.

खार-net; thorn; envy; spine; bramble.

खारा-hard water; alkaline.

खारिक-fruit of date tree.

खारिज-expelled; different; excluded; rejected; exempted; dismissed.

खारी-a kind of salt.

खाल[1]-a canal; moat; watercourse; trench.

खाल[2]-skin; hide; a bellows.

खालसा-a section of .

खाला-low.

खाला-low; lower.

खालिक़-the Creator.

ख़ालिस-pure; genuine; unadulterated.

खाली-empty; vacant; unemployed.

ख़ाविंद-lord, husband, master.

खास-special; proper; particular; peculiar; specific; private; principal; pure; excellent.

खासकर especially; in particular.

खासगी-one's own; personal.

खासा-very; particularly.

खासियत-quality; peculiarity; property.

ख़ाहमख़ाह-aimlessly; uselessly.

ख़ाहिश-longing; desire.

खिंच-a pull.

खिचड़वार-a festival falling on the day.

खिचड़ी-a dish prepared from pulse and rice boiled together; a mixture of two language; a jargon; a mixed heap; hotchpotch.

खिचाव-a pull; tenseness; a drag; retraction.

खिजलाहट-vexation; irritation.

खिज़ाब-a hair-dye.

ख़िज़ाँ-autumn.

खिड़की-a window; trap-door; casement; shutter.

ख़िताब-a prize; title (a rank).

खिदमत-duty; service; to serve.

खिन्न-sad; sore; wearied; exhausted; glum; unhappy; gloomy.

खिपना-to be abraded; to be worn off.

खियाना-to feed; to cause to eat.

खिराज-tribute; a tax.

खिरिसा-a dish made with beestings.

खिलअत-a robe of honour bestowed by a king.

खिलकौरी-frolic; play.

खिलना-to blossom; to be delighted; to flower; to blow.

खिलाड़ी-playful; mischievous; funny; sportive; frolicsome.

खिलाफ-opposition; succession.

खिलौना-a plaything; toy; a thing to amuse; a trifling thing.

खिल्ली-a betel-leaf with lime; a nail.

खिल्लू-a playful person.

खिसकना-to slip away.

खिसाना-to be abashed; to giggle.

खिसारा-loss; damage; legal cost of a case.

खिसी-rashness; shame.

खिसौंहाँ-looking fretful or peevish; ashamed.

खींचना-to drag; to pull; to draw (as a sword).

खीन-weak.

खीर-a dish made of rice, milk and sugar boiled together.

खीरा-a cucumber.

खीरी-the udder of a beast.

खील-parched rice or grain.

खीली-jest.

खीवन-intoxication.

खीस-beestings.

खीसा-a pocket; a bag.

खुंबी-mushroom.

खुंभी[1]-toadstool; fungus; a mushroom.

खुंभी[2]-a gold band; gold stud or ear ornament.

खुक्ख-empty-handed; having nothing; poor.

खुखरी-Gurkha's knife.

खुजली-itchiness; mange.

खुटक-apprehension; anxiety; care.

खुटका-apprehension.

खुट-चाल-vicious or wrong conduct.

खुटपन-flaw; defect.

खुटाना-to be brought to an end; to be finished.

खुटिला-a kind of ear-ring, an ear ornament.

खुट्टी-a crisp kind of sweetmeat.

खुत्थी-wealth; pawn; property.

खुद-self.

खुदकाश्त-land cultivated by the landowner himself.

खुदगरजी-egotism; selfishness.

खुदना-to be excavated; to be engraved; to be dug; to be carved.

खुदरा-miscellaneous objects; small ordinary things.

खुदा-the Almighty; God.

खुदी-arrogance; pride; vanity; egotism; conceit.

खुनकी-coolness; slight chill.

खुनखुना-a rattle; a toy for babies.

खुनस-animosity; dislike; spite; envy; ill-will.

खुनसाना-to be angry.

खुनसी-filled with ill-will.

खुफिया-secret; a detective of the police.-a spy.

खुबना-to penetrate.

खुभना-to penetrate; to pierce.

खुम-a large jar; wine jar.

खुमान-of long life.

खुमार-intoxication; weariness felt after intoxicating or nigh vigil.

खुरंड-the scab or crust on a healing wound.

खुर-horse's hoof; a cloven hoof.

खुरक-apprehension; anxiety.

खुरचन-a kind of sweetmeat; a scrape; pot-scarping.

खुरचाल-misconduct; wickedness; maliciousness.

खुरजी-a saddle-bag; bag or sack for equipment or goods.

खुरट-a disease of cattle.

खुरतार-a beat of hoof.

खुरदरा-uneven; rough.

खुरपा-scrapingorweedinginstrument.

खुरमा-a kind of very light sweetmeat; date fruit.

खुरराँटा-snore.

खुरहा-mouth and foot disease (in cattle).

खुराँट-colloq. ragged; very old; crafty; experienced; cunning.

खुराक-a single dose of medicine; one meal of the day; daily food; rations.

खुराफ़ात-quarrel; abusive language; tumult; brawling disturbance.

खुरिया-the knee-bone; a cup-shaped container.

खुरेंच-scratch.

खुर्रम-glad.

खुर्रा-uneven; rough; coarse (as fibre, stringing).

खुर्राट-cunning; artful; experienced; crafty; old.

खुर्शंद-contended.

खुलना-to be untied; to be opened; to be cracked.

खुलकर without obstruction; in the presence of all; without secrecy.

खुला-open; naked; wide; loose.

खुलासा-summary; sketch; gist; brief; upshot.

खुली खान-quarry.

खुश-cheerful; merry; happy; pleased.

खुसर-फुसर whispering.

खुसिया-the testicles.

खुसूसन especially.

खूँखार-fearful; cure; ferocious; terrible.

खूँट[1]-corner-stone (of a foundation); part; share.

खूँट[2]-ear-wax.

खूँटा-a stake; a tent-pin.

खूँटा-a stake; a tent-pin.

खूँद-pawing of a horse in going over a short place.

खूझा-the fibrous part within a fruit.

खूड़-a furrow.

खूद-less; residue; dregs; refuse; sediment.

खून-blood; murder.

खूब-well; good; pleasant; excellent; beautiful; amiable.

खूबसूरत-beautiful; graceful; handsome; amiable; elegant.

खूबानी-a fig or dried apricot.

खूबी-excellence; goodness; quality; speciality.

खूसट-old; dry; worn out (a person); decrepit; useless; worthless.

खेचर-a bird; a heavenly body; something moving in the sky; a demigod.

खेटक[1]-a village.

खेटक[2]-hunting.

खेड़ा-a small village.

खेढ़ी-placenta (of womb) a kind of Indian steel.

खेत-a field; place for rearing animals; ground; land; battlefield; farm; blade of sword.

खेतिया-farmer; a cultivator.

खेतिहर-farmer; an agriculturist; a cultivator.

खेद-sorrow; melancholy; gloominess; weariness; grief.

खेदना-to pursue; to drive away; to hunt; to chase.

खेदा-lassitude; grief; depression; distress; regret.

खेदित-sorrowful; sad; pained.

खेना to pass through; to row; to punt; to endure (suffering).

खेप-the quantity of a thing which is carried at one time; a voyage or trip.

खेम-welfare.

खेमटा-a kind of song; a partic; metre.

खेमा-booth; marquee; tent; pavilion; tabernacle.

खेरना-to flow; to run.

खेरा-small village; hamlet.

खेल-game; freak; fun; sport; gambol; play.

खेलक-a player.

खेलत-sportive; playing.

खेलाना-to keep engaged; to cause to play; to play with.

खेलौना-toy.

खेवक-boatman; rover.

खेवट-a rover; a boatman; a village paper in which shares of each partner of a village are record or entered.

खेवैया-wharfage; work of rowing.

खेस-a woven figured fabric; a thick cotton sheet; damask.

खेसारि-a kind of pulse.

खेह-dust.

खै-dust; dirt; ashes.

खैनी-chewing tobacco, mixed with lime.

खैर-all right; very good; let it be so.

खैरात-charity; alms.

खैरियत-good fortune; well-being.

खोंच-scratch; a cut or rent in cloth.

खोंचड़-rascal; a idle fellow or lazy.

खोंचा-the long bamboo of a fowler for catching birds.

खोंटा-defective; counterfeit; false.

खोंता-a bird's nest.

खोंपा-a storehouse (for straw).

खोंसना-to pierce; to thrust.

खो-cave; cavern.

खोई-the dry part of sugarcane after its juice has been extracted.

खोखला-excavated; empty; containing nothing; hollow.

खोखा-a boy.

खोखी-a girl.

खोज-enquiry; quest; search; investigation.

खोजा-a respectable person; a chieftain; a eunuch serving in the harem; servant.

खोजी-enquiring; searching.

खोट-defect; flaw; blemish; vice; deception; adulterated.

खोड़-an unlucky moment; the anger or curse of a god or spirit.

खोड़र-a hollow in a tree.

खोडौ-defective.

खोद-investigation; digging.

खोदना-to dig; to delve; to scoop; to scratch; to engrave.

खोदरा-pock marked.

खोदविनोद-an investigation; a thorough search.

खोनचा-a hawker's case or tray.

खोना-to get rid of; to lose; to do away with; to squander.

खोपड़ी-the skull; pate.

खोपरा-the brain; coconut kernel or shell.

खोम-host; assembly.

खोय-habit.

खोर-a narrow lane; a trough for feeding cattle; a bath; a manger.

खोरना-to bathe.

खोरा-lame.

खोराक-a dose of medicine.

खोरि-defect; blemish; flaw; a narrow lane.

खोरी-a narrow valley; a lane or alley.

खोल[1]-a cavity; shell; thick sheet of cloth.

खोल[2]-slot; a hollow; mortice.

खोली-a small room.

खोह-a cave; an abyss; a pit; a cavern; a crypt.

खौंरा-rot (among sheep).

खौफ-fear; terror; dread.

खौलन-act of boiling.

ख्यात-reputed; famous; celebrated; renowned.

ख्याल-mind; attention; fancy; imagination; memory.

ख्वाजा-a master; governor; chieftain; a Mohammedan ; a nobleman.

ख्वाब-a dream; a nap; a sleep.

ख्वार-vile, wretched; base.

ख्वाह-or; if not; either; whether.

ख्वाहिश-desire; wish; request; intention.

ग

ग-The third consonant of the Devnagari alphabet.

गंगा-the sacred river of India the the sacred water of the .

गंज[1]-a store; a grain market; heap; hoard; pile.

गंज[2]-a complaint of the scalp; baldness.

गँजना[1]-to disrespect; to destroy; to treat with contempt; to abuse.

गँजना[2]-to pile up.

गंजिया-sickle; a bag in which grass-cutter keeps grass; a wallet of an artisan.

गंजी[1]-heap; pile.

गंजी[2]-a woollen vest.

गँठ-a pickpocket.

गँठिया-a type of disease.

गँठीला-brawny; nodular; knotty; muscular.

गंड-the temple; the cheek.

गंडक-an amulet worn on the neck.

गंडा-a knotted string tied round the neck as a charm; a group of four cowries; a knot.

गँडासा-a chopper for crop stalks.

गँडेरी-a mini segment cut off from sugarcane.

गंतव्य-to be gone (by).-destination.

गंद-filth; stench; to use foul language; a smell.

गंदगी-impurity; dirtiness; foulness.

गंदना-a spice which is similar to garlic.

गँदला-dirty; foul; filthy; muddy; turbid.

गंदा-filthy; obscure; grime; dirty.

गंदुम-wheat.

गंध-smell; fragrance; scent; perfume; a bad smell.

गंधक-brimstone; sulphur.

गंधर्व-a demigod; a celestial musician; horse; a deer; the soul after death and previous of its being born again; a caste of singer.

गँधाना-to give out foul smell.

गंधबिरोजा-resin which is extracted from pine trees.

गंधार-a country.

गंधी-a seller or maker of perfumes.

गंभारी-a kind of large tree.

गंभीर-serious; thoughtful; earnest; solemn; dignified.

गँव-device; method; occasion; desire; intention.

गँवई-having to do with a village or villagers; rustic.

गँवर-a group or crowd of yokels.

गँवाऊ-wasteful; prodigal.

गँवाना-to get rid of; to waste; to lose; to spend fruitlessly.

गँवार-a villager; ignorant person; uncouth.

गँस-enmity; animosity; a knot; taunt; sarcasm.

गगन-the sky; the regions beyond the world; space.

गगरी-a water pot.

गच्चा-to incur dishonour; a setback.

गछना-to walk; to move.

गज[1]-an elephant; the number eight; a demon.

गज[2]-a yard; a measure of three feet; a kind of arrow.

गजगाह-a string of several tassels which is suspended on an elephant's neck.

गजदंत-a peg fixed in the wall, an elephant's tooth; ivory.

गजदान-rut of an elephant.

गजपति-the driver of master of an elephant.

गजपाटल-lampblack.

गज़ब-extreme or excess; disastrous thing.

गजर-chimes; the four ; chimes. at early dawn.

गजरा-a thick woven garland of flowers; a kind of silk cloth; armlet; a bracelet.

गज़ल-a poem of partic, metrical type on or including conventionally; an amatory theme.

गजा-a drum-sick.

गजाजन-an epithet of the God .

गजाना-to ferment; to blend.

गजाल-a kind of fish.

गज़ी-thin rough cloth which is hand-spun and hand-woven; a female elephant.

गज्जर-swampy ground.

गज्झा-store; heat; treasure; thick froth.

गटगट-close friendship; sexual intercourse; topsy-turvy.

ग़टरगूँ-sound of sporting pigeon.

गट्टा-the wrist joint; or the ankle joint; pastern (of a horse).

गट्ठर-a large bundle; a bale; a large package; parcel.

गठड़ी-bundle.

गठन-constitution; construction; texture.

गठबंध पत्र-pack.

गठरी-bundle; a parcel; package; truss; packet; stored wealth.

गठाना-to be joined.

गठित-strongly built.

गठिया-gout; rheumatism.

गठिवन-a kind of tree of average size.

गठीला-compact; knotty; well-built (person).

गठौंद-money tied up in bag or bundle; cash to be deposited.

गड़ंग-vanity; arrogance; pride; self-praise.

गड़-a boundary; a partition wall; a ditch; a landmark.

गड़ना-to penetrate or to be driven; to stick; to pierce; to sink; to be buried; to be a source of irritation.

गड़प्पा-a place of deception; a ditch; misleading.

गड़बड़-disorder; muddle; confusion; disturbance.

गड़रिया-a shepherd.

गड़हा-a hole; a pit.

गड़ही-a puddle.

गड़ा-a mass; an accumulation; a heap.

गड़ायत-pinching; piercing.

गड़ारा-a cart-track.

गड़ारी-a circular line; a spool; a boundary; a reel; a pulley.

गड़ासा-chopper.

गडुई-a water-pot with a curved short spout.

गड़ोलना-a child's go-cart.

गड़ौंना-a kind of betel leaf.

गड्ड-bunch; a bundle; collection.

गड्ढा-a depression in earth; a hollow; a ditch; a pit.

गढ़ंत-artificial; fabricated; imaginary.

गढ़-a fort; a castle; a battery.

गढ़ई-a small pond or tank; a pit.

गढ़त-construction; structure.

गढ़न-fashioning; making; workmanship.

गढ़ाई-shaping; making; workmanship; fashioning.

गण-gang; multitude; group; troop; flock.

गणतंत्र-republic.

गणद्रव्य-commonwealth; public property.

गणन-collection; counting.

गणिका-a dancing girl; a prostitute.

गणित-mathematics; arithmetic.

गणित्र-calculator.

गणेश-the son of God and ; represented as a fat man with an elephant's head.

गण्यता-credit.

गत-gone; dead; past.

गतांक-past; bad.

गति-going; movement; motion.

गतिया-a piece of cloth for covering a child.

गतिक-dynamic.

गतिशीलता-mobility.

गते-गते-by degrees; slowly.

गत्ता-inferior kind of cardboard; pasteboard.

गथ-capital; price; fund.

गद-a thudding sound.

गदका-a wooden stick.

गदगोल-turmoil; a stirring up.

गदबदा-plump.

गदबदाना-to rejoice.

गदना-to narrate; to tell; to relate; to weave together.

ग़दर-revolt; revolution; rebellion.

गदराहट-near ripeness (of fruit).

गदला-dirty; foul; impure; muddy (as water).

गदहा-an ass.

गदहूल-a lotus.

गदा-an Indian club; a mace; a club.

गदाई-wretched.

गदाधर-an epithet of .

गदेल-a baby.

गदेला-a thick bed or cover; a cushion.

गदोरी-palm of the hand.

गद्द-delighted; very happy; greatly.

गद्दा-a mattress; a large padded cushion.

गद्दार-an apostate; a traitor.

गधा-ass.

गधापन-stupidity; foolishness.

गधी-a she-ass.

गनना-to count.

गनहेल-a kind of oats.

गनाना-to cause to be counted.

ग़नी-rich; a rich person.

गनीम-a plunderer; an enemy; a robber.

गन्ना-sugarcane.

गप-gossip; chat; prattle; tattle; false report; rumour; hearsay; sound produced by suddenly swallowing something.

गपकना-to gobble; to swallow hastily; to gulp.

गपड़चौथ-useless talk.

गपना-to gossip; to gulp; to tattle; to prattle.

गपोड़ा-a serious gossip.

गप्प-a gossip.

गप्फा-a big morsel; full advantage or favour; gain.

ग़फ़लत-carelessness; negligence; mistake; error; swoon.

गबदा-colloq. plump.

ग़बन- embezzlement; misappropriation (of money).

गबरू-young; simple; of budding youth.

गब्बर-proud; slow; vain; arrogant; dilatory in answering; precious.

गब्भा-a quilt.

गभस्ति-ray; the Sun; arm; hand.

गम[1]-approach; access.

गम[2]-sorrow; grief; woe; care; anxiety.

गमक-deep tone or sound (as of a or a drum).

गमछा-a napkin; a towel.

गमन-the act of going; sexual relations; gait.

गमना-to walk; to go; to attend; to thing; to be sorry.

गमनीय-to be crossed or traversed; accessible; attainable; passable.

गमला-a flower-pot.

ग़मज़-flirtatious glance; a wink.

गमाना-to lose.

गमार-stupid; uncivilised.

ग़मी-time of sorrow; death; mourning.

गम्मत-object of amusement or linking; amusement.

गम्य-approachable; attainable; accessible; fit for coition.

गम्यता-practicability; accessibility.

गयंद-a big elephant.

गय-sky; wealth; life; son; a house; an elephant.

गयशिर-the sky; firmament.

गया[1]-destroyed; broken down; past; worthless.

गया[2]-the city of in (an importance place of Hindu pilgrimage).

गरकाव-drowned in water.

ग़रमज-tower on a mound; deck of a boat; battlement; scaffold; huge; ponderous.

गरगरा-a pulley.

गरज[1]-a roaring; bellowing; the noise of thunder.

गरज[2]-need; view; end; object; business; interest; concern; necessity; want; wish; use.

गरट्ठ-a group.

गरदन-the neck; nape.

गरदनी-a blow on the neck; covering for the neck and upper body of a horse.

गरना-to be squeezed.

गरनाल-an old type of gun of wide calibre.

गरभाना-growing of ears in paddy plant; to be pregnant.

गरम-warm; burning; hot; fiery; zealous; sweltering; ardent; active; choleric; pungent.

गरमागरमी-exchange of hot words.

गरमाना-to become warm; to become hot.

गरमी-heat, warmth.

गरराना-to roar; to howl.

गरल-poison.

गरा-neck.

गराज-need.

गराड़ी-a pulley; windlass; an appliance for twisting thread.

गरामी-of high repute; respected.

गराना-to cause to squeeze.

गराव-bundle of fodder; a sheaf; a chopper.

गरिमा-prestige; weight; dignity; excellence; importance; self-importance; vanity.

गरिया-eminence; importance; greatness; weight; boast; pride; self-esteem.

गरियाना-to scold; to abuse.

गरियार-stubborn.

गरियारी-stubbornness, obstinacy.

गरिष्ठ-indigestible; heavy.

गरी-the kernel or internal part of a coconut; the edible part of a nut.

गरीब-poor; humble; meek; mild; penniless.

गरीयस-weight; heavy; great; eminent; glorious.

गरूड़-eagle; large species of heron; a large vulture; the vehicle of ; a kind of battle array.

गरू-weighty; heavy.

गरूर-vanity; pride.

गरेर-to surround; to lay siege to.

गरोह-gang; group.

गर्ग-a bull.

गर्ज-thunder.

गर्जन-roaring; the sound of thundering or rumbling; bellowing.

गर्त्त-a pit; gulf; a ditch; chasm.

गर्द-dirt; dust.

गर्दभ-a donkey; an ass.

गर्दा-dust.

गर्दिश-aimlessly; wandering; adversity; a revolution.

गर्भ-womb; foetus; nucleus; embryo; the interior; pregnancy; the inside or middle.

गर्भगृह-the central yard of a house; the central room of a house; the room in a temple.

गर्भपात-abortion; miscarriage; failure of scheme.

गर्भवती-pregnant.

गर्भबीज-ovum.

गर्भस्व-a child in womb.

गर्भस्त्राव-abortion; micarriage.

गर्भधान-impregnation; conception; a ceremony performed by Hindus when a women has conceived (become pregnant).

गर्भाशय-uterus.

गर्म-hot.

गर्रा-mud.

गर्व-conceit; vanity; arrogance; elation; pride; boast.

गर्वित-given cause for pride; haughty.

गर्हण-censure; reproach.

गर्ह्य-base; censurable; detestable.

गहर्‌य-mean.

गल-the neck; the throat.

गलगंज-noise; uproar; tumult.

गलगला-wet.

गलछट-the gullet.

गलझप-the iron chain tied round an elephant's neck.

गलत-untrue; incorrect; wrong; erroneous; false; to prove to be incorrect; misunderstanding.

गलतंस-dying without issue.

ग़लतान-wallowing; rolling.

गलती-mistake; error; deception; misconception.

गलन-decaying; melting.

गलनांक-melting point.

गला-the voice; gullet; funnel.

गलाई-dissolving.

गलाऊ-soluble; fusible.

ग़लाज़त-grossness; filth; coarseness.

ग़लाना-to melt; to waste; to fuse; to thaw; to liquefy.

गलार-a species of mynah; the rose-ringed parakeet.

गलाव-solution (of a solid in a liquid).

गलित-dropped; melted.

गलियारा-a passage; lane; corridor; passageway.

गली-an alley; a narrow pass between mountains; a lane.

गलीचा-carpet.

गलीज-filthy; dirty; impure.

गल्प-herd; a tale; a flock; story.

गवय-the white-footed antelope or deer.

गवाक्ष-skylight; small window.

गवार-tolerable; acceptable; digestible.

गवाह-a witness; to a statement.

गवेजा-prattling; gossip.

गवेरुक-ruddle; red chalk.

गवेल-of a village; rustic.

गवेषना-research; investigation.

गवैया-a singer.

गश्त-a going round patrolling; wandering; a walk; a tour.

गसीला-mixed together; compact; inter-twined closely interwoven.

गह-a handle.

गहक-excitement; zeal.

गहकना-to be pleased; to be in earnest; to be intoxicated.

गहकी-a customer.

गहगड्ड-heavy; deep.

गहगहा-enthusiastic; excited.

गहगहे-with pomp; with zeal.

गहन-a dense place; a thicket; forest; hiding-place; cave.

गहना-jewellery; ornament; pledge; pawn; mortgage.

गहनि-obstinacy; a hold.

गहर-delay.-difficult; perplexing; intricate.

गहरा-deep; intimate heavy; weighty; harsh; cruel (a blow).

गहराई-depth; profundity; pathos.

गहराना-to make deep.

गहरु-procrastination; delay.

गहल-a bunch of grapes.

गहूरी-demurrage.

गहेला-vain; proud; mad; rustic; obstinate; foolish.

गाँज-an accumulation; a hoard; a heap.

गाँजना-to churn; to stir.

गाँजर-a kind of grass.

गाँजा-hemp leaves, flower, head or buds.

गाँठ-a knob; a knot; boss; gnarl; bob; tie; loop; node; bulb; gland.

गाँठना-to knot; to string or to thread; to fasten; to mend (as shoe fabric); to dispose; to arrange; to compose.

गाँड-anus.

गाँथना-to string; to intertwine; to reduce to subjection.

गांधारी-name of mother of ; belonging to or connected with .

गाँस-jealously; difficulty; enmity.

गाँसी-enmity.

गाहक-a customer.

गाच-fine cellular cloth in wrought with silk flowers.

गाछ-a tree; a bush.

गाज[1]-froth; foam; scum.

गाज[2]-the noise of thunder; anger; thunderbolt; lighting; roaring.

गाज[3]-a glass bangle.

ग़ाजी-a brave man; a hero among Mohammedans who fights for his religion.

गाटा-a plot of land; the yoking of bullocks (as for work in a mill).

गाड़-a sheep.

गाड़र-a sheep.

गाड़ा-a large cart.

गाड़ी-conveyance; bus; truck; car; cart; carriage; train.

गाढ़ना[1]-to shape; to hammer out; to forge.

गाढ़ना[2]-to bury; to lay.

गाढ़ा-thick; dense; turbid; close; muddy; solid; coarse.

गाढ़े well; arduously; forcibly.

गात-the body.

गात्र-the body; a limb.

गाथ-a song of praise; a song.

गायक-a singer; musician; chanter of scriptural texts.

गादड़-faint-hearted; coward.-a jackal.

गादा-unripe or green harvest; unripe grain.

गादुर-the flying fox (a bat) or flying squirrel.

गाध-depth of water; situation; place; bottom of a river; flow of a river.

गान-a song; singing.

गाना-to sing the praises of; to chant; to sing.

गाफ़िल-careless; senseless; stupid; imprudent.

गाबदू-stupid.

गाभ-pregnancy of cattle.

गाभा-the inner part of a plantain leaf; new unopened leaf of a plant.

गाभिन-pregnant (said of cattle); gravid.

गामी-moving on; going.

गायक-singer.

गायब-lost; vanished; absent; disappeared; missing.

गायिका-a female singer.

गार-kneaded mud.

गारत-destroyed; devastated.

गारथ-a watch; a sentry; a guard or constable.

गारना-to milk; to rub; to press; to squeeze or to wring out.

गारा-kneaded mud; mortar.

गार्ड-a guard.

गारो-vanity; pride; eminence; arrogance.

गाल-cheek; joke; prattle; jowl; mouthful; middle part.

गाला-a pad of cotton for spinning; a ball of carded cotton.

गालिब-victorious; eminent; excellent; distinguished.

गालना-to converse; to speak; to talk.

ग़ालीचा-a small carpet.

गालू-colloq. boastful; garrulous.

गावकुशी-the killing of a cow.

गावघप-fraudulent; deceitful.

गावतंकिया-a large stuffed pillow or bolster.

गावदी-stupid; bovine.

गावना-to sing.

गासिया-housing for a saddle.

गाह-a time; occasion; a place.

गाह[1]-a crocodile; one who seizes.

गाह[2]-tale.

गाहकताई-appreciation.

गाहन-a dip in water; bathing in water of a river.

गाहना-to thrash; to take a dip; a tread upon corn; to agitate; to disturb.

गाहे sometime or other.

गिंजाई-a type of centipede common in the rainy season.

गिंदर-an insect which attacks growing cereal crops.

गिउ-the neck.

गिजगिजा-soft and juicy (as ripe fruit).

ग़िज़ा-diet; food; provisions; victuals.

गिटकिरी-a trill (in singing).

गिट्टक-solid piece of stone; brick or metal.

गिट्टा-piece; the ankle point; a hard lump.-a dwarf.

गिनती-calculation; counting; enumeration; reckoning.

गिब्बन-a kind of ape or monkey; gibbon.

गिमटी-a heavy, figured cotton cloth.

गियाह-a kind of horse.

गिरई-fish.

गिरगिट-chameleon.

गिरगिरी-a toy; a child's fiddle.

गिरदा-a round pillow; anything round.

गिरफ्त-capture; seizing; grasp; power.

गिरफ्तार-captured; arrested; seized; captivated.

गिरमिट-a gimlet.

गिरमिटिया-indentured labourer.

गिरवी-mortgage.

गिरस्ती-family life.

गिरह-a joint; a knot.

गिरहकट-a pick-pocket.

गिरहबाज-a pigeon which turns up its body while flying in the air.

गिरही-residence; a house.

गिराँ-dear; precious; costly; heavy; unpleasant; disagreeable.

गिरा-voice; speech; poetry; things said; a name of .

गिराऊ-ready to fall; fit to be pulled down.

गिराना-to throw or to knock down; to cause to fall; to destroy; to disgrace.

गिरासना-to torment; to tease.

गिरि-a mountain; a hill.

गिरिराज-the Himalayas; a big mountain.

गिरो-pawned; mortgaged.

गिरोह-party; a group; band (of people).

गिर्द-around; round.

गिर्दावार-an inspector of police or customs; a wanderer.

गिलगिला-wet; moist; slimy; viscous.

गिलगिलाया-the jay bird.

गिलगिली-a species of horse.

गिलट-gilt.

गिलटी-a swelling of the glands; a tumour; a gland.

गिलना-to swallow.

गिलम-a thick quilt; a soft smooth woollen carpet.

गिलमिल-a kind of cloth.

गिलहरी-squirrel.

गिला-lamentation; complaint; reproach.

गिलाफ-a pillow case; scabbard; prepuce; sheath.

गिलावा-cement; mortar.

गिलास-a glass; a tumbler (glass or metal); a mug.

गिलौरी-a prepared and folded betel leaf.

गींजना-to form or develop a crease; to crumple; to destroy the folds of cloth.

गी-a song; a tune; a stain; sonnet; fame; glory; singing; a hymn.

गीत-sing; a song of praise.

गीता-a narration; the theological episode of the called .

गीति-song; vocal music.

गीदड़-a coward; a jackal.

गीदड़ी-female jackal.

गीदी-coward; stupid; block-head; faint-hearted.

गीबत-backbiting; absence.

गीर्ण-praised; eulogised.

गीदवी-the goddess .

गीर्षति-a learned man.

गीला-wet; moist; damp; humid.

गीस्पति-a learned man.

गुँगा-dump.

गुंचा-enjoyment; a bud; blossom.

गुंज-shrub.

गुंजक-buzzer.

गुंजन-an echo.

गुंजनिकेतन-buzzing bee.

गुंजरना-to buzz; to hum like a bee; to roar.

गुंजान-dense; compact; thick.

गुंजाइश-capacity; profit; margin; accommodation.

गुंठा-a kind of pony.

गुंठित-veiled.

गुंडा-lout; bully; a dissolute person.

गुँथना-to cause to be kneaded; to cause to be plaited; braided.

गुनाई-the wages or work for kneading something.

गुंफ-bunch; entanglement.

गुंफन-stringing together; twining.

गुंफा-cave.

गुंफित-woven; twined; strung.

गुंबज-cupola; a vault.

गुंबा-a protuberance on the head causes by hurt.

गुंभी-shoot or young branch of a plant; a sprout.

गुइयाँ-a female friend; one of a team of a players.

गुगगल-a thorny tree.

गुच्ची-very small; tiny.-a type of child's play; a small pit made by boys while playing with stick and ball.

गुच्छ-bunch; cluster.

गुच्छा-bunch; knot; bouquet.

गुज़र-passing; access; passage; the passage of time; existence; life.

गुजरात-the state of India.

गुजरान-livelihood; sustenance.

गुजरिया-one who takes the parts of a woman in a dance; a milkmaid.

गुजरी-an ornament for the twist; a bracelet.

गुज़श्ता-the past.

गुज़ार-causing to pass; performing; format; paying.

गुज़ारा-course of life; employment; a living; ferry; food; passage.

गुज़ारिश-request; petition; representation.

गुज्झा-hidden; secret.-a dowel.

गुझरौट-crease made in cloth; part of a woman's belly round the navel.

गुट-a faction; a group.

गुटकना to bolt; to gulp.

गुटका-a track; a handbook; a small ball.

गुटरगूँ-sound of cooing.

गुटिका-pebble; a pill.

गुट्ट-a band; a gang; a clique; assembly league.

गुट्ठल-of fruit containing a big stone; foolish; block-headed; stupid.

गुठला-cyst; a large lump.

गुठली-kernel; the stone of a fruit.

गुड़ंबा-raw mangoes boiled and put into syrup.

गुड़-raw sugar; molasses; treacle.

गुड़रू-a particular bird.

गुड़ाई-hoeing.

गुड़ाकू-tobacco mixed with molasses used in smoking.

गुड़िया-a doll; child's puppet.

गुढ़ा-thwarts (of a boat).

गुण-quality; property; attainment; attribute; worth; merit; talent; virtue.

गुणक-a multiplier.

गुणकारी-potential; beneficial; effective.

गुणगौरी-a woman whose husband is alive.

गुणज्ञ-one who recognises the merits of others; meritorious.

गुणन-multiplication; multiplying.

गुणवान्-possessing good qualities; talented.

गुणागुण-quality; merit.

गुणानुक्रम-order or merit.

गुणानुवाद-applause; encomium; praise; eulogy.

गुणित-multiplied.

गुणी-having good qualities; having skills or talents.

गुत्थमगुत्था-entanglement; quarrelling; dispute; turmoil; wrangle.

गुथन-a confused state; a tangle; entanglement.

गुथना-to be plaited or braided; to be strung; to be threaded; to be tangled.

गुथवाँ-plaited; strung together; interlaced.

गुद-anus.

गुदगुदा-fleshy; plump; soft.

गुदड़िया-patched or tattered clothes.

गुदड़ी-a patched quilt; a beggar's bedding.

गुदना-to be pricked or punctured; to be tattooed.

गुदराना-to make a request.

गुदरैन-repeating a lesson learnt; examination.

गुदा-anus.

गुदाज़-fleshy; plump; soft.

गुदाम-godown; warehouse.

गुदार-plump; pulpy; fleshy.

गुद्दा-pulp; kernel; nucleus; the neck; flesh on the palm of hand.

गुनगुन-humming; mumbling; buzzing; muttering.

गुना-multiplicative quality.

गुनाह-sin; fault; guilt.

गुनिया-a carpenter's square.

गुप-secret; hidden; dark; blind.

गुप्ता-a concubine.

गुप्ति-act of protecting; work of concealing or hiding; a prison; a cave.

गुप्ती-a sword-stick.

गुप्फा-wreath; tassel; bunch (as of flowers).

गुफा-place of retreat; a cave.

गुफ्तगू-conversation; talk.

गुबरैला-a type of beetle whose colour is black and lives in dung.

गुबार-dirt; vexation; affliction; dust; perplexity.

गुब्बारा-a balloon.

गुभना-to be pricked pin-ched.

गुभी-sprout; shoot.

गुम-hidden; missing; lost.

गुमची-a kind of wild Indian liquorice.

गुमटा-lump; swelling.

गुमड़ा-a bruise; a swelling; lump; tumour.

गुमना-to be lost; to be disappear.

गुमनाम-nameless; anonymous; having no name.

गुमर-arrogance; vanity; pride; a concealed; emotion; a whisper.

गुमराह-wandering; depraved; treading on an evil path; erring.

गुमान-distrust; pride; suspicion.

गुमानी-to lose.

गुमाश्ता-manager of a mercantile firm; an agent.

गुम्मज-vault; cupola; a dome.

गुर teacher; mentor.

गुरगा-a servant; an attendant; a henchman; a spy; an emissary; one sent on a mission.

गुरगाबी-a kind of shoe or slipper having the toe turned up; a toeless shoe.

गुरथी-a crease; a fold.

गुरदा-bladder; kidney.

गुरमुख-initiated by one's preceptor or Guru.

गुरबना-to dig up; to weed; to hoe.

गुरसी-whiteness; faimness; complexion.

गुराब-a wagon which is employed for carrying a cannon.

गुरिद-a mace; a kind of club.

गुरु-a teacher; a master; a spiritual guide; a religious instructor; a tutor.

गुरुकुल-teaching institution which is kept up by a tutor; a residential.

गुरुच-creeper used in medicine; a parasitic.

गुरुजन-venerable or eminent men; elderly person.

गुरुत्व केन्द्र-the centre of gravity of an object.

गुर्गा-a spy; a servant.

गुर्ज-a cudgel; a mace.

गुर्दा-kidney; courage.

गुर्राना-to roar; to growl; to snarl; to hoot; to grunt; to grumble; to part.

गुर्री-parched barley.

गुर्विणी-pregnant.

गुलकंद-a conserve prepared from rose leaves.

गुलकारी-the painting of flowers; flowering.

गुलखर-a plant which bears blue flowers.

गुलगुली-tickling; tingling; a kind of fish.

गुलचा-a light stroke on the cheeks given in affection.

गुलचाँदनी-a white flower that opens at night.

गुलछर्रा-riotous; merry-making; revelry.

गुलजार-a garden.

गुलझटी-perplexity; a tangle.

गुलड़ी-a small ring-shaped; cake of cow dung.

गुलदस्ता-a bouquet; a bunch of flowers; a nosegay.

गुलदाउदी-chrysanthemum.

गुलदान-bouquet; a vase for a nosegay.

गुलदार-a kind of needle work; a kind of white pigeon; flowery.

गुलदुपहरिया-a plant which bears bell-shaped red flowers.

गुलनार-the flower of a pomegranate.

गुलबदन-a kind of striped silken cloth.

गुलबन्द-neck-cloth; muffler; ruffle; vandyke; tie; scarf.

गुलबहार-the daisy.

गुलमेख-a nail with a studded head; tack.

गुललाला-a kind of plant.

गुलशन-a place of enjoyment or pleasure; a garden.

गुलशब्बो-the tuber-rose.

गुलहरी-a fruit of tree.

गुलाई-roundness.

गुलाब-the rose.

गुलाम-a slave; a servant; a bondsman.

गुलामी-slavery; to be slave.

गुलाल-a farinaceous red powder which is used on festival to throw on each other.

गुलिस्तां-a garden of roses.

गुलू-the neck; throat.

गुलेल-a pellet-blow; catapult.

गुलौरा-soft.

गुल्फ-the ankle bone.

गुल्म-a division of an army; a kind of shrub; a cluster of plants; enlargement of skin.

गुल्लक-container for ready money; a niche in a wall used for keeping money.

गुल्लाला-a kind of flower of deep red colour.

गुल्ली-comb of a bee's hive containing honey; a stone of a fruit; a short stick used in the game of tip-cat; a kind of domestic pigeon; a ball.

गुस्ताख-insolent; rude; arrogant; brash.

गुस्ताख़ी-rudeness; arrogance; presumption; want of politeness.

गुस्सा-anger; wrath; rage.

गुस्सैल-quick tempered.

गुह[1]-a horse; a cave; the heart; an epithet of .

गुह[2]-to thread.

गुहना-to enlace; to interweave; to entwine.

गुहराना-to shout; to call aloud.

गुहाँजनी-a style of the eye.

गुहा-a den; a cave; a secret or mysterious place; cavity.

गुहार-humble appeal.

गुहारना-to entreat for help or justice.

गुहिका-cavity.

गुहय-concealable; private; the pudendum.

गुहेरा-a kind of poisonous lizard.

गुह्य-hidden; secret; mysterious esoteric.

गूँगा-speechless; dump; mute.

गूँच[1]-an echo; a reverberation.

गूँच[2]-a kind of fish (freshwater shark).

गूँज-echo; hollow sound; buzzing, roar.

गूँथना-to string; to braid; to knead; to take; to stitch.

गूँधना-to weave; to knack; to thread; to string.

गूगेर-a milkman; a dairy-man; a cowherd.

गूजर-a man of the community; a cowherd; milkman.

गूँझा-hidden; secret.

गूढ़ा-thwarts of a boat.

गूढ़ाक्षर-hiero-glyph.

गूदड़-rags; a bundle of old tattered clothes.

गूदा-pulp; pith; kernel; marrow; brain; cramp; essential portion of a thing.

गूथना-to knead.

गून-hawser (of a boat); a rope.

गूल-an irrigation channel.

गूलर-a wild fig tree.

गूलू-a large deciduous tree.

गृहड़िया-a manure-heap.

गृध्र-a vulture; the name of a mountain.

गृध्रसी-sciatica.

गृह-residence; a house; dwelling; family; abode.

गृहिणी-lady or mistress of a house.

गृहदहन-burning of a house; arson.

गृहदेवता-family god; tutelary; deity.

गृहपति-a householder; the head of a family.

गृहयुद्ध-civil war; family feud of hostility.

गृहसचिव-Home Secretary.

गृहस्थाश्रम-the title of a householder.

गृहस्थी-house-wifery; the duties of a house holder; husbandry.

गृहस्वामी-the head of a family; a housekeeper.

गृहिणी-wife; the mistress of a house.

गृहीत-caught; attacked; taken; seized; acquired; understood; grasped.

गह्यसूत्र-the treatise dealing with the performance of religious rites.

गेंगला-silly; simple.

गेंठी-an edible tuber.

गेंड-the leave of a sugarcane; boundary.

गेंडुरी-coiling of a snake; a coil of rope; turban.

गेंद-a ball.

गेंदवा-a pillow.

गेंदा-a marigold.

गेंदुआ-bolster; a pillow.

गेंदुक-a ball.

गेड़ी-a boy's game.

गेदा-an infant; an unfledged bird; nestling.

गेरना-to surround.

गेय-fit to be sung.

गेरुई-a red blight (affecting corn).

गेरू-a red clay soil; ruddle; red ochre.

गेसू-lock (of hair); a ringlet.

गेह-house; home.

गेहनी-wife; the mistress of a house.

गेही-a householder.

गेहूँअन-name of a particular poisonous snake having a light brown skin.

गेहूँ-wheat.

गैंडा-a rhinoceros.

गैंता-a pickaxe.

गैन-way; passage.

गैब-the future.

गैबी-hidden; invisible.

गैयर-an elephant.

गैया-a cow.

ग़ैर-other; different; foreign.

ग़ैरत-shame; bashfulness; sense of self-respect of honour.

गैरिक-gold; ruddle; ochre.

गैल-path; road.

गैलड़-a stepson; the son of a woman by a former marriage.

गैलहू-a passer-by; a traveller.

गोइड़-fields near a village; the outskirts of a village.

गोंचड़ी-a tick (on cattle).

गोंठा-dried cow-dung.

गोंडरा-a circular ring.

गोंडा-a small village; an enclosure for keeping cattle.

गोंद-gum; mastic; birdlime.

गोंदनी-a reed.

गोंदनी-a reed or rush (used in making mats).

गोंदरी-a water weed; mat made of this weed; a kind of moss.

गोइंठा-a cow-dung cake; cow-dung.

गोई[1]-a pair, (or yoke) of oxen; pair (as of people working together).

गोई[2]-speaking.

गोकर्ण-a kind of deer; a mule.

गोकि although.

गोकुल-a cow-house; a flock of cows; a herd of cattle.

गोकोस-the distance to which a cow's bellowing can be heard.

गोक्षुर-a kind of ornament for the twist; briar; bramble; thistle; a thin lace of gold or silver.

गोखा-skylight; a loop hole.

गोग्रास-a portion of cooked food given to the cow.

गोचना-to stop; to seize; to catch.

गोज-the wind passing through the anus.

गोजई-mixture of wheat and barley.

गोजर-a centipede.

गोजी-a big stick or staff.

गोझनवट-the border of dhoti worn by woman.

गोझा-a thorny grass which springs up during the rainy season; a kind of sweetmeat.

गोट-border of garment; hem; welt.

गोठ-an assembly; a cow house; an excursion; a trip.

गोड़-leg; the foot; knee.

गोड़इत-a sentinel; the village watchman.

गोड़ना-to hoe; to break up.

गोड़ा-leg of a chair or bed.

गोड़ाई-the work or wages paid for hoeing a field.

गोड़ापाई-repeated coming and going in a place.

गोड़ारी-a shoe; the foot-part of a bedstead.

गोढ़ना-to scratch; to scrape; to dig; to excavate; to hollow out; to scrape out.

गोढर-weeds picked up in a field (by a harrow).

गोणी-a pannier for beast of burden. a tow-foldsack.

गोत-an exogamous subdivision of a caste group; family; lineage; stock.

गोता-immersion; dipping; a dive.

गोताखोर-a diver.

गोती-of the same family or blood.

गोत्र-sub-division of a caste group; an exogamous.

गोदंती-a kind of gem.

गोद-embrace; adoption; the lap.

गोदनहारी-a woman whose occupation is tattooing.

गोदना-to tattoo; to puncture.

गोदनी-an instrument used in tattooing.

गोदाम-a godown; a storehouse; warehouse; granary.

गोदी-dock.

गोधन-a herd of cows; property in cattle; a kind of arrow.

गोधा-a leather fence which is worn by archers on the left hand; iguana.

गोधूलि-evening; twilight (dusk).

गोनस-a kind of jewel; a kind of snake.

गोना-to conceal.-one who carries a bog of corn on his back.

गोनी-hemp; flax; sack.

गोप-a king; a cowherd; a milkman; the chieftain of a village.

गोपन-hiding; protection; guarding; concealing.

गोपनीय-confidential.

गोपिका-cowherd's wife.

गोपुच्छ-a kind of tapering necklace; a tail of a cow.

गोपुर-heaven; the gate of a city or fort.

गोप्य-needing to be protected or preserved; needing to be kept secret or hidden.

गोफा-a new shoot let.

गोबरैला-a dung-betel.

गोबी-cabbage; cauliflower.

गोभल-the name of a sage.

गोभी-a kind of vegetable; cabbage; cauliflower.

गोमक्खी-a gadfly.

गोमुख-the mouth of a cow; a conch-shell with a mouth like that of a cow; a kind of trumpet.

गोमुत्र-the urine of cow.

गोमद, गोमेदक-a precious yellowish-red hue.

गोयंदा-spy; informer.

गोया supposing; granting.

गोर-a grave.

गोरखइमली-a very large tree.

गोरखधंधा-an entangling or perplexing business; a Chinese puzzle.

गोरखनाथ-name of a legendary yogi; founder of the panth.

गोरखर-a wild ass; zebra; onager.

गोरखा-a Gurkha.

गोरज-dirt flying from the hooves of a cow.

गोरा-fair-complexioned; attractive; light-skinned.

गोरिल्ला-the gorilla.

गोरी-a woman with fair-complexion; beautiful women.

गोरू-cattle horned beasts.

गोलंदाज-a bomber; a gunner; a marksman.

गोलंबर-a round; globular object; cupola; arch.

गोल-round; globular.

गोलक-a bag or box for keeping money in.

गोलची-a goalkeeper.

गोलमाल-confusion; disturbance.

गोलामिर्च-black pepper.

गोलयंत्र-an observatory.

गोलयोग-disorder; confusion.

गोला-a ball; a cannon ball; wild pigeon; orb; a large beam of wood; a globe; sphere.

गोलाई-roundness; a circular surround.

गोलाध्यय-the science of spheres.

गोलाधारी-bombardment.

गोलार-globular; spherical; globe; round.

गोलार्ध-hemisphere.

गोली-bullet; marble; pill; globule; pellet; gunshot.

गोव-to conceal; to hide.

गोवा-cow-dung; manure.

गोवन्द-herd.

गोशा-corner; private place; direction.

गोशाला-enclosure or cattle; neat-house; byre.

गोश्त-meat; flash; a soup made with meat.

गोष्ठ-byre; cow-pen.

गोष्ठी-seminar; assembly; forum; discourse; conversation.

गोष्पद-a small amount; cow's hoof.

गोसाई-a saint; a disciple of ; monarch; God.

गोस्वामी-a saint.

गोह-a guana; a lizard.

गोहत्या-the slaughter or killing of a cow.

गोहन-one making up a group; companion; associate.

गोहरा[1]-cow-dung cake.

गोहरा[2]-to call to; to call out to.

गोहरौर-a pile of cow-dung cakes.

गोहानी-well-manure land; land near a village.

गोहार-a cry of help; an outcry; alarm; tumult.

गोहुवन-a large snake; boa constrictor.

गोहूँ-wheat.

गोहूना-a large snake.

गोही-secrecy; privacy; secret conversation.

गोंछी-a hole; waterlogged land.

गौंडी-a musical mode; a kind or rum distilled from treacle.

गौगा-uproar; noise.

गौचरी-a grazing ground for cattle near a village.

गौदुमा-conical; tapering.

गौनहाई-the bringing home of one's wife.

गौनहार-the bride who accompanies her husband to her father-in-law's house.

गौना-the ceremony in Hindus of taking a bride to her husband's house for the first time.

गौरव-dignity; gravity; venerability; honour; repute; prestige; grandeur; having to do with guru; weight.

गौरवित-honoured; dignified; venerable; invested with gravity.

गौरांग-the God ; Lord .

गौरा-a fair-skinned woman.

गौरिया-a kind of black-bird; a hubble-dubble made of clay.

गौरी-a name of goddess .

गौरैया-a hen sparrow.

गौल्मिक-an officer controlling thirty soldiers.

गौहर-hidden virtue; essence; a pearl.

गौहारी rich; manure land.

ग्रंथ-a book; a literary; composition; volume; a word.

ग्रंथकर्ता-a writer of a book; a literary man.

ग्रंथचुंबन-cursory reading of a book on a subject.

ग्रंथचोर-a plagiarist.

ग्रंथ-पढ़ना-to study; bookish; academic.

ग्रंथपूजा-biblio-latry.

ग्रंथमाला-a series of books.

ग्रंथरक्षागृह-archive.

ग्रंथसंधि-a section of a book; a chapter; a canto.

ग्रंथविद्या-bibliography.

ग्रंथसाहब-the religious book of the Sikhs.

ग्रंथसूची-catalogue.

ग्रंथालय-a library.

ग्रंथि-a gland; complex; a fixation; constriction.

ग्रस-to devour.

ग्रसना-to tease; to torment; to hold in a bad manner.

ग्रस्त-swallowed; devoured; seized.

ग्रसनी-pharynx.

ग्रसिका-oesophagus; gullet.

ग्रह-a planet; orb; star; eclipse.

ग्रहण-eclipse of the Sun or Moon; seizing.

ग्रहणशील-receptive.

ग्रहणधिकार-lien.

ग्रहणी-dysentery.

ग्रहणीय-acceptable; to be taken.

ग्रहदशा-the influence of stars on a men's fate; ill-luck; misfortune.

ग्रहपति-the Sun.

ग्रहपथ-the orbit of a planet.

ग्रंडील-huge; large; very high; grand; gigantic.

ग्राम[1]-collection; group; troop; village.

ग्राम[2]-gramme; centigramme.

ग्रामिक-rustic; rural.

ग्रामी-villager.

ग्रामीण-rural; rustic; vulgar.

ग्रामोफोन-a gramophone.

ग्राम्य-domestic; pertaining to a village; foolish; vulgar.

ग्राह-a crocodile; an alligator.

ग्राहक-a purchaser; customer; subscriber; a buyer.

ग्राहित्र-receiver.

ग्राही-receiving; valuing; taking.

ग्राह्य-acceptable; admissible; comprehensive; worthy of being received.

ग्रीखम-summer.

ग्रीव-the neck; nape of the neck.

ग्रीवा-the neck; the nape.

ग्रीष्म-summer; heat; warmth; the hot season of the year.

ग्रैव-having to do with the neck.

ग्लानि-depression of mind; sluggishness; lassitude.

ग्वारपाठा-the aloe plant.

ग्वारफली-a kind of vegetable.

ग्वाल-milkman.

ग्वालन-milk woman.

ग्वाला-a milker; milkman; cowherd; a man of community.

ग्वालिन-a milkman; a kind of insect appearing in the rainy season.

ग्वैठना-to twist; to bend; to turn; to distort.

ग्वैडों-near by near.

घ-The fourth consonant of the Devnagari alphabet.

घँगोल-white lotus; a water-lily.

घँघोरना-to impure water or anything.

घंट-an earthen pot tied to a tree in performance of funeral rites; a jug.

घंटा-chime; a clock; an hour; a bell; a period or session.

घंटिका-small bells attached to an ornament; a small bell.

घंटी-the sound of a bell; a small bell; a small metal pot.

घई-support; saddle; stay; a whirlpool; an eddy.

घघरवेल-a kind of creeper.

घघरा-a long loose skirt worn round the lions.

घट-a jug; a water pot.

घटक-a marriage broker or go-between; accomplishing; messenger; representative.

घटका-the rattling sound in the throat of a dying person.

घटती-diminution; deficiency; defalcation; decrease; lessening; degradation.

घटन-occurring; happening; forming; making accomplishing; making.

घटना[1]-event; incident; a happening.

घटना[2]-to decrease; to be reduced; to lessen; to be deducted.

घटनीय-able or likely to happen; possible; probable.

घटबढ़-variation; fluctuation.

घटवाना-to cause to be decreased.

घटवार-a wharf owner; boatman; a wharfinger.

घटा-a troop; a forbidding assemblage; a dense cloud.

घटाई-decrease; decline; diminution; degradation.

घटाव-diminution; reduction; subtraction; mitigation; retrenchment; decrease.

घटिका-a water-jar; water-clock; a jar.

घटित-happened; prepared; made; chanced.

घटिया-inferior; of poor quality.

घटुक, घटोत्कच-dishonest; cunning; fraudulent; artful; the name of son.

घटौती-rebate.

घट्टा-loss; a breach; gap; a wound.

घट्ठा-hard tumour on the body made by a rub; corn on the feet; a gap; an opening.

घड़त-to make.

घड़नई-a raft which is made of inverted pitches for fording small rivers.

घड़ना-to forge; to fabricate.

घड़ा-an earthen pot; a pail; a pitcher; a crock; a jug.

घड़िया-a crucible in which goldsmith melt gold or silver.

घड़ियाल-crocodile or gavial.

घड़ी-an instrument to measure time; a watch.

घड़ोला-a small earthen pot.

घड़ौंची-a stool for placing a jug of water.

घत-a cheat; deceiver; ambuscade.

घन-sledge-hammer; cloud; crowd; assembly; bell; gong.

घनकोण-solid angle.

घनगरज-a kind of cannon; thundering of clouds.

घनता-thickness; solidity.

घनघनाना-to clink; to jingle; to murmur; to rumble (as machinery).

घनघोर-roaring of clouds; loud sounding; fearful; terrible; very thick; deep.

घनचक्कर-a dullard; a stupid fellow; wandering; lurking.

घनता-denseness; thickness; hardness; firmness; impenetrability.

घनत्व-density.

घनफल-volume; the cubic contents of a solid.

घनमूल-the cube-root.

घनश्याम-black clouds.

घनसार-mercury; camphor.

घना-dense; thick; heavy; coarse; impenetrable.

घनाक्षरी-written in close characters.

घनापन-density.

घनिष्ठ-compact; thick; intimate; close; neighbouring.

घनीभूत-grumous; solid.

घने-many, several.

घनेरा-much, many.

घनेश-a kind of bird.

घपची-clutch with both hands; a grasp.

घपला-disorder; entanglement; perplexity; turmoil; duplicity; fraud.

घबड़ाना-to embarrass.

घबराना-to be confused; to be embarrassed; to be flustered; to be perplexed.

घबराहट-disorder; perplexity; flurry; confusion.

घमंड-pride; arrogance; conceit; vanity.

घमकना-to roar; to produce a grave sound.-to give a blow with a fist.

घमका-the noise of a blow.

घमर-a sound as of a drum.

घमरौला-crowd; turmoil; confusion; affray.

घमस-heat; warmth; sultriness of weather.

घमसान-a battle; a skirmish; a fierce fight.

घमाका-the sound produced by a heavy blow.

घमाघम-sound of lively activity; sound of repeated blows.

घमाना-to bask in the Sun; to warm oneself in the Sun.

घमोई-a kind of prickly plant having yellow flowers.

घमोरी-small pimples which appears on the body in sultry days; prickly heat.

घर-a house; dwelling; building; tenement; family; residence; compartment; birthplace.

घरघर in very home.

घरजाया-a slave who is born in the house.

घरदासी-the mistress of house; wife (slave of house).

घरद्वार-a household; a dwelling place; house.

घरफोड़ना-to create a family feud quarrel.

घरफोरी-a woman who creates quarrels in the family.

घरबसा-husband; paramour.

घरबार-family; one's household goods; household affairs; anxieties of a household.

घरवाल-household goods.

घरवाला-husband; master of a house.

घरसा-friction.

घरहाई-a woman who creates disturbance in the family.

घराऊ-personnel; domestic.

घराती-colloq. belonging to a bride's wedding party; one of the party.

घराना-a household; a family.

घरिया-a crucible of goldsmith; a small pot.

घरीक for a short time; a while.

घरेलू-domestic; personal; tame; prepared at home.

घरैया-domestic; intimate; personal.

घरौंदा-a play house (built by children); a small or frail house.

घरौंधा-a toy house.

घर्म-the heat of the Sun; perspiration.

घर्रा-the rattling sound in the throat of a dying person; agony; a king of engine; pang.

घर्राटा-a snore.

घर्षण-grinding; attrition; friction; rubbing.

घलना-to tumble; to fall; to come to blows; to be discharge from a missile.

घलुआ-given a buyer additional to his purchase.

घवरि-a bunch of fruits.

घसकना-to lapse; to glide; to slip; to steal.

घसकाना-to agitate; to remove from a place.

घसखुदा-a grass-cutter; a foolish person; an idle person.

घसिटना-to be dragged or pulled.

घसियारा-a scraper or cutter of grass; seller of grass.

घसीट-dragging; track; trace (of dragged along); scrubbed writing.

घसीटना-to trail; to drag; to pull hard; to hug; to include forcibly; to scribble; to lug.

घसेरा-a grass cutter.

घहनाना-to peal or sound forth as a bell; to tinkle.

घहराना-to thunder; to rumble; to bellow; to roar; to surge (of clouds).

घहरानि-a thundering or pealing sound; a roar.

घहरारा-a roar; a loud sound.

घाँ-space between two fingers.

घाँघर-a loose skirt which is worn round the lion.

घाँह-direction.

घाइ-wound; hurt.

घाई[1]-a turn; side; direction; a time.

घाई[2]-the angle or space between two fingers.

घाऊघप-improvident; heedless; spendthrift.

घाग-cunning person.

घाघ-experienced; clever; cunning.

घाघरा-ankle-length skirt; an ample; a loose skirt which is worn by woman round the lion.

घाघस-a kind of hen.

घाट-a landing place; ferry; deception blade of a sword.

घाटरोह-hindrance or obstruction of wharfage.

घाटा-loss; a reduction; decline; a decrease; fall (of price); shortfall.

घाटी-a mountain pass; a valley; a slope.

घात-push; stroke; harm; killing; slaughter; multiple; product; a blow; a bruise.

घातक-killing; destructive; savage (an animal); murderous (as of blow); damaging.

घातन-killing; murdering.

घाता-additional thrown in addition to a buyer's purchase.

घाती-murderous; ruinous; harmful; treacherous.

घातुक-nocuous; ruinous; murderous; pestiferous.

घान-the quantity thrown in at one time in a mill; boiled or fried at a time; stroke; a blow.

घानी-batch; outrun; output of a mill.

घाबरा-confused; perplexed; astounded; bewildered.

घाम-heat and light of the Sun; glare; sunstroke; oppressiveness; difficulty; sultriness.

घायल-hurt; injured; wounded; smitten.

घालक-a killer; one who destroys or lays waste.

घास-grass; fodder; hay; straw.-one who scrapes up grass for fodder. -grass and chaff, fodder. refuse.

घिनाना-to feel disgusted for; to have an aversion for.

घिरना-to be surrounded; to be filled; to be accumulated; to be collected around.

घिरनी-a wheel or instrument for twisting ropes; a pulley; the tumbling pigeon.

घिराई-work of surrounding.

घिरायँद-stench of urine.

घिसकना-to slide; to steer; to slip; to move along.

घिसन-friction; rubbing; damage.

घिसना-to rub; to wear out.

घिस-पिस-mutual friendship; close contact.

घिसाई-the work or wages for rubbing or smoothing an object; hard labour.

घिसाव-friction; abrasion; rubbing.

घिस्सा-thrust push; friction; attrition; a drag; a kick; a trick in wrestling.

घी-butter clarified by boiling and straining.

घुग्घी-a piece of blanket of cloth folded like a cone which villages put on their heads to protect themselves from rain or sun.

घुग्घु-an owl.

घुघुआना to mew like a cat; to hoot like a owl.

घुटकना-to bolt; to embezzle; to gulp down.

घुटन-suffocation; sultriness; choking; oppressiveness.

घुटना[1]-to be polished; to be rubbed.

घुटना[2]-the knee; region of the knee.

घुटन्ना-trousers.

घुटवाना-to cause to be rubbed; to be shaved; to be tonsure.

घुटाई-cost or charge of polishing or shaving; smoothness; polishing.

घुट्टी-a digestive medicine given to new born babies.

घुड़कना-to browbeat; to frown at; to reprimand.

घुड़की-growling; scolding; snarling; reprimand; rebuke.

घुड़कीबाज-bully.

घुड़बहल-a chariot which is drawn by horses.

घुणाक्षर न्याय-a happening by chance; a chance product.

घुन-a woodlouse; a weevil.

घुनना-to be attacked by weevils; to be consumed (as by illness; grief).

घुन्ना-malicious; sullen; spiteful; secretive.

घुप-pitch-dark; obscure.

घुप्प-dense; thick (of darkness).

घुमंतू-always moving; restless.

घुमक्कड़-a rover; vagabond; straggler; a tomboy.

घुमटा-giddiness.

घुमड़-accumulation of raining water.

घुमड़ना-to gather; to grow thick (as of clouds).

घुमड़ी-turning; spinning; a whirlpool.

घुमान-a whirl; a maze; a meander; a turn.

घुमाना-to revolve; to swirl; to rotate; to spin; to circulate; to roll.

घुमाव-a turning; curvature; spin; sweep.

घुरघुरा-a mole-cricket.

घुरना-to sound; to ring.

घुर्मित-roaming; wandering.

घुलन-dissolving; mixing; melting.

घुलना-to be dissolved in a liquid; to be melted; to be lean and thin; to be liquified; to waste.

घुलावट-act of dissolving.

घुसना-to step in; to go in; to penetrate; to enter to pierce; to intrude; to thrust into.

घुसाना-to penetrate; to obtrude.

घुसेड़ना-to cause to penetrate.

घूँगची-small red and black seed.

घूँगर-curly hair.

घूँगरू-a set of small jingling bells worn around the ankles during a dance performance.

घूँघट-a veil which conceals the face.

घूँघनी-wheat, gram or peas soaked and boiled with spices.

घूँघर-a type of ring in hair.

घूँट-a sip; a draught.

घूँटना-to swallow; to gulp.

घूँटी-a medicine given to new-born babied for clearing the bowels.

घूर[1]-a rubbish heap; trash; a manure pit; a fire of dung or rubbish.

घूर[2]-a stare; a glare; frown.

घूरना-to ogle; to stare; to gloat; to roam.

घूरा-a dung-heap; a temporary fireplace; stove.

घूर्ण-rotation.

घूस[1]-a bandicoot rat.

घूस[2]-a bribe.

घृणा-aversion; hatred; abhorrence; disdain.

घृताची-clarified butter.

घेंटा-a piglet.

घेंघरा-an unripe pod.

घेंघा-a swelling in the neck; goitre.

घेतला-sandal; slipper.

घेर-circuit; circumference; boundary.

घेरना-to encircle; to surround; to hedge in; to confine.

घेरनी-the handle of a spinning wheel.

घेरवा-a mortgage in which land is held as security and in payment of the interest.

घेरा-circumference; enclosure; skirt; fence.

घेराव-encirclement.

घेवर-a kind of sweetmeat.

घैया-the cream accumulated from fresh milk.

घैर, घैरू, घैरो-infamy; secret complaint; a slander; calumny.

घोंगा-snail.

घोंघा-conch; slug; snail; oyster.

घोंपना-to pierce; to penetrate; to stitch badly.

घोंसला-a bird's nest; nidus.

घोखना-to repeat; to learn by heart; to commit to memory; to reiterate.

घोघा-a kind of worm.

घोट-a horse.

घोटना-to rub for smothering and polishing; to learn a lesson by heart; to grind to powder; to pulverize; to rebuke; to stifle.

घोटाई-the work of wages which is paid for polishing.

घोटाला-confusion (in affairs); disorder; scandal.

घोड़दौड़-a horse-race; a place of horse racing.

घोड़सवार-rider; ranger.

घोड़साल-a stable; mews.

घोड़ा-a horse; trigger; hammer (of a gun); a character in chess.

घोड़ा गाड़ी-a carriage which is drawn by horses.

घोड़ानस-a strong gristle at the ankle of a person.

घोड़िया-a small mare; a bracket or peg for the wall.

घोड़ी-a female horse.

घोपा-a way of folding a blanket over the head against cold or rain.

घोर[1]-frightful; terrible; awesome; extreme; intense; deep; huge; violent; harsh; vehement.

घोर[2]-to make a rumbling.

घोरता-frightfulness; vehemence; intensity; awesomeness.

घोरिला-a hobby horse.

घोरी-filthy; detestable.

घोल-a solution; emulsion.

घोलना-to mix in (with a liquid); to dissolve; to melt; to shake.

घोष-sound; roaring.

घोषक-an announcer.

घोषणा-a declaration; announcement.

घोषित-announced; proclaimed.

घोषित मूल्य-declared valuation.

घोसिन-the wife of a herdsman.

घोसी-a Mohammedan milkman.

घौद-cluster (of grapes, bananas); bunch.

घौरी-a cluster; bunch.

घ्न-striking; killing; destroying.

घ्राण-the nose; smelling; odour.

घ्रात-sniffed; smelt; smelled.

ङ

ङ-(*na*) The fifth consonant of the Devnagari alphabet, the nasal letter of the guttural group, it is never used as an initial letter in a word.

च

च-The sixth consonant of the Devnagari alphabet and the first letter of the palatal class.

च-a thief; a tortoise; the moon; a wicked person.

चंक्र-complete; whole; entire.

चक्रमण-wandering; roaming about here and there.

चंग-a paper kite; crooked or bent; Jew's harp; a musical instrument resembling a tambourine; a streamer attached to a kite.

चंगना-to tighten; to draw; to tease; to pull; to torment.

चंगा-sound, right (the heart, or way or thought), well, good; pure; healthy.

चंगुल-claws (of a wild beast); talons (of a bird of prey); grasp; clutch; clutching hands.

चंचल-moving; shaking; trembling; inconstant; fickle; giddy; playful; naughty; transient; quick; active; unsteady; restless; ephemeral.

चंडू-a place where smokers gathers to smoke; a preparation of opium smoked for intoxication; perfectly false statement.

चंद-a few; some.

चंदक-the moon; moon light; an ornament which is worn on the forehead; a setting on the nose-ring; a kind of fish.

चंदन-sandalwood; an ornament which is worn on the head.

चंदनौता-a kind of lower garment worn by women.

चंदराना-to beguile; to deceive.

चँदला-bald.

चँदवर-glabrous; bald-headed.

चँदवा-a small canopy or wing crown; top (as of a hat).

चंदा-the moon; subscription; contribution.

चंदावती-a kind of song.

चंदिक, चंदिनि, चंदिनी-moonlight.

चँदिया-colloq. the crown of the head.

चँदिर-the moon.

चंदेरी-moon; elephant; a costly cotton cloth.

चंदेल-a caste.

चंद्र-the moon; water; gold; diamond; camphor.

चंद्रक-the moon; nail; camphor; a circular object.

चंद्रकला-one sixteenth part of the moon's circumference; an ornament worn on the heat.

चंद्रकान्त-the moon-stone.

चंद्रकान्ता-night; the name of the wife of moon.

चंद्रधनु-the rainbow sometimes seen at night.

चंद्रप्रभा-the moonlight.

चंद्रबिब-the disk of the moon.

चंद्रमणि-the moon-stone.

चंद्रमा-the moon.

चंद्रलोक-the sphere of the moon.

चंद्रवार-Monday.

चंद्रहार-a kind of necklace.

चंद्रहास-a sword.

चन्द्रा-wise; intelligent; moonlight; a canopy.

चंद्रिका-moonlight; the eyes of peacock's tail; cardamom; an ornament of head; a goddess.

चन्द्रोदय-the rising of the moon; an medicine; canopy.

चम्पई-of the colour of flower; deep yellow.

चँप-to crouch; to creep; to be pressed or trodden down; to lie hidden.

चंपई-having the colour of the flower; yellowish; golden; orange.

चंपक-a garland of flowers; a necklace.

चंपत-invisible; vanished; lying concealed.

चंपा-a yellow fragrant flower.

चँपी-massage; shampoo.

चंबल-an ebb; an appliance for lifting the water of a dike for irrigation.

चँबेली-jasmine.

चँवर-a flapper made of the tail of wild ox which is waved over the head to drive away flies; a servant who waves this flappers; a whisk.

चंसुर-a medicinal plant.

चउहट्ट-a crossing of four roads.

चउतरा-a platform.

चक-a kind of toy for boys; a plot of ground; wheel; discuss; a small village; abundance.

चकई[1]-child's toy resembling a yo-yo.

चकई[2]-the female bird.

चकचका-resplendent; shining.

चकचकी-an old type of Indian tumbrel.

चकचाना-to have glaring effects produced in eyes.

चकचाल-rotation; a whirl.

चकचौंध-dazzling effect; dazzlement.

चकचौंहना-to gaze at something with fixed look.

चकता-a scar; a slice; a patch.

चकती-a round or squarish piece (as of cloth, leather or metal); plate; lump; a patch.

चकत्ता-a scar; the mark which is made by biting or flogging; a blotch on the skin.

चकना-to startle; to be afraid; to be amazed.

चकनाचूर-broken into fragments; much weary; bruised.

चकफेरी-wandering in a circuitous path.

चकबंदी-marking the boundaries of plots of land.

चकमक-flint.

चकमा-trick; loss; damage; deception.

चकद-a kind of lark; a kind of sparrow.

चकरबा-uproar; quarrel.

चकरवा-a difficult situation; perplexity.

चकरा-an eddy.

चकराना-to revolve; to be confused; to be amazed; to be surprised; to feel dizzy.

चकरानी-a woman servant.

चकलई-breadth.

चकला-a district; residence of prostitute; pastry-board; mill.

चकलाना-to expand; to widen or make broad.

चकलेदार-an officer who has the charge to collect revenue in landed property.

चकल्लस-turmoil; uproar; fuss.

चकवाना-to be amazed.

चकवी-a female bird.

चकसेनी-a kind of medicinal plant.

चकहा-a wheel.

चक्रपाल-an officer who collect revenue of landed properties.

चक्रपूजा-a special kind of worship performed by

चक्रफल-a missile with a globular point.

चक्रबंधु-the Sun.

चक्रबान्धव-an epithet of Sun.

चक्रमंडल-reel; a kind of dance in a circle.

चक्रमुख-a boar; a pig.

चक्रवर्ती-an emperor; a universal monarch.

चक्रवात-a whirlwind; a cyclone.

चक्रवृद्धि-compound interest.

चक्रव्यूह-an array of soldiers in the form of a square or circle.

चक्रांत-a secret intrigue.

चक्रांश-three hundred and sixtieth part of a circle.

चक्राकार-circular.

चक्राट-a cheat; a juggler.

चक्रावल-a disease of horses legs.

चक्री-a wielder of discus ; the village priest; a potter; a snake; a spy; an oilman; an emperor.

चक्रीय-circular; cyclical; ring-shaped.

चक्षु-the eye; quarrel; discord; variance.

चक्षुष्य-beneficial to the eyes; good-looking; beautiful; ocular.

चख़-uproar; quarrelling.

चखना-to cause to taste.

चखाचखी-quarrel; discord; strife; variance.

चखाहा-colloq. a herdsman.

चखिया-quarrelsome.

चखु-the eye.

चखोड़ा-the black mark on baby's head made by Hindu woman to preserve baby from influence of an evil eye.

चखौती-delicacy; a savoury or tasty morsel.

चगड़-clever; cunning.

चचर-ploughed after lying fallow (land).

चचा-the paternal uncle.

चचींडा-the snake-gourd.

चचेरा-descended from a paternal uncle.

चचोड़ना-to suck.

चट instantly; quickly; at once.

चटक[1]-briskly; cleverly; adroitly.

चटक[2]-a kind of sparrow.

चटकना-to make a sound of breaking up; to snap; to be split; to crack; to be burst.

चटकनी-the bolt of a door.

चटकवाई-quickness.

चटकारा-the sound made by licking something; glittering; lustrous; agile; fast.

चटकाली-a flight of birds.

चटकी-an earthen pot with wide mouth.

चटकीला-splendid; bright; showy; charming; delightful; gaudy; meretricious; pungent; tasty; sharp.

चटखनी-a latch; bolt.

चटखारना-relishing experience of the tongue.

चटखारा-a clack of the tongue with the palate.

चटना-to be tasted; voracious.

चटनी-sauce; condiment; to reduce to a fine powder.

चटपट smartly; quickly.

चटपटा-delicious; pungent; saucy.

चटपटी-quickness; smartness; restlessness.

चट्टान-a rock; a crag; a piece of rock or mineral.

चट्टी[1]-an open-heeled sandal.

चट्टी[2]-shortcoming; lack; loss (as in trade); damage; expense; fine; charge.

चड्ढा-a fool; a clown.

चड़-बड़-chattering; babbling.

चड़ाक-snapped; broken.

चड्डा-the upper thigh.

चड्डी-underwear; a type of loincloth.

चड्ढी-mounting; riding; a children's game of piggyback.

चढ़त-an offering to a God.

चढ़ती-rise; advance; increase; superiority.

चढ़न-mounting; ascending.

चढ़ाऊ-capable of being climbed.

चढ़ाना-to mount; to help in ascending; to cause to ascend or climb.

चढ़ाव-rise; ascension; ascent; acclivity; flood.

चढ़ैत-one who mounts; a mounted soldier; a horseman.

चढ़ैया-a climber; one who ascends; one who lifts; a horsemen.

चढ़ौवा-a shoe having a high heel.

चण्ड-strong; hard; fierce; irritable; ferocious; arrogant.

चण्डकर-having strong rays.

चण्डता-fierceness; ferociousness; arrogance.

चण्डदीधिति-the Sun.

चण्डा-quarrelsome; arrogant.

चण्डातक-a woman's bodice.

चण्डालता-wickedness; villainy.

चण्डालिनी-a wicked woman.

चण्डिका-goddess .

चण्डीपति-an epithet of lord .

चण्डेश्वर-one of the horrible form of lord .

चतुरंग-an army consisting of horses; chariots and infantry; chess; elephant.

चतुर-active; quick; skilful; clever; sagacious; adroit; shrewd; cunning.

चतुरता-shrewdness; cleverness.

चतुराई-quickness; cleverness; alertness; dexterity; skill; cunning; shrewdness.

चतुरस्त्र-four-sided.

चतुर्गण-quadruple; of four qualities; four fold.

चतुर्थ-fourth.

चतुर्वर्गीय-quadratic.

चतुर्दशी-the fourteenth day of lunar month.

चतुर्दिक-the four quarters.

चतुर्भुज-four-sides (figure); quadrilateral; tetragon.

चतुर्भुजा-a goddess.

चतुर्भुजी-the four-armed one; the goddess .

चतुर्मास-the four months of the rainy season.

चतुर्मुख-four-faced.

चतुर्वर्ग-the four human pursuits; sensual enjoyment and salvation; wealth; virtue.

चतुष्कोण-having four angles; quadrangular.

चतुष्टय-an aggregate of four things.

चतुष्तय-having four folds or four parts; a quartet.

चतुष्पथ-a place where four roads meet.

चतुष्पद-four-footed.

चतुष्पदा-a stanza consisting of four lines.

चत्वर-a place where four roads meet.

चनक-gram.

चनकना-to burst up as the husk of a seed.

चन्दन-sandalwood.

चन्दनहार-an ornament which is worn round the neck.

चन्द्र-the moon; diamond; camphor; pearl with rosy tinge.

चन्द्रक-the halo of light round the moon; the moon; camphor; a kind of song.

चन्द्रकला-the moonlight.

चन्द्रकान्त-the moon-gem; lily.

चन्द्रकान्ता-the wife of moon.

चन्द्रगोलिका-moonlight.

चन्द्रद्युति-sandal; moonlight.

चन्द्रधनु-the rainbow which is sometimes seen at night when the moon is shining.

चन्द्रप्रभा-moonlight; camphor.

चन्द्रबंधु-a conch; lily.

चन्द्रवधू-an insect of brilliant red colour; lady-bird.

चन्द्रबाण-a kind of crescent-shaped arrow.

चन्द्रबाला-small cardamom; moonlight.

चन्द्रबिन्दु-the nasal sound which is represented by placing the sign over a letter in Devnagari script.

चन्द्रभा-the light of the moon's rays.

चन्द्रवंशी-one who is born in the lunar race.

चन्द्रवार-Monday.

चन्द्रवाला-a bigger variety of cardamom.

चन्द्रहास-sword; scimitar.

चन्द्रा-small cardamom; a canopy.

चन्द्रिका-jasmine flower; moonlight; name of goddess; an ornament for the head.

चन्द्रोदय-a canopy; the rising of the moon; a medicine of this name.

चकपन-a close-fitting jacket.

चकपना-to stick someone.

चककुलिश-difficulty; a difficult situation.

चपटा-flat; pressed flat; shallow and broad.

चपटाना-to press flat or even.

चपड़ना-to evade; to slip away.

चपड़ा-a kind of red insect; shellac.

चपड़ासी-a peon; an orderly.

चपत-a slap; push; loss.

चपना-to be pressed; to be squeezed; to be crushed; compressed; to be abashed; to be intimated.

चपल-tremulous; restless; unsteady; active; agile; swift; inconstant; volatile; fickle.-an unsteady person.

चपलता-variability; fickleness; nimbleness; frivolity; flippancy.

चपलाना-to move; to oscillate.-to stir; to waver.

चपली-slippers.

चपाती-a thin cake of bread.

चपेट-a slap; a blow; attack.

चप्पा-a fourth part; span; a small portion; a hand's breadth.

चप्पी-massaging the limbs.

चप्पू-a paddle; a oar.

चफाल-a piece of ground which is surrounded by a bog.

चबक-a shoot or throb of pain.

चबकना-to feel severe pain.

चबकी-braided silk or wool used for tying a woman's hair.

चबना-to be chewed.-gristle; cartilage.

चबाना-to chew; to munch; to masticate.

चबारा-a room in the uppermost storey of a house.

चबूतरा-terrace; platform; stand; rostrum; dais; stage.

चबेना-parched grain; something to be chewed.

चबोड़-bruised.

चभक-stinging; pricking.

चभना-to be crushed or chewed.

चभोरना-to dip; to drown in water; to drench.

चमक-glitter; a flash; sparkle; gleam; splendour; brilliance; a sudden or startled impulse (as of fear).

चमकनी-an irritable woman.

चमकारा-brilliant; dazzling.

चमकारी-bright.

चमकीला-brilliant; glittering; splendid; sparkling.

चमकौवल-work of burnishing; ogling; coquetting.

चमक्की-a coquettish woman; a termagant; a lewd woman.

चमगीदड़-a bat; a vampire.

चम-चम a sweetmeat.

चमचमाना-to shine; to glitter; to spark; to brighten.

चमचा-a large spoon; a ladle; flatterer.

चमची-a small spoon; spatula.

चमजुई-anything the incessantly accompanies some one; a kind of dog-flea.

चमटा-tongs; pincer.

चमड़ा-skin; leather; hide.

चमड़ी-skin.

चमत्कार-wonder; amazement; astonishment; surprise; splendour.

चमत्कारिक-wonderful.

चमत्कारित-astonishing nature or quality.

चमत्कारी-amazing; marvellous; astonishing; wonderful; unusual.

चमत्कृत-astonished.

चमत्कृति-wonder; surprise.

चमन-a place lush or abounding in flowers; a flower garden.

चमरख-a piece of leather fitted in a spinning wheel through which the thread passes.

चमरशिखा-the crest of horse's head.

चमरावत-a leather-worker's fee or payment in kind.

चमरी-a yak cow.

चमला-a begging bowl.

चमस-a sacrificial pot in the form of a large spoon.

चमाइन-a village midwife.

चमीकर-a gold-mine.

चमू-a squadron; a fleet; division of an army.

चमेलिया-of the colour of Jasmine flower.

चमेली-the Jasmine.

चमोकन-a body louse.

चमोटी-a whip; flog.

चमौवा-cheap leather shoe.

चम्मच-a spoon.

चय-heap; mass; multitude, collection; mound; boundary wall; a fort; foundation of a house; platform.

चयन-selection.

चयापचय-metabolism.

चर-a secret messenger; a spy; sound made when tearing cloth.

चरक-white leprosy.

चरकटा-a chaff-cutter.

चरका-a scratch loss; a slight wound; trick; fraud.

चरख-a spinning wheel; a revolving wheel; a lathe.

चरखा-a revolving wheel; a spinning wheel; a reel.

चरचना-to anoint body with sandal paste.

चरट-a wagtail.

चरड़-चरड़-a crackling sound.

चरचारी-one who censures; a prattler.

चरजना-to cheat; to make an inference; to seduce.

चरण-the foot; a line of poverty; root; clan; order; custom; a quarter part of anything.

चरबा-a sketch; a copy; counterfoil (of receipt).

चरबी-fat; suet; grease; tallow.

चरम-final; ultimate; last.

चरवाई-wages paid for grazing the animal.

चरवान-to cause to graze.

चरवाहा-shepherd; a herdsman.

चरस-an intoxicating drug prepared from the flower of hemp; a large bucket of leather used in irrigation; a wild peacock; length of 210 cubits used in measuring land.

चरसा-a large leather bucket or bag.

चरसी[1]-one who smokes.

चरसी[2]-one who irrigates a field with a leather bucket.

चरा-grazing; pasture.

चराई-the work or wages paid for grazing; pasturage.

चरान-pasture land.

चराना-to pasture; to graze; to entice by prattling; to make a fool of.

चरावर-useless gossip.

चरित-character; conduct; disposition of mind; occupation; work; demeanour; an account of the deeds of any one.

चरितार्थ-contented; successful; gratified; satisfied.

चरित्तर-trick; mimicry; coquetry.

चरित्र-behaviour; manner; conduct; ways; an account of a person life; a biography.

चरी-green plant which are used as fodder for cattle; a grazing ground.

चरुअ-a large earthen pot.

चरुखला-a spinning wheel.

चरुपात्र-a pot in which food for sacrifice is cooked.

चरेरा-rough and hard; harsh.

चरोखर-pasture; a meadow; .

चरोतर-life tenancy.

चर्खा-a jenny.

चर्चन-a rumour; a hearsay.

चर्चरी-a song sung in the spring season; merry-making; clapping of hands.

चर्चा-report; rumour; talk; remark; mention; hearsay; smearing the body with an unguent.

चर्चित-discussed; smeared.

चर्पट-the palm of the hand; a slap on the face.

चर्पटी-a kind of thin cake.

चर्पर-acrid.

चर्भटी-cucumber.

चर्भटा-report; talk; a kind of song.

चर्म-leather; tanner; shield.

चर्मकार-a shoe-maker; a tanner; a cobbler.

चर्मकील-piles.

चर्मचक्षु-ordinary sight (as opposed to inner sight).

चर्मचटका-a flying-fox; a bat.

चर्मचित्रक-leprosy.

चर्मज-hair; blood.

चर्मण्वती-the plantain tree; a river.

चर्मतरंग-wrinkles which appears on the skin.

चर्मदंड-a whip or strap made of leather.

चर्मदूषिका-a leather whip or thong; ringworm.

चर्मदेहा-a kind of bagpipe.

चर्मपादुका-leather shoes.

चर्मपीडिका-a kind of measles or smallpox.

चर्मपुट-a large bottle of leather.

चर्मप्रभेदिका-a chisel for leather cutting.

चर्मबंध-a thong of leather.

चर्मपय-full of leather; leathery.

चर्ममुण्डा-the goddess .

चर्मार-shoe maker; cobbler.

चर्मी-made of lather.

चर्य-able to be done or performed by a person.

चर्या-manner of behaviour; work; occupation; an activity or routine.

चर्राना-to ache; to smart; to burst.

चर्री-an ironical remark.

चर्वण-something which is chewed; parched cereals or grain; masticating.

चर्वित-repeating of something already told or done.

चल-movable; mobile; unsteady; inconstant; transient.

चलचलाव-starting on a journey; departure; death.

चलाचल-inconstant; unsteady.

चलचूक-trick; fraud; a cunningness.

चलंता-valid; current coin saleable.

चलता-going; continuous; current; prevalent; workable.

चलती-sphere of action; authority; influence.

चलन-moving; proceeding; gait; mien; trembling.

चलना-to proceed; to walk; to pass; to pace.

चलनी-sieve; riddle.

चलपत्र-the Indian holy fig tree.

चलविचल-misplaced; put in disorder; deranged.

चलवैया-one who causes to move; one who moves; one who walks or goes about much.

चला-earth; lightning; the goddess .

चलाऊ-durable; lasting; serving; adequate; make shift; allowing completion (as of a task).

चलाक-cunning; clever.

चलाका-lightning.

चलाचल-motion to and fro; inconstant.

चलान-prosecution; an invoice holder.

चलाना-to set in motion; to stir; to move; to cause to pass; to drive; to impel; to propel; to actuate.

चलायमान-in motion; newly under way (as a vehicle).

चलाव-a journey; habit.

चलावा-custom.

चलित-movable; unsteady; wavering; fickle; moving.

चलैया-motion; second marriage; custom; behaviour.

चलौना-a stick (for turning a spinning-wheel); a ladle (for stirring).

चवर्ग-the palatal.

चवा-wind which is blowing in all directions.

चवाई-a defamer; a slanderer; a back-biter.

चवाव-hearsay; rumour; slander; defame.

चव्य-a pepper plant; a medicine.

चश्म-the organ of sight; the eye.

चश्मा-spectacle; eye-glasses; a spring; a fountain.

चष-the eye.

चषक-wine-cup; a drinking-vessel.

चषचोल-the eyelid.

चषति-border of cloth.

चस-to be divided or split.

चसक-throbbing pain; ache.

चसका-an ardent desire; habit; taste; pleasure; relish.

चसना-to be joined together; to burn or split.

चस्का-addiction; inclination; taste; relish; ardent desire; habit; vice.

चस्पाँ-sticking or stuck; adhering.

चह-pier-head (at a river crossing); a platform.

चहक-warbling of singing of birds.

चहचहा-singing (of birds); warbling; chatter; merriment; chirping; loud laughter.

चहचहिया-whistler; warbler.

चहना-to wish; to like; to look.

चहबच्चा-a sump; a drainage; a cistern; a cesspool.

चहर-merriment; jollity; tumult; uproar.

चहल[1]-festivity; merriment.

चहल[2]-a heavy damp soil not needing ploughing; a moist; loam.

चाँडिल-strong; powerful; obstinate; excessive; impertinent.

चाँद-the moon; a crescent shaped ornament; the middle part of cranium.

चाँदतारा-a kind of fine muslin on which stars of coloured silk are woven; a kind of kite.

चाँदना-moonlight; light.

चाँदनी-moonlight; white cloth spread over a carpet; bed-sheet; a canopy.

चाँदा-a particular marked point.

चाँदी-silver; argent.

चाँदीला-a bald person.

चाँद्र-pertaining to or influenced by the moon.

चांद्रमास-a lunar month.

चाँप-a bow; arc; sound (food).

चाँपना-to compel; to press.

चाँवल-rice.

चाइयाँ-tricky (customer).

चाई[1]-scurf; scab; mange.

चाई[2]-a cunning trickster; name of a community of low status.

चाक-a wheel; a potter's wheel; a pulley.

चाकना-to affix distinctive marks on an object; to draw the boundary lines.

चाकर-servant.

चाकरी-attendance; service.

चाकू-a pocket-knife.

चाक्षुष-perceived by sight; visual examination; pertaining to eye.

चाख-the eye.

चाखना-to taste.

चाचर-fuss; making revelry; disturbance; rioting; a song sung at the Holy festival.

चाचा-paternal Uncle.

चाची-paternal Aunt.

चाट-propensity; an appetiser; licking; tasting; a taste; relish taste of inclination.

चाटी-pitcher; churn; an earthen vessel.

चाटु-flattery; favourable conversation.

चाटू-gluttonous; greedy; discriminating.

चांड-desire; wish.

चाड़ी-slander.

चाढ़ा-beloved by one; an object of love.

चातक-a kind of cuckoo which is supposed to drink only drops of rain.

चातुर-clever.

चातुरिक-a charioteer.

चातुरी-cleverness; accomplishment; skill.

चातुर्य-wisdom; skill; dexterity; cleverness.

चादर-a sheet; a coverlet; a tick; mantle, veil; counterpane; valance.

चाप[1]-a bow; a bend of bow.

चाप[2]-footsteps; the sound of footsteps; pressure; pressing.

चापजरीब-a kind of measurement of a field.

चापट-bran; husk.

चापड़-level devastated; flattened by being pressed or squeeze; ruined.

चापदंड-the stick used for propelling a thing forward.

चापना-to press; to clasp.

चापलूस-sycophant; a flatterer.

चापल्य-quickness of movement; fickleness; volatility (of temperament); mobility.

चापी-the God ; an archer.

चापू-a kind of hilly goat with a soft fur.

चाफन्द-a kind of fishing net.

चाब-molar teeth; a kind of medicinal plant and its fruit.

चाबना-to masticate; to eat food; to chew.

चाबी-a key; to lock; a wedge; to wind up (as a clock).

चाबुक-a scourge; a whip; a crop; a thrash; lash; exciting talk; hunter.

चाम-hide; leather; skin.

चामर-a fly-whisk.

चाय-tea.

चायक-desirous; willing.

चार-four; several; some.

चारक-a spy; a secret messenger.

चारखाना-chequered cloth.

चारजामा-saddle-cloth.

चारदा-a quadruped.

चारदीवारी-an enclosure; a courtyard.

चारपाई-a bedstead.

चारबाग-a square garden.

चारवा-quadruped; cattle.

चारा-food for cattle; fodder; provender; posture; forage.

चारित-behaving; conducting.

चरित्र-traditional rites; habit; conduct.

चारी-moving; going; conducting; acting; behaving; roaming.

चारु-welcome; lovely; graceful; elegant; agreeable; name of ' son.

चारुफला-creeper of grapes; vine.

चारुहासी-a woman laughing beautifully.

चालू-current; in progress; continuing; in working order; available; active.

चाल्ह-a kind of fish.

चाव-desire; ambition; ardent; affection; favour; enthusiasm; merriment; contentiousness; pleasure; eagerness; love.

चावल-rice; cooked rice; a grain-like rice.

चाशनी-a taste; a syrup; flavour (as of one substance with another); to watch (boiling) syrup.

चाष-the blue jay; eye.

चास-to plough; one ploughing (of a field).

चासा-a cultivator; a farmer; a ploughman.

चाह-desire; wish; eagerness; need; choice; fancy; will; volition; longing; affection; fondness.

चाहक-owing; due.

चाहत-desire.

चाहना-to desire; to need; to want; to demand; to love; to look; to like; to want.

चाहा-sandpiper; a snipe.

चाहि moreover than.

चाहिए-should; must.

चाहे whether, either, or; whichever.

चिआँ-the see of tamarind fruit.

चिउँटा-the black and of bigger species.

चिंगना-chicken; a small boy; a chick.

चिंगारी-spark.

चिंघाड़-scream; trumpeting (of an elephant); shrieking.

चिंजा-the Sun; a boy.

चिजी-daughter.

चिड़-a kind of dance.

चिंतक-one feeling concern; a thinker.

चिंतन-thinking; reflection; study.

चिंता-care; anxiety; thought; worry; reflection; doubt; consideration; contemplation; recollection; risk; danger; fever; concern.

चिंतायमान-immersed in thought; thoughtful.

चिंतित-perplexed; preoccupied; anxious; concerned.

चिंत्य-doubtful; reflective.

चिंदी-fragment; a piece; scrap.

चिपान्जी-the chimpanzee.

चिउंडा-flattened rice.

चिकना-slippery; smooth.

चिकनिया-well-groomed; spruce.

चिकरना-to cry aloud; to scream; to shriek.

चिकवा-one who sells meat; meat-seller; a butcher.

चिकार-a squeak.

चिकारा a ravine deer.

चिंकारा-an instrument of the type of the .

चिंकारी-a stinging insect like a mosquito.

चिकित्सक-a doctor; one who gives medical treatment.

चिकित्सा-medical treatment; healing; therapy; hospital; sanatorium; clinic.

चिकित्सित-cured; healed.

चिकिल-marsh; bog.

चिकीर्षा-desire to do a thing.

चिकुर-the hair of the head; a lock of hair; mountain; creeper animal.

चिकोता-blotch; rash.

चिक्कट-greasy; filthy; oily.

चिक्कणी-betel nut.

चिक्कस-finely ground meal.

चिखर-husk of grain.

चिखुर-a squirrel.

चिखुरन-weeded; a weed.

चिखुरी-the female squirrel.

चिखौनी-the act of tasting; a thing for tasting.

चिचड़ा-a medicinal plant of this name; the snake-gourd.

चिचिंड़ी-a tick or louse which sticks to the bodies of cattle.

चिचाना-the hawk.

चिचियाना-to shriek; to scream; to cry aloud.

चिजारा-a mason.

चिट-bit; clip; shred; a piece; a piece of paper.

चिटकना to be irritated; to be fretful; to crack; to be annoyed.

चिटकनी-a latch.

चिटकारा-a scar; a clack produced by the tongue on eating acid food; a speck.

चिटनवीस-an agent; a scribe; a writer.

चिट्टा-clear; bright; white light coloured.

चिट्ठा-an account-book; a memorandum of accounts; rough account; a day book; pay or wages disbursed; account of expense; detailed account of anything from which nothing has been hidden.

चिट्ठी-letter; note; billet; favour; document; an order.

चिड़-irritation; huff.

चिड़चिड़ा-fretful; touchy; irritable; short-tempered; a type of bird.

चिड़ना-to irritate.

चिड़वा-flattened rice.

चिड़ा-a cock-sparrow; a cock bird.

चिड़िया-a bird; anything of the from of a bird; an suite of cards; an impossible thing; a very wealthy person; a very beautiful woman.

चिड़ियाखाना-a zoo; an aviary.

चिड़िहार-a fowler.

चिढ़ना-to be irritated.

चित-intuition; the soul; knowledge (of God).

चितकबरा-speckled; spotted; dappled; variegated.

चित्कार-sudden scream; loud shriek.

चितचोर-heart-alluring; heart-stealing; beloved.

चितभंग-absent mindedness; inattention; fretfulness; disinterestedness.

चितरोख-a kind of bird.

चितवन-glance; a look; sight.

चिता-place of burning the dead; a funeral pile; pyre.

चिताखा-to warn.

चिताना-to caution; to warn; to remind; to intimate; to suggest; to instruct; to kindle fire.

चितेरा-a painter.

चित्त-reflection the soul; the mind; though; the heart.

चित्तभूमि-the five aspects of phases of mind according to Yoga philosophy.

चित्तविक्षेप-mental fickleness or inconstancy.

चित्तविभ्रम-madness; derangement of mind.

चित्ती-mark; spot; stain; freckle; scar; a speckled cowrie shell; a small white specked bird; a kind of snake.

चित्र-painting; a picture; diagram; figure; wonder; a spot; delineation; likeness; the sky.

चित्रक-an artist; a painter; an ornamental or sectarian mark on the forehead.

चित्रकला-the art of painting.

चित्रकार-a painter; a artist.

चित्रगुप्त-the god of death; the recording angel of .

चित्रण-tracing; drawing; delineating (as a character in a novel).

चित्रपट-the board or cloth on which a portrait is painted.

चित्रमद-the falling in love with a woman or man by seeing her or his portrait.

चित्रमृग-the spotted deer.

चित्रयोग-the art of changing the physical condition of person.

चित्ररथ-an epithet of the Sun.

चित्रलेखा-a portrait; a painter's pen or brush.

चित्रवर्ण-the peacock.

चित्रविचित्र-variegated; motley.

चित्रशाला-a picture gallery; a picture room.

चित्रहस्त-a single stroke with a weapon.

चित्रांग-spotted; variegated.

चित्रिणी-a women of talent and beauty with pictures; the second division of women.

चिथड़ा-shred; tatter; a rag.

चिद-the principle of thought; pure intelligence.

चिनक-a burning pain.

चिनगारी-embers; a spark; a scintilla.

चिनना-to cause to be select; to construct a wall.

चिनार-a kind of tall beautiful tree.

चिन्मय-all intelligence; spiritual.

चिन्हार-a acquaintance.

चिन्हारी-recognition.

चिपक-stickiness; cohesion; adhesion.

चिपकना-to cohere; to cling; to cause to adhere to; to stick.

चिपकू-a hanger-on; hanging on.

चिपटना-to adhere to; to stick to.

चिपड़ी, चिपरी-a dried cake of cow dung used as fuel.

चिप्पड़-patch; a piece.

चिमटना-to embrace; to cling to; to hold fast; to follow incessantly.

चिमटी-forceps; tweezers.

चिमड़ा-elastic; flexible; leathery; ductile.

चियाँ-a tamarind seed.

चिरंजीव-long-lived (a benediction, may you live long).

चिर-lasting for a long time. for a long time.

चिरई-bird.

चिरकना-to pass excreta in small amounts.

चिरकीन-dirty; foul.

चिरकुट-piece; a tattered garment; a bit.

चिरंजीवी-immortal; lasting for a long time.

चिरना-cut or torn; to be split; to splinter; to tear.

चिरवाई-the wage which is paid for cutting; tearing of sawing wood.

चिराँद-the smell of burning leather; flesh.

चिरस्थायी-permanent; perpetual.

चिरस्मरणीय-memorable; remarkable; adorable.

चिराई-sawing; price paid for sawing or splitting (wood).

चिराग-a lamp; a light.

चिरातन-ancient; old.

चिराँयध-the smell of burnt hair or leather.

चिरायता-wormwood, the plant which is used in medicine.

चिराव-slit; tear; cut; split wood (for fuel).

चिरिया-a bird.

चिरिहार-a fowler.

चिरौटा-a cock bird.

चिर्क-filth; dirt.

चिर्मिठा-wild liquorice.

चिलक-brilliance; glitter; a shooting; pain; a stitch (from running).

चिलगोजा-fruit of the pine tree of tubular form.

चिलचिल-glittering.

चिलड़ा-a fried pulse cake.

चिलता-a kind of helmet.

चिलबिल-a kind of large plant or tree.

चिलबिला, चिलबिल्ला restless; wanton; uneasy; agile.

चिलम-the part of a hubble-bubble in which fire and tobacco are placed for smoking.

चिलमन-a curtain of split bamboo sticks.

चिलवाई-muddy place (as at a well mouth).

चिल्लड़-an insect like louse; nit.

चिल्लपों-hubbub; clamour.

चिल्लर-a louse.

चिल्ला-gold threads on the borders of a turban; a period of forty days; a wild tree; a bow-string; pulse; pastry.

चिल्लाना-to cry out loudly; to shout; to scream; to yelp; to whine (as dogs); to make an outcry.

चिल्ली-a kind of small insect; thunderbolt; lightning.

चिल्हवाँस-snare for a bird (a kite).

चिवाना-a cremation site.

चिहुँकना-to startle.

चिहूँटना-to prick the vital part of the body; to pinch with fingers.

चिह्न-spot; mark; scar; stain; prints; impression (as of the feet).

चिह्नित-spotted; marked; stained; to figure; to sign; to spot; to stain.

चीं, चींचीं-warbling of birds.

चींगा-a young bird.

चींचपड़-speaking something against or in opposition.

चींटा-a large black ant.

चींटी-an ant.

चींथना-to pieces; to tear.

चींदी-a washer of leather or other material.

चींकट-sticky object; grease; residue.

चीकना-to roar or scream; to cry aloud.

चीख-shriek; screech; a scream.

चीखर, चीखल-slime; mud.

चीखुर-a squirrel.

चीज़-a thing; an article; an item; a commodity; a precious object.

चीड़-a fir or pine tree.

चीत-the planet.

चीतना-to brood; to think; to come to senses.

चीतल-the axis or spotted deer; name of the fish; a large spotted snake resembling the python.

चीता-a tiger; a leopard; a panther; thought; idea; understanding; wisdom; desire; a kind of medicinal plant.

चीत्कार-scream; shriek.

चीथड़ा-a rag.

चीथना-to crush; to tear to pieces.

चीदा-selected.

चीन[1]-China, the country of the Chinese.

चीन[2]-a kind of small miller.

चीनक-China camphor.

चीनना-to recognize.

चीना-a kind of rice; a resident of China.

चीनी-sugar, the language of China; Chinese.

चीपड़-secretion of the eye.

चीमटा-tongs.

चीमड़-elastic.

चीर[1]-bark of a tree; cloth; rag; rip; udder of a cow; garb of an ascetic; a rent; a splint; a strip.

चीर[2], **चरम**-a rag; the skin of a antelope.

चीरना-to tear; to split; to cut; to lance; to saw; to form; to create; to acquire by dubious means.

चीरफाड़-vivisection; surgical operation.

चीरा-incision; a cut; wound.

चीर्ण-split or torn.

चील-a kite.

चीलड़-a kind of louse.

चीला-a fried cake of pulse-meal.

चीलू-a fresh apricot.

चीवर-garment of an ascetic (the upper garment of the a Buddhist).

चीवरी-a beggar; a monk.

चीस-a shooting or throbbing pain; to ache; to shoot with pain; to throb.

चुँगना-to feed on; to peck.

चुंगल-talon; a handful; claw; to be brought under control of some one.

चुंगी-duty; a portion of produce; toll or levy on produce that entering a town.

चुंघाना-to cause to sip.

चुंडा-a well.

चुड़ित-wearing a knot of hairs on the head.

चुंधा-with small eyes; purblind.

चुंबक-a magnet; a lode-stone.

चुंबन-a kiss; a salute; osculation.

चुंबा-to kiss.

चुंबित-loved; touched; kissed.

चुंबी-a lover; one who kisses.

चुआई-the work of percolating or dripping.

चुआन-draining; dripping; a tank; reservoir; a surface depression into which water drains.

चुआना-to disburse; to complete; to quit; to satisfy; to repay; to render.

चुकंदर-a beet root; a tuberous vegetable.

चुकटा-a handful.

चुकटी-a pinch.

चुकाई-agreement; settlement.

चुकाना-to disburse; to complete; to adjust; to quit; to satisfy; to repay; to render.

चुक्कड़-a small earthen cup used for drinking water.

चुक्क-a kind of vinegar prepared from the juice of some fruits; sourness; sorrel.

चुगद-a fool; a blockhead; a stupid person; a owl.

चुग़ना-to pick at; to feed on (of birds); to pick out; to select; to cull.

चुग़ल-informer; a slanderer; a tale-bearer.

चुगलखोरी-backbiting.

चुगली-informing; slander; tale-bearing.

चुगाई-act of picking.

चुगाना-to cause to peck.

चुचाना-to cause to be drenched; to drip; to leak; to ooze as a liquid.

चुचुकना-to dry up and become wrinkled.

चुटक-a whip; a lash.

चुटकना-to pinch; to nip; to bite; (of a snake); to break; to pluck; to whip.

चुटकला-an epigram; a pleasantry; a witty remark; a humorous talk; a nostrum.

चुटकी-a snap with fingers; the trigger of a gun; a snapping with the fingers; a pinch.

चुटपुट-stray; minor.

चुटपुटिया-a children's firework.

चुटला-braid.

चुटिया-a coil of hair; a lock of hair left on the otherwise shaven head (men); top-knot (women).

चुटीला-injured; bruised; wounded; best; excellent.

चुटैल-wounded; hurt.

चुड़िहारा-a seller of bangles of glass.

चुड़ैल-a hag; a female giant; a hobgoblin; a termagant (woman); a shrew.

चुड्ड-vagina; vulva.

चुड्डो-a whore.

चुन-powder; flour.

चुनचुनाहट-a burning pain.

चुनट, चुनन crease; shrink; a rumple; ruffles.

चुनना-to choose; to pluck; to gather; to glean; to pick or peck at; to cull; to discard; to elect; to arrange.

चुनाँचे since, because.

चुनाई-the work or wages of closing a door with bricks.

चुनाव-election; choice; pick; selection.

चुनावट-a frill; a crease; rumple; wrinkle; a tuck; gather (in cloth).

चुनिंदा-chosen; selected.

चुनौटिया-pleated; tucked cloth; gathered.

चुनौटी-a small pot for keeping lime which is to be chewed with betel.

चुनौती-incitement; a challenge; selecting (the fittest man for a task); encouragement; instigation.

चुन्नी-a small ruby; precious stone; fragment of corn; sawdust; spangle; a star.

चुप-still; mute; silent.

चुपका, चपकी-silent; hush; reticence; still.

चुपके quietly; stealthily; silently.

चुपचाप-quiet; silent;

चुपड़ना-to anoint; to palliate; to flatter; to soothe.

चुपड़वाँ-oily; greasy; oiled.

चुपाना-to keep silence.

चुप्पा-silent; quite; taciturn.

चुबलाना-colloq. to chew or to savour food with swallowing it.

चुभकना-to duck; to plunge.

चुभन-a piercing pain.

चुभाना-to caused to be pierced or stuck in.

चुम्मा-a kiss.

चुम्बन-the act of kissing.

चुर-den of a wild beast.

चुरकुट, चुरचुस-broken to fragments; powdered.

चुरचुरा-crisp; crumbling; crunchy.

चुरचुरी-sediment; dregs.

चुरना-to be boiled or crooked; to have a secret council.

चुरमुर-a crunching or crackling sound.

चुरवाना-to cause to be stolen.

चुरस-crease in cloth.

चुराना-to rob; to steal; to conceal; to filch; to pilfer.

चुरी-bracelet; bangle; an ornament of wrist.

चुरु-hallowed palm.

चुरुट-cigar; cheroot.

चुल-itching; lust; fidgetiness.

चुलबुल-restlessness; fidgetiness; liveliness; flirtatiousness.

चुलबुला-restless; fidgety; lively; flirtatious.

चुलाना-to percolate; to ooze; to cause to drip.

चुलाव-a rice dish without meat.

चुल्ली-a chimney of stove; a fire-place.

चुल्लु-hollowed man; handful of a liquid.

चुवाना-to leak; to drip.

चुसकी-a mouthful of water or other liquid; a sip; a suck; pull (as at a pipe).

चुसक्कड़-one who is in the habit of sucking a tippler; drinker.

चुस्की-a mouthful of drink; a pull of smoking.

चुसना-to be sucked; to be emptied; to be exploited; to be absorbed.

चुसनी-feeding bottle for babies; a child's coral.

चुसान-absorption.

चुसाना-to cause to be sucked.

चुस्त-active; tight; narrow; strong; fleet.

चुस्ती-quickeness; alertness; dexterity; ingenuity.

चुहचुही-a very small bird of deep black colour.

चुहटना-to crush with feet; to trample; to bruise.

चुहल-merriment; naughtiness.

चुहलिया-funny (a person); comical.

चुहिया-a small mouse.

चुहुँटना-to embrace.

चूँ-a slight noise or sound; the noise of passing wind; a squeak; creak; chirp; twitter.

चूँकि because.

चूँट-to nip; to pluck; to break.

चूँदर-a particular cloth sheet.

चूक-mistake; error; default; deception; blunder; fault; fraud.

चूकना-to miss; to fail; to mistake; to blunder.

चूका[1]-wild sorrel.

चूका[2]-a kind of large earthen milk-pot having capacity of five litres.

चूख-to suck.

चूचुक, चूंची-pap; nipple teat.

चूजा-a chicken.

चूड़ा-a single lock of hair left on the crown of the heat at the tonsure ceremony; the top; crest.

चूड़ाकरण, चूड़ाकर्म-the tonsure ceremony among Hindus.

चूड़ामणि-a jewel worn in the crest of a diadem.-best; most excellent.

चूड़िया-a kind of striped cloth.

चूड़ी-a bangle of glass; lac; record of a gramophone.

चूड़ीदार-long trousers which crumble into plaits on wearing; of the form of rings.

चूत-vulva.

चूतड़-the buttock; the rump; bum.

चूतिया-a blockhead; stupid fellow.

चूतियापन-folly; idiocy.

चून-meal; flour.

चूना[1]-slaked lime.

चूना[2]-to drop; to drip (liquid); to leak; to ooze; to be distilled; to fall.

चूनादानी-a small box for keeping lime which is used for betel for chewing.

चूनी-fragments of corn; a small ruby.

चूनेदार-calcareous.

चूमन-kissing.

चूमना-to kiss; to caress; to salute.

चूमा-a kiss.

चूर-small fragments; filling; powder. -to be engrossed; to be intoxicated (to excess); bruised; absorbed.

चूरन-digestive powder.

चूरना-to break to pieces; to reduce to powder.

चूरमा-crumbled bread or bread crumbs fried in and mixed with sugar.

चूरा-sawdust; a broken part; a fragment; filings.

चूर्ण-fragmented substance; powder; a digestive power (composed of ground spices, dried mangoes, lime).

चूर्णन-pulverization.

चूल[1]-crest; top; the hair of the head.

चूल[2]-pivot (as of a door, in its socket on a threshold); a dovetail; wedge.

चूल्हा-a stove; hearth.

चूषक-sucker.

चूषण-act of sipping.

चूसना-to suck; to dip; to drink; to sip; to absorb; to merge; to kiss; to appropriate.

चूहड़ा-a sweeper; an outcast.

चूहा-rat; mouse; a kind of ornament of arm.

चूहाड़ी-a scavenger; a sweeper (of roads).

चूहिया-a small mouse.

चेंगड़ा-a young child.

चेंच-a kind of vegetable.

चेंचें-useless gossip; warbling of birds.

चेंचला-an unfledged bird; nestling.

चेंडा-young; little.

चेंपें-outcry; murmur.

चेकितान-an epithet of .

चेचक-small-pox.

चेट-a servant; a slave; a husband; a buffoon.

चेटक-anxiety; thought; care.

चेटकी-a servant; spy; a miracle; jugglery.

चेटी-a maid servant; a female servant.

चेत-consciousness; senses; wits; alertness.

चेतना-to awake; to be or to become conscious; to be aroused; to be or to become aware.

चेता-one who thinks; reflects or is conscious.

चेतावनी-a warning; reminder; caution.

चेतिका-funeral pyre.

चेना-a kind of wild vegetable; millet.

चेरा-a servant; a pupil; disciple.

चेराई-attendance; service.

चेष्टा-effort; exertion; attempt; endeavour; activity; action or movement of the body; gesture; impulse.

चेस्टर-a kind of overcoat.

चेहरा-face; front part of anything; countenance; a mask.

चैत-the first month of the Hindu year.

चैतन्य-the soul; perception; rationality; intelligence.

चैत्य-a house; a temple; a building; the place where a sacrifice is performed; a cenotaph; the image of Buddha; a funeral pyre.

चैन-relief; rest; ease; repose; tranquillity.

चैल-garment; clothes.

चैला, चैली-pieces of split wood used for burning; silver; chips.

चोंक-mark of teeth which is made by kissing.

चोंकली-abrasive; sharp.

चोंकर-chaff; bran.

चोंच-beak; bill.

चोंडा-a small well sunk for the sake of irrigation.

चोंथ-cow dung which is excreted at a single time.

चोंथना-to scratch; to pluck.

चोंधर-dim-sighted; purblind; stupid; foolish.

चोआ-a perfume prepared by mixing several ingredients.

चोइयाँ-scurf; scale.

चोई-husk of lentils.

चोकंदर-beet; lettuce; sugar-beet artichoke.

चोकर-barley; bran; husk or refuse of wheat.

चोख-quickness; alertness.

चोखा-pure; good; genuine; delightful; excellent; beautiful; honest; sincere; sharp; keen; pungent; clear.

चोगा-a long cloak.

चोग़ा-a long, loose knee-length cloak.

चोचला- blandishments; coquettishness.

चोज-admirable or wonderful remark; a subtle or pointed; an epigram.

चोजी-subtle; nice.

चोट-stroke; blow; swap; stuck; a hurt; wound; bruise; attach; stratagem; deception.

चोटी-braided hairs of women; a lock of hair on the crown of head; tasselled tag with which women braid their hairs; an ornament for the head; pinnacle; summit; crest; top.

चोटीपोटी-flattery.

चोट्टा-a pilferer.

चोड़-bodice; a jacket; a corset; a pair of stay.

चोदक-stimulator; instigator.

चोदना-to have sexual intercourse with (of a man).

चोदू-constantly wanting sexual intercourse; lascivious.

चोप-eagerness; enthusiasm; earnest desire; wish; hope; ardent; exultation; zeal.

चोबा-a small iron nail.

चोर-a thief; a swindler; a pilferer; a burglar; a house-breaker; a hidden spot.

चोरकट-a swindler; a robber.

चोरदर्वाजा-the back-door of a house.

चोरपुष्प-medicinal grass.

चोरबाजार-black-market.

चोरमहल-a apartment where kings keeps their concubines.

चोरमिहीचनी-a game of hide and seek.

चोरी-robbery; theft; concealment.

चोल चोलना-a bodice; a helmet; armour of head.

चोला-the body; the ceremony of putting clothes on the body of a new-born baby; a long robe worn by ascetics.

चोसा-a rasp.

चोसना-to rasp wood; horn.

चोहला-a large wooden balk (tied to necks of dangerous cattle).

चौंक-a sudden start.

चौंकना-to start up in sleep; to be alert; to be astonished; to startle.

चौंगा-wheedling; cajole; to coax.

चौंडू-fool; an idiot.

चौंथ-dazzling effect of light on the eyes.

चौंथना-to snatch or to tear.

चौंराना-to sweep; to drive away flies with a .

चौंषरौं-quadruped; a rat.

चौंसठ-sixty-four. 64.

चौ-four; a measure for weighing pearls.

चौआना-to be astonished.

चौक-a square plot of ground; a courtyard; a square platform; a big alter.

चौकड़ा-a group of total of four; division of a crop between tenant and landowner in proportions of one quarter and three-quarters.

चौकड़ी-a group of total of four (objects or people); a bound; leap (as of a deer, with all four legs together); a bounce.

चौकन्ना-alert; watchful; cautious; sly.

चौकस-careful; alert; watchful.

चौकसी-watchfulness.

चौका-a square slab of stone; a round pastry-board; a group of four similar objects; a playing card having four pips; a row of four incisors; an ornament for the head; the clean and washed place where Hindus cook their food and eat.

चौकी-a bench for sitting; a stool; a table; a chair; a police station; a watch-house; custom-house; an offering to a God; an ornament for the neck; a small pastry-board; a guard's post.

चौकीदार-a watchman; a guard; a sentry.

चौकीदारी-the work of a watchman; the wages of a watchman paid for keeping a watch.

चौकोना-square; four-sided.

चौकोर-four-sided; quadrangular.

चौखट-a door-frame; a panel; a door-sill.

चौखा-a place where four boundaries of villages meets.

चौगिर्द all round; on all sides.

चौगुना . quadruplicate; fourfold.

चौगोड़िया-a kind of a high stool.

चौगोशिया-four-cornered.

चौघड़-the molar (grinding) tooth in men.

चौघड़ी-a small box with partitions for holding cloves; cardamom.

चौघोड़ी-a carriage which is drawn by four horses.

चौबन्द-talk of calumny or slander.

चौड़ा-broad; wide; ample; an open, or a remote area.

चौड़ाई-width; breadth; extension; expansion.

चौथ-a fourth part; the fourth day of a lunar fortnight; a tribute levied by the on North Indian rulers.

चौथपन-the fourth stage of life (supposed to begin from the seventy-fifth year).

चौथा-fourth; an observance taking place on the fourth day after a death, when gifts and clothes or money are given to the widow or son of the deceased.

चौथी-the fourth day; an observance taking place on the fourth day of marriage.

चौदस-the fourteenth day of a lunar month according to Hindu calendar.

चौदाँत-a fight of two elephant.

चौधरी-the headman of a village; a leader of a community or occupational group; an honorific title.

चौपट-ruined; spoiled; destroyed; flat; plain; opened on all sides unguarded.

चौपड़-a game played with dice on a cloth or board of cross-shaped layout; the form of a cross; a temple courtyard.

चौपत-crease in cloth.

चौपतिया-kind of grass vegetable.

चौपथ-the junction of four roads.

चौपाई-a quatrain (usually printed as two rhyming lines of verse, each containing sixteen or metrical, instants).

चौपाड़ा-a resting place for villagers; a small shed.

चौपाया-cattle; a quadruped; neat; stock.

चौपाल-an assembly room, or covered assembly place in a village.

चौपैया-one who has four legs.

चौबन्दी-a kind of tight under garment; bodice.

चौबगला-of four sides.

चौबर-stout; bold; sturdy.

चौबाई-a hurricane; the blowing of wind from all directions.

चौबारा-an open room built on the roof of a house; an open shed; an attic. a fourth time; fourthly.

चौबे-community.

चौमसिया-appearing in the four months of the rainy season.

चौमासा-the four months of the rainy season beginning from ; a song which is sung in the rainy season.

चौमुख all round; on all sides.

चौमुहानी-a place where four roads meets.

चौरंग-a sword-exercise; cutting the four legs on an animal with one stroke of sword.

चौरस-level; even; flat; square.

चौरसाई-evenness; levelness.

चौरा-a platform; the place where a Hindu widows is immolated; an alter; the platform raised over the grave of a saint.

चौराहा-a cross-road; a quadrivial.

चौरेठा-rice ground with water; rice-meal.

चौल-the tonsure ceremony.

चौलड़ा-necklace made of four strings.

चौला-a kind of bean.

चौस-land four times ploughed.

चौसर-a game played with oblong dice; a necklace made of four strings.

चौसरिया-fraudulent.

चौसरी-an ornament which worn tightly round a woman's neck and behind.

चौहट्ट, चौहट्टा-a market on a cross road.

चौहड़-the jaw-bone.

चौहद्दी-boundary of the four sides of a field.

चौहरा-fourfold; having four folds.

चौहैं on all sides; around.

च्युत-oozed; dropped; fallen; degraded.

च्यूँटा-a big black ant.

च्यूँटी-an ant.

छ-The seventh consonant of the Devnagari alphabet and the second letter of the palatal class.

छंकाना-to cause to strain to to filter.

छंग-heart; bosom; lap.

छंगा-having six fingers or six toes.

छँगुली-sixth finger; little finger.

छँछनाना-to simmer; to sound.

छँछीरी-a sweetmeat prepared from milk.

छँटना-to be separated on being cut; to be taken away; to be left after selection; to be removed; to be lean and thin.

छँटनी-cutting backret; renchment.

छँटाव-selection; removal; clearing of grain.

छँडना-to vomit.

छंडाना-to snatch; to take away a thing by force.

छंद[1]-trickery; ingenuity; deceit.

छंद[2]-a wrist ornament.

छँदना-to hobbled (an animal); to be fettered.

छंलछंद (छंछद)-trick; cheating; fraud; deception.

छंदोभंग-error in versification, according to the rules of prosody (in rhetoric).

छंदोबद्ध-in the form of a verse.

छँहा-to rest in the shade; to be shaded.

छई[1]-tuberculosis.

छई[2]-the young generation; children.

छः-six.

छकड़ा-truck; car; cart; wagon; van.

छकड़ी-a set of six.

छकना-to be satisfied or gratified; to be harassed; to be astonished; to be afflicted; to be intoxicated; to be troubled; to be cheated.

छकुर-a division (as of crop) with one-sixth assigned to the land-holder.

छक्कड़-a slap; a blow.

छक्का-a group of six; the sixth at cards; a fraud.

छगड़ा-a goat.

छगन-a word of endearment; a baby; darling.

छगरा-a goat.

छगरी-a small goat.

छछिया-a skimmer (a for buttermilk).

छछुंदर-a mole; a must-rat; a kind of amulet; a kind of firework.

छछूंदरी-a vole.

छजना-to befitting; to be attractive; to be embellishing.

छज्जा-a gallery; a balcony; an overhand (in building); bottom of a cart.

छटंकी-a weight of one (nearly fifty grams); a very small thing.

छटकना-to slip (from the hand or grasp); to become out of control.

छटपटाना-to struggle; to be restless; to toss; to flounder; to toss and tumble about.

छटाँक-a sixteenth of (apporx. two ounces).

छटा-glory; brilliance; splendour; lustre; refulgence; beauty; lightning.

छठ-the sixth day of the lunar fortnight.

छठी-the ceremony performed on the sixth day after child-birth.

छड़[1]-a pole; stalk; stubble; rod; bar; a fishing rod; stem.

छड़[2]-a fragrant grass.

छड़ना-to separate husk from grain by beating or pounding.

छड़ा-apart; separate; single.

छड़िया-a porter; a gate-keeper; a watch.

छड़ी-a cane; a rod; a wand; a stick; a verge.

छड़ीला-a spice used in manufacturing tobacco; kind of fragrant moss.

छत-roof; floor; terrace; cloth stretch across a roof; a wound.

छतना-an umbrella made of bark or leaves.

छतनार-umbrella or mushroom-shaped; flattish.

छतरी-an umbrella; an ornamental pavilion; a frame set on a bamboo for pigeons; to canopy over the grave.

छतारा-a guitar.

छतिवन-a medicinal plant.

छत्तीसा a lewd woman who pretends to be chaste.

छत्तर-an umbrella.

छत्ता-seed case of lotus; a covered footpath; an umbrella.

छत्र-an umbrella; a parasol; protection; a mushroom.

छत्रक-a fungus; a mushroom.

छत्रा-a shelter or house used for distributing cooked food to beggars; mushroom.

छत्री-wing of bird; a covering; a leaf; a cover.

छंद-a leaf; a covering; a wing.

छद्म-pretext; trick; disguise; stratagem; fraud; hypocrisy.

छद्मी-deceptive.

छनक-a tinkling or jingling sound.

छनछवि-lightning.

छनना-a filter.

छननी-a strainer.

छनाई-percolation.

छन्न-covered; concealed.

छन्ना-a piece of cloth used for sifting; filter.

छन्नी-sieve.

छप-squelching or splashing sound (as of an object falling into water or mud); splattering (of rain); splashing (of water); washing.

छपकली-lizard.

छपद-a wasp; a bee.

छपन-secret; hidden.

छपना-to be stamped or printed; to be marked; to be polished; to be vaccinated.

छपरी-a small hut.

छपाई-work of printing or stamping; wages paid for printing; method of printing.

छपैया-a printer.

छप्पर-a thatched roof; a hovel; a booth; a small pit; a big slab of stone.

छाल-skin; peel; bark; rind; a kind of sweet.

छालटी-cloth prepared from the bark of certain trees.

छालना-to sift with a sieve.

छाला-a blister; a pimple; skin; a pustule.

छलिया, छाली-betel nut.

छावनी-encampment; thatch; cantonment.

छावा-a young pig.

छिंउकी-a kind of small ant; a pinching insect; gnat.

छिंकाना-to be surrounded; to be stopped; checked.

छिंछ-a current of water; splash of water.

छिंडाना-to take by force; to snatch; to seize; suddenly.

छिगुनी, छिगुली-the little finger.

छिछकारना-to sprinkle.

छिछड़ा-waster meat fragments.

छिछोरपन, छिछोरापन-childishness; meanness.

छिछोरा-shallow; frivolous; superficial; triviality; worthlessness.

छिजना-to lessen; to waste.

छिजाना-to decrease; to lessen; to cause to waste or wear away.

छिटकना-to be diffused; to be scattered; to be vanished; to be dispersed.

छिटका-a splash.

छिटवा-a bamboo basket.

छिड़कना-to scatter; to sprinkle; to spill; to patter; to powder.

छिड़ना-to commence; to begin; to be started; to start the battle.

छितनी-a broken basket; a small bamboo shallow basket.

छितरना-to be scattered.

छितराना-to shatter; to stew; to scatter; to discriminate; to disperse; to fling; to shuffle; to spread; to ramify; to intersperse; to straggle.

छिदना-to be pierced.

छिद्र-a hole; a gap; an opening; crack; a pore; a defect.

छिन-moment; instantly.

छिनक-an instant.

छिनकना-to blow the nose for expelling mucus.

छिनछवि-lighting.

छिनना-to be snatched; to be seized.

छिनरा-a man of bad character.

छिनाल-lewd (woman); a trollop; a harlot; adulterous.

छिनालपन-adultery (of a woman); prostitution.

छिन्न-divided; cut; rent; a dock; dispersed; destroyed; scattered.

छिपकली-a lizard; a common house-lizard; a kind of ear ornament.

छिपटी-a chip; shaving; splinter.

छिपना-to be concealed; to be hidden; to be absent; to withdraw.

छिपाव-secrecy; privacy; hiding; concealment.

छिया-excrement; to act in a vile away.

छिरकरना-to scatter; to sprinkle.

छिरेटा-a kind of small medicinal creeper.

छिलका-husk; peel; skin; shell; coat; bark; rind crust.

छिलना-to be shelled; to be barked; to be rough or sore (the throat); to be scraped or scratched.

छींका-a net; a rope bridge; a muzzle (for cattle); a hanging basket (for food).

छींट-fine drops especially of water; a kind of cloth; calico.

छींटना-to scatter; to sprinkle.

छींटा-a casual glance; splash; a slop; spot made by a drop of water; a dose of intoxicating drug; ironical remark.

छींबी-a pod.

छी expressing disgust or dislike.

छीका-a network in the form of a cup which is fitted on to the mouth of a bullock; network of strings for hanging anything in; a lattice window; a hanging bridge; a swing.

छीछड़ा-skinny part of meat; tough flash of an animal.

छीछालेदर-ruin; destruction.

छीज-damage; loss; deterioration; swindling; wasting or wearing away.

छीजना-to lessen; to decrease; to pine or waste away.

छीति-decrease; loss.

छीदा-thin; sparse (of texture or composition); widely separated.

छीनना-to take possession of; to deprive; to ramp; to pluck; to snatch up; to take out.

छीना झपटी-extortion; forcible seizing.

छीप-whitish spots of discoloration; a mark; impression.

छीपी-a cloth printer.

छीर-border of cloth.

छीलन-paring; shaving; scraping.

छुँगली-colloq. the little finger.

छुई-मुई-the sensitive plant; the mimosa plant.

छुगनु-small bells attached to an ornament.

छुचकारना-to worship; to honour.

छुच्छ-hollow; empty.

छुच्छी-a hose pipe; thin ring.

छुछमछली-a tadpole.

छुछूंदर-a particular firework.

छुट-relaxation.

छुटका-to open; to release; to leave; to undo; to slip from.

छुटकारा-release; deliverance; discharge; exemption; acquittal; escape.

छुटपन-childhood; infancy.

छुटपना-infancy.

छुटभैया-a person of little importance.

छुटौती-remission (of a sum due); a ransom.

छुट्टा-free; alone; not bound.

छुट्टी-leave or absence; holiday; leisure; cessation; discharge; freedom.

छुड़ाई-releasing; discharging; setting free; liberation; dismissal; rescue; ransom.

छुडौती-ransom remission (of a payment).

छुत्-hunger.

छुतहा-unclean; contagious; not usable or touchable.

छुतिहर-ceremonially unclean.

छुतिहा-calumniated; untouchable; sinful; defiled or polluted by touching.

छुद्राबलि-tiny bells.

छुधा-hunger.

छुभित-agitated; perplexed.

छुरदार-fine sharp edge of an instrument as of a razor.

छुरा-a razor.

छुरित-glitter of lighting; a kind of dance.

छुरी-a knife; dagger; scalpel.

छुलकना-to make water slowly.

छुहना-to be touched; to be coloured or painted.

छुहारा-a dried sweet date.

छुँछा-hollow; empty; vacant; mean; despicable; wretched; poor.

छू-an incantation; the act of blowing or uttering.

छुछक-a ceremony observed after childbirth generally after forth days after the birth; gifts given on this occasion by the mother's father.

छूछा-empty; without substance; shallow; facile; contemptible; base.

छूछी-needle case; a thin tube; socket (for a screw).

छूट-relaxation; remission; exemption; discount; freedom; rebate.

छूटना-to be discharged; to be got rid of; to be liberated; to be abandoned.

छूत-touch; infection; contamination; contagion; defilement.

छूना-to touch; to smear; to feel.

छूहना-to whitewash; to daub.

छूही-a pile of cow dung; worthless.

छेंक-to confiscate property; requisition of commodities.

छेंकन-interruption; detention; stoppage; confiscation.

छेक[1]-a cut; wound.

छेक[2]-urbane; clever.

छेकला-a hole.

छेटा-obstruction; stoppage.

छेड़-irritating; teasing; vexing; pinching; quarrel.

छेड़खानी-act of provoking; stricture; molestation; exciting.

छेड़ना-to touch; to adjust; to handle; to tune (an instrument); to activate; to instigate; to begin (a war, a quarrel).

छेद-a hole; an opening; gap; crack.

छेदक-boring or cutting (tool); destroyer; a divisor (in mathematics).

छेना-cheese; curd.

छेनी-a chisel; a gouge.

छेमकरी-auspicious.

छेर-a goat.

छेरना-to have diarrhoea (an animal).

छेरी-a nanny-goat.

छेव-a wound; a cut; a mark; misfortune; deception; stratagem; artifice.

छेवना-to cut; to pierce; to lance; to wound; to bleed (a palm tree).

छैना-to be worn out; to fray; to go bad; to turn (as milk).

छैया-a child; a boy.

छैल-a fop; a dandy; a beau.

छैला-modish; find-looking; handsome.

छोआ-molasses.

छोंडा-a churn which is used for making butter.

छोकड़ा, छोकरा-a boy; a page; a youngster; lad; brat.

छोकड़ी, छोकरी-a girl.

छोटा-small; junior; lesser; younger; minor; inferior; contemptible.

छोटी इलायची-cardamom.

छोड़ना-to let go; to renounce; to forsake; to omit.

छोनि-the earth.

छोप-a thick coating; the work of plastering a wall with mud; hurt; secrecy; defence.

छोभ-perplexity; agitation.

छोम-soft; smooth.

छोर[1]-border; edge; end; bank.

छोर[2]-to free; to release; to take off; to put aside; to seize; to snatch.

छोराना-release from bondage; to untie; to snatch; to take dispossess.

छोराछोरी-boys and girls; act of snatching away something form another.

छोल-a scraping; a shaving; a scratch; graze; covering.

छोलदारी-a small gable tent.

छोलना-to cut; to skim; to pare; to scrape; to reveal.

छोह-kindness; pity; love; affection; compassion.

छोहना-to show affection; to love; to pity.

छोहरा-lad.

छोहरी-lass.

छोहा-to feel affection or love.

छोहाना-to fondle; to pity; to love; to show kindness.

छोही-affectionate; loving.

छौंक-taste; flavour; seasoning.

छौंना-the young one of an animal.

ज

ज-The eight consonant of the Devnagari alphabet and the third letter of the palatal class.

ज-poison; oil; devil; father; the god ; the conqueror of death.

जंग-rust.

जंग-a warlike person; battle; war; fight.

जंगम-living; movable; moving.

जंगरा-lintel after the seeds have been removed; the dry stalk of pea.

जंगरैत-hard working; industrious; laborious.

जंगल-jungle; forest; woods; wooded or scrub country; wild; lonely; a wild or uninhabited region.

जंगला-a balustrade; a grating; a railing; a latticework.

जंगली-wild animals; forested; wooded.

ज़ँगाना-to rust.

ज़ंगार-copper sulphate; oxide of copper; verdigris.

जंगारी-of blue colour.

जंगाली-a kind of bright silken cloth of blue colour.

जंघा-thigh; hip; haunch; leg; shank.

जंघार-a boil appearing on the thigh of man.

जंघिया-knickers; half-pants; short breeches.

जँचना-to appear; to pass a test or examination; to be examined.

जँचवैया-appraiser; tester; examiner.

जंजल-entangled; old and tattered; useless.

जंजाल-perplexity; embarrassment; difficulty; trouble.

जंजाली-causing trouble (a person).

ज़ंजीर-a fetter; a chain.

जंड-the custom among Hindus of entertaining the bridegroom's father and his relations at the end of marriage.

जंत-rope; thong; tie (as used in lashing timbers or bamboos).

जंतर-an instrument; an amulet; an implement.

जंतरी-an appliance for drawing gold or silver wire; an almanac.

जँतसार-a place where grinding (of meal is done).

जँतसारी-a kind of song sung by women while grinding grain.

जंता-a wire-gauze; an instrument.

जंतु-a creature; an animal.

जंतुघ्न-insecticidal.; killer of animals or insects.

जंत्र-a instrument; a magic square; a machine; a amulet.

जंत्री-a calendar; an almanac; a musical instrument.

जंद-the holy scriptures of the ; the language in which these are written.

जंदरा-a board as used in trenching up earth; a kind of rake.

जंपना-to talk to; to speak.

जंबक-a jackal.

जंबीर-a kind of sour lemon of big variety.

जंबु-the black plum; the rose-apple.

जंबुक-a jackal.

जंबूर-an old type of small cannon (Indian).

जंबूरक-a small gun or cannon carried on a camel.

जंबूरची-a soldier in charge of cannons.

जंभ-the jaw.

जंभाई-gape; rictus; yawn.

जंभारि-the thunderbolt; fire.

जई-oats; small species of barley.

जईफ-infirm; old; weak.

जईफ़ी-old age; senility; infirmity; weakness.

जकन्द-a bound; a leap.

ज़क-defeat; humiliation; injury; loss; disgrace.

जकड़-work of tightening; to make fast.

जकना-to be astonished; to utter words while perplexed.

ज़कात-portion of property given as alms; tax; levy.

जकुट-a dog.

जक्की-a kind of sweet singing bird.

जक्षण-food.

जक्ष्मा-tuberculosis.

जखम-a wound; a cut.

जखीरा-repository; a treasury; a store-house; collection.

जखेंडा-multitude.

ज़ख्म-bruise; wound.

जग-the world; the universe; cosmos; nature; people; a religious sacrifice.

जगच्चक्षु-the Sun.

जगजगा-glittering; shining; lustrous; bright.

जगजोनि-the creator of the world ; the earth.

जगड़बाल-useless embellishment; foppery.

जगत-the high platform surrounding a well.

जगतसेठ-a very rich man; a multimillionaire.

जगतसाक्षी-the Sun.

जगरा-molasses which is prepared from palm juice.

जगह-place; locality; room; station; occasion; post; service.

जगा-जोत-brilliance; brightness; splendour.

जगाना-to awake; to raise; to arouse from sleep; to call up; to knock up; to kindle fire; to bring to senses; to invoke.

जग्मि-the air.

जघन-the hip and loins; the buttocks.

जघन्य-low; vile; base.

जंगम-going from one place to another; moving; infantry; poison of venomous insect; reptiles.

जंगल-a jungle or forest.

जङ्घा-buttocks; thigh.

जङ्गल-an ambassador; a spy.

जचना-to be examined; to be guessed; to be tied; to be proved.

जच्चा-a woman in child-bed.

जच्छ-a demigod.

जज-a Judge.

जजबात-mood; desire; feeling; longing.

जजमान a host.

जजी-the post of a Judge; a Judge's court.

जजीरा-an Island.

जज्ब-misappropriation; absorption.

जज्बा-feeling; emotion; passion.

जज्बात-feelings; emotions.

जटना-to snatch; to cheat; to rob by deceiving.

जटल-gossiping; prattling; tattling; quibbling.

जटा-a mass of twisted or braided hair; tangles roots or suckers; matter hair (as worn by ascetics, and attributed to the God).

जटाना-to be deceived or cheated.

जटायु-the name of the king of Vultures.

जटाल-having matted locks of hair on the head.

जटाव-potter's clay.

जटित-tangled; set or studded with jewels.

जटिल-matted; complicated; tangled; involved; cruel.

जठर-the abdomen; the stomach.

जठेरा-elder; senior; eldest.

जड़-senseless; numb; inert; material; irrational; immovable; unfeeling; heavy; stupid. saturnine; idotic; dumb.

जड़न-the act of setting (jewels).

जड़ना-to join; to strike; fit; to set with jewels; to inlay.

जड़बुद्धि-imbecile; dolt; idiot; wood-hearted; numskulls.

जड़भरत-a dull stupid person.

जड़वी-shoots of rice when first springing from the ground.

जड़ावर-winter dress; warm clothes; warm in winter.

जड़ित-inlaid; studded; set.

जड़िया-goldsmith; a jewellers.

जड़ी-any root used medically.

जडुल-a freckle or mark on the skin.

जड़ैया-the ague; a fever accompanied with shivering.

जतन-an attempt.

जताना-to inform; to remind; to warn; to admonish; to caution; to make known.

जतुक-asafoetida; lac; birthmark on the body.

जतुपुत्रक-one of the chessmen.

जतुमुक-hut made of lac.

जतुरस-a kind of dye prepared from lac.

जत्था-group; batch.

जत्रु-the collar-bone.

जदवार-a herb which is an antidote for poison.

जदीद-new recent; modern; newly cut off.

जद्द-strong; brave; much.

जनवास-a meeting; a resting place for the public; an assembly.

जनवासा-living quarters of the bridegroom's party (at the time of marriage).

जनवल्लभ-one who is loved by every one.

जनश्रुत-famous; renowned.

जनश्रुति-tidings; rumour; hearsay.

जनसंख्या-census; population.

जनहित-beneficial to the people.

जना-midwifery; payment or cost of midwife's service; a midwife.

जनाई-the remuneration given to a midwife.

जनाचार-dead body; hearse; bier; coffin.

जनाजा-a bier.

जनानखाना-seraglio; harem.

जनाना-to generate; to confirm; to give birth to; to help; to intimate; to assist.

जनाब-a title of respect.

जनार्दन-an epithet of Lord .

जनाव-report; intimation.

जनि-a female; mother; wife; motherland; birth; no; never; nevertheless.

जनून-mental disturbance; possession by a madness.

जनूब-the South.

जनेऊ-the sacred thread of a ; the ceremony in which is sacred thread is worn.

जनेत-the company which follows the bridegroom at the time of wedding.

जनेता-father.

जनेवा-a hardy fodder grass used in land reclamation; a kind of fragrant grass which grows with crops.

जनेश-a monarch; a king; a sovereign.

जनेष्टा-turmeric.

जनैया-an informer.

जनोक्ति-a proverb.

जन्तु-a creature; an animal; the insect which lives in a sonch-shell.

जन्तुका-lac.

जन्तुघ्न-insectivorous; destroying life (of a creature).

जंतुफल-the fruit of a Gular tree.

जन्नत-paradise.

जन्म-birth; nativity; production; life; genesis; lifetime; existence.

जन्मक्षेत्र-the place where one is born; mother-land.

जन्मज्येष्ठ-prior in birth.

जन्मपत्र-nativity; a horoscope; birth chart.

जन्मभूमि-motherland; native place; home.

जन्मविधवा-a woman who is widowed in the early years of her married life.

जन्मशय्या-the cot on which a baby is born.

जन्मस्थान-the place of one's birth; birth place.

जन्मान्ध-born blind; blind since the very birth.

जन्माष्टमी-the eight day of the dark half of on which Lord was born.

जन्मी-a living creature.

जन्यु-fire; life; .

जप-the silent repetition of a ; muttering of prayers; worshipping.

जपजी-a religious text of the Sikhs.

जपनी-sword-stick for counting ; a rosary.

जपरायण-engaged in prayers.

जफ़ा-rudeness; roughness; oppression; injustice; harshness; cruelty.

ज़फ़ीर-a whistling sound.

ज़फ़ील-a whistle; sound produced by a whistle.

जब-when; at whatever time.

जबड़ा-the jaw.

जबर-powerful; vigorous; strong; violent.

जबर-compulsion; force.

जबरजद्द-a kind of emerald.

जबरदस्त-strong; vigorous; violent; powerful.

जबरदस्ती-injustice; violence; oppression.

जबरन् by compulsion; forcibly.

जबरा-powerful; strong

जबह-slaughter.

जबहा-courage; spirit.

जबान-dialect; the tongue; conversation; promise; language; speech.

ज़बानी-unwritten; oral; traditional.
जबाब-answer.
जबार-neighbourhood.
ज़बून-deficient; bad.
जबाबदेह-accountable; responsible; liable; subject.
ज़ब्त-control; restraint.
जभन-copulation; coition.
जमकात, जमकातर-a whirlpool.
जमकूड़ा-a mat worn over the shoulders to keep of rain.
जमघट-crowd; throng; assembly; multitude.
जमडाढ़-a kind of dagger.
जमदग्नि-the name of a sage.
जमना-to be coagulated; to be frozen; to be congealed; to be fixed; to clot.
जमनिका-musical prologue.
जबवट-the wooden foundation of a well.
जमनौत-a very small percentage paid to one who is surely for some amount.
जमहूर-a populace; a community; a state; nation.
जमहाई-yawning; a gaping.
जमा-accumulation; credit; capital; amounts deposited; rent for land.
जमाई-a son-in-law.
जमाखर्च-income and expenses; settlement of an account.
जमाजत्था-property and cash.
जमात-a class; a community.
जमादार-head of a group of sweepers.
ज़मानत-bond; security; surety; guarantee.
ज़माना-period; time; an age; the world.
जमाबंदी-paper in which the amount of rent of each tenant is entered; a village.
जमामार-one who misappropriates the property of others.
जमाल-charm; elegance; beauty.
जमाल-गोटा-a small cultivated tree and its fruit (used as a purgative).
जमाव-accumulation; crowd; multitude.
ज़मी-earth.
जमीन-land; the earth; ground; soil; substratum.
ज़मीर-mind; heart; thought.
जमुकना-to be brought in contact or close together.
जमुर्रद-emerald.
जमूरक, जमूरा-a kind of small cannon.
जमैयत-society; community.
जमोग-assignment of liabilities by mutual consent.
जमोट-wooden cylinder used in formation the foundation of a masonry well.

जम्बाल-mire; bog; marsh; a kind of sweet smelling grass.

जम्बालिनी-a river; lotus flower of small size.

जम्बी-a kind of mint; basil plant.

जम्ब-an island.

जम्बुक-a jackal; the tree and its fruit.

जम्बुल-a disease of the ear.

जम्बुका-raisin.

जम्बूरची-one who handle a cannon.

जम्बूरा-a swivel; small pliers.

जम्भक-yawning.-the god or .

जम्भन-cohabitation; sexual intercourse; yawning.

जयंत-triumphant; victorious.

जयन्ती-a birthday celebration; a jubilee; a flag; banner.

जय-victory; conquest; gain; profit.

जयद-triumphant; victorious.

जयध्वज-banner of victory.

जयपत्र-a bond of victory.

जयमाला-the garland of victory.

जययज्ञ-horse-sacrifice.

जयश्री-the goddess of victory.

जयस्तम्भ-the monument erected to commemorate a victory.

जयस्मारक-a trophy.

जया-the victorious; a title of several deities.

जयाञ्जन-colly-rium.

ज़र-silver; gold; money; wealth.

जर[1]-fever.

जर[2]-a root.

जर[3]-to burn; to flame; to suffer from fever.

जरई-oats.

जरकटी-a bird of prey.

ज़रकस, जरकसी-a kind of golden tassel.

जरख़ेज-fertile; productive (land).

जरजर-crushed; decrepit.

जरठ-infirm; decrepit; decayed; old; harsh; cruel.

जरतार-wire of gold and silver.

जरत्-ancient; old; advanced in years.

जरती-an old woman; a hag.

ज़रद-pale; yellow.

जरदा-scented tobacco eaten with betel leaf; a dish of rice; a yellow horse.

जरदालू-apricot.

जरदी-yolk of an egg; yellowness.

जरदुश्त-propounder of a religion of Persia.

जरदोज़ी-needlework; embroidery.

जरना-to suffer from fever; to be feverish.

जरनि-a burning sensation; pain; a pang.

ज़रब-stroke; wound; blow.

ज़रबफ्त-embroidered silk.

ज़रब-injury; damage; hurt; loss; ruin.

ज़रर-damage; harm.

जरल-a kind of beautiful evergreen shrub.

जरांकुश-a kind of fragrant grass used in medicine.

जरा[1]-infirmity; old age; decrepitude.

जरा[2]-to kindle; to burn.

ज़रा-less; little; a small amount.

ज़राभीरु-Cupid.

ज़राफ़त-facetiousness; wit.

जरायु-the womb; the outer skin of the embryo placenta.

जरायुज-man and other animals born from the womb.

जराह-a surgeon.

जरिया-medium; connection; influence; agency; cause.

जरी-a cloth woven with gold thread.

जरीब-a surveyor's measuring chain (of fifty-five yards).

जरीबाना-fine.

जरुथ-loose of flabby flesh; skinniness.

जरूर necessarily; certainly; unavoidably; of course.

जर्कबर्क-brilliant; shinning; gaudy.

जरेला-a kind of rice.

जर्जर-decayed; archaic.

जहर-poison; venom.

जहरबाद-a carbuncle.

जहरमोहरा-a kind of green stone supposed to be an antidote to poison.

जहरीला-venomous; poisonous.

जहाँ-world.

जहाज़-a vessel; a ship; craft.

जहान-the world.

जहालत-ignorance;illiteracy;imperfect knowledge; barba-rousness.

जहीं in the very place.

जहीन-sagacious; ingenious; intelligent; wise.

जांग-a species of horse.

जाँगड़-minstrel; a bard.

जाँगर-strength of body.

जाँगलू-savage; rustic; wild.

जाँघ-the thigh.

जाँघिया-shorts.

जाँच-trail; test; question; inspection; survey; search; investigation; enquiry.

जाँचक-a beggar.

जाँत, जाँता-to grind corn; a stone.

जाँब-plum; rose-apple.

जाँबर-departure.

जा-mother; wife of husband's younger brother.

जाई-a daughter.

जाकड़-a deposit; a purchase on credit; to sell something on approval.

जाग-awakening.

जागता-manifest.

जागतीजोत-the miraculous power of deity which is manifest.

जागना-to awake; to be careful; to rise; to get up from bed.

जागरण-wakefulness, vigil; awareness.

जागरित-wide-awake; alert; watchful; brisk; vigilant.

जागरूक-aware; alert.

जागी-a minstrel; a bard.

जागीर-a rent-free grant given by Government as a reward for some services; manor; grant prebend.

जागृति-wakefulness; awakening; vigilance.

जाचक-a beggar.

जाचना-to entreat; to implore; to be earnestly.

जाजरा-old and torn up; rotten.

जाज़िब-attracting; drawing; absorbent.

जाजिम-a printed bedsheet; a floor-cloth, a carpet.

जाजुलन-rage.

जाज्वल्य-lustrous; shining; blazing; glittering.

जाज्वल्यमान-raging; burning.

जाट-the name of a northwest Indian community (chiefly of cultivators).

जाटलि-name of a tree similar to the tree.

जाठ-the wooden axis of a sugar-mill or oil-mill which crushes corn or cane; the post placed in the centre of a tank.

जाड़-root (of the teeth); a molar tooth.

जाड़ा-cold; (also) the cold season.

जाड्य-want of sensational; apathy; stupidity; senselessness; insensibility; inactivity.

जात-person; caste; the body.

जातक-a newborn child.-an anthology of Buddhist stories.

जातकर्म-the ceremony performed on the birth of a child.

जातकोप-inflamed; angry.

जातपाँत-people of the same caste; relatives.

जातबल-vigorous; strong.

जातवेदस्-fire; the sun; god.

जातवेश्म-a lying-in chamber.

जातश्रम-fatigued; tired.

जातस्नेह-enamoured.

जाता-daughter; a girl.

जातपस्य-one to whom a son or daughter is born.

जाताश्रु-having eyes filled with tears.

जाति-birth; life; race; sex; lineage; parentage; state; tribe; caste; set; quality; genus; species; nature; family; sort; quality; kind; name; order; nation; section; peoples; clan; community; breed.

ज़ाती-essential; personal; intrinsic.

जातुक-asafoetida.

जातुधान-a demon.

जातसपति-an ephitet of Lord .

जादुई-magical.-magic wand.

जादू-spell; charm; enchantment; incantation; sorcery; glamour; necromancy; magic; black art; witchery; witchcraft.

जादूगर-a magician; a wizard; a sorcerer; a warlock; an enchanter; a conjurer.

जान[1]-understanding; life; sprit; intelligence; strength; essence; a sweet-heart; an object of love.

जान[2]-acquaintance; knowledge; understanding; opinion.

जानकारी-familiarity; knowledge.

जानदार-having life; animate.

जानकी-title of ; daughter of .

जानना-to understand; to know; to ascertain; to learn; to perceive; to recognise; to suppose; to consider; to know how to.

जानपद-a country; a territory; inhabitant of a country; people in general.

जानमनि-a very learned or wise person.

जानराय-an experienced person.

जानवर-an animal; a beast; a living creature; a fool; a boor.

जाना-to depart; to go; to resort; to betake; to wend; to repair.

जानि-sweet-heart; wife.

जानिब-direction; side.

जानी-beloved; dear; animate; a mortal enemy; a fast of intimate friend.

जानु suppose.

जानू-thigh.

जाप-repeating an incantation or the name of a deity; a rosary.

जापा-delivery; childbirth; place of confinement.

जापान-Japan.

जाफ-fainting; swoon; weariness; exhaustion.

जाफत-a feast; a dinner party.

ज़ाफरान-safron.

जाफ़री-a bamboo screen or lattice; lattice-work.

जाफा-increase.

जाबिर-despotic; tyrannical.

जाबी-muzzle (for small cattle); a child's network purse (tied to the waist).

ज़ाब्ता-rule; regulation.

जाम[1]-a period of three hours; a rose-apple; a cup; a bowl.

जाम[2]-to arise; to be produced; to germinate.

जामगी-wick which is used firing cannon.

जामदानी-a box; a trunk (for clothes).

जामन-rennet used in coagulating milk.

जामा-a garment; a rainment; a robe.

जामाता-a son-in-law.

जामिक-a guard; a sentinel.

जामिन, जमिनदार-a surety; a security against loss or damage.

जामुन-the rose-apple.

जामेय-sister's son.

जामेवार-a shawl the whole surface of which is decorated with silken needlework; calico.

जाम्बव-vinegar prepared from black plum.

जाय unserviceable; in vain; useless.

ज़ायका-flavour; taste; savour.

ज़ायचा-horoscope; nativity.

ज़ायज-suitable; fitting; proper.

जायज़ा-examination; scrutiny; verification; checking; account; report.

जायद-more; abundant.

जायदाद-estate; property; effects; assets; resources; wealth.

जायफल-nutmeg; mace.

जायल-ruined; lost.

जाया-a wife.

ज़ाया-perishing; to waste.

जार-a lover; a paramour; an adulterer.

जारक-consuming; burning; digestive.

जारज-a bastard; an illegitimate child; misbegotten.

जारण-consuming; burning.

जारिणी-a woman of loose character; an adultress.

जारी-proceeding; running; current; in force; customary.

जारु-placenta after birth.

जालंधर-dropsy.

जालंध-a peep-hole; a small latticed window in a house.

जाल-a net; a lattice grating; lattice window; network; mesh; a web; a tangle; illusion; deception.

जाला-a web; cataract.

जालिका-a fine net; network.

ज़ालिम-tyrannical; cruel; oppressive.

जालिया-a cheat; a deceiver.

जाली[1]-network; netting; criss-cross; a net; muzzle (for a bullock); material to open weave; muslin; gauge; lace; a lattice; trellis; grating; screen.

जाली[2]-forged; counterfeit; false; spurious; fictitious; perjured (testimony).

जावक-a red paint with which ladies paint their feet.

जावित्री-mace (fibrous covering of the nutmeg, used as an aromatic spice and also medicinally).

जासूस-a spy; an emissary; scout; a detective.

जाहि to whom.

ज़ाहिद-one who abstains; a devout person; a recluse; zealot.

जाहिर-obvious; clear; plain; manifest; evident; apparent; open; known.

जाहिल-evidently; openly; apparently; seemingly.

ज़ाहिल-forgetful; negligent.

जाही-a kind of fragrant flower like jasmine; a king of firework.

जिन्द-a ghost; an apparition; a spectre.

जिंदगी-duration of life; age.

जिंदा-alive; living.

जिंस-kind; species; merchandise; goods; wares; crop; produce; movable articles; things.

जिउकिया-one who is engaged in a profession; a trader.

ज़िक-mention; report account.

जिगजिगिया-a flatterer.

जिगजिगी-coaxing; beseeching.

जिगर-the liver; the heart; mind; vital part of body; life; courage; sap; essence.

जिगरी-intimate; friendly.

जिगिन-a kind of big tree growing on mountains.

जिगीषा-desire for victory; excellence; superiority.

जिच-helpless; tired; weary; deadlock.

जिजिया-sister.

ज़िज़िया-a poll-tax levied on non-Muslim living under Muslim government (as during the Delhi Sultanate, and most of the Empire).

जिजी-a foster-mother; a wet nurse for a baby.

जिजीविषा-desire to live.

जिज्ञासा-inquiring; asking; search; inquest.

जिज्ञासु-curious; inquisitive.

जिठानी-wife of elder brother.

जित्-victorious; conquering.

जितना a much as; however; much.

जितनेमि-devoid of wrath.

जितात्मा-self-controlled.

जिताष्टमी-a fast which is observed on the eighth day of the dark half of by those women who have children.

जित्वर-victorious; triumphant.

जिद-obstinacy; persistence; resolution; enmity.

जिद्द-obstinate.

ज़िद्दी-stubborn; obstinate; wilful; persistent.

जिधर wherever; whither.

जिन-; the sun; Buddha.

जिनिस-commodity.

जिन्न-a demon; a headstrong or resolute person.

ज़िबह-to slaughter.

जिमखाना-a gymkhana; a gymnasium.

जिमाना-to feed; to receive to a meal; to entertain.

जिमि & like; as; just as.

जिम्मा-trust; charge; duty; service; obligation; superintendence.

ज़िम्मेवार-responsible.

जियरा-decrease; loss; damage; diminution.

ज़ियाफ़त-a feast; hospitality.

ज़ियारत-visiting (a shrine); pilgrimage.

जिरगा-group; collection; assembly of person.

जिरह-cross-questioning; wrangle.

जिला-glitter; polish.

ज़िला-division of country; district.

जिलाना-to give life; to bring back to life; to foster; to vivify; to vitalize; to protect life.

जिल्द-binding of a book; a separate volume of books; skin; leather; hide.

जिल्लत-disgrace; insult; dishonour; misfortune; baseness.

जिस upon whom; or which; whereupon; whomever; whatever; someone or other.

जिस्ता-twenty-four sheets of paper; a quire of paper.

जिस्म-the body.

ज़िहन-brain; mind; intellect.

जिहाद-a war fought by against unbelievers; a religious war; uvular; guttural.

जिहानक-annihilation or destruction of the world.

जिहालत-illiteracy; folly.

जिहासा-desire to abandon.

जिह्म-mean; wicked; unhappy.

जह्वल-eager; greedy.

जिह्वा-the tongue.

जिह्वालौल्य-greediness.

जिह्वाविद्-a fire-fly.

जी[1]-soul; spirit; life; mind; self courage; determination; thought.

जी[2] an expression of respect or of affection (used with proper names); an expression of assent; yes; true.

जीउ-life creature.

जीजा-husband of one's elder sister.

जीट-boasting.

जीत-victory; mastery; success; gain; benefit.

जीतव-life; lifetime.

जीता-living; alive; over; more than the exact weight of a thing.

जीताल-arrowroot.

जीन-a saddle; a kind of thick cloth; drill.

ज़ीनत-elegance; beauty; ornament; decoration.

जीना-to live; to be alive; to subsist; to be happy; to be pleased.

ज़ीना-ladder; a flight of stairs, or of steps.

जीभ-the tongue.

जीभूत-a mountain; cloud; the sun.

जीमड़-a particular tree.

जीमना-to partake of food.

जीयति-life; spirit.

जीयदान-protection of life.

जीर-saffron; cummin seed; sword; armour.

ज़ीरक-cummin seed.

जीरा-cummin seed; pollen contained in a flower.

जीर्ण-old; ragged; ancient; hackneyed; withered; effete; decayed; broken-down; trite; time-worn.

जील-a high note or tone; the treble; a soft, or low note.

जीव-life; soul; spirit; existence; a creature; an animal.

जीवट-bold; resolute; courage; spirit; resolution.

जीवड़ा-life; the soul.

जीवत्-alive; living.

जीवदान-gift of life; saving anyone's life.

जीवधारी-having life; animate.

जीवन-existence; breath; time; life; subsistence; animation livelihood; profession; living; beloved one; water; air.

जीवन-चरित्र-life; biography.

जीवनमृत-moribund; inert.

जीवन-धन-one who is most dear; support of life.

जीवन-बूटी-a plant which is supposed to have the power of reanimating a dead person.

जीवयोनि-animate creature; a living being.

जीव-रसायन-bio-chemistry; the chemistry of biological process and substance.

जीवलोक-the earth.

जीववृत्ति-the business of cattle farming.

जीवशून्य-lifeless; dead.

जीवसंक्रमण-transfer of soul from one body to another.

जीवसुता-the woman whose son is alive.

जीवस्थान-the vital part of the body; the heart.

जीवहत्या (हिंसा)-the killing of living beings.

जीवविद्या-a living creature; an animal great or small.

जीवाणु-microbe.

जीवात्मा-the spiritual essence in man; the individual soul.

जीवाश्म-fossil.

जीविका-livelihood; means of subsistence; occupation.

जीवेश-the supreme spirt; God; the Almighty.

जुग-emotion; impulse; a kind of tree.

जुंबिश-movement; motion.

जुआ[1]-a yoke.

जुआ[2]-play; gambling.

जुआचोर-a cheat; a deceiver.

जुआर-millet; spring-tide; flood tide.

जुआरा-the area of land which is tilled in a day.

जुआरी-a gambler.

जुकाम-a cold (in head or throat).

जुखना-to be weighed or measured.

जुग-a period; age; epoch; generation.

जुगजुगाना-to twinkle; to flicker; condition to be slightly improved.

जुगजुगी-a kind of small bird.

जुगत-idea.

जुगनी, जुगनू a fire-fly; a glow-worm; a heart-shaped necklace.

जुगवना, जुगाना-to a mass; to gather; to accumulate; to hoard; to keep with care.

जुगाड़-provision.

जुगादरी-ancient; very old.

जुगाल-cud (of ruminants).

जुगाली-chewing the cud.

जुगुप्सा-disgust; censure; abuse; loathing.

जुज-a part; a portion; form of a book.

जुजबी-very few; rare.

जुज्झ-battle.

जुझाऊ-truculent; quarrelsome; martial; military.

जुझार-a fighter; a warrior.

जुट-a batch; a pair.

जुटली-with matted hairs.

जुटवाँ-twin; germinate.

जुट्टी-small bundle (as of grass); pile (of flat object).

जुड़ना-to be united; to be joined; to cohabit; to assemble; to be grouped together; to attend to a work.

जुडपित्ती-a skin complaint causing itching and blotchiness.

जुड़वाँ-twin.

जुतना-to be attached; to be yoked; to drudge; to be ploughed; to toil.

जुताई-cultivation; wages for ploughing; ploughing.

जुताऊ-arable.

जुतियाना-to beat with a shoe; to treat with contempt.

जुत्थ-youth.

जुदा-different; apart; various; severally; separate; distinct.

जुदाई-separation; parting; absence; estrangement; distinction; difference.

जुनून-frenzy.

जुन्हरी-millet.

जुन्हाई, जुन्हैया-moonlight.

जुमला-a sentence; a clause.

जुमा-day of the congregation; Friday.

जुमेरात-Thursday.

जुमिल-a kind of horse.

जुरअत-courage.

जुरझुरी-slow fever; feverishness.

जुरमाना-fine; forfeit.

जुर्म-fault; crime; sin.

जुर्रत-daring; courage.

जुर्रा-a male hawk.

जुर्राब-a sock.

जुल-deceit; trick; cheating; a fraud.

जुलाई-the month of July.

जुलाब-a purgative medicine.

जुलाहा-a weaver .

जुलूस-procession; a demonstration.

जुल्फ-curling of hair; a ringlet.

जुल्म-wickedness; injustice; tyranny; an outrageous act (of wickedness); extortion; cruelty.

जुल्मत-darkness.

जुवाँ-louse.

जुवारा-the threads of wires which are stretched over the bridge of a musical instrument.

जुस्तजू-investigation; searching; enquiry.

जुहाना-to furnish; to accumulate; to equip.

जुहार-salutation; greeting; a formal mode of salutation or obeisance.

जुही-a jasmine.

जूँ-a louse.

जूआ-a yoke. the handle of a stone handmill; gambling.

जूज-a word which is used to frighten children.

जूझ-struggle; battle; fighting; war.

जूझना-to fight; to die by fighting; to quarrel.

जूट-the matted or twisted hair of an ascetic or the God Shiva.

जूठन-remnants of food; an object previously used by another (and so made impure and unfit for use).

जूठा-what is left off after eating.

जूड़-cold.

जूड़ा-a plait; a tress; a tuft; a braid; a circular support placed under a jug.

जूड़ी-an ague; fever; a shivering fit.

जूता-shoe; boot; slipper.

जूताखोर-beaten with shoe or slippers; degraded; shameless; despised; mean.

जूती-shoe worn by ladies; slippers.

जून[1]-old.-time; a particular time; a meal-time.

जून[2]-June.

जूना (जूइना)-twisted rope or grass used in cleansing utensils.

जूप-yoke; gambling.

जूमना-to be gathered or accumulated; together.

जूरना-to join; to attack.

जूरा-hair knot; a tress.

जूला-a tract of land sixteen in area.

जूलाई-July.

जूस-broth; cooking-water from vegetables; juice from cocked fruit.

जूसताख-evens and odds: name of a game.

जूहड़-a yoke attached to a plough.

जूही-a kind of jasmine; a kind of fireworks.

जेंवन-taking one's meal; taking food; eating.

जेंवना-devour; eat.

जेंवनार-feast.

जेठ-the third month of the Hindu year; brother-in-law; elder brother of one's husband.

जेठा-eldest; senior; very old; best; chief; most excellent.

जेठानी-the wife of a husband's elder brother.

जेठीमधु-liquorice.

जेठौत, जेठौता-the son of husband's elder brother.

जेतव्य-conquerable.

जेब-a pocket.

जेबी-handy; small; tiny.

जेर-the membrane in which foetus develops.

जेरपाई-slippers of women.

जेरबार-afflicted; troubled.

जेरी-the stick of a grazier.

जेल-prison; jail; trouble; difficulty.

जेलर-a jailer.

जेली-a pitchfork made of wood used in turning over sheaves of corn in threshing.

जेवड़ा-cord; a rope.

ज़ेवर-jewels; ornaments.

जेवरात jewellery; ornaments.

जेवरी-rope; string; cord.

जेष्ठ-the month of .

जेहड़-a pile of water-pots carried one on top of the other on a woman's head.

ज़ेहन-genius; intellect; memory; recollection.

जेहर-an ornament which is worn on the ankles.

जैजैवन्ती-a song which is sung in the morning.

जैत-name of a musical mode; name of a

जैतवार-a conqueror; a victor.

जैतून-olive tree; its fruit.

जैत्र-victorious; the olive tree.

जैन-one who is a follower of the sect.

जैफर-nutmeg.

ज़ैल-rear or lower part. as follows; as below.

जैव-pertaining to living creatures.

जैविकी-biology.

जैयद-weighty; heavy; very rich.

जैलदार-superintendent of several villages.

जैसा-similar to; as according as; in the manner.

जों-in the manner; in which.

जोंक-a leech.

जोंकी-a nail which is pointed at both ends.

जोंधरी-millet.

जोंधया-moonlight.

जो although; if; when.

जोइ-wife.

जोइसी-an astrologer.

जोख-measuring; weight.

जोखना-to ascertain the weight of a thing; to weigh.

जोखाई-the perquisite of a man who weighs.

जोखिम-enterprise; peril; danger; risk.

जोगड़ा-a sceptic; a false ascetic; a deceiver.

जोगसाधन-to practice Yog.

जोगानल-fire which is created by miraculous power.

जोगिन-a female ascetic.

जोगिया-the name of a colour.

जोगीड़ा-a kind of song; a small band of singers.

जोटा-a pair.

जोटी-a twin; an equal; a similar object.

जोड़-union; a join; connection; joint; patch; a part added; an addition; addition; total pair; mate; equal match; a rhyme (between woods); suit (of clothes).

जोड़ती-addition; reckoning; calculation.

जोड़ना-to rejoin; to supplement; to interlace; to connect; to affix; to link; to join; to unite.

जोरू-a wife.

जोलाहल-fire; flame.

जोली-mate; a partner; an equal contemporary.

जोवना-to observe; to search; to wait for; to make a search.

जोलाहा-webster; weaver.

जोश-effervescence; heat; zeal; passion; fermentation; emotion.

जोशन-armour; a silver or gold ornament or armlet.

जोशीला-zealous; enthusiastic.

जोष, जोषिता-a female or wife of an astrologer.

जोह-search; favour; assistance; expectation.

जोहड़-small pool or lake as formed in a dry river-bed.

जोहार-obeisance; salutation.

जौंकना-to abuse; to scold.

जौख-an army; an assembly; a flight of birds.

जौंची-a smut in barley and wheat which prevents the grains developing.

जौड़ा-a high platform used for keeping watch on crops.

जौंरा-भौंरा-great pleasure; delight.

जौनार-land used for a crop of sugar-cane following a barely crop.

जौर-wrong-doing; injustice; violence.

जौलानी-quickness; alertness.

जौहर-a precious stone; a jewel; the ancient custom among according to which their ladies in order to save their honour from the conquering enemy hurled themselves on a burning pyre; self-sacrifice.

जौहरी-a jeweller; the person who test the merits and demerits of a thing.

ज्यादती-abundance; excess; increase; tyranny.

ज्यादा-more; too much.

ज्येष्ठ[1]-senior; eldest; best; chief; most excellent.

ज्येष्ठ[2]-the month ; May-June.

ज्योति[1]-brilliance; light; radiance.

ज्योति[2]-astronomy; astrology.

ज्योतिष्मती-the night.

ज्योतिष्मान्-resplendent; radiant; splendid.

ज्योत्सना-moonlight; a moonlight night.

ज्योनार-diner; banquet; feat; junket.

ज्योरी-rope; twine.

ज्योहत, ज्योहर-suicide.

ज्वर-fever; a high temperature.

ज्वरांकुश-a medicine which is used to remove fever; a kind of fragrant grass.

ज्वरित-feverish; suffering from fever.

ज्वलंत-lustrous; very clear; shining.

ज्वल-flame; splendour.

ज्वलनशील-inflammable.

ज्वार[1]-flood-tide; tide.

ज्वार[2]-an Indian corn; millet; the flood tide.

ज्वालक-burner.

ज्वाला-light; heat; blaze; flame.

ज्वालावक्त्र-the epithet of or .

ज्वालाहलदी-a kind of turmeric used of colouring clothes.

ज्वालेश्वर-an ancient place of pilgrimage.

झ

झ-The ninth consonant of the Devnagari alphabet and the fourth letter of the palatal class.

झं-a sound.

झंकना-to weep; to lament.

झंकार-resonance (as of a) chirping (as of a cricket); sharp cry (as of a peacock); a ringing.

झंकृत-resounding.

झँख-to lament.

झँखना-to weep; to bewail; to lament; to shudder.

झंखाड़-thorny undergrowth; a dense thicket; a leafless tree.

झँगरा-a round basket which is made of bamboo.

झँगा-frock.

झँगुला-loose frock.

झंझकार-ringing; clinking.

झंझट-difficulty; trouble; wrangle; perplexity; worry.

झंझन-ringing; rattling sound.

झंझर-earthen vessel for water.

झँझरी-small water pitcher.

झंझा-a strong wind or gale accompanied with rain; a hurricane; wind with rain.

झँझार-flame of fire.

झंझावात-strong surface wind.

झँझिया-a small cymbal.

झँझोड़ना-to pull and tear; to worry (as an animal its prey); to give a shaking to; to shake.

झंडा-a streamer; a banner; an ensign; a flat; a standard; colours.

झँडूला-of thick leaves foliage; of a child whose tonsure ceremony has not been performed.

झंप-a tossing; an ornament for a horse's neck; a jump.

झँपरी-the cover which is used for a palanquin.

झँपान-a kind of covered sedan chair.

झँपोला-a small basket.

झँवकार-black; brownish.

झँवा-implement to rub.

झँसना-to rub oil on the soles of feet; to snatch away something by tricks or fraud.

झउवा-small basket; a hod.

झक[1]-obsession; craze; whim; caprice.

झक[2]-shining; bright; clear; clean; white.

झक[3]-to chatter; to babble; to complain or to regret; constantly.

झकझेलना-to give a push; to jerk.

झकझोर-a strong jerk.

झकड़ी-earthen vessel used in milking.

झकना-to chatter; to prattle; to speak improperly in wrath.

झकाझक-shining; glittering; lustrous; polished.

झकुराना-to move to and fro; to oscillate; to toss; to waver.

झकोर-shaking; a blast of wind.

झक्क-glittering; shining.

झक्कड़[1]-squall; violent storm; a blast.

झक्कड़[2]-perverse; stubborn.

झक्की-crazy; whimsical; prattling.

झखी-fish.

झगझगायमान-shining; resplendent; lustrous.

झगड़ना-to quarrel; to wrangle; to argue; to squabble.

झगड़ा-variance; dispute; contention; scramble; affray; squabble; controversy.

झगड़ालू-disputatious; quarrelsome; contentious; obstreperous; querulous; oppressive; pugnacious.

झगर-a kind of bird.

झगला-a loose garment for covering babies.

झगा-a long, loose garment (specially worn by very young children).

झंकार-the buzzing of bees; a tinkling sound.

झज्झर-a porous water-jug.

झझक-an unpleasant smell.

झझकना-to hesitate.

झझका-to cause one to feel a sudden hesitation; fear.

झझरी-porous; perforated; grated; latticed.

झझलका-early dawn; break of day.

झट-quickness; quick. quickly; at once. this very moment.

झटक-a toss; jerk.

झटकना-to jerk; to jolt; to wrench; to shake; to be shaken; to be worn.

झटका-a push; a jolt; a jerk; a jostle; a twist; mode of beheading an animal with one stroke.

झटकारना-to toss; to give a jerk; to shake off; to flint.

झटपट-quickly; very soon; hastily; immediately; swiftly.

झटास-squall; driving rain.

झटिति speedily; in an instant; straight way; forthwith.

झड़-a bust.

झड़ना-to fall off in small fragments; to drop; to be discharged.

झड़प-fighting; sparring; brawl; a cock-fight.

झड़ाक soon; immediately.

झड़ाझड़ continuously; incessantly; immediately.

झड़ाना-to cause to be cast to an evil spirit.

झड़ी-a shower; continuous rain.

झन-the sound of vessels of metal striking against each other.

झनकार-jingling; buzzing; clang; rattle; humming.

झन्नाहट-stinginess; pungent.

झप hastily; quickly; instantly; immediately.

झपक-a closing or lowering of the eyelids for a short moment.

झपकी-drowsiness; blinking of the eyes; a nap; doze.

झपकौहा-drowsy; snoozing; dozing; intoxicated.

झपट-a spring; leap; swoop of a beast of bird of prey.

झपट्टा-an assault; a snatch; a swoop; a sally; a spring.

झपना-to close the eyes.

झपस-clustering of shrubs.

झपसना *v.i.*-the spreading of bush with thick foliage.

झपाक-quickness; haste.

झपास-a downpour.

झपासिया-fraudulent; deceitful.

झपित-winking; sleepy; dozing.

झपिया-a kind of necklace.

झपेट-attack.

झप्पड़-a slap.

झबझबी-a kind of ear-ring.

झबरा-covered with long entangled hairs.

झबरीला, झबरैरा having entangled hairs.

झबार, झबारि-a skirmish; a brawl; a quarrel.

झबिया-a woman's arm ornament.

झबूक-shine.

झब्बा-a tassel; epaulet; a bunch of gold thread.

झमक-glitter; radiance; jangle; flash.

झमकार-shedding rain clouds.

झम-झम-tinkling of bells; sound of raining.

झमना-to be bent; to be pressed.

झमाका-a heavy shower; coquettishness.

झमूरा-a lovely child.

झमेला-entanglement; mess; trouble; wrangle.

झम्प-somersault; a lap; an ornament worn on the neck of a horse; a monkey.

झरखना-to admonish; to reprove in a mild manner.

झरना-to flow; to cascade; to trickle; to drip; to ooze; to run.

झरप-a push; a stroke; a blow; quickness; a screen.

झरबेर-a gooseberry; sloe; a strawberry.

झरहरा-porous; gauzy.

झरा-a kind of paddy which grows in a field full of water.

झराझर incessantly; continuously; without a break.

झरित-dissolved.

झरुआ-a kind of grass.

झरोखा-loophole; casement; a small aperture; window.

झर्झर-a small drum; cymbal; an iron ladle.

झर्झरा-a prostitute; a concubine; a harlot.

झर्झरी-a cymbal.

झर्झरीक-a picture; body.

झर्रा-the tailor-bird.

झल-heat; radiance; glare; sharpness (taste, smell); fierce emotion; desire; frenzy.

झलक-glitter; blaze; brightness; blink; glimpse; glance; reflection of light; refulgence.

झलका-a blister.

झलकी-a short radio play or dramatic sketch.

झलना-a kind of sweetmeat.

झलराना-to scatter about; to spread; to flicker.

झलहाया-burning with strong emotion.

झलाईगर-welder.

झलाबोर-embroidery; splendour.

झलि-the betel-nut.

झल्ल-insanity; madness.

झल्लक-tymbal which is made of pewter.

झल्लकण्ठ-a kind of pigeon.

झल्लरा-a cymbal; perspiration; baby's hairs.

झल्ला[1]-a large basket.

झल्ला[2]-hot-tempered; crazed.

झल्लाना-to be displeased or irritated; to be fretful; to annoy.

झल्लिका-a towel; cloth used for wiping the body; splendour.

झब/झष-fish; alligator; heat; jungle; the twelfth sign of zodiac; an epithet of Cupid.

झषनिकेतन-a pond of water; the sea ocean.

झषराज-crocodile; alligator.

झषांक-the god of love; the God .

झषाशन-a kind of fish; seal.

झहरना-to blink with pain; to feel weariness.-to fret; to torment.

झाँक-work of peeping.

झाँकना-to peep; to peer; to glance; to put one's head out (from a door or window); to look in (Briefly); to pay a brief visit.

झाँकी-a glimpse; view; a sight; an exhibition; display.

झाँख-a kind of huge deer.

झाँखना-to irritate.

झाँगला-a loose garment.

झाँगा-a child's loose garment.

झाँझ-a cymbal; rage; anger; passion; roguery; wickedness; a dry pond.

झाँझड़ी, झाँझन-an anklet.

झाँझर-leaky; perforated.

झाँट-pubes hairs of genitals; a worthless object.

झाँप-cover (as of a basket); a made work shade; screen or shutter.

झाँपना-to cover; to hide; to veil.

झाँवना-to wash hands and feet with a burnt brick.

झाँवर-marshy land.

झाँवली-wink; ogle; a side glance; coquetry.

झाँस-pungency.

झाँसना-to pilfer; to deceive.

झाँसा-fraud; deception.

झाई-shadow.

झाउ-the tree.

झाग-foam; froth; scum.

झाझर-dry pond; rage.

झाड़-a bush; shrub; a brake; a bramble; a chandelier.

झाड़खंड-a jungle; wood; forest.

झाड़झंखाड़-brambles; worthless objects.

झाड़दार-thick; thorny.

झाड़न-sweepings; dust; rubbish; a duster; cloth.

झाड़ना-to sweep; to brush; to clean; to knock off; to remove; to dash; to brag; to snatch away by force.

झाड़फूँक-exorcism; hocus-pocus; jugglery.

झाड़ी-brake; covert; thicket; shrub; bush; brushwood.

झाड़ू-a swab; a mop; a broom; a broomstick; a comet.

झापड़-a blow with the open hand.

झापा-a narrow-mouthed.

झाबर, झाबा-marshy land; a basket.

झाम-a tassel or ornament (that swings or glitters).

झामक-pumice; burnt brick.

झामर-a kind of anklet.

झामी-fraudulent; deceptive.

झार-heat; burning.

झारना-to comb or dress hair; to pound; to separate.

झारा[1]-a sieve.

झारा[2]-burning; heat.

झारी-a small pitcher or ewer with a slender neck and a spout attached to it.

झालर-pane; flounce; fringe; frill; trimmings; tatting.

झालरी[1]-a garland.

झालरी[2]-cymbals.

झाला-spider's web.

झालि-incessant rains.

झिंगवा-a kind of small fish.

झिंगा-small fish.

झिंझिना-an earthen pot which is pierced with holes in which a light is kept.

झिंझोटी-a kind of song.

झिक-to look; to glance.

झिझक-a sudden start (of the emotions); being at a loss; hesitation; fear; shyness; reserve; timidity.

झिडगक-cucumber.

झिडिगनी-a large forest tree.

झिरझिर-very thin; gauzy; full of tiny holes.

झिरि, झिरिका-a beetle; a cricket; a grasshopper.

झिरी-a small hole; a rent.

झिरीं-a hole dug up in the earth to stop the overflow of water of a stream.

झिलँगा-worn; ragged; an old bed with loose or broken stringing.

झिलना-to enter; to penetrate forcibly; to be satisfied; to be engrossed; to be endured.

झिलम-coat of mail; armour;

झिलमिल-a kind of gauze; flickering light; a hanging shutter; armour.

झिल्लड़-thin and gauzy.

झिल्ली[1]-a membrane; lining; film; parchment; cataract; a chrysalis.

झिल्ली[2]-a cricket.

झींकना-agitate.

झींका-the quantity of corn thrown in a grinding mill.

झींखना-to lament; to repent; to be vexed.-description of one's trouble.

झींगट-boatman.

झींगर-cricket.

झींगा-a kind of small fish; shrimp; a kind of corn.

झुंड-a flock of animals or birds; a troop; herd; swarm.

झुकना-to droop; to stoop; to bow; to be angry; to cringe; to sag.

झुकमुक-blinding darkness; pitch dark.

झुकराना-to toss; to oscillate.

झुका-half mast; bent.

झुकाना-to cause to stoop; to bend; to decline; to trend; to lean; to deflect; to tilt.

झुकार-blast of wind.

झुकाव-state of being bend down; slope curvature; stoop.

झुंगिया-a hut.

झुटपुटा-dawn; twilight.

झुटुंग-with loose or undressed locks of hair.

झुट्ठल in pretence or in fun.

झुठकाना-to fraud; to deceive.

झुण्ट-protuberance; a pillar; bulging condition.

झुन-a kind of small bird.

झुनक-to tinkle.

झुनकार-fine; gauzy; thin.

झुनझुना-a child's rattle.

झुबझुबी-an ornament worn on the ear.

झुमका-a bell shaped pendant of an ear-ring; cluster.

झुमकी-an ear ring.

झुमरा-a blacksmith's sledge hammer.

झुमरि-a kind of song.

झुमाऊ-oscillating; swinging.

झुमाना-to cause to oscillate.

झुरझुरी-shivering; quivering.

झुरना-to shrivel; to waste away; to wither; to fade.

झुरमुट-a cluster of shrubs; an assembly; a crowd; a multitude; a piece of cloth twisted round the head.

झुरबन-residue which is obtained from drying a thing.

झुर्री-a wrinkle; pucker; fold.

झुलना-a nose-ring fitted with a bunch of pearls.

झुलमुला-dawn; a flare of light.

झुलवा-a swing.

झुलसन-scorching; scorching heat.

झुलाना-to rock; to swing; to dandle; to cause to swing; to keep in suspense.

झुहिरना-burden.

झूँक-a thrust.

झूँकटी-a small thicket.

झूँका-a push; a blast.

झूँखना-to lament.

झूँझना . to struggle.

झूँझल-annoyance; peevishness.

झूँठर-field, yielding a double crop.

झूंदी-a lot of land as part of a copartnery tenure.

झूँसना-to lament.

झूट-a lie.

झूठ-lie; falsehood; fiction.

झूठन-leaving of food, drinks etc.

झूठमूठ uselessly; falsely; deceptively.

झूठा-lying; false; insincere; hypocritical; illusory; unsound.

झूना-a kind of muslin.

झूपा-heap; collection; pile.

झूम-a nap; the act of swinging or oscillating.

झूमक, झूमका-a kind of song; a pendant of an earring.

झूमड़, झामड़-coquetry; useless prolixity.

झूमना-to wave; to swing; to move to and fro; to toss the head; to slumber; to gather.

झूमर-an ornament for the forehead or side of the head (a number of series of chains, forming a fringe); a type of song (sung at festival or marriages).

झूरना-to pound; to grind.

झूरा-drought; famine.

झूल-body; clothes for cattle housing, dresses which does not fit on the body; a kind of gymnastic.

झूलना-to wobble; to swing; to oscillate; to dangle; to linger in suspense.

झूलरि-a small swinging rope.

झूला-a swing; a swinging rope; a loose garment of rustic for female; a blast of wind; suspension bridge; hammock.

झूली-a cloth used as a winnowing fan.

झेंपना-to be ashamed.

झेरना-to begin; to commence; to endure.

झेरा-disturbance.

झेल-a light push; delay; hindrance; work of removing water while swimming.

झेलना-to bear; to endure; to tolerate; to undergo; to experience.

झोंक-tension; push; blast of wind; stab; rubs; commencement of a work.

झोंकना-to throw; to push violently; to spend money lavishly.

झोंकवा-a stoker.

झोंका-a blast; a puff; collision; gust; current.

झोंकी-responsibility; fear of harm; liability; risk.

झोंझ-nest (of a bird); refuge; swelling.

झोंकल-anger; wrath; fretfulness; hot displeasure.

झोंटा, झोंटी-a bundle of grass which can be grasped in a hand; a lock of long hairs; a push given to a swing.

झोंपड़ा-a hut (built of earth or clay and roofed with thatch, reeds); a shed.

झोंपड़ी-a small cottage of hovel.

झोंटिग-one who has long standing hairs on the head.

झोकंड-fireplace of a sugar-boiling house.

झोड़-betel-nut; palm.

झोना-to set in motion as a wheel; or a process.

झोरई-full of broth or soup.

झोरना-to shake; to beat.

झोरि, झोरी-a wallet; the stomach; a kind of bread.

झोल-sou; broth; inflammation; womb; placenta.

झोला[1]-sack one closed with a draw-string; a bag.

झोला[2]-a blast of wind either hot or cold harmful to crops and vegetation

झोली-a bag; sack; a pouch; wallet; the loose portion of a garment held out to receive.

झौंझट-quarrel.

झौंद-stomach; a belly.

झौंर-cluster (as of fruit); a bunch; a thicket; a group.

झौंरना-to reverberate; to echo; to resound.

झौ-flame; fire; heat.

झौड़-a quarrel; clash; row.

झौना-a large open basket made of tamarisk twigs.

झौर-dispute; controversy; wrangling; uproar.

झौहाना-to be angry; to be fretful; to make a great noise.

ञ

ञ-The tenth consonant of the Devnagari alphabet and the fifth letter of the palatal class.

ट

ट-The eleventh consonant of the Devnagari alphabet and the first letter of the cerebral class.

टंक-a coin; pearl weighing 21¼ ; pole axe; a weight equal to four about four grams; a sculptor's chisel.

टंकक-silver coin; typist.

टंकण-a typewriter.

टँकना-to be sewn on; to be stitched; to be joined or attached.

टंकशाला-mint.

टंका-silver weight a rupee; a copper coin.

टंकार-to join by sewing; to stitch a patch; to be pounded.

टँकित्र-typewriter.

टंकी-a kind of song; a large tub for storing water or oil.

टंकोर-twang of a bow; a light blow.

टंकोरी-a small balance for weighing gold or silver.

टँगड़ी-the leg; the lower leg.

टँगना-the rope on which clothes are hung up to be dried.

टँगरी-foot.

टंगाव-hanging; suspension.

टैच-sewing; stitching.

टटघंट-worshipping an idol with tinkling of bells.

टटका-unused; fresh; recent; lately begun; new.

टटल-बटल-topsy-turvy.

टटरी[1]-hedge; fence; screen.

टटरी[2]-crown of head.

टटवानी-a pony; mare.

टटाना-to be dried; to ache (the limbs or body).

टटिया-hedge.

टटीरी-sand piper.

टटुआ-a pony.

टटुई-a small pony.

टटोना-to grope in the dark.

टटोल-groping; feeling.

टटोलना-to feel with the hand; to touch; to grope in the dark; to finger.

टटोवा-a wheel; a pulley.

टट्टनी-a lizard.

टट्र-a bamboo or wickerwork frame or screen; a shutter.

टट्टी-balustrade; fence; hedge; fence; privy; latrine.

टट्टर-the sound of a clarionet (a wind instrument).

टट्टू-a pony.

टठिया-a flat metal; earthen dish.

टड़िया-an ornament which is worn on the arm.

टन्-ton; a weight of about twenty eight mound about 1045 kilograms.

टनक-a clashing or ringing sound; a tinkling.

टनमना-healthy; of good health.

टना-clitoris.

टनाका-peal; jingle.-strong (heat of the sun).

टनेल्-a tunnel.

टनाटन-continuous ringing of several bells.

टप-cover; a drop; an ear stud; sound which is made by the dripping water; hood of a phaeton or landau.

टपक-dripping; sound of dripping.

टपना-to leap; to jump (over or across); to wait (unfit, or with hopes unfulfilled).

टपाटप incessantly; continuously; successively.

टपाना-to cause to leap or to bound; to keep (one) waiting.

टप्पर-a thatch.

टब-a tub; a cistern which is used for storing water.

टब्बर-family; clan.

टमकी-a small drum; a gong.

टमटम-a tandem; a gig.

टमटी-a kind of vessel.

टमाटर-tomato.

टर-a cry; croak of a frog; chatter; scream; shout.

टरकना-disappear; to abscond; to make off secretly.

टरकाना-to evade.

टरटराना-to chatter; to speak insolently; to prattle.

टर्रटर्र-noise of frog.

टर्रा-stubborn; refractory; insistent (on a point, a view); vicious; a horse.

टर्राना-to quack; to chatter; to gamble; to murmur.

टर्रू-a child's toy which makes a crock like a frog's.

टलन-anxiety; trouble.

टलहा-of poor quality metal.

टल्ली-a species of bamboo.

टवर्ग-the group of five cerebral letters.

टवाई-useless wandering.

टस-sound of heavy being moved.

टसक-throbbing or shooting pain in the body.

टसकना-to move; to stir; to shake; to be moved; to shed tears.

टसन-quarrel; dispute.

टसना-to split; to crack.

टसर-tosser; coarse silk.

टसुआ-tears.

टहना-the branch of a tree.

टहनी-a small branch; twig.

टहल-attendance; service; duty; business; task; work.

टहलना-to walk up and down; to go for a walk.

टहलनी-a woman-in-waiting; a female servant.

टहलुआ, टहलू-a servant; an attendant; a valet.

टहाका-a push with hand or foot; a thrust.

टही-a plot; a stratagem.

टहोका-a light blow or kick; an impulse; nudge; shock;

टाँक-a weight of about four mashas; the point of a pen; mode of writing; approximation; approach.

टाँकन-riveting; soldering.

टाँका-a solder; a stitch; a tub made of stone; a patchwork; a cistern to store water.

टाँग-the leg.

टाँगना-to hang up on; to hand a person.

टांगा-a kind of two-wheeled; an axe.

टाँगी-an adze or axe.

टाँच-tortuous behaviour; a piece of cloth which can stitch to any ragged cloth.

टाँची-a long thin bag of cloth in which coins are felled up and which is tucked on to the waist.

टाँट-the skull; cranium.

टाड़-an ornament worn on the upper arm.

टाड़ा-a pot for ghi.

टान-tension.

टाप-hoof (of a horse); sound of hooves; to paw or to beat the ground (a horse, with its hooves).

टापरा-a thatched house or hut.

टापा-a leap; spring; to jump ahead; away.

टापू-an island; shoal (in a river).

टाबर-a boy; family.

टामक-a large drum.

टाल-a rick; a heap; a stack; a trick in wrestling; evasion; a shop of firewood; chaff; a procurer.

टालना-to turn away; to make excuse; to send away; to prevaricate.

टाला-half.

टाली-bells which are fastened on the neck of cattle; an agile young cow.

टाहली-a man-servant.

टिंड-a vegetable like cabbage.

टिंडा-a creeper and its fruit; a kind of gherkin.

टिकट-a postage stamp; a label; a billet; a railway ticket.

टिकटिक[1]-a clacking of the tongue to urge on an animal.

टिकटिक[2]-ticking as of a watch.

टिकठी-a three-legged stool; a framework of bamboo; bier; triangular framework to which a person is tied to be flogged.

टिकड़ा-a disk; a thick bread which is fried on fire.

टिकना-to stop; to abide; to lodge; to tarry; to continue to stay; to sojourn; to be deposited at the bottom; to be useful for someone for a time.

टिकरी-a fried savoury pastry.

टिकली-a small round cake; a small tablet of coloured glass often gummed on the forehead of Indian women.

टिकाऊ-durable; lasting; firm; abiding; strong; permanent; stable.

टिकान-stay; residence; lodge; stability; continuance.

टिकानी-cross-bars of a cart frame.

टिकाव-stay; sojourn; residence; lodging.

टिकिया-round object as of dough ready for baking; a small flat cake of bread.

टिकुरा-a mound.

टिकुला-a spangle.

टिकैत-the prince who is an heir apparent; a chief.

टिकोरा-a small unripe mango.

टिकौना-base; support.

टिक्कड़-a thick cake of bread; a large tablet.

टिक्की-a round, flat piece; a small bread-cake.

टिघलना-to be melted.

टिचन-ready and correct.

टिटिहरी-a peewit; a sandpiper; a lapwing.

टिटिहारोर-shout; clamour.

टिट्टिभ-lapwing or a sandpiper.

टिड्डा-a grasshopper.

टिड्डी-a grasshopper or locust.

टिड़बिड़ंगा-uneven; rugged; irregular.

टिपका-a drop-dip.

टिपकारी-the connection of one stone or brick with another made by lapping the one over the other; a bond.

टिपटिप-sound made by the fall of water in drops.

टिपारा-a crown-shaped cap of Indians.

टिपारी-a box or basket.

टिपोर-boasting.

टिपुर-pride; arrogance; false show; ostentation.

टिप्पणी-annotation; comment; scholium; gloss note.

टिप्पी-mark which is made by the tip of a finger.

टिब्बा-rising ground; a hill.

टिमाक-ostentation; finery; airs.

टिरफिस-peevishness; fretfulness; obstinacy.

टिर्राना-to croak; to grumble.

टिलवा-a kind of wooden piece; a pigmy; a man of small stature.

टिल्ल-a push; a thrust.

टिसुआ-tears.

टिहुकना-to tremble; to shudder.

टीक-a close-fitting ornament worn on the neck.

टीकना-to mark the forehead with a distinctive mark.

टीका-annotation; commentary; note; remark; comment; footnote; mark made on the forehead with sandal paste; an ornament for the head.

टीन-sheet of tinned iron; a pannikin.

टीप-pressure; raising of voice in singing; hit; bond.

टीपन-horoscope; nativity.

टीपना-to press; to squeeze; to press in mortar; plater; to massage.

टीबा-raising ground; sand bank.

टीला-a hillock; mound.

टीस-a throbbing pain in a part of body; a throb.

टुँगना-to gnaw fine leaves.

टुंच-useless; mean.

टुंटा, टुंडा-stumpy; amputated.

टुंड-stump (of a branch, a tree, a limb); a leafless branch or tree; mutilated or physically defective; a hand, branch, that has been cut off.

टुंडी-the naval; stump of a arm; the arm excluding the hands.

टुइयाँ-a small parrot; tiny; dwarfish.

टुक-trivial; insignificant; small.

टुकड़गदा-a beggar.

टुकड़तोड़-one who is supported by another.

टुकड़ा-a piece; bit; scrap; fragment; a part; section.

टुकड़ी, टुकरी-a small piece; a fragment; a lice; multitude; part of an army; piece from cloth.

टुघलाना-to chew food slowly; to ruminate.

टुच्चा-base; worthless; degrading.

टुटका-a magical charm; an amulet.

टुटपूँजिया-a man of small means of income, education etc.

टुंडी-naval; a small piece.

टुनकार-chiming of a clock.

टुनगा-point of a sprig or twig; a small branch.

टुपकना-to backbite; to bite slowly; to sting.

टुर्रा-a small fragment; a particle (of sand); a slice.

टुसियाना-to bud.

टूँ-sound of making wind.

टूँकना, टूँगना-to eat in small bits; to nibble.

टूँड-the nozzle on the mouth of insects; the pointed portion of an ear of corn.

टुँडी-naval.

टूक, टूकर-an atom; a piece; a bit; a particle; a fragment.

टूका-fourth part of bread; a bit; peace.

टूट-breaking; rupture; fracture; loss; harm; deficiency; a mistake in writing; passage.

टूटन-breaking; fracture; pain in body; a fragment.

टूटना-to break; to burst; to fall; to shiver; to wreck; to make a sudden attack; to come by chance; to be separated; to be weak.

टूठना-to be pacified; to be satisfied or appeased.

टूठनि-satisfaction.

टूम-an ornament; finery.

टूमना-to make sarcastic remarks; to push.

टेंगना, टेंगरा-a kind of fish.

टेंट-the fold of the loin-cloth, pod of cotton.

टेंटा-a large bird (the grey).

टेंटुआ-the windpipe; the throat.

टेउकी-support which is placed on this bottom of a jug.

टेक-support; block; habit; stay; obstruction.

टेकर-rising ground; hillock.

टेकरा-a small hill; a hillock; a mound.

टेकला-persistence.

टेकानी-a linchpin.

टेकी-trustworthy; reliable.

टेकुआ-an awl; a spindle; a reamer.

टेघरना-to melt.

टेटका-an ornament worn on the ear.

टेटी-haughty behaviour; displeasure.

टेटुआ-a throttle.

टेड़-crookedness.

टेड़ा-the trunk of a tree.

टेंढ़-twist; bend; cunningness; haughtiness.

टेढ़बिड़ंगा-irregular; uneven.

टेढ़ा-bent; irregular; uneven; crooked; perplexing; difficult.

टेढे obliquely; crookedly.

टेना-to sharpen; to whet.

टेनी-tiny and small, table; the stone by which something make sharp.

टेम-flame; light.

टेमन-a kind of snake.

टेर[1]-shout; call; a high-pitched note (in singing); to call; to raise; the voice; to implore.

टेर[2]-spent; passed.

टेरना-to sing in a loud tone; to accomplish; to execute; to finish; spend.

टेरनि-calling.

टेरा-squinted.

टेला-marriage ceremony; marriage custom.

टेव-a habit; a way.

टेवकी-a smallest sail of a ship.

टेवैया-one who sharpens the edge of tool; a sharpener.

टेसू-the tree and its blossoms; a kind of play of boys.

टेहला-ceremony.

टैयां-a kind of small flat conch shell.

टोंक-intervene.

टोंका-corner; border; frill; end.

टोंचना-to prick; to pierce.

टोंटा-a spout fitted to a pot for drawing off water; a jet.

टोंटी-a spout; ferrule; cock; tap.

टोइयाँ-a kind of small parrot.

टोई-joint of a reed.

टोंगा-tonga.

टोंगू-a kind of small parrot.

टोंट-the beak of bird.

टोक-obstruction; interruption; influence of evil eye.

टोकरा-large wickerwork basket; a shallow basket; punnet; a coop.

टोकरी-a basket.

टोका-chopper.

टोकारा-suggestion; to bring to notice; to remind.

टोकसी-half a sherd of a coconut fruit.

टोटका-a magical practice; a black earthen pot placed in a field to avert the evil eye; amulet.

टोटकेहाई-a woman who performs a charm.

टोटा-deficiency; loss; part; remnant; a cartridge.

टोड़ा[1]-a neck chain; a bag or purse; a wrist ornament; an anklet with bells.

टोड़ा[2]-projecting part of a roof or wall.

टोना-magic; enchantment; glamour; witchcraft; black art; a kind of song; a bird of prey.

टोप-a large hat; hood; a helmet; thimble.

टोपी-a cap; hat; tiara; crown.

टोर-a hatchet; an axe.

टोरना-to cut to pieces; to break; to remove the eyes on account of shame.

टोरा-balance which is used for weighing silk.

टोर्रा-an atom; a particle; hard irregular grain.

टोरू-a particle; an atom.

टोल-party band; a group; quarter (of a village).

टोला-part of a town or city; quarter; a pebble; a piece of stone.

टोली-a group; band; party; quarter or a town or village.

टोबा-a group of several houses in a place.

टोवना-to grope in the dark; to touch with the hand.

टोवा-the boat-man who sounds the depth the a river.

टोह-searching; investigating.

टोहना-to feel for; to touch; to search.

टोहना-to seek; to be search of.

टोहिया-on who makes a search; a spy.

टौरना-to make a search; to investigate; to assay.

टौरिया-a hillock.

ठ

ठ The twelfth consonant of the Devnagari alphabet and the second letter of the cerebral class.

ठंठ-familyless; branchless (tree).

ठंठार-empty; vacant.

ठंठी-the cow which gives milk even when her calf is dead.

ठंठपाल-poor; penniless.

ठंड-cold.

ठंडई-a cold drink.

ठंडक-satisfaction; happiness; coldness; relief from disease.

ठंडा-wintry; cold; chilly; passionless.

ठंडाई-coldness.

ठंडी-colloq. smallpox.

ठ-cypher; loud roar.

ठई-stopped; settled.

ठक-stunned; the sound of knocking or hammering.

ठकठौवा-a kind of cymbal used by beggars.

ठकार-name of the letter

ठकुआ-a kind of sweetened .

ठकुराइन-landlady; a queen; mistress.

ठकुराई-supremacy; authority; the rank; office or status of a

ठकोरी-a stick support in the form of T which is used by mendicant to sit on.

ठक्कर-knocking together of two things; a collision.

ठग-swindler; villain; a cheat; a robber; a thug; member of a secret gang of robbers and murderers.

ठगई-cheating; knavery; robbing; theft.

ठगना-to dupe; to rob; to cheat; to swindle.

ठगमूरी-intoxication used by thugs to make their victim senseless.

ठगमोदक-intoxicated sweetmeats impregnated with narcotic drugs used by thugs to make their victim senseless.

ठगोरी-charm; spell; cheating; imposture.

ठट-a crowd; throng.

ठटकीला-gaudy; orna-mented.

ठटनि-construction; formation; structure.

ठटोली-fun; joking.

ठट्ठ-company; crowd; community.

ठट्ठा-a joke; a laugh; guffaw; a trifle; an easy matter.

ठठकना-to shrink; to stop; to draw back; to shrivel.

ठठना-to be fixed; to be firm; to be decked; arrayed.

ठठरी-skeleton; framework; pier; thatching of a hut.

ठठाना-to be rampant; to hold sway.

ठठेर-grandeur.

ठठेरा-a coppersmith; tinsmith; brazier.

ठठोल, ठठोलिया-a jester; a bantered; a humorist.

ठड्डा-a framework; the lengthwise stick of a paper kite; the backbone.

ठढ़ा-erect; standing.

ठढ़िया-a wooden mortar used for pounding paddy.

ठनगन-persistent or repeated demand for a gift.

ठनठनगोपाल-a penniless person; a worthless object.

ठनना-to be determined on; to be launched; to break out; to begin; to arise; to appear.

ठपका-a dash; a stroke.

ठप-closed; suspended; finished.

ठपना-to fix on the mind; to settle anything.

ठप्प colloq. a conclusive ending.

ठप्पा-a stamp; die; printer's block; type.

ठमक-recoil; stoppage; lingering; halt; break in motion; elasticity.

ठयना-to begin with a resolve; to make a firm determination; to finish; to settle; to establish.

ठरन-severe cold.

ठरमरुआ-half-dead with cold.

ठरिया-a simple kind of Hookah having a short; straight stem.

ठर्रा-thick yarn; a big half-bakes brick; a kind of cheap spirituous liquor.

ठलुआ-out of work.

ठवनी-mode of sitting or standing; position of body.

ठवर-room; place; space.

ठस-thick; solid; compact; strong; heavy; weight; slow; of dull sound; miserly.

ठसक-vanity; pride; ostentation.

ठसका-dry cough; a dash.

ठसमठस-crammed.

ठस्सा-pride; dry cough.

ठहना-a place of rest; space; interval; kitchen.

ठहर-a place; spot; kitchen.

ठहरना-to stop; to halt; to tarry; to rest; to remain; to wait; to cause, to stand; to stay; to live; to dwell.

ठहराऊ-fixed; firm; stable; lasting; durable.

ठहराव-stability (as of a situation).

ठहरो-wo! wait.

ठहाका-guffaw; a loud laugh.

ठांहिया-place.

ठाँ-residence.

ठाउँ-station; place; residence.

ठाठँ-dry; not giving mild (said of a cow); sapless.

ठांठा-healthy; fit.

ठाँय-sound of a bang, crash or shot; place; station; residence; quarrel.

ठाँव-station; residence; place.

ठाँस-coughing.

ठाँसना-to cram; to stuff; to press vigorously.

ठा-to determine; to intend.

ठाऊं-place.

ठाकुर-lord; god; idol; leader; master; chief.

ठाट[1]-splendour; splendid display.

ठाट[2]-to be harnessed, provided with (as a vehicle with animal to pull it).

ठाटबाट-splendour; pomp; gaudiness; show.

ठाटर-a framework of bamboo; the body.

ठाटी-multitude; assembly.

ठाड़ा in an upright position.

ठाठ-splendour.

ठाठा-hump of a bull.

ठाढ़ा-standing; erect; entire; proved; created; straight; steep.

ठादर-crawl; skirmish.

ठान-plunging into an activity.

ठानना-to determine; to intent; to settle; to resolve.

ठाना-to settle; to establish; to found.

ठाम-residence; place; situation; establishment.

ठायँ-destination; place.

ठार[1]-a place.

ठार[2]-frost; extremely cold.

ठाल-leisure.

ठाला-want of income; unemployment.

ठाली-unoccupied; idle.

ठावँ-place.

ठासा-an instrument for twisting a sheet of metal.

ठाहर-station; place; halting place; residence.

ठिंगना-unusual short of stature.

ठिक-a small piece of metal.

ठिकठौना-settlement; adjustment; arrangement.

ठिकड़ा-a shard.

ठिकना-stay.

ठिकरा-a shard; a fragment of an earthen vessel.

ठिकरी-a pebble.

ठिकाना-location; place; station; abode; residence; dwelling; destination; sustenance; arrangement.

ठिठक-embarrassment; uneasiness; perplexity.

ठुड्डी[1]-the chin.

ठुड्डी[2]-a cob for corn with the grains removed; a grain of corn unburst on roasting.

ठुनकना-to tap with the fingers.

ठुनठुन-the weeping and sobbing of a child.

ठुमका-dwarfish, of low stature.

ठुमुक-the act of walking with a graceful air.

ठुमरी-a type of song for two voices; a type of song.

ठुर्री-semi-parched cereal.

ठुस-dense.

ठुसकना-to whisper; to weep.

ठुसकी-sound of making wind.

ठुसना-to be crammed or stuffed in a small piece.

ठूंग-the bill or beak of a bird; the act of pecking.

ठूंठ-snag; stump; stum.

ठूँसना-to force down or in; to thrust or to cram; to eat greedily; to pack in (food).

ठेंगा-a small club; a thumb; to reject or deny something indecently.

ठेंठी-wax of the ear; plug of cotton in the ear; a stopper.

ठेंपी-a plug; a stopper.

ठेक-a support.

ठेका-place of rest; support; push; hit; rhythm; plug; stopper; contract.

ठेकाई-printing of borders in cloth or calico.

ठेकेदार-contractor.

ठेगना-to stop; to subtract; to take support.

ठेघा-a support.

ठेठ-pure; genuine; real; true; actual; informal; idiomatic speech.

ठेगी-plug; cork stopper.

ठेला-push; stroke; barrow; trolley; wheel-barrow; a rush.

ठेली-trolley; barrow.

ठेस-knock; push; percussion.

ठेसना-to knock; to dash against; to prod.

ठेसरा-a jeer; a taunt.

ठेहरी-the lower portion of a door; a support.

ठेही-sugarcane which is cut into small pieces.

ठेहुका-the cattle whose hind feed strike against each other while walking.

ठेहुना-the knee.

ठैकर-a kind of sour fruit like the lemon.

ठैन-residence; abode.

ठोंग-a peck; a blow struck with the bent fingers.

ठोंठ-beak; bill.

ठोंठी-pod of gram; pea.

ठोंसा-a stamp or mould for making metal ornaments.

ठो used after a number.

ठोक-a blow.

ठोकना-to hammer home; to strike; to drive in as a peg.

ठोकर-blow; stroke; kick; percussion; stumbling; block; toe of shoes; a smart blow.

ठोकरा-stiff; hard.

ठोकवा-a pancake as flattened by hand.

ठोका-an ornament which is worn on the twist.

ठोट-stupid.

ठोठ-foolish; insipid.

ठोठरा-empty; hollow.

ठोड़ी-the chin.

ठोढ़ी-the chin.

ठोप-a drop; to drip.

ठोर-kind of sweetmeat; a bird's beak; bill.

ठोला-a small pot.

ठोस-solid; dense; firm; sound; serving.

ठोहना-to investigate; to search.

ठोहर-scarcity.

ठौका-the place where water is lifted for irrigation.

ठौनी-place; locality.

ठौर-place; locality; room residence; chance.

ड-The thirteenth consonant of the alphabet and the third letter of the cerebral class.

डंक-point; nib of a pen; a cutting or wounding remark.

डंकना-to roar; to cry loud.

डंका-a kettle drum; a big drum; to speak openly.

डँकिनी-demoness.

डँगज्वर-dengue fever.

डँगवारा-mutual assistance between farmers consisting in the loan of oxen and ploughs without charge.

डंटैया-a molester.

डंठल-grasses; stem of cereals; stalk.

डंठा-stalks of a grain.

डँठी-stalk.

डंड-cudgel; a stick; the arm.

डँडवत-prostrated.

डँडवारा-a low boundary wall or fence of a field.

डंडवी-one who pays a fine as punishment.

डंडा-a pole; bar; a staff; beam of a pair of scales.

डंडाल-a kettle-drum.

डँडिया-a striped sari as worn at the festival.

डंडी-handle; beam of a scale; shaft; the thin stick; a twig of a plant which bears flowers.

डंडीर-a straight line.

डंडोरना-to make a search.

डंबर-gaudiness; ostentation; coquetry.

डँवरुआ-gout.

डँस-a gadfly.

डँसना-sting.

डक-a kind of strong thick cloth.

डकई-a species of plantain.

डकरना-to bellow; to low.

डकार-roaring; a belch; bellowing.

डकैत-one of a band of robbers; a robber.

डकैती-piracy; robbery; robbing.

डग-a step or stride;

डगडगाना-to quiver; to shake; to tremble; to stagger.

डगर-road; path.

डगरा-path; way.

डगा-the stick which is used for beating a drum.

डट-mark; sign.

डटना-to stop; to stay; to stand still; to stand firmly.

डट्ठा-a stopper; plug.

डढ्ढार-having a long beard; brave; courageous; valiant.

डढ़-to burn.

डढन-a kind of fish.

डढ़ना-to scorch; to burn.

डढ़ही-a kind of fish.

डढ़ियल-having beard.

डढ्ढना-to burn.

डपट-a rebuke; shouting; rushing forward; galloping.

डपोरशंख-one who makes big promises but does nothing.

डप्पू-vast; huge.

डफ-a drum; tambourine used by singers.

डफली-a small drum.

डफार-to make a great outcry.

डफाली-a drum player.

डफोरना-to challenge.

डब-a pouch; pocket.

डबकना-to drip; to let fall in drops; to throb with pain.

डबका-fear; apprehension.

डबकौंह-tearful.

डबकौहाँ-filled with tears; agitated; perplexed.

डबडबाना-(eyes) to be filled with tears.

डबरी[1]-pool of water; a ditch.

डबरी[2]-an earthen water-cup; bowl.

डबी-small box.

डब्बा-a railway wagon; bogie; a tin box; a box fitted with a lid.

डभकना-to float and sink in water alternately; to have eyes filled with tears.

डभका-water which has been just drawn from a well.

डभकी-a kind of dish made of pulse.

डमरू-a tabor or small drum shaped like an hour-glass.

डमाडोल-with no fixed abode; shilly-shally.

डबन-work of flying in the air.

डयन-a litter; flight.

डर-fear; terror; dread; awe.

डरउनी-menace.

डरपोक-fear.

डरावना-fearsome; causing fear; formidable; deterrent; intimidating.

डरावा-anything told to frighten; a piece of wood tied to the branch of a tree which when moved strikes against a branch and terrifies birds.

डरिया-a small branch.

डरीला-full of branches or twigs.

डरेया-fearful; awful.

डरेस-a kind of cloth.

डरैला-fearsome.

डल-a piece; a fragment; a bit.

डलई-a basket.

डलना-to be thrown in.

डला-a piece; a fragment; a wicker-work basket.

डलिया-a small basket; a pottle; a scuttle.

डली-a small piece; a lump; bit; a betel nut.

डल्लक-a basket made of cane or bamboo.

डस-the string by which scales are suspended in a balance; the threads at the end of a piece of cloth which are not woven.

डसना-to bite; to sting (as a snake, a scorpion).

डहक-to sob; to cry out; to roar; to break down as in tears.

डहका-to deceive.

डहडहा-fresh; green; blooming; cheerful; joyful.

डहना[1]-a bird's feather.

डहना[2]-to be jealous; to burn; to envy; to be reduced to ashes.

डहर-way; path; road; a track; the milky way.

डहरना-to roam; to walk.

डहरा[1]-marshy ground; low.

डहरा[2]-to turn the eyes towards one.

डहार-one who torments.

डाँक-to leap across or over.

डाँकना-to leap over; to bestride; to retch; to vomit.

डाँकिनी-female robber.

डाँकू-robber.

डाँगर-a beast; a low caste.

डाँट-subjugation; government; menacing; threatening; molestation; objurgation.

डाँवरी-daughter; girl.

डाँवरू-a tiger cub.

डाँवाडोल-unsteady; fluctuating; wandering; fickle.

डाँस-a large mosquito; a gad-fly.

डा suffix (form nouns having potentially dimin) force .

डाइन-hag; a demoness; witch; a shrewish or ugly old woman.

डाक-post; a stage-coach; a bid in auction sale.

डाकखाना-a post-office.

डाकगाड़ी-a mail train.

डाकघर-a post-office; post mark.

डाकना[1]-to vomit; to retch; to discharge from stomach; to bestride.

डाकना[2]-to jump over; to leap over; to vault.

डाक-बंगला-Dak-bungalow.

डाकर-a rich clay soil.

डाका-robbery; plunder; spoliation.

डाकिन, डाकिनी-female robber; a hellcat; succumb as a witch.

डाकिया-a postman.

डाकू-robber; bandit; dacoit; highwayman.

डाकोर-the god .

डाक्टर-a doctor; a person trained in western medicine; teacher of some subject.

डाख-a tree.

डागा-the stick which is used for beating a drum.

डाची-a young female camel that has calved once.

डाट-plug; stop; keystone; wedge; archway.

डाटना-to stop up; to cram; to support; to eat greedily; to pack full.

डाटना-to scold.

डाढ़-a molar tooth; fang (of a wild animal).

डाढ़ना-to burn.

डाढ़ा-extreme anguish; intense pain; wood-fire.

डाढ़ी-tuft; beard.

डाब-a sword belt; an unripe fruit of coconut.

डाबक-low ground where water collects; marshy ground; a pool of water; puddle; a small tank or ditch for water.

डाबा-a box.

डाभ-a kind of grass; mango blossom; fresh green coconut.

डाभक-water which has been just drawn from a well.

डाभर-agitation; display; ostentation; pitch.

डामर[1]-resin of the tree; a torch using pitch.

डामर[2]-marshy ground.

डायन-witch; hag.

डार-a bough; a branch; a stalk; a small basket.

डाल[1]-a branch.

डाल[2]-a basket; a gift; gift to a bride.

डाली-a wide, flat basket; a basket or tray of flowers; fruit.

डाबरा-a son; a child.

डाबरी-a daughter.

डास-to spread; to make a bed.

डासन-a bedding.

डासना-to spread a bed.

डासनी-a bedstead.

डाह-jealously; envy; heart burning; hatred; malice; enmity.

डाहना-to trouble; to tease; to torment; to perplex.

डाही-jealous; envious; malicious; ill-willed.

डाहुक-spiteful; teasing; a type of bird.

डिंगर-a fat man; a rascal; a scoundrel; a slave; a rogue.

डिंगल-an archaising form of early Language.

डिंब-skirmish; quarrel; an egg; a ball; uterus; bladder; lungs; a nugget; a fish.

डिंभ[1]-a child.

डिंभ[2]-vanity; pride.

डिंभक-larva.

डिभिया-ostentatious; arrogant; proud; haughty.

डिम्ब-fear; foetus; egg; rout; uproar; spleen.

डिम्बक-a child; boy.

डिम्बज-one born from an egg.

डिम्बाहब-a war in which the king of the land does not participate.

डिम्भ-a child; a fool; a calf.

डिल-a skein of wool.

डिल्ला-hump of an ox.

डियट-candelabrum.

डिंगिया-a boaster.

डीक-cataract of the eyes.

डीठ-look; glance; view; vision; knowledge.

डीठना-to come in sight.

डीठबंध-a juggler; a conjurer.

डीठिमठी-witchcraft; evil eyes.

डीतर-one who follows another.

डीबुआ-a.

डीमडाम-gaudiness; coquetry.

डील-size; bulk; stature.

डुंग-a heap; mould; a hillock; a small hill.

डुक-a blow with the fist.

डुकड़ी-a two horse cart.

डुकरिया-an old woman.

डुकियाना-to give a blow to someone with the fist.

डुक्कर-a boar.

डुण्डुभ-a water-snake.

डुपटना-to crease cloth.

डुबकी-a dish made of pulse; submersion; a dip; a plunge.

डुबान-a deep place; depth; a plunge.

डुबाना-to dip; to duck; to immerse into water; to swamp; to destroy; to ruin; to demolish.

डुबाव-depth to drown into.

डुब्बी-a dip.

डुभा-a large cup or small vessel to eat from.

डुरी-a string.

डुलना-to walk with a enticing gait.

डुलाना-to move; to shake; to remove; to revolve; to give motion to.

डूँगर-hillock; a hill.

डूँगरी-a small hill; hillock.

डूँडा-a bullock with one horn or with broken or defective horns.

डूगर-a hillock; a mound.

डूबना-to dive to; to plunge; to set in the horizon; to sing; to sag; to subside.

डूमर-a fig-tree

डेंगा-a float; a raft.

डेंडहा-a water-serpent.

डेंढ-one and a half.

डेकारना-to belch.

डेग-a cauldron; a retort; a still; copper.

डेगची-copper; a kettle.

डेरा-residence; abode; tent; pavilion.

डेल-lump, piece; clod.

डेला-the eyeball; the white of the eye.

डेली-a fowler's basket.

डेवढ़, डेवढ़ा-one and a half; half as much again.

डेवढ़ी-threshold; vestibule.

डेहरी-a household grain-store; threshold.

डैना-pinion; wing.

डोंगरा-a shower before the beginning of the rainy season.

डोंगा-a small open boat; a canoe.

डोंगी-canoe.

डोंडहा-water-snake.

डोंडा-cartridge for a rifle; a large cardamom.

डोंडी-a small pod or seed-capsule.

डोई-a wooden spoon or ladle.

डोकरा-a weak old person; also used for father.

डोकरी-an old women.

डोकिया, डोकी-a small wooden cup or flat dish.

डोडो-the duck- like bird Dodo which is now extinct.

डोनी-small boat.

डोब, डोबा-a plunge; a dive; a dip; a reservoir.

डोम-the sweeper or scavenger class among the Hindus.

डोमकौआ-the black crow.

डोमड़ा-sweeper.

डोमनी-woman of a community; the wife of a

डोर-rope; thread; string; line.

डोरा-thread; cord; string; stripe; line; the cutting edge of sword; a ladle with long handle; blood-vessels of the conjunctiva of the eye distended by intoxication.

डोरिया-striped material muslin.

डोरी-cord; string; rope; thread; entanglement; lace.

डोरे accompanying; together.

डोल-a bucket; an iron pot for drawing water from a well.

डोलची-a small bucket; a small basket.

डोलना-to wander; to roam; to ramble; to move; to swing.

डोला-a litter carried by porters as used to convey a bride to the house of her parents-in-law.

डोलना-to move; to remove; to rock; to make a man run away; a reel.

डोली-hearse; bier.

डोसा-a south Indian dish (rice pancake).

डोहरा-a large ladle or spoon.

डोड़सा-pimple; papilla; acne; virus.

डौंज-a boundary mark; a platform in a field from which crops can be watched.

डौंडी-a proclamation by beat of drum; to make a public proclamation; a proclamation of victory.

डौआ-a spoon made of wood.

डौल-manner; form; mode; shape; framework; method; appearance; figure; image.

डौलडाल-artifice; trick.

डौलना-to bring into shape; to form into a model.

डौला-the wrist.

ड्योढ़ा-one and a half.

ड्योढ़ी-the main gate of a house; a vestibule; frame of a gate; a porch.

ड्योढ़ीदार-a doorkeeper; a porter.

ढ

ढ-The fourteenth consonant of the alphabet and the fourth letter of the cerebral class.

ढ-a big drum; a dog; sound.

ढँकना-to cover.

ढंग-pretext; sort; posture; tread; structure; mannerism; mode; method.

ढंगलाना-to cause to stumble.

ढंगी-cunning; crafty; witty.

ढंढार-very old.

ढंढोई-scum of boiling sugarcane juice.

ढँढोर-flame of fire.

ढंढोरची-a public crier.

ढँढोरा-a drum which is used by a public crier.

ढकना-a lid; a cover.

ढकनिया-a small lid.

ढकनी-a small cover or lid.

ढका-blow; a push; a big drum.

ढकिल-a furious attack.

ढकेलना-to drive; to hurtle; to push; to press against; do dash.

ढकोसना-to gulp food or drink.

ढकोसला-dissimulation; hypocrisy.

ढक्कन-a cover; lid.

ढक्का-a big drum.

ढंकण-moss.

ढचर-vain show; affectedness.

ढटींगड़-sturdy; burly.

ढद्ढा-big and clumsy.

ढड्ढी-female prattler; a talkative old woman.

ढप्पू-extensive; very large.

ढब-manner; way; means.

ढबरी-land lying under water for part of the year.

ढबीला-elegant; graceful.

ढब्बूस-heavy; clumsy; fat.

ढबूस-fat; corpulent.

ढरकना-to descend; to flow as a liquid; to roll; to recline.

ढरकाना-to tilt; to pour; to make a liquid flow; to roll.

ढरकी-shuttle (of a loom).

ढरहरना-to slip; to bend.

ढरहरी-a kind of small-cake or baked dough.

ढर्रा-manner; way; style; attitudes.

ढलक-rolling; spilling; inclining; tilting.

ढलका-running over or spilling as of a watering eye.

ढलना-to recline; to decline; to roll; to flow; to be poured out; to be engaged; to be pleased; to be moulded into shape.

ढलमल-unsteady; shaking; tottering; wavering.

ढलवाँ-prepared by being moulded.

ढलाई-moulding; casting; wages of casting.

ढलैत-a soldier who wields a shield.

ढलैया-foundryman; a caster.

ढवाना-to cause to be destroyed or demolished.

ढहना-to fall or tumble down (as a house); to be ruined; to be destroyed.

ढहरी-a big pot or vessel of clay.

ढाँकना-to cover.

ढाँच-frame work.

ढाँचा-structure; style; plan; framework; form; system.

ढाँपना-to cover up; to shut; to hide; to conceal.

ढाँस-a cough in animals; noise of cough.

ढाँसना-to cough (animal).

ढाई-two and a half.

ढाक-the tree.

ढाका-the city of .

ढाठा-a strip of cloth tied over the head or generally used by dacoits to conceal this identity.

ढाढ़स-comfort; encouragement; solace; confidence; consolation.

ढाढ़ी-a kind of Mohammedan minstrel.

ढाना-to destroy; to demolish; to pull to the ground.

ढापना to cover.

ढाबर-a pool of dirty water.

ढार-declivity; gradient; slope; construction.

ढारना-to ruin; to demolish; to devastate; to destroy.

ढाबा-a place where snacks or meals are sold; broad caves to a house (beneath which people can sit).

ढामक-sound of a drum.

ढाल[1]-a shield.

ढाल[2]-manner; habit; slope; incline; cast; mould; form; way.

ढालना-to pour out; to drink an intoxicating drug; to mould; to cast; to shape; to found; to speak tauntingly.

ढालवाँ, ढाल sloping; cast as a metal.

ढाली-carrying a shield.

ढास-a robber.

ढासना-a support; a pillow; a set with a support.

ढाह-severely broken or eroded ground.

ढाहना-to destroy; to demolish; to ruin; to pull down.

ढाहा-steep; slope or bank as of a river.

ढिंढोर-to search through; to stir up.

ढिंढोरना-to chum; to make a search within a pot with hands.

ढिंढोरा-proclamation by beat of drum.

ढिकलना-to be pushed.

ढिग near; close to.

ढिंगाड़-heap; pile; store.

ढिठाई-impudence; pertness; presumption; saucity; petulance.

ढिबरी-nut; a socket; a mould.

ढिमका such a person.

ढिलाई-sluggishness; laziness; looseness.

ढिल्लड़-lazy; negligent; a person who work as a moulder.

ढिसर-to collapse; to be given up a worthy intention.

ढींगर-a robust person; a husband or paramour.

ढींढा-pot-bellied; pregnancy; protuberant.

ढीट-a mark; a line.

ढीठ-insolent; rude; bold; fearless; stubborn; brash; presumptuous.

ढीम-a big slab of stone; a clod of earth.

ढील-relaxation; looseness; laziness; slackness; delay; inattention; sluggishness

ढीलना-to relax; to loose; to let loose (animal).

ढीला-loose; slack; relaxed; flabby.

ढीह-a mound; high bank over a river.

ढुंढ-a robber; a thug.

ढुंढा-the name of a witch.

ढुकना-to enter; to penetrate; to pierce; to make a sudden attack; to conceal or hide an object from view.

ढुकली-a water lifting appliance.

ढुड़-the hip; to give one a cross-throw in wrestling.

ढुरकना-to slip off; to totter; to incline; to stumble.

ढुरना-to totter; to oscillate; to wave; to slip; to be engaged in work; to incline; to be pleased; to be happy; to glow.

ढुरहुरी-track; path; footpath; slipping; tottering.

ढुलकना-to slip; to slide; to drop; to fall over or down; to roll; to drip.

ढुलाना-to spill; to cause to be carried; to cause to tumble; to let fall; to incline; to swing.

ढुलाई-freight; cartridge.

ढूँढ-search; investigation.

ढूँढना-to search; to investigate; to spot.

ढूक-to lurk; to peep; to go into; to eavesdrop.

ढूह-a mound; ground intersected by ravines.

ढेंक-a kind of bird that lives by the side of water.

ढेंकली-an appliance in the form of a seesaw for lifting water; an appliance for pounding paddy.

ढेंकी-an appliance for pounding corn.

ढेंपुनी-pointed end of corn; nipple of female breast.

ढेंकली-an apparatus for drawing water lever supported on an upright, with a bucket attached to on end and a counterpoise weight at the other; an apparatus for pounding grain.

ढेंका-a machine for pounding oil-seeds or husking grain; a beam serving as a door-bar.

ढेंखर-a bundle of thorns tied together used as a makeshift harrow; and in threshing grain.

ढेंगा-a heavy stick or piece of wood.

ढेंडस-the plant called okra; lady's finger.

ढेंढ-one and a half.

ढेंढी-heap.

ढेंपी-lump.

ढेंरा-cross-eyed; squinting.

ढेड-stupid.

ढेड़-a heap.

ढेढ-a crow; a name of a community of low status whose members work with hides.

ढेढा-a pod or seed-capsule.

ढेन-a cow.

ढेपा-a lump (as of clay); a clod.

ढेबरी-nut socket.

ढेर-a heap; pile; abundance.

ढेरा-a wheel-shaped woo-den framework having two or three intersecting arms used for twisting thread or twine; a framework used to hold open the mouth of a leather water-bucket.

ढेरी-a pile; a heap; an accumulation.

ढेलवाँस-a sling.

ढेला-a clod; a lump of earth; a fragment; ball of the eye; a kind of paddy.

ढोंका-a small piece of stone; clot; clod; rubble.

ढोंग-trick; fraud; deceit; delusion.

ढोंगी-deceitful; fraudulent; deceptive; mountebank.

ढोंडी[1]-a grass which grows in rice-field and chokes young plants.

ढोंडी[2]-a girl.

ढोंढ-a bud; a pod of cotton-seed plant.

ढोंढा-a pod or seed-capsule.

ढोक-large mouthful.

ढोकना-to gulp large amount of; to gulp down.

ढोका-a small piece as a lump of salt; a flat piece of stone; blinkers.

ढोटा-child; boy; son.

ढोटी-girl; daughter.

ढोना-to carry; to bear on head or shoulder; to subsist; to maintain.

ढोबरा-hole as in a pot or in wall.

ढोरना-to pour out; to cause to roll on the ground.

ढोरा-a worm found in rotten fruits.

ढोरी-eagerness; ardour; ardent; devotion.

ढोल-a drum; tympanum of the ear; a kettle drum.

ढोलक-a small drum.

ढोलकिया-a drummer.

ढोलकी-a small drum.

ढोलन-friend; lover.

ढोलना-an amulet of the shape of a drum.

ढोलनी-a swing which is used for babies.

ढोलाई-transport; the work of transportation.

ढोलिया-drummer.

ढोली-a bundle of two hundred betel leaves; a jest.

ढौंचा-four and a half; the four and a half time table.

ढौंसना-to acclaim in merriment or joke.

ढौरी-repetition of anything.

ण

ण-The fifteenth consonant of the Devnagari alphabet and the fifth letter of the cerebral class.

त

त-The sixteenth consonant of the Devnagari alphabet and the first letter of the dental class.

त-a boat; virtue; a thief; falsehood; tail; lap; an untouchable; foetus; a gem.

तं-a boat; virute moral.

तंग-tight; harried; distressed; narrow; shot of, wanting.

तंगदस्त-miserly; poor.

तंगदिल-close-fisted; miserly; small-hearted.

तंगहाल-poor; hard up; tight.

तंगा-a kind of tree; a copper coin worth half an anna (three naye paise).

तंगी-cramped conditions; narrowness; tightness; scarcity; stinginess; poverty.

तंज-mockery; sneer.

तंजब-fine musline.

तंड-dancing.

तंडुल-rice.

तंत-thread; string; wire of a musical instrument; attachment; strong desire.

तंति-cord; line; string as of a bow; a weaver.

तंतु-thread; fibre; filament; tissue.

तंतुवादक-one who plays on a stringed musical instrument.

तंतुवाद्य-stringed instrument.

तंत्र-system; machinery.

तंत्रण-administration; government; regulation.

तंत्रवाय-weaver.

तंत्रिका-nerve.

तंत्री-srtings or wires which are used in musical instrument; sinews; cord; a guitar.

तंदुरुस्त-healthy; hale; hearty; having a good health.

तंदुरुस्ती-healthiness; health.

तंदूर-Indian oven.

तंदूरी-baked in a .

तंदेही-labour; attempt; exertion; warning.

तंद्रा-dormancy; sleepiness; lethargy.

तंद्रालस-weariness; lassitude.

तंद्रालु-drowsy; sleepy; lethargic.

तंद्रित-sleepy.

तंबा-king of loose trousers.

तंबाकू-tobacco.

तंबीह-advice; instruction; admonition; reproof.

तंबू tent.

तंबूरा-Indian type of guitar.

तँबोली-betel-leaf seller.

तक to; upto; until; as far as; even.

तक़दीर-fate; lot; luck.

तकना-to see or look; to wait or wait for.

तकनीक-technique.

तकमा-medal.

तकरार-quarrel; wrangle.

तक़रीबन almost; about; approximately.

तक़रीर-speech; lecture.

तकला-spindle.

तकली-small spindle.

तकलीफ़-trouble; hardship; dearth.

[illegible]ल्लुफ़-formal procedure; formality.

[illegible]-division (*Maths*).

[illegible] strong request.

तक़ावी-advance given to peasants.

तकिया-pillow; cushion; support; abode a mendicant; shelter.

तकुआ-spindle; distaff.

तक्र-buttermilk.

तक्षण-act of sculpting wood, stone etc.

तख़मीना-estimate; appraisal.

तख़ल्लुस-pseudonym; pen-name.

तख़्त-plank; throne.

तख़्ती-small plank/board.

तगड़ा-strong; powerful; sturdy.

तग़मा-medal.

तगार-reservoir of water used for watering bricks, preparing mortar etc.

तजना-to abandon/give up.

तजर्बा-experience.

तजर्बेकार-experienced.

तेजवीज़-plan; proposal.

तट-bank; shore; coast.

तटबंध-embankment.

तटरक्षक-coastguard.

तटवर्ती-situated on a bank/coast; coastal; littoral.

तटस्थ-situated on a bank/coast; neutral.

तड़कना-to crack.

तड़क-भड़क-pomp and show; pompousness; ostentation.

तड़का-dawn; daybreak; seasoning (with spices).

तड़के early in morning.

तड़तड़ाता-making a cracking sound.

तड़तड़ाना-(one) to split/break with a cracking noise.

तड़प-agonizing pain; pining; instantaneous reaction; glittering splendour; to writhe in pain.

तड़पना-to feel agonizing pain; to writhe in pain.

तड़पाना to cause writhing pain.

तड़बंदी-formation of cliques.

तड़ाक-snap; instantly; successively; cracking sound.

तड़ाक-फड़ाक at once; instantaneously.

तड़ाका-cracking noise made by something splitting/breaking; loud report.

तड़ाग-pond; tank.

तड़ातड़ in quick succession.

तड़ातड़ी-hurry and scurry.

तड़ी-slap. dodge.

ततैया-wasp.

तत्काल-immediately; instantaneously; on the spur of the moment.

तत्कालीन-contemporary.

तत्क्षण at once; immediately; instantly.

तत्क्षणिक-instantaneous.

तत्त्व-element; substance; factor; truth; reality.

तत्त्वज्ञान-knowledge of reality; metaphysical knowledge; philosophy.

तद्देशीय-of that country; indigenous.

तद्धित-secondary derivatives in Grammar; suffixes which form such derivatives.

तद्भव्-born of that.-a word of some other language accepted in a modified form, as from (English) 'lantern'.

तद्यपि

तद्रूप-alike; similar; identical.

तद्रूपता-likeness; similarity; identity.

तद्वत्-alike; similar (to that etc.)

तन-body.

तनख़ाह-pay; salary.

तनना-to be stretched.

तनय-son.

तनया-daughter.

तनसुख-a kind of fine muslin.

तनहा-single; alone; solitary.

तनहाई-loneliness; solitude.

तना-stem; trunk.

तनातनी-tension; strained relationship; tenseness.

तनावग्रस्त-strained; worried; ter

तनावपूर्ण-tense.

तनिक-a little; sight.

तनी-string for tying garments, etc.

तनु-lean and thin.

तनूकरण-dilution.

तन्मय-absorbed; engrossed.

तन्मयता-absorption; concentration.

तन्मात्र-infinitesimal; merge in quality.

तन्य-ductile; elastic.

तन्यता-ductility; elasticity.

तन्वंगी-a slender; delicate woman; sylph.

तन्वी-a slender woman; sylph.

तप-austerity; practice of austerity; penance; fire; heat; summer season; fever.

तपन-heat; burning sensation.

तपश्यर्चा-practice of austerity; asceticism.

तपस्या-penance; austerities; self-mortification.

तपस्विनी-female of

तपस्वी-ascetic; hermit.

तपा-ascetic

तपाक-with enthusiasm and promptitude.

तपा-तपाया-tried and seasoned.

तपाना-to heat; to inflict suffering on one's body (to gain spiritual ends).

तपित-heated; hot.

तपिश-heat.

तपेदिक-tuberculosis.

तपोधन-austerity personified; a great ascetic.

तपोनिधि-a great ascetic.

तपोनिष्ठ-engrossed in austerities.

तपोबल-prowess stained by austerity, power (spiritual).

तपोभूमि-ground sanctified by austerities.

तपोमय-ascetical.

तपोमूर्ति-austerity personified; a great ascetic.

तपोवन-forest sanctified by austerities.

तप्त-heated; flushed with rage.

तफ़तीश-probe.

तफ़रीह-amusement; merriment; recreation.

तफ़सील-particulars; details.

तब-then; at that time; therefore; for this reason.

तबक-layer; thin metallic leaf; broad shallow dish; a superstitious practice to ward off evil spirits.

तबक़गर-one who prepares metallic leaves.

तबक़ा-large piece of land; layer; any class of men.

तबदील-(object) altered or changed; (person) transferred.

तबर-axe.

तबल-large drum.

तबला-two piece drum.

तबलावादक-table player.

तबादला-transfer.

तबाह-ruined; destroyed.

तबाही-ruination; havoc; mayhem.

तबीयत-mood; condition.

तबीयतदार-sportive; large-hearted.

तबेला-stable.

तभी-at that time; right then.

तमंचा-revolver.

तम-darkness.

तमग़ा-medal.

तमचर-demon.

तमतमाना-to become red due to anger, sun etc.

तमन्ना-aspiration.

तमस-darkness.

तमाकू tobacco.

तमाचा-slap.

तमादी-limitation of time.

तमाम-entire; whole; all.

तमाल-an Indian tree.

तमावरण-black-out.

तमाशबीन-viewer; spectator; one who is fond of seeing shows.

तमाशा-show; display; fun.

तमाशाई-spectator.

तलाक़-the legal ending of a marriage; divorce.

तलाक़शुदा-divorced.

तलातल-one of the nether region according to Hindu mythology.

तलाश-search; quest; investigation.

तलाशना-to search/investigate.

तलाशी-a search.

तली-bottom; palm of the hand; sole of a foot.

तले-immediately under; beneath; below.

तलैया-small pond.

तलौंछ-sediment; dregs.

तल्ला-storey.

तल्लीन-engrossed; absorbed.

तल्लीनता-engrossment.

तवक़्क़ो-expectation.

तवज्जेह-attention.

तवर्ग-(the letters).

तवा-a circular iron plate used for cooking purpose, griddle, disc; gramophone record.

तवाज़ा-hospitality.

तवायफ़-prostitute; harlot.

तवारीख़-history.

तवालत-elongation; lengthening; botheration; entanglement.

तवी-small disc.

तश्तरी-plate; saucer.

तसक़ीन-consolation; solace; satisfaction.

तसदीक़-attestation; confirmation.

तसबीह-rosary.

तसमा-shoe-string.

तसला-big shallow pan.

तसलीम-salutations; greetings; admission; acceptance.

तसल्ली-solace; consolation; satisfaction.

तस्कर-smuggler.

तस्करता-act or state of smuggling.

तस्करी-smuggling.

तस्वीर-picture; painting; photograph.

तह-layer; fold; bottom; bed.

तहक़ीक़ात-probe; investigation.

तहख़ाना-basement; cellar.

तहज़ीब-civilisation; mannerliness.

तहत-working in the control of somebody; under.

तहबंद-loincloth.

तहमत-loincloth.

तहरी-a dish made of rice cooked with vegetables etc.

तहलका-furore; turmoil.

तहस-नहस-ruined; destroyed; devastated.

तहसील-realisation of dues; amount so realised; an administrative division of a district; office of such a division.

तहसीलदार-presiding officer of such a division; collector.

तहसीलदारी-status or office of a collector.

तहसीलना-to collect (dues).

तहाँ at that place; there only.

तहाना-to fold (up); to wrap.

तहाशा-care; fear; apprehension.

तही-layer; fold.

ताँगा-a horse-carriage.

तांडव नृत्य-violent dance (of).

ताँत-gut; string; bowstring; string of a musical instrument; a weaver's appliance.

ताँता-chain; succession; train.

तांत्रिक-pertaining to the Science/Art.

ताँबई-to the colour/hue of copper.

ताँबा-copper.

ताँबिया-big; shallow vessel of copper.

तांबूल-betel-leaf.

ता to form abstract nouns from adjectives as

ताई-slight fever; fever accompanied by cold; aunt; wife of father's elder brother.

ताईद-confirmation; support.

ताऊ-uncle; father's elder brother.

ताऊन-plague.

ताक-look-out.

ताक़-niche; alcove.

ताक-झाँक-act of snooping.

ताक़त-strength; might; power; capacity.

ताक़तवर-strong; powerful; mighty.

ताकना-to peep; to snoop; stare; to look to somebody to provide something.

ताकि so that; in order that.

ताकीद-enjoining; cautioning.

ताखा-niche; alcove.

तागड़ी-chain worn round the waist as an ornament.

तागना-to stitch; to sew in long stitches.

तागा-thread.

ताज-crown; diadem.

ताज़गी-freshness.

ताजमहल-famous mausoleum of built by the Emperor in memory of his wife.

ताज़ा-newly made or produced; fresh; recently experienced; rice; cool.

ताज़ापन-freshness; newness.

ताज़िया-model of the tomb of carried in a procession by during the .

ताज़ीरात-ए-हिंद-Indian Penal Code.

ताज़ीरी-punitive.

ताड़-toddy tree; a beating/reprimand.

ताड़न-giving a blow; upbraiding; punishment; multiplication; admonition.

ताड़ना-reprimand.

ताड़पत्र-leaf of a toddy tree.

ताड़ी-toddy.

तात-father; respectable person; word of endearment for a close relation.

ताताथेई-timing with the feet in dance; dance.

तातार-the region in central Asia.

तातारी-pertaining to the region.

तातील-holiday; vacation.

तात्कालिक-immediate; instantaneous.

तात्त्विक-substantial; elemental.

तात्पर्य-import; meaning; significance; purpose.

तादात्म्य-identity; oneness.

तादाद-number; count; quantity.

तादृश-similar; identical.

तानपूरा-an Indian type of guitar.

ताना-taunt; sarcasm; warp.

तानारीरी-unimpressive music; unimpressive/useless talk.

तानाशाह-dictator.

ताप-heat; fever; warmth; grief.

तापक्रम-temperature.

तापन-act or state of heating; sun.

तापमान-temperature.

ताप-लहरी-heat-wave.

तापविद्युत-electricity developed by the action of heat; thermoelectricity.

तापस-ascetic.

तापसी-pertaining to asceticism.

तापित-heated; afflicted; troubled.

तापीय-thermal.

तापोपचार-heat treatment.

ताफ़्ता-a kind of muslin in which the warp and woof are of different colour.

ताब-heat; warmth; gloss; strength; power of endurance.

ताबड़-तोड़ in quick succession; non-stop.

ताबूत-coffin.

ताबेदार-subservient; servile.

तामचीनी-enamel.

तामझाम-paraphernalia; pomp and show.

तामड़ा-of the colour of copper.

तामस-dark.-ignorance.

तामीर-building; construction.

तामील-execution; service.

ताम्र-copper.

ताम्रपट्ट-plate made of copper.

ताम्रयुग-copper age.

ताम्रवर्ण-copper-coloured.

तायफ़ा-band of dancers.-prostitute.

तार-wire; string; telegram; chain; series.

तारक-redeemer; saviour; star; asterisk.

तारकश-one who draws wires.

तारघर-telegraph office.

तारजाली-wire gauge.

तारण-crossing over; getting over a difficulty; redemption; deliverance from worldly worries; salvation.

तारतम्य-sequence; continuity; order.

तारना-to take across; to help cross over; to deliver from worldly worries; to exempt from future transmigration.

तारपत्र-postgram.

तारपीन-turpentine.

तारल्य-liquidity.

तारसप्तक-highest septet in Music.

तारांकित-starred.

तारा-star; pupil (of the eye).

तारागण-stars.

तारापथ-path of star; sky.

तारामंडल-constellation.

तारिका-small star; actress; film-actress.

तारीक-black; dark.

तारीख़-date.

तारीफ़-praise; compliment.

तारुण्य-youth; young age.

तार्किक-logical.

ताल-palm of the hand; clapping; pool; pond; tank.

तालबद्ध-rhymthic.

ताल-बेताल out of tune; discordant.

ताल-मेल-cohesion; harmony; coordination; concord.

तालव्य-palatal.

ताला-lock; padlock.

तालाब-tank; pond; pool.

तालिका-list; inventory.

ताली-key; clapping; applause.

तालीम-education.

तालू-palate.

ताल्लुक़-relationship; connection.

ताल्लुक़ा-an area of land for a specific purpose; estate.

ताल्लुक़ेदार-owner of an estate; landlord.

ताव-heat; wrath; great anger; sheet (of paper).

तावदार-(person) impulsive; (object) stiff and resplendent.

तावान-penalty; compensation.

तावीज़-amulet; talisman.

ताश-playing cards.

ताशा-kettledrum.

तासीर-effect; property (of some medicine, drug etc.)

तास्सुब-fanaticism; bigotry.

ताहम-yet; still; inspite of this/that.

तिकड़म-stratagem; trickery; knack.

तिकड़मी-wily; crafty.

तिकड़ा-trio.

तिकोना-triangular; three cornered.

तिक्त-pungent; acrid.

तिगुना-triple; treble; threefold.

तिजरा-intermittent fever; recurring every third day.

तिजारत-trade; commerce.

तिजोरी-safe; chest.

तितर-बितर-helter-skelter; scattered; topsy-turvy.

तितली-butterfly; glamour girl; minx.

तितलौकी-bitter; gourd.

तितिक्षा-endurance; fortitude.

तिथि-date

तिथि-पत्र-calendar.

तिन-those.

तिनका-straw.

तिन्नी-a kind of thin rice.

तिपाई-tripod; tea-poy; three-legged stool.

तिबारा-(for the) third time.

तिब्बत-Tibet.

तिब्बती-pertaining to Tibet.

तिमंज़िला-three-storeyed.

तिमाही-produced or occurring once every three months; quarterly.

तिमिंगिल-huge whale.

तिमिर-darkness.

तिमिरमय-full of darkness.

तिमिरारि-the Sun.

तिमुहानी-junction of three roads/ meeting place of three paths.

तिय-woman; wife.

तिरंगा-tri-coloured.

तिरछा-slanting; oblique.
तिरपट-bent; crooked.
तिरपटा-squint-eyed.
तिरपाल-tarpaulin; awning.
तिरसठ-sixty-three 63.
तिरस्कार-contempt; humiliation; disdain; disregard.
तिरस्कृत-humiliated; disdained; disregarded.
तिरानबे-ninety-three 93.
तिरासी-eighty-three. 83.
तिराहा-junction of three paths/roads.
तिरोधान-disappearance; vanishing; concealment.
तिरौंदा-float.
तिर्यक-slanting; (gram) oblique.
तिलंगा-inhabitant of region; a soldier of Indian army; a king of big kite.
तिलंगाना-, a region in South India.
तिलंगी-inhabitant of ; language of .
तिल-sesame.
तिलक-an ornamental mark on the forehead
तिलकना-to slip; (clay) to crack on being dried.
तिलकुट-a sweetmeal prepared of sesame and molasses/sugar.
तिलचट्टा-cockroach.
तिलचावली-mixture of sesame seed and rice.
तिलमिलाना-to get wild with rage; to be painfully restless; to be dazzled.
तिलहन-oil seed.
तिलांजलि-abandonment.
तिलिस्म-magical spell; enchantment; a structure based on a spell; enchantment or subtle devices.
तिलिस्मी-magical; talismanic.
तिलौंछ-offensive smell of cooking oil.
तिलौटी-a pudding made of sesame seed and pulse (horse bean).
तिल्ला-gold or silver thread; border made of such thread.
तिल्ली-spleen.
तिस that; which.
तिसरैत-a third person (other than the two parties to a dispute); owner of a third share of an estate.
तिहत्तर-seventy-three. 73.
तीक्ष्ण-pungent; sharp; severe; piercing; incisive; shrill; harsh; acute; keen.
तीखा-sharp; biting.
तीखापन-sate of quality of being.
तीज-third day of each half of the lunar month.
तीतर-partridge.
तीता-acrid; bitter; pungent.
तीन-three.
तीय-woman.

तीरंदाज-archer.

तीरंदाजी-archery.

तीर-arrow.

तीरस्थ-situated on the bank.

तीर्थ-a sacred place of pilgrimage; a holy bathing place.

तीर्थयात्रा-pilgrimage.

तीर्थयात्री-pilgrim.

तीर्थराज-the king of the sacred places of pilgrimage.

तीली-spoke; knitting needle; thin rod; matchstick.

तीव्र-intense; terrible; rapid; sharp; quick; brisk; energetic; nimble.

तीव्रता-state or quality of being quick; intensity; sharpness; keenness; quickness; swiftness.

तीस-thirty.

तीसी-linseed.

तुंग-lofty; high; tall.

तुंगता-height; altitude; eminence.

तुंड-snout; trunk (of an elephant).

तुंद-belly; stomach.

तुंबा-gourd; scooped gourd used as a pot.

तुक-rhyme; point.

तुकबंद-rhymester.

तुकबंदी-rhyming; versification.

तुक्का-an arrow blunt at one end; wild guess or venture.

तुच्छ-insignificant; mean; trifling; trivial.

तुच्छता-insignificance.

तुझ inflective form of (thou)

तुझे (to) thee/you.

तुड़वाई-act or state of breaking or charge/wages paid for the same.

तुड़वाना-to cause to break/demolish; to cause to pluck.

तुतलाना-to lisp/stutter.

तुनक-state of being quick tempered.

तुनकना-to get into temper; to take offence at trifles.

तुनक-मिज़ाज- quick-tempered; petulant.

तुम you.

तुमुल-tumultuous; uproarious.

तुम्हारा-your; yours.

तुम्हीं-you alone; only you.

तुरंग-horse.

तुरंत-at once; immediately; forthwith; quickly.

तुरंता-an Indian intoxicant.

तुरंती-urgent.

तुरकी-Turkey; language of Turkey.

तुरपन-a kind of hand-stitching (with long stitches).

तुरबत-tomb.

तुरही-clarion; trumpet; bugle.

तुरीय-fourth (stage).

तुरुप-trump.

तुर्क-Turk. (*fem.*)

तुर्किन-Turkish woman.

तुर्की-of Turkey.

तुर्रा-crest; lock of curly hair; ornamental tassel worn on a turban; peculiarity; peculiar incongruity.

तुलना-comparison; similarity.

तुलनात्मक-involving comparison; comparative.

तुलनीय-suitable to be compared with.

तुलवाई-act or state of weighing or wages paid for the same.

तुलसी-basil.

तुला-scales; balance; Libra; the seventh sign of the zodiac.

तुलाई-act or state of weighting or wages paid for the same; light quilt.

तुलादंड-beam of a balance.

तुलादान-gift of metal or grain equivalent to one's weight.

तुलित-weighed.

तुल्य-equivalent; equal.

तुल्यता-equivalence.

तुषार-frost; mist.

तुषारदंश-frost-bite.

तुष्ट-contented; satisfied; appeased; pleased; gratified.

तुष्टता-satisfaction; appeasement; gratification.

तुहिन-frost; snow; mist.

तूँबा-bitter gourd.

तू thou.

तूणीर-quiver.

तूतिया-blue; vitriol; copper sulphate.

तूती-a kind of small singing bird; a kind of small musical pipe.

तूफ़ान-storm; typhoon; hurricane.

तूफ़ानी-tempestuous; stormy.

तूमड़ी-hollowed out gourd used by snake-charmers as a musical pipe.

तूमतड़ाक-coquetry; gaudiness; fashion.

तूमना-to card (cotton); to reduce to shreds by piecing cotton; to rub down with fingers; to disclose (a secret) completely.

तूमार-prolixity; fuss.

तूर-large drum.

तूर्य-tabor; tumbrel.

तूल-prolongation.

तूलना-to lubricate the wheels of a vehicle.

तूलिका-painter's brush.

तूली-painter's brush.

तूस-husk; a kind of fine wool; blanket made of the same.

तृण-blade of grass; straw.

तृणमय-grassy; made of straw.

तृणवत्-like grass; insignificant; trivial.

तृतीय-third.

तृतीयांश-one-third (part).

तृतीया-third day of each half of a lunar month.

तृतीयाश्रम-third stage of (a Hindu's) life life of retirement.

तृप्त-satisfied; contented.

तृप्ति-satisfaction; contentment.

तृषा-thirst.

तृषातुर-very thirsty.

तृषालु-thirsty.

तृष्णा-thirst; greed; longing; craving.

तेंदुआ-leopard.

तेग़-sword; cutlass.

तेज-lustre; effulgence; glow; verve; enthusiasm.

तेज़-sharp; sharp-edged; piercing; penetrating; loud; fast; violent; hard; pungent; bright.

तेज़-तर्रार-sharp and short-tempered; fast-paced.

तेजपात-bay leaf.

तेजवंत-glorious; virile; strong; mighty; shining; brilliant.

तेजस्विता-glory; radiance; lustre; stateliness.

तेजस्वी-glorious; radiant; lustrous.

तेज़ाब-acid.

तेज़ी-sharpness; quickness; swiftness; intensity; pungency; dearness.

तेजोमय-brilliant; glorious; effulgent.

तेरस-thirteenth day of each half of a lunar month.

तेरह-thirteen.

तेरा-thy; thine.

तेल-oil.

तेलकूप-oil well.

तेलहा-oiled; pertaining to oil; (seed) containing oil.

तेलिन-wife of an oilmen; female oil-seller.

तेलियर-a bird having a black body with white spots.

तेलिया-oily; pertaining to oil; containing oil; of a light dark oily colour.

तेली-oilman; oil seller.

तेलुगु-the language of in South India.

तेवर-eyebrow; scowl.

तेहरा-threefold; triplicate.

तेहवार-festival.

तेहा-anger wrath; pride; vainglory; vehemence.

तेही-a short-tempered person; vainglorious person.

तै-settled; decided.

तैनात-appointed; engaged; posting (on guard).

तैयार-ready.

तैयारी-preparation.

तैरना-to swim; to float.

तैराई-act or state of swimming/ floating.

तैराक-swimmer.

तैलंग-former name of in South India.

तैल-pertaining to oil.

तैलचित्र-oil painting.

तैलपोत-oil tanker.

तैलरंग-oil colour.

तैश-wrath; anger.

तैसा-similar; akin; like that.

तैसे in a similar or same way.

तोंद-tummy; pot-belly.

तो then.

तोड़-onslaught as of water or wind; antidote; encounter.

तोड़-जोड़-stratagem; device.

तोड़ना-to break (stone, glass etc.); to pluck (flower, fruit etc.); to damage (watch, machine etc.); to violate (law; principle etc.); to cancel (an office; post etc.); to break off; to win over; to get small change (for a bigger coin; currency).

तोड़-फोड़-secretly carried-out damage to buildings, machine etc.; sabotage.

तोड़-मरोड़-perversion; distortion; mutilation.

तोड़ा-scarcity; dearth; a kind of bangle; a bag containing a thousand rupees.

तोतला-lisping.

तोता-parrot.

तोती-female of parrot.

तोतेचश्म-faceless.

तोतेचश्मी-facelessness.

तोप-cannon; gun.

तोपख़ाना-artillery.

तोपची-gunner.

तोपना-to cover (vessel, plate etc.) to cover up (pit, cavity etc.) to bury.

तोबा-vow to desist from doing something again.

तोय-water

तोरण-festoon; arch.

तोरण-पथ-archway.

तोल-weight.

तोलन-act or state of weighing.

तोलना-to weight.

तोलवाना-to cause to weight.

तोला-an Indian measure of weight equal to about 11.7 gms.

तोश-mattress.

तोष-satisfaction; contentment; appeasement; gratification,

तोहफ़ा-present; gift.

तौंसना-to be scorched.

तौक़-neck-ring.

तौफ़ीक-capacity; status.

तौर-way; manner.

तौर-तरीका-conduct; ways.

तौलाई-act or state of weighing; charged paid for weighing.

तौलिया-towel.

तौहीन-contempt; insult; disrespect.

त्यक्त-abandoned; forsaken; abnegated; rejected.

त्याग-abandonment; relinquishment; abnegation; sacrifice.

त्याग-पत्र-(letter of) resignation.

त्यागी-one who sacrifices.

त्याज्य-renounceable; worth relinquishing; fit to be given up.

त्यों like that.

त्योरस-year before last; year after next.

त्योरी-angry look; frown.

त्योहार-festival.

त्योहारी-tip given on a festival.

त्रय-triad; third; all three; the number 'three'.

त्रयताप-all the three kinds of sorrows; physical; ordained and spiritual.

त्रयी-triplicate.

त्रयोदशी-thirteenth day of each half of a lunar month.

त्रस्त-frightened; terrified; tormented.

त्राण-shelter; protection.

त्राता-protector; defender; redeemer; saviour.

त्रास-dread; fear; terror.

त्रासकारक-dreadful; frightening.

त्रासदिक-of tragedy; tragic; causing sadness.

त्रासदी-a terrible event that causes great sadness; tragedy.

त्रासदीय-pertaining to a tragedy.

त्रासिक-dreadful.

त्राहि help! help! save!

त्राहिमाम help me! save me ! protect me!

त्रिक-three.

त्रिकाल-all three times (past, present and future); all three times (morning; noon and evening).

त्रिकालज्ञ-the Omniscient God, the knower of the events of all times.

त्रिकालदर्शी-seer.

त्रिकोण triangle.

त्रिकोणमिति-Trigonometry.

त्रिगुण-the three principle qualities of human nature.

त्रिगुणित-multiplied by three.

त्रिज्या-radius.

त्रिदंड-a staff which is an insignia of a hermit/recluse.

त्रिदंडी-recluse.

त्रिदोष-the three humours of the body.

त्रिनेत्र-(lit.) having three eyes; Lord .

त्रिपक्षीय-tripartite.

त्रिपिटक-a religious book of Buddhism containing the teachings of Lord Buddha.

त्रिपुंड-a mark of three horizontal lines made on the forehead.

त्रिपुरारि-Lord .

त्रिभुज-triangle.

त्रिभुवन-the three worlds (heaven, earth, under world).

त्रिया-woman.

त्रिलोक-the three worlds.

त्रिलोकीनाथ-God, the Lord of three worlds.

त्रुटि-detect; deficiency; fault; error; flaw.

त्रुटिपूर्ण-defective; imperfect.

त्रुटिहीन-faultless; impeccable.

त्रैकाल्य-all the three stages of life : childhood; youth; old age.

त्रैवार्षिक-triennial.

त्वचा-outer covering of the body of a person; skin.

त्वचारोपण-skin graft.

त्वदीय your, yours, thine.

त्वरण-acceleration.

त्वरा-quickness; numbness.

त्वरित-accelerated; speedy.

थ

थ-The seventeenth consonant of the alphabet and the second letter of the dental class.

थ-auspiciousness; fear; a mountain; a hill.

थंब-pillar; a stay; support.

थकन growing tired.

थकान-fatigue; weariness; tiredness.

थका-माँदा-weary and exhausted.

थकावट-weariness; fatigue; exhaustion.

थक्का-lump; tired.

थन-udder; nipple.

थनेली-inflammation of udder/breast.

थपक-pat/tap.

थपकी-a pat.

थपेड़ा-buffet; blow given with the hand.

थपोड़ी-clapping.

थप्पड़-slap.

थमना-to stop/cease/stay.

थमाना-to hand over; to make one hold.

थर-layer; den.

थरथर shuddering; trembling.

थरथराना-to tremble; shudder.

थल-place; land.

थलकना-(outer skin) to loosen.

थलचर-land animal.

थल-सेना-

थलीय-pertaining to land.

थवई-mason.

थाँग-place where thieves hide.

था-was, wast.

थाई-inhabitant of Thai; stationary.

थाक-pile.

थाती-something inherited; all one's belongings.

थान-place; abode; residence; full length of cloth.

थाना-police station.

थानी-a householder.

थानेदार-office-in-charge of a police station, usually a sub-inspector (of police).

थाप-clap; a light hit with an open hand.

थापा-impression of the palm of hand; mould as that of a brick; heap; subscription given for worship.

थापी-flat mallet used by masons and potters; patting on the back for encouragement.

थाल-big flat metallic dish.

थाली-flat metallic dish.

थाह-depth.

थाहना-to estimate the depth; to probe into the depth (of).

थिएटर-theatre.

थिगली-patch stitched on clothes to cover holes.

थियासोफ़िस्ट-Theosophist.

थिर-still; tranquil; stable; fixed.

थिरक-gliding dance.

थिरकना-to dance lightly; to glide.

थिरता-stillness; stability.

थी-was. (female of)

थुक्का-फ़जीहत-scurrilous wrangling; censure and calumny.

थुड़ी . contemptuous disapprobation/ reproof.

थुथकार-(ono.) calumny; public censure.

थुथना-snout.

थुलथुल-flabby; corpulent.

थूक-spittle; sputum.

थूकना-to spit.

थूथन-snout of an animal.

थूनी-prop; support.

थूहर-a plant of the species of Euphorbia.

थैला-bag; sack.

थैली-pouch.

थोक-wholesale; bulk.

थोक विक्रेता-wholesaler.

थोड़ा-little; not much; some; meagre; slight.

थोथा-hollow; worthless; insubstantial.

थोपना-to plaster (roughly), as mud on a wall; to throw the responsibility (on someone); to impose or inflict.

थोबड़ा-snout; a person's nose.

द-The eighteenth consonant of the alphabet and the third letter of the dental class.

दंग-taken aback; dumbfounded.

दंगई-rioter.

दंगल-a crowd; an assembly; wrestling tournament.

दंगली-having to do with a contest; quarrelsome; aggressive.

दंगा-disturbance; riot.

दंगाई-quarrelsome; pungnacious.

दंगाग्रस्त-violence-torn.

दंगेबाज-given to lawless activities; riotous.

दंगेबाजी-lawless activities; disturbance of peace; riotousness.

दंगैत-quarrelsome.

दंड-stick; punishment; fine; penalty; staff; rod.

दंडक-name of a forest in South India in which according to tradition resided for some-time.

दंडदास-one who is made a slave on account of non-payment of line imposed on him.

दंडधर-ruler king; , the God of death; one equipped with a staff.

दंडन-punishing; punishment.

दंडनायक-the general of an army; a governor or king.

दंडनीय-punishable.

दंडपाणि-one who maintains law and order; , the God of death.

दंडवत-a mode of salutation by prostrating on the ground; obeisance; a bow.

दंड-संहिता-penal code.

दंडात्मक-pertaining to punishment; punitive.

दंडादेश-sentence.

दंडाधिकारी-magistrate.

दंडित-penalized; punished.

दंडी-one equipped with a staff; an ascetic who always keep a staff; doorkeeper; king.

दंत-tooth.

दंतकथा-legend; hearsay.

दंतकार-dentist.

दंतकारी-dentistry.

दँतखोदनी-tooth pick.

दंत-चिकित्सक-dentist.

दंत-चिकित्सा-dentistry.

दंतछद-teeth marks.

दंत-पीड़ा-toothache.

दंत-विज्ञान-odon-tology.

दंत-विहीन-toothless.

दंतावली-denture.

दंती-elephant.

दंतुला-having big teeth.

दंत्य-dental.

दंपति-husband and wife.
दंपती-husband and wife.
दंभ-vanity; conceit.
दंभी-vain; conceited.
दँवरी-trampling of reaped harvest by bullocks for separating corn from chaff.
दंश-sting; spite; bite.
दंशन-stinging; biting.
दई-destiny.
दक़ियानूस- old-fashioned; conservative.
दक़ियानूसी-old-fashioned; age old (custom, practice etc.).
दक्खिन-south.
दक्खिनी-southern.
दक्ष-adept; dexterous; adroit; efficient; expert; skilful.
दक्षता-dexterity; adroitness; efficiency; expertness.
दक्षिण-South; right.
दक्षिण-पंथ-right-wing.
दक्षिणा-honorarium paid to a preceptor or priest.
दक्षिणायन-winter solstice.
दक्षिणावृर्त-clockwise.
दक्षिणी-Southern.
दख़लंदाज़-(one) who meddles/ interferes.
दख़लंदाज़ी-interference; meddling.
दख़ल-occupation; meddling; interference.
दख़लकार-occupant.
दगड़-kettledrum.
दग़ा-treachery; deception; cheating
दग़ीला-speckled; stained (fruit etc.); branded.
दग़ेबाज-treacherous; deceitful
दग़ेबाजी-treachery; deceitfulness.
दग़ैल-blemished; tainted; sullied (person or character).
दग्ध-burnt; scorched.
दचक-jolt; jerk; bump.
दचकना-to jolt/jerk (as a vehicle in motion).
दचकेदार-jolty; jerky.
दढ़ियल-bearded.
दत्त-given; donated; paid.
दत्तक-adopted.
दत्तकग्रहण-adoption.
दत्तकग्राही-one who adopts.
दत्तकपिता-adopted/adoptive father.
दत्तकमाता-adopted/adoptive mother.
दत्तक-विधान-law of adoption.
दत्तकीय-pertaining to adoption.
दत्तचित्त-concentrated; fully attentive (to some work).
ददिहाल-family of paternal grandfather or his residence.
ददोड़ा, ददोरा-swelling; bump.

दद्रु-ringworm.

दधि-curd.

दन-loud report; sound produced by the firing of a gun, cannon etc.

दनदनाना-to start producing noise suddenly and continuously (said to guns and cannons); to make merry.

दनादन with the sound of a cannonade; in quick succession; incessantly.

दनुज-demon.

दफ़न-burial.

दफ़नाना-to place a dead body into a grave; to bury; to forget something completely.

दफ़ा-time.

दफ़्तर-office.

दफ़्तरशाही-bureaucracy.

दफ़्तरी-book-binder.

दफ़्तरीख़ाना-book-binding shop.

दफ़्ती-card-board.

दबंग-bold; fearless; undaunted; strong-headed.

दबकना-hide.

दबदबा-awe; overwhelming influence; dignity.

दबाऊ-weighty in the front.

दबाना-to press down; to suppress/ repress/subdue.

दबाव-pressure; coercion; duress.

दबैल-under influence/control/ subjection.

दबोचना-to seize suddenly; to hide/ conceal.

दब्बू-meek.

दब्बूपन-meekness.

दम-breadth; instant; moment.

दमक-glimmer; glitter; brilliance; glow.

दमकना-to glimmer/glitter/glow/ shine.

दमकल-water-pump; fire engine; staying power; stamina; fire-brigade.

दमकला-oven (in which coal is used).

दमख़म-staying power; strength; prowess; stamina; firmness; sharpness (of the edge of a sword).

दमड़ी-mite; one-eight of a (old Indian currency).

दमदमा-bunker.

दमदार-virile; powerful; firm; strong; stout; fully capable.

दम-दिलासा-encouragement; consolation.

दमन-oppression; suppression; repression.

दमनकारी-oppressive; suppressive; repressive.

दमनचक्र-wheel of repression.

दमनशील-suppressive; repressive; coercive.

दमनात्मक-oppressive; coercive.

दमनीय-tamable; suppressible.

दम-पट्टी-false hope.

दम-बुत्ता-bluff.

दमसाज-pal; faithful friend.

दमा-an illness which causes difficulty in breathing; asthma.

दमाद-daughter's husband.

दमादम in quick succession.

दमामा-kettledrum.

दमित-suppressed; oppressed (person); pressurised.

दयनीय-pitiable; miserable; wretched.

दया-mercy; pity.

दया-दृष्टि-attitude of kindness/ favour.

दयानत-honesty; fair-mindedness.

दयानतदार-honest; truthful.

दयानतदारी-generosity; honesty.

दयानिधान-a very good person/ benefactor; God.

दयापात्र-object of pity; favour.

दयामय-full of compassion; merciful; benevolent.

दयार्द्र-full of tenderness/kindness/ benevolence.

दयालु-humane; kind; compassionate; magnanimous.

दयालुता-kind-hearted-ness; benignity; graciousness.

दयावान-kind; compassionate; tender-hearted.

दयाशील-kind; compassionate.

दर-rate.

दरकना-to crack; to be split.

दरकार-need; necessity.

दरकिनार let alone.

दरख़ास्त-application; request.

दरख़ास्ती-pertaining to an application.

दरख़्त-tree.

दरगाह-threshold; court; tomb; place of worship.

दरगुज़र-passed; that which has happened/occurred.

दरज-crack; clef; fissure.

दरजन-dozen.

दरजा-rank; standard; class.

दरज़िन-female tailor; wife of a tailor.

दरज़ी-tailor.

दरज़ीख़ाना-tailoring house.

दरज़ीगीरी-work or calling of a tailor.

दरजेबंदी-grading; classification.

दरजेवार according to class / grade / standard; class-wise; gradewise.

दरद-pain.

दरदरा-half-grounded coarse.

दरदीला-compassionate; kind-hearted (person); compassionate (song, grounds etc.); touching; pathetic.

दरना-to grind coarsely; to destroy/ ruin/devastate/ravage.

दरबान-doorkeeper; watchman.

दरबानी-doorkeeping; watch-manship.

दरबार-king's court; royal court.

दरबारदारी-sycophancy; courtiership.

दरमियान-middle.

दरमियान के between; among.

दरवाज़ा-door; gate.

दरशाना-to show; to explain; to depict.

दर-हक़ीक़त in fact; indeed; in reality.

दराज़-drawer (of a table, wardrobe etc.)

दरार-crack; crevice; split; fissure; rift.

दरिंदा-flesh-eating animal; carnivore.

दरिद्र-poor; indigent; miserable; poverty-stricken.

दरिद्रता-poverty.

दरिद्रनारायण-a poor person.

दरिद्री-poor; wretched; shabby; unfortunate.

दरिया-river.

दरियाई-pertaining to a river.

दरियादिल-liberal; kind; large-hearted; generous.

दरियादिली-liberality; kindness; large-heart :dness; generously; magnanimity.

दरियाफ़्त-to inquire and find out; to enquire; to investigate.

दरी-carpet; ravine.

दरीबा-wholesale market.

दरेसी-dressing; preparing (ground, building) for final touches.

दर्ज-entered; noted; recorded (in a book, register etc.).

दर्जा-class; grade; order or division; standard.

दर्जी-one who stitches clothes.

दर्द-pain; ache; affliction; pathos; sympathy.

दर्दनाक-pitiful; woeful; awful.

दर्दमंद-sympathetic; compassionate.

दर्प-arrogance.

दर्पण-mirror; looking glass.

दर्रा-(mountain) pass; coarse powder (as of cereals).

दर्शक-spectator; on-looker.

दर्शक-कक्ष-visitor's lobby.

दर्शकगण-spectators; assemblage of spectators.

दर्शक-दीर्घा-visitor's gallery.

दर्शन-sight; view; Philosophy.

दर्शी-observing; seeing.

दल-party; clique; group; assembly; batch; flock; leaf; thickness.

दलक-quivering; tremor.

दलकना-to quiver.

दलगत-party wise.

दलदल-bog; marsh; quagmire.

दलदला-quaggy; boggy; marshy.

दलदार-plump; fleshy.

दलन-crushing.

दलना-to grind coarsely.

दलबंदी-party-politics; groupism; factionism.

दलबदल-defection.

दलबदलू-defector.

दलबादल-conglomeration/mass of clouds; contingent of followers and companions.

दलवाना-to have something ground coarsely.

दलहन-cereals used as pulse.

दलादली-groupism; partyism.

दलान-portico.

दलाल-commission agent; broker; middleman; tout; pimp.

दलाली-commission of a broker; brokerage; broker's vocation.

दलित-depressed; downtrodden.

दलिद्दर-poverty.

दलील-argument; plea.

दलेल-army exercise; drill; penalty parade.

दवा-medicine; drug; remedy; cure.

दवाख़ाना-dispensary.

दवात-inkpot.

दवा-दारू-medical treatment.

दवामी-permanent.

दश-ten. 10.

दशक-decade.

दशन-tooth.

दशनच्छद-lip.

दशभुज-decagon.

दशम-tenth.

दशमलव-decimal.

दशमलवकरण-decimalisation.

दशमिक-decimal; denary.

दशहरा-tenth day of bright half of lunar month of

दशा-state; condition; plight.

दशानुकूलन-acclimatization.

दशाब्द-ten years.

दशाब्दी-period of ten year; decade.

दशावतार-the ten incarnation of Lord (Hindu Mythology).

दशाह-period of ten days; tenth day after death.

दशी-decade.

दस-ten.

दसनंबरी-offender; criminal.

दस्तंदाज़-(one) who interferes/ meddles.

दस्तंदाज़ी-interference/meddling.

दस्त-hand; loose motion.

दस्तक-slight blow with the hand; a knock; demand note for payment of rent in default; tax; toll.

दस्तकार-artisan; craftsman.

दस्तख़त-signature.

दस्तख़ती-signed; pertaining to signature.

दस्तरख़ान-dining cloth.

दस्ता-handle; squad; squadron; quire (of paper).

दस्ताना-hand-glove; gauntlet.

दस्तावर-purgative; cathartic.

दस्तावेज़-document; deed.

दस्तावेज़ी-documentary.

दस्ती-pertaining to hand; handy; sent through some person; small handle; handy torch; small pen-stand.

दस्तूर-custom; practice.

दस्तूरी-commission; customary discount; perquisite.

दस्यु-bandit; robber.

दस्युता-banditry; robbery.

दस्युवृत्ति-robbery/banditry as a means of livelihood.

दहक-blaze.

दहकना-to blaze; to burn with a red-hot flame.

दहकाना-to blaze; to cause to blaze; to agitate.

दहन-combustion; burning.

दहनशील-combustible.

दहनशीलता-combustibility.

दहना-to burn.

दहल-fright; over-awe.

दहलना-to be frightened/overawed.

दहला-ten of playing cards.

दहलाना-to over-awe.

दहलीज़-door-sill; threshold.

दहशत-terror; alarm.

दहशतगर्द-terrorist.

दहशतगर्दी-terrorism; an act of terrorism.

दहाई-state of being ten times; ten's place in writing numerals; set of ten things.

दहाड़-roar of a lion; roar.

दहाड़ना-to roar; to cry loud.

दहाना-(big) mouth (of a river); mouth of a water bag; curb of the bridle of a horse; drain; gutter.

दही-curd; yoghurt.

दहेज-dowry.

दहेड़ी-curd-pot.

दाँत-tooth

दाँता-tooth of comb, saw etc.; dent.

दाँता-किटकिट-quarrel; wrangle.

दाँती-sickle.

दाँतेदार-dentate; jagged; dented.

दाँना-to separate seed (of crop).

दांपतिक-marital; conjugal.

दांपत्य-marital relationship.

दाँव-stake; device; wrestling skill/trick.

दाँव-पेच-tactics; manoeuvres.

दाई-nurse; midwife.

दाईगिरी-midwifery.

दाऊ-elder brother.

दाक्षिणात्य-southern.

दाख-grape; raisin; currant.

दाख़िल-entered; inserted; admitted.

दाता-donor; giver.

दातार-giver; a big donor.

दातुन, दातौन-fibrous twig used as a tooth-brush.

दाद-ringworm; complaint; well-deserved praise.

दादरा-a variety of Indian music.

दादा-paternal grandfather; elder brother; leader of gang; hoodlum; gangster.

दादागीरी-hooliganism; gangsterism; leadership.

दादी-grandmother; father's mother.

दादुर-frog.

दान-act of giving; donation; charity; alms.

दानपत्र-deed of gift.

दानपात्र-offertory box.

दान-पेटी-offertory box.

दानव-demon; giant.

दानवी-demonic.

दानवीर-very generous; munificent as prince.

दानशील-charitable; munificent; beneficent.

दानशीलता-munificence.

दाना-grain; bead; pimple.

दाना-चीनी-crystal sugar.

दाना-पानी-food and fodder; sustenance; livelihood.

दानी-charitable; generous; munificent.

दानेदार-granular.

दाप-over-bearing display of superiority, arrogance, pride.

दाब-pressure; paper-weight; weight.

दाबना-to press; to keep under (one's) control / restraint; to keep in check; to bury.

दाम-price; cost; value; expense; garland; heap.

दामन-the skirt of a garment.

दामाद-son-in-law.

दामादी-pertaining to a son-in-law; like that of a son-in-law.-state of being a son-in-law.

दामिनी-lightning.

दामी-expensive; costly; precious.

दामोदर-Lord

दाय-due; or worth giving.-charity; liability; inherited wealth; dowry; wedding present.

दायभाग-portion of paternal property which one is to get on division.

दायभागी-heir; inheritor.

दायर-wandering; roaming; current; filed (as a lawsuit).

दायाँ-right.

दायागत-hereditary; ancestral.

दायाधिकार-inheritance.

दायाधिकारी-inheritor.

दायित्व-liability; obligation; onus.

दायित्वबोध-sense of responsibility.

दायी bestower; giver.

दार denoting possession or quality.

दारचीनी-cinnamon.

दारण-surgery; operation; instrument of operation.

दारा-wife.

दारिद्रय-poverty; pauperism; indigence.

दारी denoting vocation, practice etc.

दारु-pine tree.

दारुण-severe; extreme; dreadful.

दारुणता-severity; dreadfulness; ghastliness; awfulness.

दारुहलदी-a king of turmeric.

दारू-medicine; alcohol; gunpowder.

दारोग़ा-inspector; supervisor.

दारोमदार-dependence; all entire.

दार्शनिक-philosophical.

दार्शनिकता-philosophic attitude.

दाल-pulse; lentil.

दालचीनी-cinnamon.

दाल-दलिया-coarse of food; poor man's diet.

दालमोठ-mixture of fried pulses (a kind of snack).

दाल-रोटी-sustenance; livelihood.

दालान-covered inner terrace (usually facing a courtyard).

दाव-jungle; wood; trick.

दावत-feast; banquet.

दावतनामा-written invitation (for a dinner).

दावनी-an ornament worn on the forehead.

दावा-claim; suit.

दावेदार-one who makes a claim; claimant.

दावेदारी-assertion of a claim.

दास-slave; serf; servant.

दासता-slavery; servility; serfdom; subjection.

दासत्व-

दासप्रथा-system of slavery; serfdom.

दासभाव-servitude.

दासानुदास-very humble servant.

दासी-female slave; maid-servant; slave girl.

दास्ताँ, दास्तान-story; tale; narrative.

दास्य-slavery; servitude.

दाह-burning; cremation; mental agony.

दाहक-caustic; inflammatory.

दाहकर्म-funeral rite(s).

दाहक्रिया-cremation.

दाहन-burning.

दाहना-to burn; to torment/torture.

दाह-संस्कार-funeral rite(s).

दाहिना-right.

दाहिने to the right.

दाह्य-combustible; inflammable.

दिउली-small earthen cup; tiny cup of tinsel used in embroidery; scab of a wound.

दिक-direction.

दिक़्क़त-difficulty; hardship; source of trouble.

दिक़्क़त-तलब-arduous; troublesome; vexatious.

दिक्सूचक-compass.

दिखना-to appear; to be in sight; to be seen; to be visible.

दिखलाई-act of showing; remuneration.

दिखलाना-to show.

दिखाई-act of showing.

दिखाऊ-showy; ostentatious.

दिखाना-to show; to display.

दिखावट-mere show; ostentation; pomposity.

दिखावटी-showy; ostentatious.

दिखावा-ostentation; display; pomp; show.

दिगंत-horizon.

दिगंबर-naked.-a sect of

दिगंबरता-nakedness.

दिगंश-azimuth.

दिगंशीय-pertaining to azimuth.

दिग्गज-one of the eight mythological elephant which support the earth.

दिग्दर्शक-(mariner's) compass; director.

दिग्दर्शन-direction guidance.

दिग्भ्रम-error about direction; loss of bearing.

दिग्मंडल-all the directions combined.

दिग्विंदु-cardinal point.

दिग्विजय-conquest of the world.

दिग्विजयी-having conquered the whole world.

दिग्व्याप्त-all-pervading.

दिन-day; daytime.

दिनकर-Sun.

दिनचर्या-daily routine.

दिन-ब-दिन day by day.

दिनमणि-Sun.

दिनमान-length/duration of the day (from Sunrise to Sunset).

दिनराज-Sun.

दिन-रात-day and night.

दिनांक-date.

दिनांकित-dated.

दिनांध-day-blind.

दिनातीत-out of date.

दिनीं-old, that which has been kept for a long time.

दिनेश-Sun.

दिनौंधी-day-blindness.

दिमाग़-brain.

दिमाग़-चट-very talkative; boring.

दिमाग़दार-brainy; very intelligent; intellectual; proud; vain.

दिमाग़ी-metal.

दिल-heart.

दिलकश-alluring; attractive.

दिलचस्प-amusing; interesting.

दिलचस्पी-interest; interestedness.

दिलजमई-conviction.

दिलजला-afflicted; tormented.

दिलजोई-consolation.

दिलदार-affectionate; generous; liberal.

दिलदारी-generosity; affectionateness; liberality.

दिलपसंद-pleasing to the heart; attractive; charming.

दिलफेंक-easily succumbing to glamour; indiscriminately loving.

दिलबर-beloved; dearly; loved.

दिलरुबा-bewitching; charming; enchanting.

दिलवाना-to cause to give.

दिलवाला-large-hearted and courageous.

दिलाना-to cause to be given.

दिलावर-courageous; brave.

दिलासा-solace; consolation.

दिली-pertaining to the heart; hearty; cordial; intimate.

दिलेर-bold; courageous; brave; daring.

दिलेरी-courage; bravery.

दिल्लगी-jest; joke; fun.

दिल्लगीबाज-jester; joker.

दिल्लगीबाज़ी-jocularity.

दिल्ला-panel of a door.

दिल्लेबंदी-process of panelling.

दिवंगत-no longer alive; late; deceased.

दिवस-day.

दिवांध-day-blind.

दिवांधता-day-blindness.

दिवाकर-Sun.

दिवाना-mad person.

दिवाल-one who gives; giver.

दिवाला-bankruptcy; insolvency.

दिवालिया-bankrupt; insolvent.

दिवाली-the festival of the Hindus when illuminations are held on houses.

दिवास्वप्न-day-dream; reverie.

दिव्य-heavenly; divine; celestial; brilliant; charming; attractive; fascinating.

दिव्यदृष्टि-divine insight.

दिव्यपरीक्षा-ordeal.

दिव्यपुरुष-divine being.

दिव्यमूर्ति-divine figure.

दिशा-direction.

दिशा-निर्देश-direction; guidance.

दिशाभ्रम-loss of direction.

दिशाशूल-inauspicious time for starting on a journey in a particular direction.

दिशाहीन-without any line of action.

दिसंबर-December.

दिसंबरी of or pertaining to December.

दिसावर-place from which goods are ordered for.

दिसावरी-of or pertaining to

दिहाड़ी-day; period of time during the day a labourer is expected to work; remuneration paid for the same.

दीक्षक-preceptor.

दीक्षण-initiation.

दीक्षणीय-esoteric.

दीक्षांत-end of an academic session.

दीक्षा-initiation; ceremonial introduction into some cult, sect etc.

दीक्षित-initiated; consecrated.

दीखना-to be visible; to appear.

दीठ-eye.

दीदा-eye.

दीदार-sight; vision.

दीदी-elder sister.

दीन-humble; indigent; destitute.

दीनता-humility; indigence; destitution.

दीनदयालु-merciful.

दीनदार-religious-minded; devout.

दीनदारी- religious-mindedness; devoutness.

दीन-दुनिया-this world and the next.

दीनबंधु-friend of the poor; God.

दीनहीन-destitute.

दीनानाथ-protector of the poor; God.

दीप-lamp.

दीपक-lamp.

दीपघर-lamp-house.

दीपमाला-row/series of lights.

दीपशिखा-flame of a lamp.

दीपाधार-lamp-stand.

दीपावली-row of lights; the festival of light.

दीपित-luminous; illuminated.

दीपोत्सव-festival of illumination.

दीप्त-illuminated.

दीप्ति-luminosity; glow; lustre; brightness.

दीमक-white ant; termite.

दीयट-lamp stand.

दीया-lamp.

दीयासलाई-match stick.

दीर्घ-long; sustained.

दीर्घकाय-tall and bulky; gigantic.

दीर्घकालिक-for a long time.

दीर्घजीवी-long-lived.

दीर्घसूत्री-dilatory; slow; lethargic.

दीर्घा-gallery.

दीर्घायु-long-lived.

दीर्घीकरण-elongation.

दीवट-lamp-stand.

दीवाना-nympholeptic.

दीवानापन-craziness, nympholepsy.

दीवानी-of civil.

दीवार-wall.

दीवाली-the Hindu festival of lights.

दुंदुभि-kettledrum.

दुंबा-a kind of ram.

दुःख, दुख-sorrow; grief; distress; regret.

दुःखद, दुखद-unfortunate; painful; sorrowful; distressing.

दुःखदाता, दुखदाता-one who causes pain or sorrow.

दुःख-भरा-painful; sorrowful.

दुःखभोग-suffering.

दुःखमय-full of sorrow / grief / agony.

दुःख-सुख-pleasure and pain; happiness and sorrow.

दुःखांत-tragic; with a tragic end.

दुःखांतिका-tragedy; tragic drama.

दुःखित-distressed; grief-stricken.

दुःखी, दुखी-grief-stricken; distressed; melancholic; sad; gloomy; (a person) who suffer (from an illness or deficiency).

दुःस्वप्न-nightmare.

दुअन्नी-two- coin (old currency).

दुआ-benediction; blessing; prayer.

दुआबा-region lying between two rivers; the land between the and the

दुकड़हा-(thing) of low quality; cheap; (person) low; mean.

दुकड़ी-pair; carriage drawn by two horses; two rupees; the two cards.

दुकान-shop.

दुकानदार-shopkeeper.

दुकानदारी-vocation of a shopkeeper; shop-keeping; haggling (over price).

दुकाल-paucity; scarcity; famine.

दुकूल-cloth; fine cloth.

दुकेला-having a companion.

दुक्कड़-a kind of drum; a pair of large boats tied together.

दुख-sorrow.

दुखड़ा-sorrowful story; saga of suffering.

दुखता-painful; sore.

दुखना-to hurt/ache.

दुखाना-to cause pain; to inflict suffering.

दुखित-distressed; grief-stricken; melancholic.

दुखिया-(one) who has suffered, afflicted with sorrow.

दुगना-double; redoubled; two fold.

दुगाना-duet.

दुग्ध-milk.

दुग्धमापक-lacto-meter.

दुग्धशाला

दुग्धशर्करा-milk sugar; lactose.

दुचित्ता-fickle-minded; not firm; wavering of two minds; distracted.

दुचित्ती-fickle-mindedness.

दुटूक-proposal/reply in concise; plain words.

दुढालू-having two slopes.

दुत Off ! Away ! Be gone !

दुतकार-reproof; reprimand; upbraiding.

दुतकारना-to reproach/reprimand/reprove/upbraid/scold.

दुतरफ़ा-two-way; bilateral.

दुतल्ला-two-storeyed.

दुद्धी-a type of grass.

दुधमुँहा-unweaned.

दुधहँड़ी-large pot for keeping milk.

दुधार-giving milk.

दुधारू-

दुधिया-of or pertaining to milk; containing a good dose of milk; like milk.-chalk; a kind of grass.

दूधैल-with a liberal yield of milk.

दुनाली-double-barrelled.

दुनिया-world

दुनियादार-worldly; worldly-wise; pragmatic.

दुनियादारी-wordily behaviour/worldliness.

दुनियासाज़-worldly-wise; tactful.

दुपट्टा-linen wrapper.

दुपल्ला-having two layers.

दुपहर-moon.

दुफ़सला-yielding two crops; having two meanings; ambiguous.

दुबकना-to quail.

दुबला-lean.

दुबलाना-to become lean/emaciated.

दुबलापन-leanness.

दुबारा-once more; for a second time; again.

दुभाषिया-one who knows two languages; bilingual; an interpreter.

दुमंजिला-double-storeyed.

दुम-tail.

दुमदार-having a tail; tailed.

दुमुँहाँ-having two mouths.

दुरंगा-of two colours; bicoloured; double-faced (person); cunning; deceitful.

दुर्, दुर pooh! tut!

दुरदुराना-to pooh-pooh.

दुरभिसंधि-conspiracy; collusion.

दुरमुट, दुरमुस-an implement for pounding pavements.

दुरवस्था-sad plight; sorry state; bad shape.

दुराग्रह-intransigence; wilfulness.

दुराग्रही-intransigent; wilful.

दुराचार-bad or immoral behaviour; misconduct.

दुराचारी-immoral; wicked; licentious; vile.

दुरात्मा-vile; wicked.

दुराना-to keep away; to hide.

दुराराध्य-difficult to please; fastidious.

दुरारोह-steep.

दुराव-concealment.

दुराश्य-malevolence; bad motive.

दुराशा-false hope; a thing that is impossible to catch or reach, will-o-the-wisp.

दुरुख़ा-double-edged; two faced.

दुरुत्साहक-abettor.

दुरुत्साहन-abetment.

दुरुपयोग-misuse; ill-use.

दुरुस्त-right; correct; in a proper condition.

दुरूह-abstruse; difficult to understand; obscure.

दुर्गंध-foul smell; stink; stench.

दुर्ग-fort; citadel.

दुर्गत-troubled; oppressed; poor; calamitous.

दुर्गति-plight; terrible plight; catastrophe; misery.

दुर्गपाल-principal officer of a fort; fort-guard.

दुर्गम-impassable; unapproachable; inaccessible; abstruse; difficult; impregnable.

दुर्गा-; goddess of prowess.

दुर्जन-villain; scoundrel; rascal; knave; rogue; base fellow.

दुर्जनता-villainy; wickedness; roguery.

दुर्जेय-impregnable; formidable.

दुर्दमनीय-impregnable; invincible.

दुर्दम्य-impregnable; invincible.

दुर्दशा-adversity; misery; sad; condition; plight.

दुर्दांत-impregnable; invincible; unable to be subdued.

दुर्दिन-bad days; hard times; a day overcast with clouds; cloudy day.

दुर्दैव-disaster; mishap; bad luck; misfortune.

दुर्बल-weak; lean; slender; infirm.

दुर्बलता-weakness; leanness.

दुर्बुद्धि-foolish; stupid; evil-minded; wicked; perverse.

दुर्बोध-incomprehensible; abstruse; obscure.

दुर्भाग्य-ill-luck; mis-fortunate.

दुर्भाव-ill will; antagonism; malevolence.

दुर्भावना-ill will; hostile feeling.

दुर्भावपूर्ण-malevolent.

दुर्भिक्ष-famine; paucity; scarcity.

दुर्भीति-phobia.

दुश्चरित्र-of bad character. -misconduct; immorality; depravity.

दुश्मन-enemy; foe.

दुश्मनी-animosity; enmity; hostility.

दुष्कर-difficult to execute / perform; arduous; hard.

दुष्कर्म-misdeed; wrong; vice; sin.

दुष्कीर्ति-infamy; disreputation.

दुष्कृत्य-misdeed; wrong.

दुष्ट-wicked; evil-mindedly; knavish; vicious; vile.

दुष्प्रकृति-ill-natured; short-tempered; wicked; low; mean.

दुष्प्रभाव-bad influence; ill effect.

दुष्प्रयोग-mis-application; misuse.

दुष्प्रवृत्ति-unwholesome trend; undesirable tendency; mean disposition; low mentality.

दुष्प्राप्य-scarce; rare.

दुष्प्राप्यता-scarcity.

दुसराना-to stay or do the same thing again; to repeat.

दुसूती-a thick cloth of two sheets.

दुस्तर-arduous; difficult; difficult to cross; impassable; insurmountable.

दुहत्थड़ with both hands.

दुहत्था-provided with two handles.

दुहत्थी-done with the two hands joined together.

दुहना-to milk; to squeeze out.

दुहराना-to revise; to repeat.

दुहाई-invocation; act of milking; wages paid for milking.

दुहाजू-(one) who marries a second time (when the first spouse is dead).

दुहाना-to cause (a cow etc.) to be milked.

दुहाव-period of lactation of a milch cattle; wages paid for milking.

दुहिता-daughter.

दुहेला-difficult; painful.

दुआ-second.

दूगुन-double.

दूज-second day of each half of a lunar month.

दूत-envoy; emissary; messenger.

दूतकर्म-office or duty of an envoy.

दूतावास-legation; consulate; embassy.

दूती-female messenger; go-between; procures.

दूध-milk; the whitish juice of certain plants/tree.

दूध-पिलाई-wet nurse; feeding bottle.

दूध-पूत-wealth and progeny.

दूध-भाई-any one of several children suckled by the same woman.

दुधवाला-milk-vendor; milkman.

दूधिया-made of milk; milky; milk-white; lactiferous.

दून-act or state of doubling.

दूना-double; two fold.

दूब-a kind of grass.

दूबदू-face to face; in straight contest.

दूबर-wanting vigour; weak; feeble.

दूभर-uncomfortable; difficult.

दूरंदेश-far-sighted; sagacious.

दूर far away; remote; distant.

दूरगामी-which can go far; far-reaching; long-term.

दूरत्व-distance; remoteness.

दूरदर्शक-telescope.

दूरदर्शिता-farsight; farsightedness; sagacity.

दूरबीन-binocular; telescope.

दूरभाष-telephone.

दूरमुद्रक-teleprinter.

दूरलेख-telegram.

दूरलेखी-telegraphic.

दूरवर्ती-distant; remote.

दूरवीक्षक-telescope.

दूरसंचार-tele-communication.

दूरस्थ-distant; remote.

दूरस्थित-distant.

दूरागत-coming from a far.

दूरी-distance; lack of friendly feelings in relation.

दूरीकरण-act or state of removing/turning away.

दूर्वा-soft green grass.

दूल्हा-bridegroom.

दूषण-fault; blame; contamination; pollution.

दूषित-faulty; defective; defiled; polluted; contaminated; sullied.

दूसरा-second; other; another.

दूहना-to milk (a cow etc.).

दृगंबु-tear.

दृग-eye; power of vision.

दृढ़-firm; steady; rigid; flexible.

दृढ़ता-firmness; steadiness; rigidity; inflexibility.

दृढांग-firm-bodied; stout; corpulent.

दृढ़ोक्ति-assertion; averment.

दृश्य-visible; visual.

दृश्यता-visibility; visuality.

दृश्यमान-visible; perceptible; visual.

दृष्ट-seen; visible; apparent.

दृष्टांत-instance; example; illustration.

दृष्टि-eyesight; vision; view; look.

दृष्टिकोण-viewpoint; angle of vision; aspect.

दृष्टिक्षेप-glance.

दृष्टिगत-viewed; seen.

दृष्टिगोचर-perceptible; visible.

दृष्टिदोष-defect in sight; oversight.

दृष्टिपटल-retina.

दृष्टिपात-glance.

देखनहारा-one who looks after of takes care of.

देखना-to see / look / notice; to watch; to look after; to search; to look into; be careful.

देखना-भालना-to look carefully; to look after; to supervise.

देखना-समझना-to explore.

देख-रेख-care; guidance; supervision.

देखा-देखी-nodding acquaintance; blind imitation.

देखो look; behold !

देग़-cauldron; big cooking pot; kettle.

देग़चा-kettle; cooking pot.

देग़ची-small cauldron; small kettle.

देदीप्यमान-refulgent; brilliant; resplendent; splendid; glorious.

देन-act of giving; gift; liability.

देनदार-debtor.

देनदारी-liability; indebtedness.

देन-लेन-banking business; giving and taking.

देनहारा-(one) who gives.

देना-to give; provide; grant or bestow; to pay; to confer.

देना-पावना-assets and liabilities (in cash).

देना-लेना-assets and liabilities (in cash); relation.

देय-due; payable.

देयता-liability.

देयादेय-assets and liabilities.

देर-delay; time

देर-सबेर sooner or later.

देरी-delay; tardiness.

देव-God; deity; giant.

देवकथा-myth.

देवकन्या-nymph.

देवगण-pantheon; assistants of gods.

देवगृह-abode/residence of a deity; temple.

देवता-deity

देवतुल्य-godlike; godliness.

देवत्व-divinity; godliness.

देवदार-cedar.

देवदासी-dancing girl; harlot; prostitute.

देवदूत-messenger of gods; angel.

देवनागरी-original name of alphabet.

देवबाला-celestial damsel; nymph.

देवभाषा-language of gods; Sanskrit.

देवयान-celestial plane/vehicle.

देवयोनि-divine form of life.

देवर-husband's younger brother.

देवराज-king of Gods; lord .

देवरानी-wife of husband's elder bother.

देवलोक-abode of gods; heaven; paradise.

देववाणी-oracle; tongue of gods; Sanskrit.

देववाद-belief in the gods.

देवस्थान-residence/abode of gods; temple.

देवांगना-wife of a deity or celestial damsel.

देवाल-giver; one who pays.

देवालय-seat of a deity; temple.

देवी-goddess; lady.

देवोत्थान-the eleventh day of the bright fortnight of the month of when lord is supposed to be awakened.

देवाद्यान-celestial garden.

देवोपासना-worship of gods.

देश-country; region; space.

देशिक-confined / pertaining to the country; internal.

देशी-native; indigenous.

देस-country.

देसावर-foreign country; place from which goods are sent.

देसावरी-pertaining to

देसी-native; indigenous.

देह-body.

देहकर्मी-sex-worker.

देहत्याग-end of the physical existence; death.

देहधर्म-physical functions of the body.

देहधारी-possessing a body; corporeal.

देहली-threshold.

देह-व्यापार-act of offering oneself for sex in return for money; prostitution.

देहांत-demise; death; expiry.

देहात-village; country.

देहाती-of a village; rustic; rural;

देहात्म-body and soul.

देहात्मवाद-materialism.

देहात्मवादी-materialistic.

देहावसान-demise; death.

दैत्य-demon; giant.

दैत्याकार-demon-like; huge; gigantic; colossal.

दैनिक-daily; newspaper published every day.

दैनिकी-diary.

दैन्य-poverty; pauperism; humility.

दैया-destiny; fate.

दैव-fate; destiny.

दैवकृत-providential.

दैवगति-course of events as ordained by destiny; providence.

दैवज्ञ-fortune-teller; astrologer; diviner.

दैवयोग-chance; contingency.

देवात् by chance; accidentally.

दैवी-pertaining to gods; divine.

दैहिक-physical; bodily; corporeal.

दैहिकी-Physiology.

दो-two.

दोअन्नी-a two- coin (old currency).

दोग़ला-cross-breed; born out of wedlock; illegitimate; not pure; mixed; bastard; two faced.

दोग़लापन-state of quality of being

दोज़ख-hell.

दोज़खी-of or like hell; hellish.

दोटूक-clearly and definitely; categorically.

दोतरफ़ा-two-sided.

दो दिला-having two minds; of a divided mind.

दोनाली-double-barrelled.

दोना-leaf-cup; leaf-bowl.

दोनों the two; both.

दोनो-of two things, persons etc.; both.

दोपहर-noon.

दोबारा second time.

दोमट-loam.

दोमुँहा-two-mouthed; having two mouths; deceitful.

दोयम-second-rate; second (in serial, order or merit).

दोरंगा-of two colours; double-dealing.

दोरसा-having two kinds of flavour or taste.

दोरुख़ा-double faced.

दोलक-pendulum.

दोलन-oscillation.

दोलायमान-oscillating; oscillatory; wavering; swinging.

दो शब्द-few words spoken or written about someone or something.

दोष-harm; blemish; defect; fault; charge; blame; guilt.

दोषमुक्त-guiltless.

दोषयुक्त-defective; faulty.

दोषारोप-charge; blame.

दोषारोपण-accusation; allegation; charging; blaming.

दोषी-at fault; guilty; culprit.

दोसाला-biennial.

दोसूती-

दोस्त-friend; intimate companion.

दोस्ताना-friendly.

दोस्ती-friendship; friendliness.

दोहन-milking; exploitation.

दोहरा-having two folds.

दोहराना-to make (something) two-fold; to revise; to recapitulate; to repeat / reiterate.

दोहराव-revision; repetition.

दोहा-couplet.

दोहाई-

दौंचना-to crush / pound; to thrash / beat.

दौड़-foot-race; race; run.

दौड़-धूप-bustle; hectic activity.

दौड़ना-to run; to rush; to run about.

दौड़-भाग-hurried activity; hustle.

दौड़ादौड़ी-hurry and scurry.

दौड़ाना-to cause to run; to make (someone) run; to despatch on errand.

दौर-cycle of times; wheel of fortune; turn of life; stage; phase; course (wine).

दौरा-tour; paroxysm; a large basket.

दौरान-duration; period.

दौरी-small basket.

दौर्बल्य-weakness; debility.

दौलत-wealth; riches.

दौलतख़ाना-residence (euphemistic).

दौलतमंद-rich; wealthy.

दौहित्र-daughter's son.

द्युति-light; lustre; glow; radiance; brilliance; splendour.

द्युतिमान-radiant; lustrous; brilliant.

द्युत-gambling.

द्यूतक्रीड़ा-gambling (as a sport).

द्यूतवृत्ति-gambling (as a vocation); habitual gambling.

द्योतक-indicative; illustrative; exemplifying; depicting; explaining.

द्योतन-indication; illustration; revelation; exemplification; manifestation.

द्योतित indicated; illustrated; illuminated; lighted.

द्रव-liquid; fluid.

द्रवण melting.

द्रवणशील-prone of liquefy; liquefiable.

द्रवणीय-liquefiable.

द्रवता-liquidity; fluidity.

द्रविड़-; a region in South India; an inhabitant of the region, a .

द्रवित melted; moved (by emotion).

द्रव्य-matter; money; wealth; substance.

द्रव्यमय-material; substantial.

द्रव्यमान-mass.

द्रष्टव्य-worth seeing; worth taking a note of; notable worth consulting.

द्रष्टा-spectator; seer; looker-on; sage.

द्राक्ष-शर्करा-glucose.

द्राक्षा-grape.

द्रावक-liquefying.

द्राविड़-of or pertaining to the .

द्रुत-fast; swift; quick; rapid.

द्रुतगति-fast moving; swift.

द्रुतगामी-going fast; swift.

द्रुम-tree.

द्रोण-a and instructor of and as per Hindu mythology.

द्रोणी-trough; basin.

द्रोह-rebellion; revolt; hostility; spite; malevolence

द्रोही-rebellious; revolting; hostile.

दंवद्व-duel; struggle; conflict; hubbub; hullabaloo; uproar; quarrel.

दंवद्वी-prone to quarrel; quarrelsome; troublesome.

द्वय-two.

द्वादश-twelve.

द्वादशी-twelfth day of each half of a lunar month.

द्वापर-the third era of Hindu mythology.

द्वार-door; gate; entrance; opening; outlet; means.

द्वारचार-ceremony performed at the door of the bride when the marriage party arrives.

द्वारपाल-doorkeeper; warder-guard; doorman; gatekeeper.

द्वारा, के-by through; through the agency of.

द्वि-two.

द्विगु-owner of two cows.

द्विगुण-double; two-fold.

द्विज-twice-born.

द्वितंत्र-diarchy.

द्वितीय-second.

द्वितीयक-second; duplicate.

द्वितीया-second day of each half of the lunar month; accusative case.

द्वित्व-duplication; duplication of a consonant in a word; repetition.

द्विदृष्टि-double vision.

द्विधा in two ways; in two parts.

द्विधार्थकता-ambiguity.

द्विपक्षी-

द्विपक्षीय-bilateral; bipartite.

द्विपद-having two feet, a human being; comprising two words, compound word; binomial (Maths).

द्विपदी-couplet.

द्विभाजन-dividing into two equal parts; bisection.

द्विभाषी-having or using two languages; bilingual.

द्विरागमन-coming (of a bride to her husband's house) second time after marriage.

द्विरुक्त-repeated; mentioned twice; reiterated.

द्विलिंगी-hermaphrodite; bisexual.

द्विवार्षिक-biennial.

द्विविध-of two kinds. in two ways.

द्विविम-two-dimensional.

द्विविवाह-bigamy.

द्विसदनात्मक-bicameral.

द्वीप-island.

द्वीपपुंज-archipelago.

द्वीपसमूह-a group of many islands; archipelago.

द्वीपी-insular; living in an island.

द्वेष-ill-will; malice; animosity; rancorous feeling.

द्वेषपूर्ण-malicious.

द्वेषवश out of malice.

द्वेषी-filled with ill-will; malicious; inimical; hostile.

द्वैत-dualism; duality.

द्वैध-distinction between two things; double-dealing.

द्वैध शासन-government vested is two supreme rulers; diarchy.

द्वैवार्षिक-biennial.

ध-The nineteenth consonant of the and Sanskrit alphabet and the fourth letter of the dental of class.

धंधा-occupation; employment; profession; vocation; prostitution.

धंधोर-a flame of light; a blace; a flare.

धँसना-to penetrate into; to subside / sink; to get thrust / stuck into.

धँसान-sinking / subsidence of land; immersion (of a statue).

धँसाना-to thrust into.

धँसाव-pit.

धक-palpitation; agitation; excitement; a louse.

धकापेल-jostling; pell-mell.

धकेलना-to shove; to push (down).

धक्कमधक्का-jostling; shoving and pushing.

धक्का-shove; impact; shock; push; setback.

धक्काड़-prolific.

धगड़ा-paramour.

धगड़ी-adulteress; paramour (woman).

धगवरी-(a woman) who is loved by her husband; an unchaste woman.

धचका-jerk.

धज-splendid appearance or attire; imposing manner or style; posture; outward appearance; mien.

धजीला-folded; gaudy; beautiful; pompous.

धज्जी-shred; smithereens; strip.

धट-the seventh sign of the Zodiac; Libar.

धड़-trunk; the main part of the human body apart from the head.

धड़क-shyness; fright (as on the stage).

धड़कन-throbbing; palpitation; pulsation.

धड़कना-to palpitate / throb / flutter.

धड़का-apprehension; scarecrow; palpitation of the heart.

धड़धड़-thudding sound.

धड़धड़ाना-to do something with a thudding sound; to do something all of a sudden.

धड़ल्ला-thudding sound.

धड़ा-a substitute for a weight; balancing substance.

धड़ाका-bang; crash; explosion.

धड़ाधड़ in quick succession.

धड़ी-a weight of five seers; roughly equal to 4½ kg; mark of any substance used for the beautification of lips.

धड़ेबन्दी-arraying armies for a show-down.

धत, धत् pooh! pooh!

धता-shunting off.

धतूरा-thorn-apple.

धधक-blaze.

धन-money; wealth; riches; property.

धनकुबेर-multi-millionaire.

धनचिन्ह-plus sign (+).

धन-जन-life and property

धन-तेरस-thirteenth day of the dark half of the month of the Hindu calender, dedicated to , the goddess of wealth.

धन-दौलत-wealth; pelf; money and possessions.

धनधान्य-wealth and plenty; affluence; prosperity.

धन-पक्ष-credit side.

धनपति-god of wealth.

धन-पिशाच-extremely stingy; over-greedy.

धनमद-intoxication/pride of wealth.

धनराशि-sum; amount.

धनलोलुप-greedy; avaricious.

धनलोलुपता-an excessive desire for wealth; greed; avarice.

धनवंत-rich; wealthy; money/monied.

धनवान, धनवान्-rich; wealthy; made of money; moneyed.

धन-विधेयक-money-bill.

धन-संपत्ति-wealth; money and possessions.

धनहीन-poor; money-less.

धनाढ्य-rich; wealthy; moneyed.

धनादेश-money order.

धनिक-rich; wealthy; moneyed.

धनिकतंत्र-plutocracy.

धनिया-coriander seed.

धनी-rich; wealthy; moneyed; well-to-do.

धनी-मानी-rich and respected; prosperous.

धनु-bow; ninth sign of the zodiac.

धनुर्धारी-skilled in archery; bowman.

धनुर्वात-tetanus.

धनुर्विद्या-archery.

धनुष-bow; arch.

धनुष-टंकार-twang of a bow-string; tetanus.

धन्ना सेठ-moneyed/wealthy man.

धन्य-blessed; blissful.

धन्यवाद-प्रकाशन-the expression of gratitude.

धन्वा-bow.

धन्वी-bowman; archer; skilled/clever in archery.

धप-light thud.

धब्बा-stain; spot; blemish; slur; blot.

धम-bang; thud.

धमकना-thumping; to have a shooting pain.

धमकाना-to intimidation; threat.

धमकी-intimidation; threat.

धमन-pumping of air; bellows.

धमन-भट्ठी-blast furnace.

धमनी-artery.

धमाका-loud bang / report; blast.

धमाचौकड़ी-furore; frisk; gambols.

धमाधम (ono.) with a thumping sound; in quick succession.

धर-(one) who holds / supports.

धरण-beam.

धरणी-earth.

धरणीधर-the mythological king of snakes who upholds the earth on his thousand hoods.

धरता-one who holds.

धरती-earth.

धरना-to place.

धरनी-beam.

धर-पकड़-rounding up; arrest.

धरमी-religious; pertaining to religion.

धरहरा-minaret.

धरा-earth.

धरातल-surface; earth.

धरातलीय-superficial.

धराधिप-king; ruler.

धराधीश-king; ruler.

धराना-to knock out (something out of someone).

धराशायी-floored-fallen flat; razed to the ground.

धरित्री-earth.

धरेला-keep (man).

धरेली-concubine; kept woman; mistress.

धरोहर-anything given or kept in trust; pledge.

धर्म-duty; function; intrinsic quality or property; religion.

धर्म-कर्म-religious or virtuous acts / conduct.

धर्म-काँटा-universally accepted standard balance; sacrosanct balance.

धर्मक्षेत्र-(place where was fought).

धर्मखाता-charity (account).

धर्मगुरु-religious preceptor; priest.

धर्मग्रंथ-religious / sacred book; holy scripture.

धर्मच्युत-fallen (in the religious or moral sense); deviated from duty.

धर्मज्ञ-well-versed in the principles of religion.

धर्मतंत्र-hierarchy; theocracy.

धर्मदर्शन-philosophy of religion; theology.

धर्म-धक्का-suffering caused by following the path of religion.

धर्मध्वज-

धर्मध्वजी-hypocrite.

धर्मनिरपेक्ष-secular.

धर्मनिरपेक्षता-secularism.

धर्मनिष्ठ-pious; devout; virtuous.

धर्मनिष्ठा-religious faith; devoutness.

धर्मपत्नी-wife (legally married).

धर्मपरायण-deeply religious; devoted to religious observances; religious minded; guided by a true sense of duty; conscientious.

धर्मपरायणता- religiousness; devoutness.

धर्म-परिवर्तक-convert.

धर्म-परिवर्तन-(religious) conversion.

धर्मपिता-godfather.

धर्मपुत्र-godson.

धर्मपुस्तक-religious book.

धर्मबुद्धि-moral or religious conscience.

धर्मभीरु-god-fearing; very religious; scrupulous.

धर्ममाता-godmother.

धर्मयुग-, the first age according to Hindu mythology; golden age.

धर्मयुद्ध-war of righteousness; crusade; just war.

धर्मराज-follower of religious tenets.

धर्म-विधान-canon; law.

धर्मवीर-one who is always prepared to follow the religious tenets; dauntless fighter for a religious cause.

धर्मव्रती-follower of or avowed to religious tenets.

धर्मशाला-pilgrim's rest house; inn.

धर्मशास्त्र-(books of) theology.

धर्मशास्त्री-theologian; theologist.

धर्मशील-pious; religious; virtuous.

धर्मसंकट-dilemma; quandary.

धर्मसभा-synod.

धर्मस्थ-well-placed in religion.

धर्मस्व-charitable.

धर्मांध-fanatical.

धर्मांधता-fanaticism.

धर्माचरण-religious conduct.

धर्माचार्य-high priest; preceptor.

धर्मात्मा-pious; virtuous.

धर्मादा-money set apart for charitable purposes; charitable endowment.

धर्माधर्म-moral consideration; discrimination between just and unjust.

धर्माधिकार-pre-lacy.

धर्माधिकारी-prelate.

धर्मार्थ-charitable. for charitable/ religious purposes.

धर्मिष्ठ-pious; religious; virtuous.

धर्मी-religious; religious minded.

धर्मोन्माद-theo-mania.

धर्मोपदेश-sermon; religious discourse.

धवल-white; clear; bright; without blemish; fair; a kind of disease.

धवलता-whiteness; clearness; brightness; fairness.

धवला-white cow.

धवलित-white (ned); brightened.

धसक-act or state of subsidence (as of land); depression; sinking of heart due to fright; constant dry cough due to pungent smell as of tobacco powder.

धसकना-to subside; to feel depressed; (heart) to sink due to fear; jealously.

धसका-a disease of lungs; dry cough; bronchitis.

धसना-to be ruined or destroyed.

धाँधली-dishonest act; unfair/ improper dealing bodering on arbitrariness; arbitrary conduct.

धाँधलीबाज-(one) who indulges.

धाँय-धाँय-thumping sound as that produced in cannonading; cannonade.

धाँस-irritating smell like that of tobacco powder or leaves.

धाँसना-to cough like a horse.

धाक-sway; predominance; commanding; influence.

धाकड़-famed; notorious; inspiring awe; strong of body.

धागा-thread.

धाड़-attack of robbers; a crowd; a multitude.

धातविक-metallic.

धाता meaning preserver; supporter; sustainer; protector.

धातु-metal; root (of a verb).

धातुकर्म-metalwork.

धातुकर्मी-metallurgist.

धातुपिंड-(usually brick shaped) lump of metal; (gold or silver) cast in a mould.

धातुमल-residue matter when metal is extracted from ore; slag.

धातुयुग-metallic age.

धातु-विज्ञान-metallurgy.

धातृका-nurse.

धात्री-wet-nurse.

धात्री-विद्या-obstetrics.

धात्वर्थ-root meaning (of a Sanskrit verb).

धात्विक-metallic.

धान-paddy; rice in the husk.

धाना-to run.

धानी-light green; receptacle; stand.

धान्य-grain.

धान्यागार-granary; barn.

धाम-abode; residence; seat of a deity.

धाय-wet-nurse.

धार-edge of a weapon; sharpness; current; flow.

धारक-one who holds; holder; bearer.

धारदार-sharp-edged.

धारना-to put on; to wear; to borrow.

धारा-current. stream; river; article section.

धाराप्रवाह-glib; fluent. fluently; non-stop.

धारावाहिक-serialised, serial.

धारित-that/which has been held.

धारी-(one) who holds; stripe; line; streak.

धारोष्ण-(milk) fresh from the udders; fresh and tepid.

धार्मिक-religious; pious.

धार्य-that which can be held; that which should be held.

धार्यत्व-act or state of supporting, wearing etc.

धावक-runner.

धावन-running.

धावा-attack; raid; charge.

धिक, धिक् term of contempt; pooh! fie!

धिक्कार-upbraid; rebuke; reproach; disdain; condemnation.

धिक्कारना-to upbraid/reproach/rebuke/curse/censure.

धिग्दंड-reprimand; admonition.

धींगाधींगी-improper dealing bodering on high-handedness.

धी-intellect; knowledge; erudition; daughter.

धीमर-fisherman.

धीमा-slow; dim; low; soft.

धीमान, धीमान्-wise; sharp-witted; intelligent.

धीमे-at a slow speed; slowly; mildly; in a low tone.

धीर-patient; steady; firm.

धीरज-patience.

धीरता-patience; steadiness; firmness.

धीरे slowly; gently; softly; lightly.

धीरे-धीरे very slowly.

धीवर-fisherman.

धीवरी-fisher-woman; fish-line.

धुँआ-smoke.

धुँआना-to be filled with smoke; to become smoky; to be disflavoured by smoke.

धुंध-fog; mist; mistiness; haze.

धुँधलका-twilight; haziness.

धुँधला-hazy; misty; obscure.

धुआँ-smoke.

धुआँकश-chimney.

धुआँधार-like a stream of smoke; fast and furious.

धुआँसा-smoky.

धुकर-पुकर-to being to palpitate.

धुत्त-besotted (with).

धुन-obsession; ruling passion; propensity; mania; tune.

धुनकना-to card (cotton).

धुनकी-carder.

धुनना-to card; to repent and lament.

धुनवाना-to cause to be carded.

धुनाई-act of carding; charges of carding.

धुनिया-carder.

धुनी-tenaciously; preserving; faddish.

धुपाना-to dry (something) in the Sun.

धुप्पल-dodge; bluff.

धुप्पलबाज-bluffer.

धुप्पलबाजी-bluffing.

धुरंधर-topping; outstanding; having mastery; pre-eminent.

धूम्र-smoke; fume.

धूम्रपान-smoking.

धूर्त-not honest or straight-forward; crafty; cunning; crooked; devious.

धूर्तता-wiliness; craftiness; cunningness.

धूर्ततापूर्ण-deceitful; full of crookedness/craftiness.

धूल-dust; dirt.

धूल-धक्कड़-dust and din.

धूल-धूसरित-steeped in dust; filled with dust.

धूलि-dust.

धूसर-of the colour of ashes; grey.

धृष्ट-insolent; impertinent; impudent; rude; reckless.

धृष्टता-insolence; impertinence; impudence.

धृष्टतापूर्ण-insolent.

धृष्टतापूर्वक insolently.

धेनु-(milch) cow.

धेला-half-pice; coin.

धैर्य-patience; endurance.

धैर्यवान-having or showing patience; patient.

धैर्यशील-patient.

धैर्यशीलता-patience.

धोखा-deceit; deception; fraud; illusion; scarecrow.

धोखाधड़ी-deceit; deception; fraud.

धोखेबाज़ी-treachery; fraud; deception; cheating.

धोती-loin-cloth.

धोना-to wash/launder; to apply water to something; bathe.

धोब-clothes given to a launderer (at a time) for washing; washing.

धोबिन-washerwoman.

धोबी-washerman.

धोबी-घाट-washing place on the bank of a river; pond etc.

धोरी-general controller; chief; eminent person; bullock.

धोरे near; close by.

धौंकना-to blow with bellows; to chastise.

धौंकनी-bellows; blow-pipe.

धौंस-browbeating; threat.

धौंसा-large kettledrum.

धौरा-white; clean.

धौरी-white cow; a kind of white bird.

धौल-slap; buffet.

धौल-धप्पा-slapping and boxing; exchange of blows.

ध्यान-attention (of mind); concentration; meditation; contemplation.

ध्यान-भंग-diversion.

ध्यानमग्न-absorbed/engrossed/lost in mediation.

ध्यानावस्थित-lost in meditation.

ध्येय-goal; aim.

ध्रुपद-form of classical Indian music.

ध्रुव-pole; firm; unchanging; fixed.

ध्रुवतारा-North star; Polestar.

ध्रुवीकरण-polarisation.

ध्रुवीय-near the earth's poles; polar.

ध्वंस-destruction; devastation; ruination.

ध्वंसक-causing great destruction; devastating.

ध्वंसन-destruction; devastation; ruination; sabotage.

ध्वंसावशेष-remains; relics; ruins.

ध्वज-flag; banner.

ध्वजदंड-flag-pole; flagstaff.

ध्वजपोत-flag-ship.

ध्वजभंग-impotency.

ध्वजा-flag; ensign; banner.

ध्वजारोहण-flag-hoisting.

ध्वजोत्तोलन-flag-hoisting.

ध्वनि-sound; implied/suggested meaning.

ध्वनित-implied/suggested (meaning).

ध्वनि-तरंग-sound wave

ध्वनि-विज्ञान-phonetics; phonology.

ध्वनि-सह-sound-proof.

ध्वन्यात्मक-phonetic.

ध्वस्त-destroyed; devastated; ruined.

ध्वस्तीकरण-destruction; annihilation.

ध्वानिक-acoustic.

ध्वानिकी-acoustics.

न

न-The twentieth consonant of the and Sanskrit alphabet and the fifth letter of the dental of class.

no, not; a sign of disagreement.

नंग-private part; nakedness.

नंगटा-naked.

नंगा-exposed; nude; naked; uncovered; bare; shameless.

नंगाई-nakedness; bareness.

नंगा-झोरी-a thorough search of the clothes which an man is wearing on his body.

नंगा-नाच-disgraceful / shameless conduct.

नंगापन-shamelessness; nakedness.

नंगा-बूचा-very poor; indigent; penniless.

नंगा-भूखा-starving and penniless.

नंगालुच्चा-mean and wicked; depraved; debased.

नंद-happiness; delight.

नंदकी-black pepper.

नंदनंदन-an epithet of Lord

नंदन-a kind of verse; hapiness; delight; son; mythical garden of Lord

नंदनकानन-garden of Lord

नंदना-to be pleased or delighted; daughter.

नंदरानी-wife of Lord mother name.

नंदित-delighted; pleased.

नंदिनी-goddess daughter.

नंदी-the (carrier) bull of Lord . banyan tree.-cheerful; jovial.

नंदीश्वर-an epithet of Lord ; one of the attendent of .

नंदोई-husband of husband's sister.

नंबरदार-headman.

नंबरवार serially; by turn.

नंबरी-numbered; standard; bearing a number; patent.

नई नवेली-belle; beautiful young girl.

नक-abbreviated form of

नकचढ़ा-finicky; peevish; hard to please; grumpy; fastidious.

नकटा-one with a nose chopped off.

नकटी-female form of

नक़द-cash; ready (money).

नकद-नारायण-ready cash.

नक़दी-cash.

नक़दी-चिट्ठा-cash-book.

नक़दी-पुर्ज़ा-cash-memo.

नक़दी-रसीद-cash receipt.
नक़ब-house-breaking; burglary.
नक़ल-imitation; mimicry; copy; duplicate.
नक़लची-(one) who copies by unfair methods.-one who imitates.
नक़ल-नवीस-copyist.
नक़ली-artificial; fake; mock; forged.
नक़शा-map; chart; drawing; sketch; rough drawing.
नक़शानवीस-dra-ftsman.
नक़शी-(that) on which embroidery has been done.
नक़शेबाज-coquet.
नक़शेबाज़ी-coquetry.
नकसीर-nose-bleed.
नक़ाब-mask; veil.
नक़ाबपोश-maker.
नकार-the letter or its sound; denial; refusal.
नकारना-to deny/refuse; to dishonour (a cheque); to negate.
नकारांत-(word) ending in the letter
नकारात्मक-negative; implying denial/ refusal.
नकारात्मकता-negation.
नक़ाशना-to engrave.
नकियाना-to speak with a nasal accent.
नकेल-nose-ring; bridle.
नक्का-the eye of a needle.
नक़्क़ारखाना-kettledrum house.
नक़्क़ारची-drummer.
नक़्क़ारा-huge drum.
नक़्क़ाल-imitator; mimic; mimicker.
नक़्क़ाली-imitation; mimicry.
नक़्क़ाश-engraver; carver.
नक़्क़ाशी-engraving; carving.
नक़्क़ाशीदार-engraved; carved; etched.
नक्की-'one' or 'ace' of a gambling game; nasal accent.
नक्कीमूठ-a gambling game played by children.
नक्कू-having a large nose; conspicuously nonconforming/ unconventional.
नक्र-crocodile.
नक़्श-imprinted.
नक्षत्र-constellation (of stars); planet.
नक्षत्र-विद्या-astrology.
नक्षत्री-having good fortune; lucky; fortunate.
नख-nail of a finger; a pear like fruit.
नखक्षत-injury caused by finger nails.
नख़त-constellation.
नख़रा-flirtatious behaviour; coquetry.
नख़रीला-coquettish; prude.
नख़लिस्तान-Oasis.
नख-शिख-head to foot.
नख़ास-market.

नखियाना-to cause hurt with the finger nails.

नखी-having large nails.

नग-gem; jewel; mountain; piece; item.

नगण्य-almost negligible.

नगद-cash.

नगद-नारायण-cash money.

नगदी in cash.

नगपति-Himalayas.

नगर-city; all the people living in a city.

नगर-नारी-prostitute.

नगर-निगम-municipal corporation.

नगर-निवासी-citizen.

नगर-पालिका-municipality.

नगरप्रमुख-mayor.

नगर-महापालिका-corporation.

नगरवासी-citizen.

नगरी-town.

नगरीकरण-urbanisation.

नगरीय-of or pertaining to the city; urban.

नगाड़ा-tymbal; huge drum.

नगीना-jewel; gem.

नगीनासाज़-one who sets gems.

नगेंद्र-Himalayas.

नग्न-completely undressed; nude; naked.

नग्नता-nudity; nakedness.

नग्न-नृत्य-show of brazen-facedness; (literature) nude dance.

नग्नवाद-nudism.

नग्नवादी-nudist.

नचना-dancer.

नचनी-woman dancer.

नचाना-to make one dance; to harass/ tease.

नज़दीक-near; adjacent; close.

नज़दीकी-near.

नज़र-the power or ability to see; eyesight; view; care; gift.

नज़रबंद-interned; detained.

नज़रबंदी-detention; interment.

नज़रबाग़-pleasure garden (in the campus of a palace).

नज़रसानी-revision; reconsideration.

नज़रा-connoisseur.

नज़राना-present gift.

नज़रिया-point of view; viewpoint.

नज़ला-catarrh.

नज़ाकत-delicacy or tenderness (of body).

नजात-deliverance; riddance; liberation.

नज़ारा-spectacle; scene; view.

नज़ीर-instance; example; precedent.

नजूम-astrology; astronomy.

नजूमी-astrologer; astronomer.

नज़ूल-land belonging to Government.

नज़्म-poem.

नट-dancer; rope-dancer; acrobat; actor; impresario; stage-manager.

नटई-throat.

नटखट-mischievous; naughty; impish.

नटखटपन-mischief; naughtiness.

नटखटी-mischief; naughtiness.

नटना-to go back by one's word; to negate; to wriggle out by saying 'no'.

नटनागर-Lord

नटनी-actress.

नटराज-Lord Lord .

नटवर-Lord

नटसाल-part of a thorn or arrow which remains in the body; agony; affliction.

नटी-actress; stage manager's wife

नत-inclined; titled; bent; curved.

नतमस्तक-having head bowed down in reverence.

नति-inclination; bent.

नतिनि-daughter's daughter.

नतीजा-the effect or outcome of something; result; consequence.

नतोदर-concave.

नत्थ-

नत्थी-file.

नत्थीकरण-filing.

नथ-nose-ring; nose-rope.

नथना-nostril.

नथनी-nose-ring.

नथुना-

नद-big river.

नदारद-missing; disappeared; absent.

नदी-river; stream.

नदीतल-river-bed.

नदीमुख-mouth of a river; estuary.

ननद-husband's sister.

ननदोई-husband of husband's sister.

ननसाल-mother's paternal home.

ननिहाल-house of maternal grandfather; mother's paternal home.

ननुनच-hitch; hesitation; objection.

नन्हाँ-little.

नन्हा-tiny; wee.

नपना-to be measured.

नपाई-act or process of measurement, or charges paid therefore.

नपा-तुला-measured; exact to the core; precisely to the point.

नपुंसक-impotent; emasculated; coward.

नपुंसकता-impotency; emasculation; cowardice.

नफ़रत-very strong dislike; hatred.

नफ़री-one day's work of a labourer; one man-day; wages paid for the same.

नफ़ा-money gained in a business; profit; gain; benefit gained from something; advantage.

नफ़ासत-refinement; nicety; delicacy.

नफ़ासतपसंद-having a refined taste.

नफ़ीरी-clarinet.

नफ़ीस-excellent; fine; nice.

नबी-prophet; divine; messenger.

नब्ज़-pulse.

नब्बे-ninety. 90.

नभ-sky; firmament.

नभचर-who moves in the sky; a bird.

नभोवाणी-a voice from sky.

नम-wet; damp.

नमक-salt.

नमकख़्वार-brought up and nurtured (by someone); dependent.

नमस्य-worthy of respect.

नमाज़-(Muslim's) prayer.

नमाज़गाह-place where prayer is performed; mosque.

नमाज़ी-one who performs scrupulously.

नमित-bent; inclined; bowed.

नमी-wetness; moisture; humidity; dampness.

नमीदार-moist; humid.

नमूना-sample; example.

नम्य-(that) which can be bent; flexible.

नम्यता-flexibility.

नम्र-quiet and modest; submissive; humble.

नम्रता-modesty; humility; meekness; submissiveness.

नम्रतापूर्वक-modest; humble.

नय-policy.

नयन-eye.

नयनगोचर-perceptible; visible.

नयनाभिराम-beautiful; charming; pleasing to eyes.

नया-not existing before; fresh; different; modern; of new fashion; recent; young.

नयापन-newness; modernism; new fashion; novelty.

नर-man.

नरक-hell; inferno.

नरकट-reed.

नरक-कुंड-infernal pond; hell-pond.

नरक-भोग-damnation; undergoing the tortures of hell.

नरक-यातना-tortures of hell.

नरकवास-living in hell.

नरकवासी-dammed.

नरकुल-reed.

नरगिस-narcissus.

नरगिसी-of the colour of narcissus.

नरपति-king.

नरपशु-monster; cannibal; beastly character; ignoble man.

नरपिशाच-ogre; cannibal.

नरपुंगव-topping/best man.

नरबलि-human sacrifice.

नरभक्षी-cannibal; man-eater.

नरम-soft; gentle; moderate; smooth and delicate.

नरमा-a kind of cotton.

नरमी-softness; gentleness.

नरमेध-sacrifice of a human being.

नरवध-man-slaughter.

नरसिंहा-a king of copper horn.

नरसों-the day, two day after tomorrow; the day, two days before yesterday.

नरहत्या-murder; homicide.

नरहरि-the fourth incarnation of Lord (Hindu mythology), in the form of a half-lion; half-man.

नरिया-a kind of clay tile.

नरेंद्र-king; prince.

नरेन्द्रमंडल . chamber of princes.

नरेतर-someone different from a human being; animal beast.

नरेली-small coconut; outer covering of a coconut; a hookah made of coconut.

नरेश-king.

नरोत्तम-superb among men; best of men.

नर्तक-male dancer.

नर्तकी-female dancer; dancing girl.

नर्तन-dancing; dance.

नर्तित-danced.

नर्स-nurse.

नल-tap; pipe; tube.

नलका-hand-pump; water-tap.

नलकूप-tubewell.

नलिका-thin tube; quiver.

नलिकाकार-tubular.

नलिन-lotus; lily.

नलिनी-louts; lily; river; left nostril.

नली-tube; pipe; spout; barrel (of a gun).

नवंबर-November.

नव-new; novel; nine.

नवखंड-the ninth part of the world (Hindu mythology).

नवग्रह-the nine planets (Hindu Astrology).

नवजागरण-renaissance.

नवजात-new-born; nascent.

नवधा-of nine kinds.

नवनीत-butter.

नवम-ninth.

नवमल्लिका-jasmine.

नवयुवक-youth; young man.

नवयुवती-young/youthful girl.

नवयौवन-adolescence; youth.

नवयौवना-woman in youthful bloom.

नवरंग-novel; of a new design.

नवरत्न-nine (kinds of) precious stones; the nine gems (learned men) of the court of king .

नवरत्नी-(ornament) with nine kinds of precious stones embedded.

नवरात्र-first nine days of the bright half of the lunar months of of , dedicated to the worship of Goddess Durga; nine-day period.

नवल-novel; new.

नवलता-novelty; newness.

नववधू-newly married girl.

नवविवाहित-newly-married.

नवशिक्षु-novice.

नवसाक्षर-neo-literate.

नवागत-newly arrived.

नवान्न-new corn of a harvest.

नवाब़-baron; (Muslim feudal Lord).

नवाब़जादा-son of a ; young Lord; a person who lives luxuriously.

नवाब़ज़ादी-daughter of a .

नवाब़ी-office, status, estate etc., of a ; way of living like that of a .

नवासा-daughter's son.

नवासी-eighty-nine; daughter's daughter.

नवासीवाँ-eighty-ninth.

नवाह्न-nine-day period; novena.

नवीकरण-renovation.

नवीकृत-renovated.

नवीन-new; novel.

नवीनता-newness; novelty; recency; modernity.

नवीनीकरण-renewal.

नवीनीकृत-renewed.

नवीयन-renewal; rejuvenation.

नवीस (one) who writes; writer; scribe.

नवीसी-act or profession of writing.

नवेद-good news; invitation; invitation card/letter.

नवेला-new and handsome; fresh and young.

नवेली-young lady.

नवोढ़-newly married (man).

नवोढ़ा-newly married woman.

नव्य-new; naval; modern; recent.

नशा-intoxication.

नशाख़ोर-habitually drunk; drunkard; inebriate.

नशाख़ोरी-(habitual) drinking; drunkenness; inebriety.

नशा-पानी-intoxicants and concomitant snacks.

नशाबंदी-prohibition.

नशीन indicating 'one who sits'.

नशीला-intoxicating; inebriating.

नशेबाज़-addicted to drinking.

नशेबाज़ी-alcoholism.

नश्तर-lancet; surgical knife.

नश्वर-mortal; destructible; perishable; transitory; ephemeral; short-lived.

नष्ट-destroyed; ruined; annihilated.

नष्टप्राय-almost destroyed/ruined/annihilated/asunder.

नस-vein; sinew; nerve; thew.

नसबंदी-a kind of minor operation to prevent the release of sperms during ejaculation.

नसल-lineage; breed; race.

नसवार-snuff.

नसीब-destiny; fortune; luck.

नसीबवर-fortunate; lucky.

नसीबा-luck.

नसीबोंजला-ill-fated.

नसीम-gentle breeze.

नसूड़िया-ill-omened; inauspicious.

नसैनी-ladder; staircase.

नस्य-snuff; the rope passing through the nose of the bullock which is used for driving him.

नहछू-nail-cutting ceremony.

नहर-canal.

नहरनी-an Indian type of nail cutter.

नहरी-of or pertaining to a canal.

नहरीकरण-canalization.

नहरुआ-guinea worm.

नहला-nine of cards.

नहलाई-act or state of laving/bathing; or charges paid for the same; maid who is engaged for laving/bathing.

नहलाना to give a bath to somebody; bathe.

नहान-ablation; bathing.

नहाना-to bathe; to take a bath.

नहाना-धोना-washing and bathing.

नहिक-negative.

नहीं a sign of disagreement; no; not; or; else; otherwise.

नहूसत-inauspiciousness; gloominess.

नाँद-tub; manger.

नाइतिफ़ाक़ी-disunity; discord; disagreement.

नाइन-barber's wife; woman of barber; a cast among Hindus.

नाईं like, as.

नाई-barber.

नाक-nose; heaven; prestige.

नाक़दारी-lack of appreciation; want of proper respect; humiliation.

नाक-नक़्शा-the cut of the face; features.

नाकवाला-prestigious.

नाका-entrance (to fort, city etc.); check-post; eye (of a needle); crocodile.

नाक़ाफी-not enough; inadequate; insufficient.

नाक़ाबिल-unfit; undeserving; unworthy.

नाकाम-unsuccessful.

नाकामयाब-unsuccessful.

नाकामयाबी-failure.

नाकामी-lack of success; failure; worthlessness.

नाकारा-good-for-nothing; worthless.

नाकारापन-worthlessness.

नाक़िस-defective (object); deficient; worthless (person).

नाकेबंदी-blockade; siege.

नाक्षत्र-sidereal.

नाख़ुदा-atheistic.

नाख़ुश-displeased; angry.

नाख़ुशी-displeasure.

नाख़ून-nail (of the finger).

नाग-cobra; snake; serpent; elephant.

नागकन्या-a female of the Nag caste.

नागपाश-a noose-like weapon.

नागफनी-a kind of thorny bush; cactus.

नागफेन-saliva of a snake; opium.

नागर-civil; civic; urban.

नागराक्षर-a letter/character of alphabet.

नागराज-king cobra.

नागरिक-civil.

नागरिकता-citizenship.

नागरिक शास्त्र-civics.

नागरिक सेना-militia.

नागरी-script; characters.

नागरीकरण-transliteration into character.

नागवार-unbearable; intolerable.

नागहानी-unexpected and sudden happening.

नागा-one belonging to the tribe; a nude ascetic.

नाग़ा-gap; absence from work.

नागालैंड-a state in the northeast of India.

नागिन-female serpent; a line of hair on the back; considered inauspicious.

नागेन्द्र-large snake; big elephant.

नागेश-kind of serpents (Hindu mythology).

नाच-dance.

नाच-गाना-dancing and singing.

नाच-घर-dancing hall.

नाचना-to dance.

नाचनेवाली-dancing girl.

नाच-रंग-dancing and merry-making.

नाचीज़-insignificant; trifling.

नाज-grain.

नाज़-pride; vanity; airs; charming gestures; fondness.

नाज़बरदार-one who dances to the tune of another.

नाज़बरदारी-act or state of being

नाजायज़-illegitimate; illegal; improper; unjust.

नाज़िर-chief copyist/writer; a court official; .

नाज़ी-very cruel; harsh; severe.

नाज़ुक-soft; delicate; tender; sensitive; vulnerable; critical; precarious.

नाज़ुकमिज़ाज-peevish; touchy; irritable.

नाटक-drama; play; dramatic performance.

नाटकबाज़ी-exaggerated emotional behaviour; dramatics.

नाटकीयता-showiness; dramatics.

नाटना-to neglect/refuse; to envy.

नाटा-dwarfish; short-statured.

नाटिका-short-drama.

नाट्य-drama.

नाट्यकला-histrionics, dramatic art.

नाट्यकार-actor; playwright; dramatist.

नाट्यशाला-theatre.

नाट्यशास्त्र-dramaturgy.

नाट्यशास्त्री-dramaturgist.

नाड़ा-umbilical cord.

नाड़ी-pulse; nerve; blood vessel; vein; artery.

नाड़ी-व्रण-sinus.

नातक़ा-power of speech.

नाता-relation, relationship.

नाता-गोता-family relationship.

नाती-daughter's son.

नाते, के due to relationship; status; position; for, on behalf of.

नातेदार-relative; kinsman.

नातेदारी-relationship.

नात्सी-Nazi.

नात्सीवाद-Nazism.

नाथ-master; Lord; nose-rope.

नाथना-to pierce a nostril of a bullock, etc. and pass a string through it of driving; to bring under control; to sew/string together.

नाद-sound; musical; noise.

नादपेटी-sound-box.

नादान-ignorant; slow to understand; untelligent.

नादानी-ignorance; silliness.

नादिरशाह-Nadir Shah, a tyrannical kind of Persia, who invaded Delhi and ordered a general massacre therein.

नादिरशाही-tyrannous; high-handed.

नादिरी-tyrannical.

नादिहंद-defaulting or defaulter in payment.

नान-big; thick type of bread.

नानखताई-a kind of a sweet.

नानबाई-baker.

नाना-mother's father; maternal grandfather.

नानार्थ-(word) homonym; (object) multi-purpose.

नानी-maternal grandfather; mother's mother.

ना-नुकर-'no', negative reply.

नाप-measure; measurement; dimension.

नाप-जोख-measurement; estimation.

नाप-तौल-weightment; measurement; weight and measure.

नापना-to measure.

नापसंद-not to one's liking; unacceptable.

नापसंदगी-disapproval;unacceptability.

नापाक-impure; unclean; dirty; uncouth.

नापास-failed; not accepted; untenable.

नापित-barter.

नाफ़-navel; nucleus.

नाफ़ा-navel of a musk-deer.

नाबदान-gutter.

नाबालिग़-minor; underage.

नाबालिग़ी-minority (in age).

नाभि-navel; hub.

नाभिक-nucleus.

नामंजूर-disallowed; rejected; not accepted; refused.

नामंजूरी-rejection; disapproval; refusal.

नाम-name; reputation; fame.

नामक-bearing/having the name, called.

नामकरण-ceremony of naming a child; denomination; nomenclature.

नाम-चढ़ाई-getting (one's) name enrolled.

नामज़द-nominated.

नामज़दगी-nomination.

नाम-धातु-denominative verb.

नाम-पट्ट-signboard; nameplate.

नामराशि-namesake.

नामर्द-impotent; effeminate.

नामर्दी-impotence; impotency; eeffeminacy; cowardice.

नामलिखाई-enrolment.

नामलेवा-heir.

नामवर-famous; renowed; reputed.

नामवरी-fame; renown; repute.

नामविहीन-nameless.

नामांकन-nomination.

नामांकित-nominated.

नामांतर-alias; second name.

नामांतरण-change of name; mutation.

नामा-cash money; letter.

नामाक़ूल-undesirable/unworthy (person).

नामावली-nomenclature.

नामिका-panel (of names).

नामी-famous.

नामुआफ़िक-unsuitable; unfavourable.

नामुनासिब-improper; wrong.

नामुंमकिन-utterly impossible; not feasible.

नामुराद-whose aspirations have been not fulfilled; unlucky; unfortunate.

नाम्ना-bearing/having the name.

नायक-leader; chief; hero.

नायन-barber's wife; woman of a the barber caste among Hindus.

नायब-deputy.

नायबी-office, status, etc.; of a

नायाब-not easily available; excellent; of a very high quality.

नायिका-heroine (of a story, novel etc.); damsel; belle.

नायिका-भेद-classification of heroines in Indian literature.

नारंगी-orange.

नारकीय-hellish; diabolical.

नारा-slogan; tape (for fastening trousers); rope attached to the yoke.

नाराज़-displeased; angry.

नाराज़गी-displeasure; anger.

नारायण-Lord

नारियल-coconut.

नारी-woman.

नारी-जगत-women's world.

नारी-धर्म-duty of a woman.

नारू-louse.

नारेबाज़-sloganeer; slogan-monger.

नारेबाज़ी-sloga-neering.

नाल-pedicel; tubular stalk; tube; barrel of a gun; weaver's spindle; naval string; horse-shoe; ring of a stone used for weight lifting; charges realised by the owner of a gambling den.

नाल-कटाई-act or state of cutting the naval string of a new-bron child; or wages paid therefor.

नालबंद-farrier.

नालबंदी-act of fixing a horse-shoe to the shoes or the feet of a horse; calling of a farrier.

नाला-big drain; gutter; rivullet; water-course; water-channel.

नालायक़-unfit; worthless; incapable; unworthy.

नालायक़ी-unfitness; worthless; incapability; unworthiness; improper act; misdeed.

नालिश-lawsuit; complaint; report.

नाली-drain; sewer.

नाव-boat; ferry.

नाविक-boatman; sailor.

नाश-annihilation; destruction; ruination.

नाशक-causing destruction; ruinous; destructive.

नाशकारी-destructive; devastating.

नाशन-destroying; runing; killing.

नाशपाती-pear.

नाशवाद-nihilism.

नाशवादी-nihilist.

नाशवान, नाशवान्-perishable.

नाश्ता-breakfast; refreshment.

नास-snuff.

नासदानी-snuffcase.

नास-पीटा-totally worthless; good-for-nothing.

नासमझ-innocent; unintelligent; lacking in understanding/intelligence; dull.

नासा-nose; nostril.

नासाज़-out of sorts.

नासिका-nose.

नासिक्य-nasal; pertaining to the nose.

नासूर-sinus; fistula.

नास्तिक-one who disbelives in the existence of God, atheist.

नास्तिकता-the belief that God does not exist; atheism.

नास्तिवाद-atheism.

नास्य-nasal; pertaining to the nose.

नाहक़ in vain; to no purpose.

नाह-नूँह-negatation; expression of reluctance.

नाहर-lion; lion-hearted person.

निंदक-backbiter; slanderer; calumniator.

निंदना-to backbite/abuse/defame.

निंदनीय-censurable; opprobrious; reprehensible; condemnable.

निंदा-backbiting; censure; slander; opprobrium; reproof.

निंदा-प्रस्ताव-censure motion.

निंदा-स्तुति-censure and praise.

निंद्य-censurable; contemptible; damnable.

नि: denoting negation.

नि:शंक-fearless; dauntless.

नि:शब्द-speechless; silent (person); without sound (place).

नि:शुल्क-without any charge/fee; free.

नि:श्वास-expiration; breathing out.

नि:संकोच also.

नि:संदेह without doubt; indubitably; certainly.

नि:स्पंद-motionless; still.

नि:स्पृह-above all desired; selfless.

नि denoting down, in, into, within etc.

निअराना-to come near.

निआमत-

निकट-proximate; near; close. near.

निकट, के close to, near.

निकटतम-nearest.

निकटता-nearness; proximity.

निकटवर्ती-situated near; close-at-hand; adjacent; adjoining.

निकटस्थ-immediate; adjacent.

निकम्मा-idle; inert; good-for-nothing; worthless.

निकम्मापन-idleness.

निकर-half-pants; short.

निकल-nickle.

निकलना-to come out; to rise; to appear; to pass; to pass out; to turn out. to be subtracted.

निकलवाना-causative of to turn out.

निकष-touchstone; criterion.

निकाय-body; system.

निकालना-to take to draw out; to bring out or publish; to dismiss; to solve, as a question.

निकाला-expulsion; banishment.

निकास-act or state of coming out; source of income; outlet; egress; exit; exhaust.

निकासी-act or state of coming or going out; manufacture and sale of goods; income; toll; clearance.

निकाह-marriage (Muslim).

निकुंज-bower; arbour; grove thicket.

निकृष्ट-very inferior; of a low order; worse; worthless; vile; base.

निकृष्टता-state or quality of being ; lowliness; worthlessness.

निकेतन-residence; abode.

निकोटना-to pinch with the nails.

निक्का-tiny; dwarfish; younger.

निक्षिप्त-thrown out; abandoned; deposited; consigned; pledged.

निक्षिप्त उपवाक्य-parenthetical clause.

निक्षेप-throwing out; despatch; thing despatched; deposit; consignment; pledge.

निक्षेपण-act or state of throwing out.

निखट्टू-(one) who earns nothing; jobless; unemployed; occupied; idler.

निखट्टूपन-state or quality of being

निख़रचे without any charge for freight, postage etc.

निखरना-to brighten up; to blossom out.

निखरवाना-causative of

निखार-lustre; brightening up; blossoming out; elegance.

निखारना-to clean/cleanse.

निखिल-entire; whole; all.

निखुटना-to be exhausted; to fall short.

निगंदना-to sew (provisionally) with long stitches.

निगड़-fetters.

निगमन-deduction; incorporation.

निगमित-deduced; incorporated.

निगमागम-(Hindu) holy scriptures.

निगमीकरण-act of incorporating; incorporation.

निगरानी-vigil; surveillance; supervision; custody.

निगलना-to swallow up; to gulp down.

निगाली-smoking pipe.

निगाह-eyesight; vision; watch; guard.

निगुरा-uninitiated.

निगूढ़-abstruse; obscure; latent; secret; hidden.

निगूढ़ार्थ-hidden/subtle meaning.

निगोड़ा-idler; lazy; worthless.

निग्रह-restraint; self-control.

निघरा-homeless.

निचय-collection; fund.

निचला-lowly; lower.

निचाई-lowness; depth; meanness.

निचान-slope; state of being low.

निचुड़ना-to be squeezed.

निचोड़-epitome; extract; essence.

निचोड़ना-to squeeze/wring/extort.

निचौहाँ-bent (downward); inclined; tending to go down.

निछत्र-dethroned.

निछल-void of any trick or stratagem.

निछावर-something (specially coins) offered for warding off evil influence; sacrifice.

निज-own.

निजवाचक-reflexive.

निजी-own; personal; private.

निजीकरण- privatization; denationalization.

निजीकृत-privatized.

निठल्ला-idler; lazy; unemployed; lounger.

निठल्लापन-laziness; idleness; unemployment.

निठुर-hard-hearted; cruel.

निठुरता-hard-hearted-ness; cruelty.

निडर-fearless; undaunted.

निडरपन-fearlessness; undauntedness.

निढाल-exhausted (with fatigue or due to some other cause); languid.

नितंब-buttocks; hips.

नित daily; every day.

नितांत-excessive; extreme; absolute; downright.

नित्य every day; always.

नित्यकर्म-ceremonial routine.

नित्यचर्चा-daily routine.

नित्यता-eternity; permanence.

नित्यनियम-eternal rule.

नित्यप्रति almost daily.

नित्यशः almost daily.

नित्यसंबंध-perpetual/permanent relation.

निथरना-to be decanted/purified.

निथार-decantation; decanted substance.

निथारना-to purify by decanting; to filter (water).

निदरना-to insult/humiliate; to neglect/ignore.

निदर्शक-illustrating.
निदर्शन-illustration; example.
निदर्शित-illustrated; exemplified.
निदान-diagnosis; end; conclusion. at last; in the end.
निदानगृह-clinic.
निदानज्ञ-diagnostician.
निदानशाला-clinic.
निदान-शास्त्र-diagnostics.
निदेश-direction; directive; instruction.
निदेशक-directive.
निदेशक मंडल-board of directors.
निदेशन-direction.
निदेशात्मक-directional.
निदेशालय-directorate.
निदेशिका-directory.
निदेशित-directed.
निद्रा-sleep; slumber.
निद्रालस-drowsiness; sleepiness.
निद्रालु-sleepy; drowsy; slumberous.
निद्रित-sleeping; asleep.
निधड़क-fearless; undaunted. fearlessly; undauntedly.
निधन-demise; decease; death.
निधान-store; reservoir.
निधि-fund; treasure.
निनादित-full of sound; echoing; resonant.
निनावाँ-thrush; a disease of the mouth.
निन्यानबे-ninety nine.
निपट-absolutely.
निपटना-to be finished off; to be free after some work; to settle accounts; to evacuate.
निपटान-evacuation.
निपटाना-to dispose of; to settle.
निपटारा-settlement; disposal.
निपत्र-without or bereft of leaves.
निपात-fall; degradation; ruin; destruction; death.
निपुण-adept; proficient; skilful; expert; dextrous.
निपुणता-efficiency; proficiency; skill; sagacity; acumen.
निपूता-issueless; childless.
निपूती-woman having no issue.
निपोरना-to show one's teeth (being unable to reply).
निबंध-essay; treatise.
निबंधक-registrar.
निबंधन-typing/joining/fastening together; registration.
निब-nib.
निबद्ध-tied / joined / fastened together; registered.
निबल-weak.
निबाह-accomplishment; arrangement.
निबाहना-to maintain.
निबेड़ना-to dispose of; to settle.

निबेड़ा-disposal; settlement; solution.

निभना-to have a comfortable or friendly relationship with somebody.

निभाना-to fulfil (one's) responsibility/duty/order/promise; to get along; to carry on/pull on.

निभाव-act or state of fulfil responsibility.

निमंत्रण-invitation.

निमंत्रण-पत्र-invitation card; letter of invitation.

निमंत्रित invited.

निमकी-lemon-pickle; fried salty smallish snacks.

निमकौड़ी-seed of

निमज्जन-bathing; immersion; submersion.

निमज्जित-bathed; immersed; submerged.

निमित्त-cause reason; purpose.

निमित्त, के for, for the sake of.

निमिष-blinking (of an eye); twinkle; time taken in the twinkling of an eye.

निमीलन-winking.

निमीलित-closed; shut up.

निमेष-winking.

निमोनिया-pneumonia.

निम्न-low; under.

निम्नगा-river.

निम्नलिखित- undermentioned; following.

निम्नांकित- undermentioned; following.

नियंतव्य-that can be/should be put under control.

नियंता-controller; Supreme Controller; God.

नियंत्रक-controller.

नियंत्रण-control; restraint.

नियंत्रण-रेखा-line of control.

नियंत्रित-controlled; restrained.

नियत-destined; fated; prescribed; specified; appointed; posted; allotted.

नियतन-allotment; fixation.

नियति-destiny; fate.

नियतिवाद-determinism.

नियतिवादी-deterministic.

नियम-rule; usual practice.

नियमत: as a rule; according to rule/law; formally.

नियमन-act of regulating/controlling.

नियमबद्ध-systematized; regulated; regularized; strict.

नियम विरुद्ध-contrary to law; illegal.

नियमानुकूल-according to rule.

नियमानुसार-as per rule.

नियमावली-manual (of rules and regulations); set of rules.

नियमित-regulated; regular.

नियमितता-the state of being regular; regularity.

नियमी-(one) who leads a regulated life.

नियाज़-grace; favour.

नियामक-regulating; regulative.

नियामत-blessing; boon; bounty; favour; benevolence.

नियुक्त-appointed; posted; engaged; employed; authorised.

नियुक्ति-appointment; posting; employment.

नियोक्ता-employer.

नियोजक-employer; appointing authority; planner.

नियोजन-act of employing; planning.

नियोजनालय-employing exchange/ bureau.

नियोजित-employed; planned.

नियोज्य-employable; which can be planned.

निर् without break/continuous.

निरंक-blank; unmarked.

निरंकुश-unrestrained; absolute; despotic.

निरंकुशता-state of being unrestrained; absolutism; despotism.

निरंकुश-शासन-despotic rule/ despotism.

निरंजन-(eyes or person) without collyrium; untained; faultless; spotless; unstained.

निरंतर-continual; continuous. incessantly; continuously; non stop.

निरंतरता-continuity; non-interruption.

निरक्षर-illiterate; unlettered; uneducated.

निरक्षर भट्टाचार्य-totally illiterate fellow.

निरखना-to behold/view/see/look; to examine.

निरगुनी-without any quality.

निरत-engrossed; absorbed.

निरन्न-without food; hungry; without cereals.

निरपराध-innocent; guiltless; not guilty.

निरपवाद-without exception.

निरपेक्ष-absolute; unconcerned; indifferent.

निरपेक्षवाद-absolutism.

निरपेक्षित-unconcerned.

निरबंसी-having no posterity; issueless; childless.

निरभिमान-without pride; humble.

निरभिलाष-without any desire; above all desires; disinterested.

निरभ्र-cloudless; serene (sky).

निरर्थक-meaningless; useless; worthless; futile.

निरर्थकता- meaninglessness; worthlessness; fruitlessness.

निरवकाश-without vacant space/gap; without leisure/recess.

निरवच्छिन्न- uninterrupted; continuous; without break; clear/ obvious.

निरवधि-having no fixed period; limitless; endless; perennial.

निरवलंब-without support; helpless.

निरसन-cancellation; repeal.

निरस्त-cancelled; repealed.

निरस्त्र-unarmed; disarmed.

निरस्त्रीकरण-the act of giving up weapons; disarmament.

निरहंकार-prideless; without vanity.

निरा-sheer; absolute; pure.

निराई-act of weeding out; or charges paid therefore.

निराकरण-repudiation; contradiction; abrogation.

निराकार-formless; without form; shapeless; incorporeal.

निराकृत-repudiated; contradicted; abrogated.

निराकृति-repudiation; contradiction; abrogation.

निरादर-disrespect; insult; disgrace.

निरादरपूर्ण-disrespectful.

निराधार-baseless; groundless; unfounded; without support/prop.

निराना-to weed out.

निरापद-immune; safe; secure.

निरापदता-immunity; security.

निरामय-sound; healthy.

निरामिष-(food) without meat, egg or fish; vegetarian (food).

निराला-strange; queer; unique; peculiar; extraordinary.

निरावरण-unveiled; uncovered.

निरावृत-unveiled; uncovered.

निराश-disappointment; frustrated; hopeless; dismayed; dejected.

निराशा-disappointment; frustration; despair; dismay; pessimism.

निराशाजनक-disappointing; hopeless; depressing; discouraging; dismaying.

निराशापूर्ण-despairing.

निराशावाद-pessimism.

निराशवादी-pessimistic.

निराशोन्माद-desperation.

निराश्रय-without refuge/shelter/ protection.

निराहार-abstaining from food.

निरीक्षक-inspector; invigilator; supervisor.

निरीक्षण-observation; viewing; inspection.

निरीक्षण-गृह-inspection house.

निरीक्षणाधीन-under inspection/observation.

निरीक्षित-inspected; observed.

निरीक्ष्य-(that) which can be viewed/inspected.

निरीश्वरवाद-atheism.

निरीश्वरवादी-atheistic.-atheist.

निरीह-innocent; harmless.

निरीहता-innocence; harmlessness.

निरुक्त-etymology.

निरुक्ति-derivation.

निरुत्तर-at a loss to answer.

निरुत्साह-without enthusiasm/zeal/spirit.

निरुत्साहित-discouraged;disheartened.

निरुद्देश्य-without aim/purpose; aimless; purposeless.

निरुद्ध-obstructed; choked.

निरुद्यम-not industrious; lazy; indolent.

निरुपम-matchless; peerless; incomparable; marvellous; extraordinary.

निरुपाय-resourceless; helpless.

निरूढ़-unmarried (person); (word) established by usage; famous.

निरूपक-representative; representing; that which determines/demonstrates.

निरूपण-exposition; elucidation.

निरूपित-explained; elucidated.

निरोग-no disease.

निरोध-constraint; control; restriction; check; prevention; condom.

निर्ख़-rate.

निर्गंध-odourless; without smell.

निर्गत-issued.

निर्गम-issue; egress; exit; outlet.

निर्गुण-without attributes; without (good or bad) qualities; absolute.

निर्जन-desolate (place); uninhabited; solitary; lonely; deserted.

निर्जनता-loneliness; desolation.

निर्जर-having no old age; ever young; possessing perennial youth.

निर्जल-dry.

निर्जल व्रत-a fast which one observes without taking even water.

निर्जलीकरण-dehydration.

निर्जीव-lifeless; without life; inanimate; dead; insipid; spiritless.

निर्झर-fall; waterfall; torrent.

निर्झरिणी-small waterfall.

निर्णय-decision; judgement; verdict; finding.

निर्णयात्मक-pertaining to decision.

निर्णायक-deciding; decisive; conclusive; determinative.

निर्णायक मत-decisive vote; casting vote.

निर्णीत-decided; judged.

निर्दय-cruel; pitiless; merciless; ruthless; barbarous; hard-hearted.

निर्दयता-cruelty; pitiless-ness; mercilessness; ruthlessness.

निर्दयतापूर्ण-cruel; ruthless.

निर्दयतयापूर्वक cruelly.

निर्दयी-pitiless; merciless; ruthless.

निर्दल-not belonging to any party; independent.

निर्दिष्ट-assigned; determined; specified.

निर्देश-instruction; direction.

निर्देशक-instructor; director.

निर्देशन-instruction; direction.

निर्दोष-innocent; blameless; guiltless; not guilty (person); unblemished; flawless.

निर्द्वंद्व-(object) without dispute; uncontested; carefree; above pleasure and pain; (person) without a rival or opposer.

निर्धन-poor; have-not; indigent; unlucky.

निर्धनता-poverty; indigence; penury.

निर्धारक-assessor.

निर्धारण-assessment; ascertainment; fixation; determination.

निर्धारित-ascertained; assessed; fixed; determined; scheduled.

निर्धार्य-that which is to be ascertained.

निर्निमेष without blinking/winking.

निर्प्रश्नीय-unquestionable.

निर्बंध-unrestricted; uninhibited; free.

निर्बल-weak; infirm; feeble.

निर्बलता-weakness; infirmity.

निर्बाध-unrestricted; unobstructed; without anything blocking; free.

निर्बीज-seedless.

निर्बुद्धि-foolish; stupid.

निर्भय-fearless; intrepid; valiant; dauntless.

निर्भर-dependent.

निर्भरता-dependability; dependence.

निर्भीक-fearless; bold; intrepid; frank; audacious.

निर्भीकता-fearlessness; boldness; intrepidity; frankness.

निर्भीकतापूर्वक fearlessly.

निर्भ्रांत-(person) who has no doubts; free from doubts.

निर्भ्रांतता-doubtlessness.

निर्मम-merciless; cruel; barbarous; harsh; ruthless.

निर्ममता-heartlessness; ruthlessness; cruelty; hard-heartedness.

निर्ममतापूर्वक-ruthlessly.

निर्मल-pure; clear; clean; spotless; stainless.

निर्माण-act of building; construction; erection; manufacturing; production; making; creation; structure.

निर्माण-कार्य-construction work.

निर्माणशाला-factory; manufactory.

निर्माता-builder; constructor; manufacturer; creator; producer.

निर्मित-built; constructed; manufactured; created; produced.

निर्मुक्त-enjoying liberty; free.

निर्मूल-rootless; without root; baseless; unfounded.

निर्मेय-proble.

निर्मोही-not responsive to love; loveless; cold-hearted; harsh; cruel.

निर्यात-export.

निर्यातक-exporter.

निर्यास-exudation from plants; gum.

निर्लज्ज-shameless; brazen faced; unabashed; immodest.

निर्लज्जता-shamelessness; immodesty.

निर्लज्जापूर्ण-shameless; impudent.

निर्लज्जापूर्वक-shamelessly; indecently.

निर्लिप्त-unattached; detached.

निर्लिप्तता-state or quality of non attachment; detachment.

निर्लोभ-unselfishness.

निर्वंश-issueless; childless.

निर्वचन-etymological interpretation; interpretation.

निर्वचनीय-which is to be interpreted.

निर्वसन-naked; nude.

निर्वहन-discharge.

निर्वाचक-elector.

निर्वाचन-election.

निर्वाचित-elected.

निर्वाच्य-unutterable; (one) who can be elected.

निर्वाण-salvation; liberation.

निर्वाणी-pertaining to

निर्वात-devoid of air or gas; vacuum.

निर्वापण-extinction.

निर्वासन-deportation; banishment; exile; expulsion.

निर्वासित-deported; banished; exiled.

निर्वाह-subsistence; sustenance; maintenance.

निर्विकल्प-without any alternative/ option; concentrated.

निर्विकार-changeless; invariable; unmoved; dispassionate; stolid.

निर्विघ्न-uninterrupted; unobstructed; unimpeded; trouble free. without interruption; without any untoward incident/obstacle.

निर्विरोध-unopposed; uncontested.

निर्वेद-disgust; indifference (to the world); resignation.

निर्व्याधि-without ailment/disease; healthy.

निर्हस्तक्षेप-nonintervention.

निलंबन-suspension.

निलंबित-suspended.

निलय-residence; mansion; abode.

निवर्तन-act of returning; conclusion; closure; repeal.

निवारक-deterrent; preventive; curative.

निवारण-clearance or removal (of something undesirable); prevention; preclusion.

निवार्य-evitable; avoidable.

निवाला-morsel; mouthful.

निवास-abode; dwelling; residence; act or residing.

निवासी-inhabitant; dweller; resident.

निवास्य-fit for dwelling.

निविड़-deep; dense; thick; pitch.

निविड़ता-density; thickness.

निविदा-tender.

निविष्ट-entered; penetrated; situated.

निविष्टि-entry.

निवृत्त-freed (after doing some work); liberated; retired.

निवृत्ति-freedom (after doing some work); retirement; abstinence; abstention.

निवेदक-applicant; petitioner.

निवेदन-submission; request.

निवेदित-submitted; requested; prayed for.

निवेश-camp; residence; house; entry; investment.

निशब्द-soundless; silent; speechless.

निशा-night.

निशाकर-the moon.

निशाचर-night wanderer; demon; goblin; hobgoblin; jackal.

निशात-pleasure; enjoyment.

निशान-mark; sign; impression; flag standard; emblem; trace; clue; spot; scar.

निशानची-a good shot; marksman.

निशाना-aim; target; bull's eye.

निशानी-sign; token; gift that evokes someone memories; keepsake.

निशानेबाज़ी-marksmanship.

निशास्ता-essence of wheat.

निशि-night.

निशिदिन day and night; ever; almost always.

निश्चय-determination; resolution; decision; certitude; certainly.

निश्चयबद्ध-fully determined.

निश्चयात्मक-positive; definite; certain; absolute.

निश्चयात्मकता-certitude; definiteness; certainly.

निश्चल-motionless; stationary; immobile; immovable; firm; calm; steady; unwavering.

निश्चलता- motionlessness; immovability; steadiness; firmness; inertia; immutability.

निश्चायक-conclusive; decisive.

निश्िंचत-carefree; without worries; free from worry/anxiety.

निश्िंचतता-freedom from worry; quietude.

निश्चित-certain; definite; determined; settled; fixed; resolved.

निश्चिति-certitude; certainly.

निश्चेतक-anaesthetic.

निश्चेष्ट-motionless; still; stagnant; inactive; inert; unconscious.

निश्चेष्टा-inertia; unconsciousness.

निश्छल-without wile; sincere; guiltless; honest.

निश्वास-exhalation.

निश्शंक-fearless; dauntless; intrepid.

निषंग-quiver; an ancient trumpet.

निषाद-a primitive non Aryan tribe in India; a person belonging to this tribe; the seventh note in Indian music.

निषिद्ध-prohibited; forbidden; tabooed.

निषेधाज्ञा-injunction; stay order.

निषेधात्मक-prohibitive; negative.

निषेधाधिकार-veto.

निष्कंटक-free from thorns; unobstructed; free from troubles or damages.

निष्कपट-ingenuous; guileless; unpretentious; honest; sincere.

निष्कपटता-ingenuity; artlessness; honesty; guiltlessness; candour.

निष्कर्ष-conclusion; result; substance; essence; finding; extract; epitome.

निष्कलंक-blameless; spotless; stainless; immaculate; innocent; pure.

निष्कलुष-without blemish; spotless; stainless; clean; immaculate; innocent.

निष्काम-(person) unattached; (act) done without any desire or attachment; motiveless.

निष्काम भाव-spirit of non-attachment; desirelessness.

निष्कारण without cause/reason.

निष्कासन-expulsion; ejectment; rustication.

निष्कासित-expelled; rusticated.

निष्क्रमण-evacuation; exit.

निष्क्रय-redemption; riddance.

निष्क्रांत-evacuee.

निष्क्रिय-not active; inactive; idle; passive.

निष्क्रियता-inactivity; inertia; inaction; passivity.

निष्ठ-faithful; loyal.

निष्ठा-loyalty; allegiance; fidelity; devotion; faith; singleness or purpose.

निष्ठावान, निष्ठावान्-loyal; faithful; devoted.

निष्ठुर-heartless; cruel; callous; ruthless.

निष्ठुरता-heartlessness; cruelty; ruthlessness.

निष्णात-accomplished; skilled; adept.

नष्पंद-without vibration; motionless; unwavering; steady.

निष्पक्ष-impartial; unbiased.

निष्पक्षता-impartiality; unbiased-ness.

निष्पत्ति-completion; accomplishment; execution (of order, instruction or decision).

निष्पन्न-completed; accomplished; executed; done.

निष्पादक-one who does what he is asked to do; executive.

निष्पादन-execution.

निष्पादित-executed; accomplished.

निष्पाद्य-to be done/executed.

निष्पाप-sinless (person or act); without guilt; guiltless; innocent.

निष्प्रभ-(object) without glitter; dull; pale; lustreless; (person) disconcerted; out of countenance.

निष्प्रभाव-ineffectual; ineffective; defunct.

निष्प्रयोजन-without purpose; purposeless; aimless.

निष्प्राण-lifeless; aimless.

निसत-without essence; false.

निसर्ग-nature.

निसर्गज-natural; innate; inborn.

निसर्गतः naturally; in the natural/primitive form.

निसार-sacrificed.

निस्तत्त्व-without any substance; worthless; unsubstantial.

निस्तब्ध-stationary; still; inert; quiet; without noise; silent.

निस्तब्धता-quietude; noiselessness.

निस्तार-deliverance; redemption; riddance.

निस्तारण-rescue; delivery; going across.

निस्तारना-to take across; to rescue; to be instrumental in getting over difficulties; to release.

निस्तीर्ण-crossed over; reserved; released; delivered.

निस्तेज-lifeless; lustreless; pallid; insipid; dull.

निस्पंद-without vibration; motionless; unwavering; steady.

निस्पृह-free from or above all desires.

निस्बत-comparison.

usually followed by

निस्संकोच-unhesitating.

निस्संग-lonesome; lonely; without any desire.

निस्संतान-issueless; childless.

निस्संदेह undoubtedly; doubtlessly; surely.

निस्सरण-excretion; outflow.

निस्सहाय-helpless; without support.

निस्सार-without any substance; worthless; unsubstantial.

निस्सारक-one who draws or turns out.

निस्सारण-causing to go out; turning out.

निस्सारित-turned out.

निस्सीम-limitless; boundless.

निस्सीमता-limitlessness.

निस्सृत-extract/drawn out.

निस्स्वार्थ-selfless; unselfish.

निहंग-alone; solitary; celibate; naked.

निहत्था-unarmed.

निहाई-anvil.

निहानी-instrument used for scratching letters on wax covered surfaces; style.

निहारना-to look intently; to behold.

निहाल-perfectly satisfied; exalted; contented; happy.

निहित-vested; inherent; implied.

निहितार्थ-implied meaning; implication.

निहोरना-to entreat/solicit/beseech.

निहोरा-obligation; entreaty; solicitations.

नींद-sleep; slumber.

नींव-foundation.

नीका-good.

नीग्रो-negro.

नीच-mean; low; base; demeaning; vulgar; abject.

नीचता-meanness; baseness; lowliness; act of meanness.

नीचा-low; below the average level; not high; sloping; mean; base.

नीचाई-lowness; depth; low level.

नीचे below; underneath; under.

नीड़-nest.

नीति-ethical principle; policy.

नीतिकुशल-tactful; politic; shrewd.

नीतिज्ञ-one who tells people how to behave ethically; statesman.

नीति-निर्धारण-policy-making.

नीतिभ्रष्ट-demoralized.

नीतिशास्त्र-ethics.

नीबू-lemon.

नीबू-निचोड़-very stingy; (one) who extracts money from others mercilessly; a shylock.

नीम-the Indian tree; light (colour); mild.

नीम-हकीम-quack.

नीयत-intention; motive.

नीर-water.

नीरज-born out of water.

नीरद-cloud.

नीरव-still; quiet; silent.

नीरवता-stillness; quiet; silence.

नीरस-without juice; juiceless; insipid; dry; prosaic; uninteresting; tedious.

नीरसता-tedium.

नीरांजनी-candle stand used in ceremonious worship.

नीरा-juice of date-tree.

नीलकंठ-jay (bird); Lord .

नीलकमल-blue lotus.

नीलगाय-antelope; yak.

नीलम-sapphire.

नीलनमणि-sapphire.

नीलांबुज-blue lotus.

नीला-blue.

नीलाक्ष-blue-eyed.

नीलापन-blueness.

नीलाम-auction.

नीलामी-pertaining to auction.

नीला-सा-bluish.

नीलिमा-bluishness; blueness.

नीलोत्पल-blue lotus.

नीलोफ़र-blue lotus.

नीहार-fog; mist.

नीहारिका-nebula.

नुक़्ता-point; dot; point; issue.

नुक़्ताचीं-fault-finder.

नुक़्ताचीनी-fault-finding; carp.

नुक़रा-white-coloured horse.

नुक़सान-loss; damage; harm.

नुक़सानी-damaged.

नुक़सान माल-seconds; damaged goods or goods of an inferior quality.

नुकीला-having a sharp tip; pointed.

नुक्कड़-corner; especially turn of a street.

नुक़्स-defect; fault; flaw.

नुनखरा-saltish; saline.

नुमाइश-exhibition; display; show.

नुमाइशी-for show only; showy; ostentatious.

नुस्ख़ा-prescription; recipe.

नूतन-new; novel; modern; fresh; recent.

नूतनता-newness; novelty; modernity; modernism.

नून-salt.

नूपुर-anklet; an ornament for the ankles.

नूर-splendour; light; lustre.

नृ-man; human being.

नृत्य-dance.

नृत्यकला-art of dancing.

नृत्यशाला-dancing hall.

नृप-king; monarch.

नृशंस-atrocious; cruel; barbarous.

नृशंसता-atrocity; cruelty.

ने-attached to the nominative case in the past tense etc., of a transitive verb.

नेक-good and virtuous; goody.

नेकचलन-of good conduct.

नेकनाम-reputed; well-known; famous.

नेकनामी-good reputation; repute; good name.

नेकनीयती-good faith; honesty of purpose.

नेकी-goodness.

नेकी-बदी-good and evil.

नेग-ceremonial tip/due present.

नेज़ा-spear; lance.

नेज़ाबदार-lancer; lancer bearer.

नेता-leader; pioneer.

नेतागिरी-leadership.

नेति There is no end to this; This (God) is infinite.

नेतृत्व-leadership; hegemony.

नेतृत्वविहीन-without a leader; headless.

नेतृत्व-शक्ति-ability of leadership.

नेतृवर्ग-group of people who lead; leadership.

नेत्र-eye.

नेत्र-जल-tear.

नेत्रविज्ञान-ophthalmology.

नेत्री-woman leader.

नेनुआ-a green Indian vegetable.

नेपथ्य-green room of a theatre.

नेपाल-Nepal; an independent Hindu state situated to the north of India.

नेपाली-of or pertaining to Nepal.

नेम-rule.

नेम-धर्म-religious practices.

नेमी-(a person) who observes religious rites punctiliously.

नेवला-mongoose.

नेस्त-non-existent.

नेस्ती-lazy; indolent; ominous.

नैज-one's own; personal.

नैतिक-ethical; moral.

नैतिकता-morality.

नैत्रिक-ocular.

नैदानिक-clinical.

नैन-eye.

नैपुण्य-the state or quality of being skill; adroitness; dexterity.

नैमित्तिक-casual; occasional

नैया-boat.

नैयायिक-logician.

नैरंतर्य-continuity; uninterrupted-ness.

नैराश्य-disappointment; despair.

नैवेद्य-offering made to a deity; oblation.

नैष्ठिक-vowing all-life celibacy.

नैसर्गिक-natural; innate; inherent.

नैहर-parental home (of a woman).

नोक-point; tip.

नोक-झोंक-wordy encounter/ skirmish/taunt.

नोकदार-pointed; sharp.

नोच-खसोट-pinching and snatching; grabbing.

नोचना-to claw.

नोट-currency note; bank note; footnote.

नोट-बुक-note-book.

नोटिस-notice.

नोन-salt.

नोना-saline; saltish.

नौ-nine.-boat; ship.

नौकर-a person employed to perform household duties; servant.

नौकर-चाकर-retinue of servants.

नौकरशाह-bureaucrat.

नौकरशाही-bureaucracy.

नौकराना-tip paid to a servant.

नौकरानी-maid servant.

नौकरी-service; job.

नौकरी-पेशा-working for a firm in return of payment.

नौका-boat.

नौका-विहार-boating.

नौ-खंडा-nine-storeyed.

नौचा-youth; young man.

नौचालन-navigation.

नौची-young woman; dancing (girl) trainee.

नौजवान-young; youthful; adolescent.

नौजवानी-youth; prime of youth.

नौटंकी-village drama.

नौनिहाल-promising (boy)

नौबत-situation; state of affairs; small drum.

नौबहार-spring season.

नौबेड़ा-naval fleet; fleet of boats.

नौरंगा-nursery.

नौरत्न-(collection of) nine gems; necklace containing nine gems; a kind of sweet sauce.

नौलखा-worth nine lakhs of rupees; very precious.

नौ-विज्ञान-nautical science.

नौशी-bride.

नौसादर-ammonium chloride.

नौसिखुआ-inexperienced.-novice; fresher.

नौ-सेना-navy; armada; sea-force; navel force.

नौ-सेनापति-admiral; chief of Naval Staff.

नौ-सेवा-naval service.

नौ-सैनिक-of or pertaining to navy; one in naval service.

न्यस्त-arranged; deposited; invested.

न्याय-justice; fairness; impartiality.

न्यायकर्ता-judge; justice.

न्यायज्ञ-jurist.

न्यायतंत्र-judiciary.

न्यायत: judicially; justly; honestly; equitably.

न्यायपरायण-just; equitable; judicious.

न्यायपालिका-judiciary.

न्यायपीठ-bench; seat of justice.

न्यायपूर्ण-justified.

न्यायमूर्ति-a Supreme Court Judge.

न्यायवादी-attorney.

न्यायवान-just; equitable.

न्यायशास्त्र-jurisprudence.

न्यायांग-judiciary.

न्यायाधिकरण-tribunal.

न्यायाधीश-judge.

न्यायालय-court of justice.

न्यायिक-judicial; juridical.

न्यायी-proper; reasonable and fair (person).

न्यायाचित-that can be justified; justifiable.

न्यारा-unique; queer; uncommon; somewhat different; peculiar.

न्यास-trust; endowment; act of arranging or placing; deposit; investment.

न्यासधारी-trustee.

न्यासभंग-breach of trust

न्यून-less; insufficient; lacking; deficient.

न्यूनतम-minimum.

न्यूनता shortage; deficiency.

न्यूनम-reduction.

न्यूनाधिक-more or less.

न्योतना-to invite.

न्योता-invitation.

न्हाव-to flee.

प

प-The twenty-first consonant of the and alphabet and the first letter of the labial or class.

पंक-mud; mire; slime; bog.

पंकज-born in slime.

पंकिल-muddy; slimy; boggy.

पंक्ति-queue; a line of houses, seats, chairs etc. line; row; rank.

पंक्तिबद्ध-arrayed; arranged in a row or rows; queued.

पंख-a wing; feather; an arm of a fan.

पंखड़ी-flower-petal; blade.

पंखा-fan.

पंखी-small fan; flying insect.

पंगत-sitting for common dinner.

पंगु-invalid; cripple; lame.

पंगुता-cripplehood.

पँच-allo. of (five).

पंचक-inauspicious period during which five particular stars are in conjunction; group/set of five.

पँचखना-five-storeyed.

पँचगुना-five times.

पंचजन्य-the famous conch of Lord .

पंचतत्त्व-the five element namely earth, water, fire, air and ether.

पंचत्व-death; demise.

पंचनामा-declaration given by five (prominent) persons; written award.

पंचनिर्णय-award; judgement of an arbitrator.

पंचभुज-pentagon.

पंचभूत-the five primary elements water, earth, air, fire, ether.

पंचम-fifth note of Indian musical scale.-fifth.

पंचमांगी-fifth columnist.

पंचमी-fifth day of each half of the lunar month.

पंचमुखी-possessing five mouths.

पँचमेल-of five sorts; assorted.

पँचरंगा-five-coloured; multi-coloured.

पंथ-way; path; cult; creed; sect; school.

पंथी-traveller; follower of a sect/cult.

पंद्रह-fifteen. 15.

पँवाड़ा-saga; exaggerated description.

पँसरहट्टा-grocery market.

पंसारी-grocer.

पँसेरी-a weight of five seers; roughly 4 kg.

पकड़-hold; catch; firm grip.

पकड़ना-to hold/seize; to nab/apprehend/arrest; to entrap/snare/entangle; to catch.

पकड़वाना-causative of

पकना-to ripe/ripen; to be cooked.

पकवान-Indian type of pudding/cookie.

पकाई-act or wage of process of ripening.

पकाना-to cook; to ripen as fruit; bake, as pots in fire; to cause to suppurate, as a boil.

पकौड़ा-a piece of vegetable fried in butter.

पक्का-ripe; mature; brickbuilt; settled; confirmed.

पक्व-cooked; mature.

पक्वता-ripeness; maturity.

पक्ष-wing; fortnight; aspect; side; phase; aspect.

पक्षधर-partisan; supporter.

पक्षपात-partiality; favouritism.

पक्षपाती-partial.

पक्ष-विपक्ष-the two parties/sides to a dispute.

पक्षांतर-the other fortnight; to other party/side.

पक्षांतरण-transposition.

पक्षाघात-paralysis.

पक्षी-bird.

पक्षीय-belonging to a party; related to a wing.

पक्षीराज-eagle.

पक्षी-विज्ञान-Ornithology.

पख-feather; fortnight.-impediment; hindrance; obstacle; flaw.

पखवाड़ा-a period of two weeks; fortnight.

पखारना-to wash/cleanse.

पखावज-drum; tumbrel.

पखेरू-bird.

पख़्तून-a person whose mother tongue is .

पग-foot; step; pace.

पगडंडी-footpath; footway.

पगड़ी-turban; black money, given for obtaining possession of a premises.

पगना-to be impregnated with some syrup.

पगला-mad; insane.

पगली-mad; insane (woman)

पगहा-a rope or chain by which an animal is tied to a peg; tether.

पगार-boundary; enclosure; wall; mud prepared for building purposes; fordable river or rivulet; wages.

पगुराना-to chew the cud; to ruminate.

पगोड़ा-Buddha temple; pagoda.

पचड़ा-ado; fuss; pother; affray.

पचना-to be digested.

पचाना-to digest.

पचाव-digestion.

पचासा-set of fifty similar things; half a century; alarm bell of a jail.

पचासों-about or more than fifty.

पचासो-more than fifty; several fifties; all the fifty.

पचीसी-set of twenty-five similar things; first twenty-five years of (someone's) life.

पच्चर-wedged; chip; anything that prevents progress.

पच्चीकारी-inlaying work.

पच्चीस-

पछड़ना-to be beaten down/defeated; to be floored; to be knocked down.

पछताना-to repent/rue.

पछतावा-sorrow for wrong doing; repentance; remorse; rue; compunction.

पछना-to be scarified/tattooed.

पछवाँ-Western, coming from the West.

पछाँहीं-belonging or pertaining to the West.

पछाड़-to fall down in overbearing grief.

पछाड़ना-to beat down/defeat; to floor; to knock down; to beat out dust from a cloth.

पछोड़ना-to winnow / to separate out.

पटंबर-silken cloth.

पट-cloth; fabric; screen; gate; door; covering; pitapat sound.

पटक-throw; knocking down.

पटकना-to knock/throw down.

पटकनी-a knockdown.

पटका-sash; belt; girdle; cincture.

पटकान-a flooring; a knock down.

पटतर-equal; equivalent.

पटना-to be covered; to be filled up; to be dumped; pulling on; completion of a transaction; balancing; squaring.

पट-परिवर्तन-change of the screen or scene.

पटरा-low wooden seat; stave; plank.

पटरानी-chief queen; queen consort.

पटरी-rail; footpath; side walk; pavement; flat ruler.

पटल-screen; roof; layer; side; wooden plank; table; counter.

पटवा-embroiderer.

पटवारी-village official who maintains land records.

पटसन-jute.

पटा-an Indian weapon (of wood or iron); cudgel; low; wooden seat.

पटाई-act or state of or wages paid for the same; dumping.

पटाक-(ono.) sharp sound; thump; crash.

पटाका-cracker; slap.

पटाक्षेप-drop-scene.

पटाना-to cause to cover as a pit; to settle as a transaction; an account, purchase etc.

पटापट-with a continuous tapping sound; briskly.

पटाव-act or state of ; rubbish etc., with which a pit is covered; covering.

पटिया-slate; tile; board.

पटीलना-to bring (someone) round; to make someone agree to one's point of view; to cheat; to accomplish.

पटु-clever; skilful; adept; dexterous; expert; diligent.

पठार-plateau; table-land.

पठित-studied; read.

पड़ता-manufacturing cost.

पड़ताल-thorough inspection; investigation; search; survey.

पड़तालना-to search/investigate closely.

पड़ती-fallow land.

पड़ना-to be laid; to fall on something.

पड़ताना-maternal great grandfather.

पड़पड़ाना-to crack; to prattle/clatter.

पड़वा-calf of a buffalo.

पड़ाव-camp; halting place; halt.

पड़िया-she-calf of a buffalo.

पड़ोस-neighbourhood; vicinity.

पड़ोसी-neighbour.

पढ़त-reading.

पढ़ना-to read; to read out; to study; to receive education; to recite.

पढ़ना-लिखना-to read and write; to study.

पढ़वाना-to cause to be read.

पढ़वैया-one who reads.

पढ़ाई-reading; studying; learning at school; teaching.

पढ़ाना-to teach; to cause to read; to coach/educate/instruct.

पढ़ा-लिखा-educated.

पण-wager; stake; bet.

पणन-act of buying.

पणनीय-marketable.

पण्य-marketable.

पण्यवस्तु-commodity.

पतंग-moth; insect; paper-kite.

पतंगबाज़-kite-flier.

पतंगबाज़ी-kite-flying.

पतंगा-moth; insect.

पत-prestige; honour; dignity.

पतझड़-autumn; the fall.

पतन-fall; downfall; decline; ruin.

पतनशील-tending to fall; falling.

पतनोन्मुख-tending to fall; falling.

पत-पानी-prestige; honour.

पतला-thin; lean.

पतला-दुबला-lean and thin; weak.

पतलापन-thinness; leanness; tenuousness; wateriness (of sweat beverages, milk etc.)

पतलून-pantaloon; trousers.

पतवार-helm; rudder.

पता-address; knowing.

पताका-flag; banner.

पति-husband; lord; master.

पतित-fallen; degraded; corrupted.

पतितपावन-one who uplifts the downtrodden.

पतिता-fallen; degraded (woman).

पति-पत्नी-husband and wife.

पतियाना-to trust/rely.

पतियारा-trust; faith.

पतिव्रता-faithful to the husband. -faithful/virtuous wife.

पतीला-(large) kettle.

पतीली-container; small

पतोखा-a cup made of leaves.

पतोहू-daughter-in-law.

पत्तन-town; port-town.

पत्तर-sheet of metal.

पत्तल-leaf-plate.

पत्ता-leaf; a playing card.

पत्ती-leaf; especially small leaf; share

पत्तीदार-shareholder; partner.

पत्थर-stone.

पत्नी-wife.

पत्नीव्रत-faithfulness/fidelity to one's wife.

पत्र-leaf; letter; paper.

पत्रक-leaflet; chit; card.

पत्रकार-journalist.

पत्रकारिता-journalism.

पत्रपंजी-letter book/register; file.

पत्रपुष्प-leaves and flowers; token (representing something greater).

पत्रपेटी-letter-box.

पत्र-मित्र-pen-friend.

पत्रवाह-postman.

पत्रवाहक-letter-bearer.

पत्र-व्यवहार-the act of exchanging letters; corresponding.

पत्रा-Hindu calendar; almanac.

पत्राचार-correspondence.

पत्रावली-collection of letters, papers etc.; file.

पत्रिक-letter-paper.

पत्रिका-periodical; magazine.

पत्रिकावली-writing pad.

पत्री-horoscope.

पथ-path; way; route; course.

पथकर-toll-tax.

पथगामी-pedestrian.

पथना-passive of

पथप्रदर्शक-guide; leader.

पथप्रदर्शन-guidance.

पथभ्रष्ट-deviated from the right path.

पथरना-to be stoned/sharpened on stone/honed.

पथराना-to petrify; to be come hard like stone.

पथराव-pelting with stones.

पथरी-bladder-stone; a type of stone cup of bowl.

पथरीला-stony; littered with stones.

पथिक-way-farer; traveller; passenger.

पथेरा-brick-maker; tile-maker.

पथ्य-wholesome diet; prescribed diet.

पद-post; office; rank; work as used in phrase or sentence; word or phrase; foot; verse-line; item; part of speech.

पदक-medal.

पदकधारी-medallist.

पदक्रम-word order.

पदचाप-football.

पदचारी-pedestrian.

पदचिह्न-foot-print; foot-mark; insignia; trail.

पदच्युत-dismissed; fired; degraded.

पदच्युति-dismissal; degradation.

पदतल-sole (of foot).

पदत्याग-relinquishment of office; abdication; renunciation.

पदत्राण-shoe; footwear.

पददलित-depressed (classes); oppressed; down-trodden.

पदधारी-office-bearer; incumbent.

पदनाम-designation.

पदनामित-designated.

पदपूरण-filling in blanks.

पदबंध-phrase.

पदवी-title/degree; rank.

पदवीधारी-one who get any title.

पद-व्याख्या-parsing.

पदस्थ-office-bearer; incumbent.

पदाघात-blow with the feet; kick.

पदाति-foot-soldier; infantry-man.

पदाधिकारी-office-bearer; official.

पदाना-to tire out; to harass/vex.

पदान्वय-paraphrasing; paraphrase.

पदारविंद-lotus-like feet (an expansion of respect).

पदार्थ-matter; substance; material; word meaning.

पदाप्रण-the act of arriving (something or someone auspicious).

पदावधि-tenure; regime.

पदावनत-bowing down at someone's hallowed feet; demoted; degraded.

पदावनति-demotion.

पदावली-phraseology.

पदासीन-occupying (an) office.

पदाहत-kicked.

पदिक-foot-soldier; infantryman.

पदी-having feet/lines.

पदेन ex-officio; because of one's position; by virtue of office.

पदोड़ा-timid; cowardly.

पदोन्नत-promoted.

पदोन्नति-advancement in rank or position; promotion.

पद्धति-orderlysystemorarrangement; method; methodology; practice; custom.

पद्म-lotus.

पद्मनाभ-Lord

पद्मभूषण-a title.

पद्मविभूषण-a title.

पद्मा-goddess of wealth, .

पद्माकर-lotus lake.

पद्मासन-a particular type of cross-legged seating posture (Yog).

पद्मिनी-small lotus; beautiful woman; belle.

पद्य-verse; a stanza of a poem.

पद्यकार-versifier.

पद्यमय-versified.

पद्यात्मक-in the form of a verse.

पद्यीकरण-the art of versifying; versified from; versification.

पधारना-to come.

पन-allomorph of (betel leaf); as allomorph of in compound words. meaning quality or state; yellowness.

पनघट-the public place where from people (usually women) draw water.

पनचक्की-water-mill.

पनडुब्बा-diver.

पनडुब्बी-submarine.

पनपना-to grow; to flourish/thrive.

पनबाड़ी-betel-garden.

पनबिजली-hydro-electricity.

पनभरा-water-carrier.

पनवाड़ी-betel seller.

पनसाल-store of drinking water, from where water is distributed to traveller.

पनसाला-of five years; occurring after every five years.

पनही-footwear.

पना-beverage prepared from mango juice or tamarind etc.; width of a cloth.

पनाला-gutter/drain.

पनाह-shelter; refuge.

पनिहार-female water-carrier.

पनिहारिन-female water-carrier.

पनीर-cheese.

पनीरी-pertaining to or made of cheese.

पन्ना-emerald; leaf (of a book etc.); folio.

पन्नी-leaf of a metal; tinfoil; coloured; shining thin paper.

पपड़ियाना-to become covered with a crust.

पपड़ी-crust; scab; thin cake or some cereal.

पपड़ीला-scabby; flaky.

पपीता-papaya fruit.

पय-milk.

पयस-milk.

पयस्विनी-milch cow; wet nurse.

पयोधर-cloud.

पयोधि-ocean; sea.

परंतु on the contrary; but; in spite of this; but; however.

परंपरा-an opinion; belief or custom passed down from the past to the present; tradition; the passing of beliefs or customs from one generation to the next.

परंपरागत-of or in accordance with tradition; traditional.

परंपरानिष्ठ-orthodox; conventional.

परंपरावाद-a very great respect from traditions; traditionalism; orthodoxy; conservation.

पर-other; not one's own; on; upon; over; after. given to; feather.

परई-earthen bowl.

परकाजी-fond of helping others; benignant; benevolent.

परकार-pair of compasses/callipers.

परकीय-belonging or pertaining to someone else.

परकीया-a woman with whom a married man is having a love affair outside marriage; other woman.

परकोटा-rampart.

परख-test; examination; assay; the ability to judge correctly.

परख़चा-particle; fragment; shred.

परखना-to test/examine critically; assay.

परखी-gadget for testing corn/grain packed in sacks.

परखाई-charges paid for testing.

परगना-unit of several villages.

परगमन-adultery.

परगाछा-a kind of parasite.

परगामिनी-adulteress.

परचा-piece of paper; chit; question paper; newspaper; handbill.

परचाना-to acquaint/familiarise/habituate; to tame; to domesticate.

परची-slip; chit; lottery ticket.

परचून-grocery; provisions.

परचूनिया-grocer; retailer of provisions.

परछत्ती-a roofing (below the roof) meant for storage.

परछाँवाँ-shadow.

परछाईं-shadow; reflection.

परजन्म-next birth/rebirth.

परजवट-a system of renting out land.

परजाता-coral tree.

परजीवी-obtaining nourishment from others, parasitic.

परतंत्र-not autonomous; subjugated; sub-dued; dependent.

परतंत्रता-subjugation; dependence.

परतल-packsaddle.

परतला-shoulder belt.

परती-fallow land; uncultivated land.

परदा-screen; curtain; veil; purdah.

परदादा-great grandfather.

परदानशीन-(a woman) who observes purdah; stay-at-home.

परदापोश-(one) who covers/conceals the faults of others.

परदा-प्रथा-system of observing.

परदेदार-using or wearing a veil; veiled; curtained.

परदेदारी-veiling system.
परदेश-foreign country.
परदेशी-belonging to a foreign country; alien; exotic.
परनाना-(maternal) great grandfather.
परनानी-(maternal) great grandmother.
परनाला-drain pipe; gutter.
परपीड़न-sadism.
परपुरुष-a person other than someone's own husband.
परपोता-great grandson.
परबाल-eyelash.
परब्रह्म-The Supreme.
परम-absolute; ultimate.
परमाणु-atom.
परमाणुवाद-atomism.
परमाणुवादी-atomistic.
परमात्मा-Supreme Soul; God.
परमादेश-writ of mandamus.
परमाधिकार-prerogative.
परमानंद-bliss; blessedness.
परमार्थ-supreme good; ultimate good.
परमार्थवाद-philosophy of ultimate good.
परमार्थवादी-one who believes in the philosophy of ultimate good.
परमिट-permit; licence.
परमेश्वर-God, the Almighty.
परराष्ट्र-foreign country.
परला-of the other side.
परलोक-next/other world; heaven.
परलोकवास-existence in the next world; demise.
परलोकवासी-late; dead.
परवर-(one) who maintains.
परवरदिगार-main-tainer of all, God.
परवरिश-maintenance; nurture.
परवर्ती-later; subsequent.
परवल-an Indian green vegetable.
परवश-dependent; subservient; helpless.
परवशता-dependence; subservience; helplessness.
परवान-limit; boundary.
परवानगी-permission; leave.
परवाना-written command/order; warrant; moth; ardent/dedicated lover.
परवाह-care; heed.
परशु-battle-axe; halberd.
परसना-to serve (food).
परस्त्री-a woman, other than one's own wife.
परस्त्रीगमन-adultery.
परस्त्रीगामी-adulterer.
परस्पर mutually.-mutual; reciprocal.
परस्पर-विरोधी- conflicting; contradictory; incompatible.
परस्परता-mutuality.
परहित-benevolence; benefaction.

परहेज़-abstinence; avoidance; abstention.

परहेज़गार-one who keeps himself away from harmful things or acts; abstainer.

पराँठा-a kind of semi-fried Indian pan-cake.

पराँदा-string/ribbon for tying

परा indicating off; away; beyond etc.

पराकाष्ठा-climax; apogee; zenith; acme.

पराक्रम-valour; bravery; prowess.

पराक्रमी-valorous; valiant; intrepid; brave.

पराग-pollen.

पराग-केसर-stamen.

परागण-pollination.

पराङ्मुख-looking the other way; disinclined; indifferent; opposed; averse.

पराजय-defeat; rout; repulse.

पराजयवाद-defeatism.

पराजयवादी-defeatist.

पराजित-defeated; subjugated; vanquished.

पराजेय-defeatable.

परात-large metal dish.

पराधीन-under subjection; subservient; subject.

पराधीनता-subjection; subservience; dependence.

परान्न-food provided by others.

पराभव-defeat; subjection; subjugation; humiliation.

पराभूत-defeated; subjected; subjugated; humiliated.

परामनोविज्ञान-parapsychology.

परामर्श-consultation; advice; counsel.

परामर्शदाता-adviser; consultant; counsel; counsellor.

परामर्शदात्री-advisory.

परमर्श मंडल-advisory board.

परामर्श-शुल्क-consultation fee.

परायण-sticking/adhering to; fulfilling; discharging.

पराया-someone else's; other's.

परार्थ-other's good; benevolence; altruism.

परार्थवाद-altruism.

परार्थवादी-altruist.

परार्थी-benevolent man; altruist.

परावर्तन-retreat; withdrawal; rebounding; turning back; reflection.

परावर्तित-rebounded; reflected; withdrawn.

पराश्रय-dependence on others; subjection.

पराश्रयी-dependent on others.

पराश्रित-depended/dependent (on others).

परास-range.

परास्त-defeated; vanquished.

परिंदा-bird.

परि round; round about; well; very well; fully; completed.

परिकथा-narrative; story (especially related to vicinity).

परिकर-having girt up one's loins.

परिकर्म-make-up.

परिकलन-calculation.

परिकल्पना-presumption; hypothesis .

परिकल्पित-presumed.

परिक्रमण-revolution; going around.

परिक्रमा-round; circumambulation.

परिखा-moat.

परिगणक-calculator.

परिगणन-calculation; enumeration.

परिगणित-calculated; scheduled.

परिचय-introduction; the beginning part of a book; a book which gives important facts about something.

परिचय-पत्र-letter of introduction; identity card.

परिचर-attendant; retainer.

परिचर्चा-all-round discussion.

परिचर्या-nursing; attendance.

परिचायक-indicative; illustrative; introductory.

परिचार-nursing.

परिचारक-pertaining to nursing or attendance.

परिचारिका-nurse; female attendant.

परिचालक-conductor.

परिचालन-act of conducting; steering; operation.

परिचालित-conducted; operated.

परिचित-acquainted.

परिच्छन्न-covered all-round; fully covered.

परिच्छादन-act of covering.

परिच्छादित-covered.

परिच्छेद-chapter; section.

परिजन-retinue; kith and kin.

परिणत-transformed; changed; metamorphosed; culminated.

परिणति- transformation; metamorphosis; finale; end; culmination.

परिणय-marriage; wedding.

परिणाम-consequence; outcome; result.

परिणामी-resultant.

परिणीत-married.

परिणीता-married (woman).

परितः on all sides; around.

परितप्त-heated; anguished; in deep anguish; ardent.

परिताप-heat; anguish.

परितुष्ट-satisfied; gratified; satiated; pleased.

परितुष्टि-satisfaction; gratification; satiation.

परितोष-satisfaction; gratification; satiation.

परित्यक्त-abandoned; renounced; forsaken; rejected.

परित्यक्ता-abandoned (woman).

परित्यजन-abandoning; renouncing; forsaking.

परित्याग-abandoning; desertion; abandonment; renunciation.

परित्याज्य-deserving of being abandoned / forsaken / renounced.

परित्राण-act of saving from danger or enemy; deliverance; riddance; protection.

परित्राता-saviour; deliverer.

परिदृश्य-perspective; view.

परिधान-clothes; costume; garment.

परिधि-circumference; periphery; boundary; perimeter.

परिनिष्ठित-standard; standardised.

परिपक्व-ripe; mature.

परिपक्वता-ripeness; maturity.

परिपक्वावस्था-state of being ripe/ mature.

परिपत्र-circular; circular letter.

परिपथ-circuit.

परिपाक-assimilation; digestion; perfection; accomplishment.

परिपाटी-convention; system; method; order; tradition.

परिपार्श्व-vicinity.

परिपालन-compliance; observance; execution; implementation.

परिपुष्ट-well-nourished; well-built; well-developed.

परिपूरक-supplementary.

परिपूर्ण-replete; brimful; perfect.

परिपूर्णता-repletion; brimfulness; fullness; perfection.

परिपृच्छा-enquiry; investigation; curiosity.

परिपोषण-act of nourishing; nourishment.

परिप्रेक्ष्य-perspective.

परिप्लावित-submerged; inundated.

परिभाषा-a statement giving the exact meaning of a word, definition; exact description about the nature or extent of something; definition; technical language.

परिभाषित-defined.

परिभाष्य-definable; that which is to be defined.

परिभोग-easement.

परिभ्रमण-rotation; touring.

परिमंडल-globe; halo.

परिमल-fragrance; aroma; sweet smell.

परिमा-periphery; circumference.

परिमाण-magnitude; quantity.

परिमाणवाचक-quantitative.

परिमाप-perimeter.

परिमार्जन-complete purification; refinement; cleansing.

परिमार्जित-purified; cleansed of all impurities; refined; cleansed.

परिमित-limited; finite.

परिमिति-limit; perimeter.

परियार साल-year before last.

परियोजना-project; scheme.

परिरंभण-embrace; hug.

परिरक्षण-preservation; custody.

परिरक्षित-preserved.

परिरूप-design.

परिरेखा-periphery; outline.

परिवर्तन-change; alteration; variation; transformations.

परिवर्तनशील-changing; changeable; alterable; convertible.

परिवर्तित-changed; altered.

परिवर्ती-changing; variable.

परिवर्धन-enlargement; growth; development.

परिवर्धनीय-developable.

परिवर्धित-enlarged; developed.

परिवहन-means or system of carrying passengers or goods, transport; act of transporting; transportation; conveyance.

परिवहनीय-transportable.

परिवाद-complaint.

परिवादी-complainant.

परिवार-family; a group of things related by common characteristics; group.

परिवार-नियोजन-family planning; birth control.

परिवारवाला-(one) having a family

परिवेश-environment; surroundings.

परिवेष्टन-enclosing; encircling; wrapping.

परिव्यय-cost; outlay; expenditure.

परिव्याप्त-all-pervaded; all-pervading; overlapped .

परिव्राजक-roving ascetic.

परिशयन-hibernation.

परिशिष्ट-appendix; addenda.

परिशीलन-study from all angles; critical study.

परिशुद्ध-accurate; precise.

परिशुद्धता-accuracy; precision.

परिशुद्धि-accuracy; precision.

परिश्रम-labour; hard work; toil; exertion.

परिश्रमपूर्वक-industriously; with great pain; laboriously.

परिश्रमशील-hard-working; industrious; diligent.

परिश्रम-साध्य-toil some; laborious.

परिश्रमी-laborious; hard-working; diligent.

परिश्रांत-exhausted; tired; weary; fatigued.

परिषद, परिषद्-council; board.

परिष्कार-refinement; purification.

परिष्कृत-refined; purified.

परिष्कृति-refinement; purification.

परिसंपत्ति-assets.

परिसंपदा-assets.

परिसंवाद-symposium.

परिसज्जा-finishing; touches; finish.

परिसमापन-liquidation.

परिसमाप्त-liquidated.

परिसमाप्ति-liquidation.

परिसीमन-delimitation; demarcation.

परिसीमा-precincts; boundary; line of demarcation.

परिसीमित-limited; demarcated.

परिस्तान-fairyland.

परिस्थिति-circumstances; situation.

परिस्थिति-गत-circumstantial.

परिहार-avoidance; evasion; atonement; expiation.

परिहार्य-avoidable.

परिहास-a remark with a good humour or for amusement.

परी-nymph; fairy; elf; dream girl.

परीक्षक-examiner.

परीक्षण-testing; examining.

परीक्षा-examination; test.

परिक्षार्थी-examinee.

परीक्षित-examined; tested; tried.

परीक्ष्य-(that) which is to be examined or is under test.

परीलोक-fairy land.

परुष-hard; harsh; rigid.

परुषता-hardness; harshness.

परुषत्व-hardness; harshness.

परे away.

परे, से beyond.

परेई-dove.

परेड-parade.

परेता-big reel.

परेशान-distressed; vexed; confused; harassed; worried.

परेशानी-worry; harassment; discomfort.

परोक्ष-indirect; invisible; imperceptible.

परोपकार-act of benevolence/munificence.

परोपकारिता-benevolence; munificence.

परोपकारी-benevolent; munificent.

पर्यायवाचक-synonymous.

पर्यालोचन-critical observation.

पर्यावरण-environment.

पर्व-festival; chapter.

पर्वत-mountain.

पर्वतपृष्ठ-ridge.

पर्वतमाला-mountain chain/range.

पर्वतवासी-hillman; highlander.

पर्वत विज्ञान-Oreography.

पर्वतारोहण-mountaineering.

पर्वतारोही-mountaineer.

पर्वतीय-mountainous; hilly.

पलंग-bed; bedstead; couch.

पलंग-तोड़-lazy; indolent (person).

पलंगपोश-bedsheet.

पलंगिया-small bed

पल-moment; instant.

पलक-eyelid.

पलटन-platoon; battalion.

पलटना-to turn about or over.

पलटा-turn; return; relapse; an Indian type of cake.

पलड़ा-scale pan.

पलथी-squatting.

पलना-swing.

पलस्तर-plaster.

पलायक-absconder; fleet; runaway; escaper.

पलायन-act of absconding/fleeing.

पलायनवाद-escapism.

पलायित-ran away; escaped.

पलाश-name of a tree.

पलास-pliers.

पली-ladle for measuring liquids.

पलीता-fuse; igniter; wick.

पलीद-unclean; dirty; polluted.

पलेट-pleat.

पलेथन-dry flour used to help (to) roll kneaded flour into a cake.

पल्लव-sprout; shoot.

पल्लवग्राही-lacking profundity.

पल्लवित-full of new sprouts/green foliage; flourishing; thriving.

पल्ला-veil; purdah; the skirt of a garment; plank; shutter of a door.

पल्लू-end of a woman's wear, used as a head-cover.

पल्लेदार-labourer; porter; grain porter.

पल्लेदारी-calling of a porter; porterage.

पवन-wind; air; breeze.

पवन-चक्की-windmill.

पवन-पुत्र-lord hanuman.

पवन-भट्ठी-wind furnace.

पवर्ग-the five labial consonants of the alphabet.

पवाड़ा-bother; trouble; fuss.

पवित्र-holy; sacred; pious; pure.

पवित्रता-holiness; sanctity; purity.

पवित्रात्मा-pious/holy (person); devout; godly.

पवित्रीकरण-act of making sacred or holy; consecration.

पवित्रीकृत-consecrated.

पशम-soft fine wool.

पशमीना-cloth made of soft fine wool.

पशु-animal; beast; cattle; cruel person; brute.

पशुचर-pasture.

पशु-चिकित्सक-veterinary doctor.

पशु-चिकित्सा-veterinary science.

पशु-चिकित्सालय-veterinary hospital.

पशुचोर-cattle-lifter; cattle-thief.

पशु-जगत-animal world.

पशुता-beastliness; brutality; savagery; cruelty.

पशुधन-livestock; cattle wealth.

पशुपति-Lord of animals; God; Lord .

पशुपालन-animal husbandry; cattle breeding.

पशुबल-brute force; physical strength.

पश्च-back; later; western.

पश्चगमन-retrogression.

पश्चगामी-going backwards.

पश्चप्रभाव-after-effect.

पश्चप्रहार-backhand stroke; backstroke.

पश्चलेख-postscript.

पश्चात, के after; afterwards; following in time.

पश्चात्ताप-repentance; remorse; contrition.

पश्चार्ध-latter half; remaining/residual part.

पश्चिम-west.

पश्चिमी-westerns.

पश्चिमोत्तर-northwest (ern.)

पश्तो-Pastho, the language of Afghanistan.

पश्यतोहर-goldsmith.

पसंद-liking; choice.

पस-pus.

पसरना-to squat or lie stretched; to stretch full length.

पसली-rib.

पसार-expansion; act or state of ; expanse; verandah; yard.

पसारना-to stretch out; to spread.

पसिंजर-passenger; passenger train.

पसीजना-to melt; to be compassionate; to ooze.

पसीना-perspiration; sweat.

पसेरी-five-seer weight, approx. 4½ kg.

पसोपेश-hitch; fix.

पस्त-completely fatigued and exhausted.

पहचनवाना-to cause to be recognized.

पहचान-identification; identity; acquaintance.

पहचानना-to recognise; to know.

पहनना-to dress oneself; to put on (clothing); to wear; to don; to have it on one's body.

पहनवाना-to cause/help to wear.

पहनाना-to clothe; to cause to dress.

पहनावा-dress; costume; vestment; robe.

पहर-one-eighth part of a day; a three-hour period.

पहरा-guard; patrol.

पहरेदार-watchman; guard.

पहरेदारी-watchman-ship.

पहल-faced; initiative.

पहल-कदमी-initiative.

पहलवान-wrestler; grappler; a stout person; athlete.

पहलवानी-wrestling; vocation of wrestling.

पहला-first; former.

पहलू-facet; aspect; side; flank.

पहले-first of all; before.

पहले, के-ahead of (someone or something).

पहलेवाला-the former; previous (one).

पहले, से before; already.

पहलौटा-first-born.

पहलौटी-first delivery.

पहाड़-hill; mountain; a herculean task; a heap of anything.

पहाड़ा-multiplication table.

पहाड़ी-hilly; mountainous; pertaining to the hills.

पहिया-wheel.

पहुँच-access; reach; arrival.

पहुँचना-to reach/arrive; to approach.

पहुँचा-wrist.

पहुँचाना-to carry/convey; to see out; to conduct; to see off.

पहुँची-an ornament worn on the wrist.

पहेली-riddle; puzzle; conundrum; enigma.

पाँच-five.

पांचजन्य-a conch of Lord.

पाँचवाँ-fifth.

पाँचा-a gadget used for collecting grains etc., in the grainyard.

पांचाल-old name of a region situated in the north-west of India.

पांडित्य-scholarship; erudition; learning; wisdom.

पांडित्यपूर्ण-scholarly.

पांडित्य-प्रदर्शन-display of useless knowledge; pedantry.

पांडु-dim yellow colour.

पांडुर-jaundice.

पांडुलिपि-manuscript.

पांडुलेख-(preliminary) draft.

पाँत-line; range.

पाँयचा-a leg of a pair of trousers; foot-rest.

पाँव-foot.

पाँवड़ा-foot-rug.

पाँवड़ी-sandal; footwear; ladder; threshold.

पाँसा-a dice.

पाइट-scaffolding.

पाइप-pipe.

पाक्षिक-appearing or happening after two weeks; biweekly; fortnightly.

पाखंड-sanctimoniousness; hypocrisy.

पाखंडपूर्ण-hypocritical; full of hypocrisy; sanctimonious.

पाखंडी-sanctimonious; hypocritical.

पाख़ाना-latrine; lavatory; excreta.

पाग-sweet or medicine prepared in some syrup.

पागना-to boil in syrup.

पागल-mad; lunatic; crazy.

पागलख़ाना-an insane asylum; lunatic asylum; mental hospital.

पागलपन-madness; insanity; lunacy; mania; craziness.

पागुर-chewing of the cud by the animal.

पाचक-digestive.

पाचन-digestion.

पाचनीय-digestible.

पाछ-incision.

पाछना-to incise.

पाजामा-Indian trousers; pyjama.

पाजी-wicked; mean; vile; crooked.

पाजीपन-wickedness; rascality; crookedness; meanness.

पाज़ेब-an ornament worn on the ankles; anklet.

पाट-jute; span (of a river); plank.

पाटन-roof.

पाटना-to roof; to cover up (a pit etc.; with earth, debris, dirt and filth etc.); to heap.

पाटल-rose.

पाटा-wooden plank.

पाटी-the longer beam of a bed; slate.

पाटीगणित-Arithmetic.

पाठ-lesson; reading; recitation; text; version.

पाठकीय-of readers.

पाठचर्या-course.

पाठदोष-textual error.

पाठभेद-difference in version.

पाठमान-syllabus.

पाठशाला-school.

पाठशालीय-of or pertaining to a school etc.

पाठांतर-different version.

पाठा-sound; healthy; stout.

पाठ्य-clear enough to be read; readable; legible; fit to be read; worth reading.

पाठ्यक्रम-curriculum.

पाड़-border of a length of cloth; scaffolding; framework placed on the mouth of a well.

पाड़ा-a group of dwelling houses; locality; enclave; boundary of a field; male young of a buffalo.

पाड़ी-female young of a buffalo.

पाढ़ा-hogdeer.

पाणि-hand.

पाणिनि-famous Sanskrit grammarian of India.

पात-fall; shedding; collapse; node (Maths); leaf.

पातक-sin; guilt; misdeed.

पातकी-sinful.

पातगोभी-cabbage.

पातर-lean and thin.

पाताल-nether world; hell.

पाताल लोक-nether world.

पाताली-belonging to underground.

पातिव्रत्य-faithful devotion (to husband).

पाती-leaf; dried leaf; letter.

पात्र-worthy; deserving; eligible (person).

पात्रता-the state of being eligibility; propriety.

पात्र-सूची-list of characters in a drama; cast.

पात्री-female of *patr.*

पाथना-to daub/beat into shape/ construct.

पाथेय-provision for a journey.

पाद-foot; leg; line or fourth part of a stanza; quadrant; fourth part of a figure; wind from bowels.

पाद-टिप्पणी-footnote.

पादना-to break/pass wind.

पादप-tree.

पादपूरण-act of filling in a required/ missing line of a poem.

पाद-प्रक्षालन-washing of the feet.

पाद-प्रहार-kick.

पादरी-clergyman; missionary.

पादशाह-king; emperor.

पादशाही-pertaining to a king.

पादाक्रांत-crushed with feet.

पादाघात-kick.

पादुका-footwear; sandal.

पादोदक-water with which feet are washed; water with which the feet deity or revered person have been washed (considered sacred).

पाधा-Hindu priest.

पान-drinking; betel leaf.

पानगोष्ठी-cocktail party.

पानदान-a box for keeping betel leaves; tobacco etc.

पाना-to get; to obtain; acquire; achieve; to find.

पानी-water; lustre; juice.

पानीदार-lustrous; sensitive to honour, word etc.; honourable.

पानीदेवा-one who offers oblations to dead ancestors; son.

पानेवाला-recipient; payee.

पाप-sin; evil.

पापकर्म-sinful deed.

पापड़-a thin crisp and saltish bread.

पापपूर्ण-sinful.

पापलेन-poplin.

पापविहीन-sinless.

पापाचार-sinful conduct/way of living.

पापी-sinful; immoral.

पाबंद-bound.

पाबंदी-restriction; binding.

पामर-mean; wicked; sinful; crooked.

पामा-eczema.

पामाल-downtrodden; devastated.

पामाली-devastation.

पायँता-part of a bedstead towards the feet.

पायजामा-trousers.

पायताबा-inner sole.

पायदान-foot-rest; foot-board.

पायदार-durable; lasting.

पायदारी-durability.

पायल-an ornament worn on the ankles; anklet.

पायस-a sweet milky dish.

पाया-leg or a chair, cot etc.; pillar; foundation; prop; support.

पायी-(one) who drinks.

पारंगत-well-versed; learned; adept.

पारंपरिक-based on tradition; traditional.

पारंपरीण-traditional.

पार-opposite bank or shore.

पारखी-. connoisseur; expert.

पारचा-big; fragment; cloth; dress.

पारण-passing.

पारण-पत्र-passport.

पारतंत्र्य-dependence; freedom.

पारद-mercury; quicksilver.

पारदर्शक-transparent; evident; obvious; frank.

पारदर्शकता-transparency.

पारदर्शी-transparent.

पारना-to dump.

पारपत्र-passport.

पारभासक-translucent.

पारभासकता-translucence.

पारमाण्विक-atomic.

पारमार्थिक-pertaining to spiritual object.

पारलौकिक-pertaining to the other world; other worldly.

पारस-philosopher's stone.

पारसल-parcel.

पारसा-pious; holy; sacred.

पारसाई-piety; holiness.

पार साल-last year.

पारसी-inhabitant of Persia or Iran; Persian.

पारस्परिक-mutual; reciprocal.

पारस्परिकता-mutuality; reciprocity; familiarity.

पारा-quicksilver; mercury.

पारायण-finale; complete reading of a (religious) book.

पारावार-limit; complete reading of a (religious) book; ocean.

पारिजात-coral tree; one of the tree of paradise.

पारिणामिक-resultant; resulting; consequential.

पारित-passed.

पारितोषिक-prize; reward; gift.

पारिभाषिक-technical.

पारिभाषिकी-terminology.

पारिवारिक-familial.

पारिवारिकता-family feeling.

पारिश्रमिक- remuneration; emolument.

पारिस्थितिक-circumstantial.

पारिस्थितिकी-ecology.

पारी-turn; shift; a player's or team's turn at batting, innings.

पारेषक-transmitter.

पारेषण-transmission.

पार्क-park.

पार्ट-role.

पार्टी-a political organisation; a social event to celebrate an occasion; a person or group forming one side of a dispute or agreement.

पार्थक्य-separation; segregation; secession; distinction.

पार्थिव-earthly; terrestrial.

पार्श्व-side; flank; siding; vicinity; neighbourhood; aspect; facet.

पार्श्वगत-gone aside.

पार्श्वगायन-background singing; playback singing.

पार्श्व-टिप्पणी-marginal note.

पार्श्ववर्ती-lying alongside; adjacent.

पार्श्व-शीर्षक-marginal heading.

पार्श्व-संगीत-back-ground music; playback music.

पार्सल-parcel.

पाल denoting (one) who maintains, governs etc.

पालक-(one) who maintains and preserves.

पालकी-palanquin; sedan chair.

पालट-adopted son.

पालतू-domestic/tame/pet (animal).

पालथी-a squat.

पालन-maintaining; maintenance; observance; discharge; performance.

पालनकर्ता-god; maintainer.

पालना-to maintain/bring up.

पालना-पोसना-to bring up/nurture/foster.

पाला-frost; dealing.

पालागन-reverential greeting; asking for benediction of some venerable person by touching his feet.

पाला-पोसा-brought up; nurtured; fostered.

पालिका-maintainer (female).

पालित-maintained; brought up; nurtured; fostered; protected.

पालिश-polish.

पालिसी-policy; insurance policy.

पाली-turn; shift; innings; an Aryan language in which most of the Buddhist scriptures are written.

पाव-quarter of a seer; a little less than one-fourth of a kg.

पावक-fire.

पावती-receipt; acknowledgement.

पावती सहित-with acknowledgement due.

पावदान-footboard; footduster.

पावन-holy; sacred.

पावनता-dues.

पावनेदार-creditor.

पावर-power; energy.

पावरोटी-loaf of bread.

पावस-monsoon.

पावा-leg of a chair, cot etc.

पाश-cord; chain; noose etc.; for tying net; snare; trap.

पाशव-brutal.

पाशविक-of or pertaining to animals; beastly; brutal.

पाषाण-stone.

पाषाण काल-stone age.

पाषाण-प्रतिमा-statue in stone.

पाषाण-हृदय- stone-hearted; hardhearted; cruel.

पासंग-difference between the weights of the two pans of a balance; weight attached to counter-balance the above difference.

पास near.

पास, के in possession; close to.

पासबान-watchman; guard.

पासबानी-guarding; keeping a watch.

पासा-dice; die.

पाहन-stone.

पाहुना-guest.

पाहुनी-female guest; reception.

पाहू-guest.

पिंगल-prosody.

पिंगल शास्त्र-science of Prosody.

पिंजर-skeleton.

पिंजरा-cage; trap.

पिंजरापोल-cow-pan.

पिंड-body; lump; orb; globe.

पिंडज-born from the body; viviparous.

पिंडदान-offering/oblation of cooked rice balls to the manes.

पिंडली-calf (of the leg).

पिंडाकार-round.

पिंडिका-small body.

पिंडी-small round lump; round skein of thread.

पिचकारी-an Indian type of syringe.

पिचपिचा-adhesive; sticky; flabby watery.

पिछड़ना-to lag behind.

पिछड़ा-backward; underdeveloped.

पिछड़ापन-backwardness.

पिछलगा-

पिछलग्गु-minion; henchman; follower; hanger-on.

पिछला-back; rear; last; old; previous.

पिछवाड़ा-rear; hind part; backyard.

पिछाड़ी-rear.

पिटंत-a beating.

पिटक-basket; small box.

पिटना-to be beaten thrashed.

पिटपिटाना-to complain in a bad-tempered way; to grumble.

पिटवाना-to cause to be beaten.

पिटाई-thorough beating/thrashing; charges paid for the above.

पिटारा-a wicker-box provided with cover; pannier; chest.

पिटारी-small pannier/basket.

पिट्ठु-blind follower; lackey; henchman; minion; puppet.

पिट्ठूपन-lackeying.

पिड़कना-to express umbrage/resentment.

पिड़की-small/tiny boil.

पितर-manes; past ancestors.

पितरायँध-acridness due to contact with brass.

पितलाना-to become acrid due to contact with brass.

पिता-father; progenitor.

पितामह-paternal grandfather.

पितामही-paternal grandmother.

पितृ-paternal ancestor; father.

पितृऋण-debt owed to the ancestors.

पितृगृह-paternal home.

पितृतंत्र-patriarchal system.

पितृतुल्य-like a father.

पितृत्व-fatherhood; paternity.

पितृदेश-fatherland.

पितृपक्ष-dark fortnight of the lunar month of during which period oblations are offered to the forefathers.

पितृभक्त-devoted to the father.

पितृलोक-world of manes.

पितृहत्या-patricide; parricide.

पित्त-bile; gall.

पित्तज-caused by bile.

पित्ता-gall bladder.

पित्ताश्य-gall bladder.

पित्ती-prickly heat.

पित्तेमार-dull and full of drudgery; dull and toilsome.

पित्तोन्माद-hypochondria.

पित्र्य-pertaining or relating to the father.

पिद्दी-a tiny bird of the sparrow family.

पिन-pin.

पिनक-lethargy due to intoxication.

पिनकना-to have the jitters; to be in a drowsy condition due to a dose of opium.

पिनकी-jittery; opium addict.

पिनपिनहाँ-(child) always weeping; emaciated and sickly.

पिनपिनाना-to go on lamenting like a sickly child.

पिनाक-bow of Lord

पिनाकी-Lord .

पिन्नी-a kind of sweetmeat.

पिपरमेंट-peppermint.

पिपासा-thirst; craving; yearning.

पिपासु-thirsty; having a craving/ yearning.

पिय-lover; husband.

पियक्कड़-drunkard; boozy.

पिया-lover; husband.

पिराना-to ache; to be painful.

पिरोना-to thread.

पिलना-to be crushed in a crusher etc.

पिलपिला-lump; not stiff (specially fruit etc.); flaccid; soft; flabby.

पिलपिलाहट-flaccidity.

पिलवाना-to cause to drink.

पिलाई-act or state of or charges paid for the same.

पिलाना-to cause to drink; to let (animal) drink; to suckle; to pour (liquid) in a hole.

पिल्ला-a young dog; puppy.

पिल्लू-a worm.

पिशाच-devil; demon; evil spirit; fiend; satan; spectre.

पिशाच-पूजा-devil worship.

पिशाच-विद्या-necromancy.

पिशुन-backbiter; slanderer.

पिशुनता-backbiting; slandering.

पिष्ट-ground; powdered.

पिष्टपेषण-grinding what is already ground; doing a thing/repeating over again; repetitiousness.

पिसनहारा-one whose calling is grinding.

पिसना-to be ground/powdered; to be overworked.

पिसवाना-to cause to grind.

पिसाई-grinding; charges paid for grinding.

पिसान-flour.

पिस्तई-of the colour of pistachio; light green.

पिस्ता-pistachio nut.

पिस्तौल-pistol; revolver.

पिस्सू-flea.

पिहकना-singing of birds like the peacock or the nightingale.

पींजना-to card (cotton).

पी-melodious note of a cuckoo.

पीक-spittle.

पीकदान-spittoon.

पीच-starch usually of rice.

पीछा-back side; chase; following.

पीछे behind; at the back; in the absence of.

पीछे, के after; behind.

पीटना-to beat/thrash.

पीठ-back.-bench; chair.

पीठ-पीछे behind one's back.

पीठिका-background.

पीठी-ground (wetted) pulse/lentils.

पीड़क-causing or inflicting pain.

पीड़न-tormenting; oppressing.

पीड़ा-pain; ache; distress.

पीड़ानाशक-analgesic; pain relieving.

पीड़ाशामक-pain-relieving.

पीड़ाहारी-pain-killing; analgesic.

पीड़ित-afflicted; distressed; one who is harmed or injured; victim.

पीढ़ा-low stool; pedestal.

पीढ़ी-generation; small stool.

पीत-yellow; pallid (due to illness).

पीतता-yellowness.

पीतत्व-yellowness.

पीतल-brazen; of the colour of brass; yellow.-brass.

पीतांबरधारी-wearing yellowrobe.

पीताश्म-topaz.

पीन-corpulent; stout.

पीनक-stupefaction; drowsiness which is caused by intoxication of opium.

पीनता-bulkiness; fatness.

पीनस-a kind of cold; palanquin.

पीना-to drink; to suck; to smoke.

पीना-पिलाना-to indulge in drinking in company.

पीप-pus.

पीपल-an Indian plant; its fruit is used as a medicine.

पीपा-cask; barrel; drum; pontoon.

पीब-pus.

पीयूष-nectar; ambrosia.

पीर-aged; old.-Muslim saint.-pain.

पीरी-old age.

पीला-yellow; pale.

पीलापन-yellowness; paleness.

पीलिया-jaundice.

पीली चिट्ठी-auspicious letter.

पीली मिट्टी-yellow clay.

पीलू-a classical melody in Indian music.

पीसना-to grind; to pound.

पीहर-parental residence (of a married woman); maternal kinfolk.

पुंकेसर-stamen.

पुंगव-best; great.

पुंगीफल-betel-nut.

पुंज-group; heap or collection.

पुंजातीय-male.

पुंजित-accumulated; collected.

पुंजीभूत-accumulated; collected.

पुंडरीक-lotus (white).

पुंलिंग-denoting or representing masculine gender; masculine.

पुंश्चली-unchaste woman; woman of loose morals; adulteress.

पुंसत्व-manliness; virility.

पुआ-variety of Indian sweet; flour-cake.

पुआल-dried steams of rice plants; straw.

पुकार-call

पुकारना-to call (by name); to call out.

पुखराज-a yellow sapphire; topaz.

पुख़्ता-firm; strong; made of baked bricks (house).

पुगना-to be completed/finished.

पुगाना-to complete; to lead/take a draughtsman to the goal.

पुचकार-coddling; fondling.

पुचकारना-to coddle/fondle/caress.

पुचकारी-coddling

पुचारना-to cleanse/wipe with a wet cloth.

पुचारा-(-form of cloth used for cleansing/wiping out.

पुच्छ-tail; rear.

पुच्छल-having a tail; tailed.

पुच्छलतारा-comet.

पुछना-to be cleaned/dried.

पुछल्ला-long tail; tail piece; an unconvincing person like a tail (coming in the end); lackey; sycophant.

पुछवैया-one who asks or takes care; maintainer; caretaker.

पुजना-to be worshipped/adored/extolled.

पुजवाना-to get (oneself) worshipped/respected.

पुजाई-act of worship; remuneration paid for the same.

पुजाना-to cause to worship.

पुजापा-paraphernalia/articles used in worship.

पुजारी-(Hindu) priest; worshipper; adorer.

पुजैया-priest.

पुट-dash; seasoning.

पुटाश-potash.

पुटी-capsule; vesicle; small packet.

पुटीन-a paste for filling holes in wood; putty.

पुट्ठा-hip; buttock.

पुड़ा-large

पुड़िया-small paper packet.

पुण्य-spiritual reward of any good act; virtue; merit.

पुण्यकर्म-holy or sacred act.

पुण्यकाल-auspicious time.

पुण्यक्षेत्र-holy place.

पुण्यतिथि-death anniversary.

पुण्यफल-fruit of righteous act.

पुण्यस्मृति-reverential remembrance of some holy or great soul.

पुण्यात्मा-virtuous pious/righteous (soul).

पुण्यार्थ-charitable.

पुतला-effigy; scarecrow.

पुतली-puppet; doll; pupil (of the eye).

पुतली-घर-ṭextile factory.

पुताई-act of whitewashing cowdung plastering etc.; wages paid for the same.

पुत्र-son; male child.

पुत्रत्व-condition; worthiness etc. of being a son.

पुत्र-पौत्र-sons and grandsons.

पुत्रप्रसू-(woman) who begets a son.

पुत्रलाभ-begetting a son.

पुत्रवत, पुत्रवत् like a son.

पुत्रवती-(woman) blessed with a son.

पुत्रवधू-son's wife; daughter-in-law.

पुत्री-daughter.

पुत्रीय-pertaining or relating to a son.

पुत्रेष्टि-यज्ञ-performed in ancient India for begetting a son.

पुदीना-mint (plant and its leaves).

पुनः again.

पुनना-to filter; to abuse.

पुनरपि again and again; time and again; time and again; even then.

पुनरवलोकन-revision.

पुनरागत-come again; returned; recurred; repeated.

पुनरागमन-coming again; reincarnation.

पुनराधन-reconciliation.

पुनरावर्ती-recurring; relapsing.

पुनरावलोकन-revision; having a second look.

पुनरागमन-coming again; reincarnation.

पुनराधन-reconciliation.

पुनरारंभ-resumption.

पुनरावृति-repetition; recurrence; revision.

पुनरीक्षण-review; revision.

पुनरीक्षित-reviewed; revised.

पुनरुक्त-repeated; retold; reiterated.

पुनरुक्ति-repetition; reiteration; something that is repeated.

पुनरुत्तर-rejoinder; counter reply.

पुनरुत्थान-resurrection; renaissance.

पुनरुत्थापक-resuscitator.

पुनरुत्पादन- reproduction; regeneration.

पुनरुद्धार-renovation; restoration; resurrection.

पुनर्गठन- reorganisation; reconstitution.

पुनर्ग्रहण-retaking; resumption.

पुनर्जनन-reproduction.

पुनर्जन्म-rebirth; metempsychosis; reincarnation.

पुनर्जन्मवाद-doctrine or reincarnation.

पुनर्जीवन-rejuvenation; resurrection.

पुनर्निर्माण-rebuilding; reconstruction; reproduction; recreation; reshuffling.

पुनर्निर्मित-rebuilt; reconstructed; reproduced; recreated.

पुनर्निर्वाचन-re-election.

पुनप्ररीक्षण-re-examination; retrial.

पुनप्रवेश-act of re-entering; re-entry.

पुनप्राप्त-regained.

पुनर्मिलन-act of reuniting; reunion.

पुनर्मूल्यांकन-reassessment.

पुनर्वास-rehabilitation; resettlement.

पुनर्विचार-reconsideration; revision; review.

पुनर्विभाजन-redistribution.

पुनर्विवाह-second marriage.

पुनर्शिक्षण-re-education.

पुनर्सज्जा-redecoration.

पुनर्स्थापन-restoration; re-establishing; reinstallation.

पुनर्स्थापित-re-established; restored.

पुनश्चर्या-refresher course.

पुनि again.

पुनीत-holy; sacred; pious; pure.

पुनीतता-holiness; sacredness; piety; cleanliness.

पुरंदर-Lord , king of gods.

पुर-town; city.

पुरखा-ancestor; forefather.

पुरजन-inhabitants of a town.

पुरज़ा-chit; slip; part of a machine.

पुरज़ी-smallish chit/slip.

पुरना-to be completed/filled; to be spun.

पुरनारी-prostitute.

पुरनिया-an aged man.

पुरबिया-belonging to the east.

पुरवट-leather bucket (used in drawing water in well irrigation).

पुरवा-small village; small earthen pot. -east wind; easterly.

पुरवाई-east wind; easterly.

पुरवासी-inhabitant of a town.

पुरसा-a measure of five cubits.

पुरस्कार-reward; prize.

पुरस्कृत-rewarded.

पुरा-small village.

पुराकाल-antiquity.

पुराकालीन-ancient; antique.

पुराण-ancient; old.

पुराण-कथा-myth.

पुरातत्त्व-Archaeology.

पुरातत्त्वज्ञ-Archaeologist.

पुरातन-ancient; very old; archaic; pertaining to antiquity.

पुरातनपंथी-conservative.

पुराना-old; old-fashioned; out of date; ancient; olden; experienced; veteran; worn out; chronic.

पुरालिपि-palaeography.

पुरालिपिज्ञ-palae-ographist.

पुरालेख-epigraph.

पुरावशेष-antiquities; remnants; ruins; relics.

पुराविद्-antiquarian.

पुरावृत-chronicle; annals.

पुरी-town; city.

पुरीष-excrement; stool; faeces.

पुरुष-man.

पुरुषत्व-manhood; virility.

पुरुषवाचक-relating to masculine gender.

पुरुषार्थ-man's objective; valour; capacity.

पुरुषार्थी-self-exerting; painstaking; industrious; energetic.

पुरुषोत्तम-Supreme Being; The Almighty.

पुरुषोत्तम मास-intercalary month.

पुरोगामी-going ahead; pioneering; progressive.

पुरोहित-Hindu priest; chaplain.

पुरोहित-तंत्र-hierarchy.

पुरोंहिताई-priesthood; priest craft.

पुर्तगाल-Portugal.

पुर्तगाली-of Portugal.

पुल-bridge.

पुलक-thrill (of joy or terror).

पुलकना-to be thrilled.

पुलकावली-row of hair standing on end due to rapture.

पुलकित-thrilled; in rapture.

पुलटिस-poultice.

पुलपुला-very soft.

पुलाव-a delicious rice preparation.

पुलिंदा-bundle.

पुलिन-bank (of a river).

पुलिया-a small bridge.

पुलिस-department of police; police force.

पुलिसमैन-constable.

पुलिस-राज-police rule; tyrannous rule.

पुली-pulley.

पुश्त-back; back part; generation.

पुश्ता-embankment; prop; buttress.

पुश्ताबंदी-embankment (act); buttressing.

पुश्तैनी-hereditary; ancestral.

पुष्कर-pond; water-pond; lotus; a famous sacred pond in and only where the holy temple of Lord is situated.

पुष्करिणी-small pond; lake.

पुष्ट-well-nourished; maintained; stout; robust; energetic; healthy and powerful; confirmed.

पुष्टई-tonic; nourishment.

पुष्टता-strength; confirmation.

पुष्टि-confirmation; ratification; nourishment.

पुष्टिकर-confirmatory; nutrient; nutritious.

पुष्टिकरण-act of confirming; confirmation.

पुष्प-flower.

पुष्पक-small flower; aeroplane.

पुष्पदंड-stem of a flower.

पुष्परज-stamen.

पुष्पवर्षा-shower of flowers.

पुष्पवाटिका-flower-garden.

पुष्पशैया-bed of flowers.

पुष्पांजलि-(offering of) handful of flowers; floral tribute.

पुष्पिका-colophon.

पुष्पित-flowered; flowering.

पुष्पोद्यान-flower-garden.

पुस्तक-book.

पुस्तक-विक्रेता-bookseller.

पुस्तकाकार-book-form. in the form of a book.

पुस्तकालय-library.

पुस्तकलयाध्यक्ष-librarian.

पुस्तकीट-bookworm.

पुस्तकीय-of or pertaining to a book; bookish.

पुस्त-डाक-book-post.

पुस्तिका-booklet; handbook; pamphlet.

पूँछ-tail.

पूँजी-capital; wealth; fund.

पूँजीपति-capitalist.

पूँजीवाद-capitalism.

पूँजीवादी-capitalistic.

पूआ-a sweet cake like a bun.

पूगना-to be complete/accomplished.

पूछ-enquiry; respect; esteem.

पूछगीछ-interrogation.

पूछताछ-enquiry; interrogation.

पूछना-to ask; to enquire/interrogate; to respect.

पूजक-worshipper; votary.

पूजन-worship (ping); adoration.

पूजनविधि-form of worshipping.

पूजना-to worship/adore/revere.

पूजनीय-revered; venerable; august.

पूजा-worship; veneration.

पूजित-worshipped.

पूजोपचार-preliminaries and requisites for worship.

पूजोपहार-offering given to deity.

पूज्य-revered; venerable; honourable.

पूज्यमान, पूज्यमान्-venerable; revered; respected.

पूज्यवर-revered.

पूत-holy; sacred; septic; contaminated.

पूतिक-pious; septic; contaminating.

पूनी cotton-roll (for spinning).

पूय-pus.

पूर-pulverized fillings (for cookies); sufficiency; instalment.

पूरक-complementary; supplementary. -supplement.

पूरण-completion; filling the gaps.

पूरणीय-worth being filled up; replaceable; reparable.

पूरना-to fill to the brim.

पूरब-east.

पूरबीय-eastern.

पूरा-full; complete; entire; all; total.

पूरित-filled; completed; fulfilled.

पूरी-an Indian variety of unleavened bread fried in fat.

पूर्ण-complete; full; whole; entire.

पूर्णकाम-feeling fulfilled.

पूर्णकालिक-whole-time.

पूर्णचन्द्र-full moon.

पूर्णत:-totally; fully; entirely; completely; downright.

पूर्णतयाtotally; fully; entirely; —totally; fully; entirely;

पूर्णता-fullness; completeness; perfection.

पूर्णयोग-grand total; sum.

पूर्णविराम-fullstop.

पूर्णांक-maximum marks; whole number; integer.

पूर्णायु-complete/ripe age.

पूर्णावतार-perfect incarnation.

पूर्णाहुति-finishing touch of a or project; holocaust.

पूर्णिमा-full-moon day.

पूर्णेंदु-full-moon.

पूर्ति-supply; fulfilment; completion.

पूर्व-former. before; prior to.

पूर्वक with.

पूर्वकथित-aforesaid; above-mentioned.

पूर्वकल्पना-presupposition.

पूर्वकल्पित-presupposed.

पूर्वकालीन-of previous times.

पूर्वकृत-accomplished / committed previously.

पूर्वगत-preceding; former.

पूर्वगामी-foregoing; preceding.

पूर्वग्रह-prejudice; bias.

पूर्वज-ancestor(s); fore-father(s).

पूर्वज्ञान-pre-knowledge; fore-knowledge; foresight.

पूर्वदत्त-prepaid.

पूर्वपीठिका- background; prolegomena.

पूर्वपुरुष-forefather; ancestors; predecessors.

पूर्ववत् as before/as it was.

पूर्ववर्ती-former; previous; foregoing; preceding; pre-existing.

पूर्वसर्ग-preposition.

पूर्वागम-prosthesis.

पूर्वानुमान-forecast.

पूर्वाभास-premonition.

पूर्वाभिमुख-facing east.

पूर्वाभ्यास-rehearsal; (in game) practice.

पूर्वायोजित-pre-planned.

पूर्वार्ध-first/former half.

पूर्वाह्न-forenoon.

पूर्वी-eastern.

पूर्वोक्त-aforesaid.

पूर्वोत्तर-north east.

पूर्वोपाय-precautionary measure.

पूला-bundle of straw etc.; sheaf.

पूली-dim of

पूस-tenth month of the Hindu calendar.

पृथक्-apart; separate; distinct.

पृथक्करण-act of separating; segregation.

पृथक्ता-secession.

पृथक्तावाद-secessionism; separatism.

पृथक्तावादी-isolationist; separatist.

पृथग्वासन-apartheid.

पृथु-wide; large; great.

पृथ्वी-earth; this world.

पृष्ट-asked; enquired; irrigated.

पृष्ठ-page; back; outer surface.

पृष्ठपोषक-supporter; one who patronize.

पृष्ठभाग-background; rear part.

पृष्ठभूमि-background.

पृष्ठांकन-endorsement.

पृष्ठांकित-endorsed.

पृष्ठास्थि-backbone.

पेंग-swing; oscillation (of a swing).

पेंडुकी-dove.

पेंदा-bottom; base.

पेंशन-pension.

पेंस-pence; penny.

पेंसिल-pencil.

पेउस-first few day's milk of a milch cow after delivery.

पेखना-to look into.

पेच-screw; twist; complication.

पेचक-hand of cord.

पेचकस-screw-driver.

पेचदार-twisted; complicated; wily.

पेचवान-a kind of big ; hubble-bubble.

पेचिश-gripes; dysentery.

पेचीदगी-complication; intricacy; complexity.

पेचीदा-complicated; intricate; complex.

पेचीदापन-complication; intricacy; complexity.

पेट-belly; stomach; abdomen.

पेटा-main part of an object; middle part of an object which is to be filled up; sub-head; details of an account; detailed description.

पेटिका-small

पेटी-box; cummerbund; girdle; bag; small box; chest.

पेटीकोट-petticoat.

पेटू-greedy eater; gourmand; gluttonous; ravenous.

पेटूपन-gourmandism; voraciousness.

पेट्रोल-petrol.

पेठा-a kind of gourd; sweet made from this.

पेड़-tree.

पेड़ा-a round lump (of cheese, flour etc.); a comfit of the same.

पेडू-pelvis.

पेन-pen.

पेनी-penny; pence.

पेनीसिलिन-penicillin.

पेपर-paper; newspaper; question paper.

पेमेंट-payment.

पेय-potable; drinkable; drink; beverage.

पेरना-to crush (sugarcane, oilseeds etc.) in crushers; to press hard; to torment; to exploit; to tease; to harass.

पेराई-act or state of crushing or charges paid therefore.

पेलना-to labour hard to penetrate.

पेश-presented; forward; put forth.

पेशकार-reader; a clerk of court.

पेशकारी-calling; office or work of a

पेशगी-money paid in advance; earnest money.

पेशतर, से-before; prior to.

पेशबंद-leather belt.

पेशबंदी- pre-arrangement; anticipation.

पेशराज-mason.

पेशवा-leader; chief; title of the Prime Minister of the kings.

पेश्वाई-reception.

पेशा-profession; calling.

पेशानी-forehead.

पेशाब-urine.

पेशाबख़ाना-urinal.

पेशाब-घर-urinal.

पेशी-hearing (of a lawsuit); presentation; muscle.

पेशेवर-professional.

पेषण-pulverisation; grinding; milling.

पेस्ट-paste.

पैंजनी-tinkling ornament worn on the ankles.

पैंट-trousers.

पैंठ-market.

पैंतरा-tactics; manoeuvre; strategic move.

पैंतरेबाज-tactician; strategist.

पैंतरेबाजी-manoeuvring; strategy.

पै on; upon; yet; but; definitely.

पैकिंग-packing.

पैकेट-packet.

पैग़ंबर-prophet; divine messenger.

पैग़ंबरी-state or quality of being a prophet.

पैग़ाम-message.

पैजामा-trousers.

पैजार-shoe.

पैठ-access; reach; insight.

पैठना-to enter; to go/dive deep.

पैड-pad; writing pad.

पैड़ी-stair; step.

पैताना-lower end of a bedstead/cot.

पैतृक-hereditary; ancestral; paternal; patriarchal.

पैतृक संपत्ति-patrimony.

पैत्तिक-bilious.

पैदल-going on foot; walking; foot soldier; pawn (chess). on foot.

पैदा-born; created; to be produced/grown; earned.

पैदाइश-birth.

पैदाइशी-inborn; inherent; innate.

पैदावार-produce; yield; harvest; production.

पैना-sharp; pointed.

पैबंद-patch; botch; graft.

पैमाइश-measurement; survey.

पैमाना-scale; measure; measuring glass.

पैयाँ-foot. on foot.

पैर-foot.

पैरवी-pursuit.

पैरवीकार-pursuer; follower on; one conducting a suit on someone's behalf.

पैरा-paragraph; para.

पैरोल-parole.

पैशाच-devilish.

पैशाचिक-devilish; diabolical; satanic.

पैशाचिकता-wickedness; cruelty.

पैशाची-devilish; demoniacal.

पैशून्य-backbiting; slander.

पैसा-one-hundreath part of a rupee; money; wealth.

पैसिंजर-passenger.

पों-a kind of long horn; the sound produced by blowing it.

पोंकना-to suffer from loose stools.

पोंगा-stupid; foolish.

पोंगापंथी-idiocy; stupidity.

पोंछन-wiping; sweepings; duster.

पोंछना-to cleanse; to rub out; to wipe; to efface.-duster; wiper.

पोआ-young one of a snake.

पोखरा-pond; tank.

पोखरी-small pond; puddle.

पोगंड-a boy between five and ten.

पोच-mean; worthless; weak; timid.

पोट-bundle.

पोटली-bundle.

पोटा-capacity.

पोटाश-potash.

पोत-ship; texture; young one of a bird/beast.

पोतघाट-pier.

पोतड़ा-baby's clout; diaper.

पोतध्वंस-shipwreck.

पोतध्वंसक-torpedo.

पोतध्वज-ensign.

पोतना-to daub; to whitewash.

पोतभार-cargo.

पोता-grandson; testicle; daubing clout.

पोताई-act, state, quality, etc., of whitewashing or wages paid therefore.

पोती-grand daughter son's daughter.

पोथा-big/voluminous book; bundle of papers.

पोथी-book, specially a religious book.

पोदीना-mint.

पोप-pope.

पोपला-shrivelled.

पोर-knuckle; gnarl; part of a limb between two joints; digit of finger.

पोल-hollowness; weakness; secret.

पोला-hollow; worthless; weak.

पोशाक-uniform; dress; apparel.

पोशाकी-allowance paid in lieu of a uniform.

पोशादगी-concealment; secrecy; privacy.

पोशीदा-secret; hidden; concealed.

पोषक-nutritive.

पोषण-bringing up; rearing; nutrition; nourishment.

पोषनीय-worth being nourished/ supported/ maintainable.

पोषित-reared; supported; brought up; nourished.

पोष्य-fit to be supported/reared; (law) maintainable.

पोस-lover born of gratefulness; tameness.

पोसना-to rear/support/bring up; to tame/domesticate.

पोस्ट-post.

पोस्टर-poster.

पोस्त-poppy flower from which opium is extracted.

पोस्तीन-hide of a hairy beast; garment made of the same; paper used in binding a inner cover.

पौंचा-five and a half times; multiplication table consisting of 5½ times of integers.

पौंड-pound sterling; pound weight.

पौ-first ray of sunlight; an ace in dice.

पौढ़ना-to lie and relax.

पौत्र-grandson; son's son.

पौत्री-granddaughter.

पौद-sapling; seedling.

पौधा-plant.

पौरा-incoming.

पौराणिक-mythological.

पौरुष-of or pertaining to man.

पौरुषेय-of or pertaining to man; man-made.

पौरोहित्य-priesthood.

पौर्वात्य-of or pertaining to the east; eastern.

पौला-a kind of sandal.

पौष-tenth month of Hindu calendar.

पौष्टिक-nutritive; nutritious; restorative; alimentary.

पौष्टिकता-nutritive-ness.

पौसरा-water-booth.

पौहारी-(one) living on milk.

प्याऊ-water-booth; free water-booth (for passers-by).

प्याज़-onion; scallion.

प्याज़ी-of or pertaining to onion; of the colour of onion.

प्यादा-footman; pedestrian; foot-soldier; pawn (chess).

प्यार-love; affection.

प्यारा-dear; beloved; pleasing; lovely; beautiful; attractive.

प्याला-cup.

प्याली-small cup.

प्यास-thirst; longing; crave; desire.

प्यासा-thirsty.

प्र-indicating : 1, in front; forward; abundantly; excessively.

प्रकंप-shivering; trembling.

प्रकंपन-shivering; trembling.

प्रकंपित-shivered; trembled.

प्रकट-apparent; obvious; clear; manifest; disclosed; express.

प्रकटन-manifestation; appearance; revelation.

प्रकटीकरण-manifestation; making apparent.

प्रकरण-topic; chapter; subject.

प्रकर्ष-eminence; distinction; excellence; plenty.

प्रकल्पना-presumption; supposition.

प्रकल्पित-presumed; supposed; settled.

प्रकांड-profound; outstanding.

प्रकार-kind; type; manner; way.

प्रकार्य-special work; function.

प्रकार्यात्मक-functional.

प्रकाश-light.

प्रकाशक-bringing to light.

प्रकाशकीय-publisher's note/ statement.

प्रकाशन-bringing to light; the act of publishing; publication; a published book or magazine.

प्रकाशनीय-worth being published.

प्रकाशमान्, प्रकाशमान-luminous; shining; brilliant.

प्रकाश-स्तंभ-light house; beacon-light.

प्रकाशिकी-optics.

प्रकाशिकीय-optical.

प्रकाशित-brought to light; published.

प्रकाश्य-(that) which is to be published/brought to light.

प्रकीर्ण-miscellaneous.

प्रकीर्णक-miscellany.

प्रकृत-natural; normal; real; true.

प्रकृति-nature; temperament; habit.

प्रकृतिवाद-naturalism.

प्रकृतिवादी-naturalist.

प्रकृतिशः-in the natural state; calm and cool; composed.

प्रकृतिस्थ-in the natural state; calm and cool; composed.

प्रकृष्ट-best, A-one.

प्रकोप-wrath; fury.

प्रकोष्ठ-lobby; chamber.

प्रक्रम-order; process.

प्रक्रिया-procedure; mode; process.

प्रक्षालन-washing; cleansing; bleaching.

प्रक्षालित-washed; cleansed; bleached.

प्रक्षिप्त-hurled; thrown; projected .

प्रक्षेप-hurling; throwing.

प्रक्षेपक-projector.

प्रक्षेपास्त्र-ballistic missile.

प्रखंड-part; division; section; part; block.

प्रखर-fierce; terrific; acute; acrid; keen; sharp.

प्रखरता-fierceness; keenness; sharpness; acuteness.

प्रख्यात-eminent; famous; reputed; renowned; well-known.

प्रख्यापन-promulgation; declaration.

प्रख्यापित-promulgated; declared.

प्रगट-appear.

प्रगति-progress; advancement; development.

प्रगतिरोधी- anti-progressive; reactionary.

प्रगतिवादी-prog-ressivistic.

प्रगतिशील-progressive.

प्रगतिशीलता-progressivism; progress.

प्रगल्भ-unabashed; unhesitant; outspoken; impertinent; courageous.

प्रगल्भता-the state of being

प्रगाढ़-very thick and deep (colour); dense; firm; tight.

प्रगाढ़ता-the state or quality of being

प्रगीत-lyric; song.

प्रचंड-terrific; violent; terrible; fierce; furious.

प्रचंडता-the state of being

प्रचल-circulating; floating.

प्रचलन-prevalence; currency; vogue.

प्रचलित-current; prevalent; in use; in force; in vogue.

प्रचार-propaganda.

प्रचारक-propagandist; propagator; publisher; publicist.

प्रचारित-propagated; publicized; made known.

प्रचालक-starter; operator.

प्रचालन-operation.

प्रचुर-plentiful; abundant.

प्रचुरता-plenty; abundance.

प्रच्छन्न-hidden; latent; obscure; concealed.

प्रच्छन्नता-latency; obscurity; concealment.

प्रच्छाया-umbra.

प्रजनन-procreation; reproduction.

प्रजा-citizen; the people who are ruled by a monarch; dictator; government etc. subjects.

प्रजातंत्र-democracy.

प्रजातांत्रिक-democratic.

प्रजापति-maintainer of subjects; king.

प्रजापालक-nurture/sustainer of the subjects, king.

प्रजापालन-nurturing/sustaining the subjects.

प्रज्ञ-wise; learned; intelligent.

प्रज्ञता-wisdom; intelligence; learning.

प्रज्ञा-intellect.

प्रज्ञाचक्षु-physically blind; but gifted with the inner eye of wisdom.

प्रज्ञान-cognizance; full consciousness; know-how; practical knowledge.

प्रज्ञावाद-intellectualism.

प्रज्ञेय-cognizable.

प्रज्वलन-ignition; setting on fire; burning; blazing.

प्रज्वलित-ignited; set on fire; burnt; blazed.

प्रण-resolution; determination; vow; promise; pledge.

प्रणत-bent; bowed (down).

प्रणति-bow; salutation; obeisance; adoration.

प्रणम्य-worthy of obeisance; deserving respect.

प्रणय-love (between lovers); affection.

प्रणयन-creation; composition (of a literary work); writing.

प्रणयिनी-beloved.

प्रणयी-lover; master; lord.

प्रणव-Om, the Almighty.

प्रणाम-respectful greeting/salutation; bow.

प्रणामी-one who greets reverentially.

प्रणाली-channel; mode; way; system; custom; manner.

प्रणिधान-religious meditation/ concentration.

प्रणीत-composed (said of a literary work); written; prepared.

प्रणेता-creator; author; composer; writer.

प्रतनु-lean and thin.

प्रताड़ना-admonition; chiding.

प्रताप-glory; benedictory; influence; dignity; splendour.

प्रतापी-august; glorious; illustrious; having benedictory influence.

प्रति-copy. every; per; in opposition to something as against something; in reverse; in opposite direction.

प्रति, के in the direction of, towards.

प्रतिकार-retaliation; revenge.

प्रतिकारी-one who retaliates/takes revenge.

प्रतिकूल-opposite; contrary; perverse; against; adverse; hostile.

प्रतिकूल, के-opposite (to).

प्रतिकूलता-contrariety; opposition; hostility.

प्रतिकृति-copy of the shape of something or somebody; facsimile.

प्रतिक्रम-reverse order.

प्रतिक्रमात्, प्रतिक्रमात vice versa.

प्रतिक्रांति-counter-revolution.

प्रतिक्रियक-reactionary.

प्रतिक्रिया-reaction; repercussion; retaliation.

प्रतिक्रियात्मक-reactionary; reacting.

प्रतिक्रियावाद-reactionism.

प्रतिक्षण happening every moment.

प्रतिक्षिप्त-repulsed; recoiled.

प्रतिक्षेप-repulsion; recoil; rebound.

प्रतिक्षेपण-repelling; recoiling; rebounding.

प्रतिगामी-regressive; retrogressive.

प्रतिगृहीत-accepted.

प्रतिग्रहण-acceptance.

प्रतिग्राहक-receiver.

प्रतिग्राह्य-acceptable.

प्रतिघात-counter-blow; counter-stroke; repercussion.

प्रतिघाती-one who gives a counter-blow.

प्रतिच्छाया-reflection; image; picture.

प्रतिच्छेद-intersection.

प्रतिज्ञा-solemn; promise.

प्रतिज्ञात्मक-votive promissory.

प्रतिदत्त-returned; refunded.

प्रतिदान-return; returning; repayment; redemption.

प्रतिदिन-daily; day by day; everyday.

प्रतिद्ंवद्व-contest; conflict; duel

प्रतिद्ंवद्विता-rivalry; contest; competition.

प्रतिद्ंवद्वी-rival; competitor.

प्रतिध्वनि-echo; resonance; reverberation.

प्रतिध्वनित-echoed; resounded; reverberated.

प्रतिनिधान-deputation.

प्रतिनिधि-representative; delegate; agent.

प्रतिनिधिक-representative.

प्रतिनिधित्व-representation.

प्रतिनिर्देश-croos-reference.

प्रतिपक्ष-opposite party; opposition; hostile camp; rival side.

प्रतिपक्षता-opposition; contest; rivalry; antithesis.

प्रतिपक्षी-opponent; rival; contestant.

प्रतिपक्षीय-oppo-sitional.

प्रतिपत्ति-exposition; expounding; accomplishment; execution.

प्रतिपदा-first day of a lunar fortnight.

प्रतिपन्न-expounded; accomplished; executed.

प्रतिपरीक्षण-cross-examination.

प्रतिपादक-exponent (person); expositor.

प्रतिपादन-exposition; presentation; treatment.

प्रतिपादित-expounded.

प्रतिपाद्य-to be expounded.

प्रतिपालक-main-tainer; patron.

प्रतिपालन-maintenance; execution.

प्रतिपालनीय-maintainable.

प्रतिपालित-maintained.

प्रतिपाल्य-maintainable.

प्रतिपीड़न-reprisal.

प्रतिपुरुष-substitute; effigy.

प्रतिपूरक- complementary; compensatory.

प्रतिपूर्ति-complementary; compensatory.
प्रतिप्राप्ति-recovery.
प्रतिफल-requital; reward; retribution; result.
प्रतिफलन-culmination.
प्रतिफलित-resulted.
प्रतिबंध-restriction; ban; prohibition.
प्रतिबद्ध-committed (to).
प्रतिबद्धता-commitment.
प्रतिबिंब-reflection; image; shadow.
प्रतिबिंबिता-reflected.
प्रतिबोध-awakening; sense; comprehension.
प्रतिबोधक-one who makes (one) comprehend.
प्रतिभा-genius; talent; intellect.
प्रतिभावान-talented.
प्रतिभाशाली-talented.
प्रतिभू-surety (person).
प्रतिभूति-bail; security.
प्रतिमा-idol; statue; icon; image; figure.
प्रतिमान-model; pattern; an accepted way of being; norm.
प्रतिमा-पूजक-idol-worshipper.
प्रतिमा-पूजा-idol-worship.
प्रतिमा-भंजक-iconoclast; idol-breaker.
प्रतिमा-भंजन-iconoclasm; idol-breaking.
प्रतिमूर्ति-replica; prototype.
प्रतियोगिता-competition; rivalry; contest.
प्रतियोगी-competitor; rival; opponent.
प्रतिरक्षा-defence.
प्रतिरक्षात्मक-defensive.
प्रतिरुद्ध-obstructed; resisted.
प्रतिरूप-counterpart; image; representative; specimen.
प्रतिरूपी-representative; typical.
प्रतिरोध-resistance; obstruction.
प्रतिरोधक-offering resistance; resistant; causing obstruction.
प्रतिरोधन-act of resisting; resistance.
प्रतिरोधी-resisting.
प्रतिलिपि-copy; duplicate; facsimile.
प्रतिलिपिक-copyist.
प्रतिलेखन-transcription.
प्रतिलोम-converse; reverse; inverted; inverse; opposite.
प्रतिलोमतः-conversely; inversely.
प्रतिवर्तन-reversion; rebounding.
प्रतिवर्तित-reversed; rebounded.
प्रतिवर्ष each year; once a year; yearly
प्रतिवाद-refutation; contradiction; protest.
प्रतिवादक-(one) who contradicts/refutes/protests.
प्रतिवादी-defendant; respondent.
प्रतिवेदन-report; representation.
प्रतिवेदित-reported.

प्रतिवेश- neighbourhood; environment.

प्रतिवेशी-neighbour.

प्रतिशत-in or for every hundred.

प्रतिशतता-percentage.

प्रतिशब्द-equivalent/synonymous word; echo; resonance.

प्रतिशोध-revenge; reprisal; retaliation.

प्रतिशोधन-retaliation; repayment.

प्रतिश्याय-cold; catarrh.

प्रतिश्रुत-heard; promised; pledged.

प्रतिश्रुति-promise.

प्रतिषेध-denial; rejection.

प्रतिष्ठा-prestige; dignity; respectability.

प्रतिष्ठान-establishment; installation.

प्रतिष्ठापन-establishing; establishment; installation.

प्रतिष्ठापरक-of or relating to prestige; prestigious.

प्रतिष्ठापित-established; installed.

प्रतिष्ठावान-prestigious.

प्रतिष्ठित-reputed; renowned; distinguished; respected; prestigious; established; installed.

प्रतिसाम्य-symmetry.

प्रतिस्थापन-replacement; substitution.

प्रतिस्थापित-replaced; substituted.

प्रतिस्पर्धा-rivalry; competition; contest.

प्रतिस्पर्धात्मक-competitive.

प्रतिस्पर्धी-rival; competitor; contestant.

प्रतिहत-attacked and wounded.

प्रतिहस्ताक्षर-counter-signature.

प्रतिहार-

प्रतिहारी-chamberlain; gate-keeper; watchman; porter.

प्रतिहिंसक-(one) who retaliates.

प्रतिहिंसा-counter-violence; reprisal.

प्रतीक-symbol; mark; emblem.

प्रतीक-कथा-allegory.

प्रतीकवाद-symbolism.

प्रतीकवादी-symbolic; symbolist.

प्रतीकात्मक-symbolic.

प्रतीक्षा-wait; waiting.

प्रतीक्षालय-waiting room.

प्रतीक्षित-awaited.

प्रतीक्ष्य-(one) awaited.

प्रतीची-west.

प्रतीच्य-western.

प्रतीत-clear to the eye or mind.

प्रतीति-feeling.

प्रतीप-inverse; counter.

प्रतीयमान-apparent; evident.

प्रतीयमानत:-apparently.

प्रत्यंग-minor parts (of the body).

प्रत्यंचा-bow-ring.

प्रत्यक्ष-obvious; apparent; visible; evident; perceivable; ocular; direct

प्रत्यक्षत:-on the evidence available; prima facie.

प्रत्यक्षवाद-positivism.

प्रत्यक्षीकरण-ocular demonstration; direct perception.

प्रत्यय-suffix; idea; concept; confidence; faith; testimony.

प्रत्यय-पत्र-credentials.

प्रत्यर्प्रण-extradition.

प्रत्याक्रमण-counter attack.

प्रत्यागत-come back; returned.

प्रत्याघात-counter blow; counter-attack.

प्रत्याभिदेश-cross reference.

प्रत्याभियोग-indictment; counter accusation.

प्रत्याभूति-guarantee.

प्रत्यारोप-counter-charge; counter-accusation.

प्रत्याशा-anticipation; expectation.

प्रत्याशित-anticipated; expected.

प्रत्याशी-candidate; applicant.

प्रत्याहार-control of the senses; formula (in Sanskrit grammar).

प्रत्याहूत-recalled; called back.

प्रत्याह्वान-recalling; recall; calling back.

प्रत्युत-however; but; on the contrary; on the other hand.

प्रत्युत्तर-rejoinder; repartee.

प्रत्युदाहरण-counter example.

प्रत्युपकार-requital of obligation.

प्रत्यूष-dawn; day-break.

प्रत्येक-each; every one.

प्रथम-before all others; foremost; most important.

प्रथमतः firstly; in the first place; first of all.

प्रथमता-first priority.

प्रथमा-nominative case. (Gram.)

प्रथा-custom; practice; usage; rule.

प्रथागत-customary.

प्रधान-head; prime; general.

प्रधानतया primarily; chiefly; mainly.

प्रधानता-importance; prominence; supremacy; primacy.

प्रधानाचार्य-principal.

प्रधानाध्यापक-head master.

प्रपंच-worldly affairs; mundane affairs; trickery; detailed ceremonial.

प्रपंची-deceitful; fraudulent; scheming.

प्रपठन-recitation.

प्रपत्र-form (of application etc.).

प्रपन्न-obtained; refugee.

प्रपात-waterfall; cataract.

प्रपितामह-paternal great grandfather.

प्रपुत्र-grandson; son's son.

प्रपौत्र-great-grandson; son's grandson.

प्रफुल्ल-joyful; blossomed blooming; delighted.

प्रफुल्लित-delighted; happy.

प्रबंध-management; organisation; contrivance; thesis; dissertation.

प्रबंधक-manager; organiser; executive.

प्रबंधकीय-managerial.

प्रबल-powerful; strong; mighty; forceful or influential; staunch.

प्रबुद्ध-enlightened; awakened.

प्रबोध-enlightenment; awakening.

प्रबोधक-(one) who enlightens/rouses/awakens.

प्रबोधन-enlightening; enlightenment; awakening.

प्रभंजन-act of breaking; ruin; destruction; hurricane; storm.

प्रभव-creation; production; origin; source.

प्रभविष्णु-Lord Vishnu.

प्रभा-light; effulgence; glory.

प्रभाकर-Sun.

प्रभाग-sub-division.

प्रभात-dawn; early morning.

प्रभाती-morning song.

प्रभा-मंडल-halo.

प्रभार-charge.

प्रभारी-acting; in-charge.

प्रभाव-influence; effect; impact.

प्रभावपूर्ण-influential; potential; effective.

प्रभावशाली-influential; potential; effective; impressive; fascinating.

प्रभावहीन-devoid of influence; unimpressive.

प्रभावान्वित-impressed; influenced; charmed.

प्रभावित-impressed; influenced.

प्रभावी-influential; effective; impressive; dominated.

प्रभावोत्पादक-effective.

प्रभु-god; master; sovereign.

प्रभुता-sway; sovereignty; glory; supremacy.

प्रभुत्व-sovereignty.

प्रभूत-plentiful; abundant; ample.

प्रभृति-et cetera.

प्रभेद-distinction; difference.

प्रभेदी-distinctive.

प्रमंडल-division.

प्रमंडलाधिकारी-divisional officer.

प्रमंडलीय-divisional.

प्रमत्तत्ता-state of being प्रमत्त।

प्रमा-authoritative knowledge of reality acquired through logic and reasoning; understanding; accurate notion.

प्रमाण-testimony; proof; evidence.

प्रमाणक-voucher; certificate; testimonial.

प्रमाणकर्ता-certifier.

प्रमाणन-act of certifying; certification.

प्रमाणपत्र-certificate.

प्रमाणित-proved; certified.

प्रमाणीकरण-authentication.

प्रमाणीकृत-authenticated.

प्रमाद-intoxication (specially with power, pelf and money); carelessness; negligence.

प्रमादी-vain; intoxicated due to power and money; careless; negligent.

प्रमाप-measure; weight.

प्रमुखता-eminence; importance; prominence.

प्रमुदित-delighted; full of joy; glad; pleased.

प्रमेय-theorem.

प्रमेह-diabetes.

प्रमोद-entertainment; recreation; enjoyment.

प्रयत्न-effort; attempt; endeavour.

प्रयत्नवान-endeavouring.

प्रयत्नशील-endeavouring.

प्रयाण-march; going; departure.

प्रयास-attempt; endeavour; effort.

प्रयुक्त-used; applied.

प्रयोक्ता-user; experimenter.

प्रयोग-use; application; usage; experiment.

प्रयोगवादी-empirical.

प्रयोगशाला-laboratory.

प्रयोगी-experimenter.

प्रयोजन-purpose; aim; intention; motive.

प्रयोजनार्थी-(one) on purpose.

प्रयोजनीय-applicable; usable; requisite; suitable.

प्रयोजनीयता- purposiveness; applicability; usability; workability.

प्रयोज्य-applicable; usable.

प्ररूप-type; form.

प्ररोह-ascent; growth.

प्ररोहण-ascending; growing.

प्रलंब-that which hangs vertically; vertical; long.

प्रलयंकर-(that) which causes deluge; catastrophic; calamitous; disastrous.

प्रलय-annihilation; total devastation; end of all existence; deluge; devastating flood.

प्रलयकारी-destroyer.

प्रलाप-incoherent talk (especially due to sorrow or grief); prattle.

प्रलापी-(one) whose speech in incoherent; prattling.

प्रलेख-document; deed.

प्रलेप-ointment; salve.

प्रलोभन-temptation; allurement; seduction; inducement.

प्रवंचक-deceiver; cheat.

प्रवंचन-deception; deceitfulness.

प्रवक्ता-spokesman; lecturer.

प्रवचन-discourse.

प्रवण-inclined; bent; disposed.

प्रवणता-inclination; disposition; bend; propensity.

प्रवर-superior; senior.

प्रवर्तक-promoter; founder; innovator.

प्रवर्तन-setting in motion; starting; founding; innovation; enforcement.

प्रवर्तित-initiated

प्रवर्धन-magnification; enlargement.

प्रवर्धित-magnified; enlarged.

प्रवसन-migration.

प्रवाचक-sermonizer; preacher; instructor.

प्रवात-gale.

प्रवाद-conversation; hearsay; rumour (especially of a bad name).

प्रवाल-coral.

प्रवास-emigration.

प्रवासी-migratory; emigrant.

प्रवाह-flow; fluency; setting in flow.

प्रवाहक-one who sets in flow.

प्रवाहमान-fluent; flowing.

प्रवाहित-set in flow.

प्रविधान-statute.

प्रविधानिक-statutory.

प्रविधि-technique.

प्रविधिक-technical.

प्रविधिज्ञ-technician.

प्रविष्ट-entered; admitted.

प्रविष्टि-entry; admission.

प्रवीण-proficient; skilful; expert.

प्रवीणता-proficiency; skilfulness.

प्रवीर-very brave; best.

प्रवृत्त inclined; engaged.

प्रवृत्ति-inclination; tendency; trend.

प्रवेश-admission; entry; entrance; access.

प्रवेशद्वार-doorways; portal; entrance.

प्रवेशपत्र-pass; admission ticket/card; admit card.

प्रवेश शुल्क-admission fee.

प्रवेशिका-primer; first reader; elementary book (on subject).

प्रवेशी-entrant.

प्रवेश्य-permissible.

प्रवेश्यता-admission.

प्रव्रजन-migration.

प्रव्राजक-wandering mendicant.

प्रशंसक-one who praises; eulogist; admirer.

प्रशंसनीय- praiseworthy; commendable; laudable.

प्रशंसा-praise; admiration.

प्रशंसात्मक-laudatory.

प्रशंसित-praised; admired.

प्रशमन-pacification; soothing.

प्रशमित-pacified; soothed.

प्रशस्त-board; expansive.

प्रशस्ति-pranegyric; eulogy.

प्रशांत-tranquil; clam; quiet.

प्रशांति-tranquillity; peace; quietude.

प्रशाखा-sub-branch; offshoot; twig.

प्रशासक-administrator.

प्रशासन-administration.

प्रशासनिक-administrative.

प्रशासित-administered.

प्रशिक्षक-trainer.

प्रशिक्षण-training.

प्रशिक्षणार्थी-trainee.

प्रशिक्षित-trained.

प्रश्न-question.

प्रश्नकर्ता-a questioner; interrogator.

प्रश्नचिह्न-sign/note of interrogation (?).

प्रश्नपत्र-question paper.

प्रश्नवाचक-interrogative.

प्रश्नात्मक-interrogative.

प्रश्नावली-a list of questions to be answered; questionnaire.

प्रश्नोत्तर-question and answer.

प्रश्नोत्तरी-quiz; catechism.

प्रश्रय-encouragement; backing; support.

प्रश्रयदाता-supporter.

प्रसंग-context; topic; subject; theme.

प्रसंविदा-covenant.

प्रसन्न-happy; pleased; glad.

प्रसन्नता-happiness; pleasure; gladness; delight.

प्रसम-normal.

प्रसमता-normalcy; normality.

प्रसरण-expansion; extension.

प्रसरणशील-expansible; extensible.

प्रसरित-expanded; extended.

प्रसव-delivery (of a child).

प्रसाद-gift (from a deity); favour; blessing; benediction; boon.

प्रसादन-appeasement; gratification.

प्रसादी-offering made to a deity.

प्रसाधन-beauty/make-up aids.

प्रसारण-broadcasting; transmission; dispersing; propagating; scattering.

प्रसारित-broadcast; transmitted; dispersed; propagated; scattered.

प्रसिद्ध-well-known; famous; renowned; reputed.

प्रसिद्धि-fame; renown; esteem; repute.

प्रसुप्त dormant; asleep; hibernated.

प्रसुप्तावस्था-dormancy.

प्रसुप्ति-dormancy; hibernation.

प्रसुत-delivered; born.

पसूता-a woman who has recently delivered a baby.

प्रसूति-labour (of delivery); progeny maternity.

प्रसून-flower; blossom.

प्रस्ताव-proposal; motion; offer (in contract).

प्रस्तावक-proposer; mover (of a resolution); offerer (in a contract).

प्रस्तावना-preface; preamble; foreword.

प्रस्तावित-proposed; moved; offered.

प्रस्ताविती-offeree.

प्रस्तुत-presented; submitted; ready.

प्रस्तुति-readiness; presentation; the production of a play.

प्रस्तुतीकरण-act of presenting; presentation; the way something is presented.

प्रस्तोता-one who pre-sents; reader; registrar.

प्रस्थान-departure; setting out.

प्रस्थाना-token by way of remedy to avoid the inauspiciousness of a day of departure for a journey.

प्रस्थापक-installer.

प्रस्थापन-presentation; installation; establishment.

प्रस्थापित-installed; established.

प्रस्फूट-blossomed; manifested.

प्रस्फूटन-blossoming; manifestation.

प्रस्फुटित-blossomed; manifested.

प्रस्वेद-sweat; perspiration.

प्रस्वेदन-sweating; perspiring.

प्रहर-eighth part of day; period of three hours.

प्रहरी-sentry; watchman; guard.

प्रहसन-farce; caricature; mockery; satire; skit.

प्रहार-blow; assault; attack.

प्रहेलिका-riddle; conundrum; puzzle; enigma.

प्रांगण-atrium; courtyard.

प्रांजल-straight; plain; simple crystal clear (idea or language); lucid.

प्रांजलता-straightness; plainness; simplicity; lucidity.

प्रांत-province; prefecture; territory; region.

प्रांतीय-provincial; prefectural.

प्राइमरी-primary; elementary.

प्राइवेट-private.

प्राकट्य-appearance; manifestation.

प्राकार-boundary; fencing.

प्राकाश्य-appearance; limelight.

प्राकृतिक-natural; innate.

प्राक्कथन-foreword.

प्राक्कलन-estimation.

प्राक्कल्पना-assumption; supposition.

प्राक्कल्पित-assumed; supposed.

प्रागल्भ्य-the state or quality of being impertinence

प्राची-east; orient.

प्राचीन-very old; ancient.

प्राचीनता-antiquity.

प्राचीर-rampart; boundary wall.

प्राच्य-eastern; oriental.

प्राज्ञ-erudite; clever; wise; learned.

प्राज्ञी-wise/educated woman.

प्राण-winds of the body; life.

प्राणघात-killing; murder.

प्राणघातक-fatal; lethal.

प्राणदंड-capital punishment.

प्राणदाता-saviour; life giver.

प्राणदान-sacrifice of one' life; saving someone's life.

प्राणनाथ-husband; lord; beloved one.

प्राणपण-

प्राणप्यारा-beloved; most dear.

प्राणप्रतिष्ठा-deification of an idol.

प्राणप्रिय-most loveable.

प्राणवत्ता-vitality; spiritedness.

प्राणवान-full of life/vitality; lively.

प्राणांत-death; end of life.

प्राणांतक-fatal; causing death.

प्राणाधार-sweet-heart.

प्राणायाम-breathing exercise.

प्राणि-living being.

प्राणी-living being; animal.

प्राणेश-Lord of one's life; husband; lover.

प्राणेश्वर-

प्राणोत्सर्ग-sacrifice of one's life; martyrdom.

प्रात:-morning.

प्रात:काल-early part of the day.

प्रात:स्नान-morning bath.

प्रात:स्मरणीय-of blessed/cherished memory.

प्रात-morning.

प्रातिभ-intuitive.

प्राथमिक-primary; initial; elementary; preliminary; first; prior.

प्राथमिकता-priority; precedence; preference.

प्रांदर्शनिक-demonstrative.

प्रादुर्भाव-origin; birth; manifestation; advent; appearance.

प्रादुर्भूत-born; manifested; appeared.

प्रादेश-mandate.

प्रादेशात्मक-mandatory.

प्रादेशिक-provincial; regional; territorial.

प्राधान्य-the quality or state of being; predominance; preponderance; supremacy.

प्राधिकार-authority.

प्राधिकारी-authority (person).

प्राधिकृत-authorised.

प्राध्यापक-professor; lecturer.

प्राध्यापन-the work or profession of a teacher; teaching.

प्रापक-receiver; receipt.

प्राप्त-received; secured; acquired; obtained.

प्राप्तव्य-due; realizable; procurable.

प्राप्ति-receipt; act of receiving; income; gain; realisation; acquisition.

प्राप्त्याशा-hope of acquisition.

प्राप्य-due; obtainable; attainable; procurable; available.

प्राबल्य-dominance; force; intensity.
प्रामाणिक-authentic; reliable; credible; genuine.
प्राय: often; quite often; usually; generally; mostly.
प्रायद्वीप-peninsula.
प्रायश:-very often; usually.
प्रायश्चित-atonement; expiation.
प्रायश्चित्तात्मक-expiatory.
प्रायिक-probable.
प्रायिकता-probability.
प्रायोगिक-tentative.
प्रायोजना-project.
प्रारंभ-beginning; commencement; debut.
प्रारंभिक-preliminary; elementary; initial.
प्रारब्ध-destiny; fate.
प्रारूप-draft; proforma.
प्रार्थना-prayer.
प्रार्थना-पत्र-application.
प्रार्थनीय-worth praying/applying/ soliciting for.
प्रार्थित-requested; applied for; solicited.
प्रार्थी-suppliant.
प्रालेख-draft; proforma.
प्रालेखक-draftsman.
प्राविधान-provision; stipulation.
प्राविधिक-technical.
प्राविधिकता-technically.
प्राश्निक-of or pertaining to a question. -interrogator.
प्रासंगिक-relevant; contingent; incidental.
प्रासाद-mansion; palace.
प्रिंट-printed design.
प्रिंटिंग-printing.
प्रिय-dear; lovely; comely.
प्रियजन-dear ones.
प्रियतम-dearest; most loved; husband.
प्रियतमा-dearest lady.
प्रियतर-dearer.
प्रियता-lovely one.
प्रिया-beloved; lovely; sweetheart.
प्रियाप्रिय-pleasant and unpleasant
प्रीतम-lover.
प्रीति-love; affection; fondness.
प्रीतिगोष्ठी-tea party.
प्रीतिभोज-social dinner; banquet.
प्रेक्षक-observer; spectator; onlooker.
प्रेक्षण-act of observing/viewing/ beholding.
प्रेक्षागृह-auditorium.
प्रेक्षित-(attentively) observed.
प्रेत-spirit (of the dead); ghost; poltergeist; spectre.
प्रेतनी-woman spirit.
प्रेतबाधा-poltergeists disturbance.
प्रेतलीला-poltergeists phenomena.

प्रेतविद्या-spiritism.

प्रेतसिद्धी-necromancy.

प्रेतात्मक-pertaining to a spirit.

प्रेतात्मा-spirit of the dead.

प्रेतोन्माद-mental ailment due to the influence of evil spirit.

प्रेम-love; affection.

प्रेमपत्र-love-letter.

प्रेमपात्र-beloved one; love.

प्रेमपीड़ित-loveborn.

प्रेमपूर्वक with love.

प्रेमलीला-romance.

प्रेम-विवाह-love-marriage; love-match.

प्रेमविहीन-loveless.

प्रेम-व्यापार-love-affair.

प्रेमातुर-love-sick.

प्रेमालाप-love talk.

प्रेमालिंगन-embrace of love; affectionate hug.

प्रेमाश्रु-tears of love.

प्रेमिका-beloved one.

प्रेमी-lover.

प्रेयसी-beloved one; darling; dearie.

प्रेरक-inspiring; inspirational; motivating.

प्रेरण-inspiration.

प्रेरणा-impetus; inspiration; urge; initiative.

प्रेरणादायक-inspiring; motivating.

प्रेरणार्थक-causative.

प्रेरणा-शक्ति-motive force; inspiration.

प्रेरित-inspired; motivated; instigated; prompted.

प्रेषक-sender; despatcher.

प्रेषण-sending; remittance; transmission.

प्रेषणीय-(that) which is worth sending.

प्रेषित-transmitter.

प्रेष्य-(that) which is to be sent.

प्रेस-printing press.

प्रोक्त-declared; announced; spoken; uttered.

प्रोग्राम-programme.

प्रोटीन-protein.

प्रोत्साहन-encouragement; boosting up; stimulation.

प्रोत्साहित-encouraged; inspired.

प्रोन्नत-promoted.

प्रोन्नति-promotion.

प्रोफ़ेसर-professor.

प्रौढ़-mature; matured; middle-aged.

प्रौढ़ता-maturity; adulthood.

प्रौढ़त्व-

प्रौढ़ा-adult/elderly woman.

प्लवन-floating.

प्लांट-plan (fixed machinery).

प्लावन-submersion; plunging.

प्लावित-flooded; inundated.

प्लास्टर-plaster.

प्लुत-drenched.

प्लेग-plague.

प्लेट-plate.

प्लेटफ़ार्म-platform.

प्लैटिनम-platinum.

फ

फ-The twenty-second consonant of the Devnagari alphabet and the second letter of the labial or class.

फंका-to destroy; to crush; a quantity of an edible powder or medicine which can be contained in hollow of the palm.

फंकी-a mouthful, small piece; a small packet.

फंदा-snare; noose; trap.

फँसना-to be entrapped/ensnared; to get stuck up.

फँसाव-entrapment.

फक-suddenly.

फ़क-white; pale.

फ़कीरी-mendicancy; poverty.

फक्कड़-a rough fellow; a base person; ribald.

फ़ख्र-pride.

फगुआ-Holi festival.

फगुआना-to throw coloured water on a person at the time of the Holi festival.

फगुनाहट-the breeze of the coming spring.

फँगुहारा-people who are engaged in merrymaking and throwing coloured water on each other at the time of the Holi festival.

फजर-dawn; early morning; dawn prayer.

फ़जल-blessing; grace.

फ़जीलत-infamy; disgrace; misfortune; ill fame.

फ़जीता-disgrace; infamy.

फ़ज़ीहत-feeling of being harried and maltreated

फ़जूल-unnecessary; useless.

फट-thud; suddenly and quickly.

फटकन-chaff separated from grain in winnowing.

फटकना-to winnow; to reach.

फटकार-scolding; upbraiding.

फटकारना-to scold/upbraid/rebuke; to snap; to beat clothes for washing or cleaning.

फटन-cleavage; fissure; split; gap; crack; rift.

फटना-to be torn.

फटफटाना-to make a fluttering sound; to flutter; to flap.

फटफटिया-motorcycle.

फटा-torn.

फटेहाल-down and out; in a sorry plight; in a miserable condition.

फड़-a cloth used as a gambling board.

फड़क-throbbing; palpitation; pulsation.

फड़कना-to pulsate.

फड़फड़ाना-to flutter/flap/flicker.

फ़ड़फड़ाहट-flutter; excitement.

फड़बाज-owner of common gambling house/den.

फण-hood of a snake.

फणधर-cobra.

फणींद्र-

फ़तवा-a (religious) ruling give by a (Muslim) judge.

फ़तह-victory.

फतिंगा-moth; flying insect; hopper.

फतुही-waist-coat stuffed with cotton.

फ़न-skill; art; cunning.

फबन-state or quality to suit nicely; befittingness; suitability.

फबना-to suit nicely/fine; to become.

फ़र-fur.

फ़रक़-distance; difference; separation; deficiency.

फ़रज़-duty.

फ़रज़ी-fraud.

फ़रद-single; unequalled; sole.

फरफंद-trickery; fraud.

फ़रागत-relief; riddance.

फ़रामोश-oblivious; forgetful.

फ़रामोशी-oblivion; forgetfulness.

फ़रार-absconder.

फ़रियाद-complaint; plaint.

फ़रियादी-complainant; accuser.

फरियाना-to settle; to decide.

फ़रिश्ता-angel.

फ़रीक़-one of the contending parties (in a suit).

फ़रेब-fraud; deception; treachery.

फ़रेबी-fraudulent; treacherous; cheater.

फ़रोख्त-sold.

फ़र्क़-difference; distinction.

फ़र्ज़-duty; obligation.

फ़र्माइशी-on request; made to order.

फ़र्मान-edict; command.

फर्राटा-fluency.

फ़र्श-floor.

फ़र्शी-hubble-bubble with a long pipe.

फ़र्शी सलाम-deferential greeting.

फल-fruit; result; consequence; effect.

फलक-sheet; counter; board.

फ़लक-sky; heavens.

फलतः consequently; therefore.

फलद-fruitful; bearing fruit.

फलदायक-fruitful.

फलदार-bearing fruit.

फलना-to bear fruit; to prove auspicious; appearance of granules on any part of the body.

फलप्रद-fruitful; bearing fruit; effective; advantageous.
फल-फलार-fruit diet and the like.
फलभोग-undergoing/enjoying the result of (one's) deed.
फलयुक्त-bearing fruit; fruitful.
फलवती-fruitful.
फल-शर्करा-fruit-sugar.
फलस्वरूप-consequently.
फलस्वरूप, के-as a result.
फलहीन-fruitless.
फ़लाँ-that (specified); so and so.
फलाँग-a leap; a jump.
फलाँगना-to jump/cross over.
फ़लाना-such and such.
फलाफल-reading/forecasting about future/prognosis.
फला-फूला-prosperous.
फ़लालैन-flannel.
फलासक्त-attached to the result/fruit.
फलाहार-fruit diet.
फलाहारी-fruitarian.
फलित-resulted; resultant.
फली-bean; bean-like vegetable.
फलीदार-(plant) bearing beans.
फलीभूत-fructified; successful.
फलोत्पादक-capable of bearing fruit.
फलोत्पादकत्व-capability of bearing fruit.
फलोदय-fructification.
फ़व्वारा-fountain.
फ़सल-crop; harvest.
फ़सली-seasonal.
फ़साद-affray.
फ़सादी-quarrelsome; given to quarrels.
फ़हम-understanding; sense.
फहरना-to flutter in the air.
फहराना-to hoist. *v.i.* to wave/flutter.
फाँक-slice of melon, mango, orange etc.
फाँकना-to chuck grain into the mouth from the palms of hand; to put something powdered into the mouth.
फाँद-jump; jumping.
फाँदना-to jump/leap over.
फाँस-thorn; splinter; trap; noose.
फाँसना-to trap/entrap/ensnare.
फाँसा-lasso; trap; snare.
फाँसी-hanging.
फ़ाइबर-fibre.
फ़ाइल-file.
फ़ाइलबाज़ी-red tapism.
फ़ाइलेरिया-filaria.
फ़ाउंटेन पेन-fountain pen.
फ़ाक़ा-starvation; fast.
फ़ाक़ेमस्त-(one) who keeps cheerful even when starving.
फ़ाक़ेमस्ती-cheerfulness even in starvation.

फ़ाख़्तई-of the colour of dove; greyish brown.

फ़ाख़्ता-dove.

फाग-Holi festival; a song sung during Holi festival.

फागुन-last month of the Hindu calendar.

फागुनी-pertaining to the month of

फ़ाज़िल-more than necessary; supernumerary; extra; residual; scholarly.

फाटक-gate; entrance.

फाटका-speculation.

फाटकेबाज़-speculator.

फाटकेबाज़ी-speculation.

फाड़न-piece (of cloth, paper etc.) torn out of a bigger piece; butter-milk left over when butter is taken out fresh from yoghurt.

फाड़ना-to tear/rend/chop/split.

फ़ानूस-chandelier.

फ़ायदा-profit; gain; advantage; benefit; use; utility.

फ़ायदेमंद-profitable; advantageous; useful.

फ़ायर-fire; shooting.

फ़ायरमैन-fireman.

फ़ारम-form; farm.

फ़ारमूला-formula.

फ़ारसी-Persian (language).

फ़ारसीदाँ-one who is well-versed in Persian.

फ़ारिग relieved.

फ़ार्म-farm.

फाल-step; stride.

फ़ालतू-useless; good for nothing; superfluous.

फालसई-brownish red.

फ़ालसा-tiny fruit of the summer season.

फ़ालिज-paralysis.

फाल्गुन-last month of the Hindu calendar.

फावड़ा-spade; mattock.

फावड़ी-small spade.

फ़ाश-exposed.

फ़ासफ़ेट-phosphate.

फ़ासफ़ोरस-phosphorus.

फ़ासला-distance.

फ़ासिज़्म-fascism.

फाहा-fluffy piece of cotton (usually soaked in perfume or medicine); a piece of cotton for cleaning wounds; swab.

फ़ाहिशा-woman of easy morals.

फ़िकर-thought; reflection; care; concern; anxiety; grief.

फ़िक़रा-sentence.

फ़िक्र-anxiety; worry; perplexity.

फ़िक्रमंद-worried; anxious.

फिचकुर-foam emitted from the mouth in a hysteric swoon and the like.

फ़िट-fit.

फ़िटन-phaeton.

फ़िटर-fitter.

फ़ितना-budding (sharper); wily.

फ़ितरत-disposition; nature; mischief; wily disposition; wiliness; cunningness.

फ़ितरती-mischievous; wily; crafty; cunning.

फ़ितूर-defect.

फ़िदवी-servant; a title of modesty for oneself.

फ़िदा-enamoured; infatuated; enchanted; fascinated; charmed.

फ़िनाइल-phenyl.

फ़िनिश-finish.

फ़िरंगी-European.

फ़िरंट-opposed; angry.

फिर-afterwards; again; more-over.

फ़िरका-tribe; clan.

फिरकी-reel.

फ़िरक़ेवाराना-communal.

फिरना-to go back; to return; to go round; to turn.

फिरनी-a sweet preparation of milk, powdered, rice etc.

फिरवाना-to have (something) returned.

फिराऊ-returnable; returning.

फ़िराक़-purpose; search.

फिराना-to take around; to cause to change

फिरोजी-violet blue.

फ़िरौती-money demanded in return for the release of a kidnapped person; ransom.

फ़िलहाल for the time being; for the present.

फ़िलासफ़ी-philosophy.

फ़िलिस्तीन-Palestine.

फ़िल्म-film; reel; movie.

फ़िल्माना-to film.

फ़िल्मी-filmic.

फिस-nought.

फिसड्डी-sluggish; always being behind.

फिसलन-slipperiness.

फिसलना-to slip; to slide/skid. -slippery.

फ़िहरिस्त-list; schedule; index; inventory.

फ़ी-each.

फीका-tasteless; without saltiness or sweetness; insipid; dim.

फीकापन-tastelessness; insipidity; dimness; faintness.

फ़ीता-a narrow strip of cloth; tape; lace; ribbon; strap.

फ़ीरोज़ा-amethyst; violet blue gem.

फ़ीरोज़ी-violet blue.

फ़ील-elephant; bishop (chess).

फ़ीलख़ाना-stable for elephant.

फीलपाँव-elephantiasis.

फ़ीलवान-elephant driver.

फ़ीस-fee.

फुँकना-to burn.

फुँकनी-blow-pipe.

फुँकवाना-causative of to burn.

फुंकार-hissing sound.

फुँदना-tassel.

फुंसी-boil.

फुट-single; alone; separate.

फ़ुट-foot (measurement).

फुटकर-retail; miscellaneous; sundry.

फ़ुटनोट-footnote.

फ़ुटपाथ-footpath.

फ़ुटबाल-football.

फुटमत-difference of opinion (in a family).

फुटा-foot-rule.

फुड़िया-smallish boil.

फुदकना-to jump/skip.

फुनगी-top; summit; cockade; sprout.

फुप्फुस-lung.

फुफकार-hiss (of a snake).

फुफकारना-to hiss.

फुफेरा-pertaining to or / (father's sister).

फुर-flutter.

फुरती-activity; briskness; promptness.

फुरतीला-agile; nimble; prompt; quick.

फुरतीलापन-agility; promptness.

फ़ुरसत-leisure; rest; opportunity.

फुर्ती-agility; promptness; haste; hurry.

फ़ुर्सत-free time; respite; spare time; leisure.

फुलका-thin; load; muffin.

फुलझड़ी-a type of firework; provocative remark.

फुलवारी-flower garden.

फुलाना-to inflate; to pump in air.

फुलाव-inflation; puffing up.

फुलेल-scented oil.

फुलौरी-a fried dish made of cereal flour.

फुसफुस-whisper.

फुसफुसाना-to whisper; to speak in a hushed up/subdued tone.

फुसफुसाहट-whispering sound.

फुसलाना-to wheedle/seduce/lure/cajole.

फुहार-drizzle.

फुहारा-fountain.

फूँक-a current of air sent out of the mouth; blow.

फूँक-ताप-squandering.

फूँकना-to blow; to turn to ashes.

फूँकनी-blow-pipe.

फूँ-फाँ-pomp and show.

फूट-split; rift; discord; disunity.

mas. a large fruit of the cucumber family resembling a melon.

फूटना-to be smashed/broken. to burst.

फूफा-husband of father's sister.

फूफी-father's sister.

फूल-flower; a white metal.

फूल-गोभी-cauliflower; broccoli.

फूलदान-flower pot/vase.

फूलदार-flowery.

फूलना-to flower/blossom; to be annoyed.

फूल-माला-flower-garland.

फूली-white outgrowth in the pupil of the eye.

फूस-hay; straw.

फूहड़-sluttish; uncouth; sloven; awkward; ludicrous; stupid; mannerless.

फूहड़पन-uncouthness; slovenliness; awkwardness; stupidity.

फेंकना-to cast, throw or hurl; to emit; to offer.

फेंट-part of the folded up round the waist.-shake.

फेंटना-to beat up (as espresso coffee); to shuffle (as a pack of cards).

फेंटा-circumference of the waist; part of tucked up round the waist; girdle; short turban.

फेन-foam; froth; lather.

फेनी-a type of Indian sweet.

फेफड़ा-lung.

फेर-detour; circuitous route; curvature; complication; misconception; misunderstanding; ambiguity; miscalculation.

फेरना-to turn; twist.

फेर-बदल-reshuffle; shake up.

फेरी-round; hawking.

फेरीवाला-hawker; pedlar.

फ़ेल-failed; ploughed.

फ़ेहरिस्त-list; inventory.

फ़ैंसी-fancy.

फैलाव-expansion; stretch; span.

फ़ैशन-fashion.

फ़ैसला-adjudication; judgement; decision; settlement.

फोक-residue left after extraction.

फोकट-without any substance; without any labour or charge.

फोकटी-costing nothing.

फ़ोटो-photo.

फोड़ना-to break/smash; to burst.

फोड़ा-suppurated sore; abscess; boil; ulcer.

फ़ोता-testicle.

फ़ोन-phone; telephone.

फ़ौज-army; military force.

फ़ौजदारी-criminal; penal.

फ़ौजी-pertaining to the army/military; martial-a soldier.

फ़ौरन forthwith; immediately; at once; instantly.

फ़ौलाद-steel.

फ़ौलादी-made of pertaining to steel; stout; sturdy.

फौवारा-fountain; artificial spring of water.

ब

ब-The twenty-third consonant of the and alphabet and the third letter of the labial.

ब-the ocean; water; fragrance.

बंक-bent; curved; crooked.-bank.

बंकट-a kind of snake.

बंका-curved; bent; powerful.

बंकिम-bent; curved; croo-ked.

बंकिमा-bent; curvature; crookedness.

बंग-intoxicating hemp.

बंगरी-a bangle made of glass or lac.

बँगला-of or pertaining to Bengal. -bungalow.-Bengali language.

बंगा-a split piece of bamboo as used in basket-making.

बंगाल-Bengal (a state in the Indian Union).

बंगाली-inhabitant of Bengal.-of or pertaining to Bengal.

बंगी-one who takes .

बंजर-barren; waste land

बंजारा-a wandering grain dealer; nomad.

बंजारी-the wife of a grain-dealer.

बंटन-distribution.

बँटना-to be divided; to be shared.

बँटवारा-partition; distribution.

बँटवैया-one who divides or distributes.

बँटाई-crop sharing; distribution; partnership in crops.

बँटाधार-destructive effect; spoilage.

बंड-maided in hands or feet tailless circumcised; impotent.

बंडल-bundle.

बंडा-tailless.

बंडी-waistcoat; jacket.

बंडेरा-the support of a thatch; the beam which is placed on a shaft.

बंद-closed; stopped; blocked; shut; locked up.

बंद गोभी-cabbage.

बंदनवार-festoon of flowers/green leaves; arch.

बंदर-ape; monkey.

बंदर-धुड़की-hollow threat; bluff.

बंदर-बाँट-unequal and wrong distribution.

बंदर-भभकी-hollow threat.

बंदरवाला-monkey-showman.

बँदरिया, बंदरी-female monkey.

बंदा-human being.

बंदापरवर-protector of the human beings.

बंदिश-restriction; precautionary measure; musical pattern.

बंदी[1]-prisoner; captive; convict; bard.

बंदी[2]-shut-down; closure; holidays.

बंदीख़ाना-prison.

बंदूक़-gun.

बंदूक़ची-gunner; gunman.

बंदूक़धारी-gunner.

बंदूक़बाज़ी-firing; marksmanship.

बंदोबस्त-management; arrangement; (land) survey and settlement.

बंधक-pledge; hostage; mortgage.

बंधन-tie; bond; restriction; bondage; joint (of the body).

बंधनकारी-binding (restriction, obligation etc.).

बँधना-to be tied/fastened/ imprisoned; to be bound.-string; cord; anything used for tying.

बँधवाना-causative of tie; to cause (someone) to tie.

बँधा-tied; fastened; bound.

बंधान-(binding) tradition; stipulation; embankment.

बंधु-brother.

बँधुआ-captive; bond-man.

बंधुत्व-brotherhood.

बंधु-बांधव-relatives; kinsfolk; cousinry; friends.

बंधुभाव-kinship; fraternalism.

बंधेज-binding tradition; amount paid due to such a tradition; restriction; hindrance.

बंध्य-sterile.

बंध्यत्व-sterility.

बंध्या-barren woman.

बंपुलिस-public lavatory.

बंब-sound of ; bomb.

बंबा-waterpipe.

बंबूकाट-a kind of two wheeled vehicle, like a .

बँसवाड़ा-bamboo market; grove of bamboos.

बंसी-flute; fishing hook.

बक-heron; prattle; gossip.

बक-झक-babbling; jabbering.

बकतर-armour.

बकना-to jabber/babble.

बकबक-prattle.

बकरदाढ़ी-a short pointed beard; goatee.

बकरम-a kind of stiff cloth; .

बकरा-he-goat.

बक़रीद-an important Muslim festival.

बकलस-buckle.

बकवाद-useless or confused talk; babble; prattle.

बकवादी-babbler; prattler; talkative; garrulous.

बकवास-prattle.

बकस-box.

बकसुआ-buckle.

बकायदा according to rule.

बक़ाया-arrear (s).

बकोटना-to pinch.

बकोटा-mark of bruise made by pinching/scratching.

बक़ौल as stated by.

बक्कल-skin; bark.

बक़्क़ाल-petty grocer/shopkeeper.

बक्की-talkative; chatty.

बक्खर-cattle-pen.

बक्स-box.

बखान-description; praise; eulogy.

बखानना-to describe in detail; to eulogise at length.

बखार-barn; grain-store; granary.

बख़िया-back-stitching.

बख़ुद by oneself.

बख़ूबी beautifully; thoroughly.

बखेड़ा-complication; mess; uproar; tumult; row.

बखेड़िया-one who starts a row; quarrelsome fellow; turbulent.

बख़्तर-armour.

बख़्शना-to forgive/excuse/pardon.

बख़्शीश-tip (given after getting some work done).

बगछुट-having a free rein (said of a horse).

बग़ल-armpit; side.

बग़लगीर-seated by the side; in the embrace.

बग़लबंदी-an old-fashioned Indian jacket.

बग़ल, में, के beside.

बगला-heron.

बगला-भगत-hypocrite.

बग़ली-pertaining to the armpit/flank. -a trick in wrestling; hole made in a wall for burglary; tailor's bag for keeping gadgets etc.

बग़ावत-rebellion; revolt.

बगिया-small garden.

बगीचा-small garden; orchard.

बगूला-whirlwind.

बग़ैर, के-without.

बग्घी-four-horse carriage.

बघ-allomorph of (tiger) used in compound words.

बघनखा-tiger-claw; a weapon of the shape of a tiger-claw.

बघमाला-tiger's skin.

बघार-seasoning (of vegetables, lentils etc.) in the process of cooking.

बघारना-to season (vegetables; lentils etc.) in the process of cooking; to talk big/tall.

बचकाना-childish; highfalutin.

बचकानापन-childishness.

बचत-money saved; saving; something saved.

बचत खाता-saving account.

बचत योजना-saving scheme.

बचन-utterance.

बचना-to be saved; to remain unused; to escape; to avoid; shun.

बचपन-childhood; childishness; puerility.

बचपना-childhood.

बचा-खुचा-left over.

बचाना-to save; to spare; to defend / protect / to avoid.

बचाव-rescue; protection; safety; escape.

बचाव-कार्य-rescue; operation.

बच्चा-(usually male) child; baby; kid; young animal.

बच्चाकश-(woman) a little too fertile.

बच्ची-female child; small girl.

बच्चेदानी-the female reproductive organ; ovary.

बछचमड़ा-calf-leather; calf-skin.

बछड़ा-he-calf.

बछिया-she-calf.

बछेड़ा-colt.

बजट-budge.

बजड़ा-millet.

बजना-to ring/tinkle.

बजबजाना-to form gas and bubbles.

बजरबट्टू-a seed used (as a talisman) for warding off the evil eye.

बजरा-double-deck boat; millet.

बजरिया-small market.

बजरी-gravel.

बजवाई-remuneration paid for playing on an instrument.

बजवैया-one who plays on musical instrument.

बजा-right; proper.

बज़ाज़-clothier; cloth-merchant; draper.

बज़ाज़ा-cloth-market; drapery.

बज़ाज़ी-the calling of a cloth-merchant.

बजाना-to play; to toot; to toll; to ring.

बजाय, के instead of; in place of.

बजे-at ...... o'clock.

बझना-to tied/entangled.

बझाऊ-entangling.

बझाना-to tie/entangle.

बट-tree.

बटखरा-weight (s).

बटन-button.

बटना-to twist as a cord, rope etc.

बटमार-one who robs travellers; highwayman.

बटमारी-act of robbing travellers.

बटलोई-a round vessel used for cooking.

बटवारा-division; partition.

बटा-divided by .

बटाई-sharing of crop.

बटाऊ-traveller; wayfarer.

बटाटा-potato.

बटालियन-battalion.

बटिया-small; smooth mass of stone or clay; small pestle; foot-path.

बटी-pill or tablet; cookie.

बटुआ-money-bag; purse.

बटुरना-to be accumulated.

बटेर-he-quail.

बटेरबाज़-one who rears quails.

बटेरबाज़ी-rearing of quails (especially for quail-fighting).

बटेरिन-she-quail.

बटेरी-she-quail; display of gifts received from the bride's party.

बटोरन-sweepings.

बटोरना-to gather or collect; to accumulate.

बटोही-traveller; wayfarer.

बट्टा-a piece of stone; stone pestle; rebate; discount; brokerage; commission.

बट्टी-cake.

बड़-tree; allomorph of used in compound words.-brag.

बड़प्पन-elderliness; greatness; generosity; magnanimity; dignity.

बड़बड़-foolish talk; grumble.

बड़बड़ाना-to talk foolishly or too much; to blab.

बड़बोल-braggart.

बड़बोला-braggart.

बड़भागी-lucky; fortunate.

बड़वानल-marine fire.

बड़हार-marriage feast given by the bridal party.

बड़ा-big; large; huge; great; grand; major; elder; older; very much. -biscuit of ground pulse fried in oil etc. too much; very.

बड़ाई-greatness; praise.

बड़ी-preparation of ground pulse.

बड़ी इलायची-black cardamom.

बढ़ई-carpenter.

बढ़ईगीरी-work of vocation of a carpenter; carpentry.

बढ़ती-increase; increment; surplus.

बढ़ना-to grow; to rise; to increase; to exceed; to be extended; to advance/ progress.

बढ़नी-broom.

बढ़ा-चढ़ा-surpassing; excelling.

बढ़ाना-to increase; to raise; to extend to lengthen; to magnify/enlarge as a photograph.

बढ़ावा-incentive; encouragement.

बढ़िया-good; nice; of a high quality; excellent; splendid.

बढ़ोतरी-increase; increment; sharp rise; hike; progress.

बढ़ौती-old age.

बणिक-trader.

बतकही-conversation.

बतक्कड़-fond of talking; talkative; garrulous; chatty.

बतरस-relish/fondness for talk.

बतलाना-to point out; to signify; to appraise; to talk; to speak.

बताना-to tell; to state; to indicate; to point out.

बतासा-a roundish sugar-cake.

बतियाना-to talk/converse.

बतौर-like; just like.

बत्ती-wick; candle; light.

बत्तीदान-candlestick.

बत्तीस-thirty-two.

बत्तीसी-a full set of teeth; denture.

बथुआ-a leafy vegetable (Indian),

बद-bad. (Its comparative form is and superlative form)

बदइंतजामी-mismanagement.

बदक़िस्मत-unlucky; unfortunate; wretched.

बदक़िस्मती-ill-luck; misfortune.

बदचलन-rakish; of loose morals; depraved; corrupted.

बदलचनी-depravation; rakishness.

बदज़बान-evil-tongued; foul-mouthed.

बदज़ात-vile; wicked.

बदतमीज़-rude; unmannerly.

बदतमीज़ी-rudeness; unmannerliness; rude or obscene act.

बदतर-worse (comparative from of

बद्दुआ-curse.

बदन-body.

बदनसीबी-ill luck; misfortunate.

बदना-to bet/wager.

बदनाम-defamed; ill-famed.

बदनामी-defame; ill-famed.

बदनीयत-of ill-intent; malevolent; ill-motived.

बदनीयती-ill-tent; malevolence; bad faith.

बदपरहेज़-intemperate in habits (especially in diet).

बदपरहेज़ी-intemperance; indulgence in wrong or unbalanced diet.

बदबू-foul/bad smell; reek.

बदबूदार-reeking; stinking; foul-smelling; smelly.

बदमाश-wicked (person); scoundrel; rascal; hooligan; hoodlum.

बदमाशी-rascality; wickedness.

बदमिज़ाज-short/ill-tempered.

बदमिज़ाजी-short/ill temper.

बदरंग-of a faded colour; discoloured; of a grotesque colour; of a different/another colour (cards).

बदल-change.

बदलना-to change; alter; to exchange or replace.

बदला-revenge; reprisal; retaliation.

बदलाव-change; replacement.

बदली-cloudiness; transfer.

बदले, के in place of; instead of.

बदलौअल-exchange; alteration.

बदशक्ल-unpleasant to look at; uncouth; awkward; clumsy; ugly.

बदसुलूकी- maltreatment; misbehaviour.

बदसूरत-ugly; clumsy.

बदस्तूर as usual; as ever before; in the customary manner.

बदहज़मी-indigestion.

बदहवास-out of one's wits; bewildered; confused; perplexed.

बदहवासी-state of being out of one's wits; state of bewilderment.

बदा-fated; destined.

बदा-बदी-rivalry.

बदी-dark fortnight of the lunar month; evil.

बदौलत, की-by the grace of; through the kindness of by virtue.

बद्ध-bound; tied; fixed.

बद्धकोष्ठ-suffering from constipation.

बद्धपरिकर-girt up.

बद्धमूल-deep-rooted.

बधाई-congratulation; greetings; felicitation.

बधावा-presents sent ceremoniously as a mark of felicitation.

बधिक-hunter; fowler; killer.

बधिया-unable to hear; deaf.

बधिर-unable to hear; deaf.

बधिरता-deafness.

बन-forest; woods; jungle.

बन-कटाई-deforestation.

बनखंड-woodland.

बनचर-wild (beast); forester.

बनजारा-nomad.

बनत-design.

बनदेवी-goddess of a forest.

बनना-to become; to be made; to be built/constructed; to come into existence; to be repaired.

बनफ़्शा-a type of medicinal herb.

बनबिलाव-a wild animal of the cat family; lynx.

बनमानुष-chimpanzee.

बनवाई-act or state of or charges paid for the same.

बनवाना-causative of

बनवास-dwelling in the forest.

बनवासी-forest-dweller.

बनस्पति-vegetable.

बनाना-to make (physical or conceptual); to build/erect/construct; to befool.

बना-बनाया-ready-made; well-made.

बनाम versus.

बनाव-manner of formation; composition.

बनावट-make-up; formation; structure; construction; affectation.

बनावटी-artificial; showy; unreal.

बनिया-a person belonging to the class or caste; the trading community among the Hindus.

बनियाइन-an upper undergarment; traders wife.

बनिस्बत in comparison with.

बनैला-wild; belonging to or living in the forest.

बन्ना-bridegroom.

बन्नी-bride.

बपौती-inheritance; heritage; patrimony.

बबर-lion.

बबुआ-toy (in the shape of a boy); boy-child.

बबूल-tree.

बबूला-bubble; whirlwind.

बम-bomb; an interjection addressed to

बमकांड-bomb explosion; case of bombing.

बमगोला-bomb shell.

बमचख़-brawl; tumult; uproar.

बमबारी-bombing.

बमवर्षक-bomber.

बमवर्षा-bombing.

बयनामा-sale-deed.

बया-weaver-bird.

बयान-statement; account; description.

बयाना-earnest money.

बरई-one who sells betel leaves.

बरकत-grace; affluence.

बरकरार-in tact.

बरख़ास्त-dismissed.

बरख़ास्तगी-sack; dismissal.

बरख़िलाफ-in opposition (to).

बरगद-tree.

बरछा-spear.

बरछी-dagger.

बरज़ोर-strong; coercive; oppressive.

बरज़ोरी-strength; coercion; oppression.

बरतन-utensil; vessel.

बरतन-चौका-act of cleaning the kitchen and kitchen-wares.

बरतना-to use; to exercise; to deal with.

बरताव-treatment; behaviour; dealing.

बरदाश्त-toleration.

बरबस-forcefully; willy-nilly; spontaneously.

बरबाद-ruined; destroyed; wasted.

बरबादी-ruination; ruin; waste; wastage; devastation.

बरमा-drill (for making holes); Burma, old name of ; a country in Asia.

बरमी-small drill; language of .-inhabitant of

बरस-year.

बरसगाँठ-birth anniversary.

बरसना-to rain; to shower.

बरसात-rain; rainy season.

बरसाती-rainy; of or pertaining to rains.-porch; rain-coat.

बरसाना-to rain; to shower (upon).

बरसी-first death anniversary.

बरात-marriage procession; marriage party.

बरात घर-the place where marriage parties stay.

बराती-a person who is a member of a marriage party; a member of a marriage party.

बराबर-of the same age or size; equal; adjoining; to squander; to even. regularly; non-stop.

बराबर, के equal to, upon.

बराबरी-equality; parity.

बरामद-seized; recovered.

बरामदगी-act of recovering; recovery; things recovered.

बरामदा-verandah.

बरास्ता via.

बरी-acquitted; released.

बरौनी-eyelash.

बर्तन-utensil.

बर्ताव-treatment; behaviour.

बर्थ-berth; seat.

बर्दाश्त-power of endurance; tolerance; forbearance.

बर्नर-burner.

बर्फ़-snow; ice.

बर्फ़बारी-snowfall.

बर्फ़ानी-snowy.

बर्फ़ी-a sweetmeat of rectangular shape.

बर्फ़ीला-icy; snowy.

बर्बर-barbaric; savage.

बर्बरता-barbarism; savagery.

बर्बरतापूर्ण-barbaric; barbarous.

बर्र-wasp.

बर्राना-to gabble; to talk in one's sleep, fever etc.

बल-force; strength; power; might; vigour; stress; emphasis; any organised body; direction; twirl.

बलकना-to be visibly excited; to boil; to simmer.

बलकारक-invigorating; vitalising; restorative.

बलग़म-phlegm.

बलग़मी-phlegmatic.

बलतोड़-boil caused by the uprooting of a hair.

बल-परीक्षा-trial of strength; show-down.

बल-प्रयोग-use of force; application of force .

बल-बूता-strength.

बलवती-strong.

बलवर्धक-tonic; invigorating; restorative.

बलवर्धन-tonic; invigorating; restorative.

बलवा-riot.

बलवाई-rioter.

बलवान-powerful; stout; strong.

बल-वैभव-might and grandeur.

बलशाली-powerful; vigorous.

बलहीन-powerless; weak.

बला-evil; calamity; adversity; trouble; affliction; misery; evil; spirit.

बलाघात-emphasis; stress.

बलात् by force; forcibly.-forced.

बलात्कार-rape; the act of spoiling something.

बलात्कारी-one who commits rape; rapist.

बलाबल-strength and weakness.

बलि-something offered as a sacrifice.

बलिदान-act of sacrificing; sacrifice.

बलिदानी-sacrificer.

बलिष्ठ-very strong; stout; powerful.

बलिहारी-to fondle; to show affection.

बली-powerful; strong.

बलीवर्द-ox; bull.

बलुआ-sandy.

बलूत-oak.

बलूती-oaken.

बल्कि but; rather; on the contrary.

बल्ब-bulb.

बल्लम-lance; spear.

बल्ला-(cricket) bat; (tennis) racket.

बल्ली-long wooden staff.

बल्लेबाज़-batsman.

बल्लेबाज़ी-batting; batsmanship.

बवंडर-whirlwind; cyclone; typhoon.

बवासीर-piles.

बशर्ते provided that; only if.

बसंत-spring.

बसंती-pertaining to the spring season; yellow.

बसंदर-fire .

बस no more please; that's all; enough; sufficient; just.

बसना-to dwell/inhabit/live; to settle (down); to permeate.

बसर-to maintain oneself; to subsist.

बसाना-to inhabit; to colonise.

बसूला-adze.

बसूली-small adze.

बसेरा-shelter; dwelling.

बस्ता-bag; school bag; portmanteau.

बस्ती-habitation; colony; population.

बहँगी-load-carrying device in the shape of a scale-pan.

बहक-raving; going astray; irrelevant; talking.

बहकना-to rave; to go astray.

बहकाना-to inveigle; to lead astray; to seduce; to entice; to allure; to mislead.

बहकावा-inveiglement.

बहना-to flow; to be swept by the current.

बहनापा-sister-like relationship; sisterhood.

बहनेली-adopted sister.

बहनोई-sister's husband; brother-in-law.

बहरा-unable to hear; deaf.

बहरापन-deafness.

बहरी-a bird of the hawk family.

बहरूपिया-multifarious.

बहलना-to be agreeably diverted/amused.

बहलाना-to amuse; recreate.

बहलाव-act or state of

बहलावा-amusement; diversion.

बहस-discussion; argument.

बहस-मुबाहिसा-prolonged discussion.

बहाऊ-squandering.

बहादुर-brave; bold; valorous; adventurous.

बहादुरी-bravery; boldness; valour.

बहाना[1]-pretext; pretence.

बहाना[2]-to cause to flow; to set a float.

बहानेबाज़-(one) who is given to making excuse/pretences.

बहानेबाज़ी-state or habit of making excuses.

बहार-the season between winter and summer, spring; season of delight/affluence; charm.

बहाल-reinstated; maintained.

बहाली-reinstatement; restoration (to the original status); happiness.

बहाव-drift; flow.

बहिरंग-external.

बहिर्गत-outward.

बहिर्गमन-an act of going out; an act of leaving a meeting, conference etc., as a protest.

बहिर्जगत-outside world; this world.

बहिर्मुखी-extrovert.

बहिर्रेखा-outline.

बहिश्त-heaven.

बहिश्ती heavenly.

बहिष्करण-boycotting.

बहिष्कार-boycott; ban; taboo.

बहिष्कृत-boycotted.

बही-a register of the old type.

बही-खाता-account book.

बहु-many.

बहु-आयामी-multidimensional.

बहुखंडीय-multi-storied; having many compartments.

बहुजातीय-multi-ethnic.

बहुज्ञ-(a person) of wide knowledge; versatile; erudite; scholarly.

बहुज्ञता-state or quality of being versatility

बहुत-much; too much; abundant; plentiful; many. very; many people.

बहुतायत-abundance; plenty; excess.

बहुतेरा-many; abundant.

बहुत्व-plentiful; plurality.

बहुदर्शी-versatile; learned.

बहुदलीय-multiparty.

बहुदेशीय-multinational.

बहुधर्मी-multi-religious.

बहुधा generally; frequently; quite often; very often; in many ways.

बहुपक्षीय-multi-lateral.

बहुपठित-well-read.

बहुपत्नीक-polygamist.

बहुभाषी-multilingual; multilinguist.

बहुमत-majority.

बहुमुखी-versatile; well rounded/versed.

बहुमूल्य-precious; costly; invaluable.

बहुरंगा-multicoloured; pied; piebald.

बहुरना-to come back/return.

बहुराष्ट्रीय-multinational.

बहुरूप-multiform.

बहुरूपिया-an expert in many different forms of disguise; imposter.

बहुल-abundant; plentiful; copious.

बहुलता-abundance; plenty; plenitude.

बहुलवाद-pluralism.

बहुलवादी-of pluralism.

बहुवचन-plural.

बहुविवाह-polygamy; polyandry.

बहुश्रुत-widely informed/heard.

बहुसंख्यक-numerous.

बहुस्तरीय-multi-level.
बहू-daughter-in-law; wife.
बहेड़ा-tree and its fruit.
बहेलिया-fowler; hunter.
बाँक-(graceful) curvature/bend.
बाँकपन-crookedness; showiness; modishness; elegance; swagger; flirtatiousness.
बाँका-foppish.
बाँकापन-foppishness.
बाँग-cock-a-doodle-doo; a long cry of a cock; prayer call (by the chief of a mosque).
बाँगड़ू-uncivilized.
बाँचना-to read aloud.
बाँझ-barren (woman).
बाँझपन-barrenness (of a woman).
बाँट-division; partition.
बाँटना-to distribute; to divide/partition; to share out.
बांड-bond.
बाँदी-female slave; servant girl.
बाँध-dam, dike; embankment.
बाँधना-to bind/tie/fasten; to wrap around.
बाँधनू-pre-planned approach.
बाधंव-fraternal relation.
बाँबी-snake-bill; ant-bill.
बाँस-bamboo.
बाँसुरी-flute.
बाँसुरीवादक-flute player; flutist.
बाँह-arm; sleeve.
बाइसिकिल-bicycle.
बाई-lady; delirium.
बाईजी-prostitute.
बाएँ-towards the left; to the left.
बाएँ, के-on the left side.
बाक़ी-subtraction; remainder; balance; arrears; remaining.
बाग-rein (s).
बाग़-garden.
बाग़बान-gardener.
बाग़ी-rebel; insurgent.
बाग़ीचा-small garden.
बाघंबर-tiger skin.
बाघ-tiger.
बाछ-tip of the lip.
बाछा-calf.
बाज़-hawk; falcon. doer. bereft of; without; to few; some.
बाजरा-millet.
बाजा-musical instrument.
बाजा-गाजा-fanfare band.
बाज़ार-market; shopping area.
बाज़ार-भाव-market-rate; kerb-rate; market value.
बाज़ारी-pertaining to the market; commonplace; rude.
बाज़ारीकरण-act of marketing.
बाज़ारू-cheap and third-rate.

बाज़ी-bet; stake; turn. denoting act or action.

बाज़ीगरी-jugglery.

बाजू-arm.

बाजूबंद-armlet.

बाट-way; path; passage; weights.

बाटी-roasted, round thick dough bread.

बाड़-hedge; fence.

बाड़ा-small garden; house.

बाढ़-growth; flood; a great quantity of something.

बाण-arrow.

बाण-विद्या-archery.

बात-talk; matter; thing.

बात-चीत-conversation.

बाती-wick.

बातूनी-talkative; chatty; garrulous.

बातूनीपन-chattiness; garrulousness.

बाद-deducted; subtracted.

बाद, के after.

बादबान-sail.

बादल-cloud.

बादवाला-next; following.

बादशाह-king; ruler; king (chessman).

बादशाहत-reign; government; sovereignty.

बादाम-almond.

बादामी-of the colour of almond.

बादी-flatulent; flattening; wind-producing (in the body); flatulence.

बाधक-obstructive.

बाधा-hurdle; hindrance; obstacle; impediment; hindrance; interruption.

बाधित-obstructed; barred.

बाध्य-compelled; forced.

बाध्यता-obligation; compulsion.

बानर-monkey.

बाना-woof; dress; guise.

बानैत-bowman; archer.

बाप-father.

बाप-दादा-forefather; ancestors.

बापुरा-destitute; wretched.

बापू-father.

बाबत, की about in respect of.

बाबा-grandfather; old man; ascetic.

बाबा आदम-primitive man.

बाबुल-father.

बाबू-educated man; clerk.

बाबू जी-(form of addressing) Father! (respectable form of addressing) an elderly man.

बायकाट-boycott.

बायन-present; gift.

बायबी-strange.

बायाँ-left.

बायें-towards the left; opposite.

बारंबार again and again; repeatedly.

बार-time.

बारजा-balcony.

बारदाना-fare; food; miscellany.

बार-बार-time after time; repeatedly; time and again.

बारहदरी-a structure (usually on the upper storey of a house) having twelve entrances.

बारहवाँ-twelfth.

बारहसिंगा-stag; reindeer.

बारिश-rain; rainfall.

बारी-turn; inning; grove; small garden.

बारीक-thin; minute; subtle.

बारीकी-thinness; minuteness; subtlety.

बारूद-gunpowder.

बारूदख़ाना-ammunition store.

बारूद-घर-ammunition store.

बारूदी सुरंग-a land mine.

बारे में, के relating to; pertaining to; about.

बार्डर-border.

बाल-hair; infant; child; ear of corn; ball.

बालक-a boy; a person who behaves like a child.

बालकपन-boyhood.

बालकमानी-spring (in a watch).

बालकाल-boyhood.

बालक्रीड़ा-childish frolics.

बालगोपाल-(plural) children.

बालचर-boy scout.

बालू-sand.

बालू-कण-a bit of sand; grit.

बालूशाही-a kind of sweet.

बालेंदु-a new moon; the moon on the second night of the bright fortnight of the month; the second night rising moon.

बालोचित-childlike.

बाल्टी-bucket; pail.

बाल्य-of or pertaining to a child.

बालयकाल-childhood; adolescence.

बाल्यावस्था-infancy; childhood.

बावजूद, के in spite of.

बावड़ी-broad well with a low surface of water provided with flight of stairs.

बावनी-a set of fifty-two things; , a pack of cards; winning all the hands/tricks in or

बावरची-cook.

बावरचीख़ाना-kitchen.

बावरा-a mad man.

बावला-insane; mad; crazy.

बावली-(fem of small tank with steps all round; leading down to it.

बावेला-ballyhoo; furore; tumult; uproar.

बाशिंदा-dweller.

बास-habitation.-smell.

बासन-vessel; utensil.

बासा-abode; habitat.

बासी-having lost freshness; stale.

बाहर out; outside.

बाहर, के outside.

बाहरवाला-outside.

बाहरी-outward; outer; external; outside; outsider; external.

बाहु-arm.

बाहुबल-physical force/strength.

बाहुबली-having a muscular body.

बाहुमूल-shoulder-joint.

बाहुयुद्ध-hand to hand fight.

बाहुल्य-exuberance; plenty; abundance.

बाह्य-outward; external.

बाह्यत: externally.

बाह्यांचल-outskirts.

बाह्याचार-showy conduct.

बिंदी-dot; point; cyper; vermilion mark on the forehead.

बिंदु-dot; point; cypher.

बिंदु-चित्रण-stippling.

बिंधना-to be pierced; to be engrossed/tied up.

बिंब-disc; image.

बिंब-योजना-imagery.

बिंब-विधान-imagery.

बिआना-to give birth to; to be delivered of (said of animals).

बिकना-to be sold.

बिकल-troubled; perplexed.

बिकलता-uneasiness.

बिकवाना-to cause to sell.

बिकसना-to bloom/blossom.

बिकाऊ-for sale.

बिक्री-sale.

बिक्री-बट्टा-sale or transaction.

बिखरना-to be scattered/diffused.

बिखराव-act or state of being scattered/diffused.

बिखेरना-to scatter/diffuse.

बिगड़ना-to be angry/annoyed; to deteriorate.

बिगड़ा-worsened; spoilt; pampered.

बिगड़ी-serious and difficult conditions.

बिगड़ैल-short-tempered; peevish.

बिगाड़-rift; discord.

बिगाड़ना-to spoil; to damage; to vitiate; to ruin.

बिगाड़ू-(one) who spoils/destroys.

बिगुल-bugle.

बिचकना-to falter.

बिचकाना-to sneer.

बिचला-middle; mid.

बिचवई-mediator.

बिचौलिया-go-between; middleman.

बिच्छी-she-scorpion.

बिच्छू-scorpion.

बिछड़ना-to cease to be together.

बिछना-to be spread out.

बिछाना-to spread out.

बिछावन-bed-sheet; bedding.

बिछिया-an ornament which is worn on the toes.

बिछुआ-an ornament worn on the toe.

बिछुड़ना-to be separate; to be separated from a person.

बिछोड़ा-bereavement; deprivation.

बिछोह-painful separation; bereavement.

बिछौना-bedding; routine work.

बिजली-lightning; electricity; electric-light.

बिजली-घर-an electrical generating station; powerhouse.

बिजूखा-scarecrow.

बिजैला-seedy.

बिज्जु-an animal of the wild cat family.

बिटिया-daughter; girlie.

बिठलाना-to cause to sit.

बिठाना-to sit.

बिड़ाल-he-cat.

बिताना-to spend (time).

बित्ता-to measure with span.

बिथरना-to scatter.

बिदकना-to shy; to be alarmed.

बिदा-farewell.

बिदाई-farewell; departure; exodus.

बिदेश-a foreign country.

बिदेसिया-dweller in a foreign land; foreigner.

बिदेसी-foreigner.

बिध-concordance.

बिधना-fate; destiny.

बिन without.

बिनती-request.

बिनन-texture.

बिनना-to pick out (bad ones); to knit/weave; to select.

बिनवाना-to cause to be knitted.

बिना without; cause; plea.

बिनाई-the work of knitting and/or charges paid for the same.

बिना, के without.

बिनावट-texture.

बिनौला-cotton-seed.

बिपता-adversity; hardship; misery; affliction.

बिफरना-to be visibly annoyed.

बियाबान-wilderness; deserted spot.

बिरता-strength; backing.

बिरला-rare.

बिरवा-plant.

बिरह-separation.

बिरहा-a fold song of separation; ballad.

बिरही-(one who is) suffering the agony of separation.

बिराजना-to be seated (gracefully).

बिरादर-brother.

बिरादराना-brotherly.

बिरादरी-community.

बिराना-not one's own; to jeer; to mock.

बिल-hole; bill (for payment).

बिलकुल entire; completely.

बिलखना-to wail/lament.

बिलग-separate; detached.

बिलगाना-to separate/detach.

बिलगाव-separation; severance.

बिलटना-to be spoiled; to be reversed.

बिलटी-railway receipt.

बिलना-to be rolled into flat cakes.

बिलनी-sty.

बिलपना-to wail/lament.

बिलबिलाना-to whine; to wriggle.

बिलसना-to look fine; to suit admirably.

बिला-without having or showing something.

बिलाई-cat.

बिलाना-to be gone out of sight.

बिलार/बिलाव-tom-cat.

बिलैया-cat; bolt.

बिलोकना-to behold/see.

बिलोना-to churn (milk, curd etc.).

बिलौटा-kitten.

बिल्कुल totally; absolutely.

बिल्ला-tom-cat; badge.

बिल्ली-cat; shutter used for fastening doors.

बिल्लौर-crystal; quartz.

बिल्लौरी-crystalline; quartziferous.

बिवाई-chilblain(s).

बिस-poison.

बिसखोपड़ा-chameleon.

बिसमिल्ला-beginning.

बिसरना-to be forgotten.

बिसहा-a dog having 20 nails (supposed to be mad).

बिसात-capacity; board for displaying goods for playing chess etc.

बिसातख़ाना-general merchandise; haberdashery/drapery.

बिसाती-general merchant; haberdasher/draper.

बिसायँध-stench.

बिसारना-to forget.

बिसूरना-to sob/wail.

बिस्कुट-biscuit.

बिस्तर-bedding.

बिस्तरबंद-holdall.

बिस्वा-a measure of land; one-twentieth of a

बिहान-dawn; day-break.

बिहार-an Indian state.

बिहिश्त-paradise.

बिही-quince; smallish guava.

बींधना-to bore/perforate.

बी-wife.

बीघा-a measure of land; five-eighth of an acre.

बीच-centre; middle part.

बीच, के amidst; between.

बीच-बचाव-mediation.

बीचोबीच, के exactly or just in the middle or midway.

बीछी-female scorpion.

बीज-seed; the cause or beginning of something.

बीजक-invoice.

बीजगणित-Algebra.

बीजगणितीय-algebraic; algebraical.

बीजमंत्र-basic ; compendious formula.

बीजारोपण-sowing (seeds).

बीजी-weasel; mongoose.

बीट-bird droppings.

बीड़ा-seasoned and folded betel leaf; prepared for being taken.

बीड़ी-Indian substitute for cigarette with tobacco rolled in spl. kinds of leaves.

बीतना-to pass; to be spent; to elapse.

बीन-a classical Indian strin-ged instrument; snakecharmer's flute.

बीनना-to pick up/select/choose.

बीनाई-vision; eyesight.

बीबी-lady; elder sister; wife.

बीभत्स-horrid; loathsome; abhorrent; frightful; hideous.

बीभत्सता-horridness; loathsomeness; frightfulness.

बीम-beam.

बीमा-insurance.

बीमाकर्ता-insurer.

बीमाकृत-insured.

बीमार-sick; ill.

बीमारी-disease; illness; sickness.

बीया-seed.

बीर-bold; brave; undaunted; intrepid.

बीरन-brother.

बीर-बहूटी-velvety; insect; lady-cow; lady-fly.

बीवी-wife.

बीसी-set of twenty.

बीहड़-rough and rugged; hazardous; difficult to do; arduous.

बुँदकी-dot.

बुंदा-ear-top.

बुँदिया-a small globular Indian sweet.

बुंदीदार-dotted; spotted.

बुंदेलखंड-an area of North India.

बुंदेला-subcaste among .

बुंदेली-dialect of .

बुआ-father's sister.

बुकचा-bundle (usually of clothes).

बुकनी-powder.

बुक्का-pulverized mica.

बुख़ार-fever; irritation.
बुच्ची दाढ़ी-a sharp pointed beard.
बुज़दिल-coward.
बुजुर्ग-venerable; an elderly (person).
बुजुर्गी-elderliness; old age; seniority.
बुझना-to be extinguished; to be quenched; slaked.
बुझाना-to extinguish; to put out (fire, flame etc.); to slake.
बुड़बुड़ाना-to mutter.
बुड़भस-dotage; senility.
बुड्ढा-old; aged; old man.
बुढ़ाना-to get/grew old.
बुढ़ापा-the latter part of the life; old age.
बुढ़िया-old woman.
बुत-dump and motionless.-icon; idol.
बुतख़ाना-temple with an idol.
बुतपरस्त-idolater.
बुतपरस्ती-idolatry.
बुतशिकन-iconoclast.
बुताना-to quench.
बुताम-button.
बुत्ता-dodge.
बुदबुदाना-to effervesce/bubble; to be bubbling; to mumble.
बुदबुदाहट-effervescence.
बुद्ध-awakened; enlightened; scholarly; Lord Buddha.
बुद्धत्व-state of being
बुद्धि-intelligence; wisdom; sense; wit; knowledge.
बुद्धिकौशल-feat of wisdom.
बुद्धिगम्य-that can be discerned by mind; discernible.
बुद्धिजीवी-an intellectual.
बुद्बिल-intellectual power.
बुद्धिभ्रंश-dementia.
बुद्धिमत्ता-wisdom; intelligence.
बुद्धिमत्तापूर्ण-wise.
बुद्धिमत्तापूर्वक wisely; intelligently.
बुद्धिमानी-wisdom; an act of wisdom; sagacity; prudence.
बुद्धिरहित-void of sagacity; senseless.
बुद्धिवर्ग-intellectual class.
बुद्धिवाद-intellectualism; rationalism.
बुद्धिवादी-intellectual.
बुद्धिविभ्रम-fix; being in two minds; predicament.
बुद्धिहत-void of sagacity; senseless; upset.
बुद्धिहीन-void of sagacity; senseless; stupid; foolish.
बुद्धू-simpleton; dullard.
बुध-Wednesday; Mercury (planet).
बुधजन-scholarly people; the wise; learned.
बुधवार-Wednesday.
बुनकर-weaver.
बुनना-to knit; to weave.

बुनवाई-act of knitting/weaving; charges paid for knitting; weaving.

बुनवाना-causative of knitting.

बुनाई-texture; charges paid for knitting/weaving.

बुनावट-texture.

बुनियाद-foundation; basis.

बुनियादी-basic; serving as a foundation.

बुनियादी ढाँचा-infrastructure.

बुभुक्षा-hunger; appetite.

बुभुक्षित-hungry.

बुर-female genital organ.

बुरकना-to spray/sprinkle.

बुरक़ा-veil.

बुरक़ापोश-veiled; covered by veil.

बुरकी-enchanted dust.

बुरबक-senile.

बुरा-bad; untoward; harmful; faulty; evil.

बुराई-defect; flaw; evil; vice; discredit; bad name.

बुरादा-saw-dust.

बुरा-भला-good side and bad.

बुरुश-brush.

बुर्ज-bastion; turret; tower.

बुर्जी-*fem.* of turret.

बुर्जुआ-bourgeois.

बुर्दाफ़रोश-slave-dealer.

बुर्राक़-very bright.

बुलंद-lofty; loud.

बुलंदी-loftiness; height.

बुलडाग-bulldog.

बुलबुल-nightingale.

बुलबुला-bubble; transitory thing; unrealistic scheme.

बुलवाना-to send for; to make one speak.

बुलाक़-nose-pendant.

बुलाना-to call; to invite; to convene.

बुलावा-call; invitation.

बुलाहट-call.

बुलेटिन-bulletin.

बुसना-to become stale.

बुहारना-to sweep.

बुहारी-broom.

बूँद-drop.

बूँदा-बाँदी-rain-dropping; drizzling.

बू-foul smell.

बूआ-father's sister.

बूकना-to powder.

बूचड़-butcher.

बूचड़ख़ाना-slaughter-house.

बूचा-maimed; mutilated.

बूझ-faculty of guessing the future or factuality correctly; comprehension.

बूझना-to infer/guess correctly; to pose a riddle for solution.

बूट-boot.

बूटा-plant; design (usually on cloth).

बूटी-herb; design; pip (on a playing card).

बूटेदार-embroidered or printed cloth.

बूढ़ा-aged; old; an old man.

बूढ़ी-old woman.

बूता-capacity; to do; hold or contain something.

बू-बास-smell; characteristics.

बूरा-unrefined sugar.

बृहत्-great; greater.

बृहत्तर-greater.

बृहद्-large.

बृहस्पति-Jupiter; Thursday.

बेंच-bench.

बेंट-handle (of knife etc.).

बेंत-cane.

बे without; lacking; void.

बेअक्ल-void of wisdom; foolish; idiot; stupid.

बेअक्ली-lack of wisdom; foolishness.

बेअदब-lacking in proper respect; impertinent.

बेआब-lustreless; dull; dim.

बेआबरू-dishonoured.

बेइंतिहा-endless; without end.

बेइंसाफ़-unjust.

बेइंसाफ़ी-lack of justice; injustice.

बेइज़्ज़त-dishonoured; disgraced.

बेइज़्ज़ती-dishonour; ignominy.

बेईमान-dishonest; corrupt; fraudulent; insincere.

बेईमानी-dishonesty; deceitfulness; fraud.

बेउसूल-unprincipled.

बेएतबार-mistrusted; disingenuous.

बेएब-faultless; flawless.

बेऔलाद-issueless; childless.

बेक़द्र-unappreciative.

बेक़द्री-non-appreciation; lack of appreciation; disrespect.

बेक़रार-disconsolate; uneasy; restless.

बेक़रारी-discomfiture; disquiet; uneasiness.

बेकस-helpless.

बेकसी-helplessness.

बेक़सूर-guiltless; innocent.

बेकहा-not amenable to advice.

बेक़ाबू-uncontrollable.

बेकाम-idle; good for nothing; ineffectual; unemployed (person); having no practical use; unserviceable.

बेक़ायदा-irregular; improper; unmannerly; unlawful; illegal.

बेक़ायदे-irregularly; improperly; unmannerly.

बेकार-good-for-nothing; hopeless; useless; worthless; unemployed.

बेकारी-employment.

बेखटक-without apprehension; freely.

बेखटके-without hitch or apprehension; unhesitatingly.

बेख़बर-oblivious; unwary; heedless; uninformed; unaware.

बेख़ुदी-selflessness.

बेख़ौफ-fearless; dauntless. fearlessly.

बेग-bag.

बेगम-queen.

बेग़म-having no sorrow.

बेग़मी-of or pertaining to the queen.

बेगाना-not belonging or related to oneself; outsider; stranger.

बेगार-forced or involuntary labour; careless work.

बेगारी-forced labour.

बेगुनाह-guiltless; innocent; faultless. -an innocent person.

बेग़ैरत-lost to all sense of shame; shameless.

बेघर-homeless; without home and hearth.

बेचना-to sell/dispose.

बेचान-endorsement; sale.

बेचारा-helpless; poor.

बेचैन-listless; restless; uneasy.

बेचैनी-listlessness; restlessness; uneasiness; unrest.

बेज़बान-unable to speak; mute; voluntarily silent.

बेजा-improper; unfair; unjust.

बेज़ाब्ता-contrary to the rule of law.

बेज़ार-fed up; tired.

बेजोड़-without joints; matchless; ideal; unique.

बेटा-son.

बेटिकट-without ticket.

बेटी-daughter.

बेठन-wrapper; covering.

बेठिकाने at a wrong place.

बेड़ा-fleet; raft.

बेड़ी-boat; fetters; shackles.

बेडे horizontally.

बेडौल-disproportionate; not symmetrical; ugly; clumsy.

बेढंगा-uncouth; rough and shaggy; non-systematic; non-methodical.

बेढब-deformed; uncanny; odd sort of.

बेतकल्लुफ़-observing no formality; informal.

बेतरतीब-unsystematic; unmethodical.

बेतरह unmethodically; beyond limits.

बेतहाशा at breakneck speed; recklessly; wildly.

बेताब-uneasy.

बेताबी-uneasiness.

बेतार-wireless.

बेताल-out of tune; ghost.

बेतुका-unrhymed; absurd; grotesque; incongruous; irrelevant; bizarre; pointless.

बेतुकापन-absurdity; pointlessness.

बेदख़ल-ejected; dispossessed.

बेदख़ली-ejectment; dispossession.

बेदम-breathless; totally exhausted.

बेदर्द-hard-hearted; heartless; merciless; harsh; cruel.

बेदर्दी-mercilessness, hard-heartedness.

बेदाग़-spotless; stainless.

बेदाना-without seeds.

बेदिल-heartless; unkind.

बेदिली-half-heartedness.

बेध-hole.

बेधड़क without hitch or hesitation; dauntlessly; fearlessly.

बेधना-to pierce a hole into.

बेनज़ीर-without precedent; unprecedented.

बेनाग़ा without any absence/gap; continuously.

बेनाम-without name; nameless.

बेनामी-in another's name; .

बेपनाह-without shelter/support; shelterless.

बेपर-without feathers/wings.

बेपरदगी-state of being feathers.

बेपरदा-unveiled; uncovered; exposed.

बेपरवाह-careless; indifferent.

बेपरवाही-carelessness; indifference.

बेपेंदा-bottomless.

बेफ़ायदा-without any gain/profit; fruitless; useless.

बेफ़िकरा-carefree; without worry.

बेफ़िकरी-carelessness.

बेफ़िक्र-careless; carefree; happy-go-lucky.

बेबस-helpless.

बेबसी-helplessness; subjugation.

बेबाक-fully paid up; cleared off.

बेबुनियाद-baseless; unfounded; groundless.

बेभाव-unbounded; unlimited.

बेमज़ा-tasteless; not entertaining; insipid.

बेमतलब-pointless; meaningless. in vain; without purpose.

बेमन-uninterested; unwilling.

बेमानी-meaningless; having no meaning.

बेमिसाल-unparalleled; unique; marvellous.

बेमुरव्वत-not caring about someone's feelings; inconsiderate.

बेमेल-incongruous; odd.

बेमौका-inopportune.

बेमौक़े at a wrong occasion.

बेमौसमी-unseasonable; off-season.

बेरंग-lack-lustre.

बेर-jujube.

बेरहम-merciless; ruthless; heartless; cruel.

बेरहमी-cruelty; ruthlessness.

बेरी-jujube tree.

बेरी-बेरी-beri beri (a disease).

बेरुख़-indifferent.

बेरुख़ी-indifference; neglect.

बेरोक-unobstructed; unhindered. unhampered.

बेरोक-टोक without any hitch or hindrance; without any obstruction.

बेरोज़गार-unemployed.

बेरोज़गारी-unemployment.

बेरौनक़-lack-lustre; dull.

बेल-wood-apple; creeper.

बेलगाम-unbridled.

बेलचा-shovel.

बेलदार-manual labourer; digger.

बेलदारी-job of a labourer.

बेलन-rolling pin; cylinder; roller.

बेलना-to roll (kneaded flour into flat cakes).

बेल-बूटा-embroidery.

बेला-a kind of jasmine; time; period of time; wave; seashore; a variety of stringed instrument.

बेलाग-straight-forward; frank; impartial; detached; evident.

बेलिहाज़-having no regard and consideration.

बेली-bailee; friend; companion.

बेलौस-upright and selfless.

बेवक़ूफ़-foolish; stupid; idiot.

बेवक़ूफ़ी-foolishness; stupidity.

बेवक़्त untimely.

बेवजह without any reason.

बेवफ़ा-disloyal; faithless.

बेवफ़ाई-disloyalty; faithlessness.

बेवा-widow.

बेवाई-chilblain.

बेशऊर-unmannerly; tactless; stupid.

बेशऊरी-tactlessness; unmannerliness; stupidity.

बेशक-of course; indeed; definitely; surely; certainly; undoubtedly; without doubt.

बेशक़ीमत-precious; costly; very useful or important; valuable.

बेशक़ीमती-of great value.

बेशर्म-shameless.

बेशर्मी-shamelessness.

बेशुमार-countless; innumerable; numberless; plenty.

बेसन-gram flour; pulverised gram.

बेसनी-cake made of gram flour.

बेसबब-without cause.

बेसबरा-impatient.

बेसबरी-impatience.

बेसमझ-devoid of sense; silly; senseless.

बेसमझी-silliness; senseless.

बेसलीक़ा-mannerless; unmannerly; rude; impolite.

बेसहारा-helpless; without support/shelter.

बेसाख़्ता-involuntarily; inadvertently.

बेसिर-having no basis; illogical.

बेसिलसिले-without due order; disorderly; desultory.

बेसी-much; more; excessive.

बेसुध-unconscious; absent-minded.

बेसुधी-unconsciousness; absent-mindedness.

बेसुरा-discordant; out of tune.

बेस्वाद-tasteless; insipid.

बेहतर-better.

बेहतरी-betterment.

बेहद-excessive. excessively.

बेहन-seedling.

बेहया-shameless; obstinately; shameless.

बेहायाई-shamelessness.

बेहाथ out of hands.

बेहाल-afflicted; distressed.

बेहिसाब-incalculable. incalculably.

बेहुनर-artless; unskilled.

बेहूदगी-smuttiness; obscenity.

बेहूदा-smutty; obscene or offensive; absurd.

बेहूदापन-smuttiness; obscenity; absurdity.

बेहोश-fainted; unconscious.

बेहोशी-unconsciousness.

बैंक-bank.

बैंकर-banker.

बैंगन-eggplant; brinjal; aubergine.

बैंगनी-purple; a fried dish of brinjal slices and gram flour.

बैंड-band.

बैकुंठ-paradise.

बैज-badge.

बैट-bat (cricket).

बैटरी-battery.

बैठक-sitting/drawing room; parlour; sitting; an Indian athletic; posture.

बैकठबाज़- associative/companionable; habituated to gossiping; tricky (fellow); sharper.

बैठका-spacious sitting room.

बैठकी-a parlour.

बैठकी हड़ताल-sit-down strike.

बैठना-to sit; to take a seat; to appear.

बैठाना-to seat; to set (fracture of a bone etc.).

बैठे-ठाले

बैठे-बैठाए unexpectedly; without any warning.

बैताल-evil spirit; goblin.

बैनामा-sale-deed.

बैरंग-bearing.

बैर-enmity; hostility; ill-will.

बैरक-barrack.

बैरा-bearer (in a hotel).

बैराग-detachment from world by affairs; renunciation.

बैरागी-one who has renounced all; recluse.

बैरिस्टर-barrister-at-law.

बैरिस्टरी-work or profession of a barrister-at-law.

बैरी-an enemy.

बैरोमीटर-barometer.

बैल-bullock.

बैसाख-second month of the Hindu calendar.

बैसाखनन्दन-ass.

बैसाखी-crutches; festival observed in the month of

बोआई-act or process of sowing; wages paid for sowing.

बोआना-causative of sowing.

बोका-foolish.

बोगदा-tunnel.

बोझ-load; burden.

बोझा-load.

बोझिल-loaded; heavy; burdensome.

बोटी-slice of flesh.

बोड़ा-a kind of Indian bean.

बोतल-bottle.

बोदा-dull-headed; stupid; timid.

बोदापन-stupidity; dull-headedness; timidity.

बोध-perception;sense;enlightenment.

बोधक-indicating; (one) who imparts knowledge; signifying.

बोधगम्य-intelligible; understandable.

बोनसाई-potted dwarf tree.

बोना-to sow.

बोरना-to drown; to sink; to calumniate; to mix.

बोरसी-earthen firepot.

बोरा-sack; bag; burlap.

बोराबंदी-preparing bagfuls of grain.

बोरिया-small sack/bag; mat.

बोरिया-बिस्तर-bag and baggage; lock; stock and barrel.

बोरी-small sack/bag.

बोर्जुआ-relating to the middle class; bourgeois; a capitalist.

बोर्ड-board.

बोल-utterance.

बोल-चाल-colloquial parlance.

बोलता सिनेमा-talkie.

बोलती-power of speech.

बोलना-to speak.

बोलना-चालना-to converse; speaker.

बोलबाला-sway.

बोली-dialect; bid; sarcastic remark.

बोहनी-the first cash sale of the day (which is considered auspicious).

बोहनी-बट्टा-(first) sale transaction of the day.

बौखलाना-to speak too loudly and angrily.

बौखलाहट-state of shocked.

बौछार-shower; volley.

बौड़म-mad cap; stupid.

बौड़मता-stupidity.

बौद्ध-pertaining to Buddhism.

बौद्धिक-of person's power of reasoning; intellectual.

बौना-dwarfish; dwarf.

बौर-blossom.

बौरा-crazy.

बौराना-to go off one's head; to become crazy.

ब्याज-interest.

ब्याजख़ोर-usurer.

ब्याजख़ोरी-usury.

ब्याज-मुक्त-interest-free.

ब्यान-delivery (only in relation to animals).

ब्याना-to give birth to (said of an animal).

ब्यालू-dinner.

ब्याह-marriage; wedding.

ब्याहता-married (woman).

ब्याहना-to wed/marry.

ब्योंत-planning.

ब्योंतना-to cut the cloth as per measurement.

ब्योरा-description; details.

ब्योरेवार in details.

ब्रज-the land in the vicinity of the modern city of , where Lord passed his childhood days.

ब्रह्म-the eternal spirit; the voice of conscience.

ब्रह्मचर्य-celibacy.

ब्रह्मचारी-celibate.

ब्रह्मज्ञान-knowledge of the Supreme.

ब्रह्मतेज-divine radiance.

ब्रह्मभोज-collective feeding (of Brahmins or ascetics).

ब्रह्मरेखा-line of fate (on forehead).

ब्रह्मर्षि-seer of the spiritual reality.

ब्रह्मलेख-line of fate (which is ineffaceable).

ब्रह्मविद्या-knowledge divine.

ब्रह्मांड-universe; cosmos.

ब्रह्मांडीय-cosmic.

ब्रह्मा-Lord ; the creator/ .

ब्राह्म-of or pertaining to .

ब्राह्मण-Brahmin; the first caste among the Hindus.

ब्राह्मणत्व-Brahman-hood.

ब्राह्मणी-wife of a Brahman; woman of Brahman caste.

ब्राह्मी-a medicinal herb; an ancient Hindu script from which most of the Indian scripts are believed to be evolved.

भ-The twenty-fourth consonant of the Devnagari alphabet, it is the fourth letter of the labial or class.

भंकार-a horrible sound.

भंग-dissolution; breach; disbandment; breaking up; breakage; fracture.-an intoxicating herb.

भंगड़ा-typical folk dance.

भँगना-to be broken; to be pressed; to acknowledge defeat.

भंगराज-a kind of blackbird.

भंगार-a deep pit in which rain water gathers; straw; refuse.

भंगिमा-pose; posture.

भंगी-scavenger; swee-per.

भंगुर-breakbale; destructible; crooked; perishable; fragile.

भंगेड़ी-one who habitually takes

भंग्य-breakable.

भंजक-(one) who breaks/destroys.

भंजत-breaking; discount on changing money.

भंजन-demolition; breaking; destruction.

भँजना-to be broken into pieces; to break; to be changed into smallar coins; to be twisted or folded several times; to be divied.

भंजना-to break.

भँजाई-act or state of breaking or charges paid for the same.

भँजाना-to have a big coin changed into smaller ones; to cause to break or twist.

भंटा-aubergine; brinjal; eggplant.

भंडन-deception; wickedness; armour; war; battle.

भँड़साल-utensil-store.

भंडसाली-one having a store-house.

भंडा-secret; earthen-pot.

भंडाना-to ruin; to destroy; to frolic; to make disturbance; to prank; to devastate.

भंडाफोड़-exposure/disclosure (of someone's secrets).

भंडार-stock; store; depot.

भंडार-घर-store-house.

भंडारा-community; feast; the feast open to all.

भंडारी-cook; store-keeper; steward.

भँडैती-buffoonery.

भँभीरी-a butterfly; a dragon fly; a child's top.

भँवर-whirlpool.

भँवरा-blackbee.

भइया-brother.

भक-sound produced by a sudden outburst into a flame.

भक-भक-repeated sound of the (railway) engine.

भकभकाना-to glow intermittently with a noise; to fret and fume.

भकुआ-fumbler; tom-fool.

भकुआना-to fumble.

भकोसू-one who takes big morsels; grabber (of big chunks).

भक्त-devotee.

भक्तराज-prince among devotees.

भक्तवत्सल-fondly affectionate towards devotees.

भक्त-शिरोमणि-jewel/gem among devotees.

भक्ति-devotion.

भक्तिमार्ग-path of devotion.

भक्षक-devourer.

भक्षण-devouring.

भक्षणीय-eatable.

भक्षना-to eat; to devour; to eat up.

भक्षित-eaten; devoured; eaten up.

भक्षी-eater.

भक्ष्य-edible; eatable.

भक्ष्याभक्ष्य-edible and inedible.

भगंदर-fistula in the anus.

भग-vulva.

भगत-devotee.

भगतिन-woman devotee.

भगदड़-sudden rush of frightened people or animals; stampede; panic.

भगल-swindling; stratagem.

भगवत्-God.

भगवती-goddess.

भगवा-saffron-coloured.

भगवाकरण-saffronisation.

भगवान-God.

भगाना-to cause to run away; to drive off; to dispel.

भगिनी-sister.

भगीरथ-an ancient Indian king who brought to the earth.

भगीरथ-प्रयत्न-Herculean or heroic effort.

भगीरथ-सुता-river .

भगोड़ा-absconder; fugitive; truant; coward; shirker.

भग्गू-(person) who shirks, coward.

भग्न-broken; interrupted.

भग्नावशेष-ruins; debris; remains.

भचक-limp.

भचकना-to limp.

भजन-hymn; devotional song; prayer.

भजन-पूजन-worshipping and reciting of hymns.

भजन-भाव-spirit of devotion.

भजना-to repeat God's name with a devotional attitude.

भजनानंदी-one who enjoys singing hymns.

भजनावली-hymnal; hymn book.

भजनीक-a singer of hymns.

भजनीय-one whose name is worthy of being repeated; worth propitiation.

भट-the soy bean.

भटई-the occupation or the verse of a bard; flattery; false praise.

भटकना-to go astray; to stroll; to wander about.

भटकाना-to mislead; causative of wandering.

भटकाव-the state of being off the track.

भटियारख़ाना-abode of a inn-keeper; centre of noise and tumult; rendezvous of vulgar people.

भटियारा-inn-keeper (of a low order).

भटियारिन-wife of an inn-keeper; (woman) inn-keeper.

भट्ट-a sub-caste among Brahmins.

भट्ठा-a brick kiln; a large furnace or oven.

भट्ठी-big oven; fireplace; furnace; distillery; liquor shop; wine-shop.

भठियारा-inn-keeper.

भड़कदार-gaudy; splendid; glittering; shinning.

भड़कना-to flare up; to get enraged/provoked.

भड़काऊ-provocative.

भड़काना-to excite; to incite.

भड़कीला-ostentatious; gaudy; cheap; showy; tawdry; causing excitement.

भड़कीलापन-ostentation; tawdriness; gaudiness.

भड़भड़-dull thudding sound; discordant or tumultuous noise.

भड़भड़िया-prattler; one who can't retain a secret.

भड़भूँजा-parcher.

भड़साईं-parcher's oven.

भड़ास-pent-up feeling.

भडुआ-a musician companion of a dancing girl; broker of a prostitute; pimp; pander.

भणित-(that which is) said/uttered.

भतार-husband.

भतीजा-brother's son; nephew.

भतीजी-brother's daughter; niece.

भत्ता-allowance.

भदंत-revered; adored.

भद्द-ridicule; humiliation.

भद्दा-awkward; clumsy; uncouth; vulgar; dirty.

भद्दापन-ugliness; awkwardness; clumsiness.

भद्र-courteous; affable.

भद्रजन-noble person; gentleman.

भद्रता-nobility; generosity; politeness.

भद्रपुरुष-gentleman.

भद्रा-evil conjunction of stars.

भद्रापद-good and evil.

भद्रे-O noble lady!

भनक-low or faint ring/sound.

भनभनाहट-hum; buzz.

भब्भड़-disorderly crowd; turmoil.

भभक-flare (of a lamp, lantern etc.); foul smell; stench.

भभकना-to flare up; to emit/come out forcefully.

भभका-foul smell; stench; flare (of a lamp, lantern etc.).

भभकी-bluff; menace; threat.

भभूका-red hot.

भभूत-sacred ashes.

भयंकर-terrible; dreadful; awful; precarious.

भयंकरता-dreadfulness.

भय-fear; dread; scare.

भयत्रस्त-terror-stricken; frightened; scared.

भयप्रद-alarming; terrifying.

भयभीत-afraid; frightened; scared; terrified.

भयातुर-afraid; alarmed.

भयादोहन-blackmail.

भयानक-terrible; dreadful; dangerous.

भयानकता-dreadfulness.

भयावना-terrifying; frightening.

भयावह-vicious; alarming; appalling.

भर-fully; only.

भरण-feeding.

भरण-पोषण-support; maintenance.

भरत-full load/capacity; name of a younger brother of Lord Ram.

भरत-वाक्य-epilogue.

भरता-mash; sustainer; husband.

भरतार-husband.

भरती-recruitment; enrolment; admission; filling.

भरना-to fill in.

भरपाई-receipt acknowledging payment in full.

भरपूर-completely full/over flowing; plentiful.

भरभराना-to crash down.

भरम-illusion; credit (in a market).

भरमना-to roam/doubt/confuse.

भरम-भाव-credit (in the market).

भरमाना-to mislead/misdirect; to delude; to perplex.

भरमार-abundant; plenteous; excessive.-abundance; plenty.

भरवाई-the act of filling or charges paid for the same.

भरवाना-to have the work of stuffing; a thing made by another; to cause to load.

भरसक to one's utmost; as far as possible; will all one' might.

भरसाई-an over for parching grain.

भरा-full; loaded; fleshy.

भराई-act or state of filling up, or charged paid for the same.

भराव-act or state of filling; filling; stuffing; saturation.

भरी-an Indian measure for weighing sold, silver etc.; approximately equal to 11 grams.

भरू-one who fill.

भरोसा-reliance; trust; hope; faith; confidence.

भर्ता-sustainer; husband; lord.

भर्त्सना-admonition; reproach; upbraiding; reprimand.

भर्राटा-dull; rattling sound.

भर्राना-to whizz.

भलमनसाहत-goodness; gentleman-less; benevolence; generosity; nobility.

भला-good; gentle; noble; pleasing.

भलाई-goodness; welfare; advantage.

भलाई-बुराई-good or bad; pros and cons.

भला-चंगा-hale and hearty; stout.

भला-बुरा-good and evil; pros and cons; reproach; upbraiding; scolding.

भलामानस-good man/person; gentleman.

भली-भाँति thoroughly.

भले good; well.

भव-entity; existence; world.

भवकूप-well of life.

भवजाल-(mesh of) worldly affairs, snares of life.

भवदीय yours; yours faithfully.

भवन-building; mansion; house; premises; palace.

भवन-निर्माण-the art and science of building; tectonics.

भवसागर-the world viewed as an ocean.

भवानी-; goddess of prowess.

भवितव्य-destined; fated.

भवितव्यता-fate; the inevitable; destiny.

भविष्य-future; future tense.

भविष्य कथन-augury.

भविष्य काल-future tense (gram.)

भविष्य ज्ञान-knowledge of the future/ foresight.

भविष्यदर्शी-seer.

भविष्यद्रष्टा-seer.

भविष्य-निधि-provident fund.

भविष्य-वक्ता-fortune-teller; prophet.

भविष्यवाणी-prediction; prophecy.

भविष्यवादी-prophet; fortune-teller.

भव्य-splendid; magnificent; grand; superb; marvellous.

भव्यता-splendour; magnificence; grandeur.

भसींड़-lotus stem.

भस्म-which has been completely burnt to ashes.

भस्मवत्-ashen.

भस्मसात्-turned/reduced to ashes.

भस्मावशेष-residue in the form of ashes.

भस्मी-ashes.

भस्मीकरण-incineration.

भस्सी-dust of lime, coal etc.

भहराना-to collapse/crash down.

भाँग-Indian intoxicating leafy drug.

भाँज-fold.

भाँजना-to fold; twist; to brandish (sword etc.).

भाँजा-sister's son.

भाँजी-interruption; impediment; complaint; sister's daughter; niece.

भांड-pot; vessel.

भाँड-jester; clown; buffoon.

भाँडा-earthen vessel; pot; to be revealed (a secret, a vice).

भांडार-stock; stock-room; godown; warehouse.

भाँति-type; design.

भाँपना-to guess; to see through; to divine.

भाँय-भाँय-sound of wind produced in a desolate place.

भाँवर-circumambulation of a matrimonial fire.

भाई-brother.

भाईचारा-fraternity; social dealings between people.

भाई-दूज-the second day of bright half of .

भाई-बंद-brother; brethren; brotherhood; kin; relations.

भाई-भतीजे-(plu.) kith and kin; relations.

भाखा-language.

भाग-part; division; luck; share; portion.

भाग-दौड़-running about; hustle and bustle.

भागना-to run; to avoid (a task).

भागनेय-the sister's son.

भागफल-quotient; result of dividing.

भाग रेखा-oblique

भागीदार-co-partner; partner.

भागीदारी-partnership; participation.

भागीरथी-Ganga.

भाग्य-fate; destiny; luck.

भाग्यलक्ष्मी-Goddess of fortune/ wealth.

भाग्यवादी-fatalistic.

भाग्यवान-lucky; fortunate.

भाग्यविधाता-controller of destiny/ fate.

भाग्यहीन-luckless; unfortunate.

भाग्याधीन-depending on fate; destined.

भाग्योदय-advent of luck.

भाजक-divisor.

भाजन-pot; vessel; receptacle; act of dividing .

भाजी-vegetable.

भाज्य-divisible.

भाट-bard.

भाटा-low tide.

भाड़-parcher's oven.

भाड़ा-fare; freight; hire.

भात-boiled rice.

भाथा-quiver; big bellows.

भाथी-bellows.

भादों-sixth month of the Hindu calendar.

भाद्रपद-the month of Hindu calendar.

भान-knowledge; consciousness.

भानजा-sister's son.

भानजी-sister's daughter.

भानमती-sorceress.

भाना-to be appealing/pleasing.

भानु-Sun.

भानुसुता-the river .

भाप-steam; vapour.

भाभी-brother's wife.

भामिनी-pretty and attractive lady; peevish woman.

भार-load; burden; responsibility.

भारत-India.

भारतमाता-Mother India.

भारतवर्ष-India.

भारतवर्षीय-Indian.

भारतवासी-an Indian.

भारतीय-Indian.

भारतीयकरण-Indianisation.

भारतीयकृत-India-nised.

भारतीयता-Indianees; Indianism.

भारमुक्त-disburdened.

भारी-heavy; hefty; huge; vast; great; over-whelming; massive/ ponderous.

भारीपन-heaviness; weightiness.

भारी-भरकम-massive; hefty; voluminous and heavy.

भारोपीय-Indo-European.

भार्या-wife.

भाल-forehead.

भालना-to look intently.

भाला-spear; lance.

भालू-bear.

भाव-existence (lit.); idea; purport; gist; sentiment; emotion; rate.

भावचित्र-ideogram; ideograph.

भावज-brother's wife.

भावना-mental attitude; sentiment; imagination.

भावनात्मक-sentimental; fanciful; emotional.

भावनामय-full of sentiment/feelings.

भावप्रधान-primarily emotional; sentimental.

भावप्रवण-emotional; sentimental.

भावप्रवणता-emotional/sentimental disposition.

भावभंगी-gesture and posture.

भाव-भीनी-steeped in emotion; hearty.

भाववाचक-(gram.) abstract.

भावविभोर-overwhelmed with emotion; steeped in emotion.

भावव्यंजक-expressive.

भावव्यंजन-expression of emotion or sentiment.

भावशून्य devoid of emotion; unemotional; expressionless.

भावशून्यता-state or quality of being expressionless.

भावहरण-plagiarism.

भावहीन-without expression.

भावातिरेक-exuberance of emotion.

भावात्मक-sentimental; emotional; positive.

भावानुवाद-free translation.

भावार्थ-substance; purport.

भावावेश-impulse (of emotion).

भावी-coming; would be; pertaining to future; predestined.

भावुक-sentimental; emotional.

भावुकता- sentimentality; thoughtfulness.

भावोत्कर्ष-exaltation of emotion/ sentiment.

भावोत्तेजक-emotive/exciting.

भावोन्मत्तत्ता-state or quality of being emotional; emotional wildness.

भाषण-speech; lecture; oration.

भाषण-स्वातंत्र्य-liberty/freedom of speech.

भाषांतर-translation.

भाषांतरकार-translator.

भाषांतरण-act of translating.

भाषा-language.

भाषाई-lingual; linguistic.

भाषाबद्ध-reduced to language.

भाषायी-linguistic.

भाषावार-linguistic.

भाषा-विज्ञान-Philology; Linguistics.

भाषा-विज्ञानी-philologist.

भाषाविद्-linguist.

भाषिक-pertaining to language; lingual; linguistic.

भाषित-spoken; said; uttered; told.

भाषी-one who speaks a language.

भाषीय-lingual; linguistic.

भाष्य-annotation; an explanatory treatise; commentary.

भाष्यकार-one who interprets/ explains or advocates; exponent; commentator.

भास-effulgence; radiance.

भासना-to glitter/sparkle/gleam; to appear; to seem.

भासमान-appearing.

भासित-appeared; seemed.

भास्कर-sun.

भास्वर-radiant; effulgent.

भिंडी-ladyfinger; okra.

भिक्षा-alms.

भिक्षाटन-wandering about for alms.

भिक्षापात्र-beggar's bowl.

भिक्षावृत्ति-mendicancy.

भिक्षु-beggar; mendicant.

भिक्षुक-mendicant; beggar.

भिखमंगी-beggarly.

भिखारिणी-lady beggar.

भिखारिन-female beggar.

भिखारी-beggar.

भिखारीपन-beg-gardom.

भिगोना-to wet; to make wet.

भिजवाना-to cause to wet; to cause to send.

भिड़ंत-grappling; encounter; confrontation; collision; bout.

भिड़-wasp.

भिड़ना-to collide; to grapple (with).

भिड़ाना-causative of grapple.

भितल्ला-lining (of a cloth).

भित्ति-wall.

भित्तिचित्र-fresco; wall painting.

भिदुर-brittle.

भिनकना-to buzz.

भिनभिन-buzzing sound.

भिनभिनाना-to buzz.

भिनभिनाहट-buzzing sound.

भिन्न-different.

भिन्नता-difference; dissimilarity.

भिन्नात्मक-fractional.

भिन्नाना-to appear indignant.

भिलावाँ-marking tree; .

भिश्ती-water-carrier; one who carries water in a leather bag.

भींजना-to get wet.

भी too; also; denoting emphasis.

भीख-alms; begging.

भीगना-to get soaked; to get wet/ drenched.

भीटा-mound.

भीड़-crowd; crush; mob; throng.

भीड़-तंत्र-mob rule; ochlocracy.

भीड़-भड़क्का-thick of a crowd.

भीड़-भाड़-thick of a crowd; multitude.

भीत-afraid; wall.

भीतर in; within; inside.

भीतर, के inside.

भीतरी-internal; inner; secret.

भीति-phobia; scare.

भीना-light and delightful.

भीनी-sweet.

भीम-huge; of very great size; gigantic.

भीमकाय-enormous in size and strength; titanic.

भीरु-fearful; timid; coward.

भीरुता-timidity; shyness.

भील-a jungle tribe of central India.

भीषण-terrible; gruesome; horrible; awful.

भीषणता-gruesomeness; awfulness.

भीषिका-panic.

भीष्म-dreadful; terrible; horrible.

भुकड़ी-mould; fungus.

भुक्खड़-famished (with hunger); gluttonous.-glutton.

भुक्तभोगी-having experience of suffering.

भुखमरा-famished; dying of starvation.

भुखमरी-collective starvation; famine.

भुगतना-to suffer; face or undergo.

भुगतान-payment; disbursement.

भुगताना-to pay up.

भुच्च-idiotic; stupid.

भुच्चड़-idiotic; stupid.

भुजंग-snake.

भुज-arm; side of a geometrical figure.

भुजपाश-arm-embrace.

भुजबंध-armlet.

भुजबल-strength of the arms; physical power; prowess.

भुजा-arm; side.

भुजाली-small dagger.

भुजिया-roasted.

भुट्ठा-ear of corn.

भुतनी-hag.

भुतहा-haunted.

भुनगा-gnat; maggot; a kind of tiny flying insect.

भुनना-to be roasted; to be changed into smaller coins.

भुनभुनाना-to fret and fume; to mutter.

भुनवाई-act or state of parching or charges paid for the same.

भुनवाना-causative of parching.

भुन्नासी-a kind of locking device.

भुरकस-pulp.

भुरभुरा-friable; crisp.

भुरभुरापन-friability; crispness.

भुलक्कड़-forgetful; absent-minded.

भुलक्कड़पन- forgetfulness; negligence.

भुलवाना-to cause to forget.

भुलाना-to forget.
भुलावा-dodge; feint; illusion.
भुवन-world.
भुवनेश्वर-Lord of the world, God.
भुस-chaff.
भुसौरा-barn.
भूँकना-to bark/yelp.
भूँजना-to parch.
भूँजा-parched gram.
भू-earth; land.
भू-अभिलेख-land records.
भूकंप-earthquake.
भुकंप पीड़ित-quake-hit.
भूखंड-an extended area; track; a piece of land; plot.
भूख-appetite; hunger.
भूख-हड़ताल-hunger-strike.
भूखा-hungry.
भूगर्भ-interior/bowels of the earth.
भूगोल-Geography.
भूचाल-earthquake.
भूटान-Bhutan, a country to the north-east of India.
भूटानी-pertaining to Bhutan; the inhabitant of Bhutan; the language of Bhutan.
भूडोल-earthquake.
भूत-past; ghost; relevant.
भूतकाल-past tense.
भूतकालिक-pertaining to the past.
भूतकृदंत-past participle.
भूतनी-female ghost.
भूतपूर्व-pristine; ex-; former.
भूत-प्रेत-evil spirits.
भूत-बाधा-influence of evil spirit.
भूतल-surface of the earth; this world.
भूदान-gift of land.
भूदान-यज्ञ-donation of land as a religious act.
भूदानी-one who donates his land.
भूदेव-Brahmin.
भूधर-mountain.
भूनना-to roast/parch.
भूप-king; monarch.
भूभल-hot ash.
भूभाग-territory.
भूमंडल-globe.
भूमध्य रेखा-equator.
भूमध्य सागर-Mediterranean Sea.
भूमि-land; soil; ground.
भूमिका-introduction; preamble; prelude; preface; role; part.
भूमिगत-underground; acting in secret.
भूमिधर-a farmer who owns his own land.
भूरा-brown.
भूराजस्व-land revenue.
भूरापन-the quality, colour etc. of being brown.
भूरि-very much.

भूरेल-underground railway; subway.

भूल-mistake; error; slip.

भूल-चूक-errors and omissions.

भूलना-to forget.

भूल-भुलैया-labyrinth.

भूल-सुधार-correction of an error; rectification of a mistake.

भूला-बिसरा-forgotten through a lapse of memory.

भूला-भटका-stra-yed.

भूलोक-earth; region mundane.

भूविज्ञान-Earth Science; Geology.

भूशय्या-earth used as a bed.

भूशायी-(one) whose bed is earth, lying on the ground.

भूषण-ornament; ornamentation; decoration; embellishment.

भूषणीय-worthy of decoration.

भूषित-ornamented; decorated; embellished.

भूसंपति-estate.

भूसा-husk; hay.

भूसी-husk.

भूस्खलन-landslide.

भूस्वामी-landlord.

भृंग-black bee.

भृकुटी-eyebrow.

भृत-servant.

भृति-service; salary.

भेंगा-squint-eyed.

भेंट-gift; present; meeting.

भेंटना-to meet; to embrace.

भेंटवार्ता-interview.

भेंटस्वरूप-by way of a gift/present.

भेजना-to send; to despatch.

भेजवाना-to cause to send.

भेजा-brain.

भेड़-sheep.

भेड़-चाल-tendency to follow unthinkingly; mob-mentality.

भेड़ना-to shut/close.

भेड़ा-male-sheep; ram.

भेड़िया-wolf.

भेड़ी-sheep; ewe.

भेद-secret; mystery; difference; discrimination.

भेदक-piercing; intersecting; discriminative.

भेदन-act of piercing; intersection.

भेदना-to pierce.

भेदबुद्धि-discriminating power; faculty of discrimination.

भेदभाव-the feeling of difference; discrimination.

भेदित-pierced.

भेदिया-one who knows the secret of others; spy; confident.

भेदी-piercing; one who knows the secret.

भेद्य-pierceable; permeable; vulnerable.

भेरी-siren; drum.

भेला-lump.

भेली-a lump of molasses.

भेष-an assumed appearance.

भेषज-drug.

भेस-dress; garb; guise.

भैंस-buffalo.

भैंसा-male-buffalo.

भैंया-brother.

भैया-दूज-a Hindu festival falling on the second day of the bright fortnight of on which the brother takes a pledge to protect the honour of his sister.

भैरव-one of the melodies of Indian music; Lord .

भैरवी-one of the morning melodies of Indian music.

भैषजिकी-Pharmacy.

भोंकना-to thrust/stab/pierce.

भोंडा-clumsy; odd; awkward.

भोंडापन-clumsiness.

भोंदू-dullard; stupid.

भोंदूपन-dullardness; stupidity.

भोंपू-siren; horn.

भोंभों-the sound of the barking of dogs.

भोक्ता-consumer; one who uses/utilises.

भोग-enjoyment; suffering; pain; offering; easement.

भोगकाल-duration.

भोगना-to pay for; to suffer; to enjoy.

भोगबंधक-mortgage with possession.

भोगलिप्सा-sensuous enjoyment.

भोगवाना-causative of भ to cause to suffer.

भोगविलास-indulgence in luxury.

भोगाधिकार-right of occupancy; right of easement.

भोगी-enjoyer.

भोग्य-worth consuming/using; worth enjoying.

भोज-feast; community dinner; banquet.

भोजन-food; meal; diet.

भोजन-कक्ष-a room where meals are eaten/served; dining room.

भोजन-नलिका-food-pipe; gullet.

भोजनभट्ट-one who eats too much; gourmand; glutton.

भोजनयान-a railway coach used as a dinning room; dining car.

भोजन-वस्त्र-food and clothing.

भोजनालय-restaurant; eating-house; mess.

भोजपुरी-a dialect of spoken in Eastern U.P. and Western.
भोजी-eater.
भोज्य-eatable; edible.
भोट-the country of Bhutan.
भोटिया-(an inhabitant) of or pertaining to Bhutan.
भोथरा-obtuse; blunt; dull.
भोथरापन-obtuseness; bluntness.
भोर-morning; early morning; dawn.
भोला-simple and artless; simple-hearted.
भोलापन-simplicity and artlessness.
भोला-भाला-gullible; naive; very simple; ingenuous.
भोलेनाथ-Lord
भौं-eyebrow.
भौंकना-to bark; yelp; to howl (pej.).
भौंरा-blackbee; beetle.
भौंरी-female blackbee.
भौंह-eyebrow.
भौगोलिक-geographical.
भौगोलिकी-gazetteer.
भौचक-astonished.
भौजाई-elder brother's wife.
भौजी-elder brother's wife.
भौतिक-material; physical; mundane.
भौतिकवाद-materialism.
भौतिकवादिता-materialistic tendency.
भौतिकवादी-materialistic.
भौतिकी-physics.
भौमिकी-Geology.
भ्रंश-fall; ruin; destruction; sabotage; breach.
भ्रकुटि-eyebrow.
भ्रम-illusion; fallacy; misunderstanding; misconception; confusion.
भ्रमजनक-illusive; illusory.
भ्रमजाल-snares of illusion; worldly affairs.
भ्रमण-roaming; travelling (widely).
भ्रमणकारी-(one) who moves about; traveller; nomad.
भ्रमणशील-roving; rambling.
भ्रममूलक-illusory; misleading.
भ्रमर-blackbee.
भ्रमरी-female of blackbee.
भ्रमात्मक-illusory.
भ्रमित-illusioned; mistaken; confused.
भ्रमोत्पादक-misleading; illusory.
भ्रमोत्पादकता-illusoriness.
भ्रष्ट-corrupt; deprave; immoral.
भ्रष्टता-corruptness; corruption; depravity.
भ्रष्टाचार-corruption.
भ्रांत-mislead; mistaken.
भ्रांति-illusion; confusion.
भ्रांतिकर-deceptive; misleading; confusing.
भ्रांतिजनक-confusing; illusory.

भ्रांतिमूलक-confusing; illusory; illusive; misleading.

भ्राता-brother.

भ्रातृ-brother.

भ्रातृभाव-feeling of brotherhood; fraternity.

भ्रातृ-स्नेह-brotherly affection.

भ्रातृ-हत्या-fratricide.

भ्रात्रीय-fraternal.

भ्रामक-confusing; illusive.

भ्रू-eyebrow; pleasing movement of the eyebrow.

भ्रूण-foetus; embryo.

भ्रूणहत्या-foeticide.

भ्रूभंगिमा-the movement of the eyebrow, specially fascinating.

म

म-The twenty-fifth consonant of the or Sanskrit alphabet, it is the fifth letter of the labial or **पवर्ग** class.

मंग-the head (of a boat).

मंगत-begger.

मँगता-beggar.

मँगनी-espousal; betrothal; loan.

मंगरा-(Bihar) redging-tiles(s) (on a roof).

मंगल-Tuesday; Mars; welfare; auspicious.

मंगलकलश-a jar filled with water which is placed for worship on an auspicous occasion.

मंगलकारक-auspicious.

मंगलकारी-auspicious.

मंगलगान-song sung on ceremonial occasions.

मंगलग्रह-Mars.

मंगलघट-suspicious pitcher of water.

मंगलपाठ-

मंगलप्रद-auspicious; benedictory.

मंगलभाषण-euphemism.

मंगलभाषित-euphemistic.

मंगलवार-Tuesday.

मंगलसूत्र-the thread wrapped round the right wrist as an embled of a god's gift.

मंगलस्नान-bathing with the idea of gaining bliss.

मंगला-name of.

मंगलाचरण-prologue; invocatory/ benedictory.

मंगलामुखी-prostitute; harlot.

मंगली-born under the influence planet Mars.

मंगलोत्सव-festivity.

मँगवाना-to be brought by someone; to cause to be sent for.

मँगाना-to ask for; to send for.

मँगेतर-fiance.

मंगोल-a tribe of Central Asia.

मंच-stage; dais; podium; platform; stadium; forum.

मंचन-way of presenting a play on the stage; staging.

मंच-संकोच-stage shyness.

मंचीय-of or pertaining to the stage.

मंजन-tooth-powder.

मँजना-to get proficient/seasoned.

मंजरी-sprout.

मँजवाना-to cause to be cleansed.

मँजाई-cleansing or polishing or remuneration paid for the same.

मँजा-मँजाया-perfectly proficient.

मंजिल-storey; floor; destination.

मंजीर-anklet.

मँजीरा-a kind of cymbal.

मंजु-beautiful; pretty.

मंजुल-beautiful; pretty.

मंजुलता-beauty; prettiness.

मंजूर-approved; accepted; granted; sanctioned.

मंजूरी-acceptance; sanction.

मंजूषा-casket.

मँझधार-midstream.

मंझा-cot.

मंड-starch.

मंडन-embellishing; corroboration; support.

मंडना-to embellish/decorate; to corroborate.

मंडनात्मक-corroborative; supporting.

मंडनीय-worth corroboration; supportable.

मंडप-pavilion.

मँडराना-to hover.

मंडल-circle; halo; ring; zone; commissionary; monastery.

मंडलाकार-circular; ring-shaped.

मंडलाधिकारी-zonal officer.

मंडलायुक्त-the head of a commissionary; commissioner.

मंडली-party; team; society; association; club.

मंडलीय-pertaining to a zone; zonal.

मंडलेश्वर-head of a monastery.

मँडवा-a frame; arbour.

मंडित-adorned; embellished; decorated.

मंडी-market place; town or trade centre for specified commodities; wholesale market; bazaar.

मँडुआ-pavilion; mobile theatre.

मंडूक-frog.

मंतव्य-objective; intent.

मंत्र-hymn; any sacred verse; incantation; spell; charm; verse; esoteric formula.

मंत्रकार-composer of.

मंत्रज्ञ-one who is versed in .

मंत्रण-act of counselling/advising.

मंत्रणा-counsel; advice; deliberation.

मंत्रणाकार-counsellor; adviser.

मंत्रणा-परिषद-advisory council.

मंत्रद्रष्टा-prophet; seer.

मंत्रपाठ-recitation of .

मंत्रबल-power of

मंत्रमुग्ध-enchanted; spellbound.

मंत्रशक्ति-power of *mantra.*

मंत्रसिद्धि-power to obtain success through *mantra.*

मंत्रालय-ministry.

मंत्रित-consecrated by .

मंत्रित्व-ministership.

मंत्रि-परिषद-ministry.

मंत्रिमंडल-cabinet.

मंत्री-minister; secretary.

मंथन-churning; contemplation.

मंथर-slow; sluggish; tardy.

मंद-slow; sluggish; dim; dull; feeble; low. denoting 'endowed with' as wise.

मंदता-slowness; dimness; dullness; feebleness.

मंदबुद्धि-dull; stupid; moron; imbecile.

मंदभाग्य-not favoured by luck; unfortunate.

मंदमति-of sluggish intellect; moron; dullard.

मंदा-slow; tardy; dull.

मंदाकिनी-galaxy.

मंदाग्नि-dyspepsia; indigestion.

मंदित-retarded.

मंदिर-temple; house.

मंदी-slump; recession; depression.

मंद्र-deep.

मंशा-intent; intention/desire/ willingness.

मंसबदार-officer.

मंसूख़-annulled; revoked.

मंसूख़ी-annulment; revocation.

मग़ज़ी-hem; border.

मगद-a variety of sweetmeat.

मगदल-a variety of sweetmeat prepared from powdered pulse.

मगध-ancient name of South .

मगन-drowned.

मगर conj. but.-alligator; crocodile.

मगरमच्छ-crocodile.

मग़रिब-west.

मग़रिबी-western.

मग़रूर-proud; vain; arrogant; haughty; intolerant.

मगही-belonging to region; a kind of betel-leaf.

मग़ज़-brain.

मग्न-engrossed; delightfully; absorbed; immersed; sunk.

मग़्रिब-west.

मघवा-owl.

मघा-tenth constellation in Hindu Astronomy.

मचना-to be perpetrated/occasioned; to happen.

मचलन-act or state of

मचलना-to indulge in childish insistence; to pester.

मचला-prone to

मचलापन-childish insistence; pestering.

मचान-raised structure/platform usually for guarding farms or for game hunting; scaffold.

मचाना-to make/create.

मचिया-a low wicker stool to sit on.

मच्छ-a very big fish.

मच्छड़-mosquito.

मच्छर-mosquito.

मच्छरदानी-mosquito net/curtain.

मछली-fish.

मछलीमार-angler; fisherman.

मछुआ/मछुआरा-fisherman.

मज़दूर-labourer.

मज़दूर-संघ trade union; labour union.

मज़दूरी-wages; labour charges; calling of a labourer.

मजनूँ-celebrated lover of of tales; lovelorn person; very lean and thin person.

मज़बूत-strong; stout; sturdy person.

मज़बूती-strength; sturdiness; firmness.

मजबूर-helpless; compelled.

मजबूरन-under compulsion; in a state of helplessness.

मजबूरी-helplessness; compulsion.

मजमा-gathering.

मज़मून-subject; essay; article.

मज़म्मत-censure; upbraiding; reprimand; reproof; chiding.

मजलिस-assembly.

मजलिसी-pertaining to an assembly.

मज़हब-religion.

मज़हबी-religious.

मज़ा-fun; delight; pleasure; enjoyment.

मज़ाक-joke; ridicule; spoof.

मज़ाकन by way of fun.

मज़ाकिया-fun-loving; witty; humorous.

मज़ार-grave; tomb.

मज़ाल-courage; guts.

मजिस्ट्रेट-magistrate.

मजिस्ट्रेटी-magistracy.

मजीठ-a creeper from which red colour is prepared.

मजीठी-of the colour of red.

मज़ीद-still more.

मज़ेदार-enjoyable; pleasurable; delicious; full of relish.

मज्जन-bath; dipping; immersion.

मज्जा-marrow.

मझधार-mid-stream.

मझला-middle; of the middle.

मझोला-medium.

मटक-strut.

मटकना-to strut; to walk with airs; to move in a coquettish manner; to ogle.

मटका-large earthen pitcher.

मटकाना-to make coquettish gestures by strutting one's limbs.

मटकी-small earthen pitcher.

मटकौअल-act of making coquettish gestures.

मटक्का . flirtatious movement.

मटमैला-of the colour of earth; dust-coloured; dim.

मटर-pea.

मटरगश्त-roaming; wandering.

मटरगश्ती-roaming; wandering.

मटियामेट-completely ruined; devastated.

मटीला-dusty; dust-coloured.

मट्ठर-slow and sluggish.

मट्ठा-butter-milk.

मट्ठी-thin fried saltish pancake.

मठ-Hindu convent/monastery; abbey.

मठधारी-head of a monastery.

मठा-butter-milk.

मठाधीश-head of a monastery.

मुड़ई-hutment; cottage.

मड़ैया-hutment; cottage.

मढ़ना-to frame/mount/cover; to inflict.

मढ़वाई-act of framing or charges paid for the same.

मढ़वाना-causative of framing.

मढ़ाई-act of framing or charges paid for it.

मढ़ी-hutment; small monastery or temple.

मणि-gem-jewel.

मणिमाला-string of jewels.

मत-opinion; belief; view; vote; theory; doctrine; sect; creed.

denoting forbiddance.

मतगणना-counting of votes.

मतदाता-one who has a right to vote; voter.

मतदान-voting; polling.

मतदान-केन्द्र-polling station.

मतदान-कोष्ठ-polling booth.

मतदान-पेटिका-ballot-box.

मतपत्र-a printed slip used in secret voting; ballot.

मत-परिवर्तन-conversion.

मतभेद-difference of opinion; disagreement.

मत-मतांतर-diverse opinions.

मतलब-meaning; purport; motive; object.

मतलबी-selfish.

मतली-nausea.

मतवाला-drunk; intoxicated; insane; tipsy; one who is off his head.

मतवालापन-state or quality of being

मत-संग्रह-a survey of public opinion on a given subject; poll.

मत-स्वातंत्र्य-freedom of vote/ expression.

मतांतर-different opinion/view.

मतांतरण-difference of opinion.

मतांध-fanatic.

मतांधता-fanaticism.

मताग्रह-dogmatism.

मताग्रही-dogmatic.

मताधिकार-franchise; suffrage.

मताधिकारी-eligible voter.

मतानुयायी-adherent of a creed etc.; follower of a creed/tenet.

मतावलंबी-follower of a creed or sect.

मतारी-mother.

मति-intellect; opinion; view.

मतिभ्रंश-psychosis.

मतिभ्रम-hallucination; mental aberration.

मतिभ्रष्ट-lost to all sense of wisdom; foolish; stupid; idiot.

मतिमंद-foolish; stupid.

मतिमान-wise.

मतिहीन-foolish.

मतैक्य-unanimity; unison.

मत्त-intoxicated; drunk.

मत्ता-drunkenness.

मत्था-forehead.

मत्सर-jealously; envy.

मत्स्य-fish.

मत्स्य-उद्योग-fishing industry; fishery.

मत्स्यजीवी-fisherman.

मत्स्यविज्ञान-Ichthyology.

मथन-churning.

मथना-to churn; to beat; to skim.

मथानी-churn-shaft.

मथित-churned; mixed; probed.

मद-intoxication; pride; vanity; madness.

मदक-an intoxicant prepared from opium.

मदकची-one addicted to end.

मदकाल-a period of sexual excitement.

मदद-help; aid; assistance.

मददगार-helper.

मदन-Cupid.

मदनोत्सव-an ancient festival held in the month of and dedicated to the god of love.

मदमत्त-intoxicated; power-drunk.

मदरासी-of or pertaining to Madras Madras is a city in South India, now named as .

मदहोश-heavily intoxicated; dead drunk.

मदहोशी-drunkenness; senselessness due to intoxication.

मदांध-heavily intoxicated; blind drunk; power-blind; intoxicated with power and pelf.

मदांधता-state or quality of being

मदार-elephant; a plant also called

मदारी-juggler; trickster; showman of animals trained to perform tricks.

मदिर-intoxicating.

मदिरा-fine; liquor.

मदिरालय-public drinking house; bar.

मदोन्मत्त-drunk; intoxicated; arrogant; power-blind.

मदोन्मत्तता-drunkenness; arrogance.

मद्दा-depressed; slump.

मद्धिम-moderate; slow.

मद्य-wine; liquor.

मद्यत्याग-temperance.

मद्य-निर्माणी-distillery; brewery.

मद्य-निषेध-the state of being forbidden the manufacture, sale and consumption of alcoholic drinks; prohibition.

मद्यप-drunkard.

मद्यपान-act of drinking alcohol.

मद्यपायी-act of drinking alcohol.

मद्यसेवन-alcoholism.

मद्योन्माद-dipsomania.

मधु-honey.

मधुऋतु-spring season.

मधुकर-blackbee; mellifer.

मधुकरी-cooked articles collected as alms form different houses.

मधुकोश-honey-comb; beehive.

मधुप-blackbee.

मधुबाला-wine-maid; lady wine server.

मधुमक्खी-honey-bee.

मधुमय-sweet; charming.

मधुमास-the month which heralds the advent of spring.

मधुमेह-diabetes.

मधुयामिनी-the first night of newly married couple.

मधुर-sweet; pleasant; melodious.

मधुरता-sweetness; harmony; gaiety.

मधुरिमा-sweetness; charm; comeliness; gracefulness.

मधुवाटिका-apiary.

मधुशाला-public drinking house; bar; pub.

मधुसूदन-Lord .

मध्य-middle; mid; central.

मध्यकाल-middle age; medieval period.

मध्यकालीन-medieval.

मध्यक्रम-middle order.

मध्यपूर्व-the Middle East.

मध्यपूर्वी-Middle Eastern.

मध्यम-medium; intermediate.

मध्यमा-middle finger.

मध्यमान-mean; average.

मध्यमार्ग-middle path/course.

मध्यमार्गी-steering the middle path; centrist.

मध्ययुग-medieval era/age; middle age, middle age.

मध्ययुगीन-medieval.

मध्यरात्रि-midnight.

मध्यवर्ग-middle class; bourgeois.

मध्यवर्गीय-middle class; bourgeois.

मध्यवर्ती-middle; central intermediary.

मध्यस्थ-intermediary; mediator.

मध्यस्थता-state or quality of being mediator; mediation.

मध्यांतर-interval of time .

मध्यावकाश-recess.

मध्याह्न-the middle of the day; noon; midday.

मन:स्थिति-state of mind.

मन-Indian weight equal to forty seers; maund; roughly equal to 37 kg. mind; heart.

मनका-bead; rosary.

मनगढ़ंत-fictitious; concocted; fabricated.

मनचला-flirtatious.

मनचाहा-longed/wished/cherished for.

मनचीता-desired; thought of.

मनन-reflection; meditation.

मननशील-of reflective/meditative; temperament.

मनपंसद-to one's liking.

मनबहलाव-amusement; merriment; recreation; diversion; distraction.

मनभाया-after one's heart gratifying; pleasing; agreeable.

मनमाना-arbitrary; spontaneous; according to one's own free-will.

मनमानी-arbitrary conduct; arbitrariness; entirely voluntary.

मन-मुटाव-estrangement; strained thinking.

मनमोदक-wishful thinking; day-dreaming.

मनमोहन-charm personified; Lord .

मनमौजी-temperamental; capricious; fantastical.

मनमौजीपन-capriciousness.

मनवांछित-according to your mind.

मनवाना-to causative of

मनशा-desire; intention.

मनश्चिकित्सा-psychotherapy.

मनसा mentally.

मनसाराम-a form of addressing one's oneself.

मनसूख़-cancelled; revoked.

मनसूख़ी-cancellation; revocation.

मनसूबा-plan; design.

मनस्तत्त्व-psychic element.

मनस्ताप-remorse; mental agony; sorrow.

मनस्तोष-mental satisfaction.

मनस्वी-determined to achieve an object; strong willed.

मनहर-attractive.

मनहरण-lovely; extremely attractive; marvellous.

मनहूस-ominous; inauspicious; abominable; gloomy.

मनहूसी- ominousness; inauspiciousness; gloominess.

मना-prohibited; forbidden.

मनाई-forbiddance.

मनाना-to persuade; to bring round; to carry out; to perform.

मनाही-forbiddance; prohibition.

मनिया-glass bead.

मनिहार-bangle-seller.

मनिहारिन-woman-bangle-seller.

मनीआर्डर-money-order.

मनुज-man; offspring of .

मनुजाद-cannibal.

मनुष्य-man; human.

मनुष्य जाति-mankind; human race.

मनुष्यता-the quality of being human; humanity; human race.

मनुष्य-निर्मित-man-made.

मनुष्यभक्षी-cannibal.

मनुष्योचित-fit or suitable for people; humane.

मनुहार-appeasement.

मनोकामना-longing; desire.

मनोगत-idea.

मनोगति-tendency of the mind.

मनोग्रंथि-mental complex.

मनोदशा-condition of the mind.

मनोनयन-nomination.

मनोनिग्रह-self-control.

मनोनियोग-application of mind; attention.

मनोनीत-nominated.

मनोबल-morale; tempo.

मनोभाव-mentality.

मनोभावना-sentiment.

मनोमय-mental.

मनोमालिन्य- antagonism; estrangement; alienation.

मनोयोग-single-mindedness.

मनोरंजक-recreative; amusing; entertaining.

मनोरंजकता-state or quality of being

मनोरंजन-entertainment; recreation; amusement.

मनोरथ-long cherished desire.

मनोरम-charming; lovely; comely; attractive.

मनोरमता-charm; loveliness; comeliness; fascination.

मनोराग-a set of idea in the mind on which someone harps; mind set.

मनोराज्य-world of fancy.

मनोरोग-mental disease; psycho-pathy.

मनोरोगी-mental patient; psychopath.

मनोलीला-phantom.

मनोवांछित-longed for; aspired after.

मनोविकार-emotion; passion; psychopathy; mental disorder.

मनोविकृति-mental aberration; psychosis.

मनोविज्ञान-Psychology.

मनोविनोद-amusement; recreation; merriment.

मनोविलास-merriment.

मनोविश्लेषण-psychoanalysis.

मनोवृत्ति-mentality; disposition.

मनोवेग-impulse.

मनोवैज्ञानिक-psychological.

मनोव्यथा-mental agony.

मनोव्यापार-activity of mind; thought; conception.

मनोहर-attractive; alluring; charming.

मनोहरता-attractiveness of features; comeliness.

मनोहारी-attractive.

मनौअल-appeasement.

मनौती-vow of offering to a deity.

मन्नत-promise; vow.

मन्वंतर-tenure of in .

मम-pron. my; mine; of me.

ममता-parental/filial affection.

ममी-mummy; preserved corpse; mother.

ममेरा-of or pertaining to the maternal uncle.

मयंक-moon.

मय denoting fullness.

मयस्सर-available.

मयूख-beam; ray; flame.

मयूर-peacock.

मयूरी-female of peacock.

मरक-epidemic.

मरकज़-centre.

मरकज़ी-central.

मरकटहा-gaunt; lean; emaciated.

मरकत-emerald.

मरकहा-prone to attack usually with horns .

मरखना-prone to hit animal .

मरघट-cremation ground.

मरज़-ailment; disease.

मरज़ी-wish; consent.

मरण-death.

मरणांतक-resulting/ending in death; fatal.

मरणासन्न-one on the point of death; dying; moribund.

मरणोत्तर-posthumous.

मरतबान-jar.

मरता-on the verge of death; dying.

मरदना-to crush; to trample upon; to knead.

मरदानगी-bravery; masculinity.

मरदाना-manly; brave.

मरदानापन-masculinity.

मरदूद-condemned; contemptible.

मरन-death.

मरना-to die; to sacrifice oneself; to long keenly.

मरना-जीना-birth and death; coming to and leaving this world.

मरनी-death.

मरनी-करनी-obsequies; funeral rites.

मर-भुक्खा-famished with hunger; indigent; ravenous; furiously voracious.

मरमर-marble.

मरमरा-brittle.

मरम्मत-repair; mending.

मरम्मत-कराई-the act of repairing; charges for repairing something.

मरम्मत-तलब-requiring repairs.

मरम्मती-things for being repaired, or needing repairs.

मरसिया-elegy; song of lamentation.

मरहम-ointment.

मरहमपट्टी-dressing, bandaging.

मरहला-intricate problem.

मरहूम-late; deceased.

मरातिब-storey of a building.

मराल-swan.

मरियम-Mary, mother of Christ.

मरियल-gaunt; lean; emaciated; rickety; sickly.

मरी-epidemic resulting in many fatalities.

मरीचिका-mirage; illusion.

मरीचिमाली-Sun.

मरीची-Sun.

मरीज़-patient.

मरु-desert; barren land.

मरुद्यान-oasis.

मरुद्वीप-oasis.

मरुस्थल-desert land.

मरोड़-twist; contortion.

मरोड़ना-to twist/contort/wring.

मरोड़ी-prickly heat.

मर्कट-monkey.

मर्ज़-ailment; disease.

मर्ज़ी-wish; desire; will; pleasure.

मर्त्य-mortal.-man; body.

मर्त्यता-mortality.

मर्त्यलोक-the world of mortality; mortal world; the earthly world.

मर्द-man.

मर्दन-massaging; rubbing vigorously; crushing/trampling.

मर्दानगी-masculinity.

मर्दाना-often manly.

मर्दुमशुमारी-census.

मर्म-quintessence; essential meaning; secret; vital organ.

मर्मज्ञ-one who knows the quintessence of things; connoisseur.

मर्मप्रहार-blow at the vitals.

मर्मभेदी-heart-rending.

मर्मर-marble; rustling sound.

मर्मवेदना-deep-anguish.

मर्मव्यथा-agony in the vitals.

मर्मस्थल-vital spot; vulnerable point.

मर्मस्पर्शी-touching; moving.

मर्मांतक-poignant; that which penetrates the inner recesses of the heart.

मर्माहत-hit in the vitals.

मर्मी-one who knows someone' secret.

मर्यादा-limit; boundary line; ethical propriety; decorum; status; dignity.

मर्यादापूर्ण-decorous.

मर्यादित-limited; limited/restricted by propriety.

मर्हूम-deceased; late.

मलंग-carefree person.

मल-filth; waste matter; faecal matter; excrement.

मलकीट-worm found in faecal matter.

मलत्याग-defecation.

मलद्वार-anus.

मलना-to rub; to massage.

मलबा-debris from a ruined building; rubble; wreckage.

मलमल-a fine cotton cloth; muslin.

मलमास-intercalary month.

मलमूत्र-excreta excrement and urine.

मलय-a region in South India famous for sandalwood trees.

मलयज-sandal.

मलयालम-a religion of state in South India; language of the above region.

मलहम-ointment.

मलहम-पट्टी-dressing.

मलाई-cream; fatty part of milk; the creamy portion.

मलाट-coarse thick packing paper.

मलामत-reproof.

मलाया-peninsula in south-east Asia.

मलाल-bitter regret; anguish; remorse; compunction.

मलावरोध-constipation.

मलाशय-rectum.

मलिक-king; lord.

मलिका-queen.

मलिन-unclean; dirty; filthy; sad.

मलिनता-uncleanliness; dirtiness.

मलीदा-a sweet dish made usually of flour, rich in ghee; a soft woollen cloth.

मलेरिया-malaria.

मल्ल-wrestler; athlete.

मल्लभूमि-wrestling arena.

मल्लयुद्ध-wrestling bout.

मल्लविद्या-art of wrestling.

मल्लशाला-wrestling arena.

मल्लाह-boatman.

मल्लाही-boatmanship.

मल्लिका-a fragrant flower.

मल्हार-an Indian melody sung during the rainy season.

मवक्किल-client.

मवाद-pus.

मवेशी-cattle.

मवेशीख़ाना-cattle pen/pound.

मशक-a big water bag of leather. -mosquito; gnat.

मशक़्क़त-toil; hard labour.

मशक़्क़ती-hard-working.

मशग़ूल-occupied; busy; engaged.

मशरिक़-east.

मशरिक़ी-eastern.

मशविरा-counsel; advice.

मशहूर-famous.

मशहूरी-fame.

मशाल-torch.

मशालची-torch-bearer.

मशीन-machine.

मशीनगन-machine-gun.

मशीनमैन-machine-man.

मशीनरी-machinery; mechanism.

मश्क़-practice; exercise.

मस-the soft hair on the top lip; the beginning of moustaches.

मसक-mosquito.

मसकना-to give way said of cloth.

मसकाना-to tear; to separate; to split.

मसख़रा-jester; buffoon.

मसख़रापन-jesting.

मसख़री-jesting; jestful remark.

मसजिद-mosque.

मसनद-roundish pillow for reclining and/or cushioned seat.

मसनूई-artificial; false.

मसरफ़-purpose.

मसरूफ़-occupied; busy.

मसल-maxim; proverb.

मसलन conj. for instance/example.

मसलना-to press with great force.

मसला-problem; issue.

मसहरी-large bed; mosquito net.

मसा-wart.

मसान-cremation ground.

मसाना-urinary bladder.

मसाला-condiment; spice; something requisite; material; matter.

मसालेदार-spiced; exciting or interesting; spicy.
मसि-ink.
मसिजीवी-writer.
मसीह-Christ.
मसीहा-messiah; angel.
मसूड़ा-the gums.
मसूर-lentil.
मसूरिका-measles; chickenpox.
मसोसना-to feel woefully frustrated/ helpless.
मसौदा-draft; written preliminary sketch.
मस्जिद-mosque.
मस्त-carefree; engrossed in; intoxicated.
मस्तक-forehead; head; summit.
मस्तमौला-happy-go-lucky; easy-going.
मस्तराम-devil-may-care.
मस्ताना-easy-going; unworrying; happy-go-lucky.-to be intoxicated/ inebriated.
मस्तिष्क-brain.
मस्ती-state of being self-contained; gaiety; inebriety; inebriation.
मस्तूल-mast.
मस्सा-wart; mole.
महँगा-dear; expensive; costly.
महँगाई-dearness.
महँगाई-भत्ता-dearness allowance.
महँगी-dearness; costliness.
महंत-high priest.
महंती-priesthood.
महक-smell.
महकदार-fragrant; sweet smelling.
महकमा-department.
महाजन-high personage; great man; a person whose business is money lending; moneylender; banker.
महाजनी-pertaining to money-lender; money-leading business; accountancy; banking; script used by money-lenders.
महाजाल-large net; big trap.
महात्मा-high-souled personage; saint.
महादेव-Lord Shiv.
महादेवी-goddess ; wife of Lord .
महाद्वीप-continent.
महाद्वीपीय-continental.
महाधिवक्ता-Advocate General.
महान, महान्-great; eminent.
महानगर-metropolis.
महानगरीय-metropolitan.
महानिद्रा-sleep eternal.
महानुभाव-person of high and noble ideas; a highly respected person; illustrious; magnanimous.
महान्यायवादी-Attorney General.
महापराध-felony.
महापातक-great sin; atrocious offence.

महापातकी-great sinner; heinous offender.

महापाप-great sin.

महापापी-great sinner.

महापुरुष-great man; dignitary.

महाप्रयाण-life's journey's end.

महाप्राण-noble soul.

महाबली-mighty; exceedingly powerful.

महाबाहु-valorous.

महाब्राह्मण-a Brahmin who conduct funeral obsequies for payment .

महाभाग-one whose luck is in; lucky person; happy.

महाभारत-one of the two great epics of India; the war described therein; a big fight; a great struggle.

महाभाष्य-master commentary.

महामंडल-big division.

महामंत्र-top secret of success.

महामंत्री-general secretary.

महामना-high-minded; noble.

महामहिम-His Excellency.

महामहोपाध्याय-a title given by government for great scholarship/ academic distinction.

महामात्य-Prime Minister.

महामाया-illusion supreme.

महामारी-pestilence; epidemic.

महामुनि-pestilence; epidemic.

महायुद्ध-great war.

महारत-skill obtained by training or practice.

महारथी-the great warrior.

महाराज-emperor; cook.

महाराजाधिराज-Emperor; the Great.

महाराज्ञी-*fem.* of emperor.

महाराणा-a title of rulers of some states of India.

महारानी-the wife of an emperor; a woman emperor; empress.

महाराष्ट्र-a state in South-West India.

महाराष्ट्रीय-of or pertaining to .

महारोग-incurable and frightful disease.

महार्घ-valuable; precious; too costly.

महार्णव-great ocean.

महाल-locality.

महालय-deluge; a fortnight in which Hindus offer oblations to their deceased ancestors.

महालेखापाल-Accountant General.

महावत-elephant driver.

महावात-hurricane.

महाविद्यालय-college.

महाविपत्ति-catastrophe.

महावीर-very bravel Lord; Lord Hanuman.

महाशय-a polite form of address; gentleman.

महासभा-congress.

महासभाई-member of the congress.

महासागर-ocean.

महि-earth.

महिधर-hill; mountain.

महीन-thin; fine; sharp.

महीप-king.

महीपति-king.

महीपाल-king.

महुआ-an Indian tree bearing yellow flowers which are used for preparing liquor.

महेश-Lord Shiv.

महेश्वर-Lord Shiv.

महेश्वरी-goddess Laxmi.

महोत्सव-gala festival.

महोदय-a polite form of address for gentleman.

महोदया-a polite form of address for ladies.

महोपध्याय-great scholar or preceptor.

महौषधि-remedy for all ills; panacea.

माँ-mother.

माँग-demand; hair-parting.

माँग-जली-widow.

माँगना-to beg; to claim; to demand; to request; to ask for ; to borrow.

माँग-पत्र-order form; indent; memorandum of demands.

मांगलिक-auspicious; propitious.

माँग-सूची-a formal request for supplies.

माँझा-substance used for sharpening the kite-flying thread; size.

माँझी-boatman.

माँड़-boiled rice-water; scum.

माँड़ना-to knead flour; to separate grain from chaff.

मांडलिक-divisional.

माँड़ा-a disease of the eye.

माँद-den; lair.

माँदगी-illness; fatigue.

माँदा-ill.

मांस-meat; flesh.

मांसपेशी-muscle.

मांसभक्षी-non-vegetarian person; carnivorous animal .

मांसल-of or like flesh; fleshy.

मांसलता-fleshiness.

मांसाहार-non-vegetarian food.

मांसाहारी-non-vegetarian person; carnivorous.

माई-mother; elderly woman.

माई-बाप-all in all.

माओवादी-Maoist, one who follows the doctrine of Maotsetung.

माक़ूल-appropriate; proper; reasonable; fit.

माखन-butter.

माखन-चोर-one who enjoys pilfering butter.

माघ-eleventh month of the Hindu calendar.

माघी-pertaining to

माचिस-matches match-box.

माछ-fish.

माजरा-matter; affair; happening.

माज़ी-past.

माजून-sweetened tonic.

माटी-soil.

माठा-whey.

माणिक-ruby.

मात-mate; checkmate.

मातदिल-temperate; moderate.

मातबर-reliable; trust-worthy.

मातबरी-reliability; trust-worthiness.

मातम-mourning.

मातम-पुर्सी-offering of condolence.

मातहत-subordinate; dependent.

मातहती-subordination; dependence.

माता-mother; smallpox.

मातामह-mother's father.

मातामही-mother's mother.

मातुल-mother's brother.

मातृ-mother.

मातृक-maternal; matriarchal.

मातृका-mother; matron.

मातृतंत्र-matriarchy.

मातृत्व-motherhood; maternity.

मातृभाषा-mother-tongue.

मातृभूमि-one's native country; motherland.

मातृहत्या-matricide.

मात्र-only.

मात्रा-quantity; dosage; dose; sign, specially vowel mark; a unit of measurement as in music, prosody etc.

मात्रात्मक-quantitative.

मात्रिक-unitary.

मात्सर्य-jealously.

मात्स्य-pertaining to fish.

माथा-forehead.

माथा-पच्ची-taxing of brain.

मादक-intoxicating; spirituous.

मादकता-inebriety; intoxication.

मादरी-pertaining to maternal relation.

मादा-female animal.

माद्दा-essential element/ingredient; capability; innate capacity; pus.

माधव-name of Lord Krishna.

माधवी-a creeper bearing fragrant flowers.

माधुरी-sweetness.

माधुर्य-sweetness; melodiousness; pleasantness.

माध्य-average; mean.

माध्यम-medium.

माध्यमिक-middle; secondary; intermediary.

मान-respect; regard; dignity; reputation; feigned anger.
मानक-standard.
माननीकरण-standardization.
मानकीकृत-standardized.
मानचित्र-map; chart.
मानचित्रण-mapping.
मानचित्रावली-book of maps, atlas.
मानज-pertaining to mind.
मानदंड-criterion.
मानद-given as an honour; honorary.
मानदेय-honorarium.
मानना-to admit; to accede/accept.
माननीय-honourable; esteemed; revered.
मानने योग्य-admissible; acceptable; believable.
मानमंदिर-observatory.
मान-मनौअल-propitiation of one's feigning anger.
मानमर्दन-subduing of someone's vanity; humiliation.
मान-मर्यादा-established prestige.
मानमोचन-pacifying the angry dear one.
मानव-human.-man; human being.
मानवता-humane race; humanity; the quality of being human.
मानवतावाद-humanism.
मानवतावादी-humanistic.
मानवती-beloved; feigning to be angry.
मानवप्रेम-philanthropy.
मानव-भूगोल-philanthropy.
मानवशास्त्र-humanities.
मानवाधिकार-human rights.
मानवीकरण-humanisation.
मानवीय-human; humane.
मानवीयता-the characteristic qualities of a man.
मानवोचित-befitting a human being.
मानस-mind.
मानसरोवर-a time-honoured lake in Tibet.
मानसिक-mental.
मानसी-mental; silent worship.
मानसून-monsoon.
मानस्वर-phon. cardinal vowel.
मानहानि-defamation.
मानाभिषेक-investiture.
मानार्थ-complimentary.
मानिंद-like; similar.
मानिक-ruby.
मानिनी-wife or beloved who feigns to be angry.
मानी-proud.-meaning; purport.
मानुषिक-human.
मानुषी-human.
माने-meaning; purport.
मानो-as if; as it were.
मानोपाधि-title of honour.

मान्य-prestigious; honourable; respected; acceptable.

मान्यता-recognition; accreditation; tenet; assumption.

मान्यता-प्राप्त-recognized.

माप-measure.

मापक-meter; measurer.

मापन-measuring.

मापना-to measure.

मापनी-scale.

माफ़-forgiven; pardoned.

माफ़िक़-favourable inclined/ disposed; agreeable.

माफ़िया-a secret terrorist or criminal group; Mafia.

माफ़ी-forgiveness; pardon; freehold land.

माफ़ीदार-freeholder.

मामला-case; affair; matter.

मामा-maternal uncle.

मामी-maternal aunt.

मामूली-ordinary; commonplace.

मायका-mother's home of a married woman.

माया-God's play; illusion; wealth.

मायाजाल-web of worldly attachments.

मायामय-illusory; full of illusion.

मायावाद-illusionism.

मायावादी-illusionist.

मायावी-illusory; illusive; magical.

मायूस-disappointed; dejected.

मायूसी-disappointment; frustration; dejection; gloom.

मार-beating; range.

मारक-antidote.

मारका-mark.

मार-काट-bloody affair; bloody scuffle; carnage.

मारकीन-a kind of coarse cloth.

मारकेश-ominous conjunction of planets.

मारजार-pussy, cat.

मारण-killing.

मार-धाड़-fighting and killing; fracas; affray; onslaught.

मारना-to beat; to strike; to hit; to snatch.

मार-पीट-exchange of blows; scuffle; battery; assault.

मारफ़त, की-through; care of.

मारवाड़-a region in .

मारा-stricken; beaten; smitten.

मारामारी-scuffle; affray; hot haste.

मारी-epidemic.

मारुत-wind.

मारू-martial music.

मारे, के-on account of; because of; due to.

मार्क्सवाद-Marxism.

मार्क्सवादी-Marxist.

मार्केट-market.

मार्ग-way; route; road.

मार्ग-कर-toll-tax.

मार्गच्युत-deviated; deflection.

मार्गदर्शक-guide; superintendent.

मार्गदर्शन-guidance.

मार्गरक्षक-escort.

मार्गव्यय-travelling expenses; passage money.

मार्गशीर्ष-the ninth month of Hindu calendar.

मार्गी-traveller.

मार्च-March month.

मार्जन-cleansing; cleaning; purifying; purification; rectification; correction.

मार्जनी-broom.

मार्जित-cleansed; purified; rectified; corrected; refined.

मार्तंड-Sun.

मार्फ़िया-morphia.

मार्मिक-touching; appealing; moving; pathetic; stirring.

मार्मिकता-poignancy.

मार्शल-martial.

माल-valuable property; merchandise; stock; material; commodities; goods; revenue; stuff.

माल-अदालत-revenue court.

माल-असबाब-luggage.

मालकिन-lady of the house.

मालख़ाना-store-house.

माल-गाड़ी-goods train; freight train.

मालगुज़ार-one who pays land revenue; landlord.

मालगुज़ारी-land revenue.

मालगोदाम-railway godown; goods-shed.

माल-घर-godown.

मालटा-Malta island; a kind of citrus fruit.

मालती-a creeper yielding sweet-smelling flowers.

मालदह-a variety of mango.

मालदार-wealthy; rich.

मालपुआ-pancake.

माल बाबू-goods clerk.

माल-मता-effects; assets; wealth.

माल-मस्त-happy in one's wealth/ opulence.

माल-महकमा-department of revenue.

मालवा-Malwa, a region of .

माल-सूची-inventory of property.

माला-garland; wreath; rosary.

मालामाल-very affluent; immensely rich; opulent; wealthy.

मालिक-owner; master; boss.

मालिका-female landlord.

मालिकाना-of or pertaining to an owner; in the capacity of an owner; like an owner; proprietary.

मालिन-woman gardener; wife of a gardener; flower selling maid; second wife of a widower.

मालिन्य-dirtiness; impurity.

मालियत-value; wealth.

मालिश-massage.

माली-pertaining to finance; financial; economic; gardener.

मालूम-known.

मालूमात-pieces of information; knowledge.

माशा-an Indian measure of weight; equivalent to one-twelfth of a tola; approximately 1 gm.

माशाअल्लाह . Good God!

माशूक़-beloved.

माशूक़ा-beloved woman.

मास-month.

मासांत-end of the month.

मासानुमासिक-monthly.

मासिक-of or pertaining to a month.

मासूम-innocent; guileless.

मास्टर-master; teacher.

मास्टरी-profession/job of a teacher; expert knowledge; expertise.

मास्य-one month old; aged one month.

माह-month.

माहवार once a month; monthly.

माहवारी-occurring or appearing once every month; monthly.

माहात्म्य-greatness; glory.

माहिर-expert; dexterous; proficient; clever.

माहिरी-state of being an expert; expertness; proficiency.

माहुर-poison; venom.

माहेश्वर-pertaining to Lord the Great.

माहेश्वरी-goddess .

मिचकना-to wink.

मिचकाना-to wink/blink the eyes over and again.

मिचना-to close; specially closing of the eyes.

मिचलाना-to feel like vomiting; to nauseate.

मिचली-nausea; qualm.

मिचवाना-causative of

मिचोली-hide and seek.

मिज़ाज-temperament; disposition; mood.

मिज़ाजी-proud; vainglorious; conceited.

मिटना-to be erased/effaced; to be destroyed/ruined.

मिटाना-to erase/efface/abolish; to destroy.

मिट्टी-earth; clay; corpse.

मिट्टी का तेल-kerosene oil.

मिट्टी का दीया-mud lamp.
मिट्ठु-parrot; sweet tongued person.
मिठलोना-mild/pleasantly saltish.
मिठाई-sweet.
मिठास-sweetness.
मिडिल-middle.
मिडिलची-one who has studied upto the middle class.
मितभाषी-taciturn; one who speaks little.
मितव्यय-thrift; frugality.
मितव्ययिता-thriftiness; economy.
मितव्ययी-thrifty; economical; frugal.
मिताई-friendship.
मिताक्षर-concise.
मिताहार-austerity in food.
मिताहारी-austere in food.
मिति-system of measurement; date.
मिती-date according to the lunar month.
मिती-काटा-discount.
मित्र-friend.
मित्रता-friendship.
मित्रतापूर्ण-friendly; showing good will.
मित्रभाव-friendship; friendly; attitude; cordiality.
मित्रराष्ट्र-ally; allies.
मिथुन-Gemini sign of the zodiac; mating; couple.
मिथ्या-false; spurious; untrue.
मिथ्याचार-deceitful conduct.
मिथ्याभिमान-false pride; vainglory.
मिथ्यावादी-one who tells a lie; liar.
मिनकना-to say something almost inaudibly.
मिनट-minute.
मिनमिन-utterance; almost inaudible.
मिनिस्टर-minister.
मिनिस्टरी-ministry.
मिन्नत-supplication; entreaty.
मिमियाना-to bleat; to supplicate with servility; to grovel.
मियाँ-a Mohammedan from of address; husband.
मियाँ-मिट्ठू-self-complacent.
मियाद-time limit; validity period.
मियादी-extending over a fixed period.
मियान-scabbard; sheath.
मियाना-medium; open palanquin.
मियानी-a small storey between to main floors; mezzanine; gusset in a pyjama.
मिर्गी-epilepsy.
मिर्च-chilli.
मिर्जई-an Indian type of jacket.
मिल-mill.
मिलकर together; jointly.
मिलता-जुलता-very much alike; resembling; akin.
मिलन-union; meet; meeting.

मिलनसार-social; sociable; affable; companionable.

मिलनसारी-sociability; affability; social nature.

मिलना-to meet; to be found; to be mixed; mingled; to get/obtain/receive; to have.

मिलना-जुलना-to mix; to have social intercourse.

मिलनी-a ceremonial meet.

मिलनेवाला-acquaintance.

मिलवाना-to cause to meet.

मिला-जुला-mixed; collective.

मिलान-act or state of collation; comparison.

मिलान-कर्ता-collator.

मिलाना-to mix; to blend; to connect/join.

मिलाप-reunion; reconciliation.

मिलावट-act of mixing; adulteration; mixture; the thing admixed.

मिलावटी-adulterated.

मिलिटरी-army; the military.

मिली-भगत-collusion.

मिल्कियत-ownership; property; estate.

मिल्लत-friendship; sociability; sect.

मिशन-specific purpose; group of missionaries.

मिशनरी-one engaged in charitable works and religious teaching; missionary.

मिश्र-mixed; a sub-caste among Brahmins.

मिश्रक-a person or machine that blends; blender.

मिश्रण-mixture; compound; solution.

मिश्रित-compound; compounded; mixed; mingled.

मिष्ट-sweet.

मिष्टभाषी-sweet-tongued.

मिष्टान्न-sweets.

मिस-pretext; miss.

मिस, के-on behalf of.

मिसरा-one-half of a couplet.

मिसरी-sugar candy.

मिसरोटी-cake of mixed flour.

मिसाल-example.

मिसिल-case-file.

मिस्की-croon; humming Music.

मिस्तरी-artisan; mechanic; mason.

मिस्त्र-Egypt.

मिस्त्री-Egyptian.

मीनाकारी-enamelling.

मीनाक्षी-woman having charming eyes; fish-shaped, as it were.

मीना बाज़ार-fancy fair; .

मीनार-tower; minaret; turret.

मीमांसक-exponent; commentator.

मीमांसा-interpretative; commentation; exposition; scholarly; commentary.

मीमांसित-thoroughly expounded; commented upon.

मीमांस्य-worth exposition.

मीर-leader; chief; nobleman; winner in a game/sport.

मीर मुंशी-head clerk.

मीरासी-a member of a Muslim clan of professional folk singers and dancer; male accompanist of a singer or dancer.

मील-a unit of length equal to 1760 yards; mile.

मीलन-act of closing; act of contracting/resiling.

मीलित-closed; shut.

मीलों-at a great distance.

मीसना-uncommunicative; usually self-agonising; to mix; to crush by rubbing.

मुँगरा-wooden hammer.

मुँगौरी-tiny roundish eatable; prepared of ground pulse.

मुंड-head; skull.

मुंडन-the act of shaving the head; ceremonious tonsure.

मुँडना-to have the head shaved; to be fleeced/cheated.

मुंडमाल-garland of skulls.

मुंडविहीन-beheaded; headless.

मुंडा-shaven-headed; bald-headed; without a head/cover.

मुँड़ाई-the act of shaving the head or charges paid for the same.

मुँडाना-to get shaven.

मुंडिका-small head/skull.

मुंडित-shaved; tonsured.

मुंडी-shaven-headed woman.

मुँडेर-boundary of a field.

मुँडेरा-parapet; battlement.

मुँदना-to be closed; to come to an end.

मुँदरी-finger-ring.

मुंशियाना-charges paid to a

मुंशी-clerk; scribe.

मुंसरिम-record-keeper of a court.

मुंसिफ-presiding officer in a lower court.

मुँह-mouth; face; front part of a thing; opening of pots; vessels etc.

मुँह-चोर-shy; unwilling to be seen; bashful.

मुँह-चोरी-shyness.

मुँह-छिपाऊ-sulker; bashful.

मुँह-छुआई-insincere offer made for the sake of formality .

मुँह-जबानी orally; verbally.

मुँह-जला-a form of Indian abuse; accursed; damned.

मुँह-जोर-impudent; insolent; obstinate; rude.

मुँह-झौंसा-a form of Indian abuse; accursed; damned.

मुँह-दर-मुँह-face to face.
मुँह-दिखाई fem present offered to the bride on the occasion.
मुँह-देखनी-an Indian ritual after marriage when kins-women see the bride formally.
मुँह-फट-speaking roughly and plainly; blunt; abusive.
मुँह-बंद-unopened.
मुँह-बोला-regarded as; taken as; treated as.
मुँह-भराई-hush money; bribe; sop; process of giving hush money.
मुँह-माँगा-asked for.
मुँह-मुलाहज़ा-just for maintenance of relationship.
मुँहँ-लगा-cheeky; impertinent.
मुँहाँ-having a mouth.
मुँहाँमुँहँ to the brim; face to face.
मुँहाँसा-pimple; acne.
मुअत्तल-suspended from service.
मुअत्तली-suspension from service.
मुअन्नस-feminine.
मुआ-dead.
मुआयना-inspection.
मुआवज़ा-compensation.
मुक़त्ता-well-trimmed.
मुक़दमा-law-suit.
मुक़दमेबाज़-litigant.
मुक़दमेबाज़ी-litigation.
मुक़द्दम-ancient; primary.
मुक़द्दमा-case.
मुक़द्दर-destiny; fate; luck.
मुकद्दस-holy; sacred; pious.
मुकना-to be finished; to come to an end.
मुकम्मल-complete / completed; complete and perfect.
मुकरना-to go back upon one's word; to deny; to refuse.
मुकरी-riddle in the form of a short couplet.
मुक़र्रर-appointed; fixed.
मुकलावा-
मुक़ाबला-comparison; encounter.
मुक़ाम-halt; halting place; site; place.
मुकियाना-to give light blows with the fists for giving relief; to pummel.
मुकुंद-Lord .
मुकुट-coronet; crest; diadem; crown; tiara.
मुकुर-mirror.
मुकुल-bud.
मुकुलित-budded.
मुक्का-punch; blow given with the fist.
मुक्का-मुक्की-exchange of blows/ punches.
मुक्की-light blow of fist.
मुक्केबाज़-boxer.
मुक्केबाज़ी-boxing.

मुक्कैश-mad.

मुक्त-freed; liberated; released; emancipated; free; independent.

मुक्तकंठ-without any reserve.

मुक्तक-piece of poetry.

मुक्तकेश-having uncombed hair.

मुक्तचेता-one who has realised the secret to attain salvation.

मुक्तछंद-blank verse.

मुक्तद्वार-open door; free excess.

मुक्तवसन-naked; nude.

मुक्त-व्यापार-free trade.

मुक्तहस्त-bounteous; liberal.

मुक्ता-pearl.

मुक्तावली-string of pearls.

मुक्ति-liberation; emancipation; release; salvation; riddance; deliverance; acquittal; exemption.

मुक्तिदाता-liberator; one who gives salvation; saviour.

मुक्तिधाम-place which leads to salvation.

मुक्तिपथ-path of salvation.

मुक्तिपत्र-order of release.

मुक्ति-सेना-salvation army.

मुख-mouth; face; opening.

मुखकमल-lotus-like face; pretty face.

मुखकांति-halo of the face; radiance of the face.

मुखचित्र-frontispiece.

मुखड़ा-face.

मुख़तार-Mukhtar; legal agent.

मुख़तारनामा-power of attorney.

मुख़तारी-attorneyship.

मुखद्वार-gateway.

मुखपत्र-an organ of a particular party or group.

मुख़बिर-one who gives secret information; informer; spy.

मुखमंडल-countenance.

मुखर-cheeky; talkative; loquacious; vociferous.

मुखरता-vociferousness.

मुखरित-voiced; expressed; given vent to; resonant.

मुख़शुद्धि-cleansing of the mouth (after a meal); taking betel-leaf; clove; cardamon etc. after a meal.

मुखसुख-ease/facilityinpronunciation.

मुखाकृति-mien.

मुख़ातिब-to turn towards (someone).

मुखापेक्षी-looking at others for help; depending on others.

मुखारविंद-pretty/lovely face.

मुखारी-semblance of the face.

मुख़ालिफ़-opposition.

मुख़ालिफ़त-opposition.

मुखिया-head; headman; kingpin.

मुखी-the sunflower.
denoting orientation; oriented towards the Sun; resemblance; having a face like moon.

मुखौटा-mask; false face; countenance.

मुख़्लतिफ़-different.

मुख़्तसर-brief.

मुख्य-chief; main; key; primary; principal; leading.

मुख्यतः mainly; primarily; predominantly; pre-eminently; chiefly; principally.

मुख्यतया

मुख्यता-prominence; pre-minence.

मुख्यार्थ-denotation.

मुख्यालय-head office; headquarters.

मुगदर-Indian type of a dumbbells used in physical exercise; mallet.

मुग़ल-Moghal.

मुग़लई-after the Moghal style.

मुग़लिया-of Moghal dynasty or period.

मुग़ालता-delusion.

मुग्ध-fascinated; infautated; captivated.

मुग्धता-fascination; infatuation.

मुग्धा-innocent heroine; not yet fully mature.

मुचल्का-personal-bond.

मुच्छल-whiskered.

मुछंदर-whiskered.

मुछकटा-with clipped moustache.

मुछमुंडा-clean-shaven.

मुजरा-musical sitting by a dancing girl.

मुजरिम-accused; offender; criminal.

मुझ-me

मुझे-me; to me.

मुटका-fat (person).

मुटमरद-proud; vainglorious.

मुटमरदी-inactivity due to lassitude.

मुटाई-fattiness.

मुटाना-to fatten; to grow fat.

मुटापा-fatness; plumpness; obesity.

मुटासा-vainglorious (due to affluence).

मुटियाना-to get fat; to become arrogant.

मुट्ठा-bundle; handle.

मुट्ठी-fist.

मुठभेड़-confrontation; encounter.

मुठिया-haft; a handle or hilt.

मुठियाना-to massage with light strokes of the fist; to hold in one's fist/grip/grasp.

मुड़कना-to bend/twist.

मुड़ना-to turn (about); to return; to bend; to be twisted.

मुड़िया-head; one with a clean-shaven head.-a type of Hindi script used in Mahajani books (account).

मुतबन्ना-adopted (son).

मुतलक़ absolutely.

मुतवल्ली-guardian of a minor.

मुतवातिर-continuously.

मुतसद्दी-clerk; assistant; agent.

मुतालबा-dues; arrears.

मुतास-urge to urinate.

मुताह-temporary marriage prevalent among Muslim.

मुत्तफ़िक़-in agreement with.

मुत्तला-informed; notified.

मुदर्रिस-school teacher.

मुदर्रिसी-teaching.

मुदाख़लत-interference.

मुदित-delighted; pleased; rejoiced.

मुद्गर-an ancient weapon.

मुददआ-

मुददई-plaintiff; suitor; enemy.

मुद्दत-duration; long period/time.

मुद्दती-of a fixed duration; old; time-worn.

मुद्दा-intention; purport; proposition; issue.

मुद्र-type printing .

मुद्रण-printing.

मुद्रणालय-printing press.

मुद्रलिख-typewriter.

मुद्रा-seal; money; coin/currency; mien.

मुद्रा-बाज़ार-money market.

मुद्राशास्त्र-numismatics.

मुद्रास्फीति-inflation of currency.

मुद्रिका-finger ring; seal.

मुद्रित-printed.

मुनक्क़ा-currant.

मुनादी-announcement; proclamation.

मुनाफ़ा-profit; gain; advantage.

मुनासिब-proper; fit; just; reasonable.

मुनि-hermit; sage; saint.

मुनियाँ-a small red-coloured bird; small girl.

मुनींद्र-great hermit/sage.

मुनीम-accounts clerk; accountant; clerk.

मुनीमी-work or profession of a accountant.

मुनीश-a great hermit/sage.

मुनीश्वर-great hermit.

मुन्ना-dear child.

मुफ़लिस-poor; pauper.

मुफ़लिसी-penury; poverty.

मुफ़ीद-beneficial; useful; advantageous.

मुफ़्त-free of charge.

मुफ़्तख़ोर-social parasite.

मुफ़्तख़ोरी-habit of living on others; parasitic way of living.

मुफ़्ती-dispenser of law.

मुबारक-auspicious.

मुबारकबाद-congratulations.

मुबालग़ा-exaggeration.

मुबाहिसा-discussion.

मुमकिन-possible.

मुमताज़-selected; chosen; preferred.

मुमानियत-prohibition, forbiddance.

मुमुक्षा-aspiration for salvation.

मुमुक्षु-seeking/desiring salvation/ deliverance.

मुमूर्षा-pining for death; desire to die.

मुमूर्षु-person pining for death.

मुरंडा-dried out; very lean and thin.

मुरकी-ear-top; ear-ring; a kind of musical ornamentation around a note.

मुरग़ा-cock; fowl.

मुरग़ाबी-water-fowl.

मुरग़ी-hen.

मुरग़ी-पालन-poultry-farming.

मुरझाना-to fade/wither.

मुरदनी- lifeless/deadly/deathly stillness; funeral.

मुरदा-dead.

मुरदा-घर-mortuary.

मुरब्बा-. square.-jam; preserve.

मुरमुरा-parached and puffed rice; maize etc.

मुरमुराना-to break with a clicking sound; to crack down.

मुरलिका-flute.

मुरली-flute.

मुरलीधर-flute-player; Lord Krishna.

मुरलीमनोहर-Lord Krishna.

मुरव्वत-consideration; affability; favour; obliging disposition.

मुराद-longing; craving.

मुरारी-Lord Krishna.

मुरीद-follower; disciple.

मुर्ग़-cock.

मुलमुलाना-to blink.

मुलम्मा-veneer; coating.

मुलम्मासाज़-glider.

मुलाक़ात-meeting; acquaintance.

मुलाक़ाती-visitor; acquaintance.

मुलाज़मत-service; employment.

मुलाज़िम-employee; servant.

मुलायम soft; delicate; tender.

मुलायमियत-softness; tenderness.

मुलाहिज़ा-consideration; regard for others.

मुलेठी-liquorice.

मुल्क-country.

मुल्की-pertaining to a country.

मुल्ज़िम-accused.

मुल्तवी-postponed.

मुल्ला-Muslim priest.

मुवक्किल-client.

मुशायरा poet's meet; poetic symposium.

मुश्क-musk; odour; smell; arm.

मुश्किल-not easy; difficult; hard; tough.

मुश्की-musky.

मुश्त-fist.

मुष्टि-fist.

मुष्टि-प्रहार-hard punch; sock.
मुसम्मात-woman; lady.
मुसम्माती-pertaining to a woman.
मुसम्मी-a variety of orange.
मुसलमान-Muslim.
मुसलमानी-of a Muslim.-circumcision.
मुसल्लम-all entire; whole.
मुसल्ला-Muslim prayer-mat.
मुसाफ़िर-traveller; voyager; passenger.
मुसाफ़िरख़ाना-waiting room.
मुसाफ़िरी-travel.
मुसाहबी-sycophancy.
मुसाहिब-counsellor; sycophant.
मुसीबत-difficulty; trouble; adversity; calamity; misfortune.
मुसीबतज़दा-struck by misfortune.
मुस्कराना-to smile.
मुस्कान-smile.
मुस्टंडा-boorish; hefty fellow.
मुस्तैद-ever-ready; alert; prompt; vigilant.
मुस्तैदी-ever-readiness; alertness; vigilance.
मुस्लिम-Muslim.
मुहकमा-department.
मुहताज indigent; poor; handicapped; needy; wanting.
मुहब्बत-love; deep affection.
मुहब्बती-loving; affectionate.
मुहम्मद-praised; prophet Mohammed.
मुहम्मदी-pertaining to Mohammed; a Muslim.
मुहर-an Indian gold coin; seal; stamp.
मुहरबंद-sealed.
मुहर्रम-day of 's martyrdom a Muslim festival.
मुर्हरमी-dismal; very gloomy.
मुहर्रिर-clerk.
मुहर्रिरी-work or calling of a clerk.
मुहलत-period of time allotted for finishing a job; leisure; leave of absence from work.
मुहल्ला-locality.
मुहल्लेदार-neighbour; one living in the same locality/street.
मुहल्लेदारी-neighbour-hood; feeling of neighbourliness.
मुहाना-estuary; mouth.
मुहाल-difficult.
मुहावरा-idiom; practice.
मुहावरेदार-idiomatic.
मुहासा-pimple.
मुहिम-campaign; military expedition; arduous job.
मुहूर्त-auspicious moment.
मूँग-green gram; kidney bean.
मूँगफली-ground-nut.
मूँगा-coral.
मूँगिया-of the colour of
मूँछ-moustache.

मूँज-a kind of reed.

मूँड़-head.

मूँड़ना-to shave the head; to fleece.

मूँदना-to close/shut/cover.

मूआ-head.

मूक dump; speechless; mute; silent.

मूज़ी-tyrannical; mean; lowly; extremely miserly/stingy.

मूठ-handle; black magic.

मूड-mood.

मूढ़-idiotic; stupid; foolish; ignorant.

मूढ़ता-idiocy; stupidity; foolishness; folly; silliness.

मूत-urine.

मूतना-to pass urine; to urinate.

मूत्र-urine.

मूत्रालय-urinal.

मूत्राशय-urinary bladder.

मूर्ख-stupid; foolish.

मूर्खता-stupidity; foolishness.

मूर्च्छना, मूर्छना-modulation.

मूर्च्छा, मूर्छा-swoon; fainting.

मूर्च्छित, मूर्छित-fainted; out of senses, hysterical.

मूर्त-concrete; tangible; corporeal; personified.

मूर्तता-concreteness.

मूर्ति-idol; statue; icon.

मूर्तिमान, मूर्तिमान्-personified.

मूर्द्धन्य, मूर्धन्य-cerebral; top-ranking; renowed; leading.

मूर्द्धा, मूर्धा-cerebrum.

मूलत: originally; basically; fundamentally.

मूलतत्त्व-the basic element of a subject.

मूलधन-principal amo-unt.

मूलभूत-fundamental; basic.

मूलमंत्र-keynote.

मूल स्थान-original home; starting point; source.

मूली-radish.

मूलीय-pertaining to the root.

मूल्य-value; price; principle; standard.

मूल्य-नियंत्रण-price control.

मूल्यवान-valuable; precious; costly.

मूल्यविहीन-valueless; worthless.

मूल्यवृद्धि-hike/rise in price.

मूल्य-सूचकांक-price index.

मूल्य-सूची-price list.

मूल्यांकन-valuation; estimation.

मूल्यांकनकर्ता-valuer.

मूल्यानुसार-ad valorem.

मूषक-rat.

मूषिका-she-rat.

मूस-rat; mouse.

मूसदानी-rat-trap.

मूसना-to extort out money from someone; to steal; pilfer.

मूसल-pestle.
मूसलचंद-rustic; sturdy but idle fellow.
मूसलधार-torrential rain.
मूसला-tap-root.
मूसली-small pestle.
मूसा-mouse; Moses.
मूसाई-follower of Moses; Jew.
मृग-deer.
मृगचर्म-skin of deer; deerskin.
मृगछाला-skin of deer; deerskin.
मृगछौना-fawn.
मृगजल-mirage.
मृगतृष्णा-mirage; any hope that cannot be fulfilled.
मृगदाव-deer-park.
मृगनयनी-deer-eyed; having captivating eyes.
मृग-मरीचिका-mirage.
मृगया-the chasing and killing of birds and wild animals; hunting.
मृगी-hind.
मृणाल-stalk of the lotus plant.
मृणपात्र-earthen vessel; pot.
मृणमूर्ति-clay model.
मृत-dead; deceased; extinct.
मृतक-a dead person.
मृतक-कर्म-obsequies; last rites.
मृतजात-still-born.
मृतप्राय-about to come to an end; almost dead.
मृत-संजीवनी-a mythological herb which restores life to the dead.
मृत्तिका-earth; clay.
मृत्युंजय-immortal; Lord .
मृत्यु-death.
मृत्युकर-death duty.
मृत्युदंड-capital punishment.
मृत्यु-दर-death rate.
मृत्यु-प्रमाणक-death certificate.
मृत्युलोक-this world; mortal world.
मृत्युशय्या-death bed.
मृत्यु-संख्या-death roll.
मृत्यु-समाचार-obituary; news of the death of someone.
मृदंग-an Indian musical instrument of the percussion type.
मृदु-soft; tender; mild; sweet; gentle.
मृदुता-softness; tenderness; sweetness; gentleness.
मृदुभाषी-sweet/soft-tongued.
मृदुल-soft; tender; sweet.
मृदुलता-softness; tenderness; sweetness.
में-in; into; at; on; between among; denoting possession.
मेंगनी-dung-ball of cattle.
मेंड-ridge between two fields.
मेंडक-frog.
मेंडकी-female of frog.
मेंबर-member.

मेंबरी-membership.

मेंमें-bleat of a goat.

मेंह-rain.

मेकप-act of applying cosmetics; make-up.

मेख-smallish nail.

मेखल-girdle.

मेखला-belt.

मेगज़ीन-magazine.

मेघ-cloud.

मेघदूत-a classical Sanskrit poem of in which he addresses the cloud as a lover's messenger.

मेघनाद-thunder.

मेघाच्छन्न-over spread with clouds; clouded.

मेघाच्छादित-clouded.

मेघालय-a state in the east of India.

मेज़-table.

मेज़बान-one who receives and entertains guest, host; one who introduces and interviews guests; presenter.

मेज़बानी-generous treatment and entertainment of guest; hospitality.

मेजर-major army.

मेट-mate; foreman of labourers.

मेट्रन-matron.

मेडिकल-medical.

मेढ़ा-ram.

मेढ़ी-small braid; braiding.

मेथी-a green plant used as vegetable.

मेद-fate inside the body.

मेदा-stomach.

मेदिनी-earth.

मेधा-intellect.

मेधावी-intellectual; intelligent; wise; clever.

मेनू-menu.

मेम-madam; lady; in playing cards queen.

मेमना-lamb.

मेम-साहब-lady; your Ladyship!

मेमार-mason.

मेमोरियल-memorial.

मेयर-mayor.

मेरा-तेरा-mine and thine.

मेरी-pron. used to emphasize the speaker.

मेरु-a mythological mountain.

मेरुज्योति-auroro polaris.

मेरुदंड-backbone; spine.

मेरुदंडीय-spinal; vertebrate.

मेरु-रज्जु-spinal cord.

मेल-match; concord.

मेल-गाड़ी-mail train.

मेल-जोल-intimacy.

मेलना-to collate.

मेल-मिलाप-unison; reconciliation; coming back to friendship after estrangement.

मेल-मुलाकात-friendly association; social relationship.

मेल-मुहब्बत-mutual affection; close relationship.

मेला-fair; fete.

मेला-ठेला-festive gathering; crowdy gathering.

मेवा-dry fruit.

मेवाड़-a region in India.

मेवाड़ी-pertaining to .-dialect of .

मेष-sheep; Aries, the first sign of zodiac.

मेस-mess.

मेहँदिया-of the colour of myrtle.

मेहँदी-myrtle.

मेह-diabetes.

मेहतर-sweeper; scavenger.

मेहतरानी-female of

मेहनत-labour; toil.

मेहनत-मज़दूरी-manual labour.

मेहनताना-remuneration specially that paid to a lawyer.

मेहनती-laborious.

मेहना-taunt.

मेहमान-guest.

मेहमानदार-hospitable; host.

मेहमानदारी-hospi-tability.

मेहमानी-stay as guest.

मेहर-grace.

मेहरबान-kind; benevolent; merciful.

मेहरा-servant who does household chores, drawing water; cleansing utensils.

मेहराब-arch.

मेहरारू-woman; wife.

मेहरी-female of servant; maid-servant.

मैं-pron. I.

मैंगनीज़-manganese.

मै-wine.

मैख़ाना-liquor-shop; bar.

मैत्री-friendship; alliance; unison.

मैथिली-a dialect of spoken in region in North.

मैथुन-coitus.

मैदा-fine-flour.

मैदान-ground; plains.

मैना-a black Indian bird with a melodious voice.

मैनाक-a peak of the Himalayas.

मैयत-death.

मैया-mother.

मैल-dirt; filth; grudge; grouse.

मैलख़ोरा-dust/dirt absorbing.

मैला-dirty; filthy; nasty; defiled; foul.

मैला-कुचैला-dirty and untidy; slatternly.

मैलापन-dirtiness; filthiness.

मोक्ष-Salvation; Deliverance; .

मोखा-opening; scuttle; peehole.

मोच-sprain; twist.

मोचन-deliverance; riddance; release; acquittal.
मोचना-to get rid of; to liberate.
मोची-cobbler.
मोज़ा-sock; stocking.
मोट-bundle; bag of leather.
मोटर-motor.
मोटरकार-motor-car.
मोटर-ड्राइवर-motor-driver.
मोटर-साईकिल-motor-cycle.
मोटा-fat; rough.
मोटाई-obesity; fatness.
मोटा-झोटा-coarse; rough.
मोटा-ताज़ा-fleshy and plump.
मोटाना-to grow fat; to fatten; to become swollen-headed.
मोटापा-obesity; fatness; plumpness; corpulence.
मोठ-a kind of lentil.
मोड़-turn; bend; curve.
मोड़-तोड़-turn and twist.
मोड़ना-to turn/bend/twist.
मोतिया-of the colour of pearl.
मोतियाबंद-cataract.
मोती-pearl.
मोती-चूर-tiny sweetened balls of gram flour.
मोती-झरा-typhoid.
मोद-delight; pleasure.
मोदक-a type of Indian sweet.
मोदी-grocer.
मोम-wax.
मोमजामा-oil-cloth.
मोमबत्ती-candle-stick.
मोमिन-Muslim; Muslim weaver class.
मोमिया-mummy.
मोमियाई-a kind of black ointment.
मोमी-made of wax.
मोयन-ghee used in kneading flour.
मोर-peacock.
मोर-चंद्रिका-moon-like pattern at the end of a peacock's feather.
मोरचा-rust; battle front; a particular area of activity; front.
मोरचेबंदी-battle-array; entrenchment.
मोरछल-whist made of peacock feathers.
मोरनी-peahen.
मोरपंख-peacock feather.
मोरपंखी-of the colour of the feather of a peacock.
मोरम-a reddish pebble used in the construction of roads.
मोरमुकुट-crown made of peacock feathers.
मोरी-drain; sewer; outlet for water.
मोल-price; cost.
मोल-भाव-bargaining; horse trading.
मोह-infatuation; fascination; delusion.

मोहक-attractive; charming; fascinating; stupefying.

मोहग्रस्त-infatuated; obsessed.

मोहन-extremely charming; enchanting; alluring.

मोहना-to charm/fascinate.

मोहनिद्रा-stupor due to illusion.

मोहभंग- disenchantment; disillusionment.

मोहनी-spell; enchantment.

मोह-ममता-deep attachment; undue affection.

मोहरा-the mouth of a container; chessman; forepart of an army; vanguard.

मोहरी-mouth-like forepart of trousers or bottle etc.

मोहलत-leisure; moratorium; period of time.

मोहिनी-spell; enchantment.

मोही-fascinated; captivated; under an illusion.

मौक़ा-occasion; opportunity.

मौक्तिक-of pearls.

मौखिक-spoken; oral; verbal.

मौज-wave; fancy; caprice.

मौज-पानी-easy-life.

मौज-मज़ा-revelry; merry-making.

मौज़ा-village.

मौजी-capricious; fanciful; jovial.

मौजूँ-just; suitable; opportune; appropriate.

मौजूद-present.

मौजूदगी-presence.

मौत-end of life; death; the power that destroy life.

मौन-the state of non-speaking silence.

मौन-प्रार्थना-silent prayer.

मौनव्रत-vow of silence.

मौन-सम्मति-tacit consent.

मौन-सहमति-acquiescence; tacit concurrence.

मौर-crown; diadem; tiara; crest; coronet; blossoming of mango.

मौरूसी-hereditary.

मौलवी-scholar of Arabic, Persian or Urdu.

मौलसिरी-the plant ninsops dengi.

मौला-master; god.

मौलाना-a great Muslim scholar.

मौलिक-original; basic; elementary; fundamental.

मौलिकता-originality.

मौसम-weather; season; suitable period

मौसमी seasonal.

मौसा-husband of mother's sister.

मौसी-mother's sister.

मौसेरा-related through.

म्याऊँ-mewing of a cat .

म्यान-sheath; scabbard.

म्युज़ियम-museum.
म्युनिसिपेल्टी-municipality.
म्लान-withered; without energy or spirit; languid; gloomy.
म्लानता-state of being withered; languor; gloom.
मलेच्छ-dirty unclean; un-Indian; pagan.
म्लेच्छता-state or quality of being dirty.

य

य-The twenty-sixty, palatal consonant of the alphabet.
यंत्र-instrument; apparatus; implement; talisman; machine; amulet.
यंत्रकार-machine-maker.
यंत्रचालित-machine-operated.
यंत्रज्ञ-mechanic.
यंत्रणा-affliction; fortune; pain; anguish.
यंत्र-मंत्र-sorcery; black magic.
यंत्र-मानव-robot.
यंत्र-युग-machine-age.
यंत्र-रचना-mechanism.
यंत्रवत् mechanically; like a machine.
यंत्र-विद्या-repairing or handling machines; art of making.
यंत्र-सज्जित-mechanized.
यंत्रालय-machine-room.
यंत्रिका-gadget; small machine.
यंत्रीकरण-mechanization.
यकायक all of a sudden.
यकार-the letter or its sound.
यक़ीन-surety; confidence; certainty; faith.
यक़ीनन confidently; certainly; surely.
यकृत-liver.
यक्ष-mythological demigod.
यक्ष्मा-tuberculosis.
यजमान-host; patron of priest.
यजमानी-work or function of a host.
यजुर्वेद-the third of the four .
यजुर्वेदी-adherent of ; scholar of
यज्ञ-religious sacrifice and oblation.
यज्ञ-मंडप-a canopy prepared for performance of religious sacrifice and oblation.
यज्ञोपवीत-the sacred thread worn by the caste Hindus.
यति-ascetic; check; obstacle.
यतीम-orphan.
यतीमख़ाना-orphanage.
यतीमी-of an orphan.
यत्किंचित्-somewhat; to a small degree.
यत्न-effort; exertion; labour; device; care.
यत्नपूर्वक-with effort; with due care.

यत्नशील-making an effort; diligent; laborious.

यत्नशीलता-state or quality of being laborious.

यत्र-तत्र here and there; at several places.

यथांश-quota.

यथा as per.

यथाकथित-as mentioned; as forehead/state.

यथाक्रम-in (due) order; systematically; as scheduled.

यथाज्ञा-as per order.

यथातथ्य-exact; as it is.

यथानियम-according to rule.

यथापूर्व-as before.

यथापूर्व स्थिति-status quo.

यथामूल्य-advalorem.

यथायोग्य-suitably.

यथार्थ-real; exact; reality.

यथार्थतः really; exactly.

यथार्थता-reality; exactness; exactitude; accuracy.

यथार्थवाद-realism.

यथार्थवादी-realistic.

यथावकाश-as per leisure.

यथावत्-as before.

यथाशक्ति-as far as possible; to one's level best/capacity.

यथाशीघ्र-as soon as possible.

यथासंभव-as far as possible; in all probability.

यथासमय-in due course; in time.

यथासाध्य-as far as practicable.

यथास्थान-at the proper place.

यथास्थिति-according to the situation.

यथेष्ट-sufficient; enough; as required.

यथेष्टता-sufficiently.

यथोचित-proper; just; appropriate.

यदा when; where.

यदा-कदा occasionally; off and on.

यदि if; in case; supposing.

यद्यपि though; although; even though; in spite of.

यम-god of Death.

यमक-pun.

यमज-born together; twin.

यमदूत-messenger/angel of Death.

यमपुरी-infernal world.

यमलोक-infernal world.

यमुना-name of a river.

यवन-Mohammedan.

यवनिका-curtain.

यश-repute; renown.

यशगान-eulogy.

यशस्वी-reputed; renowned; glorious; celebrated.

यशोगाथा-narrative of glorious deeds.

यशोगान-eulogy; encomium.

यष्टि-rod; stick.

यह-this one.

यहाँ-here.

यहाँ, के-at this house/place.

यहाँवाले-local place.

यहीं-at this very place.

यही-this very; this one.

यहूदिन-Jewess.

यांत्रिक-mechanical.

यांत्रिकता-mechanism.

या-or.

याचक-suppliant; beggar.

याचना-supplication; suppliance; begging.

याचिका-petition.

याजक-sacrificing priest.

यातना-torture; bodily infliction.

यातायात-traffic; transport.

यात्रा-journey; march.

यात्री-traveller; passenger.

याद-memory.

याददाश्त-memory.

यादृच्छिक-arbitrary; random.

यान-vehicle.

यानी that is.

यापन-spending; passing.

यामिनी-night.

याम्तोत्तर-meridian.

यायावर-nomad.

यार-friend; companion; boy friend; lover.

याराना-friendly.

यारी-friendship.

यावज्जीवन throughout life; lifelong.

यावत्-as much. as far as.

युक्त-combined; joined; fitted.

युक्ति-plea; argument; device; trick.

युक्तिपूर्ण-reasonable; sound.

युक्तिपूर्वक tactfully; skilfully.

युक्तियुक्त-befitting; suitable; proper.

युक्तिसंगत reasonable; rational.

युक्तिसंगतता-reasonableness.

युग-age; era; epoch; long period.

युगपत्-simultaneous.

युग-परिवर्तन-change of the era.

युगयुगांतर-for ages after ages.

युगल-twins; pair.

युगांतर-new era.

युगांतरकारी-epoch-making.

युगीय-of a epoch.

युग्म-pair; couple.

युति-combination.

युद्ध-war; warfare; battle.

युद्धक-fighting.

युद्ध-कौशल-tactics of war; stratagem.

युद्धक्षेत्र-battle-field.

युद्धघोष-battle/war cry.

युद्धनीति-war policy/strategy.

युद्धपोत-warship.

युद्धबंदी-prisoner of war.

युद्धभूमि-battle-field.

युद्धमंत्री-Minister of war.

युद्धरत-belligerent.

युद्धविराम-ceasefire.

युद्धस्थगन-cessation of hostilities.

युद्धकांक्षी-militant.

युद्धाभ्यास-manoeuvres of war.

युयुत्सा-belligerence; enmity.

युयुत्सु-militant; belligerent; war monger.

युवक-young boy/man; youth.

युवती-young girl/woman.

युवराज-heir; apparent.

युवा-youth; young person.

युवावस्था-young age; youth; youthfulness.

यूनानी-an inhabitant of Greece.

ये-they.

येन-केन-प्रकारेण somehow or other.

यों-in this way; thus.

योग-total; grand/sum total; joining together; union; system of meditation; one of the six schools of Indian philosophy; conjunction (of stars).

योगक्षेम-welfare.

योगदान-participation; contribution.

योगफल-sum; result of addition.

योगबल-power acquired through *Yoga.*

योगशास्त्र-treatise on *Yoga.*

योगात्मक-pertaining to *Yoga.*

योगाभ्यास-practice of *Yoga.*

योगासन-posture adopted in practising *Yoga.*

योगिनी-female of *Yogi.*

योगी-ascetic; yogi.

योग्य-able; capable; worthy.

योग्य, के to be equal to or capable for; up to.

योग्यता-ability; capability; fitness.

योग्यतापूर्वक ably; meritoriously.

योजक-which unites/joins; connective; conjunction.

योजक-चिह्न-hyphen.

योजन-joining; union; a measure of distance; roughly 13 kilometres.

योजना-project; scheme; plan.

योजना आयोग-Planning Commission.

योजनाबद्ध-planned; preplanned.

योजिका-hyphen.

योजित-planned/projected.

योद्धा-warrior.

योनि-vagina; female organ; form of life.

यौगिक-compound.

यौन-sexual.

यौनता-sexuality.

यौनतृप्ति-sexual gratification.

यौनधर्म-sexual function.

यौन-भावना-sexual urge.

यौनमत्त-feeling sexual desire; sexy.

यौनमत्ता-sexiness.

यौनाचारी-sex-indulgent; morally lax.

यौनिकी-Sexology.

यौवन-youth; adolescence; heyday.

यौवनकाल-period of youth.

यौवनारंभ-beginning of youth; puberty.

यौवनावस्था-youth age.

र

र-The twenty-seventh cerebral consonant of the alphabet; it is the second of the semivowels.

रंक-penniless; poor.

रंग-hue; dye; colour; complexion; paint.

रंगक्षेत्र-stage.

रंग-ढंग-conduct; way.

रंगत-complexion; tint; tinge; shade.

रँगना-to colour/dye.

रंग-बिरंगा-of various colours; multi-coloured; motley.

रंगभूमि-theatre.

रंगभेद-apartheid; colour bar.

रंगमंच-stage.

रंगमंचीय-theatrical; stagy.

रंगमंडप-theatre.

रंगमहल-theatre.

रंग-रँगीला-jovial; colourful and gay.

रंगरली-revelry.

रंगरूट-novice; recruit.

रंग-रूप-complexion; the colour and general appearance of the skin especially of the face.

रंगरेज़-dyer.

रंगरेली-

रंग-रोग़न-paint and varnish.

रँगवाना-causative of to cause to be dyed.

रंगशाला-theatre; stage.

रंगसाज़-painter.

रंगसाज़ी-painting.

रँगाई-colouring; painting; act of process of dying, or charges paid for the same.

रंगारंग-variegated; colourful.

रंगीन-colourful; coloured.

रंगीनी-colourfulness.

रँगीला-gay; sportive; colourful; jovial.

रँगीलापन-gaiety; sportiveness; colourfulness.

रंगोली-pictures made on the ground with coloured powders.

रँगौधी-colourblind-ness.

रंज-sorrow; grief.

रंजक-pigment; dye-stuff.

रंजन-dyeing; entertainment.

रंजित-dyed; coloured.

रंजिश-ill-feeling; malice.

रंजीदा-sad; gloomy.

रँडापा-widowhood.

रंडी-prostitute; harlot.

रंडीबाज़-one who wenches with prostitute.

रंडीबाज़ी-habit of wenching with prostitutes.

रँडुआ-widower.

रँडुआपन-state of being a widower.

रँदना-to plane (carpentry).

रंदा-planer.

रंधन-cooking.

रंध्र-pore; orifice.

रंभा-a celestial nymph; prostitute; harlot; iron rod, chiselled at one end, used for digging holes

रँभाना-to bellow (cow, buffalo etc.).

रइयत-subject; peasant.

रई-churning stick.

रईस-wealthy; prosperous.

रईसज़ादा-scion of a nobleman.

रईसी-richness; riches; nobility.

रक़बा-area.

रक़म-amount; sum; capital; goodly sum; ornament.

रकाब-stirrup.

रकाबी-disc; plate.

रकार-the letter or its sound.

रकारांत-(word) ending in

रक्त-blood; blood-red.

रक्त-कणिका-blood-corpuscle.

रक्त-क्षीणता-anaemia.

रक्तचाप-blood-pressure.

रक्तदाता-donor of blood; blood-donor.

रक्तदान-donation of blood.

रक्तपात-bloodshed; carnage.

रक्तपायी-blood-sucker.-leech.

रक्तपिपासु-bloodthirsty.

रक्तरंजित-blood-stained; bloody; involving bloodshed.

रक्तवर्ण-blood-red.

रक्तस्राव-haemorrhage; bleeding.

रक्ताभ-ruddy; having red tinge.

रक्तिम-red-coloured.

रक्षक-defender; protector; saviour; guard.

रक्षण-protection; defence.

रक्षा-protection; defence.

रक्षा-कवच-safeguard; armour.

रक्षात्मक-defensive; protective.

रक्षाबंधन-a Hindu festival held on the full moon day of sisters tie a sacramental thread on the wrist of their brothers, the latter guarantee them life-long protection.

रक्षार्थ, के-for protection or defence.

रक्षित-protected.

रक्ष्य-worth protecting/defending/ life-long protection.

रखना-to put/place; to lay; to keep; to appoint; to maintain.

रखनी-kept woman.

रख-रखाव-maintenance; upkeep.

रखवाना-to cause to place/appoint/maintain, etc.

रखवाला-caretaker; guard; watchman.

रखवाली-guarding; watchmanship.

रखाना-to guard.

रखेल-a kept wife or a person.

रखेली-concubine; kept woman.

रग-nerve.

रगड़-friction.

रगड़ना-to rub.

रगड़वाना-causative of rubbing.

रगड़ा-rub; rubbing.

रग-पट्ठा-veins and muscles.

रग-रेशा-the fibres of a leaf; the various parts within the body.

रगेदना-to chase away.

रघु-the primeval ancestor of the ancient solar dynasty of India.

रघुकुल-the solar dynasty starting with

रघुनंदन-Ram, the greatgrandson of

रचना-construction; composition; formation; to construct; to compose; to fabricate.

रचनात्मक-constructive.

रचनाधर्मिता-constructive nature.

रचनाधर्मी-having constructive nature.

रचयिता-author; composer.

रचित-constructed; composed; compiled.

रज-dust; blood of menstruation.

रजत-silver.

रजत-जयंती-silver jubilee.

रजतपट-silver screen.

रजतमान-silver standard.

रजनी-night.

रजनीकर-moon.

रजनीचर-nocturnal being; demon.

रजनीपति-moon.

रजनीश-moon.

रजवाड़ा-erstwhile princely state of India.

रजस्वला-woman in her menstrual period.

रज़ा-wish; desire; consent; permission.

रज़ाई-quilt.

रज़ाकार-volunteer.

रज़ामंद-agreed.

रज़ामंदी-consent; agreement.

रजिस्टर-register.

रजिस्ट्रार-registrar.

रजिस्ट्री-registration.

रजोगुण-the second of the three constituent qualities of all the material objects.

रजोधर्म-menses.

रजोनिवृति-menopause.

रज्जु-rope; cord; string.

रटंत-learning by rote; repetitiousness.

रटंत-विद्या-the process of learning by study rather than by understanding.

रट-continual repetition; reiteration.

रटन-repeating.

रटना-to cram; to learn by rote.

रडार-radar.

रड़क-irritating sensation (due to some foreign matter).

रड़कना-to produce irritating pain.

रण-battle; war; combat.

रणकौशल-tactics of war; stratagem.

रणक्षेत्र-battle-field.

रणचंडी-Goddess of war .

रणछोड़-Lord

रणधीर-steady warrior.

रणस्थल-battle-field.

रणांगण-battle-zone.

रत-engaged; busy; absorbed.

रतजगा-keeping awake/vigil the whole night usually for devotional purposes, singing etc.

रतनारा-ruddy; red.

रतनारी-(eyes) with veins reddened.

रति-conjugal love; love; cohabitation; affection.

रतिक्रिया-cohabitation; copulation.

रतिभाव-sentiment of love/affection.

रतिशास्त्र-Sexology.

रतौंध-night-blind; nyctalopic.

रतौंधी-night-blindness; nyctalopia.

रत्ती-an Indian weight; approximately equal to 1.2 mg.

रत्न-jewel; gem; the most extraordinary/talented.

रत्नकार-jeweller.

रत्नाकर-ocean; sea.

रथ-chariot.

रथवान-charioteer.

रथवाह-charioteer.

रथी-charioteer.

रथ्या-roadway.

रद-tooth.

रदक्षत-tooth-mark.

रद्द-cancelled.

रद्दा-rubbing stroke with the arm; layer.

रद्दी-of very poor/inferior quality; worthless; waste paper; something discarded as junk; waste material.

रद्दोबदल-alteration; modification; change.

रन-run (cricket).

रनिवास-harem; seraglio.

रपट-report.

रपटना-slippery.-to slip/skid.

रपटीला-slippery.

रफ़-rough.

रफ़ता-रफ़ता-gradually; slowly.

रफ़ल-shawl; woollen wrapper.

रफ़ा-shunted away.

रफ़ा-दफ़ा-settled and finished; done away with.

रफ़ू-darning.

रफ़ूगर-darner.

रफ़ूगरी-calling of darner.

रफ़ू-चक्कर-disappeared; run away.

रफ़्तार-speed.

रब-God.

रबड़-rubber.

रबड़ी-thick sweetened milk.

रबी-spring crop; crop.

रब्त-ज़ब्त-mixing together; close association.

रमक-flavour.

रमचेरा-attendant.

रमज़ान-ninth month of the Muslim calendar.

रमण-amorous activity/dalliance; cohabitation; merriment.

रमणी-(lovely) young woman.

रमणीक-pleasing; attractive; inviting.

रमणीकता-state or quality of being

रमणीय-pleasant and enjoyable; elegant; charming; fascinating.

रमणीयता-state or quality of being pleasant and enjoyable.

रमता-roving; roaming; wandering.

रमता जोगी-roving mendicant; wandering .

रमना-to rove; to be engrossed; lawn; pleasant spot for roaming.

रमल-future-telling by a throw of dice; geomancy.

रमा-Goddess of wealth.

रम्मी-a game of cards in which players try to form sets or sequences of cards; rummy.

रम्य-pleasant.

रलना-to get mixed up; as a child in a crowd.

रव-sound; noise; uproar; tumult.

रवन्ना-passage/transit permit; waybill.

रवाँ-fit; proper; accurate.

रवा-crystal.

रवानगी-departure.

रवाना-departed; set out.

रवानी-flow; fluency.

रवि-Sun.

रवि-उच्च-aphelion.

रवि-नीच-perihelion.

रविमार्ग-ecliptic.

रविवार-Sunday.

रविश-aisle/path between flower beds; movement.

रवेदार-granular; crystalline.

रवैया-way of doing something; style; way of dealing with someone; behaviour; conduct.

रशियन-Russian.

रश्मि-beam; ray.

रस-juice; essence; sap (of tree); extract; relish; flavour; interest.

रसगुल्ला-an Indian sweet made from cheese.

रसज्ञ-connoisseur.

रसद-provisions; supplies

रसदार-containing a lot of juice; juicy.

रसदारु-sap wood; resinous wood.

रसना-tongue.

रसभंग-interruption of relish.

रसभरा-full of juice; juicy.

रसभरी-raspberry.

रसमय-juicy.

रसशास्त्र-Chemistry.

रससिद्ध-expert in preparing medicinal extracts.

रसहीन-sapless.

रसा-soup of meat, vegetable etc.; broth; juice.

रसाई-approach.

रसातल-nether world; hell; Hedges; under world.

रसात्मक-juicy; giving pleasure.

रसायन-chemistry.

रसायनज्ञ-chemist.

रसायनशाला-chemical laboratory.

रसायनशास्त्र-(science of) Chemistry.

रसायनशास्त्री-chemist; one well-versed in Chemistry.

रसाल-mango.

रसास्वादन-tasting; relishing.

रसिक-getting pleasure from poetry, drama etc.; jolly person.

रसिकता-liking or enjoyment of poetry, drama etc.

रसिया-a man of taste; one with aesthetic sense; a type of folk song.

रसीद-receipt.

रसीदी टिकट-revenue stamp.

रसीला-juicy; delicious.

रसूल-divine messenger; prophet.

रसेदार-having broth.

रसोइया-cook; chef.

रसोई-cooking; cuisine; kitchen.

रसोई-घर-kitchen.

रसौली-tumour.

रस्म-custom; practice; formality.

रस्म-रिवाज़-conventions; customs and practices.

रस्मी-ceremonial.

रस्सा-rope.

रस्साकशी-tug-of-war.

रस्सी-rope string; cord.

रहन-mortgage; way of living.

रहन-सहन-way of living.

रहट-Persian wheel (used for drawing water from a well).

रहना-to live; to stay; to remain.

रहम-kindness; pity; compassion; benevolence.

रहमदिल-kind; merciful; compassionate; benevolent.

रहस्य-secret; inexplicable event; mystery.

रहस्यपूर्ण-mysterious; arcane; mystic.

रहस्य-भरा-mysterious.

रहस्यमय-mysterious; arcane.

रहस्यवाद-mysticism.

रहस्यवादी-of or based on mysticism; mystical; mystic.

रहस्यात्मक-mystical; mysterious.

रहस्योद्घाटन-revelation of a mystery.

रहा-सहा-all that remained; residual; left over.

रहित-bereft; less; devoid.

रहीम-kind; God.

राँगा-tin.

राँड-widow.

राँधना-to cook (lentil, rice etc.).

राइफ़ल-rifle.

राई-small seeds of mustard used as condiment.

राका-the night of the full moon.

राकेट-rocket.

राकेट-विद्या-rocketry.

राकेश-moon.

राक्षस-goblin; devil; demon; giant; monster; wicked person; badly behaved person.

राक्षसी-devilish; demoniac.-demoness.

राख-ash; ashes.

राखदान-ash-tray.

राखी-sacred thread tied by the sister on the wrist of her brother who guarantees life-long protection to her.

राग-melody; tune; passion; attachment.

रागदारी-classical way of singing.

रागरंग-merry-making; enjoyment.

रागिनी-a kind of melody.

रागी-filled with love/attachment.

राछ-a weaver's tool.

राज-state; dominion; rule; administration; kingdom; reign; mason.

राजकन्या-princess.

राजकर्ता-statesman.

राजकाज-state affairs.

राजकीय-of or pertaining to the state; of the government; governmental; princely; managed by the state.

राजकुमार-prince.

राजकुमारी-princess.

राजकुल-royal family.

राजकोष-royal treasury.

राजगद्दी-throne; enthronement.

राजगीर-mason.

राजगीरी-masonry.

राजगृह-palace; royal mansion.

राजचिह्न-insignia of royalty.
राजतंत्र-monarchy; polity.
राजतंत्रवादी-royalist.
राजतिलक-coronation.
राजत्व-kindship; reign.
राजदंड-sceptre; punishment awarded by the king.
राजदूत-ambassador.
राजदूतावास-embassy; consulate.
राजद्रोह-treason; sedition; disloyalty.
राजद्रोही-seditionist; disloyal.
राजधानी-the seat of a government of the country; capital; metropolis; a place associated with a particular activity; capital.
राजधानीय-metropolitan.
राजनय-diplomacy.
राजनयिक-diplomatic; diplomat.
राजनीति-politics.
राजनीतिक-political.
राजनीतिकरण-politicization.
राजनीतिज्ञ-politician; statesman.
राजनीति-शास्त्र-Political Science.
राजनेता-statesman.
राजनैतिक-political.
राजपत्र-gazette; charter.
राजपत्रित-gazetted.
राजपथ-highway.
राजपद state/government post.
राज-पाट-empire and its paraphernalia.
राज-पुरुष-state official.
राजप्रासाद-palace.
राजभक्त-loyal to the ruler or country. -loyalist.
राजभवन-government house.
राजभाषा-official language of a country.
राजमद-the vanity of being in power and pelf.
राजमहल-royal palace.
राजमहिषी-queen.
राजमार्ग-highway.
राजयक्ष्मा-tuberculosis.
राजयोग-combination of stars predicting rise to the throne.
राजरोग-long-drawn ailment.
राजर्षि-saintly king.
राजलक्ष्मी-goddess of royal grandeur;.
राजवंश-royal family; dynastic.
राजवंशीय-public finance.
राजविद्रोह-insurrection; anarchy.
राजविप्लव-privy purse.
राजवृत्ति-privy purse.
राजवैद्य-king's physician.
राज-व्यवस्था-polity.
राजशाही-royal; kingly; stately.
राजश्री-royal grandeur.
राजसत्ता-regal power; sovereignty.
राजसभा-royal court; royal assembly.
राज-सिंहासन-royal throne.

राजसी-princely; royal; gaudy.

राजस्थान-a State in the Indian Union.

राजस्थानी-of or pertaining of; language of Rajasthan; a resident of Rajasthan.

राजस्व-revenue.

राजा-king; good.

राजाज्ञा-royal/regal order.

राजाधिराज-emperor.

राज़ी-agreed; agreeable; willing.

राज़ी-खुशी happily peacefully.

राज़ीनामा-agreement.

राजीव-lotus; elephant.

राजेन्द्र-emperor.

राज्ञी-queen consort.

राज्य-rule; state.

राज्यकाल-reign; ruling period.

राज्यक्षेत्र-territory.

राज्यतंत्र-the form of government; polity.

राज्य-परिषद-council of state.

राज्यपाल-governor.

राज्यविप्लव-rebellion; coup d' etat.

राजव्यवस्था-polity.

राज्यसंघ-confederation.

राज्यसभा-council of State; Upper House.

राज्याभिषिक्त-enthroned.

राज्यभिषेक- coronation; enthronement.

राज्यारोहण-accession to the throne.

राढ़-quarrel; fracas; dispute.

राणा-king of Nepal; member of royal family.

रात-night.

रात की रानी-queen of the night; a very fragrant flower which blooms in the night.

रातिब-one day's food for cattle.

रात्रि-night.

रात्रिकालीन-night time.

रात्रिचर-demon; nocturnal being.

राधा-favourite of Lord .

राधिका-consort; queen.

राब-molasses.

राबिश-waste material of the building mortar.

राम-कहानी-episode of one's life.

रामदाना-a king of sago.

रामनवमी-birthday of God Ram.

राम भरोसे to the mercy of god.

रामरज-yellow ochre.

रामरस-salt.

रामराज्य-rule of Ram; ideal rule; utopia.

राम-राम-greeting; valediction; valedictory remark.

रामलीला-dramatic pageant of the .

रामसखा-chum of Ram.

रामायण-(epic).

राय-opinion; king.

रायज-prevalent; customary.

रायता-a saltish dish prepared with curd and vegetables.

रायबहादुर-title of (British rule).

रायल-royal size (of paper).

रायसाहब-title of Saheb (British rule).

रार-quarrel; dispute.

राल[1]-resin.

राल[2]-spittle.

राव-king; a member of a royal family.

रावटी-small tent.

रावत-small king; chieftain; warrior.

रावण-demon king of Lanka.

रावल-title of certain princes.

राशन-ration.

राशि-amount; quantity; zodiac sign.

राशिनाम-name given to a child soon after birth; in accordance with the position of stars on the horoscope.

राष्ट्र-nation.

राष्ट्रकवि-national poet.

राष्ट्रगान-national anthem.

राष्ट्रगीत-national anthem.

राष्ट्रचिह्न-national emblem.

राष्ट्रध्वज-national flag.

राष्ट्रपति-President.

राष्ट्र-परिषद-National Council.

राष्ट्रभाषा-national language; .

राष्ट्रमंडल-Commonwealth.

राष्ट्रवाद-nationalism.

राष्ट्रवादी-nationalist.

राष्ट्रव्यापी-nation-wide.

राष्ट्रसंघ-United Nations Organisation; U.N.O.

राष्ट्रीकरण-nationalisation.

राष्ट्रीकृत-nationalized.

राष्ट्रीय-national.

राष्ट्रीयता-nationality; nationalism.

रास-favourable; beneficial; circular dance associated with Lord ; reins.

रासधारी-a performer who dramatises the episodes of Lord on the stage.

रास-मंडली-band of performers of

रासायनिक-chemical.

रासो-poetic life-history of a king.

रास्त-right.

रास्ता-path; way; road; route; passage.

रास्ता-चलता-wayfarer; passer-by.

रास्ती-forbearance.

राह-path; way.

राह-ख़र्च-travelling expenses.

राहगीर-wayfarer.

राह-चलता-passer-by; wayfarer.

राहज़न-highwayman.

राहज़नी-highway robbery.

राहत . respite; relief.

राह-रस्म-social dealings/intercourse.

राही-one who goes on a journey specially by foot; wayfarer.

राहु-the mythical monster who swallows up the moon and the sun and thus causes their eclipses; (someone) pestilent.

राहु-केतु-ever-pestering enemies.

रिंच-wrench.

रिंद-nonconformist; an easy-going person.

रिंदा-roguish; devilish; wicked; mean; wretched.

रिआयत-concession; remission; relaxation.

रिआयती-concessional.

रिआया-subjects; people.

रिकशा-rickshaw.

रिक्त-empty; vacant; blank.

रिक्तता-void; vacuum; vacancy.

रिक्थ-legacy.

रिक्शा-rickshaw.

रिक्शेवाला-rickshaw puller.

रिज़क-livelihood.

रिज़र्व-reserved.

रिझाना-to allure/captivate/entice/please.

रिझाव-captivation; lure.

रिटायर-retired.

रिड़कना-to churn; to suffer from a lingering disease.

रिपु-enemy; foe; antagonist.

रिपुता-enmity; hostility.

रिपोर्ट-report.

रिर्पोटर-reporter.

रिबन-ribbon.

रिम-ream; edge of a wheel; rim.

रिमझिम-light drizzle.

रियाज़-exercise; exertion; practice.

रियासत-former Indian princely state; estate; state; regality.

रियासती-princely; stately.

रिरियाना-to whimper; to implore/beseech abjectly.

रिवाज-custom; practice; vogue.

रिवाल्वर-revolver.

रिश्वत-bribe.

रिश्वतख़ोर-(one) who is used to taking bribes; bribe.

रिश्वतख़ोरी-the giving or taking of bribes; bribery.

रिश्ता-relation; relationship.

रिश्तेदार-relative; relation; kinsman.

रिश्तेदारी-kinship; relationship.

रिस-anger; wrath; indignation.

रिसना-to ooze/drizzle/leak.

रिसाना-to get angry.

रिसाला-platoon; journal.

रिहर्सल rehearsal.

रिहा-released; acquitted; freed.

रिहाइश-residence.

रिहाइशी-residential.

रिहाई-release; discharge; acquittal.

रीं-रीं-whimpering sound.

रीछ-bear.

रीझ-overbearing interest.

रीठा-soap-nut.

रीढ़-backbone; spine.

रीढ़दार-backbones; spiny.

रीढ़हीन-lacking backbone; spineless; lacking courage or resolution.

रीता-empty; vacant.

रीतापन-emptiness; vacantness.

रीति-रिवाज-customs and manners; rites and rituals.

रीतिक-formal.

रीम-500 sheets of paper; ream.

रील-reel (of thread etc.).

रुंड-torso.

रुँधना-to be choked.

रुआँ-fuzz; soft hair on the body.

रुआब-influence.

रुई-cotton.

रुईदार-stuffed with cotton.

रुकना-to stop; to stay.

रुकवाना-to cause to stop.

रुकाव-state of being blocked.

रुकावट-hindrance; obstacle; obstruction.

रुक़्क़ा-chit; note; document.

रुक्ष-harsh; rough; ruffled; unkempt (hair).

रुख़-attitude; trend; face; facet; frontage; rook/castle (in chess).

रुख़सत-leave (of absence); permission of leave.

रुख़सती-departure.

रुखाई-curtness; bluntness.

रुखानी-chisel.

रुग्न-indisposed; ailing; ill; unwell; sick.

रुचि-illness; liking; taste; relish.

रुचिकर-inspiring interest; extremely interesting; relishing.

रुचिर-slightly; winsome; attractive; sweet; pleasing; winning.

रुझान-bent; proclivity; inclination; propensity.

रुतबा-position; status; rank.

रुतबेवाला-of high official position or rank.

रुदन-lamentation; weeping; bewailing.

रुद्ध-blocked; choked; impeded.

रुद्र-dreadful; awful; fearful.

रुद्रता-dreadfulness; awfulness.

रुद्राक्ष-seed of a tree used for making rosaries worn by .

रुद्राणी-goddess .

रुधिर-blood.

रुधिरस्राव-bleeding; haemorrhage.

रुनझुन-tinkle/tinkling sound.

रुनाई-redness; ruddiness.

रुपएवाला-having a lot of money; wealthy.

रुपया-rupee; money.

रुपया-पैसा-money; wealth.

रुपल्ली-money.

रुपहला-silvery.

रुबाई-quatrain; four-foot poem.

रुलाई-wailing; weeping.

रुलाना-to cause to weep.

रुष्ट-displeased; offended; angry; enraged; indignant.

रुष्टता-displeasure; anger; indignation.

रुसवाई-ill-fame; disrepute.

रुसूख़-social contact(s).

रुस्तम-(a legendary warrior of Persia).

रुस्तम-ए-हिंद-Hero of India.

रूई-cotton.

रूखा-not smooth; rough; dry; harsh; blunt.

रूखापन-roughness; dryness (of person); bluntness.

रूठना-to be displeased; to show displeasure.

रूढ़-conventional; prevalent; traditional.

रूढ़ार्थ-conventional meaning.

रूढ़ि-convention; tradition.

रूढ़िगत-conventional; traditional.

रूढ़िग्रस्त-conservative.

रूढ़िवाद-conservatism; conventionalism; conformism.

रूप-beauty; charm; shape; form; size; appearance; form.

रूपक-metaphor; bluff; a kind of dramatic play; allegory.

रूपगर्वित-proud of (one's) beauty.

रूप-तालिका-(Gram) paradigm.

रूप-रेखा-outline; contour; synopsis; design.

रूपवंत-beautiful; handsome; charming.

रूपवती-(woman) of beautiful features; a beauty; damsel.

रूपवान-handsome; pretty.

रूप-विज्ञान-morphology.

रूप-सज्जा-make-up; beautification.

रूप-साधन-declension.

रूपसी-beautiful (woman).

रूपांतर-transformation; adaptation.

रूपांतरकार-adapter.

रूपांतरण-transformation; transfiguration; adaptation (of a literary piece).

रूपा-silver.

रूपायन-giving a shape.

रूपायित-shaped.

रूपी-denoting shape or figure.

रूबरू-in the presence of in front of; face to face.

रूमाल-handkerchief; scarf.

रूमाली-children's underwear; privy cover.

रू-रिआयत-concession; leniency; consideration.

रूल-ruler; rule; regulation.

रूलदार-ruled.

रूलर-ruler; scale.

रूसी-Russian; Russian language; scurf; dandruff.

रूह-soul; inner being.

रेंकना-to bray.

रेंगना-to creep/crawl/plod.

रेंट-snot; mucus of nose; nasal discharge.

रेंड-castor plant.

रेख-line; mark.

रेखांकन-underlining; demarcation.

रेखांकित-underlined; demarcated; crossed.

रेखा-line.

रेखाकार-linear.-sketcher.

रेखाकृति-line-drawing; sketch.

रेखागणित-Geometry.

रेखाचित्र-line-drawing; diagram; sketch.

रेखा-चित्रण-drawing a diagram; sketching.

रेखिका-dash (—).

रेखित lined; delineated; demarcated; furrowed.

रेखीय-linear.

रेगमाल-sand-paper.

रेगिस्तान-desert.

रेगिस्तानी-of or pertaining to a desert; sandy.

रेचक-purgative.

रेचन-purgation; purging (of bowels).

रेज़गारी-money in small units.

रेट-rate; price.

रेडियम-radium.

रेडियो-radio.

रेढ़-ruin; devastation.

रेणु-sand.

रेत-sand.

रेतना-to file/rasp.

रेता-sand.

रेती-file; sandbank; (expanse of) sand.

रेतीला-sandy.

रेल-railway; rail.

रेलगाड़ी-railway train.

रेलपथ-rail track.

रेल-पेल-melee; bustle; exuberance.

रेल-मंत्री-Railway Minister.

रेल-मार्ग-railroad; railway.

रेलवे-railway.

रेलवे लाइन-railway line.

रेला-a rush.

रेलिंग-railing.

रेवड़-flock.

रेवड़ी-a hard crisp sweetmeat.

रेशम-silk.

रेशमी-silken.

रेशा-fibre.

रेशेदार-made of fibres; fibrous.

रेस्टोराँ-restaurant.

रेह-whitish soil for cleansing purposes.

रेहन-pledge; mortgage; hypothecation.

रेहनेदार-mortgagee.

रेहननामा-mortgage deed.

रैन-night.

रैन-बसेरा-a place for taking shelter at night; night shelter.

रैयत-public; subjects.

रोंगटा-small and soft hair on the body.

रोंआँ-small and soft hair on the body; fur.

रोआसा-on the point of weeping almost in tears.

रोंएँदार-hairy.

रोक-restraint; restriction; ban; prohibition; prevention; embargo; matrimonial engagement.

रोक-टोक-too much of restriction/ proscription.

रोकड़-cash in hand.

रोकड़-बही-cash-book.

रोकड़-बाक़ी-cash-balance.

रोकड़िया-cashier.

रोक-थाम-prevention; check; preventive measure.

रोकना-to stop; stem; to prevent/ hinder/check; to detain; to avert; to restrain.

रोग-disease; sickness; illness; malady.

रोगग्रस्त-diseased; ailing.

रोग़न-paint; lacquer.

रोग़नदार-lacquered.

रोगनाशक-preventive; prophylactic.

रोग़नी-smeared with oil or ghee.

रोगशय्या-sick-bed.

रोगाणु-germs of a disease; microbe.

रोगी-sick; patient.

रोगी-कक्ष-patients's ward.

रोचक-interesting; pleasant; sweet.

रोचकता-quality of being interesting; interest; sweetness.

रोज़-day. daily.

रोज़गार-business; occupation; profession.

रोज़गारी-businessman.

रोज़नामचा-diary.

रोज़मर्रा daily; everyday.

रोज़ा-fast.

रोज़ाना daily.

रोज़ी-livelihood.

रोज़ी-रोटी-means of livelihood.

रोटी-loaf (of a bread); meal.

रोड़ा-piece of stone/brick; pebble; impediment.

रोड़ी-small pebble.

रोदन-weeping; crying; lamentation.

रोध-blockade.

रोना-pathetic and painful episode of one's life; to weep.

रोना-कलपना-to grieve over; to wail; to bemoan.

रोना-धोना-

रोना-पीटना-to cry and wail loudly.

रोनी सूरत-one who habitually expresses one's sorrow or disappointment for something.

रोपक-planter; transplanter.

रोपण-planting.

रोपना-to plant/implant/transplant.

रोपनी-transplanting.

रोपाई-act or process of planting.

रोपित-planted; transplanted; sown; affixed.

रोब-overpowering; influence; awe.

रोब-दाब-awe.

रोबदार-awe-inspiring; highly influential.

रोबीला-awe-inspiring.

रोम-soft hair on the body; fur.

रोमहर्षक-horrid.

रोमांच-sensation; a feeling of excitement; thrill.

रोमांचक-causing excitement; thrilling.

रोमांचित-thrilled.

रोमानी-romantic.

रोमावली-soft hair on the body.

रोर-hubbub; uproar; tumult.

रोल-role.

रोलना-to stir with the fingers; to earn.

रोलर-roller.

रोली-a mixture of turmeric and lime powder used for auspicious purposes.

रोशन-lit up; lighted; bright; shining; manifest.

रोशनदान-ventilator.

रोशनाई-ink.

रोशनी-light; illumination.

रोष-resentment.

रोहण-ascending; mounting climbing.

रोहू-a kind of fish.

रौंदना-to trample down; to crush down.

रौ-flow; impulsive mood.

रौज़ा-mausoleum.

रौद्र-dreadful; fearful; horrible; terrible.

रौनक़-lustre; brightness; shinning; hustle-bustle.

रौरव-dreadful; terrible; horrible.

रौला-uproar; tumult.

ल-The twenty-eighth consonant of the alphabet; it belongs to dental class and it is the third of the semivowels.

लंक-pile; heap.

लंका-(island).

लंकिनी-evil spirit; witch.

लंकेश-king of Lanka.

लंग-limp; lameness.

लंगड़-anchor.

लँगड़ा-limp; lame; crippled.

लँगड़ाना-to limp.

लँगड़ापन-limping; lameness.

लँगड़ा बुखार-dengue fever.

लँगड़ा-लूला-crippled (person); lame and maimed.

लंगर-a thread with a weight at one end (toy); anchor; a place where free meal is served to all the sundry.

लंगूर-gibbon; an Indian ape having a black face and a long tail.

लँगोट-a type of under garment.

लँगोटा-a small loin-cloth used as an under garment in India.

लचक-elasticity (of objects); flexibility; adaptability (of persons, laws etc.).

लचकदार-elastic; flexible.

लचकना-to resile; spring back; to bend.

लचना-to bend; to come down in one's attitude.

लचर-weak; loose.

लचीला-elastic; flexible (constitution).

लच्छा-hank; skein; a kind of sweetmeat in the form of threads (thicky coiled).

लच्छेदार-charming/fascinating (talk).

लजाना-to be shy; to blush; to be ashamed.

लजालू-bashful.

लज़ीज़-delicious; tasty.

लजीला-bashful.

लजीलापन-bashfulness.

लज्जा-bashfulness; modesty; shame; prestige.

लज्जाजनक-shaming; shameful.

लज्जालु-bashful; shy; shameful.

लज्जावती-bashful; shy (woman).

लज्जावान-bashful.

लज्जाशील-modest and humble; bashful; coy.

लज्जाहीन-brazen; shameless; impudent.

लट-lock of hair.

लटक-affected movement; bend; impulse.

लटकन-pendent; pendulum; locket; a kind of flower or its seed which yields a reddish colour.

लटकना-to hang; to swing; to sag/ bend; to be in suspense.

लटका-device; compendious formulas; tip; mannerism; coquetry.

लटकाना-to hang/suspend; to keep waiting; to delay; to keep in suspense; to dangle.

लटकौआ-that which can be suspended/hung.

लटना-to become lean and thin.

लटपटा-staggering; loose (garment) scattered about; emaciated lean and thin; playful; humorous; incoherent.

लटपटाना-to stagger; stumble; to falter while walking.

लट्टू-a toy that spins round and round whirling; (electric) bulb.

लट्ठ-stick; cudgel.

लट्ठबाज़-skilled in wielding a

लट्ठबाज़ी-skill in wielding a

लट्ठमलट्ठा-battling with sticks.

लट्ठमार-uncivil; crude.

लट्ठा-a rod measuring 5½ cubits; log; raft.

लड़-strand; string.

लड़कपन-the state of being a baby; childhood; childishness; silliness.

लड़क-बुद्धि-childish mentality.

लड़का-body.

लड़का-बाला-issue(s).

लड़की-girl.

लड़कीवाला-member of the bride's party; one who has a daughter.

लड़केवाला-member of the bridegroom's party; one who has a son.

लड़खड़ाना to move or walk as if about to fall; to stagger; to falter; to fall; collapse.

लड़खड़ाहट-staggering gait; tottering state.

लड़ना-to fight; to collide.

लड़ना-झगड़ना-to quarrel.

लड़ना-भिड़ना-to quarrel.

लड़ाई-fight; battle; war; clash.

लड़ाई-झगड़ा-broil; quarrel.

लड़ाईबंदी-cessation of hostilities and ceasefire.

लड़ाका-fighter.

लड़ाकू-quarrelsome; militant; bellicose.-a militant; fighter.

लड़ाना-to cause to fight.

लड़ी-string; chain.

लड़ैत-skilled fighter; quarrelsome.

लड़ैता-beloved.

लड्डू-a round Indian sweet; zero; cypher.

लत-habit; bat habit; addiction; whim.

लतख़ोर-used to receiving kicks; habituated to kicks; mean.

लतख़ोरा-door-mat.

लतर-a creeper.

लता-creeper.

लताड़-heavy scolding; upbraiding; reproof; insult.

लताड़ना-to press with feet for relieving pain; to scold/upbraid/reprove.

लतियल-in the habit of kicking; liable to kick.

लतियाना-to give a kicking; to kick; to trample by foot.

लतीफ़ा-witticism.

लत्ता-rag; tatter.

लत्ती-leg.-addict.

लथपथ-besmeared; wet.

लथाड़-reproof.

लथाड़ना-to scold/reproof.

लथेड़ना-to mark dirty by rough and wrong use.

लदन-load.

लदना-to be loaded; to be sentenced to rigorous imprisonment; to be laden (with fruits).

लदवाना-to cause to load.

लदाई-act of loading or charges paid therefor.

लदाऊ-(beast) meant for loading, (beast) of burden.

लदान-process of loading; load.

लदा-फँदा-overloaded; overladen; overburdened.

लदाव-load; cargo.

लद्दू-beast of burden.

लद्धड़-slow; lethargic; lazy.

लद्धड़पन-slowness; lethargy.

लनतरानी-vain boasting.

लप-elasticity.

लपक-state or quality of being elastic.

लपकना-to rush forward; to catch.

लपका-pilferer.

लपझप-unsteady; odd and uncouth.

लपट-flame; blaze.

लपटीला-sticky.

लपना-to bend/sag.

लपलपाना-to be bent again and again; to resile.

लपलपाहट-act or quality of

लपसी-a variety of (sweet dish); a sticky substance; porridge.

लपेट-fold; twist; winding; involvement; ambiguity.

लपेटन-folding; winding; cover; wrapper.

लपेटना-to fold/roll up; to implicate/entangle.

लपेटवाँ-which can be folded/twisted/wound.

लपेटा-fold; twist.

लप्पड़-slap with the full palm.

लफ़ंगा-loafer; rogue; roguish; vagabond.

लफ़्ज़-word.

लफ़्ज़ी-pertaining to a word.

लफ़्फ़ाज़-verbose; accustomed to using high-sounding words.

लफ़्फ़ाज़ी-verbosity; act or state of being

लब-lip.

लबड़-धोंधों-mess; confusion; row.

लबनी-an earthen pot in which toddy is collected from a palm tree.

लबाड़-babbling.

लबाड़िया-used to talking unnecessarily.

लबादा-over-garment; cloak; gown; robe.

लबाब-essence; gist.

लबालब-full to the brim; brimming.

लबेद-something not sanctioned by scriptures; useless talk thing.

लब्ध-got; attained; acquired.

लब्धप्रतिष्ठ-reputed; renowned.

लब्धि-attainment; quotient (maths).

लभ्य-available; attainable.

लमतड़ंग-lean and lanky; tall.

लमहा-moment.

लय-rhythm; tune.

लयन-act or state of being merged.

ललक-longing; craving; intense; desire.

ललकना-to long for; to crave.

ललकार-challenge; gage.

ललकारना-to challenge; to abet (someone); to assault/murder.

ललचना-to be tempted/allured.

ललचाना-to tempt; to allure; to entice.

ललचौहाँ-reddish.

ललन-sweet baby.

ललना-beautiful lady.

ललमुँहाँ-red-faced.

लला-sweet child (boy).

ललाई-redness; flush of face.

ललाट-forehead.

ललाम-beautiful; charming.

ललित-fine; pretty; comely.

ललिता-a melody in Indian music.

लली-sweet girl.

ललौहाँ-reddish.

लल्ला-an affectionate form of addressing a boy.

लल्लो-tongue.

लल्लो-चप्पो-flattery; servility.

लवंग-clove.

लवंग-लता-clover creeper; a variety of Indian sweet.

लव-tiny.

लवण-salt.

लवणता-salinity; comeliness.

लवणित-salted.

लवना-to harvest a crop.

लवलासी-yearning to establish a love connection.

लवलीन-absorbed; engrossed.

लवलेश-iota.

लवा-a bird allied to the lark; parched rice.

लवाज़्मा-accoutrement; paraphernalia.

लवारा-calf.

लवेरी-milch cow.

लशकर-army; host; multitude.

लशकरी-martial; soldierly.-soldier.

लस-stickiness; adhesiveness.

लसदार-sticky; viscid; clammy.

लसना-to paste; as a stamp on an envelope.

लसलसा-gluey; sticky; adhesive.

लसलसाना-to be gluey/sticky/ adhesive.

लसलसाहट-glueyness; stickiness; adhesiveness.

लसी-temptation.

लसीला-sticky; gluey; adhesive.

लसीलापन-stickiness; adhesiveness.

लसोड़ा-a tree, or its fruit.

लस्टम-पस्टम haphazardly; in a disorderly manner.

लस्त-fagged; fatigued; exhausted.

लस्त-पस्त-totally exhausted; weary.

लस्सी-drink yogurt.

लहँगा-a long loose skirt worn by women in India.

लहँड़ा-flock; herd.

लहँदी-a dialect spoken in West Punjab.

लहक-blaze; glare.

लहकना-to blaze/glare.

लहकारना-to excite; to excite a dog to attack someone.

लहजा-tone; intonation; manner of speech.

लहनदार-creditor.

लहना-dues; collection.

लहमा-moment.

लहर-wave; impulse.

लहरदार-wavy; undulatory.

लहर-बहर-merrymaking; enjoyment; affluence; prosperity.

लहरा-wave; merrymaking; enjoyment.

लहराना-to wave/undulate.

लहरिएदार-wavy; rippling; corrugated.

लहरिया-wavy line; tilde.

लहरी-whimsical; fanciful.

लहलहाना-to be verdant/bloom (said of fields and foliage); to flourish/ bloom.

लहसुन-garlic, .

लहसुनिया-cat's eye; a variety of grey-coloured precious stone.

लहालोट-enamoured; fascinated; extremely pleased.

लहू-blood.

लहू-लुहान-smeared with/bathed with blood.

लाँग-the part of the dhoti tucked up at the back.

लाँघना-to cross over; to jump over; to transgress/overstep.

लांछन-stigma; stain; blemish.

लाइट-light.

लाइन-a long thin mark; line; queue; railway line; business; profession.

लाइनदार-lined.

लाइब्रेरियन-librarian.

लाइब्रेरी-library.

लाइलाज-incurable; irremediable.

लाइसेंस-licence.

लाई-लुतरी-backbiting; telltale.

लाउडस्पीकर-loudspeaker.

लाकेट-locket.

लाक्षणिक-figurative; metaphoric (al).

लाक्षा-sealing wax; lac.

लाक्षागृह-house of lac.

लाख-a hundred thousand; lac.

लाखा-colour made from lac.

लाखी-of the colour of lac.

लाग-approach; subtle device.

लाग-डाट-rivalry; competition.

लागत-cost; investment.

लाग-लपेट-hidden meaning/ implication.

लागू-applicable (of rules); accustomed to haunt.

लाघव-brevity; shortness.

लाचार-helpless; poor.

लाचारी-helplessness.

लाज-honour; prestige; bashfulness; shyness.

लाजवंत-shy; bashful.

लाजवंती-bashful (blonde); shy woman; touch-me-not.

लाजवाब-having no equal; matchless; incomparable; unique; speechless; answerless.

लाज़िम-compulsory; obligatory.

लाट-a tall tower; steeple.

लाटरी-lottery.

लाठी-lathi; staff.

लाठी-चार्ज-lathi-charge.

लाड़-(excessive) fondness; caressing.

लाड़ला-darling; beloved.

लात-leg.

लातीनी-Latin.

लाद-belly; entrails.

लादना-to put a load on; to load; to cause to do something under pressure; force.

लाद-फाँद-parching and loading.

लादी-load of a beast; big lot; burden.

लान-lawn.

लानत-damnation; reproach.

लानत-मलामत-reproach; reproof.

लाना-to bring/fetch.

लापता-missing; (person) whose whereabouts are unknown/ missing; untraceable.

लापरवाह-careless; negligent.

लापरवाही-lack of proper care; carelessness; negligence.

लाभ-profit; gain; attainment; benefit; advantage.

लाभकर-worthwhile; profitable.

लाभकारक-causing profit.

लाभदायक-profitable; gainful; lucrative; paying; beneficial; advantageous.

लाभप्रद-useful.

लाभांश-a share of profit paid to a shareholder; dividend.

लाभालाभ-profit and loss.

लाम-army; war/battle front.

लामबंदी-mobilization.

लामा-Tibetan Buddhist priest.

लायक़-able; capable; befitting; worthy; fit; competent.

लायक़ियत-ability.

लायक़ी-ability.

लार-saliva.

लार-गद्दी-bit.

लारी-lorry.

लाल-red; carbuncle (gem); son; ruby; a variety of a tender and small bird.

लालच-greed; temptation; avarice.

लालची-greedy; avaricious.

लालटेन-lantern; lamp.

लालन-bringing up.

लाल पगड़ी-(lit. red turban) police.

लाल परी-(lit. red nymph) wine.

लाल फीता-red tape; circumlocution.

लाल बुझक्कड़-village wiseacre.

लाल मिर्च-chilli.

लालसा-yearning; craving; cherished desire; aspiration.

लाल सागर-Red Sea.

लाल सुर्ख़-wildly red.

लाला-a term of respect a form of respectful address; a variety of red flower.

लालायित-eager; anxious; desirous.

लालित्य-charm; grace; winsomeness.

लालिमा-ruddiness; reddishness.

लाली-redness; glow; radiance; repute; honour.

लाले-lack; shortage.

लावण्य-charm; loveliness; elegance.

लावनी-a kind of fold song.

लाव-लश्कर-an army with its retinue and followers.

लावा-parched rice; lava (volcano).

लावारिस-(person) heirless; (object) unclaimed.

लावारिसी-state of being heirless.

लाश-dead body; corpse; carcass.

लासा-an adhesive; birdlime; lure; bait.

लासानी-peerless; matchless; unique.

लास्य-a spontaneous female dance.

लाही-grain insect; parched rice.

लिंग-gender; male organ.

लिंग-पूजा-phallus worship.

लिंग-शरीर-ethereal body.

लिंगायत-the adherents of which wear a golden/silver on their arm.

लिंगेंद्रिय-male organ; penis.

लिंगोपासना-phallicism.

लिंटर-lintel.

लिए, के-for, for the sake of; in the order to.

लिक्खाड़-voracious writer (often used derogatorily).

लिखत-writing.

लिखत-पढ़त-(written) deed; document.

लिखना-to write; to note down.

लिखना-पढ़ना-reading and writing.

लिखवाई-causing to write or remuneration paid therefore.

लिखवाना-to cause to write.

लिखा-written.

लिखाई-act or process of copying or writing to dictation or remuneration paid therefor.

लिखाई-पढ़ाई-education; studies.

लिखा-पढ़ा-educated; literate.

लिखा-पढ़ी-reduction to written form; correspondence (of letters).

लिखावट-hand-writing.

लिखित-written; reduced to black and white; documentary.

लिटर-litre.

लिट्टी-small biscuits made of flour spherical ball of flour baked on fire.

लिथड़ना-to be be-smeared.

लिपटना-to cling (to); to be engrossed; to embrace.

लिपटाना-causative of engrossed.

लिपना-to be plastered/coated; to be smeared.

लिपवाना-causative of

लिपाई-act/process of white-washing or charges paid for the same.

लिपाई-पुताई-plastering and white-washing.

लिपा-पुता-plastered and white-washed.

लिपि-script; writing.

लिपिक-clerk; writer.

लिपिकार-clerk; scribe; copyist.

लिपिबद्ध-written; reduced to black and white.

लिपि विज्ञान-scriptology.

लिपिशास्त्र-scriptology.

लिप्त-closely connected; embroiled; involved; engrossed; united.

लिप्तता-involvement; embroilment.

लिप्यंतरण-transliteration.

लिप्सा-greed; lure; lust.

लिप्सु-greedy; lustful.

लिफ़ाफ़ा-envelope; outer covering.

लिफ़ाफ़िया-not durable.

लिफ़्ट-lift.

लिबड़ना-to be smeared.

लिबलिबा-too soft to touch.

लिबलिबी-trigger.

लिबास-dress; attire; uniform.

लियाक़त-ability; capability.

लिया-बेची-buying and selling.

लिवाना-to cause to bring.

लिसलिसा-viscous.

लिसलिसापन-viscosity.

लिसोड़ा-the fruit or its tree.

लिस्ट-list.

लिहाज़- consideration; considerateness; respect; point of view; modesty.

लिहाज़ा therefore; hence; and so.

लिहाड़ा-rough and ready (person); mean; contemptible.

लिहाड़ी-ridicule; mockery; derision.

लिहाफ़-quilt.

लीक-line; track; rut (of a wheel).

लीख-a type of tiny whitish louse.

लीग-league (institution); measure of distance; roughly equivalent to 5 kilometres.

लीचड़-sluggish; lethargic; mean (in money matters); stingy.

लीचड़पन-state or quality of being

लीची-a tree and its fruit.

लीडर-leader.

लीडरी-leadership.

लीन-dissolved; merged; mingled; absorbed; engrossed; rapt.

लीपना-to plaster/coat/besmear; to swear.

लीपना-पोतना-to plaster/coat and whitewash/paint.

लीपा-पोती-clumsy whitewashing; patching up; deceptive actions or words intended to conceal someone's error; whitewash.

लीलना-to swallow/devour.

लीला-frolicsome/illusory creation (of God); sportive display; fun and frolic.

लीलापुरुष-Lord who revelled in fun and frolic.

लीलाप्रिय-Lord who was fond of sportive display.

लीवर-lever (of a gadget).

लुंगी-an Indian type of loin cloth.

लुंचन-pulling off (hair etc.); pulling out (feathers etc.).

लुंज crippled.

लुंजपुंज-wholly or badly crippled.

लुंठन-rolling.

लुंठित-rolled.

लुंड-torso; trunk; dead body without arms, legs or head.

लुंड-मुंड-headless or maimed (body); bundled up.

लुंडा-tailless (lamb, bird etc.).

लुंडी-roundish ball of thread.

लुआठा-a long piece of wood with one end burning, embers.

लुआब-sticky pith.

लुआबदार-sticky.

लुक-shining paint; flame.

लुकना-to prevent oneself from being seen; to hide; to go underground.

लुकना-छिपना-to hide.

लुक़मा-morsel.

लुक़मान-a legendary Arab physician.

लुका-छिपी-children's game in which children hides and one child try to find them; hide and seek.

लुकाना-छिपाना-to conceal from being seen or known about.

लुकाव-छिपाव-act of concealing; concealment.

लुगदी-pulp; paper pulp.

लुगाई-woman; wife; kept woman; concubine.

लुगाईबाज़-womanizer.

लुच्चा-wicked (person); scoundrel; villain; rogue.

लुच्चापन-wickedness; villainy; roguery.

लुच्ची-a big biscuit made of fine wheat flour.

लुटना-to be robbed/looted/plundered.

लुटाना-to squander; to spend lavishly; to give away indiscriminately.

लुटिया-diminutive of

लुटेरा-robber; plunderer; bandit.

लुटेरापन-robbery; banditry.

लुढ़कना-to roll down; to die; to be upset/toppled; to tumble down.

लुढ़काना-causative of roll down.

लुतरा-telltale; backbiter.

लुतरापन-habit of telling tales/backbiting.

लुत्फ़-enjoyment; pleasure; fun.

लुनना-to reap.

लुनाई-reaping or wages paid therofore.

लुनेरा-reaper

लुप्त-disappeared; vanished; extinct; obsolete; omitted.

लुब्बे-लुबाब-essence; pith; gist; sum and substance.

लुभाना-to be charmed/lured/enticed/attracted.

लुभावना-charming; fascinating; attractive.

लुहार-blacksmith.

लुहारी-craft or calling of a blacksmith.

लू-heat wave; sunstroke.

लूका-flame; burning piece of wood; meteor.

लूट-pillage; loot.

लूट-खसोट-act of plundering; plunder; goods seized by plundering; plunder.

लूटना-to rob/plunder/loot/despoil/ravage.

लूट-पाट-plundering and destruction; looting and ruination.

लूट-मार-plundering and massacre.

लूता-spider.

लूम-loom.

लूला-with a maimed/dismembered hand.

लूलू-fool.

लेंस-lens.

लेंहड़ा-herd.

लेई-an adhesive preparation of fine flour (used in book-binding); paste.

लेई-पूँजी-entire assets.

लेकिन but; however.

लेक्चर-lecture.

लेक्चरबाज़ी-habit or lecturing; habitual lecturing.

लेख-writing; handwriting; article; treatise; composition; essay; deed; document.

लेखक-writer; author; clerk.

लेखन-act of writing; profession of a writer.

लेखन सामग्री-stationery.

लेखनी-an instrument for writing specially with ink; pen.

लेखपाल-record-keeper; patwari.

लेखबद्ध-reduced to writing.

लेखमाला-series of articles.

लेखा-account; calculation.

लेखा-जोखा-calculation of accounts.

लेखा-परीक्षक-auditor.

लेखा-परीक्षण-auditing.

लेखा-बही-account book; ledger.

लेखिका-woman writer; authoress.

लेख्य-worthy to be noted down.

लेट-late.

लेटना-to lie (down); to lay oneself down.

ले-दे-give and take.

लेनदार-creditor.

लेन-देन-give-and-take; social dealings; financial transaction.

लेना-to accept; to take; to claim; to get.

लेना-देना-transaction; relation.

लेप-liniment; coating; plaster; ointment.

लेपन-anointing; applying liniment; plastering; coating.

लेपना-to anoint/coat.

लेफ़्टिनेंट-lieutenant.

लेबिल-label.

लेमनचूस-lemon-juice.

लेमनेड-lemonade.

लेवा-one who takes.

लेश-bit; whit; modicum.

लेस-adhesiveness; stickiness.

लेसदार-adhesive; sticky; gluey.

लेह-jelly-type preparation.

लैंगिक-sexual.

लैला-legendary heroine of a famous tale.

लैस-fully-equipped; fitted.

लोंदा-wet lump; dough.

लो Now see this one! What a surprise! Take this! This beats! This is topping!

लोई-dough; a thin woollen shawl or wrapper.

लोक-world; people.

लोककंटक-public nuisance.

लोककथा-folk tale.

लोकगीत-folk song.

लोकतंत्र-democracy.

लोकतंत्री-democrat.

लोकतांत्रिक-democratic.

लोकना-to catch (a dropping ball, fruit etc.).

लोकनाट्य-folk play.

लोकनिंदा-public censure.

लोकनीति-folk ethics.

लोकनृत्य-folk-dance.

लोकप्रिय-popular; in vogue.

लोकप्रियता-popularity.

लोकरंजन-entertainment of the public.

लोक-लज्जा-regard for public opinion.

लोकवादी-public-spirited.

लोकसंग्रह-mobilisation of the people.

लोकसभा-house of the people; the lower house of the Indian Parliament.

लोकसेवा-public service.

लोकहित-public interest.

लोकाचार-popular custom; ethos.

लोकापमान-disapprobation of the public.

लोकापवाद-adverse public opinion; public slander.

लोकोक्ति-popular saying.

लोकोत्तर-supernatural; unworldly; ethereal.

लोकोपकार-philanthropy; public well-being.

लोकोपकारी-philanthropic.

लोकोपचार-social formality.

लोकोपयोगी-popular; useful for the people.

लोग-men; public; people; fold.

लोग-बाग-common people.
लोच-elasticity; flexibility; tenderness.
लोचदार-elastic; flexible.
लोचन-eye.
लोट-rolling.
लोटन-a kind of pigeon.
लोट-पोट-rolling; weltering.
लोटा-an Indian type of water vessel.
लोथ-corpse; dead body.
लोथड़ा-lump of flesh.
लोन-salt.
लोना-saltish; saline.
लोप-the state of being vanished; disappearance; a letter (of the alphabet) which is understood.
लोफ़र-loafer; vagabond.
लोबान-a tree gum used as incense.
लोबिया-cow pea.
लोभ-greed; rapacity.
लोभी-greedy; rapacious.
लोभीपन-greediness; avarice.
लोम-soft hair on the body; fur.
लोमड़ी-fox.
लोमनाशक-depilatory.
लोमहर्षक-horrifying.
लोरी-lullaby.
लोलक-pendant.
लोलित-oscillated.
लोलुप-covetous; avaricious; greedy.
लोलुपता-covetousness.
लोहाँगी-a bamboo with an iron bar at one end.
लोहा-iron.
लोहार-blacksmith.
लोहारी-blacksmith's work or calling.
लोहित-red; scarlet.
लोहू-blood.
लौंग-clove; nose-stud.
लौंडा-lad; boy.
लौंडापन-boyishness.
लौंडिया-lass; girl.
लौंडी-servant/slave girl.
लौंडेबाज़-sodomite.
लौंडेबाज़ी-sodomy; paedophilia.
लौंद-intercalary month.
लौ-flame; glow; love; devotion.
लौआ-gourd; pumpkin.
लौकिक-worldly; mundane.
लौकिकता-worldliness.
लौकी-bottle gourd; pumpkin.
लौट-return.
लौटना-to return; to come back.
लौट-पौट-act of turning over.
लौट-फेर-interchange; substantial derangement.
लौटाना-to give back; to return.
लौह-iron.
लौहचूर्ण-iron filings.
लौहपुरुष-iron-man.
लौहयुग-iron age.

व-The twenty-ninth dento-labial consonant of alphabet; it is the fourth of the semivowels.

वंक-bent; crooked; curved.

वंकट-curved; crooked; impassable; difficult; arduous.

वंग-Bengal.

वंगज-vermilion; brass; an organ.

वंगदेश-State of (undivided) Bengal.

वंगभंग-Partition of Bengal in pre-independence India.

वंगीय-of or pertaining to Bengal.

वंचक-crafty; swindler; deceitful; cheat; fraudulent.

वंचकता-wangling; deceitfulness; fraud.

वंचन-deprivation; deception.

वंचित-deprived; deceived; cheated.

वंटक-distributor.

वंटन-distribution.

वंदन-adoration; obeisance.

वंदनवार-wreathe of green leaves (hung up on auspicious occasions).

वंदना-adoration; obeisance; salutation.

वंदनीय-adorable; worthy of obeisance/reverence.

वंदी-prisoner; captive.

वंदीगृह-prison.

वंद्य-adorable.

वंध्य-sterile.

वहन-act of carrying; transportation.

वहनीय-transportable.

वहम-false notion; misconception; delusion.

वहमी-(one who is) prone to delusion; superstitious (person).

वहशत-craziness; mania; savagery; savage conduct.

वहशियाना-savage; wild.

वहशी-savage; barbarous/cruel (person).

वहशीपन-barbarity; savagery.

वहाँ there; thither; yonder.

वहीं at that very place; right there.

वही-the same.

वांछनीय-desirable.

वांछनीयता-desirability.

वांछा-desire; wish.

वांछित-desired.

वा or.

वाक़ई in reality; really; indeed; infect; truly speaking.

वाक़फ़ीयत-acquaintance.

वाक़ा-event; happening; fact.

वाक़िफ़-familiar; conversant.

वाक्-speech.

वाक्चतुर-clever in talking; conversant; eloquent.

वाक्छल-fraudulent talk/speech; a speech calculated to defraud/deceive; glibness; sophistry.

वाक्पटु-skilled in the art of talking; eloquent.

वाक्पटुता-the art of using language in an impressive way; eloquence; gift of the gab.

वाक्य-sentence.

वाक्यांश-phrase.

वाक्या-event; happening.

वाग्जाल-grand eloquence; insincere but impressive speech or writing; rhetoric.

वाग्दत्त-(object) plighted/pledged.

वाग्दत्ता-(woman) betrothed/engaged.

वाग्दान-betrothal; engagement.

वाग्मिता-oratory.

वाग्मी-orator; eloquent.

वाग्युद्ध-war of words.

वाग्विदग्ध-

वाग्विलास-delightful conversation; grandiloquence.

वाग्विलासी-grandiloquent.

वाङ्मय-literature.

वाचक-narrator. as in **वाचक।**

वाचन-reading.

वाचनालय-reading room.

वाचस्पति-profound scholar.

वाचाल-talkative; prattler; garrulous.

वाचालता-talkativeness; prattling; grarrulousness.

वाच्य-the form of the verb that shows the relation of the subject (or object) to the verb.

वाच्यार्थ-literal meaning.

वाजिब-right; proper; just; appropriate; reasonable.

वाजी-horse.

वाटिका-small garden.

वाणिज्य-trade; commerce.

वाणी-speech; voice; language.

वात-one of the three/four humours of the body; wind.

वातचक्र-whirlwind.

वातज-(ailment) caused by

वातानुकूलन-air-conditioning.

वातानुकूलित-air-conditioned.

वातायन-ventilator.

वातावरण-atmosphere; environment.

वातुल-talkative; gabbler; garrulous.

वात्या-gale.

वात्सल्य-parental affection.

वात्सल्यपूर्ण-affectionate.

वाद-ism; suit (law court); argument.

वादक-instrumentalist.

वादन-playing on a musical instrument.

वाद-प्रतिवाद-argument and counter-argument; discussion; debate; discourse.

वाद-विवाद-discussion; controversy; debate.

वाद-विषय-issue.
वादा-promise.
वादा-ख़िलाफ़ी-breach of promise.
वादी-complainant; plaintiff.
वाद्य-musical instrument.
वाद्यवृंद-orchestra.
वाद्यसंगीत-instrumental music.
वानप्रस्थ-a person in his third stage of life (Hindu system).
वानर-ape; monkey.
वानस्पतिक-pertaining to vegetation.
वानस्पत्य-vegetation.
वापन-sowing.
वापस-returned.
वापसी-act of returning.
वापी-tank.
वाम-left (side).
वामपक्ष-left side; left wing.
वामपक्षी-leftist; left-winger; of or pertaining to the left wing/side.
वाममार्ग-a cult.
वाममार्गी-belonging to
वामा-woman.
वामावर्त-anti-clockwise; counter-clockwise.
वायदा-promise.
वायन-presents of sweets to relatives on auspicious occasions.
वायलिन-violin.
वायव-aerial.
वायवीय-aerial; pneumatic.
वायस-crow.
वायु-air.
वायु-दाब-air pressure.
वायु-पंप-air pump.
वायु-परिवर्तन-climatic change.
वायुबल-air-force.
वायु-भार-atmospheric pressure.
वायुमार्ग-air-route.
वायुयान-aeroplane.
वायु-सेना-air-force.
वायु-सेवा-air-service.
वायु-स्नान-air bath.
वायुहीन-destitute/devoid of air.
वारंट-warrant.
वारंवार frequently; time and again; repeatedly.
वारंवारता-frequency.
वार-day; stroke.
वार-signifying direction or manner.
वारण-banning; prohibition.
वारदात-mishap; accident.
वारना-to sacrifice (on someone).
वारनिश-varnish.
वार-पार-this end and that.
वारांगना-harlot; prostitute.
वाराणसी-holy city of Uttar Pradesh.
वाराणसेय-of or pertaining to
वारा-न्यारा-final settlement of issues.
वाराह-wild boar.

वारि-water.

वारिज-water-born; lotus.

वारिद-cloud.

वारिधर-cloud.

वारिधि-ocean.

वारिस-heir.

वारुणी-wine.

वार्ड-ward.

वार्डन-warden.

वार्ता-conversation; talk; negotiation.

वार्ताकार-speaker; talker.

वार्तालाप-parley; conversation (usually amiable).

वार्धक्य-old age; senility.

वार्षिक-yearly; annual.

वार्षिकी-annuity.

वार्षिकोत्सव-anniversary.

वाला equivalent to 'er'; as in receiver

वाली female of

वावैला-furore; uproar; tumult.

वाष्प-steam.

वासंतिक-pertaining to the spring season.

वासंती-related to spring.

वास-abode; residence; habitation; smell.

वासना-craving; longing; sexual love or desire.

वासस्थान-abode; residence.

वासित-perfumed.

वासी-dweller; inhabitant.

वासुकि-an ancient God (myth).

वासुदेव-Lord ; son of ; tree.

वास्कट-waistcoat.

वास्तव-factual; actual; real.

वास्तविक-real; actual; defacto.

वास्तविकता-reality; actuality.

वास्ता-dealing.

वास्तु-building.

वास्तु-कला-architecture.

वास्तुकार-architect.

वास्ते, के-for the sake of; for the purpose of.

वाह-excellent; well done; bravo!

वाहक-bearer.

वाहन-that which carries; vehicle.

वाहनिक-one who rears beasts of burden.

वाहवाही-applause; cheer.

वाहिका-vein.

वाहिनी-a division of the army.

वाहियात-good-for-nothing; vulgar (talk); undesirable (person); worthless (object); nonsense.

वाही-तबाही-baseless; nonsense.

वाह्य-portable; external; outward.

वाह्लीक-an ancient region to the north-east of India; modern .

विंदु-point; dot; drop.

विंध्य-a range of mountains in central India.

वि-denoting separation, contrariety, intensity etc.

विकच-without hair.

विकट-horrible; monstrous; formidable; onerous.

विकराल-monstrous; formidable.

विकरालता-monstrosity; formidability; formidableness.

विकर्ण-diagonal .

विकर्णत:-diagonally.

विकर्षण-repulsion; aversion.

विकल-restless; uneasy; not at east; agitated; perturbed.

विकलता-restlessness.

विकलांग-handicapped; disabled.

विकल्प-option; alternative.

विकसना-to flourish; to develop; to blossom/bloom.

विकसित-developed; blossomed/ bloomed/budded.

विकार-change (smacking of deterioration); deviation (from a natural state); transformation.

विकारी-changeable; variable; declinable.

विकास-development; growth; evolution.

विकासवादी- evolutionary; evolutionist.

विकासशील-developing.

विकासशीलता-developability.

विकासोन्मुख-developing.

विकिट-wicket (cricket).

विकिरण-radiation.

विकिरणशील-radioactive.

विकिरणशीलता-radioactivity.

विकीर्ण-scattered; disseminated; diffused.

विकृत-deformed; distorted; changed.

विकृति-deformity; distortion; abnormality.

विकृष्ट-thrown back; repulsed.

विकेंद्रण-decentralisation.

विकेंद्रित-decentralised.

विकेंद्रीकरण-act of decentralising; decentralisation.

विकेश-bald; bald-headed.

विक्रम-valour; valiance.

विक्रमी-valorous; valiant.

विक्रय-sale.

विक्रय-कला-salesmanship.

विक्रय-केन्द्र-shopping centre.

विक्रांत-valorous; valiant.

विक्रेता-seller; salesman.

विक्रेय-saleable; marketable.

विक्रेयता-saleability; marketability.

विक्षत-wounded and mutilated.

विक्षिप्त-insane; demented.

विक्षिप्तता-insanity; dementia.

विक्षुब्ध-agitated; perturbed; perplexed; turbulent.

विक्षेप-projection; deflection.

विक्षोभ-agitation; perturbation; turbulence.

विक्षोभित-agitated; perplexed.

विखंड-split up; divided into parts.

विखंडन-splitting; breaking up.

विखंडित-split up; divided into parts.

विख्यात-renowned; well-known; distinguished.

विख्याति-renown; repute; fame; celebrity.

विख्यापन-advertisement.

विख्यापित-advertised.

विगत-past; previous.

विगलन-melting; fusion.

विगलित-melted; fused.

विगुण-devoid of merit; useless.

विग्रह-disintegration; squabble; tiff; idol.

विग्रही-quarrelsome; bellicose.

विघटन- decomposition; disintegration; dissolution.

विघटनकारी-causing disruption; disruptive.

विघटनशील-disin-tegrable.

विघटित-decomposed; disintegrated; dissolved.

विघ्न-hindrance; obstacle; impediment; interference.

विघ्नकारी-impeding; obstructing.

विघ्ननाशक-(that) which counters or removes impediments.

विचक्षण-very sagacious; far-sagacious; farsighted; proficient.

विचक्षणता-sagacity; farsightedness.

विचरण-rambling; wandering; variation .

विचलन-deviation.

विचलित-deviated; upset.

विचार-idea; thought; view; consideration.

विचारक-thinker; ideologist; philosopher.

विचार-गोष्ठी-symposium or meeting for exchange of thoughts.

विचारणा-contemplation; reasoning.

विचारणीय-worth consideration/ considering; worth being given a thought to; ponderable.

विचारधारा-ideology; line of thinking.

विचारना-to think (over).

विचारपति-judge.

विचारपूर्ण-full of thought; thoughtful; well-considered.

विचारपूर्वक-thoug-htfully.

विचारमग्न-absorbed/engrossed in thought; pensive.

विचारवान-man of thought; thoughtful; sober.

विचार-विनिमय-exchange of ideas.

विचार-विमर्श- deliberation; consultation.

विचार-शक्ति-power of thinking; reasoning; intellect.

विचारशील-showing careful thought; rational; thoughtful; contemplative.

विचारशीलता-thoug-htfulness.

विचार-स्वातंत्र्य-freedom of thought.

विचारहीन-devoid of thought/ common sense; thoughtless.

विचाराधीन-under consideration; pending.

विचारोत्तेजक-thought provoking/ exciting/instigating.

विचारोत्पादक-thought provoking/ alluring.

विचार्य-worth considering.

विचित्र-strange; fantastic; curious; peculiar; weird; funny.

विचित्रता-strangeness; queerness.

विधर्मी-belonging to a religion other than one's own; heretic.

विधवा-widow.

विधवापन-widow-hood.

विधवाश्रम-widow's home.

विधा-form; type.

विधाता-creator; providence.

विधान-constitution; legislation.

विधायक-lawmaker; legislator.

विधायन-legislation; enactment.

विधायिका-legislature.

विधारणा-prejudice.

विधारित-prejudiced.

विधि-method; mode; system; law; ways; activities; movements.

विधिक-legal.

विधिकता-legality.

विधिज्ञ-one who knows law; lawyer; legal expert.

विधितः by law; lawfully.

विधि-निषेध-do's and dont's.

विधिपूर्वक methodically.

विधिभंग-breach of law.

विधिमान्य-legally acceptable; valid.

विधिवक्ता-barrister-at-law.

विधिवत् lawfully; legally; duly; methodically.

विधि-विधान-rules and regulations.

विधिविहित-(as) prescribed by law.

विधिवेत्ता-expert in law; jurist.

विधि-व्यवस्था-law and order.

विधिशास्त्र-Science of law; jurisprudence.

विधिशास्त्री-jurist.

विधिसंगत-in conformity with law/ rules; consistent with the law.

विधिसम्मत-in accordance with law; supported by law.

विधिहीन-unsystematic.

विधुर-widower.

विधेयक-bill (legislative).

विध्वंस-destruction; devastation; desolation; demolition.

विध्वंसक-destructive; subversive.

विध्वस्त-destroyed; ruined; devastated.

विनत-bowed low; bowing low; modest.

विनति-act of bowing; entreaty; submission.

विनती-entreaty.

विनम्र-modest; humble.

विनम्रता-meekness; courtesy.

विनम्रतापूर्ण-full of modesty; modest; humble.

विनम्रतापूर्वक modestly; humbly.

विनय-modesty; humility.

विनयपूर्वक humbly.

विनयशील-modest; humble.

विनयशीलता-modesty; humility.

विनयी-polite; modest.

विनश्वर-perishable; destructible; transitory.

विनष्ट-perished; ruined; destroyed; devastated.

विनायक-God.

विनाश-destruction all round; devastation; ruination.

विनाशक-destructive.

विनाशकारी-destructive; devastating; deadly.

विनाशी-destructive.

विनिधान-allocation.

विनिमय-exchange; barter.

विनिमेय-exchangeable.

विनिमेयता-exchangeability.

विनियंत्रण-act of decontrolling or state of being decontrolled; decontrol.

विनियंत्रित-decontrolled.

विनियम-regulation.

विनियोग-appropriation; investment.

विनिश्चय-decision.

विनिश्चायक-deciding.

विनिश्चित-decided.

विनिषिद्ध-contraband.

विनीत-bowing; modest; submissive; humble.

विनीतता-modesty; submissiveness.

विनोद-amusement; humour.

विनोदपूर्ण-humorous; witty; jocund.

विनोदप्रिय-humorous; jocular.

विनोदवृत्ति-humorous temperament.

विनोदशील-humorous.

विनोदशीलता- humorousness; humorous temperament.

विनोदी-humorous; jocular; jocund.

विनयस्त-arranged; installed; set in order.

विन्यास-arrangement; setting; marshalling.

विपक्ष-opposite party; opponent; opposition party.

विपक्षी-opponent.

विपण-market.

विपणन-marketing.

विपण्य-marketable.

विपण्यता-marketability.

विपत्ति-hardship; woe; adversity; calamity; catastrophe.

विपथ-wrong path.

विपथगामी-(one) going the wrong way; aberrant.

विपथन-aberration.

विपद्-hardship; woe.

विपदा-hardship; adversity.

विपन्न-distressed; afflicted.

विपन्नावस्था-state of distress.

विपरीत-contrary; opposite.

विपरीतता-contrariety; opposition.

विपर्ण-without leaves.

विपर्यय-transposition; reversal.

विपर्यस्त-disarranged.

विपर्याय-antonym.

विपर्यास-reversal; interchange.

विपल-one-sixtieth part of a moment.

विपाक-ripening; maturity.

विपिन-forest; woods.

विपुत्र-issueless; childless.

विपुल-abundant; immense; ample; plenty; huge.

विपुलता-abundance; hugeness; immensity.

विप्र-Brahmin.

विप्रलंभ-separation (of lovers).

विप्लव-revolt; rebellion; uprising; panic; insurrection.

विप्लवकारी-revolting; rebellious.

विप्लवी-revolting; rebellious.

विफल-fruitless; futile; failed; unsuccessful.

विफलता-failure; ill-success.

विबुद्ध-wise (man).

विबोधन-awakening.

विभक्त-separated; divided; partitioned.

विभक्ति-postposition; division; partition.

विभव-wealth; riches; prosperity; affluence; pelf; pomp.

विभा-lustre; radiance; brilliance.

विभाकर-sun.

विभाग-division; portion; department.

विभागीय-departmental.

विभाजक-dividing.

विभाजित-divided; portioned.

विभाज्य-divisible.
विभाव-that which gives fillip to emotion.
विभावना-imagination; supposition.
विभावरी-night.
विभाषा-dialect.
विभिन्न-of different kinds; diverse; various.
विभिन्नता-diversity; variety.
विभीषण-younger brother of Ravana, held as traitor by some people.
विभीषिका-dread; horror; terror; scarecrow.
विभु-omnipresent; all pervading; omnipotent; almighty; omniscient; extensively wise.
विभुता-omnipresence; omnipotence.
विभूति-(sacred) ash; grandeur; great personality; personage.
विभूषण-ornament; embellishment.
विभूषित-ornamented; embellished; adorned.
विभेद-sub-division; divisiveness.
विभेदक- discriminating; discriminatory.
विभेदक चिह्न-differentiating sign; sign of discrimination.
विभेदकारी-discriminating; divisive; causing disunity.
विभेदन-splitting; differentiation.
विभेद्य-pierceable; distinguishable.
विभो-O, Almighty!
विभोर-filled with joy.
विभ्रंश-destruction.
विभ्रम-delusion; confusion; perplexity; paranoia.
विभ्रमित-mystified.
विभ्रांत-confused; perplexed.
विभ्रांति-confusion; perplexity; hallucination.
विमंडित-embellished; adorned.
विमति-dissent; disagreement.
विमर्दन-pounding; crushing.
विमर्दित-pounded; crushed.
विमर्श-consultation; consideration; deliberation.
विमल-limpid; crystal clear; pure; immaculate; flawless; spotless.
विमलता-limpidity; purity; flawlessness.
विमा-dimension.
विमाता-step-mother.
विमातीय-step-motherly.
विमान-aeroplane.
विमानक्षेत्र-airfield.
विमानचालक-pilot.
विमानचालन-aviation.
विमानपत्तन-airport.
विमान-परिचारिका-airhostess.
विमानवाहक-aircraft carrier.

विमिश्रित-mixed; mingled.

विमीय-dimensional.

विमुक्त-released; freed; liberated; emancipated; exempted.

विमुक्ति-release; freedom; liberation; emancipation; exemption.

विमुख-turned away (from).

विमुखता-state or quality of being aversion.

विमुग्धकारी-infatuating; charming.

विमोचन-release; liberation; emancipation.

विमोचित-released; liberated; emancipated.

वियुक्त-separated.

वियुक्ति-separation.

वियोगजन्य-generated by separation.

वियोग-शृंगार-description of the pangs of separation from the beloved .

वियोगांत-ending in separation; having a tragic finale.

वियोगात्मक-analytic; separative; analytical.

वियोगी-separated from the beloved one.

वियोजन-separation; subtraction.

वियोजिका-hyphen.

वियोजित-separated; subtracted .

विरंजक-bleaching.

विरंजन-bleaching.

विरंजित-bleached.

विरक्त-detached (from worldly affairs).

विरक्ति-detachment; aversion.

विरचना-to compose/compile.

विरचित-composed; written; produced.

विरत-refrained; desisted.

विरति-refrainment; desistance.

विरल-rare.

विरस-insipid; tasteless.

विरसता-insipidity; tastelessness.

विरह-separating; parting.

विरहाग्नि-agony/anguish of separation.

विरही-(one) separated from the loved one.

विराग-detachment.

विरागी-(one) detached.

विराजना-to take seat; to be seated.

विराजमान-occupying a seat (of honour); present.

विराजित-gracing with one's presence.

विराट-large-scale; gigantic.

विराम-the action or act of stopping; stop; cessation; rest; an interval between periods of work; break; pause; full-stop.

विराम-चिह्न-punctuation mark.

विराम-संधि-truce; armistice.

विरमावस्था-position of rest.
विरासत-heritage; inheritance.
विरुद-eulogy; panegyric.
विरुदावली-chain of panegyrics; long-drawn eulogy.
विरुद्ध-adverse; hostile; contrary; opposite.
विरूद्ध, के against.
विरूप-malformed; uncouth; ugly.
विरूपण-disfiguration; deformation.
विरूपता-deformity.
विरूपित-disfigured; deformed.
विरूपी-disfigured; deformed.
विरेचक-laxative; purgative.
विरेचन-purgation.
विरेचित-purged.
विरोध-opposition; objection; hostility.
विरोधात्मक-adversative; contradictory.
विरोधाभास-paradox; apparent contradiction.
विरोधी-contrary; hostile.
विरोधी-anti-counter.
विलंब-delay.
विलंबन-delaying; postponement.
विलंबित-late; delayed.
विलक्षण-peculiar; queer; odd; remarkable.
विलक्षणता-peculiarity; oddity; quirk; remarkability; queerness.
विलग-separated; disjointed.
विलगाव-aloofness; isolation; separation.
विलय-dissolution; merger.
विलयन-dissolution; merger. .
विलाप-wailing; lamentation; moaning.
विलायत-England; any European country.
विलास-indulgence and enjoyment of rich and comfortable living; merriment; luxury.
विलास-प्रिय-excessively fond of comfort and luxury.
विलासमय-luxurious.
विलासिता-indulgence in gay life.
विलासी-pleasure-seeking.
विलीन-absorbed; merged; vanished; disappeared.
विलुप्त-disappeared; vanished; no longer used.
विलेख-legal document; deed.
विलेप-ointment.
विलेपन-anointing.
विलेय-soluble.
विलेयता-solubility.
विलेयशील-soluble.
विलोकन-act of beholding.
विलोकना-to behold/see.
विलोकनीय-worth beholding/seeing.
विलोकित-beheld; seen; viewed.

विलोड़न-act of churning; through study.
विलोड़ित-churned; thoroughly studied.
विलोप-extinction; effacement; disappearance.
विलोपन-causing to disappear; elimination.
विलोपित-disappeared; effaced; eliminated.
विलोम-converse; reverse; inverse; opposite; contrary.
विलोमता-reversion.
विलोमित-reversed.
विल्व-wood-apple tree and its fruit.
विल्व-पत्र-leaf of wood-apple tree.
विवक्षित-implied.
विवर-cavity; hole.
विवरण-description; account; particulars; statement; explanation.
विवरणिका-brochure.
विवरणी-return (of income tax etc.).
विवर्ण-faded; dimmed; pale.
विवर्त-round.
विवर्तन-going round.
विवश-helpless; compelled; forced.
विवशता-helplessness; compulsion.
विवस्त्र-naked.
विवाचक-arbitrator.
विवाचन-arbitration.
विवाद-dispute; controversy; litigation.
विवादग्रस्त-controversial; disputed; under dispute/controversy.
विवादात्मक-controversial; disputable.
विवादास्पद-controversial.
विवादित-disputed.
विवादी-discordant.-disputant.
विवाद्य-disputable; questionable.
विवाह-marriage; wedding; union.
विवाह-योग्य-marriageable.
विवाह-विच्छेद-divorce.
विवाहित-married.
विवाहोत्सव-marriage celebration.
विविक्त-isolated.
विविक्ति-isolation.
विविध-miscellaneous; diverse; various.
विविधता-diversity; variety.
विवृत-open.
विवृति-interpretation; commentary.
विवेक-faculty of reasoning; discretion.
विवेकाधीन-discretionary.
विवेकी-prudent; discreet.
विवेचक-discriminating.
विवेचन-discrimination; critical appreciation; discussion.
विवेचना-expatiation; detailed discussion.

विवेचनीय-worth discussion; discussible; debatable.

विवेचित-discussed.

विवेच्य-worth discussion.

विशद-elaborate.

विशाख-without branches; branchless.

विशारद-proficient; versed in.

विशाल-grand; colossal; gigantic; huge.

विशालता-grandeur; hugeness; enormity.

विशिष्ट-particular; specific; prominent; remarkable.

विशिष्टता-speciality; highlight; singularity.

विशुद्ध-pure; unmixed; genuine.

विशुद्धता-purity; genuineness.

विशुद्धि-purification; purity.

विशुद्धीकरण-purification.

विशूचिका-cholera.

विशृंखल-disarrayed; disorderly; scattered.

विशेष-special; particular; specific.

विशेषक-characteristic.

विशेषज्ञ-specialist.

विशेषज्ञता-specialisation.

विशेषण-adjective; epithet; attribute.

विशेषतः-especially.

विशेषता-speciality; characteristic feature; trait.

विशेषता-रहित-having no trait or characteristic.

विशेषांक-special number/issue (of a newspaper, periodical etc.).

विशेषाधिकार-privilege; prerogative.

विशेषाधिकारी-special officer.

विशेषित-qualified by an epithet.

विशेषीकरण-specialization.

विशेषीकृत-specialised.

विशेष्य-that which is qualified; a noun which is qualified by an adjective.

विश्रांत-reposed; relaxed.

विश्रांति-relaxation.

विश्रांति-काल-recess; interval; period of rest.

विश्राम-rest; repose; relaxation.

विश्राम-कक्ष-rest room; lounge.

विश्रामालय-retiring room.

विश्रुत-renowned; famous; reputed.

विश्रुति-renown; fame; repute.

विश्लिष्ट-analysed.

विश्लेषण-analysis.

विश्लेषणात्मक-analytical.

विश्लेषित-analysed.

विश्वंभर-God, the All supporting.

विश्व-universe; world.

विश्वक-universal.

विश्वकर्मा-God, the Architect of the Universe.

विश्वकोश-encyclopaedia.

विश्वजनीन-universal.

विश्वजनीनता-universality.

विश्व-प्रसिद्ध-world-renowned.

विश्वविजय-conquest of the world.

विश्वविजयी-conqueror of the world.

विश्वविद्यालय-university.

विश्वव्यापी-world-wide universal.

विश्वसन-believing; relying; trusting.

विश्वसनीय-credible; reliable; trustworthy.

विश्वसनीयता-credibility.

विश्वसुन्दरी-the woman adjudged most beautiful in a world beauty contest; beauty queen.

विश्वस्त-relied on; reliable.

विश्वस्तता-reliability.

विश्वात्मा-God, the Universal Spirit.

विश्वास-belief; confidence; trust; faith; assurance.

विश्वासघात-perfidy; betrayal; treachery; deception.

विश्वासघाती-betrayer; traitor.

विश्वासपात्र-fit to be trusted; reliable; trustworthy (person).

विश्वासी-believer; trustful; faithful; trustworthy; reliable.

विश्वेश्वर-God, Master of Universe.

विष-poison.

विषघ्न-antidote.

विषण्ण-gloomy; melancholy; saddening; depressing.

विषण्णता-gloominess; melancholy

विषद-poisonous.

विषधर-(poisonous) snake.

विषनाशक-alexi-morphic.

विषम-uneven; rough; odd; difficult; intricate; adverse. '

विषमता-unevenness; roughness; dissimilarity; contrast.

विषय-subject; subject matter; theme; matter; topic.

विषयक-concerning; pertaining.

विषयरत-engrossed in sensual pleasures.

विषयलोलुप-voluptuous; sensual.

विषय-वस्तु-subject matter.

विषय-वासना-sensuality.

विषय-सुख-sensual pleasure.

विषय-सूची-table of contents.

विषयांतर-diversion; digression.

विषयानुक्रमणिका-subject index.

विषयासक्त-given or attached to sensual pleasures.

विषयासक्ति-attachment to sensual pleasures.

विषयी-sensual; carnal; debauched; voluptuous; licentious.

विष विज्ञान-toxicology.

विषहर-anti-venom.

विषहीन-non-poisonous.

विषाक्त-poisonous; toxic.

विषाक्तता-toxicity, poisonousness.

विषाण-horn (of a beast); tusk (of a boar etc.).

विषाणु-virus.

विषाद-despondency; gloom; sadness; melancholy; sorrow; grief.

विषादजनक-causing melancholy.

विषादपूर्ण-melancholic; gloomy.

विषादमय-gloomy; sorrowful.

विषादयुक्त-having or showing loss of hope; despondent.

विषुव-equinox.

विषुवत्-equatorial.

विषुवत् वृत्त-equator.

विषूचिका-cholera.

विषैला-poisonous; venomous.

विष्ठा-excrement; faeces.

विष्णु-Lord , the preserver.

विसंक्रमण-disinfection.

विसंगत-inconsistent; irrelevant; incoherent; discrepant.

विसंगति-inconsistency; irrelevancy; incoherence; discrepancy.

विसंघटित-disorganised; disarranged.

विसदृश-dissimilar.

विसम्मत-dissenting.

विसम्मति-dissent.

विसरण-diffusion.

विसरणशील-diffusive.

विसर्जन-abandonment; giving up; disposal; dispersal.

विसर्जित-dispersed; disposed.

विसर्पण-meandering.

विस्तरण-extension.

विस्तार-extent; extension; expansion; expanse.

विस्तारक-expansive.

विस्तारपूर्वक-in detail; extensively; elaborately.

विस्तारवाद-the doctrine of expanding the territory of one's own country; expansionism.

विस्तारवादी-expansionist.

विस्तार्य-that can be expanded; expandible.

विस्तृत-extensive; extended; broad; spacious; wide; detailed; all-round.

विस्तृति-extension; expansion.

विस्थापन-displacement.

विस्थापित-displaced; displaced person.

विस्थिति-crisis.

विस्फारण-spreading out.

विस्फारित-spread out.

विस्फीति-deflation.

विस्फोट-blast; explosion.

विस्फोटक-explosive.

विस्मय-amazement; astonishment; surprise.

विस्यमकारी-causing amazement; amazing; astonishing; wonderful.

विस्मयाकुल-wonder-struck; amazed.

विस्मरण-forgetting; oblivion; forgetfulness.

विस्मरणशील-oblivious; forgetful.

विस्मरणशीलता-forgetfulness.

विस्मित-amazed; astonished; wonder-struck.

विस्मृत-forgotten; lost to memory; gone into oblivion.

विस्मृति-forgetfulness; oblivion.

विस्वर-disharmonious voice; discordant note.

विस्वरता-disharmony; discord.

विहंग-bird.

विहंगम-bird.

विहग-bird.

विहसन-laughing.

विहसित-laughed at.

विहाग-a classical Indian melody.

विहान-day-break; dawn.

विंहार-roaming for pleasure; merrymaking; amusement; Buddhist monastery.

विहार-स्थली-pleasure resort.

विहारी-one who wanders of pleasure.

विहित-enjoined; ordained.

विहीन-bereft of; without.

विह्वल-agonisingly perturbed; vexed.

वीचि-ripple; wave.

वीचिमाली-ocean.

वीतरागी-having overcome attachment.

वीथी-street; track.

वी.पी.पी.-V.P.P. (value payable post).

वीभत्स-astonished.

वीर-brave; gallant; daring; valiant.

वीरगति-heroic end.

वीरगाथा-a narrative depicting heroic achievement

वीरचक्र-an award given for gallantry in war.

वीरता-bravery; gallantry; heroism.

वीरतापूर्ण-brave; valiant; heroic.

वीरतापूर्वक valiantly; bravely; heroically.

वीरपूजा-hero-worship.

वीरप्रसू-mother of the brave.

वीर-विहीन-bereft of the brave.

वीरांगना-heroine; valiant woman.

वीरान-desolate; deserted.

वीराना-desolate/deserted place.

वीरासन-heroic posture.

वीरेंद्र-the bravest of the brave.

वीरोचित-befitting/becoming a hero.

वीर्य-semen.

वीर्यपात-discharge of semen.

वीर्यवत्ता-virility.

वीर्यवान्-virile; potent.

वुज़ू-Muslim practice of performing ablutions before offering prayer.

वुजूद-existence; being.
वृंत-stem; stalk.
वृंद-congregation; assemblage; group.
वृंदगान-chorus.
वृंदवादन-orchestration.
वृक्क-kidney.
वृक्ष-tree.
वृक्ष-पंक्ति-row of trees.
वृक्षरोपण-plantation of tree.
वृक्षवासी-arboreal.
वृक्षहीन-treeless.
वृक्ष्य-of or pertaining to a tree.
वृत्त-circle; description; account.
वृतचित्र-documentary film.
वृत्तांत-description; narrative; account; story.
वृत्ताकार-circular.
वृत्ति-vocation; calling (for sustenance; livelihood); disposition; mentality.
वृत्ति-कर profession tax.
वृत्तीय-pertaining to a circle; vocational; professional.
वृथा in vain; uselessly.
वृद्ध-aged; elderly; old man.
वृद्धा-old woman.
वृद्धावस्था-old age; senility.
वृद्धि-increase; enhancement; growth.
वृश्चिक-scorpion.
वृष-bull.
वृषभ-bull; Taurus; the second sign of zodiac.
वृष्टि-rain.
वृष्टिकाल-rainy season.
वृष्टिपात-rainfall.
वृहस्पति-the name of a day.
वे-those.
वेग-velocity; speed.
वेगपूर्ण-moving quickly; fast.
वेगपूर्वक speedily; fast.
वेगमापी-speedometer.
वेगवती-female of (swift).
वेगवान-fleet; swift.
वेणी braid (of hair).
वेणु-flute.
वेतन-pay; salary.
वेतनभोगी-salaried; stipendiary.
वेतनमान-scale of pay; pay-scale.
वेतन-वृद्धि-increment; increase in salary.
वेताल-evil-spirit.
वेत्ता-a person having knowledge of something. proficient; well-versed.
वेदज्ञ-one who is well-versed in the .
वेदना-agony; affliction; torment.
वेदनाहर-that relieves pain.
वेदपाठ-recitation of the *Veda*.
वेदपाठी-reciter of the *Veda*.
वेदमंत्र-hymn.

वेदवाक्य-truth; unquestionable truth; gospel truth.

वेदसम्मत-sanctioned by the .

वेदांग-one of the six branches of the *Veda.*

वेदांत-highest form of philosophy as per the *Veda.*

वेदिका-small altar.

वेदी-altar (as sanctioned by the).

वेदोक्त-ordained by the .

वेधक-one who pierces; perforator.

वेधन-act of piercing; perforation; observation.

वेधनीय-pierceable; perforable.

वेधशाला-observatory; a building wherefrom stars, planets can be observed by the scientists.

वेधित-pierced; perforated.

वेधी-piercing.

वेला-time; moment.

वेश-dress; costume; apparel; guise.

वेशधारी-in the guise.

वेशभूषा-garments; apparel and get-up etc.

वेश्या-a woman who offers herself to somebody in return for money; prostitute.

वेश्यागमन-prostitution.

वेश्यागामी-one who is in the habit of going to prostitutes.

वेश्यालय-brothel.

वेश्यावृत्ति-the practice of working as a prostitute; prostitution.

वेष्टन-wrapping; enveloping; wrapper; envelope.

वैकुंठ-abode; heaven.

वैकुंठ-लोक-paradise.

वैचारिक-ideological.

वैचारिकी-ideology.

वैजयंती-trophy.

वैज्ञानिक-scientific; scientist.

वैज्ञानिकता-scientific approach/ attitude.

वैटिकन-Roman Catholic Church; Vatican.

वैतनिक-stipendiary; salaried; paid.

वैतरणिक-distributive.

वैतरणी-legendary river which flows between this world and the world hereafter.

वैताल-evil spirit; goblin.

वैतालिक-magician.

वैतालीय-pertaining to evil spirit.

वैदिक-pertaining or related to the *Veda.*

वैदुष्य-scholarship; learning.

वैदूर्य-a precious stone; beryl.

वैदेशिक-foreign; pertaining to a foreign country.

वैदेही-daughter of Sita.

वैद्य-physician.

वैदयक-system of medicine.

वैद्यराज-topmost physician.

वैध-legally accepted; affected or used; valid; legitimate.

वैधता-validity; legitimacy.

वैधर्मिक-irreligious.

वैधानिक-constitutional.

वैफल्य-failure.

वैभव-grandeur; magnificence; wealth and glory.

वैभवशाली-grand; magnificent; wealthy and glorious.

वैभागिक-departmental.

वैभाषिक-dialectal.

वैभिन्नय-variety.

वैमत्य-discordance.

वैमनस्य-animosity; rancour.

वैमात्र-step-motherly.

वैमानिक-aeronautical; pilot.

वैमानिकी-aeronautics.

वैयक्तिक-personal; individual.

वैयक्तिकता-individuality.

वैयाकरण-an expert in grammar; grammarian.

वैर-enmity.

वैरागी-(one) who has renounced mundane affairs; recluse; mendicant.

वैराग्य-dispassion; non-attachment; renunciation.

वैराग्य-भाव-spirit of renunciation.

वैरी-foe; enemy.

वैवाहिक-matrimonial.

वैशाख-second month of the calendar.

वैशाखनंदन-donkey; ass.

वैशेषिक-one of the six systems of Indian Philosophy.

वैश्य-third of the four castes of Hindu social system; its main profession is business.

वैषम्य-difference.

वैष्णव-devotee of Lord ; an orthodox sect among the Hindus.

व्यंजित-expressed.

व्यक्त-explicit; expressed; manifested.

व्यक्ति-person; individual.

व्यक्तिगत-personal; individual.

व्यक्तित्व-personality; individuality.

व्यक्तिनिष्ठ-subjective.

व्यक्तिवादी-individualistic.

व्यक्तिकरण- individualisation; personalisation.

व्यग्र-restless; perturbed; bewildered; perplexed.

व्यग्रता-restlessness; perturbation; perplexity.

व्यजन-hand fan; act of fanning.

व्यतिक्रम-violation of established/ traditional order; deviation.

व्यतिरेक-distinction by contrast; contradistinction.

व्यतिरेकी-contrastive.

व्यतीत-passed; past (time).

व्यत्यय-reversion of order; reversal.

व्यथा-anguish; agony.

व्यथित-in agony.

व्यभिचार-adultery; fornication.

व्यभिचारिणी-adulteress; lewd woman.

व्यभिचारी-going astray; straying; deviating or diverging from; erring.

व्यभिचारी भाव-a transitory feeling.

व्यय-expenditure; expense; expending.

व्ययसाध्य-high-priced; expensive; costly.

व्यर्थता-uselessness; futility.

व्यवकलन-subtraction.

व्यवकलित-subtracted.

व्यवच्छिन्न-separated.

व्यवच्छेद-separation.

व्यवच्छेदन-dissection.

व्यवधान-hindrance; impediment; obstruction; interruption.

व्यवसाय-vocation; calling; profession; occupation; trade; business.

व्यवसायिक-professional.

व्यवस्था-arrangement; management; system; order; ruling.

व्यवस्थापक-manager; organiser.

व्यवस्थापन- organisation; management.

व्यस्थापिका-legislature.

व्यवस्था-स्थापन-establishment of order.

व्यवस्थित-organised; well-managed; systematised; methodical.

व्यवस्थिति-system; method.

व्यवहार-behaviour; dealing; use; practice.

व्यवहार-कुशल-practical; wordlywise; dextrous.

व्यवहार-कुशलता-wordily/practical wisdom; adroitness.

व्यवहार-चतुर-pragmatic.

व्यवहारत:-practically.

व्यवहार-बुद्धि-practical wisdom.

व्यवहार्य-practicable; feasible.

व्यवहार्यता-practicability; feasibility; savvy.

व्यवहृत-used; retolised.

व्यष्टि-individual.

व्यष्टिवाद-individualism.

व्यष्टिवादी- individualistic; individualist.

व्यसन-addiction; evil habit; hobby.

व्यसनी-addict.

व्यस्त-busy; engaged; occupied.

व्याकरण-Grammar; a book of grammar.

व्याकरण-सम्मत-conforming to the rules of grammar; grammatical.

व्याकरणिक-grammatical.

व्याकुल-agitated; perturbed; restless.

व्याकुलता-perturbation; restlessness.

व्याख्या-explanation; elaboration; expatiation.

व्याख्याकार-commentator; interpreter.

व्याख्यात्मक-explanatory; annotated.

व्याख्यान-lecture; speech.

व्याख्येय-fit to be explained/annotated.

व्याघात-blow; stroke; hindrance; obstruction; obstacle.

व्याघ्र-tiger.

व्याघ्रचर्म-tiger-skin.

व्याघ्रमुखी-tiger-faced.

व्याज-pretext; pretence; interest.

व्याजनिंदा-ironical censure.

व्याजस्तुति-ironical commendation.

व्याजोक्ति-ironical statement.

व्याध-hunter; fowler.

व्याधि-ailment; malady; disease.

व्याधिनाशक-antidote.

व्याधि-मंदिर-abode of ailment human body.

व्याधिहर-antidote.

व्यापक-pervading; pervasive; extensive; widespread; comprehensive.

व्यापकता-pervasiveness; extent; comprehensiveness.

व्यापना-to pervade; to spread through/over.

व्यापार-business; trade; trading.

व्यापार-कर-trade-tax.

व्यापार-चक्र-trade-cycle.

व्यापार-चिह्न-trade-mark.

व्यापार-तुला-balance of trade.

व्यापार-संघ-mercantile association.

व्यापारिक-commercial; mercantile.

व्यापारी-trader; tradesman; merchant; businessman; dealer.

व्यापित-pervaded.

व्यापी-pervading; pervasive.

व्याप्त-pervaded; permeated.

व्याप्ति-pervasiveness; pervasion.

व्याप्य-pervasive.

व्यामोह-infatuation; fascination; bewilderment; embarrassment.

व्यामोहित-infatuated; fascinated.

व्यायाम-physical exercise; bodily exercise; athletic.

व्यायामशाला-gymnasium.

व्यायामी-athlete.

व्याल-snake.

व्यावसायिक-professional; vocational; occupational; pertaining to business.

व्यावहारिक-practical; realistic; down-to-earth; applied.

व्यावहारिकता-the state or quality of being practical or realistic; practically.

व्यास-diameter; an ancient Hindu writer of legendary epics; a river in the Punjab; professional religious discoverer.

व्यासपीठ-pulpit.

व्यासीय-diametrical.

व्युत्क्रमण-reversal; reciprocation.

व्युत्पत्ति-derivation; etymology.

व्युत्पत्तिक-derivative; etymological.

व्युत्पन्न-derived; derivative.

व्युत्पन्नमति-ready wit; witty.

व्युत्पादन-etymological derivation.

व्यूह-battle array; disposition.

व्यूहबद्ध-strategically arrayed.

व्योम-sky; space.

व्योमगंगा-Milky Way.

व्योमचारी-sky-going/faring.

व्रजन-roaming; wandering.

व्रण-wound.

व्रत-vow; pledge; fast.

व्रती-(one) who has taken a vow/ pledge; (one) who is observing/ keeping a fast.

व्रीड़ा-bashfulness; modesty.

श

श The thirtieth palatal consonant of the alphabet.

शंकनीय-questionable; doubtful.

शंका-apprehension; doubt.

शंकाकुल-perturbed by doubt.

शंकाजनक-(that) which raises suspicion/doubt.

शंका-निवारण-removing a doubt.

शंका-निवृत्ति-removal of a doubt.

शंकालु-inclined to doubt; (a person) of a suspicious disposition.

शंकाशील-of a suspicious nature.

शंका-समाधान-clearing up an objection or doubt.

शंकित-alarmed; apprehensive; full of doubt/suspicions.

शंकु-peg; cone.

शंख-conch.

शंखध्वनि-sound of a conch.

शंखिनी-one of the categories of women according to sexology.

शंबु-snail.

शऊर-manners; wisdom; mannerliness; shrewdness.

शक-uncertainty;suspicion; the tribe which invaded India in the Ist century B.C.

शकट-cart.

शकर-sugar.

शकरकंद-sweet potato.

शकरकंदी-sweet potato.

शकुंत-bird.

शकुन-omen; augury; bird; auspicious sign.

शकुन-विचार-augury.

शकुनी-soothsayer; augur.

शक्कर-sugar.

शक्की-sceptical; whimsical; of a doubting/suspicious nature.

शक्की-मिज़ाज-of doubting nature.

शक्ति-power; physical strength; might; energy; Goddess of power.

शक्ल-सूरत-appearance; looks.

शख़्स-person; individual.

शख़्सियत-personality; individuality.

शग़ल-hobby; pastime; occupation.

शगुन-an auspicious ceremony performed as a token; token of betrothal ceremony given by the bride's party.

शगुनिया-augur; diviner.

शगूफ़ा-bud; blossom; squib; utterance calculated to let off a quarrel.

शजरा-genealogical table/tree; map of rural holdings.

शटर-a shutter.

शठ-wicked; rogue; knave; cunning.

शठता-roguery; wickedness; knavery.

शत-hundred.

शतक-one hundred; a score of one hundred runs by one batsman in an innings.

शतदल-lotus.

शतपति-centenarian.

शतपद-centipede.

शतरंज-chess.

शतरंजी-chessboard; carpet with a chessboard design.

शतवार्षिकी-centenary.

शतशः in a hundred ways.

शताब्दी-century; 100 years; centenary.

शतायु-100 years old; centenarian.

शती-a period of 100 years; century.

शत्रु-enemy; foe; opponent; antagonist.

शत्रुता-enmity; hostility; animosity.

शत्रुतापूर्ण-inimical; hostile.

शनाख़्त-identification.

शनि-Saturn; the seventh of the nine planets; Saturday.

शनिवार-Saturday.

शनिश्चर-Saturday.

शनैः-शनैः gradually; by degrees.

शपथ-oath; swearing.

शपथ-ग्रहण-oath-taking.

शपथ-पत्र-an affidavit.

शपथपूर्वक on oath; under oath.

शफ़तालू-a kind of peach; nectarine.

शबनम-dew.

शबनमी-sheet suspended over the bed to keep off the dew.

शब्द-word.

शब्दकार-coiner of words.

शब्दकोश-dictionary; lexicon.

शब्दक्रम-word-order.

शब्दगत-related with the word.

शब्दचयन-act of collecting or selecting words; words selected to express an idea; wording.

शब्दचित्र-word-sketch.

शब्दजाल-word-trap; circumlocution.

शब्दब्रह्म-God as the Word.

शब्दभेद-part of speech.

शब्दवेधी बाण-arrow which allows the tract of a sound.

शब्दशः verbatim.

शब्दशक्ति-word-power; force of a word.

शब्दसंग्रह-collection of words.

शब्दसूची-list of words.

शब्दसौष्ठव-elegance of words.

शब्दहीन-speechless; finding no words to say.

शब्दाडंबर-circumlocution.

शब्दातीत-beyond words/description.

शब्दानुवाद-literal translation.

शब्दानुशासन-Grammar; grammatical discipline.

शब्दान्वय-parsing.

शब्दार्थ-word meaning; literal meaning.

शब्दालंकार-embellishment of words.

शब्दावली-list of words in proper order; terminology; wording.

शम-tranquillity/peace of mind.

शमन-act of extinguishing; slaking.

शमशीर-sword.

शमा-burning candle/lamp.

शमादान-candle-stand; lamp-stand.

शमित-extinguished; slaked; allayed; quenched.

शयन-sleeping; turning in.

शयन-कक्ष-bed-room.

शयनागार-bed-chamber.

शयनिका-bunk; sleeping berth.

शय्या-bedstead; bed; couch.

शय्याग्रस्त-bed-ridden.

शय्याव्रण-bed-sore.

शर-arrow.

शरच्चंद-autumnal moon.

शरच्चंद्रिका-autumnal moonlight.

शरण-refuge; shelter; asylum.

शरणस्थल-sanctuary; refuge.

शरणागत-(one) who has come to seed shelter; refugee.

शरणागति-approach for shelter.

शरणार्थिन-female of refugee.

शरणार्थी-refugee.

शरणालय-asylum; refuge.

शरण्य-seeking/needing shelter.

शरत-autumn.

शरत्काल-autumn season.

शरद-autumn.
शरदऋतु-autumn.
शरीफ़ा-custard apple.
शरीर-naughty; mischievous.-body.
शरीरत्याग-demise; death.
शरीरधारी-incarnate.
शरीररक्षक-bodyguard.
शरीरविज्ञान-Physiology.
शरीरवैज्ञानी-physiologist.
शरीरवैज्ञानिक-physiological.
शरीरांत-death; demise.
शरीरी-physical; corporal; corporeal.
शर्करा-sugar.
शर्त-condition; terms.
शर्तिया surely; certainly; assuredly.
शर्म-shame; shyness.
शर्मनाक-shameful; disgraceful.
शर्मिंदगी-shame; discomfiture.
शर्मिंदा-ashamed.
शर्मीला-shy; bashful; modest.
शर्मीलापन-shyness; bashfulness; modesty.
शलक-scale (of fish).
शलग़म-turnip.
शलभ-moth.
शलाका-rod; spoke.
शल्य-thorn; surgical instrument.
शल्यकर्म-surgery.
शल्यकार-surgeon.
शल्यक्रिया-surgical operation.
शल्यचिकित्सा-surgery; (surgical) operation.
शव-dead body; corpse.
शवच्छेदन-autopsy.
शवदाह-cremation.
शव-परीक्षा-postmortem examination.
शव-पेटी-coffin.
शवशाला-mortuary.
शवसंस्कार-(last) funeral rites.
शशक-rabbit.
शशांक-moon.
शशि-moon.
शस्त्र-weapon; arms; a mean of getting the better of someone.
शस्त्रजीवी-professional warrior.
शस्त्रधारी-armed soldier; warrior.
शस्त्रविद्या-science of arms; Military Science.
शस्त्रसज्जित-armed; equipped with arms.
शस्त्रागार arsenal; armoury.
शस्त्राभ्यास-military exercise.
शस्त्रास्त्र-arms and weapons.
शहंशाह-king of kings; emperor.
शहंशाही-pertaining to a emperor; royal; regal; kingly; state of being a emperor; reign of a emperor.
शह-check (in chess); lift; incitement.
शहज़ादा-prince.
शहज़ादी-princess.

शहतीर-beam.

शहतूत-mulberry tree and its fruit.

शहद-honey.

शहनाई-an Indian clarionet; oboe.

शहबाला-a young boy who accompanies the bridegroom.

शहर-town; city.

शहरी-belonging to a city or town; urban.

शहसवार-horse-rider; horse-man.

शहसवारी-horsemanship.

शहादत-testimony; evidence; martyr's suffering or death; martyrdom.

शहाना-royal; regal; majestic.

शहीद-one who is made to suffer or killed because of his religious beliefs; martyr.

शांत-tranquil; calm; serene; peaceful; silent; quiet.

शांतचित्त-calm by nature; of a peaceful mind.

शांति-tranquillity; calm; peace; silence.

शांतिकुंज-bower of peace.

शांतिदायक-tranquillizing; pacifying; peace-giving.

शांतिपूर्ण-peaceful.

शांतिपूर्वक peacefully.

शांति-प्रक्रिया-peace process.

शांतिप्रिय-peace-loving; peaceable; peaceful.

शांतिभंग-breach of peace.

शांतिमय-peaceful.

शांतिवार्ता-peace talks; peace negotiations.

शांति-संधि-peace treaty.

शांति-सेना-peace-force.

शाक-(leafy) vegetable.

शाकाहार-vegetarian food; vegetarian diet.

शाकाहारी-vegetarian; herbivorous (animal).

शाकीय-herbaceous.

शाक्त-worshipper of Goddess of Power/Energy.

शाख़-a branch of a tree; a branch of any business firm; a division of a larger system; offshoot.

शाखा-branch; school (of though).

शागिर्द-pupil; disciple.

शागिर्दी-pupilage; discipleship.

शातिर-extremely bad; vile.

शादी-marriage.

शान-pomp; splendour; grandeur; grace.

शानदार-magnificent; splendid; grand; great.

शानबान-magnificence; grandeur.

शाप-curse; imprecation.

शापग्रस्त-cursed; accursed.

शाबाश-Bravo, Well Done.

शाबाशी-applause (for cheering up).

शाब्दिक-verbal; literal.

शाम-evening.

शामत-ill-luck.

शाम-सबेरे-in the very near future; occasionally; almost all the time.

शामियाना-canopy.

शामिल-included.

शायक-arrow.

शायद-perhaps.

शायर-(Urdu) poet.

शायराना-poetic; poet-like.

शायरी-(Urdu) poetry.

शायिका-railway sleeper; sleeping birth.

शायी-prostrate; lying down.

शारद-autumnal.

शारदा-Goddess of learning.

शारदीय-autumnal.

शारीर-bodily; physical.

शारीरिक-bodily; physical.

शार्क-shark.

शार्दूल-lion; tiger.

शाल-shawl; sal tree.

शाला-house.

शालिनी-female of

शाली denoting possession.

शालीन-graceful; serene; decent.

शालीनता-grace; gracefulness; sobriety; decency.

शावक-young one of an animal or bird.

शाश्वत-eternal; perpetual; everlasting.

शाश्वतता-eternity; perpetuality; perpetuity.

शासक-ruler.

शासकीय-official; governmental.

शासन-governance; government; rule.

शासन-तंत्र-system of government; government.

शासन-निकाय-governing body.

शासन-प्रणाली/व्यवस्था-system of government.

शासन-सूत्र-power of governing.

शासनिक-governmental.

शासित-ruled; governed.

शास्ति-sanction; provision for enforcing obedience to law.

शास्त्र-branch of knowledge; scripture.

शास्त्रज्ञ-one who knows the scriptures; scholar.

शास्त्र-विज्ञान-prescription of the scriptures.

शास्त्रार्थ-debate on the scriptures or interpretation thereof.

शास्त्री-scholar of the scriptures.

शीघ्र-speedily; quickly; soon.

शीघ्रगामी-speedy; quick.

शीघ्रता-quickness; swiftness; promptness.

शीघ्रतापूर्वक-quickly; promptly; rapidly.

शीघ्रपात-quick ejaculation (in coitus).

शीत-cold; frigid.

शीतक-cooler.

शीत कटिबंध-frigid zone.

शीतकाल-winter season.

शीतकालीन-wintry; of winter.

शीतयुद्ध-cold war.

शीतल-cool; cold.

शीतलता-coolness; coldness.

शीतल-पाटी-straw mat.

शीत-लहरी-cold wave.

शीतला-smallpox; goddess of smallpox.

शीतागार-cold storage.

शीतोष्ण-temperate; moderate.

शीत्कार-hissing sound (due to excessive cold).

शीरा-thick syrup produced when sugar is refined; molasses; treacle; syrup.

शीर्ष-apex; summit; top.

शीर्षक-heading; title; headline (in a newspaper).

शीर्षविंदु-apex; vertical point; zenith.

शीर्षस्थ-highest in position; topmost; top-ranking.

शीर्षस्थान-top position.

शील-disposition; (deferential) modesty; propriety.

शीलभंग-outrage of modesty; rape.

शीलवती-(woman) deferentially modest.

शीलवान-deferentially modest.

शीश-head.

शीशम-rosewood.

शीशमहल-house of mirrors.

शीशा-glass; mirror; looking glass.

शीशी-phial.

शुंड-trunk (of an elephant).

शुक-parrot.

शुकनासिका-(woman) having a parrotlike nose.

शुक्ति-oyster.

शुक्र-semen; planet Venus; Friday; thanks.

शुक्रगुज़ार-grateful; thankful.

शुक्रवार-Friday.

शुक्राणु-spermatozoan.

शुक्राना-money offered by way of thanksgiving.

शुक्राशय-ovary.

शुक्रिया-thanks.

शुक्ल-white.

शुचि-pure; sacred.

शुचिता-cleanliness; purity; sanctity.

शुतुरमुर्ग़-ostrich.

शुद्ध-pure; unadulterated; chaste; accurate; genuine; correct; right; net.

शुद्धता-purity; accuracy.

शुद्धतावाद-purism.

शुद्धतावादी-purist.

शुद्धात्मा-pure in/of heart.

शुद्धि-purification; correction; rectitude.

शुद्धिपत्र-errata; corrigendum.

शुद्धीकरण-purification.

शुभंकर-mascot.

शुभ-auspicious; good.

शुभचिंतक-benevolent; well-wisher.

शुभाकांक्षी-well-wisher; well-wishing.

शुभागमन-gracious arrival.

शुभाशीष-gracious benediction.

शुभाशुभ-good and evil; auspicious and inauspicious.

शुभ्र-white; bright; radiant.

शुभ्रता-radiance; brightness.

शुमार-count.

शुरुआत-beginning.

शुरुआती-of or at the beginning; initial; preliminary.

शुरू-beginning;start;commencement.

शुल्क-fee; subscription; duty.

शुश्रूषा-nursing.

शुष्क-dry; arid.

शूक-bristle.

शूकर-pig; boar.

शूटिंग-shooting of a film.

शूद्र-a member of a the lowest of the four classes of Hindu society.

शून्य-empty; vacant.

शून्यक-vacuum.

शून्यता-nothingness; voidness; void.

शून्यभाव-vacant look.

शून्यवाद-nihilism.

शून्यवादी-nihilistic.

शूर-brave; valorous; gallant.

शूरता-bravery; valour; gallantry.

शूरवीर-valiant (person).

शूल-prong; thorn; stabbing pain.

शूलना-to inflict pain; to torture.

शृंखला-chain; series.

शृंखलाबद्ध-arrayed in series.

शृंखलित-arranged like a chain.

शृंग-summit; peak; horn.

शृंगार-make-up; adornment; ornamentation.

शृंगार रस-most important of the nine sentiments depicting romance and love in Indian poetics.

शृंगारिक-amatory; amorous; erotic.

शृंगारिकता-eroticism; amorousness.

शृंगारी-pertaining to make-up; erotic; amatory.

शृंगी-horned.

शृगाल-jackal.

शेख़-one of the four subdivisions amongst Muslims.

शेख़ीबाज़-boastful; vainglorious.

शेख़ीबाज़ी-boastfulness.

शेड-shed; shade.

शेयर-share.

शेर-tiger; couplet in poetry.

शेरदिल-lion-hearted; fearless.

शेरबच्चा-dauntless; fearless person.

शेरबबर-lion.

शेरमर्द-he-man; masculine man.

शेरवानी-a long fitting coat.

शेष-remainder; residue; rest; outstanding; balance.

शेषनाग-(in Hindu mythology) thousand-headed serpent who is supposed to support the earth on his head.

शेषशायी-Lord who is supposed to sleep over

शेषांश-remaining part.

शै-thing.

शैक्षणिक-academic.

शैक्षिक-educational.

शैतान-naughty; mischievous.

शैतानी-Satanic; mischievous.

शैथिल्य-laxity; looseness; lethargy; relaxation.

शैल-rock.

शैलराज-Himalayas.

शैली-style; method; mode.

शैलीकार-one who has a distinctive style; stylist.

शैलीबद्ध-stylised.

शैलेंद्र-Himalayas.

शैव-of or pertaining to Lord-Lord devotee.

शैवाल-moss; algae.

शैशव-infancy; childhood.

शोक-sorrow; grief; distress; mourning; dolour.

शोकगीत-elegy.

शोकग्रस्त-crushed with sorrow; grief-stricken; bereaved.

शोकमग्न-overcome with grief.

शोकमय-sorrowful; woeful; mournful.

शोकविह्वल-overcome with grief.

शोकसंतप्त-bereaved.

शोकसंदेश-message of condolence.

शोकसभा-condolence meeting.

शोकाकुल-overwhelmed with grief; bereaved.

शोकातुर-overwhelmed with grief; inconsolable; woeful.

शोख़-impertinent; insolent; rude; aggressive; offensive.

शोख़ी-impertinence; insolence.

शोचनीय-critical; causing anxiety; deplorable.

शोचनीयता-state of quality of being critical.

शिलष्टता-state or quality of being united.

श्लीपद-elephantiasis.

श्लील-refined; not vulgar.

श्लेष-pun; equivoque; paronomasia.

श्लेष्मा-phlegm; catarrh.

श्लोक-couplet; hymn.

श्लोकबद्ध-versified.

श्वदंत-canine tooth.

श्वन-a dog.

श्वसन-act of breathing/respiration.

श्वसुर-father-in-law.

श्वान-dog.

श्वास-breath; asthma.

श्वास-नली-bronchial pipe.

श्वास-प्रश्वास-inhaling and exhaling.

श्वासरोध-suffocation.

श्वेत-white.

श्वेतपत्र-white paper.

श्वेत-श्याम-black and white.

श्वेतसार-starch.

श्वेतांबर-white clothes; one of the two principal sects amongs.

ष

ष-The thirty-first cerebral consonant of the alphabet, and second of the four sibilants of the alphabet.

षंड-a eunuch; an impotent person; a name of ; bull; bullock.

षकार-the letter or its sound.

षकारांत-(word) ending in

षट्-six; the six acts enjoined on a Brahmin; the number of 6.

षट्ऋतु-the six seasons of the year (summer, rains, autumn, winter, frigid and spring).

षट्कोण-a six-angled figure; a six-angle; a hexagon.

षट्चक्र-six mysterious (cycles) of the body, according to

षटतिला-the eleventh day of the dark half of Magha.

षटमद-having six legs.

षटरस-six main tastes (sweet, saline, bitter, pungent, astringent, sour).

षटशास्त्र-the six main strains in music

षडंग-the six supplementary branches of sacred science . the six parts of body . arms, legs, head and waist.

षड्यंत्र-conspiracy; plot; intrigue.

षड्यंत्रकारी-conspirator.

षटरस-the six prominent tastes.

षडानन-Lord.

षणमासिक-six-monthly.

षष्टिपूर्ति-completion of sixty years of age.

षष्ठी-sixth day after birth; possessive case .

षोडश-sixteen; 16.

षोडशी-belle of blooming sixteen.

षष्ठीवन-spitting.

स

स-The thirty-second cerebral consonant of the alphabet, .

संकट-jeopardy; distress; trouble; adversity; crisis.

संकटकाल-period of crisis.

संकटकालीन-pertaining to a crisis.

संकटपूर्ण-distressing; critical; adverse.

संकटमय-critical.

संकटापन्न-in trouble; in distress.

संकर-cross; hybrid.

संकरज . cross-breed.

संकरण-cross-breeding.

संकरता-miscegenation; hybridity.

सँकरा-narrow.

संकलन-collection; compilation.

संकलकर्ता-compiler.

संकलित-compiled.

संकल्प-determination; resolve.

संकल्पना-notion; concept.

संकल्पवाची-conceptual.

संकल्पित-resolved.

संकाय-faculty (in an academic institution).

संकायाध्यक्ष-Dean of a faculty.

संकीर्ण-parochial; narrow.

संकीर्णता-parochialism; narrowness.

संकीर्तन-congregational singing (of devotional songs).

संकुचित-narrow; contracted; parochial.

संकुल-crowded; congested.

संकुलता-crowding; congestion.

संकेंद्रण-concentration.

संकेंद्रित-concentrated.

संकेत-signal; hint.

संकेतक-pointer.

संकेत-लिपि-notational script.

संकेतित-signalled; hinted; indicated.

संकोच-contraction; shyness; bashfulness; hesitation; hitch.

संक्रमण-transition; infection.

संक्रांति-transition; transition of the sun from one constellation to another.

संक्रामक-infectious.

संक्रिया-operation; process.

संज्ञाहीन-unconscious.

संज्ञाहीनता-unconsciousness.

संड-bull.

सँड़सी-household forceps; pincers; pliers.

संडा-stout; carefree fellow (smacking of mischievousness).

संडास-latrine in the form of a pit.

संत-saintly; saint; ascetic; mendicant.

संत-चरित-biography of a saint; hagiology.

संत-चरित्र-saintly character.

संतत-continuous (in space).

संतति-progeny; offspring.

संतति-निग्रह-birth-control.

संतति-निरोध-birth-control.

संत-पूजा-saint-worship.

संतप्त-grieved; stricken (with grief).

संतरण-crossing the Rubicon.

संतरा-tangerine; orange (India).

संतरी-sentry; armed guard.

संत-सुलभ-saintly.

संतान-issue; offspring; progeny.

संताप-grief; anguish; agony; woe; remorse; compunction.

संतुलन-balance; counter balance; equilibrium.

संतुष्ट-satisfied; gratified.

संतृप्त-satiated; well-satisfied.

संतृप्ति-satiation; saturation.

संतोष-satisfaction; contentment.

संतोषजनक-satisfactory; satisfying.

संतोषप्रद्र-satisfactory.

संतोषी-contented.

संत्रस्त-tormented; tortured; terrorised.

संत्रास-torment; torture; terror.

संदर्भ-context; reference.

संदर्भ-ग्रंथ-reference book.

संदर्भ-साहित्य-reference literature.

संदर्श-perspective.

संदर्शिका-guide-book.

संदल-sandal (wood).

संदिग्ध-doubtful; dubious; suspicious.

संदिग्धता-dubiety; doubtfulness.

संदूक़-box.

संदेश-message; tidings; information; news.

संदेशवाहक-messenger.

संदेशहर-messenger.

सँदेसा-message.

संदेह-suspicion; doubt.

संदेहजनक-suspicious; doubtful.

संधान-aiming; searching.

संधि-conjunction (of two different entities); joint; union of two sounds (Gram.); treaty; hole; knot.

संधिपत्र-deed/document of treaty.

संधि-विच्छेद-annulment of treaty; separation of the constituents in a conjunct word.

संधिशोथ-arthritis.

संध्या-evening; twilight; dusk; evening prayer.

संध्यावंदन-evening prayer.

संध्योपासना-evening prayer; evening worship.

संन्यास-the fourth and the last stage of a Hindu's life typifying renunciation of family, its affairs and also home; renunciation.

संपत्ति-wealth; pelf; riches; property; possession; effects; attainments.

संपत्ति-कर-wealth/property tax.

संपत्तिवान-wealthy.

संपदा-wealth; property; resources.

संपन्न-endowed with plenty; prosperous; affluent; accomplished; completed; fulfilled.

संपन्नता-plenty; prosperity; affluence.

संपरीक्षण-scrutiny.

संपर्क-contact; liaison.

संपर्क-स्थापन-establishment of contact.

संपात-coincidence; contact.

संपातिक-coincident.

संपाती-coincident; the name of elder the brother of

संपादक-editor.

संपादकत्व-editor-ship.

संपादक-मंडल-editorial board.

संपादन-editing; accomplishment; carrying out.

संपादिका-female of editor.

संपादित-edited; accomplished.

संपाद्य-(that) which is to be edited/accomplished.

संपीड़न-compression.

संपीड़ित-compressed.

संपुट-hollow of a receptacle; cavity.

संपुटिका-capsule.

संपुष्ट-confirmed; certified.

संपुष्टि-confirmation; certification.

संपूरक-complementary.

संपूर्ण-entire; whole; complete; completed; finished.

सँपेरा-snake-charmer.

सँपोला-young one of a snake.

संप्रदाय-community; (religious) sect; school (of thought).

संप्रभु-sovereign.

संप्रभुता-sovereignty.

संप्रेक्षक-despatcher; one who transmits.

संप्रेषण-transmission.

संप्रेषणीय-transmissible.

संप्रेषित-transmitted.

संप्रेष्य-that which is transmitted.

संबंध-relation; connection; relationship; contact; betrothal.

संबल-mainstay; support.

संबोधन-address; vocative case.

संबोधित-addressed.

संभरक-supplier.

संभरण-supply.

सँभलना-to pull oneself together; to come to one's self/senses; to recover; to recuperate.
संभव-possible.
संभवतः possibly; probably.
सँभाल-looking after; care; upkeep.
सँभालना-to take care of; to look after.
सँभाला-the last flicker.
संभावना-possibility; likelihood.
संभावित-probable.
संभावी-probable.
संभाव्य-probable.
संभाषी-speaker.
संभाष्य-appropriate to conversation.
संभोग-cohabitation; coitus.
संभोगी-(male) (one) who indulges in sex.
संभोग्य-(female) fit for sex.
संभोजन-common dinner.
संभ्रम-confusion; perplexity.
संयंत्र-fixed machinery; plant.
संयत-restrained; controlled; disciplined; subdued.
संयम-restraint; discipline.
संयमित-disciplined.
संयमी-moderate; disciplined; sober; temperate.
संयुक्त-joint; united.
संयुक्त खाता-joint account.
संयुक्त राष्ट्र-United Nations.
संयुक्त वाक्य-compound sentence.
संयुक्त व्यंजन-compound consonant.
संयुक्त सरकार-coalition government.
संयुत-conjunct.
संयुति-conjunction.
संयोग-coincidence; chance.
संयोगवशात् by mere coincidence.
संयोजन-combination.
संयोजित-combined.
संयोज्य-that which can be mixed/ combined; combinable.
संरक्षक-patron; guardian; supporter.
संरक्षित-patronised; protected; preserved.
संरक्षित राज्य-protectorate.
संरचना-structure; composition; construction.
संरचनात्मक-structural.
संराधन-conciliation.
संरेखन-alignment.
संरोध-blockade.
संलग्न-attached; appended; annexed.
संवरण-choice; selection; resistance.
सँवरना-to appear in a right/choice make-up.
सँवरिया-the darkish one; Lord Krishna.
संवर्ग-cadre.
संवर्धक-magnifying.

संवर्धन-enlargement; magnification; nourishment; culture.

संवर्धित-enlarged; magnified; cultured.

संवहन-carrying; conduction.

संवातन-ventilation.

संवाद-message; dialogue; conservation; news; communication.

संवादक-reporter.

संवाददाता-correspondent.

संवादशील-communicative.

संवादहर-messenger.

संवादिता-correspondence; the exchange of information and ideas; communication.

संवादी-corresponding; concordant.

सँवारना-to make-up; to arrange/put in proper order.

संवाहक-conductor.

संवाहन-conduction.

संवाही-conductor.

संवितरण-disbursement.

संविदा-contract.

संविधान-constitution.

संविधानवाद-constitutionalism.

संविधान-सभा-constituent; assembly.

संविधानिक-constitutional.

संविधि-a rule or law passed by an institution or Parliament; statute.

संविधिक-statutory.

संविभाग-portfolio.

संविहित-constituted.

संवीक्षक-scrutinizer.

संवीक्षा-scrutiny.

संवृत-closed.

संवृद्धि-growth; development.

संवेग-momentum.

संवेदन-sensation.

संवेदनशील-sensitive.

संवेदनहारी-anaesthetic.

संवेदना-condolence; the deep feeling of sharing the suffering of another.

संवेदिक-sensory.

संवेदित-perceived through senses.

संवेदी-sympathetic.

संवेद्य-fit to be experienced; worthy of being informed.

संवेष्टक-packer.

संवेष्टन-packing.

संवेष्टित-packed.

संवैधानिक-constitutional.

संशय-doubt; suspicion; uncertainty.

संशयवाद-scepticism.

संशयवादी-sceptic.

संशयात्मक-doubtful; uncertain.

संशयालु-sceptic; doubting.

संशयी-given to doubting; sceptic.

संशोधक-corrective.

संशोधनवाद-revisionism.

संश्रय-alliance.

संश्रित-allied.

संश्लिष्ट-synthesised; synthetic; mixed up.

संसक्त-cohesive.

संसक्ति-cohesion.

संसद-parliament.

संसदीय-parliamentary; admissible in parliament.

संसर्ग-contact; association.

संसर्गज-born out of association; contagious.

संसार-world.

संसृति-world.

संसेचन-insemination.

संस्करण-edition.

संस्कारहीन-uncultured; unrefined.

संस्कारित-cultured.

संस्कृति-culture.

संस्तर-bed.

संस्तवन- commendation; recommendation.

संस्तुत-recommended.

संस्तुति-recommendation.

संस्था-institution; a very familiar person in some activity.

संस्थागत-institutional.

संस्थान-institute.

संस्थापक-founder.

संस्थापना-establishment.

संस्पर्श-touch; contact.

संस्मरण-reminiscences; memories.

संहत-compact; consolidated.

संहति-compactness; state of being consolidated.

संहार-annihilation; carnage.

संहित-accumulated; codified.

संहिता-a set of rules or laws arranged in a system; statute-book; code.

संहिताकरण-codification.

संहिति-accumulation.

स denoting 'with' as with love; likeness or quality, as like, similar, equal.

सइयाँ-lover; husband.

सईस-one who cleans and looks after horses; groom.

सईसी-work or function of a groom.

सकंटक-thorny.

सकता-state of being dumb-founded.

सकना-to be able to.

सकरकंद-sweet potato.

सकरकंदी-sweet potato.

सकरपारा-a kind of lozenge-shaped sweet.

सकरुण-compassionate.

सकर्मक-transitive.

सकल-all; whole; entire; gross; total.

सकाम-impelled by desire; purposeful; motivated; purposive.

सकार-the letter or its sound.

सकारना-to honour.

सकारे-at day-break; in the early morning.

सकुचना-bashful.

सकुचाना-to feel embarrassed; to hesitate; to feel shy.

सकुल-with kith and kin.

सकोरा-earthen cup.

सक़्क़ा-water-carrier.

सक्रियता-activity.

सक्षम-competent; capable.

सक्षमता-competence; capability.

सखरा-cooked in water.

सखरी-food cooked in water.

सखा-chum; pal; intimate friend.

सखी-chum (girl).

सखी भाव-friendly feeling or attitude in which a male devotee reacts as the wife of his lord.

सख़्त-hard; rigorous; strict; harsh; dire; serious; stiff.

सख्य-feeling of being chummy.

सख्य-भाव- companionably; friendliness.

सगा-real; sibling; born of the same parents.

सगाई-betrothal; engagement; remarriage of widow or divorcee.

सगुण-possessed of attributes; endowed with qualities.

सगुनिया-soothsayer.

सगुनौती-augury.

सगोत्र-of the same caste.

सगोत्रता-kinship; the state of being of the same caste.

सग्गड़-hand-cart.

सघन-dense; thick; intensive.

सघनता-denseness; thickness; intensity.

सच-true; real; right.

सचमुच truly; really; in fact; verily; actually; indeed.

सचल-moving; movable; mobile.

सच-सच-complete truth.

सचाई-truthfulness; truth; veracity.

सचान-falcon; hawk.

सचित्र-pictorial; illustrated.

सचिव-secretary.

सचिवालय-a secretary's place of work; secretariat; the staff of secretary's office; body of secretaries.

सचेत-alert; cautious; conscious.

सचेतक-an official of a political party who maintains discipline among its members in legislative debates; whip.

सचेतन-conscious.

सचेष्ट-active; endeavouring.

सचेष्टता-activeness; activity.

सच्चरित्र-of good moral character; virtuous.

सच्चा-truthful; true; sincere.

सच्चाई-truthness.

सच्चापन-truthfulness; truth.

सज-style; orientation.

सजग-wakeful; awake; cautious; attentive.

सजगता-wakefulness; cautiousness.

सजना-to appear in make-up; to be embellished/adorned/bedecked/decorated/dressed; to shine forth.

सजनी-sweet chum.

सजल-hydrous; aqueous; tearful.

सज़ा-punishment; penalty.

सज़ा-ए-मौत-capital punishment.

सजात-of the same sort of type.

सजाति-of same caste.

सजातीय-of one and the same class/caste; homogenous.

सजा-धजा-made-up and adorned.

सजाना-to embellish/adorn/decorate; to arrange in proper order; to put (things) shipshape.

सज़ायाफ़्ता-convicted.

सजाव-decoration.

सजावट-decoration; ornamentation.

सजावटी-that makes something look more beautiful; decorative.

सजीला-winsome; graceful.

सजीव-live full of life; vivacious.

सजीवता-liveliness; vivacity.

सज्जन-gentleman; good-man.

सज्जनता-goodness, gentlemanliness.

सज्जा-decoration; equipment.

सज्जित-decorated; adorned; equipped.

सज्जी-saltpetre.

सझिया-partner.

सटकना-to give the slip; to slip away.

सटना-to be contiguous; to stick/adhere.

सटीक-to the point; apt; supplied with explanatory notes; annotated.

सटोरिया-speculator.

सट्टा-speculation.

सट्टी-market-place.

सट्टेबाज़-speculator.

सठियाना-to be in dotage; to be senile.

सठियाव-dotage; senility.

सड़क-road.

सड़न-putrefaction; decomposition.

सड़ना-to rot/decompose.

सड़सी-pair of tongs; forceps.

सड़ा-putrefied; decomposed.

सड़ाना-to cause to putrefy; to decompose.

सड़ायँध-stench; foul smell due to putrefaction; disagreeable smell.

सड़ियल-rotten; decaying; putrid; good for nothing; worthless.

सतगुना-seven times.

सतगुरु-a good preceptor or teacher; God.

सतजुग-the golden age of period.

सतत-continual; continuous (in time); constant; perpetual.

सतथ्य-with facts; factual.

सतमासा-of seven months.

सतरंगा-of seven colours.

सतर-line; row.

सतर्क-alert; cautious; careful.

सतर्कता-alertness; cautiousness.

सतलड़ा-having seven chains; necklace with seven chains.

सतवंती-(woman) faithful to her husband and true to her duties.

सतसई-collection of seven hundred of a poet.

सतह-the uppermost level of land; surface; level.

सताना-to oppress/victimize/torment/torture.-victimization.

सतालुई-light red; crimson.

सतालू-peach.

सतावर-asparagus.

सती-chaste woman, especially true to her husband.

सती-प्रथा-the tradition of being cremated with the dead body of the husband on the funeral pyre.

सतीत्व-chastity; fidelity to one's husband.

सतीत्व-भंग-loss of (one's) chastity.

सतीत्व-हरण-spoliation of (someone's) chastity.

सती-साध्वी-fully loyal to (one's) husband.

सती-सावित्री-extremely loyal to (one's) husband.

सतोगुण-first of the three qualities according to the Hindu Philosophy of life; representing purity and goodness.

सतगुणी-one in whom the quality of

सत्कर्म-virtuous deed.

सत्कार-courteous welcome.

सत्कीर्ति-good name; renown; repute; fame.

सत्त-essence; extract; power; strength.

सत्तांतरण-transference of power or authority.

सत्ता-existence; power; the 'seven' of playing cards.

सत्ताधारी-(person) in power/authority.

सत्तारूढ़-in power or authority.

सत्ता-संघर्ष-power-struggle.

सत्तू-parched gram or barley; pulverised and used as an edible.

सत्त्व-existence.

सत्त्वहीन-void of essence.

सत्पथ-path of truth; right path.

सत्पात्र-deserving/worthy person.

सत्प्रयास-a sincere effort.

सत्फल-excellent result.

सत्य-true.

सत्यकाम-seeker of truth.

सत्यत: verily; truly.

सत्यता-truthfulness; reality.

सत्यदर्शी-seer of truth.

सत्यनारायण-God, the Truth.

सत्यनिष्ठ-loyal to Truth.

सत्यपरायण-devoted to Truth.

सत्यभाषी-true in word.

सत्यवादी-scrupulously true in word.

सत्यशील-truthful by nature.

सत्यशीलता-truthfulness.

सत्यांकन-ratification.

सत्यांकित-ratified.

सत्याग्रह-insistence on truth; a nonviolent struggle offered to uphold the truth; passive resistance.

सत्यानाश-total ruination; destruction.

सत्यानाशी-ruinous; completely destructive.

सत्यापक-one who verifies.

सत्यापन-verification.

सत्यापित-verified.

सत्ययुग-the first age according to Indian mythology; golden age.

सत्र-session period of time having definite limits.

सत्र-न्यायालय-session court.

सत्रांत-end of the session.

सत्रांश-term (in an academic institution).

सत्रावसान-prorogation (of an assembly); conclusion of a session.

सत्वर-fast; swiftly; quickly.

सत्वरता-swiftness; fastness.

सत्संग-company of the good; religious assembly.

सत्समागम-confluence of the good and the great.

सद good.

सदन-house.

सदन-त्याग-walk-out; leaving the house.

सदमा-shock; trauma.

सदय-filled with kindness/compassion.

सदयता-state or quality of being compassionate.

सदरी-sleeveless jacket.

सदस्य-member.

सदस्यता-membership.

सदा always; ever; cry; *spl.* mendicant's cry.

सदाक़त-truthfulness.

सदाचरण-good conduct.

सदाचार-good conduct; righteousness.

सदाचारिता-righteousness.

सदाचारी-of good conduct; righteous.

सदापर्णी-evergreen.

सदाबहार-evergreen.

सदारत-chairmanship; presidentship.

सदावर्त-distributing food to the poor on a permanent basis.

सदाशयता-bonafides; genuineness.

सदिश-vector (Maths.).

सदी-century.

सदुपदेश-good counsel.

सदुपयोग-god use; proper use.

सदृश-like; alike; partial similar; analogous.

सदृशता-likeness; resemblance; partial similarity.

सदेह bodily; physically.

सदैव always; ever; forever.

सदोष-faulty; defective; having shortcomings.

सद् good.

सद्गति-better state/condition; salvation.

सद्गुण-good trait; virtue.

सद्गुणी-possessing good traits; virtuous.

सदगुरु-worthy preceptor.

सद्भाव-good will; kindly feeling.

सद्यः just a moment ago; a moment back; forthwith.

सद्यःकृत-just performed/done.

सद्वृत्ति-righteous disposition; right type of attitude.

सधना-to be well accomplished; to be well practised; to be well-trained; correct aiming.

सधन्यवाद thankfully.

सधर्मी-co-religionist; having similar function.

सधवा-(woman) whose husband is alive.

सधाना-to cause to be trained.

सन-hemp; sound (resembling a hissing noise) produced by an object moving swiftly; year.

सनई-hemp.

सनक-fad; whim; vagary; mania; craze.

सनकना-to go crazy.

सनदयाफ़्ता-certificate-holder.

सनना-to be besmeared; to be kneaded.

सनम-a person who is much loved; dear one; darling.

सनसन-hissing/swishing sound.

सनसनाना-to produce a swishing sound; to rustle.

सनसनी-sensation; thrill; excitement.

सनसनीखेज़-sensational; thrilling; exciting; whizzing.

सनातन-eternal; perpetual; traditional.

सनातम धर्म-Religion Eternal; conservation/orthodox Hinduism.

सनातन धर्मी-(one) who follows

सनातनी-eternal; of or pertaining to

सनाथ-endowed with a patron; blessed with a protector.

सनीचर-Saturn; Saturday.

सन्-Anno Domini.

सन्न-stunned.

सन्नद्धता-preparedness.

सन्नाटा-stillness complete.

सन्निकट close by; very near; in close proximity.

सन्निकटता-nearness; proximity; approximation.

सन्निकर्ष-close proximity.

सन्निपात-disorder of the three humours.

सन्निविष्ट-inserted; included.

सन्निवेश-inclusion; insertion.

सन्निहित-included; implied.

सन्मान-honour.

सन्मार्ग-path of righteousness/virtue; right/moral course.

सन्मुख-front.

सपक्ष-having wings; belonging to same party; winged.

सपत्नी-co-wife.

सपत्नीक along with (one's) wife.

सपना-dream.

सपरदायी-accompanist of a dancing girl.

सपरना-to pull through.

सपरिकर with attendants/ paraphernalia.

सपरिवार with family.

सपरेटा-skimmed milk.

सपर्ण-having leaves; leafy.

सपाट-flat; plane; smooth; even.

सपाटा-speed.

सपिंड-collateral.

सपुर्द-deposit.

सपुर्दगी-deposited.

सपूत-worthy son.

सपेरा-snake-charmer.

सपोला-young snake.

सप्त-seven, 7.

सप्तक-group of seven; septat/ septette; gamut (Music).

सप्तपदी-seven bridal steps round the fire.

सप्तमी-seventh day of each lunar half month.

सप्तमी विभक्ति-sign of locative case (Gram.).

सप्तर्षि-Ursa Major; the Great Bear.

सप्तलोक-the seven worlds.

सप्तस्वर-the seven notes of music.

सप्ताह-week.

सप्ताहांत-weekend.

सफ़र-journey; travel.

सफ़र-ख़र्च-travel expenses.

सफ़रनामा-description of a journey.

सफ़र-मैना-sappers and miners.

सफ़री-suitable for (purposes of a) journey.

सफल-successful; fruitful.

सफलता-success; fruitfulness; achievement.

सफलीभूत-successful; fruitful; thriving.

सफ़ा-clean.-page; folio.

सफ़ाई-cleanliness; tidiness; cleansing; explanation; clarification; defence.

सफ़ाई-पक्ष-defence party/side.

सफ़ाया-clean sweep.

सफ़ेद-white.

सफ़ेदा-white lead; a variety of mango; a kind of tree.

सफ़ेदी-whiteness; albumen (of egg).

सब-all; denoting 'under' as in sub-inspector.

सबक़-lesson.

सब-कुछ-everything.

सबब-cause; reason.

सबरी-an iron-rod used for house breaking; jemmy.

सबल-strong; powerful.

सबलता-strength; power.

सबूत-proof; evidence.

सबेरा-morning.

सबेरे in the morning.

सब्ज़-green.

सब्ज़ी-herbage; vegetable.

सब्ज़ी-मंडी-vegetable market.

सब्ज़ीवाला-vegetable vendor; green-grocer.

सब्बल-crowbar.

सब्र-patience.

सभा-assembly; meeting.

सभागृह-assembly chamber/room.

सभात्याग-a sudden angry departure from a meeting; walk-out.

सभापति-chairman.

सभापतित्व-chairmanship.

सभा-भवन-assembly hall.

सभा-मंच-dais.

सभा-मंडप-pavilion.

सभासद-member of an assembly; councillor.

सभी-all; everybody.

सभ्य-civilized; civil.

सभ्यता-civilization; civility; courtesy.

समंजन-adjustment.

समंजित-adjusted.

सम-equal; even.

समकक्ष-of the same level; on the same footing of the same stature.

समकारी-equalising.

समकालिक- synchronous; contemporary; coeval.

समकोण-right angle.

समकोणिक-right-angled.

समक्ष before.

समग्र-entire; whole.

समग्रता-entirely; totality.

समग्र युद्ध-total war.

समजातीय- homogeneous; homologous; of the same species.

समजातीयता-homogeneity; homology.

समझ-intelligence; intellect; understanding; sense; comprehension.

समझदार-sensible; wise.

समझना-to understand/follow; to make out; to comprehend; to realize; to consider; to know; act of understanding.

समझ-बूझ-prudence; shrewdness.

समझाना-to make (someone) understand; to explain; to instruct; to advise; to bring round by persuasion.

समझौता-compromise; agreement; pact; compounding.

समतल-level; even; plane; smooth.

समतलन-levelling.

समता-equality; parity.

समतुलन-equilibrium; equipoise.

समतुलित-equipoised.

समतोलन-act of balancing.

समदर्शिता-the state or quality of being non-discriminating; even-handed.

समदर्शी-non-discriminating; even-eyed.

समदृष्टि-even-handed-ness.

समधिक-exceeding.

समधिन-mother-in-law of son/ daughter.

समधियाना-residence or household of the father-in-law of son/daughter.

समध्वनिक-homonym.

समन-summons.

समाँ-time atmosphere.

समांग-homogeneous.

समांगता-homogeneity.

समांतर-parallel.

समांतरता-parallelism.

समाई-capacity; room.

सभाकलन-integration.

समागत-welcome stranger.

समागम-arrival; meeting; assembly or gathering.

समाघात-blow; percussion.

समाचार-news.

समाचारदाता-news reporter.

समाचार-पत्र-newspaper.

समाचार-फ़िल्म-newsreel.

समाचारवाचक-newsman.

समाचारिक-pertaining to news.
समाज-society; company.
समाजवाद-socialism.
समाजवादी-socialistic.
समाज-विरोधी-antisocial.
समाजशास्त्र-Sociology.
समाजशास्त्री-sociologist.
समाजशास्त्रीय-sociological.
समाजशील-sociable.
समाज-सुधार-social reform.
समाज-सेवक-social worker.
समाज-सेवा-social service.
समाज-सेविका-woman social worker.
समाज-सेवी-social worker.
समाजी-social.
समाजीकरण-socialization.
समादर-reverence; veneration; respect.
समादरणीय-reverend.
समादिष्ट-commanded.
समादृत-revered.
समादेश-command; writ.
समाधान-solution (of a problem); satisfaction; satisfying explanation.
समाधि-transcendental meditation; trance; tomb; grave.
समाधिमग्न- experiencing transcendental knowledge.
समाधि-लेख-epitaph.
समाधि-शिला-tomb-stone.
समाधिस्थ-in a state of trance/ meditation.
समान-equal; similar; like; uniformity.
समानता-equality; similarity; likeness.
समानांतर-parallel.
समानांतरता-parallelism.
समाना-to pervade in; to fill (in its entirety); to occupy all space in.
समानाधिकरण-apposition.
समानार्थ-(words) having similar meanings; equivalent.
समानार्थक-equivalent.
समानार्थकता-similarity in meaning; equivalence.
समानुपात-proportion.
समानुपातिक-proportional.
समापन-winding up; closing up; ending; completion.
समापवर्तक-common factor.
समापवर्त्य-common multiple.
समापिका क्रिया-finite verb.
समाप्त-finished; ended.
समाप्तप्राय-almost finished; moribund.
समाप्ति-conclusion; expiry; end; finish; expiration; extinction.
समाप्य-which can be finished/ended.
समायुक्त-adjusted.
समायोजक-adjuster.
समायोजन-adjustment.
समायोजित-adjusted.

समारंभ-happy beginning; commencement; initiation.

समारोह-celebration; function; festive event; ceremony.

समार्थ-equivalent in meaning.

समार्थक-equivalent (word).

समालोचक-reviewer; critic.

समालोचन-act of reviewing.

समालोचना-review; criticism.

समावर्तन-returning from after completion of studies.

समाविष्ट-incorporated; included; entered.

समावृत-enclosed; attached.

समावेश-incorporation; inclusion.

समाशोधन-clearing.

समास-compound; compound word (Gram.).

समास-बहुल-full of compound words.

समासीन-seated.

समाहरण-collecting.

समाहर्ता-collector.

समाहार-collection; accumulation.

समाहित-collected; merged (into); included (in).

समिति-a body of persons appointed or elected for some specified function; committee; society.

समिति-कक्ष-committee room.

समिधा-fire-wood used as fuel in sacrificial fire.

समीकरण-equation; equalisation; assimilation.

समीकार-equaliser.

समीकृत-equalised.

समीक्षक-reviewer; commentator.

समीक्षण-reviewing; commenting.

समीक्षा-act of viewing again; review; a critical discussion dealing with a book; review.

समीक्षाकार-reviewer; commentator.

समीक्ष्य-worth reviewing/ commenting; under review.

समीचीन-appropriate; proper; right; befitting.

समीप-near; close by.

समीपतम-nearest.

समीपता-nearness; proximity.

समीपस्थ-near (by); proximate.

समीपी-near

समीर-breeze.

समुंदर-ocean.

समुचित-appropriate; suitable.

समुचितता-appropriateness; fitness.

समुच्चय-collection; set; compilation.

समुच्चयार्थक-collective.

समुज्जवल-effulgent.

समुदाय-association; commune; community; group.

समुद्यत-just ready; quite ready.

समुद्र-sea; ocean.

समुद्र-कंप-sea-quake.

समुद्र-तट-coast; sea-beach; sea-shore; sea-board.

समुद्र-तटीय-coastal.

समुद्र-तल-sea-level.

समुद्र-तली-sea-bed; sea-bottom.

समुद्र-देवता-Oceanus.

समुद्र-पत्तन-sea-port.

समुद्र-मंथन-churning of the sea (Indian Mythology).

समुद्र-यात्रा-voyage.

समुद्र-यात्री-sea-farer.

समुद्रवर्ती-littoral.

समुद्र-विज्ञान-Oceanography.

समुद्राभिमुख-sea-ward.

समुद्री-oceanic.

समुद्री-गाय-sea-cow.

समुद्री-डाकू-pirate; sea-robber.

समुद्री ताक़त-sea power; a country with a strong navy.

समुद्री तार-cable.

समुद्रीय-oceanic.

समुन्नत-raised high; elevated; developed.

समुपस्थित-elevation; development.

समुपस्थित-appeared.

समुपस्थिति-appearance; presence.

समूचा-whole; all entire.

समूल-total. from the root.

समूह-multitude; concourse; assemblage; crowd; group.

समूहन-grouping.

समूहवाचक-collective.

समृद्ध-prosperous; rich; affluent.

समृद्धि-prosperity; affluence; richness.

समेकता-consolidation; integration.

समेकन-fusion; consolidation.

समेकनीय-fusible.

समेकित-consolidated.

समेटना-to gather; to roll up.

समेत with; along with.

समोना-to mix together inextricably.

समोसा-an Indian variety of saltish pastry, usually triangular in shape.

सम्मत-sanctioned by.

सम्मति-opinion; view; assent; consent.

सम्मन-summons.

सम्मान-honour; esteem; respect.

सम्मानीय-honourable; respected.

सम्मानपूर्ण-honourable; respectful.

सम्मानसूचक-honorific.

सम्मानार्थ in honour (of).

सम्मानित-esteemed; respected; honoured; revered.

सम्मान्य-honourable.

सम्मित-symmetrical ; resembling.

सम्मिलन-combining; joining; mingling; meet; get-together.

सम्मिलित-combined; joint; mingled; included.

सम्मिश्र-complex.

सम्मिश्रण-compounding; combining; admixture; mixing up.

सम्मिश्रित-compounded; combined; mixed up.

सम्मुख, के in front of; facing each other; face to face.

सम्मेय-of the same size; commensurate.

सम्मेलन-conference; convention.

सम्मोह-fascination; charm.

सम्मोहक-fascinating; charming; attractive.

सम्मोहन-charm; fascination.

सम्मोहन विद्या-hypnotism.

सम्मोहनास्त्र-hypnotising.

सम्मोहनी-that which hypnotises; hypnotising agent.

सम्मोहित-hypnotised.

सम्यक-through; comprehensive; all-around; proper; appropriate.

सम्राज्ञी-empress.

सम्राट-emperor.

सम्हलना-to be alert.

सयानपन-cleverness; dexterity.

सयाना-grown up; shrewd; clever.

सयानापन-shrewdness; cleverness.

सयापा-a chant of lamentation.

सरंध्र-porous.

सर-victorious; hand in game.

सरकंडा-a kind of reed.

सरकना-to move a little; to crawl; to move slowly.

सरकस-circus.

सरकार-government.

सरकारी-official; pertaining to government; governmental.

सरख़त-deed; written agreement.

सरगना-(ring) leader; chieftain.

सरगम-gamut (Music).

सरगर्मी-zeal and enthusiasm.

सरगी-meal taken at early dawn immediately before commencing a fast.

सरणी-line; row; table.

सरताज-topping.

सरदार-chief; chieftain; leader; member of Sikh community.

सरदारी-leadership.

सरना-to be accomplished.

सरनाम-well-known; renowned; famed; reputed.

सरनामा-form of addressing (on top of a letter).

सरपंच-chief arbiter.

सरपट-galloping; at a gallop.

सरपत-a kind of reed.

सरपरस्त-guardian; patron.

सरपरस्ती-guardianship; patronage.

सरमाएदारी-state or quality of being a capitalist; capitalism.

सरमाया-capital; total assets; estate.

सरमायेदार-capitalist.

सरल-simple; easy; straight.

सरलता-simplicity; easiness; straightness.

सरल संगीत-light music.

सरलीकरण-simplification.

सरलीकृत-simplified.

सरस-juicy; watery; tasty; delicious; full of tender sentiments; fascinating; attractive.

सरसना-to flourish/prosper; to look lovely/charming.

सरसब्ज़-in full bloom; verdant.

सरसर-sound produced by a snake, air etc.; whilst in movement; rustle.

सरसराना-to produce a sound as that of the movement of air, snake and the like.

सरसराहट-sound produced by the movement of air, snake and the like, rustle.

सरसरी-cursory; summary.

सरसाम-delirium.

सरसिज-lotus.

सरसिरुह-louts.

सरसी-waterpool; pond.

सरसों-mustard (seed or plant).

सरस्वती-Goddess of Learning.

सरहज-wife of brother-in-law.

सरहद-border; boundary; frontier.

सरहदी-pertaining to the frontier.

सरापना-to curse.

सरापा-complete set of clothes.

सराफ़-jeweller.

सराफ़ा-a place where bankers transact business.

सराफ़ी-banking; money changing.

सराय-inn; tavern; caravan-serai.

सरासर totally; wholly.

सराहना-to praise/laud; to commend.

सराहनीय-worthy of praise; praise-worthy; laudable; commendable.

सरिता-stream; river.

सरिया-iron bar.

सरिश्ता-a department of an administrative machinery.

सरिश्तेदार-official incharge of a administrative machinery.

सरिश्तेदारी-office or tenure of a administrative machinery.

सरिस-similar; alike; equal.

सरीखा, के-like; similar; to.

सरीसृप-crawling/creeping insects or the like; reptiles.

सरीसृप-विज्ञान-Herpetology.

सरूप-alike; similar; beautiful; guise.
सरूपता-likeness; similarity; semblance; comeliness; beauty.
सरूर-slight inebriation; intoxication.
सरेआम publicly.
सरे दरबार in open court.
सरे बाज़ार publicly; openly.
सरे शाम early in the evening; at the start of evening.
सरेस-gelatine; glue.
सरो-cypress tree.
सरोकार-concern; connection; dealings.
सरोज-lotus.
सरोतर-befitting from beginning to end.
सरोद-an Indian musical instrument resembling a guitar.
सरोरुह-lotus.
सरोवर-lake; pond; pool.
सरोष angrily; wrathfully.
सरौता-instrument for cutting betels nuts; nut-cracker.
सर्ग-canto; chapter.
सर्जन-creation; surgeon.
सर्जनहार-creator.
सर्जनात्मक-creative.
सर्जरी-surgery.
सर्द-cold.
सर्दख़ाना-cool room (in the basement).
सर्दा-a variety of melon.
सर्दी-cold; winter.
सर्प-snake.
सर्पण-creeping/crawling (like a serpent).
सर्पदंत-fang of a snake.
सर्पदंश-snakebite; wound caused by snakebite.
सर्पिणी-female of snake.
सर्पित-crept; crawled.
सर्पिल-serpentine.
सर्पी-crawling; creeping.
सर्फ़-spent.
सर्फ़ा-expenditure.
सर्राटा-fast; swiftly; very fast speed.
सर्राफ़-bullion merchant.
सर्राफ़ा-bullion market.
सर्राफ़ी-calling of a bullion merchant.
सर्व-all; whole; entire.
सर्वकाम-full of desires.
सर्वगत-all-pervasive.
सर्वग्रास-total eclipse.
सर्वग्रासी-all-devouring.
सर्वचारी-rolling all round.
सर्वजन-persons; one and all; everybody.
सर्वजनीन-pertaining to all.
सर्वजित-all-conquering.
सर्वजीवी-whose father; grand-father and great-grand-father are all alive.

सर्वज्ञ-omniscient.

सर्वज्ञता-omniscience.

सर्वतः all round; on all sides; in every respect.

सर्वता-wholeness; entirety.

सर्वतोभद्र-auspicious all around.

सर्वतोमुखी-all-round; versatile.

सर्वत्र-everywhere; at every place; in all cases.

सर्वथा-totally; completely; entirely.

सर्वदर्शी-all-seeing; seer all-round.

सर्वदलीय-of or pertaining to all parties; all-party.

सर्वदा ever; ever more; always.

सर्वनाम-pronoun.

सर्वनाश-complete ruination; utter/ total destruction.

सर्वनाशी-utterly destructive; completely ruinous.

सर्वनियंता-Controller Supreme.

सर्वप्रयोज्य-all-purpose.

सर्वप्रिय-dear to all; love by all; darling of one and all.

सर्वभक्षी-omnivorous; devouring anything.

सर्वमंगला-Goddess.

सर्वमान्य-accepted by all.

सर्वव्यापक-omnipresent; all-pervading.

सर्वशक्तिमान-all-powerful; almighty; omnipotent.

सर्वश्री-Messrs.

सर्वश्रेष्ठ-best of all.

सर्वसंहार-utter annihilation.

सर्वसम्मत-unanimous.

सर्वसम्मती-unanimity.

सर्वसाधारण-common people; public; populace.

सर्वस्व-one's all.

सर्वस्वाहा-ruined entirely.

सर्वस्वीकृत-unanimous.

सर्वहर-all-usurping usurper all round.

सर्वहारा-member of proletariat; proletariat.

सर्वहारा वर्ग-the lower labouring classes; proletariat.

सर्वहित-public good; common weal.

सर्वांग-all components (of the body).

सर्वांगपूर्ण-full and complete in all respects.

सर्वांगीण-all-round.

सर्वांतर्यामी-all-pervading (God).

सर्वात्मा-Soul Universal.

सर्वाधिक-greatest in number; surpassing every one.

सर्वाधिकार-all rights; full powers.

सर्वार्थ-all purposes.

सर्वार्थ-साधन-fulfilling of all purposes.

सर्वेक्षक-surveyor.

सर्वेक्षण-surveying.

सर्वेश्वर-Supreme Lord; Lord of all.

सर्वे-सर्वा-all in all.

सर्वोच्च-supreme; highest in place or rank.

सर्वोत्तम-supreme; best of all; the very best.

सर्वोदय-uplift of one and all.

सर्वोपकारी-benevolent to all.

सर्वोपयोगी-useful to all.

सर्वोपरि-above all; supreme.

सलई-pine tree.

सलज्ज-coy; bashful.

सलना-to be bored/pierced.

सलमा-gold and silver thread used in embroidery.

सलवार-a kind of trousers (worn by women, especially in Punjab).

सलसलाना-to feel itching sensation; to rub gently with fingers.

सलसलाहट-itching sensation.

सलहज-wife of brother-in-law; wife of wife's brother.

सलाई-pointed longish stick rod for applying collyrium to the eyes; match-stick.

सलाख़-thin long metallic bar.

सलाद-salad.

सलाम-Muslim form of salutation.

सलामत-(fully) alive; safe.

सलामती-state or quality of being fully alive.

सलामी-salutation; formal salutation (military in particular); gratification (in cash).

सलामी बल्लेबाज-an opening batsman.

सलाह-advice; counsel.

सलाहकार-counsellor; advisor.

सलिल-water.

सलीक़ा-etiquette; good manners.

सलीक़ेदार-mannerly; possessing good manners.

सलीता-a kind of tough and stout cloth.

सलीपर-(pair of) slippers.

सलीब-cross.

सलीम-simple-hearted.

सलीस-(language) easy to understand; simple and cultured (language).

सलूक-behaviour; social dealings; treatment; the good done; obligation.

सलूका-a jacket worn by women.

सलोना-comely; winsome; charming; saltish.

सलोनापन-state or quality of being comely.

सल्तनत-sultanate; dominion; kingdom; reign.

सवर्ण-having the same colour; (words) having the same spelling.

सवर्णता-state or quality of being

सवर्ण हिन्दू-a Hindu belonging to one of the upper three castes.

सवा-one and a quarter.

सवाक-gifted with the talking faculty/ speech; which can talk.

सवाब-(Heavenly) reward for deeds meritorious; religious/virtuous deed.

सवाया-one and a quarter times.

सवार-mounted; rider.

सवारी-act of state of riding; passenger; cavalcade.

सवाल-an inquiry to obtain information; question; demand; a subject of debate or dispute; issue; problem.

सवाल-जवाब-question and answer; argumentation.

सवालिया-interrogative.

सविता-Sun.

सविनय-humble; modest. humbly.

सविनय अवज्ञा-civil disobedience.

सविनय निवेदन-humble submission.

सविस्तर in detail.

सवेरा-morning.

सवैया-one and a quarter; multiplication table of one and a quarter time of natural numbers; a kind of metre in poetry.

सशंकित-alarmed due to suspicion.

सशक्त-powerful; dominant; forceful.

सशक्तता-forcefulness; power.

सशक्तीकरण-an act of making powerful; empowerment.

सशपथ-an oath.

सशरीर-physically; bodily.

सशस्त्र-armed.

सशुल्क ad paying fee/subscription.

सश्रम-fatigued; tired; rigorous.

ससीम-limited; finite.

ससुर-father-in-law.

ससुरा-the expression 'father-in-law' used as a form of abuse.

ससुराल-place or residence of the in-laws.

सस्ता-low in price; cheap; inexpensive.

सस्नेह with love; with loving regards.

सस्मित-smiling; with a smile playing on the lips.

सस्य-crops.

सह indicating 'with', 'along with', equivalent of 'co-'.

सह-अपराधी-accomplice.

सह-अभिनेता-co-star.

सह-अस्तित्व-co-existence.

सहकर्मी-co-worker.

सहकार-cooperation.

सहकार-समिति-cooperative society.

सहकारिता-cooperation.

सहकारी-co-operative.

सहगमन-going along with (somebody); self-immolation on the pyre of the husband.

सहगान-chorus.

सहगामिनी-who gets along with (someone); wife; mate.

सहचर-associate; companion; running mate.

सहचरी-fairsex associate or companion.

सहचार-going along; together; association.

सहचारी-associate; companion.

सहज-easy (that) which comes easily.

सहज ज्ञान-instinctive/innate knowledge; intuition.

सहजता-state of being easy; easiness.

सहजन्मा-born together of the same mother; a brother one of twins, triplets etc.

सहज बुद्धि-natural wit; innate sense.

सहज भाव-innate tendency.

सहजवृत्ति-instinct.

सहजात-born together of the same mother; a brother one of twins, triplets etc.; natural; innate; inborn.

सहता-bearable.

सहधर्मिणी-wife.

सहधर्मी-having a common duty; having the same intrinsic quality.

सहन-courtyard; act or state of enduring/bearing/tolerating.

सहन-शक्ति-power of forbearance; forbearing; tolerant.

सहनशील-having tolerance; forbearing; to-learnt.

सहनशीलता-forbearance; tolerance.

सहना-to endure/bear/tolerate; to abide by; to suffer; to put up with.

सहनिदेशक-co-director.

सहनीय-bearable; tolerable.

सहपाठी-class fellow.

सहभागी-copartner.

सहभोज-a dinner; community dinner.

सहभोजी-mess-mate.

सहमत-concurred; agreed.

सहमति-concurrence; assent.

सहमना-to get scared/alarmed/ frightened.

सहमरण-dying together.

सहयात्री-co-traveller; fellow passenger.

सहयोग-cooperation; collaboration.

सहयोगी-associated.

सहयोजन-co-option.

सहयोजित-co-opted.

सहर-morning.

सहरा-jungle; forest.

सहराई-wild.

सहरी-a kind of fish; early breakfast (usually taken before dawn).

सहलाना-to rub gently.

सहलेखक-coauthor.

सहवर्ती- contemporaneous; contemporary.

सहवास-living together; co-dwelling; cohabitation.

सहवासी-co-dweller.

सहशिक्षा-coeducation.

सहसंपादक-coeditor.

सहसंबंध-co-relation.

सहसा suddenly; all of a sudden.

सहस्र-thousand.

सहस्रदल-thousand-petalled lotus.

सहस्राब्द-a millennium.

सहस्राब्दि-a millennium.

सहानुभूति-sympathy.

सहाय-helper.

सहायक-assistant; aide; helper.

सहायक नदी-tributary.

सहायता-aid; help; assistance.

सहारना-to endure/tolerate.

सहारा-support; prop.

सहारे के-with the support of.

सहालग-period considered auspicious for (Hindu) weddings.

सहिजन-a kind of large tree whose long beans and flowers are used as a vegetable.

सहित, के-with; along with; together with.

सहिष्णु-meek and forbearing; tolerant.

सहिष्णुता-state or quality of being ; tolerance.

सही-right; correct; true; fit; testimony; attestation; a mark put beside an item or sum to show that its has been checked.

सही-सलामत-not harmed or injured; unscathed; safe.

सही-सही correctly.

सहूलियत-facility; amenity.

सहृदय-warm-hearted; good-hearted; gentle; affectionate; having a (literary) taste.

सहृदयता- warm-heartedness; humaneness.

सहेजना-to check/collate/tally.

सहेली-female companion.

सहोदर-sibling; (one's) own brother.

सह्य-bearable; endurable; tolerable.

सह्यता-endurance; tolerance.

साँई-lord; master; husband; God; a title used for a Mohammadan mendicant.

साँकल-chain-like hasp for fastening the door.

सांकेतिक-relating to a symbol; serving as a symbol; symbolic.

सांकेतिक भाषा-code language.

सांख्य-numerical; knowledge.

सांख्यिकी-Science of Statistics.

सांख्यिकीय-statistical.

सांग-

सांगोपांग wholly; together with parts; all entire.

सांघातिक-deadly; mortal; lethal.

साँझ-evening.

साँट-mark of abrasion left on the body caused by a lash.

साँटा-whip/lash made of twisted cloth.

साँठ-गाँठ-complicity; unholy alliance; intrigue.

साँठी-capital.

साँड़-bull.

साँड़नी-fast-going she-camel; dromedary.

साँडनी-सवार-messenger who rides a she-camel; dromedaries.

सांत-ending; finite; limited.

सांत्वना-solace; consolation.

सांध्य-of or pertaining to the evening.

सांध्यकाल-evening time.

सांध्यगोष्ठी-evening meet.

सांध्यवेला-eventide.

साँप-serpent; snake.

सांपत्तिक-pertaining to wealth.

साँपिन-female snake.

साँपिया-of the dusty colour of a snake; dusty colour of a snake.

सांप्रतिक-current.

सांप्रदायिक-communal.

सांप्रदायिकता-communalism.

साँबर-South-Indian spiced curry.

साँभर-salt prepared from this lake; a type of Indian antelope.

सांवत्सरिक-pertaining to

साँवला-having a dark complexion; swarthy.

साँवलापन-swarthiness.

साँवलिया-(swarthy complexioned) lover.

साँवाँ-a variety of rice.

सांश्लेशिक-synthetic.

साँस-breath.

साँसत-agony (as in suffocation).

सांसद-member of the Parliament.

साँसा-breath; life.

सांसारिक-worldly; mundane; materialistic.

सांसारिकता-worldliness.

सांस्कृतिक-cultural.

सांस्थानिक-institutional.

साइकिल-cycle-bike.

साइत-moment; auspicious moment.

साइनबोर्ड-sign-board.

साई-advance; earnest; money.

साईस-groom; syce.

साईसी-work or post of a groom.

साएदार-shady.

साका-era.

साकारता-state or quality of being shaped.

सकारोपासना-idol worship.

साकिन-resident/inhabitant of.

साक़ी-server of wine; beloved; one who serves drinks.

साक्ष-having an axis; endowed with eyes; possessing eyes.

साक्षर-able to read and write; literate.

साक्षरता-literacy.

साक्षात-personified, in flesh and blood.

साक्षात्कार-being face to face; interview.

साक्षात्कारी-(one) who seeks interview.

साक्षी-witness; eye-witness; deponent; evidence.

साक्षीकरण-attestation.

साक्ष्य-evidence; testimony.

साक्ष्यांकित-attested.

साख-credit; goodwill; faith; trust; reputation.

साखी-witness; arbiter; arbitrator.

साखू-saltree and its wood.

साख्य-friendship; friendliness.

साग-green leaves used as vegetables; cooked vegetable preparation.

साग-पात-herbs and vegetables.

साग-भाजी-vegetables.

सागर-sea.

साग़र-cup (of wine).

सागौन-teak-wood.

साज-equipage; articles of decoration.

साज़-accoutrements; set of musical instruments.

साज-सज्जा-decoration and grandeur; equipment.

साज-सामान-equipment; furniture; luggage.

साजन-husband; lover.

साजात्य-state or quality of belonging to the same class or caste.

साज़िंदा-one who plays on a musical instrument, in the company of a dancer; accompanist.

साज़िश-conspiracy; plot; intrigue.

साज़िशी-conspiring; intriguing; conspiratorial.

साझा-partnership; co-ownership.

साझी-common.

साझेदार-copartner; co-owner; co-sharer.

साझेदारी-co-partnership; co-ownership.

साटन-satin.

साठ-sixty, 60.

साठ-गाँठ-complicity; collusion.

साठा-(person) sixty years old; of sixty years.

साठी-a kind of paddy which ripens in sixty days.

साड़ी-saree; sari; the principal outer garment of an Indian woman; especially one of artistic work.

साढ़ी-cream.

साढू-husband of wife's sister; brother-in-law.

साढ़े-plus half.

साढ़ेसाती-evil influence of planet Saturn which lasts for 7½ years, 7½ month or 7½ days.

सात-seven, 7.

सातत्य-continuity.

सातपूती-(woman) having seven sons.

सात फेरे-seven bridal rounds of the sacred fire.

सात्विक-purified; pure and pious; honest; virtuous.

सात्विकता-purity and piety.

साथ-company; association.

साथ, के-with.

साथवाला-next to; close to.

साथ-साथ together; concurrently.

साथिन-she-companion/associate.

सादगी-simplicity.

सादर-with respect; respectfully.

सादा-simple; plain.

सादा काग़ज़-a blank sheet of paper; plain or unlined paper.

सादृश्य-resemblance; likeness; similarity; analogy.

साद्यंत-entire; whole.

साध-long-cherished desire.

साधक-religiously persevering; accomplishing; effecting; completing; instrumental; one who perseveres; one who helps in accomplishing (something).

साधन-means; resources; act of accomplishment; completion.

साधना[1]-great perseverance; act performed with great perseverance; aim; practice.

साधना[2]-to accomplish; to bring (someone) round; to break in.

साधनिक-pertaining to resources.

साधनीय-worth being accomplished.

साधर्मिक-of or having the same religion.

साधार-based; having a basis/prop.

साधारण-ordinary; common; normal.

साधारणत: ordinarily.

साधारणता-state or quality of being ordinary.

साधारणीकरण-generalisation.

साधिका-female of

साधिकार-authoritative, authoritatively.

साधित-accomplished; attained.
साधु-saintly; saint; mendicant.
साधुता-saintliness; goodness; nobility; virtue; righteousness.
साधुवाद-eulogy.
साधुवृत्ति-saintly disposition; saintly way of life.
साधू-hermit; saint.
साध्य-attainable; practicable; which can be accomplished.
साध्वी-chaste and faithful (woman).
सानंद-happy; happily.
सान-whetstone; grindstone; hone.
सानना-to knead; to mix; to smear; to implicate.
सानी-matching; prepared fodder for cattle.
सानुज along with younger brother.
सानुनय humbly; modesty.
सानुप्रास-with alliteration.
सान्निध्य-proximity; closeness; neighbourhood.
सापेक्ष-relative.
सापेक्षता-state or quality of being relative.
सापेक्षतावाद-relativism.
सापेक्षवाद-relativity.
सापेक्षवादी-relativistic; of or pertaining to relativity; relativist.
सापेक्षिक-comparative.
साप्ताहिक-weekly; weekly magazine/journal.
साफ़-clear; clean; pure; frank; guileless; smooth; fair; honest; clear-cut. plainly.
साफल्य-success.
साफ़ा-a turban-like head-dress.
साबका-dealing.
साबित-proved; testified.
साबुत-entire; whole.
साबुन-soap.
साबुनदानी-soap-case.
साबूत-entire; complete; whole.
साबूदाना-sago.
साभार gratefully; thankfully.
साभिप्राय with a purpose/motive.
साभिमान with pride.
सामंजस्य-coordination.
सामंत-feudal chieftain.
सामंतवाद-feudalism.
सामंतवादी-feudalistic; feudalist.
सामंतशाही-feudalism.
सामंतिक-feudalistic.
साम-the prayers which in olden time were sung during sacrifices; sweet voice, conciliary means used in politics; gentel words.
सामग्री-collection of articles/requisites.

सामना-the part or side of something that faces forward; the main side of something; meeting; confrontation.

सामने-before.

सामने, के-in front of; before; in someone's presence or life time.

सामनेवाला-of or at the front; frontal; one who faces someone; other party; opposite party.

सामयिक-current; relating to current affairs; topical.

सामरिक-pertaining to war; martial; military.

सामर्थ्य-strength; power; capacity.

सामवेद-one of the four.

सामाजिक-social.

सामाजिकता-sociality; sociability.

सामाजीकरण-socialization.

सामान-goods; luggage.

सामान-घर-luggage-room.

सामान्य-general; common; average.

सामान्यत: generally; commonly.

सामान्यतया generally; commonly.

सामान्या-harlot; prostitute.

सामान्यीकरण-generalisation.

सामिधेनी-fountain of energy.

सामिष-non-vegetarian (dish or food).

सामी-Semitic.

सामीप्य-nearness; closeness; proximity.

सामुदायिक-pertaining to a community.

सामुद्र-marine; maritime.

सामुद्रिक-marine; maritime.

सामूहिक-collective.

साम्य-similarity; likeness; resemblance.

साम्यवाद-communism.

साम्यवादी-of or related to communism; communistic.

साम्यावस्था-equilibrium.

साम्राज्य-empire.

साम्राज्यवाद-imperialism.

साम्राज्यवादी-imperialistic; imperialist.

सायं-pertaining to evening; evening.

सायंकाल-evening; evening time.

सायक-vesperal; evening.

सायक-arrow.

सायण-a renowned commentator on the Vedas.

सायत-auspicious moment (for marriage ceremony and the like).

सायबान-shed; usually of tin.

साया-shadow; shade; petticoat.

सायुध-armed.

सारंग-a variety of deer; cloud; swan; conch.

सारंगिया-one who plays on *sarangi.*

सारंगी-an Indian stringed musical instrument.

सार-essence; quintessence; epitome; gist; substance; abstract; purport.

सारगर्भित-pregnant with meaning; pithy.

सारग्राही-competent to draw out the essence of things; connoisseur.

सारजंट-sergeant.

सारण-purging; purification.

सारणी-table (systematic arrangement in rows and columns).

सारणीकार-tabulator.

सारथी-charioteer.

सारना-to accomplish; to accomplish gracefully.

सारभाग-substance; pith essential portion; epitome.

सारभूत-substantial; essential.

सारल्य-simplicity.

सारवत्ता-substantiality; pithiness; sententiousness.

सारवान-substantial; pithy; sententious.

सारसंग्रह-digest.

सारस-crane (bird).

सारस्वत-of or pertaining to river; academic.

सारांश-the substance of some passage, speech etc.; gist; summary.

सारा-whole; entire; all.

सारिका-cuckoo.

सारिणी-table.

सारी-table; dice.

सारूप्य-similarity of form; likeness; resemblance.

सारोपा-set of clothes from head to foot.

सार्थ-meaningful. meaningfully.

सार्थक-meaningful; significant; fruitful.

सार्थकता- meaningfulness; significance; fruitfulness.

सार्थवाह-a merchant who goes abroad (obsolete).

सार्व-pertaining to all; general.

सार्वकालिक-pertaining to all times; eternal; perennial.

सार्वकालिकता-perenniality.

सार्वजनिक-public; common.

सार्वजनीकरण-universalisation.

सार्वत्रिक-existing everywhere and under all circumstances; universal.

सार्वदेशिक-pertaining to all countries; cosmopolitan.

सार्वदेशिकता-universality.

सार्वनामिक-pronominal.

सार्वभौमिक-universal; cosmopolitan.

सार्विक-general; universal.

साल-year; a kind of tree and its timber.-stiffening of nerves.

सालगिरह-birthday.

सालन-soupy preparation.

सालना-to cause piercing pain; to cause ceaseless pain.

सालस-arbiter; arbitrator.

सालसी-arbitration.

सालू-a kind of cloth of deep red colour usually worn by women on auspicious occasions.

सावधान-careful; cautious; attention.

सावधानी-carefulness; cautiousness.

सावधि-having a time-limit; timed; periodic.

सावन-fifth month of Hindu calendar; the main month of the rainy season.

सावन-भादों-the two main months of the rainy season.

सावनी-of or pertaining to *sawan.*

सावरण-covered; provided with cover.

सावित्री-the devoted wife of , who conquered a, the God of Death.

साश्चर्य-with surprise/wonder.

साष्टांग-in conjunction with eight limbs.

सास-one's husband's/wife's mother; mother-in-law.

साहचर्य-association; companionship; comradeship.

साहब-Lord; master; God; officer; boss; a vocable or response of address denoting respect; a polite term of address for a man, Sir.

साहबज़ादा-son of a lord or master.

साहबज़ादी-daughter of a lord or master.

साहबी-aristocratic; royal; lordly; state or quality of being a ; lordliness; officiousness.

साहस-courage; nerve.

साहसिक-courageous; brave.

साहसी-courageous; brave; enterprising; adventurous; valiant.

साहा-auspicious time; usually pertaining to marriage.

साहित्य-literature.

साहित्यकार-literary person; writer.

साहित्यिक-of or pertaining to literature; literary; literary person.

साहिल-coast; shore; bank.

साहिली-coastal.

साही-porcupine.

साहुल-plumb.

साहुल-सूत्र-plumb line.

साहू-wealthy person; banker.

साहूकार-money-lender; wealthy person; banker.

साहूकारा-banking business; venue of banking business.

सिंगारदार-make-up box/case.

सिंगारना-to make-up.

सिंगारहाट-red-light district; colony of brothels.

सिंगी-blow-pipe made of a horn; horn used as a flute.

सिंगौटी-receptacle made of horn; an ornament fitted on the tips of the horn.

सिंघाड़ा-water chestnut.

सिंघेला-cub of a lion.

सिंचन-irrigation; watering; sprinkling.

सिंचना-to be irrigated or watered.

सिंचवाना-to cause to be irrigated or watered.

सिंचाई-irrigation; watering; charges paid for irrigation.

सिंचित-irrigated; watered.

सिंदूर-vermilion; cinnabar.

सिंदूरदान-putting of vermilion on the head of the bride by the bridegroom.

सिंदूरदानी-small receptacle for keeping vermilion.

सिंदूरी-of or pertaining to vermilion; of vermilion colour; vermilion.

सिंधु-sea; river Indus; Sindh province.

सिंधु घाटी-Indus Valley (Punjab).

सिंधुज-born of of marine origin.

सिंह-lion; Sikhs and other warrior classes.

सिंहकेसर-name of a lion.

सिंहद्वार-main gate.

सिंहनाद-roar of a lion; war cry.

सिंहनी-female of lion.

सिंहमुखी-(house) having the frontage like the head of lion; broad in front with a narrow end.

सिंह राशि-fifth sign of the Zodiac; Leo constellation.

सिंहवत्-lion like.

सिंहवाहिनी-goddess ; riding a lion.

सिंहशावक-lionet.

सिंहस्थ-situated in leo constellation.

सिंहावलोकन-looking all around; circumspection; retrospection.

सिंहासन-throne.

सिंहोदरी-(woman) having a slim waist like that of a lion.

सिकंदर-Alexander the Great.

सिकंदरा-railway signal.

सिकटा-fragment of a broken pot.

सिकड़ी-chain (ornament); chain (bolt).

सिकता-sand.

सिकतामय-full of sand; sandy.

सिकली-act of polishing metallic objects; burnishing.

सिकलीगर-one whose occupation is doing ; burnisher.

सिकुड़न-crumple; wrinkle; crease.

सिकुड़ना-to shrink/shrivel; to contract.

सिकोड़ना-to contract; to cause to shrink/shrivel.

सिक्का-coin.

सिक्के net; without any discount or commission.

सिक्केबंद-having original seal; genuine.

सिक्त-irrigated; watered.

सिखाना-to train/instruct; to teach.

सिखाना-पढ़ाना-to tutor/coach.

सिखावन-counsel; advice.

सिगनल-signal.

सिगरेट-cigarette.

सिगड़ी-small charcoal oven for keeping one's body wam.

सिगार-cigar.

सिजदा-obeisance; bowing down in veneration.

सिजल-in good shape; tidy; seemly; nice; decent; of better quality.

सिझना-to be cooked (said of vegetables, lentils etc.).

सिझना-to cook (said of vegetables, lentils etc.).

सिटकिनी-bolt; latch.

सिटपिटाना-to be completely non-plussed/stupefied.

सिट्टी-braggting.

सिठनी-caricaturing couplets sung (by women) on ceremonial occasions.

सिड़-crankiness.

सिड़-बिल्ला-simpleton.

सिड़ी-cranky.

सिड़ीपन-crankiness.

सितंबर-September.

सित-white.

सितता-whiteness.

सितम-oppression; tyranny; cruelty.

सितमगर-cruel; oppressive.

सितली-cold sweat/perspiration.

सितार-sitar; an Indian type of guitar.

सितारवादक-(one) who plays on sitar.

सितारा-star; spangle.

सितारिया-a professional who plays on sitar.

सिद्ध-decided; proved; established; fulfilled; attained.

सिद्धकाम-having conquered (one's) desires; having fulfilled (one's) object or mission.

सिद्धपीठ-seat sacred to saintly persons.

सिद्धहस्त-adept; deft; dexterous.

सिद्धहस्तता-adeptness; deftness; dexterity.

सिद्धांजन-magic collyrium bestowing power of clairvoyance.

सिद्धांत-principle; canon; theory; doctrine.

सिद्धांतज्ञ-theorist.

सिद्धांतत:-on principle; theoretically.

सिद्धांतवाद-sticking to principles.

सिद्धांतवादी-upholder of principles; theoretician.

सिमटना-to constrict/contract; to near completion.

सियार-jackal.

सियासत-politics.

सियासी-political.

सियाह-dark.

सिर-head.

सिर-कटा-headless; beheaded.

सिरका-vinegar.

सिरकी-screen made of reeds.

सिर-खपाऊ-brain-racking.

सिरताज-crown; Lord.

सिर-दर्द-headache; worry; botheration.

सिरनामा-form of address in a letter etc.; full address of a recipient; caption of an article.

सिर-पड़ा-required to be done.

सिर-फिरा-crank; crankish.

सिर-मौर-diadem; crown of the head.

सिरहाना-side of a bed-stead where the head rests; pillow.

सिरा-the extremity of the length of something long as a thread, line, road etc.; end; top.

सिरी-head of an animal slaughtered for meat.

सिरोही-a variety of sword; a kind of bird.

सिर्फ़-with no other of the group, only; very few in number.

सिल-flat stone used for grinding purposes.

सिलपट-rendered plane by constant use.

सिल-बट्टा-stone pestle and flat stone.

सिलवट-crease; crumple.

सिलवाई-act of sewing/stitching or charges paid therefor.

सिलवाना-to get (clothes etc.) stitched/sewn.

सिलसिला-sequence; order; connection; context; continuity; recurrence.

सिलसिलेवार in orderly manner; in due order.-placed in order; orderly.

सिलाई-stitching; sewing; sewing charges.

सिला-सिलाया-made to wear; ready-made (garment).

सिलीपर-slipper; a kind of footwear; sleeper.

सिल्ला-remnants of grains left over after harvesting; gleanings.

सिल्ली-a large solid rectangular piece of metal, ice etc.; whetstone for sharpening metallic tools.

सिवँई-vermicelli.

सिवा besides; except.

सिविल-of or relating to the citizens; civil; involving civil law rather than criminal law.

सिसकन-sob; sobbing.

सिसकना-to sob.

सिसकारना-to make a hissing sound.

सिसकारी-hiss; hissing sound.

सिसकी-sob.

सिहरन-a slight shaking; tremor; thrill.

सिहरना-to shake because one feels cold, shyness or fright; to shiver.

सींक-slender twig-like stick.

सींक-सलाई-lean and thin (person).

सींकिया-lean and thin.

सींग-horn.

सींगड़ा-horned animal.

सींगी-musical pipe made or horn.

सींचना-to supply land with water by artificial means for the growth of crops; to irrigate.

सी-hissing sound.

सीकाकाई-a vegetable cleansing agent.

सीख-advice; instruction.

सीख़-broach; skewer; spit.

सीख-कबाब-kebab.

सीखचा-iron bar.

सीखना-to learn; to receive lessons.

सीखा-पढ़ा-well-instructed; tutored.

सीझना-to boil.

सीट-seat; boast; brag.

सीटना-to brag; to indulge in bravado.

सीट-पटांग-bravado; gasconade.

सीटी-whistle.

सीठा-tasteless; insipid.

सीठापन-tastelessness; insipidity.

सीठी-fibrous residual matter; dregs; refuse.

सीड़-dampness; damp; moisture.

सीढ़ी-ladder; staircase; flight of stairs.

सीढ़ीनुमा-like a flight of stairs.

सीत-cold.

सीताफल-pumpkin.

सीत्कार-sibilance.

सीध-straightness.

सीधा-straight; straight forward; simple; direct; clear; upright.

सीधा-उलटा-obverse and reverse (side).

सीधापन-simplicity; quality of being too simple.

सीधा-सादा-plain and simple; innocent.

सीधे straight-away; directly.

सीन-scene.

सीनरी-scenery.

सीना-to stitch/sew; chest/breast.

सीनाज़ोर-high-handed.

सीनाज़ोरी-high-handedness.

सीनियर-senior.

सीनेट-the main governing body of certain universities; senate; the upper house of legislative body in some countries.

सीनेटर-a member of the senate; senator.

सीप-shell of an oyster.

सीपी-small shell of an oyster; often used as a gadget.

सीमंत-one of the sixteen of Hindus; performed during the seventh or eighth month of pregnancy.

सीमांकन-demarcation.

सीमांकित-demarcated.

सीमांत-frontier; border.

सीमा-border; limit; boundary; furthest extent; limit.

सीमा-चौकी-terminal post.

सीमातिक्रमण-crossing the boundary; aggression.

सीमाबद्ध-bounded.

सीमा-रेखा-border-line.

सीमाविहीन-having no limit; limitless.

सीमा-शुल्क-duty paid on import; customs.

सीमित-limited.

सीमेंट-cement.

सीमोल्लंघन-transgression of territorial limit; violation of territory.

सीयन-line of stitches; seam.

सीर-land cultivated by the land-owner himself.

सील-damp; seal; seal; a kind of sea-animal.

सीलन-dampness; damp.

सीलना-to get damp; to affix a seal to.

सीलबंद-sealed.

सीसा-lead.

सुँघनी-snuff.

सुँघाना-to cause to smell.

सुंडा-an insect which infests vegetables.

सुंदर-beautiful; handsome; comely; pretty; lovely; charming.

सुंदरता-beauty; comeliness; prettiness.

सुंदरी-beautiful woman.

सुंबा-boring gadget.

सु denoting goodness; auspiciousness.

सुअर-pig; boar.

सुअवसर-good / favourable opportunity.

सुआ-big needle.

सुई-needle; a syringe to insert a drug in the body; hand of a watch/clock.

सुईकारी-needle work.

सुकंठ-having a good voice; melodious.

सुकर-easy to accomplish; practicable.

सुकर्म-good deed.

सुकीर्ति-renown; repute.

सुकुमार-delicate; gentle; pretty lad.

सुकुमारता-delicacy; tenderness; softness.

सुकुमारी-female of a delicacy.

सुकुल-virtuous.

सुकृति-good deed; virtuous act.

सुकृत्य-good deed; virtuous act.

सुखंडी-rickets; rachitics.

सुख-happiness; pleasure; comfort.

सुखकर-giving pleasure or comfort; pleasing; delightful.

सुखद-pleasing; pleasant; delightful.

सुख-दुःख-weal and woe; happiness and sorrow; pleasure and pain.

सुखपूर्वक happily; blithely; comfortably.

सुखभोग-enjoyment.

सुखवाद-hedonism.

सुखवादी-hedonistic; hedonist.

सुख-शांति-peace and happiness.

सुख-संपत्ति-happiness and prosperity.

सुख-सुभीता-pleasure and convenience.

सुख-सुविधा-pleasure and amenities.

सुखांत-with a happy ending; comedy.

सुखाना-to make dry; to dry up.

सुखाभास-euphoria.

सुखी-happy.

सुख्यात-famous; reputed.

सुख्याति-fame; reputation.

सुगंधि-fragrance.

सुगंधित-fragrant; aromatic.

सुगठित-well-built; compact; well-knit.

सुगति-wellbeing after death; beatitude; salvation.

सुगबुगाहट-whisper.

सुगम-easy; simple; plain; not difficult; easy to reach; accessible; passable.

सुगमता-easiness.

सुगमतापूर्वक with ease; easily.

सुगम्य-easily accessible.

सुगृही-having a good abode; having a beautiful and accomplished wife.

सुग्गा-parrot.

सुग्राहिता-sensitivity.

सुग्राही-sensitive.

सुघड़-well-built; shapely; accomplished.

सुघड़पन- accomplishment; proficiency.

सुघड़ी-auspicious moment.

सुचारु-pretty; charming.

सुचाल-right move; good ways.

सुचालाक-good conductor (of electricity); good driver.

सुचि-needle.

सुचित-serene; tranquil; at leisure.

सुजन-good man; gentleman.

सुजनता-goodness; politeness.

सुजनी-a variety of thick bedsheet.

सुजाति-of high caste; high caste.

सुजान-sagacious; sensible; wise; intelligent; clever.

सुजानता-sagacity; wisdom.

सुझाखा-having (good) eye-sight.

सुझाना-to suggest; to indicate.

सुझाव-something that is suggested; suggestion.

सुड़कना-to take liquid through the nose; to quaff (something liquid or semiliquid).

सुडौल-shapely; well-formed; well-proportioned; beautiful.

सुत-son.

सुतरां hence; therefore; as such.

सुतली-hemp or jute string.

सुतीक्ष्ण-very sharp.

सुतीक्ष्णता-state or quality of being sharp.

सुथनी-a variety of loose pyjama worn by women and girls.

सुथरा-near; clean; tidy.

सुथरापन-tidiness.

सुदर्शन-beautiful to look at; pleasing to the eye; good-looking.

सुदिन-happy times.

सुदी-bright fortnight of the lunar month.

सुदीर्घ-(very) long.

सुदूर-far off; very far; far away.

सुदूरपूर्व-Far East.

सुदृढ़-very firm; strong; rigid.

सुदेश-good country.

सुद्दा-piece of dry stool/faeces.

सुद्ध-pure.

सुध-awareness; consciousness; recollection; remembrance.

सुध-बुध-awareness.

सुधरना-to be reformed; to improve.

सुधर्मी-religious; pious.

सुधा-nectar; ambrosial beverage.

सुधाकर-moon.

सुधानिधि-moon; sea.

सुधामय-full of nectar/ambrosia.

सुधार-reform; reformation; improvement.

सुधारक-reformer.

सुधारना-to reform; to correct/improve.

सुधारालय-reformatory.

सुधि-awareness; consciousness.

सुधी-having clear intellect; intellectual.

सुनगुन-whispering rumour.

सुनना-to hear; to listen.

सुनना-गुनना-to listen and assimilate.

सुनम्य-flexible.

सुनम्यता-flexibility.

सुनयन-having a pair of lovely eyes.

सुनयना-(woman) having a pair of lovely eyes.

सुनवाई-hearing.

सुनवैया-listener, especially attentive listener.

सुनसान-lonely; desolately; quiet.

सुनहरा-with the colour of gold.

सुनहला-golden; auburn; fortune; precious.

सुनाई-the ability to hear; the capacity to hear; hearing of the law case.

सुनाना-to tell/narrate/recite.

सुनाम-good name.

सुनार-goldsmith.

सुनारिन-female goldsmith; wife of goldsmith.

सुनारी-occupation of a goldsmith; goldsmithery; good woman; wife of a goldsmith.

सुनावनी-news of the death of some kinsman.

सुनिश्चय-firm determination.

सुनिश्चित-firmly determined; definite.

सुनीति-equity; wholesome policy.

सुन्न-sensationless; void of all sensation; benumbed; insensible.

सुन्नत-circumcision.

सुन्नती-one who has been circumcised.

सुन्ना-zero; cypher.

सुन्नी-one of the two main sects of Muslims.

सुपंथ-good/right path.

सुपत्नी-good wife.

सुपथ-good/right path.

सुपथ्य-wholesome diet (prescribed for a patient).

सुपरीक्षित-well-tried.

सुपाच्य-easily digestible.

सुपाच्यता-state or quality of being digestible.

सुपात्र-well-deserving.

सुपात्रता-state or quality of being

सुपारी-betel nut; areca nut; killing contract.

सुपुत्र-dutiful son.

सुपुर्द-entrusted (to).

सुपूत-dutiful son.

सुपूती-(woman) having good/worthy sons.

सुप्त-asleep; dormant; latent.

सुप्तावस्था-state of being asleep; dormancy.

सुप्ति-sleepiness.

सुप्रतिष्ठित-renowed; well-reputed.

सुप्रभात-good morning; a morning; a harbinger of a good day.

सुप्रसिद्ध-renowed; reputed.

सुप्रसिद्धी-renown; repute.

सुफल-fruitful.

सुबह-morning.

सुबह-शाम-morning and evening.

सुबह-सवेरे-in the early morning; at dawn.

सुबाहु-having shapely arms.
सुबुक-soft; light.
सुबुकना-to sob faintly.
सुबुद्धि-good sense; better sense.
सुबोध-easily intelligible; comprehensible.
सुबोधता-intelligibility.
सुभग-lovely; charming.
सुभगा-(woman) comely; beautiful.
सुभाषिणी-sweet-tongued (woman).
सुभाषी-sweet-tongued; having the gift of the gab.
सुभिक्ष-(when alms are easily available) time of plenty; days of affluence.
सुभीता-convenience.
सुमंत्रित-well-advised; well-counselled.
सुम-hoof.
सुमति-right way of thinking; concord; harmony.
सुमधुर-deliciously sweet; very sweet; melodious.
सुमन-nice-hearted; flower.
सुमिरना-to repeat devotedly (God's) name etc.
सुमिरनी-rosary.
सुमेरु-mythological mountain (of gold).
सुयश-renown; repute.
सुयोग-happy coincidence/occasion.
सुयोग्य-worthy; very competent.
सुरंग-of good colour; of chestnut colour; reddish-brown; tunnel; mine (of dynamite).
सुरंगबुहार-mine sweeper.
सुर-god; tone; note; tune.
सुरक्षण-act of protecting well.
सुरक्षा-protection; good protection; security; defence.
सुरक्षात्मक-defensive.
सुरक्षा-परिषद-Security Council.
सुरक्षा-बल-security forces.
सुरक्षित-well-protected; defended; well-defended; reserved.
सुरक्षोपाय-safeguard.
सुरख़ाब-a bird of the heron.
सुरत-recollection; memory.
सुरतंगिणी-Milky Way.
सुरति-pleasant love-play.
सुरती-tobacco leaves turned into small flakes.
सुरदार-melodious.
सुरपति-god , king of the gods.
सुरपुर-the city where the gods dwell;-
सुरभि-fragrance; perfume.
सुरभित-fragrant; perfumed.
सुरमई-of the colour of collyrium; of saltish hue.
सुरमा-collyrium.
सुरमेदानी-small collyrium container.
सुरम्य-exquisitely charming.

सुरराज-Indra, the chief of the gods.

सुरस-juicy.-good juice.

सुरसुराना-to itch slightly; to make a sound like that of a creeping / crawling insect / animal or such like.

सुरसुरी-an insect which eats into grains; slight itch.

सुरही-a game played with 16 cowries.

सुरांगना-celestial damsel.

सुरा-wine/liquor.

सुराग़-clue; cue.

सुरागाय-yak.

सुराज्य-good government.

सुराधिप-Lord Indra; chief of the gods.

सुरानीक-army of the gods.

सुरापात्र-goblet of wine; wine-glass.

सुरापान-drinking of wine.

सुरापी-drunkard.

सुरासव-methylated spirit; celestial drink.

सुरासार-alcohol.

सुरासुर-gods and demons.

सुराही-ewer; long-necked jar, usually earthen, meant for cooling water.

सुराहीदार-long-necked.

सुरीला-melodiousness; sweetness.

सुरुचि-good taste.

सुरुचिपूर्ण-full of good taste; decorous.

सुरेंद्र-Lord Vishu; chief of the gods.

सुरेंद्रचाप-bow of Lord ; rainbow.

सुरेश-Lord.

सुरेश्वर-Lord.

सुरैत-concubine; kept mistress.

सुर्ख-red; blood-red; scarlet.

सुर्खरू-glorified/honoured.

सुर्ख़ी-redness; powder of bricks used in making brick walls; banner line in a newspaper; headline.

सुलक्षण-having traits characteristically auspicious; auspicious sign; good omen.

सुलगना-to smoulder.

सुलगाना-to ignite/kindle; to lit/light.

सुलझना-to be disentangled.

सुलझाना-to disentangle; to resolve.

सुलटा-direct; straight.

सुलतानी-of or pertaining to *Sultan*; state or office of (being) a *Sultan*.

सुलफ़ा-an intoxicant made from tobacco leaves for smoking.

सुलफ़ेबाज़-one who is addicted to smoking.

सुलफ़ेबाज़ी-habit of smoking.

सुलभ-easily available/obtainable.

सुलभता-easy availability.

सुलह-compromise; truce; treaty.

सुलहनामा-deed of compromise.

सुलह-सफ़ाई-settlement and compromise.

सुलाना-to cause to sleep; to make (someone) sleep.

सुलाभ-advantage.

सुलूक-behaviour.

सुलेश-beautiful handwriting; calligraphy.

सुवास-fragrance.

सुवासित-scented.

सुविख्यात-well-known; well-reputed; renowed.

सुविचार-good/excellent idea.

सुविज्ञ-having special knowledge; well-versed; expert.

सुविज्ञता-special knowledge; expertise.

सुविदित-well-known.

सुविधा-convenience; facility; concession.

सुविधाजनक-convenient.

सुविधाजीवी-ease-loving; easy-going.

सुविधानुसार at convenience.

सुव्यवस्था-good arrangement; good management.

सुव्यस्थित-well-arranged; well-managed.

सुशिक्षित-highly educated; lettered.

सुशील-of good disposition; courteous; well-behaved.

सुशीलता-innate quality of good disposition.

सुशोभित-graceful.

सुश्री-honorific used for women.

सुश्रुत-well-known (object).

सुषमा-natural/exquisite beauty.

सुषप्त-asleep in slumber; latent; dormant.

सुषुप्ति-slumber; dormancy.

सुषुम्ना-one of the fourteen main features of the body.

सुष्ठु-graceful; beautiful; sweetly graceful.

सुसंगत-cogent; relevant.

सुसंगति-good company; cogency; relevance.

सुसंस्कृत-well-cultured.

सुसंहत-compact.

सुसंहति-compactness.

सुसज्जित-well-decorated.

सुसमय-good days; favourable times; time of prosperity.

सुसाध्य-easily achievable/attainable.

सुस्त-lazy; idle; indolent; slow.

सुस्ताना-to take rest.

सुस्ती-laziness; idleness; indolence.

सुस्थित-well-placed; well-situated.

सुस्थिति-good situation.

सुस्थिर-well-poised; calm and balanced; steady; firmly settled.

सुस्पष्ट-clearly outlined; clear-cut.

सुस्वादु-very tasty; delicious.

सुहाग-a woman's blessed state of life when her spouse is alive.

सुहाग-रात-night of ceremonious consummation (of marriage).

सुहागा-borax.

सुहागिन-woman whose husband is alive.

सुहाना-to be pleasing/agreeable.

सुहाल-a dainty, salty preparation.

सुहावना-eye-catching; pleasant; delightful; pleasing.

सुहावनापन-state or quality of being delightful.

सुहृद-dearly loving; sincerely loving.

सुहृदय-having a good heart.

सूँघना-to smell.

सूँड-trunk (of an elephant).

सूँडी-an insect which eats into vegetables.

सूँस-porpoise.

सूअर-pig.

सूअर-बियान-giving birth to several children at a time.

सूकर-pig.

सूकरी-she-pig.

सूक्ति-quotable quote; good saying.

सूक्ष्म-minute; very small; subtle; tenuous.

सूक्ष्मता-minuteness; subtly.

सूक्ष्मदर्शी-having a keen insight; microscope.

सूक्ष्म शरीर-astral body.

सूखना-to dry; to get dry.

सूखा-dry; without warmness or feeling.-draught.

सूखी खुजली-dry itch.

सूखी खेती-dry farming.

सूखी तनख़्वाह-only cash pay (no perquisites).

सूचन-act of informing.

सूचना-information; communication; notice; notice.

सूचनापट्ट-notice board.

सूचनाप्रद-giving (useful) information; informative.

सूचना प्रौद्योगिकी-Information Technology.

सूचनालय-information centre.

सूचनीय-worth communicating; communicable.

सूचिका-needle.

सूचित-informed.

सूची-needle; inventory.

सूचीपत्र-catalogue.

सूचीभेद्य-very dense.

सूजन-swelling; inflammation.

सूजना-to swell.

सूजा-a kind of long and thick stitching needle; distaff; awl.

सूज़ाक-gonorrhoea.

सूजी-granulated wheat; semolina.

सूझ-insight; perception; penetrating insight; striking idea.

सूझना-to be visible; to occur; to come to mind; to strike.

सूझ-बूझ-imagination and wisdom.

सूझ-बूझवाला-having insight; discerning.

सूट-puff (of smoke).

सूटकेस-suit-case.

सूटा-pull.

सूत-cotton yarn; thread.

सूतक-state of temporary untouch-ability due to some birth or death in the family.

सूता-thread.

सूतिका-flying-in woman.

सूतिकागार-lying-in ward.

सूती-made from cotton.

सूत्र-formula; aphorism; clue; source.

सूत्रकार-one who formulates aphorisms.

सूत्रधार-state-manager (in old Sanskrit dramas).

सूत्रपात-commencement; beginning.

सूथन-a type of trousers worn by women, especially in Punjab.

सूद-interest (or principal).

सूदख़ोर-a person who lends money at an exorbitant rate of interest; usurer.

सूदख़ोरी-the practice of lending money at an exorbitant rate of interest; usury.

सूदन-destroyer; dear; endearing.

सूदी-pertaining to interest; (sum) earned as interest; (principal) yielding interest.

सूना-lonely; unfrequented.

सूनापन-loneliness.

सूप-a handy gadget/appliance used for winnowing grain and the like.

सूफ़ियाना-plain but befittingly beautiful; sophisticated.

सूफ़ी-believer of the cult of mysticism among Muslims.

सूफ़ी-संप्रदाय-sect of among Muslims.

सूबा-province.

सूबेदार-governor of a province; a non-commissioned officer in the Indian army.

सूम-miserly; penurious; miser.

सूमड़ा-unwilling to spend or give; niggardly; a stingy person; niggard.

सूमपन, सूमपना-miserliness; niggardliness.

सूमो-Japanese wrestling.

सूर-blind.
सूरज-Sun.
सूरज-घड़ी-sun-dial.
सूरजमुखी-sun-flower.
सूरत-appearance; countenance; face; situation; form.
सूरत-शक्ल-face and looks.
सूरत-हराम-of deceptive looks.
सूरन-elephant's foot; an edible root.
सूरमा-warrior; brave; fighter; hero.
सूरमापन-heroism; bravery; bravado.
सूराख़-hole; aperture.
सूर्य-Sun.
सूर्यग्रहण-solar eclipse.
सूर्यवंश-a renowned ancient Indian dynasty; solar dynasty.
सूर्यास्त-sunset; sundown.
सूर्योदय-sunrise.
सूर्योपासना-sun-worship.
सूली-an ancient form of capital punishment.
सूहा-bright red.
सृजन-The Creation.
सृजनहार-The Creator (of the world).
सृष्ट-created; produced.
सृष्टि-the creation.
सृष्टिकर्ता-Creator.
सृष्टि-विज्ञान-cosmology.
सेंक-fomentation; warmth.
सेंकना-to foment; to bake; roast.
सेंकाई-fomentation.
सेंटा-lower end of a reed (often used as a pen).
सेंतमेंत में gratis; free of cost/charge.
सेंद्रिय-organic.
सेंध-hole made in a house for burglary.
सेंधा नमक-common salt as a solid mineral; rock-salt.
सेंधिया-house-breaker; burglar.
सेंसर-censor.
से from; to; with; through; by; since; for; than.
से अधिक-more than.
सेकंड-second; one-sixtieth part of a minute.
सेक्रेटरी-secretary.
सेचन-irrigation; watering.
सेचित-irrigated.
सेज-luxurious bed.
सेट-set (of articles).
सेठ-wealthy/moneyed person.
सेतु-bridge.
सेतुबंध-dam; serving as a bridge; construction of a bridge.
सेना-army; to serve; to attend upon; to dance attendance on.
सेनाधिकारी-military officer.
सेनाधिपति-commander-in-chief.
सेनाध्यक्ष-chief of the army.
सेनानायक-general.

सेनानी-commanding officer.

सेनापति-commander.

से पहले before.

सेब-apple.

सेम-bean.

सेमल-silk cotton tree.

सेर-seer (an Indian unit of weight, a little over two pounds).

सेरा-smaller arm of bedstead.

सेरी-denoting weight in seers.

सेल-special sale/clearance of goods.

सेलखड़ी-soap-stone; talc.

सेलटैक्स-sales tax.

सेव-a salty preparation (gram flour, shredded and fried).

सेवई-vermicelli.

सेवक-servant; worker.

सेवकधर्म-duty of a *sevak*.

सेवकाई-service attendance.

सेवड़ा-salty preparation (long rectangular fried solids of wheat flour).

सेवन-use.

सेवन-विधि-method of use.

सेवा-service.

सेवाकाल-period of service.

सेवा-टहल-attendance and service.

सेवादार-one who serves as a religious duty (among Sikhs).

सेवाधर्म-service as duty.

सेवानिवृत्त-having retired from work.

सेवानिवृत्ति-retirement.

सेवापंजी-service-book.

सेवाभाव-spirit of service.

सेवावृत्ति-spirit of service.

सेवा-सुश्रूषा-attendance (on a patient) and nursing.

सेविका-a female servant.

सेवित-attended upon (person); used (object).

सेवी-server.

सेव्य-fit to be served; worth being served.

सेहरा bridegroom's chaplet; eulogical verse composed for a wedding.

सेहराबंदी-ceremony of putting on the bridegroom's chaplet.

सेहरी-a variety of small fish.

सैकड़ा-hundred.

सैकड़े in units of hundred.

सैकड़ों-hundred (of).

सैकत-pertaining to ; sandy.

सैद्धांतिक-pertaining to principle; theoretical.

सैनिक-soldier.

सैनिकीकरण-militarisation.

सैन्यवाद-militarism.

सैयाँ-husband; lover.

सैयाद-fowler.

सैर-the act of walking; roving; outing; pleasure trip; picnic.

सैर-सपाटा-excursion; roving for joy.

सैला-wedge.

सैलानी-tourist; excursionist; rover.

सैलानीपन-habit of roving.

सैलाब-flood.

सैलाबी-pertaining to flood.

सैलून-saloon; barber's shop; special carriage, meant for some high dignitary.

सोंटा-stout walking stick.

सोंठ-dried ginger.

सोंधा-having a light, pleasing (particularly earthen) smell.

सोंधापन-light; pleasing smell.

सो-so.

सोआ-a variety of leafy vegetable.

सोख़ना-to suck/absorb/soak.

सोख़्ता-blotting paper.

सोग-mourning.

सोगवारी-period of mourning.

सोच-consideration; anxiety.

सोचना-to think; to suppose or consider.

सोच-विचार-deliberation; due thought.

सोडा-soda.

सोडावाटर-soda-water.

सोता-spring (of water).

सोद्देश्य-purposeful; tendentious.

सोनचिरैया-a bird with gold-coloured; plumage; golden goose.

सोनल-golden.

सोना-gold; to sleep; sleeping.

सोपाधि-conditional; with a condition.

सोपान-staircase; flight of stairs.

सोपानित-stepped.

सोफ़ा-sofa.

सोफ़ासेट (-set) sofa set.

सोम-an ancient creeper; moon; elixir.

सोमरस-celestial beverage from the creeper; elixir.

सोमवती अमावस्या-last day of the dark half of a lunar month, when it falls on a Monday.

सोमवार-Monday.

सोमवारी-of or pertaining to Monday; held/observed on Monday.

सोयाबीन-soyabean.

सोलह-sixteen. 16.

सोलह सिंगार-an Indian style of make-up in all its sixteen traditional forms.

सोल्लास with enthusiasm tinged with joy.

सोहन-comely.

सोहन-पपड़ी-a variety of Indian sweet.

सोहन-हलुआ-a variety of Indian pudding.

सोहना-beautiful; to appear comely.

सोहबत-company; association; society.

सोहर-a variety of songs sung on auspicious occasions, child birth.

सौंदर्य-beauty; loveliness.

सौंदर्यवाद-aestheticism.

सौंदर्यवादी-aesthetic.

सौंदर्यशास्त्र-aesthetics.

सौंपना-to entrust.

सौंफ-fennel.

सौ-hundred; century.

सौकर्य-state or quality of being ; convenience.

सौकुमार्य-young-age.

सौख्य-comfortability; pleasure.

सौगात-some special present for someone brought from outside.

सौगाती-pertaining to speical present.

सौत-second wife; co-wife.

सौतिया-pertaining to a co-wife.

सौतेला-begotten form a step-mother.

सौदा-transaction; bargain; deal; marketing; sundry household articles of day-to-day consumption.

सौदाई-maniac (usually in love).

सौदागर-businessman; merchant; tradesman (usually from outside).

सौदागर बच्चा-born businessman.

सौदागरी-tradesman-ship.

सौदामिनी-lightning.

सौदा-सुल्फ़-transaction.

सौदेबाज़-bargainer; higgler; haggler.

सौदेबाज़ी-bargaining; horse trading.

सौध-mansion; palace.

सौभाग्य-good fortune.

सौभाग्यवती-(woman) whose husband is alive.

सौभाग्यशालिनी-(woman) of good fortune.

सौभाग्यशाली-fortunate; of good fortune.

सौभाग्याकांक्षिणी-maid (betrothed) seeking the happy state of married womanhood.

सौम्य-amiable; serene; placid; tranquil.

सौम्यता-amiability; serenity; placidity; tranquillity.

सौर-solar; pertaining to the Sun.

सौर जगत-solar system.

सौर दिवस-solar day.

सौरभ-fragrance; sweet smell; mango.

सौर मंडल-solar system.

सौर मास-solar month.

सौर वर्ष-solar year.

सौराष्ट-ancient name of *Saurashtra*; a region in the western part of India.

सौरी-lying-in chamber.

सौवाँ-hundredth.

सौष्ठव-grace; elegance; charm.

सौहार्द-warm and cordial relations; amity.

सौहार्दपूर्ण-pleasant and friendly; cordial.

सौहार्दपूवक cordially.

स्कंध-shoulder.

स्कूल-school.

स्कूली-pertaining to a school.

स्क्रू-screw.

स्खलन-falling down; deviation from the right path; discharge; emission.

स्खलित-from

स्टांप-stamp.

स्टाक-stock.

स्टाफ़-staff.

स्टाल-stall.

स्टीम-steam.

स्तंभन-शक्ति-power of retention.

स्तंभित-dazed/astounded/stunned/ bewildered.

स्तन-breast; udder.

स्तनधारी-mammal.

स्तनपान-breast-sucking.

स्तनपायी-breast-sucking (animal); mammal.

स्तनी-mammalian.

स्तन्य-pertaining to breast.

स्तबक-bunch of flowers; bouquet.

स्तब्ध-stunned; stupefied dumb-founded.

स्तर-level; standard; stature; fold; layer.

स्तरण-stratification.

स्तरी-pertaining to level/stature.

स्तुति-reverential praise; eulogy.

स्तुत्य-praiseworthy; laudable.

स्तूप-mound; stupa.

स्तोता-one who offers reverential praise; panegyrist.

स्तोत्र-hymn; eulogy of a god/goddess.

स्त्रियोचित-behaving women.

स्त्रियोपयोगी-useful to women.

स्त्री-woman; female; wife.

स्त्रीत्व-womanhood.

स्त्री-धन-property bestowed to woman (principally on the occasion of her wedding).

स्त्री-धर्म-inherent duty of a woman.

स्त्री-राज्य-gynarchy.

स्त्रीलिंग-feminine gender.

स्त्रैण-effeminate.

स्त्रैणता-effeminacy.

स्थगन-adjournment; postponement.

स्थगित-adjourned; postponed.

स्थल-place; site; venue; land.

स्थलचर-living on land; terrestrial.

स्थलज-born on land.

स्थल-डमरूमध्य-isthmus.

स्थल-मार्ग-land route.

स्थल-युद्ध-land warfare.

स्थल-सेना-army; land force.

स्थली-(picturesque) spot.

स्थलीय-pertaining to land.

स्थविर-steady; venerable.

स्थान-place; locality; spot.

स्थानांतर-transfer.

स्थानांतरण-act of transferring; transference.

स्थानांतरित-transferred.

स्थानापत्ति-substitution; replacement.

स्थानापन्न-that acts or serves in place of another.

स्थानीय-local.

स्थापक-founder.

स्थापत्य-architecture (art); design and style of building.

स्थापन-act of founding; establishment; installation.

स्थापना-founding; establishment; installation.

स्थापना-दिवस-foundation day; installation day.

स्थापनीय-worth founding/ establishing/installing.

स्थापित-founded; established; installed.

स्थायित्व-stability; permanence.

स्थायी-stable; durable; lasting; permanent.

स्थायीकरण-confirmation; fixation.

स्थायी कोष-reserve fund.

स्थायी भाव-enduring emotion/spirit.

स्थायी समिति-standing committee.

स्थावर-immovable; fixed.

स्थित-situated.

स्थितप्रज्ञ-of unperturbed disposition.

स्थितप्रज्ञता-state or quality of being

स्थितिशील-static; conservative.

स्थिर-fixed; stable; stationery; immovable; motionless; firm; stabilized.

स्थिरता-the quality or state of being stable; stability.

स्थिरीकरण-the act of stabilizing or the state of being stabilized.

स्थूल-bulky; fat.

स्थूलकाय-bulky; having a bulky body.

स्थूलता-fatness; bulkiness.

स्थूलबुद्धि-dull-headed.

स्थूलमति-unintelligent.

स्थैतिक-static.

स्थैतिकी-static; the branch of physics.

स्नात-bathed.

स्नातक-graduate.

स्नातकोत्तर-postgraduate.

स्नान-bath.

स्नानगृह-bathroom.

स्नानगार-bathroom.

स्नानोदक-water meant for a bath.

स्नायविक-pertaining to nerves; nervous.

स्नायु-nerve; tendon; sinew.

स्नायु-तंत्र-nervous system.

स्निग्ध-oily; lubricative; smooth; glossy.

स्निग्धता-oiliness; smoothness.

स्नेह-affection; love; oily substance.

स्नेहक-lubricant.

स्नेहन-lubrication.

स्नेहपाशा-bond of love; tie of love.

स्नेहमयी-(woman) full of affection; affectionate; loving; kind.

स्नेही-affectionate; loving.

स्पंज-sponge.

स्पंदन-vibration; pulsation; throbbing.

स्पंदित-pulsated.

स्पर्धा-emulation; rivalry.

स्पर्धी-rival; competitor.

स्पर्श-touch; contact; (Gram.) stop.

स्पर्शजन्य-arising from touch; contagious.

स्पर्शनीय-tangible.

स्पर्शनीयता-tangibility.

स्पर्श-रेखा-tangent line (Maths.).

स्पर्श-बिन्दु-point of contact.

स्पर्श-संघर्षी-affricate (Ling.).

स्पर्शी-touching.

स्पर्शेंद्रिय-sense-organ of touch; skin.

स्पष्ट-clear; obvious; evident; free from doubt or confusion; explicit; frank; honest.

स्पष्टतः clearly; evidently; plainly; explicitly.

स्पष्टतया-clearly; evidently; plainly; explicitly.

स्पष्टवादिता-frankness in speaking; outspokenness.

स्पष्टीवादी-one who talks straight; outspoken; straightforward.

स्पष्टीकृत-clarified; explained.

स्पिरित-spirit (methylated or rectified).

स्पीकर-speaker.

स्पीड-speed.

स्पृश्य-worthy of being touched.

स्फुरण-sprouting forth; flashing on the mind; pulsating.

स्फुरना-to issue forth; to flash on the mind; to come suddenly to mind.

स्फुरित-issued forth; flashed on the mind; agility.

स्फुलिंग-spark.

स्फूर्ति-agility; liveliness; quickness.

स्फोट-eruption; bursting out; explosion.

स्फोटक-causing eruption; explosive; detonating; boil; fuse.

स्फोटकता-explosiveness.

स्फोटन-eruption; explosion; detonation.

स्फोटवाद-primordial theory of explosion.

स्फोटित-erupted; exploded; detonated.

स्मरण-recalling to mind; recollection; remembrance; memorization.

स्मरण-पत्र-memorandum; reminder.

स्मरणीय-memorable; worth remembering.

स्मारक-memorial; monument; relic.

स्मारिका-souvenir; memorandum.

स्मित-smiling; smile.

स्मिति-smile.

स्मृत-recollected; brought to memory; remembered.

स्मृति-memory; recollection; remembrance.

स्मृतिकार-author of the *smiriti*.

स्मृति-चिह्न-memento.

स्मृति-पटल-screen of the mind.

स्मृति-पत्र-reminder; memorandum.

स्यंदन-war chariot.

स्यात perhaps; possibly.

स्यापा-collective mourning; situation that evokes grief.

स्यामल-blackish; tawny.

स्यार-jackal.

स्याह-black.

स्याही-blackness; black ink; ink.

स्रवण-oozing.

स्रष्टा-creator; the God.

स्राव-discharge.

स्रोत-source; origin; spring of water.

स्लिप-slip.

स्लीपर-slippers; sleeper (rail).

स्लेज-sledge.

स्लेट-slate.

स्व denoting one's own or self. self.

स्वकर्म-one's deed(s).

स्वकीय-one's own.

स्वकीया-wedded woman devoted to her husband.

स्वगत-कथन-soliloquy.

स्वचल-automatic.

स्वचालक-self-starter.

स्वचालित-automatic.

स्वच्छंद-at liberty; free; unfettered; self-willed.

स्वच्छंदचारिणी-woman of loose morals.

स्वच्छंदचारी-self-willed; libertine.

स्वच्छंदता-freedom; the right to do as one chooses; liberty.

स्वच्छ-clean; limpid; clean and clear; pure.

स्वच्छता-cleanliness; limpidness.

स्वजन-kith and kin; near and dear relatives.

स्वजनता-kinship.

स्वजातीय-of one's own race/caste.

स्वतंत्र-independent; free; self-governed.

स्वतंत्रता-independence; freedom.

स्वतंत्रता-सेनानी-one who fights for independence of his country; freedom fighter.

स्वत: involuntarily; automatically.

स्वत: निर्मित-of one's own making; self-created.

स्वत: सिद्ध-obvious; self-evident.

स्वत्त्व-right; ownership.

स्वत्त्वाधिकार-ownership.

स्वत्त्वाधिकारी-owner.

स्वदेश-motherland; native land.

स्वदेशभक्त-patriot.

स्वदेशभक्ति-patriotism.

स्वदेशी-indigenous.

स्वधर्म-innate quality.

स्वधीत-studied.

स्वन-sound; noise; phoneme.

स्वनाम-धन्य-renowned through one's own name; self magnanimous.

स्वनिक-phonetic.

स्वनित-sounded; voiced.

स्वनिर्मित-made by oneself; self-made.

स्वप्न-dream.

स्वप्न-दर्शन-dream-vision.

स्पप्नदर्शी-dreamer.

स्वप्नदोष-nocturnal emission; spermatorrhoea; night pollution.

स्पप्नलोक-dreamland.

स्वप्निल-dream-like.

स्वभाव-temperament; nature; innate disposition.

स्वभावगत-habitual; wonted.

स्वभावत: by nature; naturally; by disposition.

स्वयं-myself; yourself; himself or herself; one's own self; alone (without help). automatically.

स्वयंतथ्य-axiom.

स्वयंपाकी-one who cooks his own food; one who eats food cooked only by his ownself, one who does not take food cooked by another.

स्वयंप्रमाण-self-proved; which needs no testimony.

स्वयंभू-self-born; God.

स्वयंवर-ceremony prevalent in ancient India in which the bride chose her husband herself.

स्वयंवरा-maiden who selects her husband herself.

स्वयंसिद्ध-axiomatic.

स्वयंसेवक-volunteer, one who serves others voluntarily; scout.

स्वर-vowel; voice; tone; tune; intonation.

स्वर-यंत्र-larynx.

स्वर-लिपि-musical notation.

स्वर-संधि-union of adjacent vowels.

स्वर-साधन-constant practice and training of voice and tone (Music).

स्वरांत-(word) ending in a vowel.

स्वरागम-introduction of a vowel.

स्वराघात-accent.

स्वराजी-votary of movement.

स्वराज्य-self-government; Swaraj.

स्वराष्ट्र-one's own nation.

स्वरित-one of the three ways of pronouncing vowels in the Vedas.

स्वरूप-shape; form; appearance; mask; identity.

स्वर्गगमन-departing for Heaven.

स्वर्गधाम-Heaven.

स्वर्गपुरी-Heaven.

स्वर्गलोग-Heaven.

स्वर्गवास-departure for Heaven; death.

स्वर्गवासी-the late.

स्वर्गस्थ-dwelling in Heaven; dead.

स्वर्गारोहण-ascendance into Heaven; passing away.

स्वर्गीय-heavenly; paradisiacal; late.

स्वर्गोपाम-Heavenly; Heaven.

स्वर्ण-gold.

स्वर्णकार-goldsmith.

स्वर्णकारी-calling of a goldsmith.

स्वर्णकाल-golden period; glory days.

स्वर्णज-born out of gold; made of gold.

स्वर्ण-जयंती-golden jubilee.

स्वर्णमान-gold standard.

स्वर्ण-मुद्रा-golden coin; gold-currency.

स्वर्ण-युग-golden-age.

स्वर्ण-वर्ण-of golden colour.

स्वर्णाक्षर-golden letter; letter of gold.

स्वर्णिम-golden.

स्वल्प-very little (in quantity).

स्वल्पायु-of a very short span of life.

स्वल्पाहार-small quantity of food; light refreshment.

स्वल्पहारी-one who subsists on a small quantity of food.

स्वशासन-self-government; self-rule.

स्वशासित-self-ruled.

स्वसहायता-self-help.

स्वस्तिक-a sign; flyfot.

स्वस्तिमान-auspicious self.

स्वस्तिवाचन-chanting of benedictory words/mantras.

स्वस्थ-healthy.

स्वावलंबन-self-reliance.

स्वावलंबी-self-reliant; self-dependent.

स्वास्थ्य-health.

स्वास्थ्य-रक्षा-preservation of health.

स्वास्थ्यकर-wholesome; conductive to (good) health.

स्वास्थ्य-मंत्रालय-Health Ministry.

स्वास्थ्य-मंत्री-Health Minister.

स्वास्थ्य-विज्ञान-Hygiene; science of health.

स्वीकार-act of acceptance.

स्वीकारना-to accept; to acknowledge.

स्वीकारात्मक-affirmative.

स्वीकारोक्ति-admission; acceptance; avowal; confession.

स्वीकार्य-acceptable; worth accepting.

स्वीकृत-accepted; admitted; acknowledged.

स्वीकृति-assent; acceptance; admission.

स्वेच्छया of one's own volition; according to one's own with; at one's free-will.

स्वेच्छा-one's own volition/wish.

स्वेच्छाचार-wilful conduct.

स्वेच्छाचारिता-wilfulness.

स्वेच्छाचारी-self-willed.

स्वेटर-sweater.

स्वेद-perspiration; sweat.

स्वेदज-born of perspiration.

स्वेदन-act of perspiring.

स्वेदित-perspired.

स्वैच्छिक-following one's own volition/wish.

स्वैर-uncontrolled; unrestrained.

स्वैराचार-unrestrained conduct.

स्वैराचारी-self-willed; libertine.

ह

ह-The thirtieth palatal consonant of the alphabet; it is very often inaccuracy interchanged with or in Hindi.

हँकवा-one who drives.

हँकवाना-to scare away (cattle etc.); to halloo; to cause to drive.

हँकवैया-one who directs the course (of cattle etc.).

हँकुआ-one who partakes in a

हंगामा-uproar; tumult; furore.

हंगामी-uproarious; tumultuous.

हंटर-lash; whip.

हंडा-metallic container (usually of brass) for storing water etc.

हँडिया-a glass jug for holding a candle; a small earthern pot.

हंडिया-small earthen pot used for cooking purposes.

हंतव्य-who deserves being killed.

हंता-murderer; killer.

हंस-goose; swan; soul.

हंसगामिनी-(woman) possessing the graceful gait of a swan.

हँसना-to laugh at; to laugh; to deride/ridicule.

हँसना-खेलना-merry making.

हँसना-बोलना-to exchange pleasantries.

हँसना-हँसाना-to be joyous and to spread an atmosphere of joy around.

हँसमुख-jolly; facetious; cheery; good-humoured; cheerful.

हँसली-collar bave.

हंसवाहिनी-goddess of Learning whose mount is a swan.

हँसाई-derision; ridicule.

हँसाना-to amuse; to make (others) laugh; to tickle.

हंसिनी-female swan/goose.

हँसिया-sickle.

हँसी-laughter; laugh; joke; fun.

हँसी-खुशी cheerfully; cheerfulness.

हँसी-खेल-joke; fun and frolic; easy joy; almost a joke.

हँसी-ठट्ठा-jesting and laughing.

हँसी-दिल्लगी-joking and jesting; wit and humour.

हँसी-मज़ाक़-joking; jesting.

हँसीला-jocular.

हँसुआ-large sickle.

हँसुली-collar-bone; an ornament worn round the neck.

हँसोड़-jocular; jocose.

हक़-right; privilege; claim; title.

हक़तलफ़ी-transgression of (one's) right.

हक़दार-rightful claimant.

हकबकाना-to be startled bewildered; confused.

हक़-मालिकाना-proprietary right.

हक़-मौरूसी-ancestral right.

हकला-stutterer; stammerer.

हकलाहट-sutttering; stammering.

हक़ीक़त-reality; truth; fact.

हक़ीकी-real.

हकीम-physician following the Greek system of medical treatment.

हकीमी-profession of a Hakeem; science or art of the Greek system of treatment.

हक्का-बक्का-taken aback; confused; bewildered.

हगना-to pass stools; to defecate; to evacuate.

हगाना-causative to pass stools.

हगास-urge to defecate.

हचक-loss of the joint grip.

हचकना-to lose the joint-grip.

हचका-mild joint/shock.

हचकोला-jolt.

हज-pilgrimage to Mecca.

हज़म-digested; misappropriated.

हज़रत-a reverential for of address, Sire.-high-souled person; roguish.

हजामत-shave and/or hair.

हज़ार-thousand.

हज़ारवाँ-thousandth.

हज़ारा-of or consisting of a thousand; metallic device for sprinkling water on plants etc.

हज़ारों-thousands; many a thousand.

हज्जाम-barber.

हटक-forbiddance.

हटकना-to forbid.

हटना-to move away/aside.

हटरी-toy-temple meant for lighting in; during the festival.

हटवाना-to cause to move away.

हटाना-to displace/remove; to oust/dismiss.

हटाना-बढ़ाना-to move this way or that.

हटिया-market.

हटौती-build of the body.

हट्ट-market.

हट्टा-कट्टा-strong in constitution; stout and sturdy.

हट्टी-shop.

हठ-stubbornness; obstinacy.

हठधर्म-bigotry.

हठधर्मी-sheer obstinacy/stubbornness.

हठ-योग-one of the six kinds of Yoga.

हठ-विद्या-Science of Yoga.

हठात्-forcibly; through sheer obstinacy; suddenly.

हठी-stubborn; obstinate.

हठीला-stubborn; obstinate; resolutely firm.

हठीलापन-state or quality of being stubborn.

हड़कंप-furore; great.

हड़क-intense craving for water by a hydrophobic patient.

हड़कना-to be instigated.

हड़काना-to instigated.

हड़काव-state of instigate.

हड़ताल-strike.

हड़ताली-a worker who is on strike; striker.

हड़पना-to swallow; to devour in big mouthfuls; to grab.

हड़प्पा-state of swallow; big chunk/lump (of food etc.).

हड़बड़-haste; rashness.

हड़बड़ाना-to make undue haste; to act precipitously.

हड़बड़िया-hasty; (one) who habitually acts precipitously; rash.

हड़बड़ी-undue haste; precipitation; hurry-scurry.

हड़हड़ाना-to make a loud sound (as in a crash down).

हड़ावल-wreath of bones.

हड़ीला-reduced to a skeleton.

हड्डी-bone.

हत-killed; murdered.

हतक-insult; disgrace.

हतभाग्य-hapless; unfortunate; unlucky.

हतवीर्य-bereft of one's prowess/masculinity.

हताश-despairing; hopeless; disappointed.

हताशा-despair; despondency.

हताहत-killed and wounded.

हतोत्साह-disheartened; dejected.

हत्था-handle; holder; impression of hand.

हत्थी-small handle.

हत्थे through (the hand of).

हत्या-murder; homicide.

हत्यारा-murderer; assassin.

हत्यारिन-murderess.

हथ of used as a prefix in compound words.

हथ-उधार-loan without the support of a written document.

हथकंडा-(lit) sleight of hand; tactics; stratagem.

हथकड़ी-handcuff; manacle; shackle.

हथकरघा-handloom.

हथकल-hand-operated machine.

हथगोला-hand-grenade.

हथछुट-who slaps even on trifles.

हथनी-she-elephant.

हथफेर-given to pinching (things) at odd places.

हथफेरी-habit of pinching (things) at odd places.

हथबना-hand-made.

हथबुना-hand-spun.

हथ-मिलाव-handshake.

हथलपक-swindler.

हथा-handle; hand.

हथिया नक्षत्र-tenth constellation of stars denoting heavy downpour.

हथियाना-to grab; wrest.

हथियार-an object used in fighting; weapon (specially of offence); tool.

हथियार-घर-armoury; arsenal.

हथियारबंद-armed; equipped with arms.

हथियारबंदी-equipped (one-self) with arms; armament.

हथेली-palm (of hand).

हथौड़ा-hammer.

हथौड़ी-small hammer.

हद-limit; boundary; bound.

हदबंदी-act of demarcating.

हदस-scare.

हदसना to be scared.

हदीस-collection of traditional sayings of Prophet Mohammed.

हनन-slaughtering; slaying; murdering.

हनना to slaughter/slay/murder/kill.

हननीय-fit to be slaughtered/slayed/murdered.

हनु-the jawbone; jaw.

हनुमान-monkey-god who helped-

हफ़्ता-week.

हफ़्तेवार-weekly.

हफ़्तेवारी-weekly.

हबर हबर-hurriedly; fastly; quickly; hastily.

हब्बा-डब्बा-breathing trouble (among children); pneumonia.

हब्शिन-*fem.* of a Negro.

हब्शी-any dark-skinned person of Africa; America; Negro.

हम-we; also replaces I generally. denoting equality, similarity etc.

हम-उम्र-of the same age.

हमजोली-chum; pal.

हमदम-very intimate friend; chum.

हमदर्द-sympathiser.

हमदर्दी-sympathy.

हमनाम-name-sake.

हमपेशा-of the same profession; co-professional.

हमप्याला-हमनिवाला-those who drink and dins together; born companions.

हमबिस्तर-one who enjoys the same bed; bedfellow; companion.

हमराह-going together.

हमराही-one who accompanies; co-traveller.

हमल-pregnancy; conception.

हमला-attack; assault.

हमलावर-assailant; invader.

हमवतन-compatriot; fellow countryman.

हमवार-even; level.

हमशक्ल-resembling in appearance; similar in looks.

हमसफ़र-fellow-traveller; fellow-passenger.

हमसाया-neighbour.

हमाम-bath room.

हमाम-दस्ता-mortar and pestle.

हमारा-our; ours; my; mine.

हमाहमी-egoism; egotism.

हमीर-हठ-dogged pertinacity.

हमें to us; we.

हमेल-a type of necklace made of coins.

हमेव-egotism.

हमेशा always; evermore.

हम्माम-bath-room; large container, provided with a tap, for keeping water hot.

हय-horse.

हयशाला-stable.

हया-innate modesty.

हयादार-innately modest/bashful.

हर-every.

हरकत-movement; motion; unbecoming / undesirable behaviour/conduct.

हरकारा-messenger (usually a postal employee); courier.

हरखना-to be delighted.

हरगिज़-never at all; on no account; absolutely not.

हरज-loss; harm; damage.

हरजा-indemnity; compensation for loss.

हरजाई-a spouse who carries on with various persons.

हरण-stealing/carrying away.

हरताल-an arsenic, used as a pigment; orpiment.

हरना to steal/carry away.

हरफ़-letter (alphabet).

हरबा-arm; weapon.

हरबोंग-turmoil; hubbub; furore; tumult.

हरम-harem; seraglio; female apartment in a palace.

हरमज़दगी-villainy; rascality.

हरहा-wolf.

हरा-green.

हराना-to defeat/beat.

हरापन-greenness.

हरा-भरा-lush with greenery; gay and flourishing.

हराम-ill-gotten; improper.

हरामख़ोर-(he) who dose not earn by the sweat of his brow.

हरामख़ोरी-subsistence on ill-gotten earnings.

हरामज़ादा-bastard; illegitimate offspring (used as an invective).

हरामी-illegitimate; born out of adulterous union (vituperative language).

हरारत-heat; warmth; temperature.

हरावल-vanguard.

हरि-Lord.

हरिजन-(lit.) God's own being; (now; in common parlance) one belonging to the scheduled class.

हरिण-dear.

हरिणी-female dear.

हरित-green.

हरिताभ-having a green shade; of a greenish hue.

हरिद्रा-turmeric.

हरियाला-greenery.

हरिस-beam of a plough.

हरीरा-a sweet preparation of pulverised almond and milk.

हरे-vocative of *hari.*

हरेक-everybody; everyone.

हर्ज-loss; harm.

हर्जाना-something given to compensate; damages; compensation.

हर्र-myrobalan.

हर्ष-joy; delight; cheer; happiness.

हर्षकारक-delighting; exhilarating.

हर्षध्वनि-cry of joy/jubilation.
हर्षातिरेक-rapture.
हर्षाश्रु-tears of joy.
हर्षित-delighted; pleased.
हर्षोन्माद-ecstasy.
हलंत-(word) ending mark in hindi.
हल्-a consonant down below which the aforesaid mark is appended.
हल-plough; solution (of a problem).
हलक़-gullet; throat.
हलकापन-lightness; shallowness.
हलका-फुलका-light in weight; without substance; not severe; intense or classical.
हलचल-stir; commotion.
हलदी-turmeric.
हलधर-ploughman; elder brother of Lord.
हलफ़-oath.
हलफ़नामा-affidavit; written statement on oath.
हलफ़ी-statement made on oath.
हलरा-to rock a baby; a cradle; to dandle; to play with a baby.
हलराना-to rock/cradle.
हलवा-a dainty Indian dish.
हलवाईन-female of confectioner.
हलवाई-confectioner.
हलवाहा-ploughman.
हलाक-killed; murdered.
हलाकान-harassed.
हलाकानी-harassment.
हलाकू-killer; murderer.
हला-भला-disposal.
हलाल-slaughtered as per Muslim convention.
हलालख़ोर-(one) who lives on well-begotten earnings; scavenger.
हलालख़ोरी-living on well-begotten; earnings.
हलाहल-deadly poison.
हलीम-forbearing; modest; humble.
हलीमा-forbearance; modesty.
हलूफ़ा-a ceremony during a wedding in which the two parties are introduced to each other.
हल्का-light.
हल्ला-noise; attack.
हल्ला-गुल्ला-hullaballoo; commotion; tumult; uproar; clamour.
हवन-ceremony in which oblations are offered to the fire-god.
हवनकुंड-prism shaped dugout vessel (with square ends) used for performing
हवन-सामग्री-the group of articles offered to fire-god.
हवलदार-sergeant.
हवस-insatiable lust; persistent and excessive desire.

हवा-air.
हवाई-of or pertaining to air; aerial.
हवाई अड्डा-aerodrome.
हवाई-चक्की-windmill.
हवाई-छतरी-air-umbrella; parachute.
हवाई-जहाज़-an aeroplane.
हवाई डाक-airmail.
हवाई यात्रा-journey by air.
हवाकश-ventilator.
हवादार-airy; well-ventilated.
हवादारी-system of ventilation.
हवा-पानी-climate.
हवा-बदल-change of climate.
हवाबाज़-air pilot.
हवा-महल-airy palace.
हवामार-anti-aircraft.
हवामार तोप-anti-aircraft gun.
हवाल-turn of events.
हवाला-reference.
हवालात-lock-up.
हवालाती-detainee.
हवाली-मवाली-associates and companions.
हवास-knowledge through sense organs.
हवि-oblation; sacrificial goat.
हवेली-mansion; palatial building; temple.
हशीश-hashish; a kind of intoxicant prepared from dried hemp.
हश्र-day of judgment; destiny; final outcome; resultant.
हसरत-innate desire.
हसीन-handsome; comely; pretty; beautiful.
हसीना-pretty young girl.
हस्त-hand; tenth constellation of stars.
हस्तकला-handicraft.
हस्तकौशल-manual skill.
हस्तक्रिया- hand-practice; masturbation.
हस्तक्षेप-interference; meddling.
हस्तगत-obtained; come into one's possession; received.
हस्तमैथुन-act of inciting one's genital organ to get sexual satisfaction; masturbation.
हस्तरेखा-line on the palm.
हस्तलाघव-skill of hand; sleight-of-hand.
हस्तलिखित-hand-written.
हस्तलिपि-handwriting.
हस्तलेख-handwriting.
हस्तशिल्प-handicraft.
हस्तांतरण-handing over; transference.
हस्तांतरणीय-transferable.
हस्तांतरणीयता-transferability.
हस्तांतरित-transferred.
हस्तांतरिती-transferee.

हस्ताक्षर-signature.

हस्ताक्षरक-signatory.

हस्ताक्षरित-signed.

हस्तामलक-crystal clear.

हस्तिनी-female elephant; fourth class of women. (Hindu Sexology).

हस्ती-elephant; individuality; personality; figure.

हस्ते, के-though the agency of.

हाँ-yes.

हाँक-calling aloud.

हाँकना-to drove; to goad.

हाँका-driving out a game by making loud noises to a spot suitable for hunting.

हाँडी-earthen pot meant mainly for cooking purposes.

हाँफना-to pant.

हा denoting sorrow or grief.

हाइफ़न-hyphen.

हाइफ़न-युक्त-hyphenated.

हाई-excessive craving.

हाई कोर्ट-High Court.

हाकिम-ruler; officer.

हाकिमाना-officer like.

हाकी-Hockey.

हाजत-call of nature.

हाजती-(person) under duress or custody.

हाज़मा-power of digestion.

हाज़िर-present.

हाज़िरजवाब-of ready wit; ready-witted.

हाज़िरबाश-ever-ready at one's service.

हाज़िरी-attendance; roll call.

हाजी-one who has been to Mecca on pilgrimage; appellation attached to the name of such a person.

हाट-market; periodical market.

हाड़-bone.

हाता-compound; enclosure.

हातिम-generous; liberal.

हाथ-hand.

हाथा-impression of the hand with turmeric etc.

हाथापाई-scuffle.

हाथी-elephant.

हाथी-दाँत-ivory.

हाथीवान-an elephant driver.

हादसा-mishap; accident.

हानि-loss; harm.

हानिकर-causing loss.

हाफ़िज़-protector; one, especially a Muslim, who has memorized the-

हाफ़िज़ा-memory.

हामिला-pregnant.

हामी-assent.

हाय-alas !-sigh/cry of a lacerated heart; insatiable hunger.

हार-defeat.

हार-जीत-defeat and victory; victory or defeat.

हारना-to be defeated.

हारमोनियम-harmonium.

हारा-denoting 'doer'.

हारिल-a greenish Indian bird.

हार्दिक-hearty; cordial; heart-felt.

हार्दिकता-heartiness.

हाल-condition; state; time that is passing; recent past.

हाल-चाल-state of affairs.

हालत-condition.

हालाँकि though; although.

हाला-liquor; wine.

हाला-चाला-earthquake.

हालात-circumstances.

हाली-ploughman.

हाव-भाव-gestures and postures (especially amorous).

हावी-domineering.

हाशिया-margin; border.

हास-laugh; laughter.

हास-परिहास-fun and laughter.

हासिल-gained; got; acquired; obtained.

हास्य-laugh; laughter; humour.

हास्यकर-humorous; provoking laughter.

हास्य-व्यंग्य-humour and satire.

हास्यास्पद-preposterous; ludicrous; ridiculous.

हास्योत्पादक-O; the tragedy!

हाहंत-O; the tragedy!

हाहाकार-cry of distress.

हाहा-हूहू-joyous hilarity.

हिंकरना-to neigh; whinny.

हिंडोला-swing adorned with a seat; merry-go-round.

हिंद-India.

हिंदी-Hindi; the national language of India.

हिंदुत्व-Hinduism.

हिंदुस्तान-India.

हिंदुस्तानी-Indian.

हिंदु-Hindu.

हिंदुकुश-a mountain range in the northern-most part of India.

हिंदूपन-spirit of Hinduism.

हिंदोस्तान-India.

हिंदोस्तानी-Indian.

हिंसक-violent (person); carnivorous (animal).

हिंसा-violence.

हिंसाचार-violence.

हिंसात्मक-violent.

हिंस्त्र-violent; ferocious.

हिकमत-Greek system of Medicine; skill; tact.

हिकमती-tactful; skilful.

हिचक-hitch; hesitation.

हिचकना-to hitch/hesitate.

हिचकिचाहट-hitch; hesitation.

हिचकी-hiccup.

हिचर-मिचर-undue hesitation; shilly-shally.

हिजड़ा-impotent; an eunuch; an ineffective man.

हिजरी-Muslim era.

हिज्जे-spelling.

हित-benefit; gain; welfare; interest.

हितकर-beneficial; salutary; useful; profitable.

हितचिंतक-well-wisher; benefactor.

हितचिंतन-well-wishing.

हिताहित-good and evil.

हितैषी-well-wisher.

हितोपदेश-teaching for (one's) good.

हिदायत-instruction.

हिनहिनाना-to neigh/whinny.

हिनहिनाहट-neighing.

हिना-myrtle.

हिनाई-of the colour of (grounded) myrtle.

हिफ़ाज़त-safety; protection.

हिम-snow; frost.

हिमगिरी-Himalayas.

हिमनदी-glacier.

हिमपात-a fall of snow snowfall.

हिममानव-snowman.

हिमयुग-ice-age.

हिमरेखा-snow-line.

हिमवर्षा-snow-fall.

हिमशैल-ice-berg.

हिमश्वेत-snow-white.

हिमांक-freezing point.

हिमाक़त-folly; stupidity.

हिमाचल-Himalayas.

हिमाच्छादित-covered with snow; snow-covered.

हिमाद्री-Himalayas.

हिमानी-glacier; avalanche.

हिमायत-support; help; backing.

हिमायती-supporter.

हिमालय-Himalayas.

हिमावृत-snow-capped.

हिमियानी-knitted purse used as a belt.

हिम्मत-courage; boldness.

हिम्मती-courageous; lose courage.

हिय-heart.

हियरा-heart.

हिया-heart; mind; breast.

हियाव-shyness; hitch.

हिरण-deer.

हिरण्य-gold.

हिरन-deer.

हिरनौटा-young of a deer.

हिरासत-duress; legal detention/custody.

हिरासती-pertaining to custody.

हिर्स-unfulfilled longing; longing due to envy or emulation.

हिलकोरा-billow; wave.

हिलगना-to be attached/entangled/joined/clung (to).

हिलना-to move/shake; to quiver.

हिलना-मिलना-to hobnob.

हिलाना-to move.

हिलाना-डुलना-to move.

हिलोर-wave; surge; undulation.

हिलोरना-to gather.

हिसाब-account; sum (in Arithmetic); calculation; estimate.

हिसाब-किताब-accounts.

हिसाबिया-calculating.

हिसाबी-pertaining to account.

हिस्सा-part; portion.

हिस्सेदार-co-sharer; shareholder; partner.

हिस्सेदारी-co-sharing; partnership.

हींग-assafoetida.

ही-only; solely; none but; indeed; exactly.

हीक-smell, rather dislikable/unpleasant.

हीन-low; destitute; denoting 'devoid' of.

हीनता-lowliness; inferiority; deficiency.

हीनत्व-inferiority complex.

हीनभावना-inferiority complex; low mentality.

हीया-heart.

हीर-pith; quintessence.

हीरक-diamond.

हीरक जयंती-diamond jubilee.

हीरा-diamond.

हीला-pretext; pretence.

हीला-हवाला-false excuse.

हीलेबाज़-pretender; one who pretends; pretending.

ही ही-titter.

हुँ-denoting assent.

हुंकार-belligerent cry; war cry.

हुंकारना-to make a belligerent cry; to chide; to rebuke.

हुँकारी-sound indicating that one is listening.

हुंडी-bill of exchange.

हुक-hook.

हुकुम-order.

हुकूमत-government; rule; suzerainty.

हुक़्क़ा-hubble-bubble.

हुक़्क़ा-पानी-social dealings/relations.

हुक्म-order; command.

हुक्मनामा-written order.

हुक्मबरदार-obeisance; servant.

हुक्मबरदारी-obeisance; obedience.

हुक्मी-imperative; mandatory; infallible; never failing.

हुजूम-crowd.

हुज़ूर-your Honour; Sir.

हुज़ूरी-sycophancy.

हुज्जत-(needless) wrangling.

हुज्जती-given to wrangling.

हुड़क-pang/heartache due to separation (said of a child).

हुड़कना-to suffer the pangs of separation (usually said of a child).

हुड़दंग-uproar; disturbance; noisy confusion; bedlam; commotion; tumult.

हुड़दंगी-playful and restive.

हुताग्नि-sacrificial fire.

हुतात्मा-martyr.

हुताशन-fire.

हुन-gold coin.

हुनर-art; skill.

हुनरमंद-skilful.-artist.

हुनरमंदी-artistry; skilfulness.

हुनरा-trained (said of a monkey).

हुमकना-to dance/frisk about.

हुमसना-to dance with/for joy.

हुमा-an imaginary bird whose shadow showers blessings.

हुमेल-a variety of necklace; especially of gold coins.

हुलसना-to express an exuberance of joy/delight.

हुलास-jubilation; snuff.

हुलिया-physical features; form; shape.

हुल्लड़-noise; uproar; furore; tumult; ballyhoo.

हुश-hush! shutup!

हुस्न-comeliness; handsomeness; prettiness; beauty.

हुस्नपरस्त-worshipper of beauty.

हुस्नपरस्ती-worship of beauty.

हूँ-am; assent; attention (to what is being said).

हूँक-cry (denoting pangs of separation) usually of a cow.

हूँठा-number which is three and a half times a given integer; multiplication table giving such numbers.

हूँस-jealously; malice; evil eye; curse.

हूँसना-to entice; to curse; to imprecate; to evoke.

हूँ-हाँ-an expression of agreement or consent.

हूक-stabbing pain born of some intense longing.

हूबहू-exactly alike; resembling on all fours.

हूर-fairy; beauty celestial; lovely damsel.

हूरना-to box; to give blows with the fist.

हूल-piercing thrust.

हूलना-to thrust piercingly.

हूश-vulgar; savage-like.

हूशपन-vulgarity.

हृतकंप-throbbing of heart; palpitation.

हृतंत्री-a musical instrument like heart.

हृदयंगम-rooted in the heart; understood.

हृदय-heart.

हृदयग्राही-captivating.

हृदय-वल्लभ-darling of the heart.

हृदयवान-having a heart.

हृदयविदारक-poignant; heart-rending.

हृदयवेधी-heart-piercing.

हृदयस्पर्शी-touching the heart; pathetic.

हृदयी-pertaining to the heart.

हृदयेश-lord of one's heart.

हृदयेश्वरी-mistress of the heart; beloved.

हृद्‌रोग-heart-disease.

हृष्ट-पुष्ट-stout and robust.

हें-हें-imploring like a sycophant.

हे-particle of address.

हेकड़-arrogant; rude.

हेकड़ी-bravado and gas-conade.

हेच-of a low order; trifling.

हेठी-especially lowering in the estimation of others.

हेडमास्टर-headmaster.

हेडमास्टरी-headmastership.

हेतु-purpose.

हेत्वाभास-fallacy (logic).

हेमंती-pertaining to winter.

हेम-gold.

हेय-interior; bad; deficient; worthless.

हेरना-to search; investigate; to gaze.

हेर-फेर-interchange of articles; manipulation; exchange; alteration.

हेरा-फेरी-moving about to and fro with some (ulterior) motive; interchange of articles with some (ulterior) motive.

हेल-मेल-hob-nobbing.

हेली-मेली-chum; hob-nobbing associate.

हेस-नेस-finalization.

हैं-are.

हैंडबैग-hand-bag.

हैंडिल-handle.

है-is.

हैज़ा-cholera.

हैट-hat.

हैरत-wonderment; astonishment.

हैरान-surprised and perplexed.

हैरानी-anxiety; perplexity; botheration.

हैवान-beast.

हैवानियत-beastliness; bestiality.

हैसियत-status; capacity.

होंठ-lip.

होटल-hotel.

होठ-lip.